Ford Pick-ups
Automotive Repair Manual

by Jeff Killingsworth
and John H Haynes

Member of the Guild of Motoring Writers

Models covered:
Ford F-150 Pick-ups
2015 through 2017
Does not include F-250 or Super Duty

ABCDE
FGHIJ
KLMNO
PQRST

Haynes Publishing Group
Sparkford Nr Yeovil
Somerset BA22 7JJ England

Haynes North America, Inc
859 Lawrence Drive
Newbury Park
California 91320 USA
www.haynes.com

Acknowledgements

Wiring diagrams provided exclusively for Haynes North America, Inc. by Haynes Pro. Technical writers who contributed to this project include Demian Hurst and Scott "Gonzo" Weaver. Mechanical work and photography was provided by Mark Henderson.

A book in the Haynes Automotive Repair Manual Series

Printed in Malaysia

ISBN-13: 978-1-62092-281-1
ISBN-10: 1-62092-281-9

Library of Congress Control Number: 2017950228

While every attempt is made to ensure that the information in this manual is correct, no liability can be accepted by the authors or publishers for loss, damage or injury caused by any errors in, or omissions from, the information given.

"Ford" and the Ford logo are registered trademarks of Ford Motor Company. Ford Motor Company is not a sponsor or affiliate of Haynes Publishing Group or Haynes North America, Inc. and is not a contributor to the content of this manual.

Contents

Introductory pages

About this manual	0-5
Introduction	0-5
Vehicle identification numbers	0-6
Recall information	0-7
Buying parts	0-9
Maintenance techniques, tools and working facilities	0-9
Booster battery (jump) starting	0-16
Jacking and towing	0-17
Automotive chemicals and lubricants	0-18
Conversion factors	0-19
Fraction/decimal/millimeter equivalents	0-20
Safety first!	0-21
Troubleshooting	0-22

Chapter 1
Tune-up and routine maintenance — 1-1

Chapter 2 Part A
V6 engines — 2A-1

Chapter 2 Part B
V8 engine — 2B-1

Chapter 2 Part C
General engine overhaul procedures — 2C-1

Chapter 3
Cooling, heating and air conditioning systems — 3-1

Chapter 4
Fuel and exhaust systems — 4A-1

Chapter 5
Engine electrical systems — 5-1

Chapter 6
Emissions and engine control systems — 6A-1

Chapter 7 Part A
Automatic transmission — 7A-1

Chapter 7 Part B
Transfer case — 7B-1

Chapter 8
Driveline — 8-1

Chapter 9
Brakes — 9-1

Chapter 10
Suspension and steering systems — 10-1

Chapter 11
Body — 11-1

Chapter 12
Chassis electrical system — 12-1

Wiring diagrams — 12-21

Index — IND-1

Haynes photographer and mechanic with a 2017 F-150 XL, 2.7L twin-turbocharged V6

About this manual

Its purpose

The purpose of this manual is to help you get the best value from your vehicle. It can do so in several ways. It can help you decide what work must be done, even if you choose to have it done by a dealer service department or a repair shop; it provides information and procedures for routine maintenance and servicing; and it offers diagnostic and repair procedures to follow when trouble occurs.

We hope you use the manual to tackle the work yourself. For many simpler jobs, doing it yourself may be quicker than arranging an appointment to get the vehicle into a shop and making the trips to leave it and pick it up. More importantly, a lot of money can be saved by avoiding the expense the shop must pass on to you to cover its labor and overhead costs. An added benefit is the sense of satisfaction and accomplishment that you feel after doing the job yourself.

Using the manual

The manual is divided into Chapters. Each Chapter is divided into numbered Sections, which are headed in bold type between horizontal lines. Each Section consists of consecutively numbered paragraphs.

The reference numbers used in illustration captions pinpoint the pertinent Section and the Step within that Section. That is, illustration 3.2 means the illustration refers to Section 3 and Step (or paragraph) 2 within that Section.

Procedures, once described in the text, are not normally repeated. When it's necessary to refer to another Chapter, the reference will be given as Chapter and Section number. Cross references given without use of the word "Chapter" apply to Sections and/or paragraphs in the same Chapter. For example, "see Section 8" means in the same Chapter.

References to the left or right side of the vehicle assume you are sitting in the driver's seat, facing forward.

Even though we have prepared this manual with extreme care, neither the publisher nor the author can accept responsibility for any errors in, or omissions from, the information given.

NOTE

A **Note** provides information necessary to properly complete a procedure or information which will make the procedure easier to understand.

CAUTION

A **Caution** provides a special procedure or special steps which must be taken while completing the procedure where the Caution is found. Not heeding a Caution can result in damage to the assembly being worked on.

WARNING

A **Warning** provides a special procedure or special steps which must be taken while completing the procedure where the Warning is found. Not heeding a Warning can result in personal injury.

Introduction

These pick-ups are offered in 2WD and 4WD models, and are available with the following trim level packages: XL, XLT, Lariat, King Ranch, Platinum, Limited (beginning in 2016), and Raptor (beginning in 2017).

Available gasoline engines are the 2.7L twin-turbo V6, 3.5L twin-turbo V6, 3.5L non-turbo V6, and the 5.0L V8. All models are equipped with the On Board Diagnostic Second-Generation (OBD-II) computerized engine management system that controls virtually every aspect of engine operation. OBD-II monitors emissions system components for signs of degradation and engine operation for any malfunction that could affect emissions, turning on the CHECK ENGINE light if any faults are detected.

Chassis layout is conventional, with the engine mounted at the front and the power being transmitted through a 6-speed automatic transmission (2017 3.5L engines are equipped with a 10-speed automatic transmission) and a driveshaft to the solid rear axle. On 4WD models, a transfer case transmits power to a front differential by way of a driveshaft and then to the front wheels through independent driveaxles.

Suspension is independent at the front of the vehicle, consisting of coil spring-over-shock absorber assemblies. The rear suspension features semi-elliptical leaf springs. All models use telescopic shock absorbers at each corner and a front and rear stabilizer bar. Both 4WD and 2WD models share the same type of suspension.

The brakes are disc-type on all four wheels, with an Anti-Lock Brake System (ABS) as standard equipment. Some models are equipped with an Electronic Parking Brake (EPB) system.

The electrically power-assisted steering gear assembly is mounted on the chassis frame rail underneath the engine.

Vehicle identification numbers

Modifications are a continuing and unpublicized process in vehicle manufacturing. Since spare parts lists and manuals are compiled on a numerical basis, the individual vehicle numbers are necessary to correctly identify the component required.

Vehicle Identification Number (VIN)

This very important identification number is stamped on a plate attached to the dashboard inside the windshield on the driver's side of the vehicle (see illustration). The VIN also appears on the Vehicle Certificate of Title and Registration. It contains information such as where and when the vehicle was manufactured, the model year and the body style.

VIN engine and model year codes

Two particularly important pieces of information found in the VIN are the engine code and the model year code. Counting from the left, the engine code letter designation is the 8th digit and the model year code letter designation is the 10th digit.

On the models covered by this manual the engine codes are:

8   3.5L V6, Dual overhead camshaft (DOHC) Twin independent Variable Cam Timing (Ti-VCT), gasoline (non-turbo)

G   3.5L V6, Dual overhead camshaft (DOHC), GTDI (Gasoline Turbo charged Direct Injection)
P   2.7L V6, Dual overhead camshaft (DOHC), GTDI (Gasoline Turbo charged Direct Injection)
F   5.0L V8, Dual overhead camshaft (DOHC), gasoline, flex fuel

On the models covered by this manual the model year codes are:
F   2015
G   2016
H   2017

Vehicle Certification Label

The Vehicle Certification Label is attached to the driver's side door pillar (see illustration). Information on this label includes the name of the manufacturer, the month and year of production, as well as information on the options with which it is equipped. This label is especially useful for matching the color and type of paint for repair work.

Engine identification number

Labels containing the engine code, engine number and build date can be found on the valve cover (see illustration). The engine number is also stamped onto a machined pad on the external surface of the engine block.

Automatic transmission identification number

On some models, the automatic transmission ID number is on a label affixed to the left side of the case (see illustration).

The transmission code is also shown on the Vehicle Certification label, under "TR."

CODE	TRASMISSION TYPE
6	6R80, 6-speed automatic
G	10R80, 10-speed automatic

The VIN is visible through the windshield on the driver's side

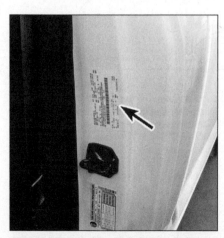

The Vehicle Certification Label is affixed to the driver's side door pillar

The engine identification label is affixed to the valve cover - 2.7L engine models shown

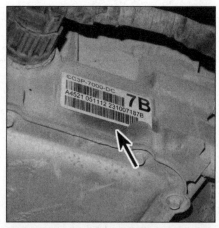

The automatic transmission identification tag is located on the left (driver's) side of the case

The transfer case identification label location

Transfer case identification number

The transfer case ID number is on a label which is affixed to the rear cover (see illustration).

Differential identification number

The differential/axle ID number is located on the Vehicle Certification Label. Some axles are also equipped with a tag on which this information is stamped.

CODE	GEAR RATIO/AXLE TYPE
15	3.15, non limited-slip
19	3.55, non limited-slip
26	3.73, non limited-slip
27	3.71, non limited-slip
L3	3.31, electronic locking differential
L4	4.10, electronic locking differential
L5	3.15, electronic locking differential
L6	3.73, electronic locking differental
L9	3.55, *electronic locking differential*

Vehicle Emissions Control Information label

This label is found in the engine compartment. See Chapter 6 for more information on this label.

Recall information

Vehicle recalls are carried out by the manufacturer in the rare event of a possible safety-related defect. The vehicle's registered owner is contacted at the address on file at the Department of Motor Vehicles and given the details of the recall. Remedial work is carried out free of charge at a dealer service department.

If you are the new owner of a used vehicle which was subject to a recall and you want to be sure that the work has been carried out, it's best to contact a dealer service department and ask about your individual vehicle - you'll need to furnish them your Vehicle Identification Number (VIN).

The table below is based on information provided by the National Highway Traffic Safety Administration (NHTSA), the body which oversees vehicle recalls in the United States. The recall database is updated constantly. For the latest information on vehicle recalls, check the NHTSA website at www. nhtsa.gov, www.safercar.gov, or call the NHTSA hotline at 1-888-327-4236.

Recall date	Recall campaign number	Model(s) affected	Concern
April 28, 2015	15V251000	2015 F-150	Some models may have loose or missing underbody heat shields. A missing underbody heat shield can lead to degradation or melting of the fuel or vapor lines, increasing the risk of a fire.
May 12, 2015	15V279000	2015 F-150	Some models may have been built with a steering upper intermediate shaft that was improperly riveted. If the intermediate shaft was improperly riveted, it could separate from the intermediate shaft flex coupling, resulting in loss of steering control and increasing the risk of a crash.
September 30, 2015	15V614000	2015 F-150	On some models equipped with Adaptive Cruise Control (ACC), while using the ACC, the vehicle may falsely detect an obstacle in its path and may unexpectedly apply the brakes. A vehicle that unexpectedly brakes increases the risk of a crash.

Recall date	Recall campaign number	Model(s) affected	Concern
December 22, 2015	15V867000	2015 F-150	On some models equipped with driver or front passenger seat belt anchorage assemblies, the pre-tensioner cable was not properly crimped. As a result, the seat belts may not properly restrain the seat occupant in the event of a crash, which could increase the risk of injury.
February 25, 2016	16V110000	2016 F-150	On some models equipped with Multi-Contour Seats (MCS), the front passenger seat Occupant Classification System (OCS) that calibrates the airbag deployment level may incorrectly classify an adult as a child when the seat massage feature is activated. If an adult is incorrectly classified as a child, the passenger frontal airbag will not deploy during a crash, increasing the risk of injury.
June 28, 2016	16V475000	2016 F-150	On some models equipped with a manual-reclining driver's seat, the seat back frame may have insufficient welds; the seat back may not adequately restrain the occupant during a crash, increasing the risk of injury.

Buying parts

Replacement parts are available from many sources, which generally fall into one of two categories - authorized dealer parts departments and independent retail auto parts stores. Our advice concerning these parts is as follows:

Retail auto parts stores: Good auto parts stores will stock frequently needed components which wear out relatively fast, such as clutch components, exhaust systems, brake parts, tune-up parts, etc. These stores often supply new or reconditioned parts on

an exchange basis, which can save a considerable amount of money. Discount auto parts stores are often very good places to buy materials and parts needed for general vehicle maintenance such as oil, grease, filters, spark plugs, belts, touch-up paint, bulbs, etc. They also usually sell tools and general accessories, have convenient hours, charge lower prices and can often be found not far from home.

Authorized dealer parts department: This is the best source for parts which are

unique to the vehicle and not generally available elsewhere (such as major engine parts, transmission parts, trim pieces, etc.).

Warranty information: If the vehicle is still covered under warranty, be sure that any replacement parts purchased - regardless of the source - do not invalidate the warranty!

To be sure of obtaining the correct parts, have engine and chassis numbers available and, if possible, take the old parts along for positive identification.

Maintenance techniques, tools and working facilities

Maintenance techniques

There are a number of techniques involved in maintenance and repair that will be referred to throughout this manual. Application of these techniques will enable the home mechanic to be more efficient, better organized and capable of performing the various tasks properly, which will ensure that the repair job is thorough and complete.

Fasteners

Fasteners are nuts, bolts, studs and screws used to hold two or more parts together. There are a few things to keep in mind when working with fasteners. Almost all of them use a locking device of some type, either a lockwasher, locknut, locking tab or thread adhesive. All threaded fasteners should be clean and straight, with undamaged threads and undamaged corners on the hex head where the wrench fits. Develop the habit of replacing all damaged nuts and bolts with new ones. Special locknuts with nylon or fiber inserts can only be used once. If they are removed, they lose their locking ability and

must be replaced with new ones.

Rusted nuts and bolts should be treated with a penetrating fluid to ease removal and prevent breakage. Some mechanics use turpentine in a spout-type oil can, which works quite well. After applying the rust penetrant, let it work for a few minutes before trying to loosen the nut or bolt. Badly rusted fasteners may have to be chiseled or sawed off or removed with a special nut breaker, available at tool stores.

If a bolt or stud breaks off in an assembly, it can be drilled and removed with a special tool commonly available for this purpose. Most automotive machine shops can perform this task, as well as other repair procedures, such as the repair of threaded holes that have been stripped out.

Flat washers and lockwashers, when removed from an assembly, should always be replaced exactly as removed. Replace any damaged washers with new ones. Never use a lockwasher on any soft metal surface (such as aluminum), thin sheet metal or plastic.

Fastener sizes

For a number of reasons, automobile manufacturers are making wider and wider use of metric fasteners. Therefore, it is important to be able to tell the difference between standard (sometimes called U.S. or SAE) and metric hardware, since they cannot be interchanged.

All bolts, whether standard or metric, are sized according to diameter, thread pitch and length. For example, a standard 1/2 - 13 x 1 bolt is 1/2 inch in diameter, has 13 threads per inch and is 1 inch long. An M12 - 1.75 x 25 metric bolt is 12 mm in diameter, has a thread pitch of 1.75 mm (the distance between threads) and is 25 mm long. The two bolts are nearly identical, and easily confused, but they are not interchangeable.

In addition to the differences in diameter, thread pitch and length, metric and standard bolts can also be distinguished by examining the bolt heads. To begin with, the distance across the flats on a standard bolt head is measured in inches, while the same dimension on a metric bolt is sized in millimeters (the same is true for nuts). As a result, a standard wrench should not be used on a metric bolt and a metric wrench should not be used on a standard bolt. Also, most standard bolts have slashes radiating out from the center of the head to denote the grade or strength of the bolt, which is an indication of the amount of torque that can be applied to it. The greater the number of slashes, the greater the strength of the bolt. Grades 0 through 5 are commonly used on automobiles. Metric bolts have a property class (grade) number, rather than a slash, molded into their heads to indicate bolt strength. In this case, the higher the number, the stronger the bolt. Property class numbers 8.8, 9.8 and 10.9 are commonly used on automobiles.

Strength markings can also be used to distinguish standard hex nuts from metric hex nuts. Many standard nuts have dots stamped into one side, while metric nuts are marked with a number. The greater the number of

dots, or the higher the number, the greater the strength of the nut.

Metric studs are also marked on their ends according to property class (grade). Larger studs are numbered (the same as metric bolts), while smaller studs carry a geometric code to denote grade.

It should be noted that many fasteners, especially Grades 0 through 2, have no distinguishing marks on them. When such is the case, the only way to determine whether it is standard or metric is to measure the thread pitch or compare it to a known fastener of the same size.

Standard fasteners are often referred to as SAE, as opposed to metric. However, it should be noted that SAE technically refers to a non-metric fine thread fastener only. Coarse thread non-metric fasteners are referred to as USS sizes.

Since fasteners of the same size (both standard and metric) may have different

strength ratings, be sure to reinstall any bolts, studs or nuts removed from your vehicle in their original locations. Also, when replacing a fastener with a new one, make sure that the new one has a strength rating equal to or greater than the original.

Tightening sequences and procedures

Most threaded fasteners should be tightened to a specific torque value (torque is the twisting force applied to a threaded component such as a nut or bolt). Overtightening the fastener can weaken it and cause it to break, while undertightening can cause it to eventually come loose. Bolts, screws and studs, depending on the material they are made of and their thread diameters, have specific torque values, many of which are noted in the Specifications at the beginning of each Chapter. Be sure to follow the torque recommen-

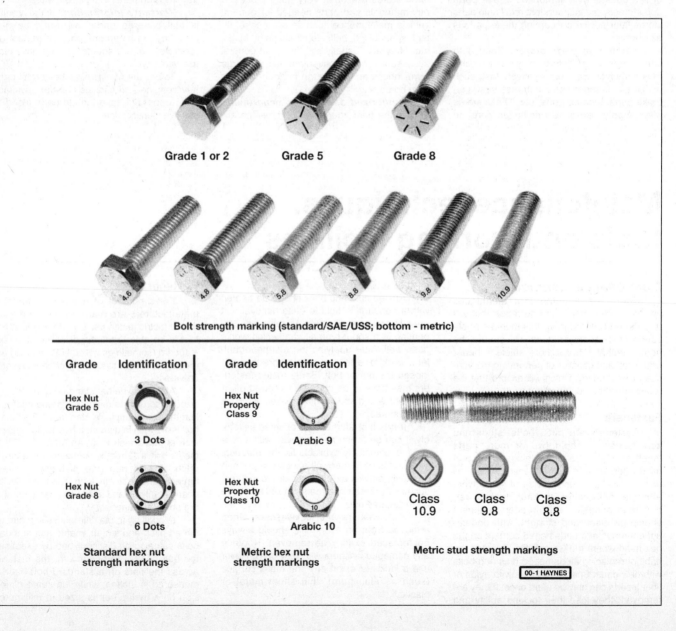

Grade 1 or 2   Grade 5   Grade 8

Bolt strength marking (standard/SAE/USS; bottom - metric)

Grade	Identification
Hex Nut Grade 5	3 Dots
Hex Nut Grade 8	6 Dots

Standard hex nut strength markings

Grade	Identification
Hex Nut Property Class 9	Arabic 9
Hex Nut Property Class 10	Arabic 10

Metric hex nut strength markings

Class 10.9   Class 9.8   Class 8.8

Metric stud strength markings

00-1 HAYNES

dations closely. For fasteners not assigned a specific torque, a general torque value chart is presented here as a guide. These torque values are for dry (unlubricated) fasteners threaded into steel or cast iron (not aluminum). As was previously mentioned, the size and grade of a fastener determine the amount of torque that can safely be applied to it. The figures listed here are approximate for Grade 2 and Grade 3 fasteners. Higher grades can tolerate higher torque values.

Fasteners laid out in a pattern, such as cylinder head bolts, oil pan bolts, differential cover bolts, etc., must be loosened or tightened in sequence to avoid warping the component. This sequence will normally be shown in the appropriate Chapter. If a specific pattern is not given, the following procedures can be used to prevent warping.

Initially, the bolts or nuts should be assembled finger-tight only. Next, they should be tightened one full turn each, in a criss-cross or diagonal pattern. After each one has been tightened one full turn, return to the first one and tighten them all one-half turn, following the same pattern. Finally, tighten each of them one-quarter turn at a time until each fastener has been tightened to the proper torque. To loosen and remove the fasteners, the procedure would be reversed.

Metric thread sizes	Ft-lbs	Nm
M-6	6 to 9	9 to 12
M-8	14 to 21	19 to 28
M-10	28 to 40	38 to 54
M-12	50 to 71	68 to 96
M-14	80 to 140	109 to 154

Pipe thread sizes		
1/8	5 to 8	7 to 10
1/4	12 to 18	17 to 24
3/8	22 to 33	30 to 44
1/2	25 to 35	34 to 47

U.S. thread sizes		
1/4 - 20	6 to 9	9 to 12
5/16 - 18	12 to 18	17 to 24
5/16 - 24	14 to 20	19 to 27
3/8 - 16	22 to 32	30 to 43
3/8 - 24	27 to 38	37 to 51
7/16 - 14	40 to 55	55 to 74
7/16 - 20	40 to 60	55 to 81
1/2 - 13	55 to 80	75 to 108

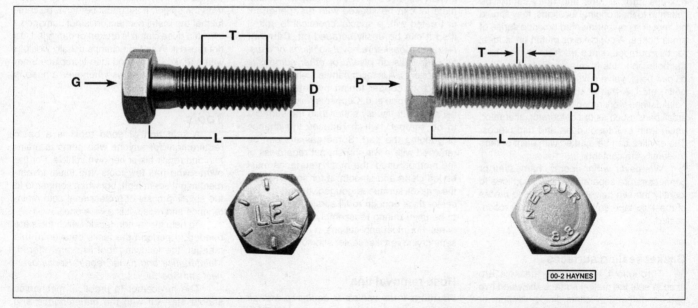

Standard (SAE and USS) bolt dimensions/grade marks

G   Grade marks (bolt strength)
L   Length (in inches)
T   Thread pitch (number of threads per inch)
D   Nominal diameter (in inches)

Metric bolt dimensions/grade marks

P   Property class (bolt strength)
L   Length (in millimeters)
T   Thread pitch (distance between threads in millimeters)
D   Diameter

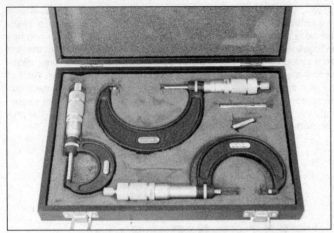

Micrometer set

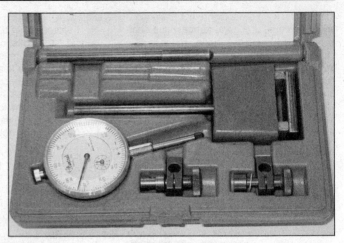

Dial indicator set

Component disassembly

Component disassembly should be done with care and purpose to help ensure that the parts go back together properly. Always keep track of the sequence in which parts are removed. Make note of special characteristics or marks on parts that can be installed more than one way, such as a grooved thrust washer on a shaft. It is a good idea to lay the disassembled parts out on a clean surface in the order that they were removed. It may also be helpful to make sketches or take instant photos of components before removal.

When removing fasteners from a component, keep track of their locations. Sometimes threading a bolt back in a part, or putting the washers and nut back on a stud, can prevent mix-ups later. If nuts and bolts cannot be returned to their original locations, they should be kept in a compartmented box or a series of small boxes. A cupcake or muffin tin is ideal for this purpose, since each cavity can hold the bolts and nuts from a particular area (i.e. oil pan bolts, valve cover bolts, engine mount bolts, etc.). A pan of this type is especially helpful when working on assemblies with very small parts, such as the carburetor, alternator, valve train or interior dash and trim pieces. The cavities can be marked with paint or tape to identify the contents.

Whenever wiring looms, harnesses or connectors are separated, it is a good idea to identify the two halves with numbered pieces of masking tape so they can be easily reconnected.

Gasket sealing surfaces

Throughout any vehicle, gaskets are used to seal the mating surfaces between two parts and keep lubricants, fluids, vacuum or pressure contained in an assembly.

Many times these gaskets are coated with a liquid or paste-type gasket sealing compound before assembly. Age, heat and pressure can sometimes cause the two parts to stick together so tightly that they are very difficult to separate. Often, the assembly can

be loosened by striking it with a soft-face hammer near the mating surfaces. A regular hammer can be used if a block of wood is placed between the hammer and the part. Do not hammer on cast parts or parts that could be easily damaged. With any particularly stubborn part, always recheck to make sure that every fastener has been removed.

Avoid using a screwdriver or bar to pry apart an assembly, as they can easily mar the gasket sealing surfaces of the parts, which must remain smooth. If prying is absolutely necessary, use an old broom handle, but keep in mind that extra clean up will be necessary if the wood splinters.

After the parts are separated, the old gasket must be carefully scraped off and the gasket surfaces cleaned. Stubborn gasket material can be soaked with rust penetrant or treated with a special chemical to soften it so it can be easily scraped off. **Caution:** *Never use gasket removal solutions or caustic chemicals on plastic or other composite components.* A scraper can be fashioned from a piece of copper tubing by flattening and sharpening one end. Copper is recommended because it is usually softer than the surfaces to be scraped, which reduces the chance of gouging the part. Some gaskets can be removed with a wire brush, but regardless of the method used, the mating surfaces must be left clean and smooth. If for some reason the gasket surface is gouged, then a gasket sealer thick enough to fill scratches will have to be used during reassembly of the components. For most applications, a non-drying (or semi-drying) gasket sealer should be used.

Hose removal tips

Warning: *If the vehicle is equipped with air conditioning, do not disconnect any of the A/C hoses without first having the system depressurized by a dealer service department or a service station.*

Hose removal precautions closely parallel gasket removal precautions. Avoid scratching or gouging the surface that the

hose mates against or the connection may leak. This is especially true for radiator hoses. Because of various chemical reactions, the rubber in hoses can bond itself to the metal spigot that the hose fits over. To remove a hose, first loosen the hose clamps that secure it to the spigot. Then, with slip-joint pliers, grab the hose at the clamp and rotate it around the spigot. Work it back and forth until it is completely free, then pull it off. Silicone or other lubricants will ease removal if they can be applied between the hose and the outside of the spigot. Apply the same lubricant to the inside of the hose and the outside of the spigot to simplify installation.

As a last resort (and if the hose is to be replaced with a new one anyway), the rubber can be slit with a knife and the hose peeled from the spigot. If this must be done, be careful that the metal connection is not damaged.

If a hose clamp is broken or damaged, do not reuse it. Wire-type clamps usually weaken with age, so it is a good idea to replace them with screw-type clamps whenever a hose is removed.

Tools

A selection of good tools is a basic requirement for anyone who plans to maintain and repair his or her own vehicle. For the owner who has few tools, the initial investment might seem high, but when compared to the spiraling costs of professional auto maintenance and repair, it is a wise one.

To help the owner decide which tools are needed to perform the tasks detailed in this manual, the following tool lists are offered: *Maintenance and minor repair, Repair/overhaul* and *Special.*

The newcomer to practical mechanics should start off with the *maintenance and minor repair* tool kit, which is adequate for the simpler jobs performed on a vehicle. Then, as confidence and experience grow, the owner can tackle more difficult tasks, buying additional tools as they are needed. Eventually the basic kit will be expanded into the *repair and overhaul* tool set. Over a period of time, the

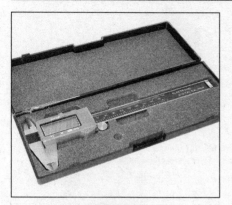

Dial caliper

Hand-operated vacuum pump

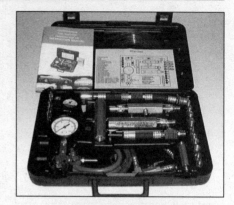

Fuel pressure gauge set

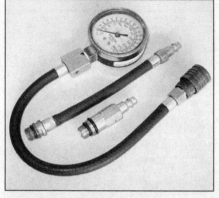

Compression gauge with spark plug hole adapter

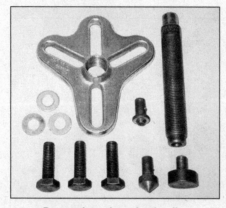

Damper/steering wheel puller

General purpose puller

Hydraulic lifter removal tool

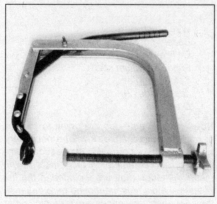

Valve spring compressor

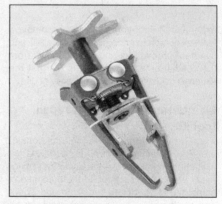

Valve spring compressor

Ridge reamer

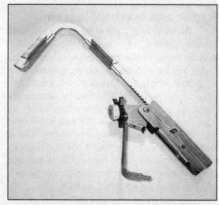

Piston ring groove cleaning tool

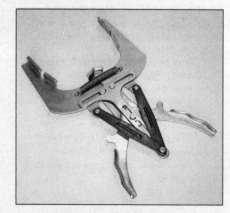

Ring removal/installation tool

Ring compressor

Cylinder hone

Brake hold-down spring tool

Torque angle gauge

Clutch plate alignment tool

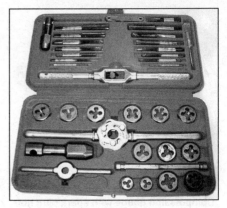

Tap and die set

experienced do-it-yourselfer will assemble a tool set complete enough for most repair and overhaul procedures and will add tools from the special category when it is felt that the expense is justified by the frequency of use.

Maintenance and minor repair tool kit

The tools in this list should be considered the minimum required for performance of routine maintenance, servicing and minor repair work. We recommend the purchase of combination wrenches (box-end and open-end combined in one wrench). While more expensive than open end wrenches, they offer the advantages of both types of wrench.

> *Combination wrench set (1/4-inch to 1 inch or 6 mm to 19 mm)*
> *Adjustable wrench, 8 inch*
> *Spark plug wrench with rubber insert*
> *Spark plug gap adjusting tool*
> *Feeler gauge set*
> *Brake bleeder wrench*
> *Standard screwdriver (5/16-inch x 6 inch)*
> *Phillips screwdriver (No. 2 x 6 inch)*
> *Combination pliers - 6 inch*
> *Hacksaw and assortment of blades*
> *Tire pressure gauge*
> *Grease gun*
> *Oil can*
> *Fine emery cloth*

> *Wire brush*
> *Battery post and cable cleaning tool*
> *Oil filter wrench*
> *Funnel (medium size)*
> *Safety goggles*
> *Jackstands (2)*
> *Drain pan*

Note: *If basic tune-ups are going to be part of routine maintenance, it will be necessary to purchase a good quality stroboscopic timing light and combination tachometer/dwell meter. Although they are included in the list of special tools, it is mentioned here because they are absolutely necessary for tuning most vehicles properly.*

Repair and overhaul tool set

These tools are essential for anyone who plans to perform major repairs and are in addition to those in the maintenance and minor repair tool kit. Included is a comprehensive set of sockets which, though expensive, are invaluable because of their versatility, especially when various extensions and drives are available. We recommend the 1/2-inch drive over the 3/8-inch drive. Although the larger drive is bulky and more expensive, it has the capacity of accepting a very wide range of large sockets. Ideally, however, the mechanic should have a 3/8-inch drive set and a 1/2-inch drive set.

> *Socket set(s)*
> *Reversible ratchet*

> *Extension - 10 inch*
> *Universal joint*
> *Torque wrench (same size drive as sockets)*
> *Ball peen hammer - 8 ounce*
> *Soft-face hammer (plastic/rubber)*
> *Standard screwdriver (1/4-inch x 6 inch)*
> *Standard screwdriver (stubby - 5/16-inch)*
> *Phillips screwdriver (No. 3 x 8 inch)*
> *Phillips screwdriver (stubby - No. 2)*
> *Pliers - vise grip*
> *Pliers - lineman's*
> *Pliers - needle nose*
> *Pliers - snap-ring (internal and external)*
> *Cold chisel - 1/2-inch*
> *Scribe*
> *Scraper (made from flattened copper tubing)*
> *Centerpunch*
> *Pin punches (1/16, 1/8, 3/16-inch)*
> *Steel rule/straightedge - 12 inch*
> *Allen wrench set (1/8 to 3/8-inch or 4 mm to 10 mm)*
> *A selection of files*
> *Wire brush (large)*
> *Jackstands (second set)*
> *Jack (scissor or hydraulic type)*

Note: *Another tool which is often useful is an electric drill with a chuck capacity of 3/8-inch and a set of good quality drill bits.*

Special tools

The tools in this list include those which are not used regularly, are expensive to buy, or which need to be used in accordance with their manufacturer's instructions. Unless these tools will be used frequently, it is not very economical to purchase many of them. A consideration would be to split the cost and use between yourself and a friend or friends. In addition, most of these tools can be obtained from a tool rental shop on a temporary basis.

This list primarily contains only those tools and instruments widely available to the public, and not those special tools produced by the vehicle manufacturer for distribution to dealer service departments. Occasionally, references to the manufacturer's special tools are included in the text of this manual. Generally, an alternative method of doing the job without the special tool is offered. However, sometimes there is no alternative to their use. Where this is the case, and the tool cannot be purchased or borrowed, the work should be turned over to the dealer service department or an automotive repair shop.

Valve spring compressor
Piston ring groove cleaning tool
Piston ring compressor
Piston ring installation tool
Cylinder compression gauge
Cylinder ridge reamer
Cylinder surfacing hone
Cylinder bore gauge
Micrometers and/or dial calipers
Hydraulic lifter removal tool
Balljoint separator
Universal-type puller
Impact screwdriver
Dial indicator set
Stroboscopic timing light (inductive pick-up)
Hand operated vacuum/pressure pump
Tachometer/dwell meter
Universal electrical multimeter
Cable hoist
Brake spring removal and installation tools
Floor jack

Buying tools

For the do-it-yourselfer who is just starting to get involved in vehicle maintenance and repair, there are a number of options available when purchasing tools. If maintenance and minor repair is the extent of the work to be done, the purchase of individual tools is satisfactory. If, on the other hand, extensive work is planned, it would be a good idea to purchase a modest tool set from one of the large retail chain stores. A set can usually be bought at a substantial savings over the individual tool prices, and they often come with a tool box. As additional tools are needed, add-on sets, individual tools and a larger tool box can be purchased to expand the tool selection. Building a tool set gradually allows the cost of the

tools to be spread over a longer period of time and gives the mechanic the freedom to choose only those tools that will actually be used.

Tool stores will often be the only source of some of the special tools that are needed, but regardless of where tools are bought, try to avoid cheap ones, especially when buying screwdrivers and sockets, because they won't last very long. The expense involved in replacing cheap tools will eventually be greater than the initial cost of quality tools.

Care and maintenance of tools

Good tools are expensive, so it makes sense to treat them with respect. Keep them clean and in usable condition and store them properly when not in use. Always wipe off any dirt, grease or metal chips before putting them away. Never leave tools lying around in the work area. Upon completion of a job, always check closely under the hood for tools that may have been left there so they won't get lost during a test drive.

Some tools, such as screwdrivers, pliers, wrenches and sockets, can be hung on a panel mounted on the garage or workshop wall, while others should be kept in a tool box or tray. Measuring instruments, gauges, meters, etc. must be carefully stored where they cannot be damaged by weather or impact from other tools.

When tools are used with care and stored properly, they will last a very long time. Even with the best of care, though, tools will wear out if used frequently. When a tool is damaged or worn out, replace it. Subsequent jobs will be safer and more enjoyable if you do.

How to repair damaged threads

Sometimes, the internal threads of a nut or bolt hole can become stripped, usually from overtightening. Stripping threads is an all-too-common occurrence, especially when working with aluminum parts, because aluminum is so soft that it easily strips out.

Usually, external or internal threads are only partially stripped. After they've been cleaned up with a tap or die, they'll still work. Sometimes, however, threads are badly damaged. When this happens, you've got three choices:

1) Drill and tap the hole to the next suitable oversize and install a larger diameter bolt, screw or stud.
2) Drill and tap the hole to accept a threaded plug, then drill and tap the plug to the original screw size. You can also buy a plug already threaded to the original size. Then you simply drill a hole to the specified size, then run the threaded plug into the hole with a bolt and jam nut. Once the plug is fully seated, remove the jam nut and bolt.

3) The third method uses a patented thread repair kit like Heli-Coil or Slimsert. These easy-to-use kits are designed to repair damaged threads in straight-through holes and blind holes. Both are available as kits which can handle a variety of sizes and thread patterns. Drill the hole, then tap it with the special included tap. Install the Heli-Coil and the hole is back to its original diameter and thread pitch.

Regardless of which method you use, be sure to proceed calmly and carefully. A little impatience or carelessness during one of these relatively simple procedures can ruin your whole day's work and cost you a bundle if you wreck an expensive part.

Working facilities

Not to be overlooked when discussing tools is the workshop. If anything more than routine maintenance is to be carried out, some sort of suitable work area is essential.

It is understood, and appreciated, that many home mechanics do not have a good workshop or garage available, and end up removing an engine or doing major repairs outside. It is recommended, however, that the overhaul or repair be completed under the cover of a roof.

A clean, flat workbench or table of comfortable working height is an absolute necessity. The workbench should be equipped with a vise that has a jaw opening of at least four inches.

As mentioned previously, some clean, dry storage space is also required for tools, as well as the lubricants, fluids, cleaning solvents, etc. which soon become necessary.

Sometimes waste oil and fluids, drained from the engine or cooling system during normal maintenance or repairs, present a disposal problem. To avoid pouring them on the ground or into a sewage system, pour the used fluids into large containers, seal them with caps and take them to an authorized disposal site or recycling center. Plastic jugs, such as old antifreeze containers, are ideal for this purpose.

Always keep a supply of old newspapers and clean rags available. Old towels are excellent for mopping up spills. Many mechanics use rolls of paper towels for most work because they are readily available and disposable. To help keep the area under the vehicle clean, a large cardboard box can be cut open and flattened to protect the garage or shop floor.

Whenever working over a painted surface, such as when leaning over a fender to service something under the hood, always cover it with an old blanket or bedspread to protect the finish. Vinyl covered pads, made especially for this purpose, are available at auto parts stores.

Booster battery (jump) starting

1   Observe these precautions when using a booster battery to start a vehicle:

 a) *Before connecting the booster battery, make sure the ignition switch is in the Off position.*
 b) *Turn off the lights, heater and other electrical loads.*
 c) *Your eyes should be shielded. Safety goggles are a good idea.*
 d) *Make sure the booster battery is the same voltage as the dead one in the vehicle.*
 e) *The two vehicles MUST NOT TOUCH each other!*
 f) *Make sure the transaxle is in Neutral (manual) or Park (automatic).*
 g) *If the booster battery is not a maintenance-free type, remove the vent caps and lay a cloth over the vent holes.*

2   Connect the red jumper cable to the positive (+) terminals of each battery (see illustration).
3   Connect one end of the black jumper cable to the negative (-) terminal of the booster battery. The other end of this cable should be connected to a good ground on the vehicle to be started, such as a bolt or bracket on the body.

4   Start the engine using the booster battery, then, with the engine running at idle speed, disconnect the jumper cables in the reverse order of connection. The vehicle with the dead battery may have to be driven for 20 minutes or more to sufficiently recharge the battery for independent starting.

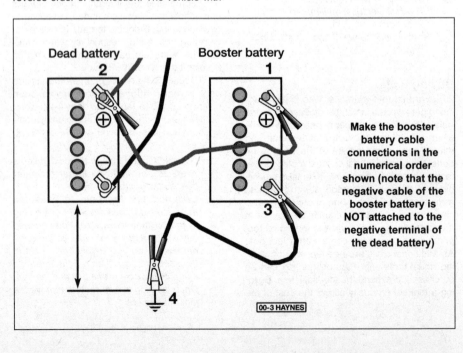

Make the booster battery cable connections in the numerical order shown (note that the negative cable of the booster battery is NOT attached to the negative terminal of the dead battery)

Jacking and towing

Jacking

Warning: *The jack supplied with the vehicle should only be used for changing a tire or placing jackstands under the frame. Never work under the vehicle or start the engine while this jack is being used as the only means of support.*

1   The vehicle should be on level ground. Place the shift lever in Park, if you have an automatic, or Reverse if you have a manual transmission. Block the wheel diagonally opposite the wheel being changed. Set the parking brake.

2   Remove the spare tire and jack from stowage. Remove the wheel cover and trim ring (if so equipped) with the tapered end of the lug nut wrench by inserting and twisting the handle and then prying against the back of the wheel cover. Loosen the wheel lug nuts about 1/4-to-1/2 turn each.

3   Place the jack under the vehicle in the indicated position (see illustrations). Turn the jack handle clockwise until the tire clears the ground. Remove the lug nuts and pull the wheel off. Replace it with the spare.

4   Install the lug nuts with the beveled edges facing in. Tighten them snugly. Don't attempt to tighten them completely until the vehicle is lowered or it could slip off the jack. Turn the jack handle counterclockwise to lower the vehicle. Remove the jack and tighten the lug nuts in a diagonal pattern.

5   Install the cover and be sure it's snapped into place all the way around.

6   Stow the tire, jack and wrench. Unblock the wheels.

Towing

Emergency towing

7   The preferred method to tow these vehicles is with all four wheels off the ground on a flat-bed car hauler. However, these vehicles (both 2WD and 4WD models) can be towed from the front, up to 50 miles, provided the transmission is placed in Neutral, the parking brake is released, the steering is unlocked, and speeds do not exceed 35 mph.

Recreational towing

Two-wheel drive models

8   Two-wheel drive models should not be towed with any wheels on the ground - damage to the vehicle or transmission can occur.

Four-wheel drive models

9   Four-wheel drive models can be towed with all four wheels on the ground by placing the transfer case in Neutral and engaging the "four-wheel-down" towing feature:

Caution: *If the "four-wheel-down" towing feature is not engaged before towing the vehicle, drivetrain components will be damaged.*

a)   *Turn the ignition key to the On position (don't start the engine). On models with (Intelligent Access (keyless ignition), push the Start/Stop button one time (don't depress the brake pedal while doing this).*

b)   *Depress the brake pedal and turn the 4WD switch to the 2H position.*

c)   *Place the shift lever in the Neutral position.*

d)   *Turn the 4WD switch from 2H to 4L and back to 2H. Do this five times within seven seconds.*

Note: *The information display should read "NEUTRAL TOW LEAVE IN N" or "NEUTRAL TOW ENABLED LEAVE TRANSMISSION IN NEUTRAL." If it doesn't, repeat the "four-wheel-down" towing engagement sequence again.*

10   Models with an ignition key: Turn the key toward the Off position as far as it will go (it won't go all the way because the shift lever is in the Neutral position. The key must be left in the ignition.

11   Models with Intelligent Access (keyless ignition): Push the Start/Stop button one time (don't depress the brake pedal). The keys can be removed from the vehicle, and the vehicle can be locked and unlocked.

Warning: *Do not disconnect the battery while the vehicle is connected to the tow vehicle and the "four-wheel-down" towing feature is engaged.*

12   To return the transfer case to the 2H position and place the vehicle into service, perform the following steps:

a)   *With the vehicle still connected to the tow vehicle, Turn the ignition key to the On position (don't start the engine). On models with Intelligent Access (keyless ignition), push the Start/Stop button once (don't depress the brake pedal).*

b)   *Now depress the brake pedal and shift the transmission out of Neutral to any other range.*

c)   *Release the brake pedal.*

d)   *The information display should now read "NEUTRAL TOW DISABLED." If not, repeat the sequence.*

13   Engage the parking brake and disconnect the vehicle from the tow vehicle.

14   Release the parking brake. Start the engine and shift to the Drive (D) position to verify that the transfer case is not still in the Neutral position.

Front jacking location

Rear jacking location

Automotive chemicals and lubricants

A number of automotive chemicals and lubricants are available for use during vehicle maintenance and repair. They include a wide variety of products ranging from cleaning solvents and degreasers to lubricants and protective sprays for rubber, plastic and vinyl.

Cleaners

Carburetor cleaner and choke cleaner is a strong solvent for gum, varnish and carbon. Most carburetor cleaners leave a dry-type lubricant film which will not harden or gum up. Because of this film it is not recommended for use on electrical components.

Brake system cleaner is used to remove brake dust, grease and brake fluid from the brake system, where clean surfaces are absolutely necessary. It leaves no residue and often eliminates brake squeal caused by contaminants.

Electrical cleaner removes oxidation, corrosion and carbon deposits from electrical contacts, restoring full current flow. It can also be used to clean spark plugs, carburetor jets, voltage regulators and other parts where an oil-free surface is desired.

Demoisturants remove water and moisture from electrical components such as alternators, voltage regulators, electrical connectors and fuse blocks. They are non-conductive and non-corrosive.

Degreasers are heavy-duty solvents used to remove grease from the outside of the engine and from chassis components. They can be sprayed or brushed on and, depending on the type, are rinsed off either with water or solvent.

Lubricants

Motor oil is the lubricant formulated for use in engines. It normally contains a wide variety of additives to prevent corrosion and reduce foaming and wear. Motor oil comes in various weights (viscosity ratings) from 0 to 50. The recommended weight of the oil depends on the season, temperature and the demands on the engine. Light oil is used in cold climates and under light load conditions. Heavy oil is used in hot climates and where high loads are encountered. Multi-viscosity oils are designed to have characteristics of both light and heavy oils and are available in a number of weights from 0W-20 to 20W-50.

Gear oil is designed to be used in differentials, manual transmissions and other areas where high-temperature lubrication is required.

Chassis and wheel bearing grease is a heavy grease used where increased loads and friction are encountered, such as for wheel bearings, balljoints, tie-rod ends and universal joints.

High-temperature wheel bearing grease is designed to withstand the extreme temperatures encountered by wheel bearings in disc brake equipped vehicles. It usually contains molybdenum disulfide (moly), which is a dry-type lubricant.

White grease is a heavy grease for metal-to-metal applications where water is a problem. White grease stays soft under both low and high temperatures (usually from -100 to +190-degrees F), and will not wash off or dilute in the presence of water.

Assembly lube is a special extreme pressure lubricant, usually containing moly, used to lubricate high-load parts (such as main and rod bearings and cam lobes) for initial start-up of a new engine. The assembly lube lubricates the parts without being squeezed out or washed away until the engine oiling system begins to function.

Silicone lubricants are used to protect rubber, plastic, vinyl and nylon parts.

Graphite lubricants are used where oils cannot be used due to contamination problems, such as in locks. The dry graphite will lubricate metal parts while remaining uncontaminated by dirt, water, oil or acids. It is electrically conductive and will not foul electrical contacts in locks such as the ignition switch.

Moly penetrants loosen and lubricate frozen, rusted and corroded fasteners and prevent future rusting or freezing.

Heat-sink grease is a special electrically non-conductive grease that is used for mounting electronic ignition modules where it is essential that heat is transferred away from the module.

Sealants

RTV sealant is one of the most widely used gasket compounds. Made from silicone, RTV is air curing, it seals, bonds, waterproofs, fills surface irregularities, remains flexible, doesn't shrink, is relatively easy to remove, and is used as a supplementary sealer with almost all low and medium temperature gaskets.

Anaerobic sealant is much like RTV in that it can be used either to seal gaskets or to form gaskets by itself. It remains flexible, is solvent resistant and fills surface imperfections. The difference between an anaerobic sealant and an RTV-type sealant is in the curing. RTV cures when exposed to air, while an anaerobic sealant cures only in the absence of air. This means that an anaerobic sealant cures only after the assembly of parts, sealing them together.

Thread and pipe sealant is used for sealing hydraulic and pneumatic fittings and vacuum lines. It is usually made from a Teflon compound, and comes in a spray, a paint-on liquid and as a wrap-around tape.

Chemicals

Anti-seize compound prevents seiz-ing, galling, cold welding, rust and corrosion in fasteners. High-temperature ant-seize, usually made with copper and graphite lubricants, is used for exhaust system and exhaust manifold bolts.

Anaerobic locking compounds are used to keep fasteners from vibrating or working loose and cure only after installation, in the absence of air. Medium strength locking compound is used for small nuts, bolts and screws that may be removed later. High-strength locking compound is for large nuts, bolts and studs which aren't removed on a regular basis.

Oil additives range from viscosity index improvers to chemical treatments that claim to reduce internal engine friction. It should be noted that most oil manufacturers caution against using additives with their oils.

Gas additives perform several functions, depending on their chemical makeup. They usually contain solvents that help dissolve gum and varnish that build up on carburetor, fuel injection and intake parts. They also serve to break down carbon deposits that form on the inside surfaces of the combustion chambers. Some additives contain upper cylinder lubricants for valves and piston rings, and others contain chemicals to remove condensation from the gas tank.

Miscellaneous

Brake fluid is specially formulated hydraulic fluid that can withstand the heat and pressure encountered in brake systems. Care must be taken so this fluid does not come in contact with painted surfaces or plastics. An opened container should always be resealed to prevent contamination by water or dirt.

Weatherstrip adhesive is used to bond weatherstripping around doors, windows and trunk lids. It is sometimes used to attach trim pieces.

Undercoating is a petroleum-based, tar-like substance that is designed to protect metal surfaces on the underside of the vehicle from corrosion. It also acts as a sound-deadening agent by insulating the bottom of the vehicle.

Waxes and polishes are used to help protect painted and plated surfaces from the weather. Different types of paint may require the use of different types of wax and polish. Some polishes utilize a chemical or abrasive cleaner to help remove the top layer of oxidized (dull) paint on older vehicles. In recent years many non-wax polishes that contain a wide variety of chemicals such as polymers and silicones have been introduced. These non-wax polishes are usually easier to apply and last longer than conventional waxes and polishes.

Conversion factors

Length (distance)

Inches (in)	X	25.4	= Millimeters (mm)	X 0.0394	= Inches (in)
Feet (ft)	X	0.305	= Meters (m)	X 3.281	= Feet (ft)
Miles	X	1.609	= Kilometers (km)	X 0.621	= Miles

Volume (capacity)

Cubic inches (cu in; in³)	X	16.387	= Cubic centimeters (cc; cm³)	X 0.061	= Cubic inches (cu in; in³)
Imperial pints (Imp pt)	X	0.568	= Liters (l)	X 1.76	= Imperial pints (Imp pt)
Imperial quarts (Imp qt)	X	1.137	= Liters (l)	X 0.88	= Imperial quarts (Imp qt)
Imperial quarts (Imp qt)	X	1.201	= US quarts (US qt)	X 0.833	= Imperial quarts (Imp qt)
US quarts (US qt)	X	0.946	= Liters (l)	X 1.057	= US quarts (US qt)
Imperial gallons (Imp gal)	X	4.546	= Liters (l)	X 0.22	= Imperial gallons (Imp gal)
Imperial gallons (Imp gal)	X	1.201	= US gallons (US gal)	X 0.833	= Imperial gallons (Imp gal)
US gallons (US gal)	X	3.785	= Liters (l)	X 0.264	= US gallons (US gal)

Mass (weight)

Ounces (oz)	X	28.35	= Grams (g)	X 0.035	= Ounces (oz)
Pounds (lb)	X	0.454	= Kilograms (kg)	X 2.205	= Pounds (lb)

Force

Ounces-force (ozf; oz)	X	0.278	= Newtons (N)	X 3.6	= Ounces-force (ozf; oz)
Pounds-force (lbf; lb)	X	4.448	= Newtons (N)	X 0.225	= Pounds-force (lbf; lb)
Newtons (N)	X	0.1	= Kilograms-force (kgf; kg)	X 9.81	= Newtons (N)

Pressure

Pounds-force per square inch (psi; lbf/in²; lb/in²)	X	0.070	= Kilograms-force per square centimeter (kgf/cm²; kg/cm²)	X 14.223	= Pounds-force per square inch (psi; lbf/in²; lb/in²)
Pounds-force per square inch (psi; lbf/in²; lb/in²)	X	0.068	= Atmospheres (atm)	X 14.696	= Pounds-force per square inch (psi; lbf/in²; lb/in²)
Pounds-force per square inch (psi; lbf/in²; lb/in²)	X	0.069	= Bars	X 14.5	= Pounds-force per square inch (psi; lbf/in²; lb/in²)
Pounds-force per square inch (psi; lbf/in²; lb/in²)	X	6.895	= Kilopascals (kPa)	X 0.145	= Pounds-force per square inch (psi; lbf/in²; lb/in²)
Kilopascals (kPa)	X	0.01	= Kilograms-force per square centimeter (kgf/cm²; kg/cm²)	X 98.1	= Kilopascals (kPa)

Torque (moment of force)

Pounds-force inches (lbf in; lb in)	X	1.152	= Kilograms-force centimeter (kgf cm; kg cm)	X 0.868	= Pounds-force inches (lbf in; lb in)
Pounds-force inches (lbf in; lb in)	X	0.113	= Newton meters (Nm)	X 8.85	= Pounds-force inches (lbf in; lb in)
Pounds-force inches (lbf in; lb in)	X	0.083	= Pounds-force feet (lbf ft; lb ft)	X 12	= Pounds-force inches (lbf in; lb in)
Pounds-force feet (lbf ft; lb ft)	X	0.138	= Kilograms-force meters (kgf m; kg m)	X 7.233	= Pounds-force feet (lbf ft; lb ft)
Pounds-force feet (lbf ft; lb ft)	X	1.356	= Newton meters (Nm)	X 0.738	= Pounds-force feet (lbf ft; lb ft)
Newton meters (Nm)	X	0.102	= Kilograms-force meters (kgf m; kg m)	X 9.804	= Newton meters (Nm)

Vacuum

Inches mercury (in. Hg)	X	3.377	= Kilopascals (kPa)	X 0.2961	= Inches mercury
Inches mercury (in. Hg)	X	25.4	= Millimeters mercury (mm Hg)	X 0.0394	= Inches mercury

Power

Horsepower (hp)	X	745.7	= Watts (W)	X 0.0013	= Horsepower (hp)

Velocity (speed)

Miles per hour (miles/hr; mph)	X	1.609	= Kilometers per hour (km/hr; kph)	X 0.621	= Miles per hour (miles/hr; mph)

Fuel consumption*

Miles per gallon, Imperial (mpg)	X	0.354	= Kilometers per liter (km/l)	X 2.825	= Miles per gallon, Imperial (mpg)
Miles per gallon, US (mpg)	X	0.425	= Kilometers per liter (km/l)	X 2.352	= Miles per gallon, US (mpg)

Temperature

Degrees Fahrenheit = (°C x 1.8) + 32

Degrees Celsius (Degrees Centigrade; °C) = (°F - 32) x 0.56

*It is common practice to convert from miles per gallon (mpg) to liters/100 kilometers (l/100km), where mpg (Imperial) x l/100 km = 282 and mpg (US) x l/100 km = 235

DECIMALS to MILLIMETERS

Decimal	mm
0.001	0.0254
0.002	0.0508
0.003	0.0762
0.004	0.1016
0.005	0.1270
0.006	0.1524
0.007	0.1778
0.008	0.2032
0.009	0.2286
0.010	0.2540
0.020	0.5080
0.030	0.7620
0.040	1.0160
0.050	1.2700
0.060	1.5240
0.070	1.7780
0.080	2.0320
0.090	2.2860
0.100	2.5400
0.110	2.7940
0.120	3.0480
0.130	3.3020
0.140	3.5560
0.150	3.8100
0.160	4.0640
0.170	4.3180
0.180	4.5720
0.190	4.8260
0.200	5.0800
0.210	5.3340
0.220	5.5880
0.230	5.8420
0.240	6.0960
0.250	6.3500
0.260	6.6040
0.270	6.8580
0.280	7.1120
0.290	7.3660
0.300	7.6200
0.310	7.8740
0.320	8.1280
0.330	8.3820
0.340	8.6360
0.350	8.8900
0.360	9.1440
0.370	9.3980
0.380	9.6520
0.390	9.9060
0.400	10.1600
0.410	10.4140
0.420	10.6680
0.430	10.9220
0.440	11.1760
0.450	11.4300
0.460	11.6840
0.470	11.9380
0.480	12.1920
0.490	12.4460

Decimal	mm
0.500	12.7000
0.510	12.9540
0.520	13.2080
0.530	13.4620
0.540	13.7160
0.550	13.9700
0.560	14.2240
0.570	14.4780
0.580	14.7320
0.590	14.9860
0.600	15.2400
0.610	15.4940
0.620	15.7480
0.630	16.0020
0.640	16.2560
0.650	16.5100
0.660	16.7640
0.670	17.0180
0.680	17.2720
0.690	17.5260
0.700	17.7800
0.710	18.0340
0.720	18.2880
0.730	18.5420
0.740	18.7960
0.750	19.0500
0.760	19.3040
0.770	19.5580
0.780	19.8120
0.790	20.0660
0.800	20.3200
0.810	20.5740
0.820	20.8280
0.830	21.0820
0.840	21.3360
0.850	21.5900
0.860	21.8440
0.870	22.0980
0.880	22.3520
0.890	22.6060
0.900	22.8600
0.910	23.1140
0.920	23.3680
0.930	23.6220
0.940	23.8760
0.950	24.1300
0.960	24.3840
0.970	24.6380
0.980	24.8920
0.990	25.1460
1.000	25.4000

FRACTIONS to DECIMALS to MILLIMETERS

Fraction	Decimal	mm	Fraction	Decimal	mm
1/64	0.0156	0.3969	33/64	0.5156	13.0969
1/32	0.0312	0.7938	17/32	0.5312	13.4938
3/64	0.0469	1.1906	35/64	0.5469	13.8906
1/16	0.0625	1.5875	9/16	0.5625	14.2875
5/64	0.0781	1.9844	37/64	0.5781	14.6844
3/32	0.0938	2.3812	19/32	0.5938	15.0812
7/64	0.1094	2.7781	39/64	0.6094	15.4781
1/8	0.1250	3.1750	5/8	0.6250	15.8750
9/64	0.1406	3.5719	41/64	0.6406	16.2719
5/32	0.1562	3.9688	21/32	0.6562	16.6688
11/64	0.1719	4.3656	43/64	0.6719	17.0656
3/16	0.1875	4.7625	11/16	0.6875	17.4625
13/64	0.2031	5.1594	45/64	0.7031	17.8594
7/32	0.2188	5.5562	23/32	0.7188	18.2562
15/64	0.2344	5.9531	47/64	0.7344	18.6531
1/4	0.2500	6.3500	3/4	0.7500	19.0500
17/64	0.2656	6.7469	49/64	0.7656	19.4469
9/32	0.2812	7.1438	25/32	0.7812	19.8438
19/64	0.2969	7.5406	51/64	0.7969	20.2406
5/16	0.3125	7.9375	13/16	0.8125	20.6375
21/64	0.3281	8.3344	53/64	0.8281	21.0344
11/32	0.3438	8.7312	27/32	0.8438	21.4312
23/64	0.3594	9.1281	55/64	0.8594	21.8281
3/8	0.3750	9.5250	7/8	0.8750	22.2250
25/64	0.3906	9.9219	57/64	0.8906	22.6219
13/32	0.4062	10.3188	29/32	0.9062	23.0188
27/64	0.4219	10.7156	59/64	0.9219	23.4156
7/16	0.4375	11.1125	15/16	0.9375	23.8125
29/64	0.4531	11.5094	61/64	0.9531	24.2094
15/32	0.4688	11.9062	31/32	0.9688	24.6062
31/64	0.4844	12.3031	63/64	0.9844	25.0031
1/2	0.5000	12.7000	1	1.0000	25.4000

Safety first!

Regardless of how enthusiastic you may be about getting on with the job at hand, take the time to ensure that your safety is not jeopardized. A moment's lack of attention can result in an accident, as can failure to observe certain simple safety precautions. The possibility of an accident will always exist, and the following points should not be considered a comprehensive list of all dangers. Rather, they are intended to make you aware of the risks and to encourage a safety conscious approach to all work you carry out on your vehicle.

Essential DOs and DON'Ts

DON'T rely on a jack when working under the vehicle. Always use approved jackstands to support the weight of the vehicle and place them under the recommended lift or support points.

DON'T attempt to loosen extremely tight fasteners (i.e. wheel lug nuts) while the vehicle is on a jack - it may fall.

DON'T start the engine without first making sure that the transmission is in Neutral (or Park where applicable) and the parking brake is set.

DON'T remove the radiator cap from a hot cooling system - let it cool or cover it with a cloth and release the pressure gradually.

DON'T attempt to drain the engine oil until you are sure it has cooled to the point that it will not burn you.

DON'T touch any part of the engine or exhaust system until it has cooled sufficiently to avoid burns.

DON'T siphon toxic liquids such as gasoline, antifreeze and brake fluid by mouth, or allow them to remain on your skin.

DON'T inhale brake lining dust - it is potentially hazardous (see *Asbestos* below).

DON'T allow spilled oil or grease to remain on the floor - wipe it up before someone slips on it.

DON'T use loose fitting wrenches or other tools which may slip and cause injury.

DON'T push on wrenches when loosening or tightening nuts or bolts. Always try to pull the wrench toward you. If the situation calls for pushing the wrench away, push with an open hand to avoid scraped knuckles if the wrench should slip.

DON'T attempt to lift a heavy component alone - get someone to help you.

DON'T rush or take unsafe shortcuts to finish a job.

DON'T allow children or animals in or around the vehicle while you are working on it.

DO wear eye protection when using power tools such as a drill, sander, bench grinder, etc. and when working under a vehicle.

DO keep loose clothing and long hair well out of the way of moving parts.

DO make sure that any hoist used has a safe working load rating adequate for the job.

DO get someone to check on you periodically when working alone on a vehicle.

DO carry out work in a logical sequence and make sure that everything is correctly assembled and tightened.

DO keep chemicals and fluids tightly capped and out of the reach of children and pets.

DO remember that your vehicle's safety affects that of yourself and others. If in doubt on any point, get professional advice.

Steering, suspension and brakes

These systems are essential to driving safety, so make sure you have a qualified shop or individual check your work. Also, compressed suspension springs can cause injury if released suddenly - be sure to use a spring compressor.

Airbags

Airbags are explosive devices that can **CAUSE** injury if they deploy while you're working on the vehicle. Follow the manufacturer's instructions to disable the airbag whenever you're working in the vicinity of airbag components.

Asbestos

Certain friction, insulating, sealing, and other products - such as brake linings, brake bands, clutch linings, torque converters, gaskets, etc. - may contain asbestos or other hazardous friction material. Extreme care must be taken to avoid inhalation of dust from such products, since it is hazardous to health. If in doubt, assume that they do contain asbestos.

Fire

Remember at all times that gasoline is highly flammable. Never smoke or have any kind of open flame around when working on a vehicle. But the risk does not end there. A spark caused by an electrical short circuit, by two metal surfaces contacting each other, or even by static electricity built up in your body under certain conditions, can ignite gasoline vapors, which in a confined space are highly explosive. Do not, under any circumstances, use gasoline for cleaning parts. Use an approved safety solvent.

Always disconnect the battery ground (-) cable at the battery before working on any part of the fuel system or electrical system. Never risk spilling fuel on a hot engine or exhaust component. It is strongly recommended that a fire extinguisher suitable for use on fuel and electrical fires be kept handy in the garage or workshop at all times. Never try to extinguish a fuel or electrical fire with water.

Fumes

Certain fumes are highly toxic and can quickly cause unconsciousness and even death if inhaled to any extent. Gasoline vapor falls into this category, as do the vapors from some cleaning solvents. Any draining or pouring of such volatile fluids should be done in a well ventilated area.

When using cleaning fluids and solvents, read the instructions on the container carefully. Never use materials from unmarked containers.

Never run the engine in an enclosed space, such as a garage. Exhaust fumes contain carbon monoxide, which is extremely poisonous. If you need to run the engine, always do so in the open air, or at least have the rear of the vehicle outside the work area.

The battery

Never create a spark or allow a bare light bulb near a battery. They normally give off a certain amount of hydrogen gas, which is highly explosive.

Always disconnect the battery ground (-) cable at the battery before working on the fuel or electrical systems.

If possible, loosen the filler caps or cover when charging the battery from an external source (this does not apply to sealed or maintenance-free batteries). Do not charge at an excessive rate or the battery may burst.

Take care when adding water to a non maintenance-free battery and when carrying a battery. The electrolyte, even when diluted, is very corrosive and should not be allowed to contact clothing or skin.

Always wear eye protection when cleaning the battery to prevent the caustic deposits from entering your eyes.

Household current

When using an electric power tool, inspection light, etc., which operates on household current, always make sure that the tool is correctly connected to its plug and that, where necessary, it is properly grounded. Do not use such items in damp conditions and, again, do not create a spark or apply excessive heat in the vicinity of fuel or fuel vapor.

Secondary ignition system voltage

A severe electric shock can result from touching certain parts of the ignition system (such as the spark plug wires) when the engine is running or being cranked, particularly if components are damp or the insulation is defective. In the case of an electronic ignition system, the secondary system voltage is much higher and could prove fatal.

Hydrofluoric acid

This extremely corrosive acid is formed when certain types of synthetic rubber, found in some O-rings, oil seals, fuel hoses, etc. are exposed to temperatures above 750-degrees F (400-degrees C). The rubber changes into a charred or sticky substance containing the acid. *Once formed, the acid remains dangerous for years. If it gets onto the skin, it may be necessary to amputate the limb concerned.*

When dealing with a vehicle which has suffered a fire, or with components salvaged from such a vehicle, wear protective gloves and discard them after use.

Troubleshooting

Contents

Symptom	Section

Engine
Alternator light fails to come on when key is turned on	13
Alternator light stays on	12
Battery will not hold a charge	11
Engine backfires	18
Engine diesels (continues to run) after being turned off	21
Engine hard to start when cold	4
Engine hard to start when hot	5
Engine lacks power	17
Engine 'lopes' while idling or idles erratically	8
Engine misses at idle speed	9
Engine misses throughout driving speed range	14
Engine rotates but will not start	2
Engine stalls	16
Engine starts but stops immediately	7
Engine surges while holding accelerator steady	19
Engine will not rotate when attempting to start	1
Excessive fuel consumption	24
Excessive oil consumption	23
Excessively high idle speed	10
Fuel odor	25
Hesitation or stumble during acceleration	15
Low oil pressure	22
Miscellaneous engine noises	26
Pinging or knocking engine sounds when engine is under load	20
Starter motor noisy or engages roughly	6
Starter motor operates without turning engine	3

Cooling system
Abnormal coolant loss	31
Corrosion	33
External coolant leakage	29
Internal coolant leakage	30
Overcooling	28
Overheating	27
Poor coolant circulation	32

Automatic transmission
Fluid leakage	37
General shift mechanism problems	34
Transmission slips, shifts rough, is noisy or has no drive in forward or reverse gears	36
Transmission will not downshift with accelerator pedal pressed to the floor	35

Transfer case
Lubricant leaks from the vent or output shaft seals	41
Noisy or jumps out of four-wheel drive Low range	40
Transfer case is difficult to shift into the desired range	38
Transfer case noisy in all gears	39

Driveshaft
Knock or clunk when the transmission is under initial load (just after transmission is put into gear)	43
Metallic grinding sound consistent with vehicle speed	44
Oil leak at seal end of driveshaft	42
Vibration	45

Axles
Brake pedal feels spongy when depressed	52
Brake pedal pulsates during brake application	55
Excessive brake pedal travel	51
Excessive effort required to stop vehicle	53
Noise	46
Noise (high-pitched squeal with the brakes applied)	50
Oil leakage	48
Pedal travels to the floor with little resistance	54
Vehicle pulls to one side during braking	49
Vibration	47

Suspension and steering systems
Lack of power assistance	61
Excessive pitching and/or rolling around corners or during braking	58
Excessive play in steering	60
Excessive tire wear (not specific to one area)	62
Excessive tire wear on inside edge	64
Excessive tire wear on outside edge	63
Excessively stiff steering	59
Shimmy, shake or vibration	57
Tire tread worn in one place	65
Vehicle pulls to one side	56

This section provides an easy reference guide to the more common problems which may occur during the operation of your vehicle. These problems and their possible causes are grouped under headings denoting various components or systems, such as Engine, Cooling system, etc. They also refer you to the chapter and/or section which deals with the problem.

Remember that successful troubleshooting is not a mysterious black art practiced only by professional mechanics. It is simply the result of the right knowledge combined with an intelligent, systematic approach to the problem. Always work by a process of elimination, starting with the simplest solution and working through to the most complex - and never overlook the obvious. Anyone can run the gas tank dry or leave the lights on overnight, so don't assume that you are exempt from such oversights.

Finally, always establish a clear idea of why a problem has occurred and take steps to ensure that it doesn't happen again. If the electrical system fails because of a poor connection, check the other connections in the system to make sure that they don't fail as well. If a particular fuse continues to blow, find out why - don't just replace one fuse after another. Remember, failure of a small component can often be indicative of potential failure or incorrect functioning of a more important component or system.

Engine

1 Engine will not rotate when attempting to start

1 Battery terminal connections loose or corroded. Check the cable terminals at the battery; tighten cable clamp and/or clean off corrosion as necessary (see Chapter 1).
2 Battery discharged or faulty. If the cable ends are clean and tight on the battery posts, turn the key to the On position and switch on the headlights or windshield wipers. If they don't operate, the battery is discharged.
3 Automatic transmission not engaged in park (P) or Neutral (N).
4 Broken, loose or disconnected wires in the starting circuit. Inspect all wires and connectors at the battery, starter solenoid and ignition switch (on steering column).
5 Starter motor pinion jammed in driveplate ring gear. Remove starter (Chapter 5) and inspect pinion and driveplate (Chapter 2A or Chapter 2B).
6 Starter solenoid faulty (Chapter 5).
7 Starter motor faulty (Chapter 5).
8 Ignition switch faulty (Chapter 12).
9 Engine seized. Try to turn the crankshaft with a large socket and breaker bar on the pulley bolt.
10 Starter relay faulty (Chapter 5).

2 Engine rotates but will not start

1 Fuel tank empty.
2 Battery discharged (engine rotates slowly).
3 Battery terminal connections loose or corroded.
4 Fuel not reaching fuel injectors. Check for clogged fuel filter or lines and defective fuel pump. Also make sure the tank vent lines aren't clogged (Chapter 4).
5 Low cylinder compression. Check as described in Chapter 2C.
6 Water in fuel. Drain tank and fill with new fuel.
7 Defective ignition coil(s) (Chapter 5).
8 Dirty or clogged fuel injector(s) (Chapter 4).
9 Wet or damaged ignition components (Chapters 1 and 5).

10 Worn, faulty or incorrectly gapped spark plugs (Chapter 1).
11 Broken, loose or disconnected wires in the starting circuit (see previous Section).
12 Broken, loose or disconnected wires at the ignition coil or faulty coil (Chapter 5).
13 Timing chain(s) failure or wear affecting valve timing (Chapter 2A or Chapter 2B).
14 Fuel injection or engine control systems failure (Chapters 4 and 6).
15 Defective MAF sensor (Chapter 6)

3 Starter motor operates without turning engine

1 Starter pinion sticking. Remove the starter (Chapter 5) and inspect.
2 Starter pinion or driveplate teeth worn or broken. Remove the inspection cover and inspect.

4 Engine hard to start when cold

1 Battery discharged or low. Check as described in Chapter 1.
2 Fuel not reaching the fuel injectors. Check the fuel filter, lines and fuel pump (Chapters 1 and 4).
3 Defective spark plugs (Chapter 1).
4 Defective engine coolant temperature sensor (Chapter 6).
5 Fuel injection or engine control systems malfunction (Chapters 4 and 6).

5 Engine hard to start when hot

1 Air filter dirty (Chapter 1).
2 Bad engine ground connection.
3 Fuel injection or engine control systems malfunction (Chapters 4 and 6).

6 Starter motor noisy or engages roughly

1 Pinion or driveplate teeth worn or broken. Remove the inspection cover on the left side of the engine and inspect.
2 Starter motor mounting bolts loose or missing.

7 Engine starts but stops immediately

1 Loose or damaged wire harness connections at distributor, coil or alternator.
2 Intake manifold vacuum leaks. Make sure all mounting bolts/nuts are tight and all vacuum hoses connected to the manifold are attached properly and in good condition.
3 Insufficient fuel pressure (see Chapter 4).
4 Fuel injection or engine control systems malfunction (Chapters 4 and 6).

8 Engine 'lopes' while idling or idles erratically

1 Vacuum leaks. Check mounting bolts at the intake manifold for tightness. Make sure that all vacuum hoses are connected and in good condition. Use a stethoscope or a length of fuel hose held against your ear to listen for vacuum leaks while the engine is running. A hissing sound will be heard. A soapy water solution will also detect leaks. Check the intake manifold gasket surfaces.
2 Plugged PCV valve or tubes (see Chapters 1 and 6).
3 Air filter clogged (Chapter 1).
4 Fuel pump not delivering sufficient fuel (Chapter 4).
5 Leaking head gasket. Perform a cylinder compression check (Chapter 2C).
6 Timing chain(s) worn (Chapter 2A or Chapter 2B).
7 Camshaft lobes worn (Chapter 2A or Chapter 2B).
8 Valves burned or otherwise leaking (Chapter 2A or Chapter 2B).
9 Ignition system not operating properly (Chapters 1 and 5).
10 Fuel injection or engine control systems malfunction (Chapters 4 and 6).

9 Engine misses at idle speed

1 Spark plugs faulty or not gapped properly (Chapter 1).
2 Fauly ignition components (Chapter 5).
3 Vacuum leaks at intake manifold or hose connections. Check as described in (Chapter 2C).

4   Low or uneven cylinder compression. Check as described in.
5   Fuel injection or engine control systems malfunction (Chapters 4 and 6).

10   Excessively high idle speed

1   Vacuum leaks at intake manifold or hose connections.
2   Fuel injection or engine control systems malfunction (Chapters 4 and 6).

11   Battery will not hold a charge

1   Alternator drivebelt defective or not adjusted properly (Chapter 1).
2   Battery cables loose or corroded (Chapter 1).
3   Alternator not charging properly (Chapter 5).
4   Loose, broken or faulty wires in the charging circuit (Chapter 5).
5   Short circuit causing a continuous drain on the battery.
6   Battery defective internally.

12   Alternator light stays on

1   Fault in alternator or charging circuit (Chapter 5).
2   Drivebelt or tensioner defective (Chapter 1).

13   Alternator light fails to come on when key is turned on

1   Defective alternator (Chapter 5).
2   Fault in the instrument cluster, PCM or BCM (Chapters 6 and 12).

14   Engine misses throughout driving speed range

1   Impurities in the fuel system. Clean system (Chapter 4).
2   Faulty or incorrectly gapped spark plugs (Chapter 1).
3   Emissions system components faulty (Chapter 6).
4   Low or uneven cylinder compression pressures. Check as described in Chapter 2C.
5   Weak or faulty ignition coil(s) (Chapter 5).
6   Vacuum leaks at intake manifold or vacuum hoses.
7   Dirty or clogged fuel injector(s) (Chapter 4).
8   Fuel injection or engine control systems malfunction (Chapters 4 and 6).

15   Hesitation or stumble during acceleration

1   Ignition system not operating properly (Chapter 5).
2   Dirty or clogged fuel injector(s) (Chapter 4).
3   Low fuel pressure. Check for proper operation of the fuel pump and for restrictions in the fuel lines (Chapter 4).
4   Fuel injection or engine control systems malfunction (Chapters 4 and 6).

16   Engine stalls

1   Idle speed incorrect (Chapter 4).
2   Emissions system components faulty (Chapter 6).
3   Faulty or incorrectly gapped spark plugs (Chapter 1).
4   Vacuum leak at the intake manifold or vacuum hoses.
5   Fuel injection or engine control systems malfunction (Chapters 4 and 6).

17   Engine lacks power

1   Faulty or incorrectly gapped spark plugs (Chapter 1).
2   Air filter dirty (Chapter 1).
3   Faulty ignition coil(s) (Chapter 5).
4   Brakes binding (Chapters 1).
5   Automatic transmission fluid level incorrect, causing slippage (Chapter 1).
6   Impurities in the fuel system (Chapter 4).
7   Use of sub-standard fuel. Fill tank with proper octane fuel.
8   Low or uneven cylinder compression pressures. Check as described in Chapter 2C.
9   Vacuum leak at intake manifold or vacuum hoses.
10   Dirty or clogged fuel injector(s) (Chapters 1 and 4).
11   Fuel injection or engine control systems malfunction (Chapters 4 and 6).
12   Restricted exhaust system (Chapter 4).

18   Engine backfires

1   Damaged valve springs or sticking valves (Chapter 2A or Chapter 2B).
2   Vacuum leak at the intake manifold or vacuum hoses.

19   Engine surges while holding accelerator steady

1   Vacuum leak at the intake manifold or vacuum hoses.
2   Restricted air filter (Chapter 1).

3   Fuel pump or pressure regulator defective (Chapter 4).
4   Fuel injection or engine control systems malfunction (Chapters 4 and 6).

20   Pinging or knocking engine sounds when engine is under load

1   Incorrect grade of fuel. Fill tank with fuel of the proper octane rating.
2   Carbon build-up in combustion chambers. Remove cylinder head(s) and clean combustion chambers (Chapter 2A or Chapter 2B).
3   Incorrect spark plugs (Chapter 1).
4   Fuel injection or engine control systems malfunction (Chapters 4 and 6).
5   Restricted exhaust system (Chapter 4).

21   Engine diesels (continues to run) after being turned off

1   Defective ignition switch (Chapter 12).
2   Faulty Powertrain Control Module (Chapter 6 ,).
3   Faulty Body Control Module.
4   Leaking fuel injector(s) (Chapter 4).

22   Low oil pressure

1   Improper grade of oil.
2   Oil pump worn or damaged (Chapter 2A or Chapter 2B).
3   Engine overheating (Chapter 3).
4   Clogged oil filter (Chapter 1).
5   Clogged oil strainer (Chapter 2A or Chapter 2B).
6   Oil pressure gauge not working properly (Chapter 2C).

23   Excessive oil consumption

1   Loose oil drain plug.
2   Loose bolts or damaged oil pan gasket (Chapter 2A or Chapter 2B).
3   Loose bolts or damaged front cover gasket (Chapter 2A or Chapter 2B).
4   Front or rear crankshaft oil seal leaking (Chapter 2A or Chapter 2B).
5   Loose bolts or damaged valve cover gasket (Chapter 2A or Chapter 2B).
6   Loose oil filter (Chapter 1).
7   Loose or damaged oil pressure switch (Chapter 2C).
8   Pistons and cylinders excessively worn (Chapter 2C).
9   Piston rings not installed correctly on pistons (Chapter 2C).
10   Worn or damaged piston rings (Chapter 2C).

11   Intake and/or exhaust valve oil seals worn or damaged (Chapter 2A or Chapter 2B).
12   Worn or damaged valves/guides (Chapter 2A or Chapter 2B).
13   Faulty or incorrect PCV valve allowing too much crankcase airflow.

24   Excessive fuel consumption

1   Dirty or clogged air filter element (Chapter 1).
2   Incorrect idle speed (Chapter 4).
3   Low tire pressure or incorrect tire size (Chapter 1).
4   Inspect for binding brakes (see Chapter 9).
5   Fuel leakage. Check all connections, lines and components in the fuel system (Chapter 4).
6   Dirty or clogged fuel injectors (Chapter 4).
7   Fuel injection or engine control systems malfunction (Chapters 1 and 6).
8   Thermostat stuck open or not installed.
9   Improperly operating transmission.

25   Fuel odor

1   Fuel leakage. Check all connections, lines and components in the fuel system (Chapter 4).
2   Fuel tank overfilled. Fill only to automatic shut-off.
3   Charcoal canister filter in Evaporative Emissions Control system clogged (Chapter 1).
4   Vapor leaks from Evaporative Emissions Control system lines (Chapter 6).

26   Miscellaneous engine noises

1   A strong dull noise that becomes more rapid as the engine accelerates indicates worn or damaged crankshaft bearings or an unevenly worn crankshaft. Replace the bearing and/or service or replace the crankshaft (Chapter 2C).
2   A similar (yet slightly higher pitched) noise to the crankshaft knocking described in the previous paragraph, that becomes more rapid as the engine accelerates, indicates worn or damaged connecting rod bearings (Chapter 2C).
3   An overlapping metallic noise that increases in intensity as the engine speed increases, yet diminishes as the engine warms up indicates abnormal piston and cylinder wear (Chapter 2C).
4   A rapid clicking noise that becomes faster as the engine accelerates indicates a worn piston pin or piston pin hole. This sound will happen each time the piston hits the highest and lowest points in the stroke (Chapter 2C).
5   A metallic clicking noise coming from the water pump indicates worn or damaged water

pump bearings or pump. Replace the water pump with a new one (Chapter 3).
6   A rapid tapping sound or clicking sound that becomes faster as the engine speed increases indicates "valve tapping." This can be identified by holding one end of a section of hose to your ear and placing the other end at different spots along the valve cover. The point where the sound is loudest indicates the problem valve. If the pushrod and rocker arm components are in good shape, you likely have a collapsed valve lifter. Changing the engine oil and adding a high viscosity oil treatment will sometimes cure a stuck lifter problem. If the problem persists, the lifters, pushrods and rocker arms must be removed for inspection (see Chapter 2A or Chapter 2B).
7   A steady metallic rattling or rapping sound coming from the area of the timing chain cover indicates a worn, damaged or out-of-adjustment timing chain. Service or replace the chain and related components (Chapter 2A or Chapter 2B).

Cooling system

27   Overheating

1   Insufficient coolant in system (Chapter 1).
2   Drivebelt defective or not adjusted properly (Chapter 1).
3   Radiator core blocked or radiator grille dirty and restricted (Chapter 3).
4   Thermostat faulty (Chapter 3).
5   Cooling fan not functioning properly (Chapter 3).
6   Expansion tank cap not maintaining proper pressure. Have cap pressure tested by a gas station or repair shop.
7   Defective water pump (Chapter 3).
8   Improper grade of engine oil.
9   Inaccurate temperature gauge (Chapter 12).
10   Blown cylinder head gasket (Chapter 2A or Chapter 2B).

28   Overcooling

1   Thermostat faulty (Chapter 3).
2   Inaccurate temperature gauge (Chapter 12).

29   External coolant leakage

1   Deteriorated or damaged hoses. Loose clamps at hose connections (Chapter 1).
2   Water pump seals defective. If this is the case, water will drip from the weep hole in the water pump body (Chapter 3).
3   Leakage from radiator core or header tank. This will require the radiator to be professionally repaired (see Chapter 3 for removal procedures).

4   Leakage from the coolant reservoir or expansion tank.
5   Engine drain plugs or water jacket freeze plugs leaking (see Chapter 1 or Chapter 2C).
6   Leak from coolant temperature switch (Chapter 3).
7   Leak from damaged gaskets or small cracks (Chapter 2A or Chapter 2B).
8   Leak from oil cooler or oil cooler adapter housing (Chapter 3).

30   Internal coolant leakage

Note: *Internal coolant leaks can usually be detected by examining the oil. Check the dipstick and underside of the engine oil filler cap for water deposits and an oil consistency like that of a milkshake.*
9   Leaking cylinder head gasket. Have the system pressure tested or remove the cylinder head (Chapter 2A or Chapter 2B) and inspect.
10   Cracked cylinder bore or cylinder head. Dismantle engine and inspect (Chapter 2C).
11   Loose cylinder head bolts (tighten as described in Chapter 2A or Chapter 2B).
12   Leakage from internal coolant pipe/hose (accessible only with intake manifold removed (Chapter 2B).
13   Leakage from internal coolant pipe/hose (gasoline engines) (accessible only with intake manifold removed (Chapter 2A).

31   Abnormal coolant loss

1   Overfilling system (Chapter 1).
2   Coolant boiling away due to overheating (see causes in Section 27).
3   Internal or external leakage (see Sections 29 and 30).
4   Faulty expansion tank cap. Have the cap pressure tested.
5   Cooling system being pressurized by engine compression. This could be due to a cracked head or block or leaking head gasket(s). Have the system tested for the presence of combustion gas in the coolant at a shop.

32   Poor coolant circulation

1   Inoperative water pump. A quick test is to pinch the top radiator hose closed with your hand while the engine is idling, then release it. You may be able to feel a surge of coolant if the pump is working properly (Chapter 3).
2   Restriction in cooling system. Drain, flush and refill the system (Chapter 1). If necessary, remove the radiator (Chapter 3) and have it reverse flushed or professionally cleaned.
3   Loose water pump drivebelt (Chapter 1).
4   Thermostat sticking (Chapter 3).
5   Insufficient coolant (Chapter 1).

33 Corrosion

1　Excessive impurities in the water. Soft, clean water is recommended. Distilled or rain-water is satisfactory.
2　Insufficient antifreeze solution (refer to Chapter 1 for the proper ratio of water to anti-freeze).
3　Infrequent flushing and draining of sys-tem. Regular flushing of the cooling system should be carried out at the specified intervals as described in Chapter 1.

Automatic transmission

34 General shift mechanism problems

1　Common problems which may be attrib-uted to a misadjusted shift cable are:
a) *Engine starting in gears other than Park or Neutral.*
b) *Indicator on shifter pointing to a gear other than the one actually being selected.*
c) *Vehicle moves when in Park.*
2　Refer to Chapter to check the transmis-sion range (TR) sensor adjustment.

35 Transmission will not downshift with accelerator pedal pressed to the floor

Since these transmissions are electronically controlled, your dealer or a professional shop with the proper equipment will have to diag-nose the probable cause.

36 Transmission slips, shifts rough, is noisy or has no drive in forward or reverse gears

1　There are many probable causes for the above problems, but the home mechanic should be concerned with only one possibility - fluid level.
2　Before taking the vehicle to a repair shop, check the level and condition of the fluid as described in Chapter 1. Correct fluid level as necessary or change the fluid and filter if needed. If the problem persists, have a pro-fessional diagnose the problem.

37 Fluid leakage

1　Automatic transmission fluid is a deep red color. Fluid leaks should not be confused with engine oil, which can easily be blown by airflow to the transmission.
2　To pinpoint a leak, first remove all built-up dirt and grime from around the transmission.

Degreasing agents and/or steam cleaning will achieve this. With the underside clean, drive the vehicle at low speeds so air flow will not blow the leak far from its source. Raise the vehicle and determine where the leak is com-ing from. Common areas of leakage are:
a) *Pan: Tighten the mounting bolts and/or replace the pan gasket as necessary (see Chapter 1).*
b) *Filler pipe: Replace the rubber seal where the pipe enters the transmission case.*
c) *Transmission oil lines: Tighten the con-nectors where the lines enter the trans-mission case and/or replace the lines.*
d) *Vent pipe: Transmission overfilled and/or water in fluid (see checking procedures, Chapter 1).*
e) *Speedometer connector: Replace the O-ring where the vehicle speed sensor enters the transmission case (Chapter 6).*

Transfer case

38 Transfer case is difficult to shift into the desired range

1　Speed may be too great to permit engagement. Stop the vehicle and shift into the desired range.
2　Shift linkage loose, bent or binding on a manual shift transfer case. Check the linkage for damage or wear and replace or lubricate as necessary (Chapter 7B).
3　Defective circuit and or range switch on electric shift transfer case (Chapter 8).
4　If the vehicle has been driven on a paved surface for some time, the driveline torque can make shifting difficult. Stop and shift into two-wheel drive on paved or hard surfaces.
5　Insufficient or incorrect grade of lubri-cant. Drain and refill the transfer case with the specified lubricant (Chapter 1).
6　Worn or damaged internal components. Disassembly and overhaul of the transfer case may be necessary (Chapter 7B).

39 Transfer case noisy in all gears

Insufficient or incorrect grade of lubricant. Drain and refill (Chapter 1).

40 Noisy or jumps out of four-wheel drive Low range

1　Transfer case not fully engaged. Stop the vehicle, shift into Neutral and then engage 4L.
2　Shift linkage loose, worn or binding. Tighten, repair or lubricate linkage as neces-sary.
3　Shift fork cracked, inserts worn or fork binding on the rail. See your dealer for a new or rebuilt unit.

41 Lubricant leaks from the vent or output shaft seals

1　Transfer case is overfilled. Drain to the proper level (Chapter 1).
2　Vent is clogged or jammed closed. Clear or replace the vent.
3　Output shaft seal incorrectly installed or damaged. Replace the seal and check con-tact surfaces for nicks and scoring.

Driveshaft

42 Oil leak at seal end of driveshaft

Defective transmission or transfer case oil seal. See Chapter for replacement proce-dures. While this is done, check the splined yoke for burrs or a rough condition which may be damaging the seal. Burrs can be removed with crocus cloth or a fine whetstone.

43 Knock or clunk when the transmission is under initial load (just after transmission is put into gear)

1　Loose or disconnected rear suspension components. Check all mounting bolts, nuts and bushings (see Chapter 10).
2　Loose driveshaft bolts. Inspect all bolts and nuts and tighten them to the specified torque.
3　Worn or damaged universal joint bear-ings (see Chapter 8).

44 Metallic grinding sound consistent with vehicle speed.

Pronounced wear in the universal joint bear-ings. Check as described in Chapter 8.

45 Vibration

Note: *Before assuming that the driveshaft is at fault, make sure the tires are perfectly bal-anced and perform the following test.*
1　Install a tachometer inside the vehicle to monitor engine speed as the vehicle is driven. Drive the vehicle and note the engine speed at which the vibration (roughness) is most pronounced. Now shift the transmission to a different gear and bring the engine speed to the same point.
2　If the vibration occurs at the same engine speed (rpm) regardless of which gear the transmission is in, the driveshaft is NOT at fault since the driveshaft speed varies.
3　If the vibration decreases or is eliminated when the transmission is in a different gear at

the same engine speed, refer to the following probable causes.

4   Bent or dented driveshaft. Inspect and replace as necessary (see Chapter 8).
5   Undercoating or built-up dirt, etc. on the driveshaft. Clean the shaft thoroughly and recheck.
6   Worn universal joint bearings. Remove and inspect (see Chapter 8).
7   Driveshaft and/or companion flange out of balance. Check for missing weights on the shaft. Remove the driveshaft (see Chapter 8) and reinstall 180-degrees from original position, then retest. Have the driveshaft professionally balanced if the problem persists.

Axles

46   Noise

1   Road noise. No corrective procedures available.
2   Tire noise. Inspect tires and check tire pressures (Chapter 1).
3   Rear wheel bearings loose, worn or damaged (Chapter 8).

47   Vibration

See probable causes under Driveshaft. Proceed under the guidelines listed for the driveshaft. If the problem persists, check the rear wheel bearings by raising the rear of the vehicle and spinning the rear wheels by hand. Listen for evidence of rough (noisy) bearings. Remove and inspect (see Chapter 8).

48   Oil leakage

1   Pinion seal damaged (see Chapter 8).
2   Axleshaft oil seals damaged (see Chapter 8).
3   Differential inspection cover leaking. Tighten the bolts or replace the gasket as required (see Chapters 1 and 8).

Brakes

49   Vehicle pulls to one side during braking

1   Defective, damaged or oil-contaminated disc brake pads on one side. Inspect as described in Chapter 9.
2   Excessive wear of brake pad material or disc on one side. Inspect and correct as necessary.
3   Loose or disconnected front suspension components. Inspect and tighten all bolts to the specified torque (Chapter 10).

4   Defective brake caliper assembly. (Chapter 9).

50   Noise (high-pitched squeal with the brakes applied)

1   Disc brake pads worn out. The noise comes from the wear sensor rubbing against the disc (does not apply to all vehicles) or the actual pad backing plate itself if the material is completely worn away. Replace the pads with new ones immediately (Chapter 9). If the pad material has worn completely away, the brake discs should be inspected for damage as described in Chapter 9.
2   Linings contaminated with dirt or grease. Replace pads or shoes.
3   Incorrect linings. Replace with correct linings.

51   Excessive brake pedal travel

1   Partial brake system failure. Inspect the entire system (Chapter 9) and correct as required.
2   Insufficient fluid in the master cylinder. Check (Chapter 1), add fluid and bleed the system if necessary (Chapter 9).
3   Problem with the anti-lock brake system (Chapter 9).

52   Brake pedal feels spongy when depressed

1   Air in the hydraulic lines. Bleed the brake system (Chapter 9).
2   Faulty flexible hoses. Inspect all system hoses and lines. Replace parts as necessary.
3   Master cylinder mounting bolts/nuts loose.
4   Master cylinder defective (Chapter 9).
5   Problem with the anti-lock brake system (Chapter 9).

53   Excessive effort required to stop vehicle

1   Power brake booster not operating properly (Chapter 9).
2   Excessively worn pads. Inspect and replace if necessary (Chapter 9).
3   One or more caliper pistons seized or sticking (Chapter 9).
4   Brake pads contaminated with oil or grease. Inspect and replace as required (Chapter 9).
5   New pads installed and not yet seated. It will take a while for the new material to seat against the disc.
6   Problem with the anti-lock brake system (Chapter 9).

54   Pedal travels to the floor with little resistance

1   Little or no fluid in the master cylinder reservoir caused by leaking caliper piston(s), loose, damaged or disconnected brake lines. Inspect the entire system and correct as necessary.
2   Worn master cylinder seals (Chapter 9).
3   Problem with the anti-lock brake system (Chapter 9).

55   Brake pedal pulsates during brake application

Disc defective. Check for excessive lateral runout and parallelism (Chapter 9). Have the disc resurfaced or replace it with a new one.

Suspension and steering systems

56   Vehicle pulls to one side

1   Tire pressures uneven (Chapter 1).
2   Defective tire (Chapter 1).
3   Excessive wear in suspension or steering components (Chapter 10).
4   Front end in need of alignment.
5   Front brakes dragging. Inspect the brakes as described in Chapters 1.

57   Shimmy, shake or vibration

1   Tire or wheel out-of-balance or out-of-round. Have professionally balanced.
2   Worn front wheel bearings (Chapter 1).
3   Shock absorbers and/or suspension components worn or damaged (Chapter 10).

58   Excessive pitching and/or rolling around corners or during braking

1   Defective shock absorbers. Replace as a set (Chapter 10).
2   Broken or weak springs and/or suspension components. Inspect as described in Chapter 10.

59   Excessively stiff steering

1   Incorrect tire pressures (Chapter 1).
2   Worn balljoints (see Chapter 10).
3   Front end out of alignment.
4   Lack of power assistance.

60 Excessive play in steering

1 Worn front wheel bearings (Chapter 1).
2 Excessive wear in suspension or steering components (Chapter 10).
3 Steering gear damaged or out of adjustment (Chapter 10).

61 Lack of power assistance

Electric motor faulty or bad connection at the steering gear (Chapter 10).

62 Excessive tire wear (not specific to one area)

1 Incorrect tire pressures (Chapter 1).
2 Tires out-of-balance. Have professionally balanced.

3 Wheels damaged. Inspect and replace as necessary.
4 Suspension or steering components excessively worn (Chapter 10).

63 Excessive tire wear on outside edge

1 Inflation pressures incorrect (Chapter 1).
2 Excessive speed in turns.
3 Front end alignment incorrect. Have professionally aligned.
4 Suspension arm bent (Chapter 10).

64 Excessive tire wear on inside edge

1 Inflation pressures incorrect (Chapter 1).
2 Front end alignment incorrect (toe-out). Have professionally aligned.

3 Loose or damaged steering components (Chapter 10).

65 Tire tread worn in one place

1 Tires out-of-balance.
2 Damaged wheel. Inspect and replace if necessary.
3 Defective tire (Chapter 1).

Chapter 1
Tune-up and routine maintenance

Contents

	Section
Air filter check and replacement	22
Automatic transmission fluid and filter change	24
Automatic transmission fluid level check	6
Battery check, maintenance and charging	9
Brake check	18
Brake fluid change	25
Cabin air filter replacement	21
Chassis lubrication	8
Cooling system check	15
Cooling system servicing (draining, flushing and refilling)	23
Differential lubricant change	30
Differential lubricant level check	20
Drivebelt check and replacement	26
Engine oil and filter change	7
Exhaust system check	12
Fluid level checks	4

	Section
Fuel system check	16
Ignition coil check and replacement	29
Introduction	2
Maintenance schedule	1
Positive Crankcase Ventilation (PCV) system check and replacement	27
Seat belt check	13
Steering and suspension check	17
Spark plug check and replacement	28
Tire and tire pressure checks	5
Tire rotation (every 6000 miles or 6 months)	11
Transfer case lubricant change (4WD models)	31
Transfer case lubricant level check (4WD models)	19
Tune-up general information	3
Underhood hose check and replacement	14
Windshield wiper blade inspection and replacement	10

Specifications

Note: *Listed here are manufacturer recommendations at the time this manual was written. Manufacturers occasionally upgrade their fluid and lubricant specifications, so check with your local auto parts store for current recommendations.*

Recommended lubricants and fluids

Engine oil
- Type .... API "certified for gasoline engines"
- Viscosity
  - Turbocharged engines .... 5W-30 Synthetic blend (USA), 5W-30 premium oil (Canada)
  - Non-turbocharged engines .... 5W-20 Synthetic blend (USA), 5W-20 premium oil (Canada)

Brake fluid .... Motorcraft DOT 4 LV high-performance brake fluid or equivalent

Automatic transmission fluid*
- 6-speed transmission .... MERCON LV automatic transmission fluid
- 10-speed transmission (Raptor model and 2017 3.5L engine) .... Motorcraft MERCON ULV automatic transmission fluid

Transfer case lubricant
- 2015 and 2016 models
  - Electronic shift-on-the-fly (ESOF) (Standard 4WD) .... Motorcraft transfer case fluid ESP-M2C166-H (XL-12) or equivalent
  - 2-Speed torque-on-demand (Automatic 4WD) .... Motorcraft MERCON LV automatic transmission fluid or equivalent
- 2017 models .... Motorcraft MERCON LV automatic transmission fluid or equivalent

Coolant .... Motorcraft Premium Orange Antifreeze/coolant VC-3DIL-B (USA); CVC-3DIL-B (Canada) or equivalent.

Rear wheel bearing grease .... Motorcraft 75W-85 Premium Synthetic Hypoid Gear Lubricant (WSS-M2C942-A) or equivalent

Chassis grease .... NLGI No. 2 lithium base grease containing polyethylene and molybdenum disulfide

Differential lubricant
- 2015 models
  - Front axle .... Motorcraft SAE 80W-90 Premium rear axle lubricant (WSP-M2C197-A) or equivalent
  - Rear axle .... Motorcraft SAE 75W-85 Premium synthetic hypoid gear lubricant (WSS-M2C942-A) or equivalent
- 2016 and 2017 models (front and rear axles) .... Motorcraft SAE 75W-85 Premium synthetic hypoid gear lubricant (WSS-M2C942-A) or equivalent

Axle shaft/seal grease .... Motorcraft Premium long-life grease (XG-1-E1), or equivalent

*Use only the recommended fluid type. Do not mix fluids.

Capacities*

Engine oil (with filter change)

2.7L/3.5L turbocharged engines	6.0 quarts
3.5L non-turbocharged engine	6.3 quarts
5.0L engine	7.7 quarts
Automatic transmission (capacity with torque converter drained)**	13 quarts
Transfer case..	1.5 quarts
Differential	
Front	3.5 pints
Rear***	5.5 pints

Cooling system

2.7L turbo engine	16.4 quarts
3.5L (non-turbo) engine	
With oil cooler	15.3 quarts
Without oil cooler	15.1 quarts
3.5L turbo engine	15.6 quarts
5.0L engine	15.85 quarts

  * The best way to determine the amount of fluid to add during a routine fluid change is to measure the amount drained. All capacities approximate. Add as necessary to bring to the appropriate level.

 ** It is important not to overfill the transmission. The capacity specified is for when the transmission and torque converter are both drained completely (dry fill). When performing an automatic transmission fluid change, the level for refilling will be significantly less.

*** 1 - With the vehicle on a level surface, the rear differential fluid level should be approximately 1/4 to 9/16-inch below the bottom of the filler plug hole.
    2 - On 8.8-inch Traction Lok axles, add 4 ounces of the specified additive friction modifier when refilling the differential: Ford part XL-3 (EST-M2C118-A) or equivalent.
    3 - The manufacturer states that the rear axle/differential is "filled for life", and the fluid should only be checked/changed when a leak is suspected or the rear axle has been submerged in water.

Brakes

Disc brake pad thickness (minimum)...	1/8-inch
Parking brake shoe lining thickness (minimum)	1/32-inch above rivet heads

Ignition system

Spark plug

Type	Motorcraft Part #12405 or equivalent
Gap	
3.5L V6 turbocharged engine	0.028 to 0.037 inch
2.7L V6 turbocharged engine	0.028 to 0.031 inch
V8 and 3.5L V6 non-turbocharged engine..................................	0.049 to 0.053 inch
Ignition timing	10-degrees BTDC (base timing - not adjustable)
Firing order	
V6 engines	1-4-2-5-3-6
V8 engine..	1-3-7-2-6-5-4-8

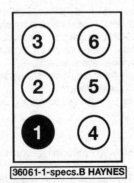

36061-1-specs.B HAYNES

Cylinder location diagram - V6 engines

5.0L V8 ENGINE
1-3-7-2-6-5-4-8

36063-02B-00.00a HAYNES

Cylinder location diagram - V8 engine

Torque specifications
Ft-lbs (unless otherwise indicated)

Note: *One foot-pound (ft-lb) of torque is equivalent to 12 inch-pounds (in-lbs) of torque. Torque values below approximately 15 foot-pounds are expressed in inch-pounds, because most foot-pound torque wrenches are not accurate at these smaller values.*

Automatic transmission	
10-speed automatic transmission fluid filter bolts	93 inch-lbs
Automatic transmission fluid pan bolts	
6-speed models	80 inch-lbs
10-speed models	
Bolts	89 inch-lbs
Stud-bolts	106 inch-lbs
Differential cover bolts	33
Engine oil drain plug (except 2.7L and 3.5L turbo engines)	20
Engine oil filter housing (canister-type, 2.7L turbo engine)	18
Drivebelt tensioner bolt(s)	
V6 models	18
V8 models	
Accessory belt (front)	35
Air conditioing compressor belt (rear)	18
Spark plugs	
5.0L engine	128 inch-lbs
All other engines	133 inch-lbs
Wheel lug nuts*	150

* The manufacturer recommends that wheel lug nuts be retightened 100 miles after being installed.

Typical engine compartment components (2.7L V6 engine shown)

1	Brake fluid reservoir	4	Engine oil filler cap	7	Windshield washer fluid reservoir
2	Air filter housing	5	Engine coolant expansion tank	8	Underhood fuse/relay block
3	Engine oil dipstick	6	Battery		

Typical engine underside components (2.7L V6 engine shown)

1	Exhaust pipe	3	Front disc brake caliper	5	Drivebelt
2	Engine oil drain plug	4	Steering gear boots	6	Radiator drain plug

Typical rear underside components

1	Muffler	3	Leaf spring	5	Differential check/fill plug
2	Driveshaft	4	Shock absorber	6	Rear disc brake caliper

1 Maintenance schedule

The following maintenance intervals are based on the assumption that the vehicle owner will be doing the maintenance or service work, as opposed to having a dealer service department or other repair shop do the work. Although the time/mileage intervals are loosely based on factory recommendations, most have been shortened to ensure, for example, that such items as lubricants

and fluids are checked/changed at intervals that promote maximum engine/driveline service life. Also, subject to the preference of the individual owner interested in keeping his or her vehicle in peak condition at all times, and with the vehicle's ultimate resale in mind, many of the maintenance procedures may be performed more often than recommended in the following schedule. We encourage such

owner initiative.

When the vehicle is new it should be serviced initially by a factory authorized dealer service department to protect the factory warranty. In many cases the initial maintenance check is done at no cost to the owner (check with your dealer service department for more information).

Every 250 miles or weekly, whichever comes first

Check the engine oil level (Section 4)
Check the engine coolant level (Section 4)
Check the windshield washer fluid level (Section 4)
Check the brake fluid level (Section 4)
Check the tires and tire pressures (Section 5)

Every 3000 miles or 3 months, whichever comes first

All items listed above, plus:
Check the automatic transmission fluid level (Section 6)
Change the engine oil and oil filter (Section 7)
Lubricate the chassis (Section 8)
Check the engine drivebelt (Section 26)

Every 6000 miles or 6 months, whichever comes first

All items listed above, plus:
Check and service the battery (Section 9)
Inspect and replace, if necessary, the windshield wiper blades (Section 10)
Rotate the tires (Section 11)
Inspect the exhaust system (Section 12)
Check the seat belt operation (Section 13)

Every 15,000 miles or 12 months, whichever comes first

All items listed above, plus:
Inspect and replace, if necessary, all underhood hoses (Section 14)
Inspect the cooling system (Section 15)

Check the fuel system (Section 16)
Inspect the steering and suspension components (Section 17)
Inspect the brakes (Section 18)
Check the transfer case lubricant level (Section 19)
Check the differential lubricant level (Section 20)

Every 30,000 miles or 24 months, whichever comes first

Replace the air filter (Section 22)*
Service the cooling system (drain, flush and refill) (Section 23)
Change the automatic transmission fluid and filter (Section 24)**
Change the brake fluid (Section 25)

Every 60,000 miles or 48 months, whichever comes first

Check the engine drivebelt (Section 26)
Check the PCV valve (Section 27)
Replace the spark plugs (Section 28)
Inspect and replace, if necessary, the ignition coils (Section 29)

Every 100,000 miles or 60 months, whichever comes first

Change the transfer case lubricant (Section 31)
Change the differential lubricant (Section 30)

* Replace more often if the vehicle is driven in dusty areas

** If the vehicle is operated in continuous stop-and-go driving or in mountainous areas, change at 15,000 miles

2   Introduction

1   This Chapter is designed to help the home mechanic maintain the Ford F-150 with the goals of maximum performance, economy, safety and reliability in mind.

2   Included is a master maintenance schedule, followed by procedures dealing specifically with each item on the schedule. Visual checks, adjustments, component replacement and other helpful items are included. Refer to the accompanying illustrations of the engine compartment and the underside of the vehicle for the locations of various components.

3   Servicing the vehicle, in accordance with the mileage/time maintenance schedule and the step-by-step procedures will result in a planned maintenance program that should produce a long and reliable service life. Keep in mind that it is a comprehensive plan, so maintaining some items but not others at the specified intervals will not produce the same results.

4   As you service the vehicle, you will discover that many of the procedures can - and should - be grouped together because of the nature of the particular procedure you're performing or because of the close proximity of two otherwise unrelated components to one another.

5   For example, if the vehicle is raised for chassis lubrication, you should inspect the exhaust, suspension, steering and fuel systems while you're under the vehicle. When you're rotating the tires, it makes good sense to check the brakes since the wheels are already removed. Finally, let's suppose you have to borrow or rent a torque wrench. Even if you only need it to tighten the spark plugs, you might as well check the torque of as many critical fasteners as time allows.

6   The first step in this maintenance program is to prepare yourself before the actual work begins. Read through all the procedures you're planning to do, then gather up all the parts and tools needed. If it looks like you might run into problems during a particular job, seek advice from a mechanic or an experienced do-it-yourselfer.

Owner's Manual and VECI label information

7   Your vehicle owner's manual was written for your year and model and contains very specific information on component locations, specifications, fuse ratings, part numbers, etc. The owner's manual is an important resource for the do-it-yourselfer to have; if one was not supplied with your vehicle, it can generally be ordered from a dealer parts department.

8   Among other important information, the Vehicle Emissions Control Information (VECI) label contains specifications and procedures for applicable tune-up adjustments (if applicable) and, in some instances, spark plug replacement (see the front of this manual for more information on the VECI label). The information on this label is the exact maintenance data recommended by the manufacturer. This data often varies by intended altitude, local emissions regulations, month of manufacture, etc.

9   This Chapter contains procedural details, safety information and more ambitious maintenance intervals than you might find in manufacturer's literature. However, you may find procedures or specifications in your owner's manual or VECI label can be considered correct, since it is specific to your particular vehicle.

3   Tune-up general information

1   The term tune-up is used in this manual to represent a combination of individual operations rather than one specific procedure.

2   If, from the time the vehicle is new, the routine maintenance schedule is followed closely and frequent checks are made of fluid levels and high wear items, as suggested throughout this manual, the engine will be kept in relatively good running condition and the need for additional work will be minimized.

3   More likely than not, however, there will be times when the engine is running poorly due to lack of regular maintenance. This is even more likely if a used vehicle, which has not received regular and frequent maintenance checks, is purchased. In such cases, an engine tune-up will be needed outside of the regular routine maintenance intervals.

4   The first step in any tune-up or diagnostic procedure to help correct a poor running engine is a cylinder compression check. A compression check (see Chapter 2) will help determine the condition of internal engine components and should be used as a guide for tune-up and repair procedures. If, for instance, a compression check indicates serious internal engine wear, a conventional tune-up will not improve the performance of the engine and would be a waste of time and money. Because of its importance, the compression check should be done by someone with the right equipment and the knowledge to use it properly.

5   The following procedures are those most often needed to bring a generally poor running engine back into a proper state of tune.

Minor tune-up

Check all engine related fluids (Section 4)
Clean, inspect and test the battery (Section 9)
Check all underhood hoses (Section 14)
Check the cooling system (Section 15)
Check the fuel system (Section 16)
Check the air filter (Section 22)

Major tune-up

All items listed under Minor tune-up, plus...
Replace the air filter (Section 22)
Check the drivebelt (Section 26)
Replace the PCV valve (Section 27)
Replace the spark plugs (Section 28)
Check the charging system (Chapter 5)

4   Fluid level checks (every 250 miles or weekly)

1   Fluids are an essential part of the lubrication, cooling, brake and windshield washer systems. Because the fluids gradually become depleted and/or contaminated during normal operation of the vehicle, they must be periodically replenished. See *Recommended lubricants and fluids* at the beginning of this Chapter before adding fluid to any of the following components.

Note: *The vehicle must be on level ground when fluid levels are checked.*

Engine oil

2   The oil level is checked with a dipstick, which is located on the left-rear side of the engine compartment (see illustration). The dipstick extends through a metal tube down into the oil pan.

3   The oil level should be checked before the vehicle has been driven, or about five minutes after the engine has been shut off. If the oil is checked immediately after driving the vehicle, some of the oil will remain in the upper part of the engine, resulting in an inaccurate reading

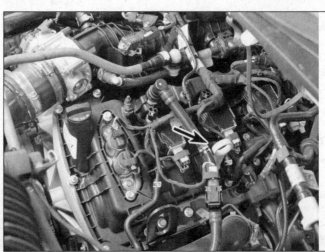

4.2 Engine oil dipstick location - 2.7L V6 engine model shown

on the dipstick. Wait about 15 minutes after the engine has been shut off before checking the oil level, to allow time for all the oil to drain into the oil pan.

4   Pull the dipstick out of the tube and wipe all the oil from the end with a clean rag or paper towel. Insert the clean dipstick all the way back into the tube and pull it out again. Note the oil at the end of the dipstick. At its highest point, the level should be at or near the MAX mark on the dipstick (see illustration). If it isn't, add the specified type of fresh oil until it is.

5   It takes approximately one quart of oil to raise the level from the MIN mark to the MAX mark on the dipstick. Do not allow the level to drop below the MIN mark or oil starvation may cause engine damage. Conversely, overfilling the engine (adding oil above the MAX mark) may cause oil fouled spark plugs, oil leaks or oil seal failures.

6   To add oil, remove the filler cap from the valve cover (see illustration). After adding oil, wait a few minutes to allow the level to stabilize, then pull out the dipstick and check the level again. Add more oil if required. Install the filler cap and tighten it by hand only.

Note: *The oil filler cap is located on the left valve cover on all V6 models and the right valve cover on V8 models*

7   Checking the oil level is an important preventive maintenance step. A consistently low oil level indicates oil leakage through damaged seals, defective gaskets or past worn rings or valve guides. If the oil looks milky in color or has water droplets in it, the cylinder head gasket(s) may be blown or the head(s) or block may be cracked. The engine should be checked immediately. The condition of the oil should also be checked. Whenever you check the oil level, slide your thumb and index finger up the dipstick before wiping off the oil. If you see small dirt or metal particles clinging to the dipstick, the oil should be changed (see Section 7).

Engine coolant

Warning: *Do not allow antifreeze to come in contact with your skin or painted surfaces of the vehicle. Flush contaminated areas immediately with plenty of water. Don't store new coolant or leave old coolant lying around where it's accessible to children or pets - they're attracted by its sweet smell. Ingestion of even a small amount of coolant can be fatal! Wipe up garage floor and drip pan spills immediately. Keep antifreeze containers covered and repair cooling system leaks as soon as they're noticed.*

8   All vehicles covered by this manual are equipped with a pressurized coolant recovery system. A plastic expansion tank located at the front of the engine compartment (on top of the cooling fan shroud) is connected by a hose to the radiator. As the engine heats up during operation, the expanding coolant fills the tank to a higher level.

Warning: *Do not remove the expansion tank cap to check the coolant level when the engine is warm!*

9   The coolant level in the tank should be checked regularly. The level in the tank varies with the temperature of the engine. When the engine is cold, the coolant level should be at or slightly above the COLD FILL mark on the reservoir. If it isn't, wrap a thick cloth around the expansion tank cap, then slowly unscrew and remove it. If coolant or steam escapes, let the engine cool down longer, then remove the cap. Add a 50/50 mixture of the specified type of antifreeze and water (see illustrations). Once the engine has reached normal operating temperature, the level will rise to the MAX mark.

10   Drive the vehicle and recheck the coolant level. Don't use rust inhibitors or additives. If only a small amount of coolant is required to bring the system up to the proper level, water can be used. However, repeated additions of water will dilute the antifreeze and water solution. In order to maintain the proper ratio of antifreeze and water, always top up the coolant level with the correct mixture. An empty plastic milk jug or bleach bottle makes an excellent container for mixing coolant.

11   If the coolant level drops consistently, inspect the radiator, hoses, filler cap, drain plugs, thermostat, and water pump (see Section 15); another possibility is a blown head gasket. If no leaks are noted, have the expansion tank cap pressure tested by a service station.

12   Check the condition of the coolant as well. It should be relatively clear. If it's brown or rust colored, the system should be drained, flushed and refilled. Even if the coolant appears to be normal, the corrosion inhibitors wear out, so it must be replaced at the specified intervals.

Brake fluid

13   The brake master cylinder is mounted on the front of the power booster unit in the engine compartment.

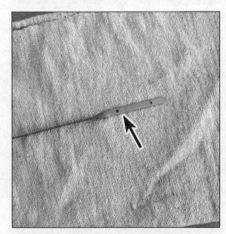

4.4 The oil level should be at or near the MAX mark on the dipstick

4.6 The oil filler cap is located on the left valve cover on V6 models

4.9a The coolant expansion tank is located at the front of the engine compartment, on top of the cooling fan shroud

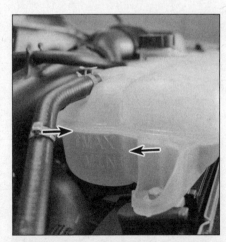

4.9b The coolant expansion tank fluid level should be kept between the MIN and MAX marks on the translucent plastic reservoir - DO NOT remove the cap until the engine has cooled completely

14   To check the brake fluid level, simply look at the MAX and MIN marks on the reservoir (see illustration). The level should be between the marks.

15   If the level is low, wipe the top of the reservoir and cap with a clean rag to prevent contamination of the brake system before unscrewing the cap.

16   Add only the specified type of brake fluid to the brake reservoir (refer to *Recommended lubricants and fluids* at the front of this Chapter or to your owner's manual). Mixing different types of brake fluid can damage the system. Fill the brake master cylinder reservoir no higher than the MAX line.

Warning: *Use caution when filling the reservoir - brake fluid can harm your eyes and damage painted surfaces. Do not use brake fluid that is more than one year old or has been left open. Brake fluid absorbs moisture from the air. Excess moisture can cause a dangerous loss of braking.*

17   While the reservoir cap is removed, inspect the master cylinder reservoir for contamination. If deposits, dirt particles or water droplets are present, the system should be drained and refilled.

18   After filling the reservoir to the proper level, make sure the cap is tightened securely to prevent fluid leakage.

19   The fluid in the brake master cylinder will drop slightly as the brake pads at each wheel wear down during normal operation. If the master cylinder requires repeated replenishing to keep it at the proper level, this is an indication of leakage in the brake system, which should be corrected immediately. If the brake system shows an indication of leakage, check all brake lines and connections, along with the calipers, wheel cylinders and brake booster (see Section 18 for more information).

20   If, upon checking the brake master cylinder fluid level, you discover the reservoir is empty or nearly empty, the system should be properly bled and refilled (see Chapter 9).

Windshield washer fluid

21   Fluid for the windshield washer system is stored in a plastic reservoir located at the right-front corner of the engine compartment (see illustration).

22   In milder climates, plain water can be used in the reservoir, but it should be kept no more than 2/3 full to allow for expansion if the water freezes. In colder climates, use windshield washer system antifreeze, available at any auto parts store, to lower the freezing point of the fluid. Mix the antifreeze with water in accordance with the manufacturer's directions on the container.

Caution: *Do not use cooling system antifreeze - it will damage the vehicle's paint.*

---

5   Tire and tire pressure checks (every 250 miles or weekly)

---

1   Periodic inspection of the tires may spare you the inconvenience of being stranded with a flat tire. It can also provide you with vital information regarding possible problems in the steering and suspension systems before major damage occurs.

2   The original tires on this vehicle are equipped with 1/2-inch wide bands that will appear when tread depth reaches 1/16-inch, at which point they can be considered worn out. Tread wear can be monitored with a simple, inexpensive device known as a tread depth indicator (see illustration).

3   Note any abnormal tread wear (see illustration). Tread pattern irregularities such as cupping, flat spots and more wear on one side than the other are indications of front end alignment and/or balance problems. If any of these conditions are noted, take the vehicle to a tire shop or service station to correct the problem.

4   Look closely for cuts, punctures and embedded nails or tacks. Sometimes a tire will hold air pressure for a short time or leak

down very slowly after a nail has embedded itself in the tread. If a slow leak persists, check the valve stem core to make sure it is tight (see illustration). Examine the tread for an object that may have embedded itself in the tire or for a "plug" that may have begun to leak (radial tire punctures are repaired with a plug that is installed in a puncture). If a puncture is suspected, it can be easily verified by spraying a solution of soapy water onto the puncture area (see illustration). The soapy solution will bubble if there is a leak. Unless the puncture is unusually large, a tire shop or service station can usually repair the tire.

5   Carefully inspect the inner sidewall of each tire for evidence of brake fluid leakage. If you see any, inspect the brakes immediately.

6   Correct air pressure adds miles to the life span of the tires, improves mileage and enhances overall ride quality. Tire pressure cannot be accurately estimated by looking at a tire, especially if it's a radial. A tire pressure gauge is essential. Keep an accurate gauge in the glove compartment. The pressure gauges attached to the nozzles of air hoses at gas stations are often inaccurate.

7   Always check tire pressure when the tires are cold. Cold, in this case, means the vehicle has not been driven over a mile in the three hours preceding a tire pressure check. A pressure rise of four to eight pounds is not uncommon once the tires are warm.

8   Unscrew the valve cap protruding from the wheel or hubcap and push the gauge firmly onto the valve stem (see illustration). Note the reading on the gauge and compare the figure to the recommended tire pressure shown on the tire placard on the driver's side door. Be sure to reinstall the valve cap to keep dirt and moisture out of the valve stem mechanism. Check all four tires and, if necessary, add enough air to bring them up to the recommended pressure.

9   Don't forget to keep the spare tire inflated to the specified pressure (refer to the pressure molded into the tire sidewall).

4.21 The windshield washer reservoir is located in the engine compartment, at the right-front corner behind the headlight housing

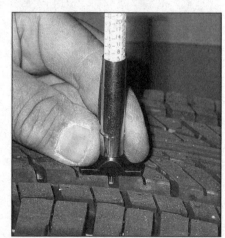

5.2 Use a tire tread depth indicator to monitor tire wear - they are available at auto parts stores and service stations and cost very little

4.14 The brake fluid level should be kept between the MIN and MAX marks on the translucent plastic reservoir

UNDERINFLATION

CUPPING

Cupping may be caused by:

- Underinflation and/or mechanical irregularities such as out-of-balance condition of wheel and/or tire, and bent or damaged wheel.
- Loose or worn steering tie-rod or steering idler arm.
- Loose, damaged or worn front suspension parts.

OVERINFLATION

INCORRECT TOE-IN OR EXTREME CAMBER

FEATHERING DUE TO MISALIGNMENT

5.3 This chart will help you determine the condition of the tires, the probable cause(s) of abnormal wear and the corrective action necessary

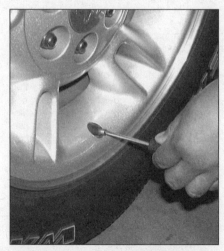

5.4a If a tire loses air on a steady basis, check the valve stem core first to make sure it's snug (special inexpensive wrenches are commonly available at auto parts stores)

5.4b If the valve stem core is tight, raise the corner of the vehicle with the low tire and spray a soapy water solution onto the tread as the tire is turned slowly - leaks will cause small bubbles to appear

5.8 To extend the life of the tires, check the air pressure at least once a week with an accurate gauge (don't forget the spare!)

6.5a Remove the transmission check/fill plug…

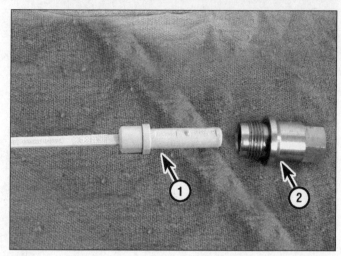

6.5b … then pull the transmission dipstick (1) out of the plug (2)

6   Automatic transmission fluid level check (every 3000 miles or 3 months)

1   The automatic transmission fluid level should be carefully maintained. Low fluid level can lead to slipping or loss of drive, while overfilling can cause foaming and loss of fluid. Either condition can cause transmission damage.

2   Since transmission fluid expands as it heats up, the fluid level should be checked when the transmission is warm (at normal operating temperature). If the vehicle has just been driven over 20 miles (32 km), the transmission can be considered warm. Allow the transmission to cool down for about 30 minutes. You can also check the transmission fluid level when the transmission is cold. If the vehicle has not been driven for over five hours and the fluid is about room temperature (70 to 95-degrees F), the transmission is cold. How-

ever, the fluid level is normally checked with the transmission warm to ensure accurate results.

Note: *If the vehicle has just been driven for a long time at high speed or in city traffic in hot weather, or if it has been pulling a trailer, an accurate fluid level reading cannot be obtained.*

3   Immediately after driving the vehicle, park it on a level surface, set the parking brake and start the engine. While the engine is idling, depress the brake pedal and move the selector lever through all the gear ranges, pausing for 5 seconds in between, beginning and ending in Park.

4   Working under the vehicle, remove the engine rear splash shield (see Section 7).

5   Remove the transmission check/fill plug from the right side of the transmission, then remove the dipstick from the plug (see illustrations).

6   With the engine still idling, wipe off the dipstick with a clean rag. Push the dipstick

all the way into the plug opening until it seats completely, then withdraw it again and note the fluid level.

7   If the transmission is cold, the level should be in the "cross-hatched" (1) range on the dipstick. If it's warm to hot, the fluid level should be in the "dotted" (2) range (see illustration). If the level is low, add the specified type of automatic transmission fluid through the fill plug opening. A hand pump, squeeze bottle or similar tool will be necessary to accomplish this.

8   Add just enough of the recommended fluid to fill the transmission to the proper level (near the top of the dotted area). It takes about one pint to raise the level from the low mark to the high mark when the fluid is hot, so add the fluid a little at a time and keep checking the level until it's correct. Also, be sure to shift through all the gears (as mentioned above) between fluid additions and checking the level.

9   Turn the engine off, install the transmission dipstick and plug, then tighten the plug securely.

10   The condition of the fluid should also be checked along with the level. If the fluid is black or a dark reddish-brown color, or if it smells burned, it should be changed (see Section 24). If you are in doubt about its condition, purchase some new fluid and compare the two for color and smell.

7   Engine oil and filter change (every 3000 miles or 3 months)

1   Frequent oil changes are the most important preventive maintenance procedures that can be done by the home mechanic. As engine oil ages, it becomes diluted and contaminated, which leads to premature engine wear.

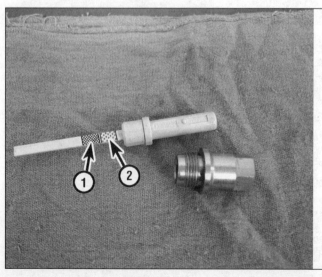

6.7 The transmission dipstick has two areas for checking the fluid level- a crosshatched area (1) and a dotted area (2). It is recommended to use the dotted area when checking the transmission fluid level, with the engine idling and the transmission at normal operating temperature.

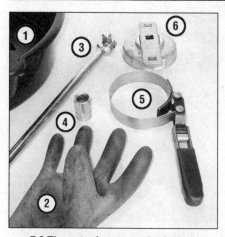

7.2 These tools are required when changing the engine oil and filter

1 **Drain pan** - *It should be fairly shallow in depth, but wide to prevent spills*
2 **Rubber gloves** - *When removing the drain plug and filter, you will get oil on your hands (the gloves will prevent burns)*
3 **Breaker bar** - *Sometimes the oil drain plug is tight, and a long breaker bar is needed to loosen it*
4 **Socket** – *To be used with the breaker bar or a ratchet (must be the correct size to fit the drain plug - six-point preferred)*
5 **Filter wrench** - *This is a metal band-type wrench, which requires clearance around the filter to be effective*
6 **Filter wrench** - *This type fits on the bottom of the filter and can be turned with a ratchet or breaker bar (different-size wrenches are available for different types of filters)*

7.6 Engine rear splash shield mounting bolt locations

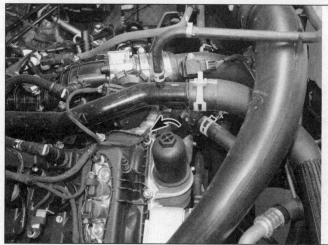

7.7 Unscrew the housing to access the oil filter element (2.7L V6 models)

2   Make sure that you have all the necessary tools before you begin this procedure (see illustration). You should also have plenty of rags or newspapers handy for mopping up oil spills.
3   Access to the oil drain plug and filter will be improved if the vehicle can be lifted on a hoist, driven onto ramps or supported by jackstands.
Warning: *Do not work under a vehicle supported only by a jack - always use jackstands!*
4   If you haven't changed the oil on this vehicle before, get under it and locate the oil drain plug and the oil filter (on some models, the filter is located in the engine compartment). The exhaust components will be warm as you work, so note how they are routed to avoid touching them when you are under the vehicle.
5   Start the engine and allow it to reach normal operating temperature - oil and sludge will flow out more easily when warm. If new oil, a filter or tools are needed, use the vehicle to go get them and warm up the engine/oil at the same time. Park on a level surface and shut off the engine when it's warmed up. Remove the oil filler cap from the valve cover.

6   Raise the vehicle and support it on jackstands. Make sure it is safely supported! Remove the engine rear splash shield (see illustration).
Caution: *Be careful not to touch the hot exhaust components.*

2.7L turbo models
7   Locate the canister-type oil filter housing at the front of the engine compartment. Rotate the filter housing counter-clockwise with a wrench (see illustration), then remove the housing and filter element from the engine. This will also allow any oil that remains in the housing to drain into the bottom of the engine oil pan.
8   Position a drain pan under the plug in the bottom of the engine, then rotate the drain plug counterclockwise 120-degrees by hand and remove the plug (see illustration). It's a good idea to wear a rubber glove while unscrewing the plug the final few turns to avoid being scalded by hot oil. It may be necessary to move the drain pan slightly as oil flow slows to a trickle. Inspect the old oil for the presence of metal particles.

9   Once all the oil has drained, wipe off the drain plug and opening on the engine oil pan. Confirming that the O-ring on the drain plug is in suitable condition, install the plug and turn it clockwise by hand until it is fully seated.

7.8 Rotate the drain plug 120 degrees (counter-clockwise) by hand, then pull out the plug and allow the oil to drain into the pan

7.10 Remove the old filter element, replace and lubricate the O-rings, then install a new filter element into the housing

1   *Filter housing*
2   *Filter element*
3   *O-rings*

7.21 Lubricate the oil filter gasket with clean engine oil before installing the filter on the engine

10   Separate the old filter element from the housing, clean the housing and replace all the O-rings (and lubricate them with a film of clean engine oil), then install a new filter element into the housing (see illustration).
11   Clean the engine mating surface of the oil filter from all old oil and sealing material. Install the filter and housing, screwing it into place, then tighten it to the torque listed in this Chapter's Specifications.
12   Remove all tools and materials from under the vehicle, being careful not to spill the oil in the drain pan, then lower the vehicle if it was raised.

5.0L, 3.5L turbo and 3.5L non-turbo engines

13   Position a drain pan under the plug in the bottom of the engine, turn the drain plug counter-clockwise with a wrench, then unscrew and remove the plug the rest of the way by hand. It's a good idea to wear a rubber glove while unscrewing the plug the final few

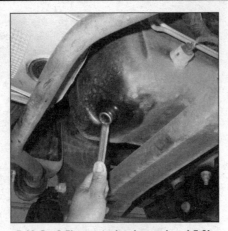

7.13 On 3.5L non-turbocharged and 5.0L models, use a proper size box-end wrench or socket to remove the oil drain plug and avoid rounding it off

turns to avoid being scalded by hot oil (see illustration).
Note: *For removing the drain plug on 3.5L turbo engines, see Step 8.*
14   It may be necessary to move the drain pan slightly as oil flow slows to a trickle. Inspect the old oil for the presence of metal particles.
15   After all the oil has drained, wipe off the drain plug with a clean rag. Any small metal particles clinging to the plug would immediately contaminate the new oil. Also clean the area around the drain plug opening.
16   Reinstall the plug and tighten it to the torque listed in this Chapter's Specifications.
17   Move the drain pan into position under the oil filter.
18   Loosen the oil filter by turning it counterclockwise with a filter wrench (see illustration).
19   Once the filter is loose, use your hands to unscrew it from the block. Empty the old oil inside the filter into the drain pan.
20   Using a clean rag, wipe off the mounting surface on the block. Also, make sure that none of the old gasket remains stuck to the mounting surface. It can be removed with a scraper if necessary.
21   Compare the old filter with the new one to make sure they are the same type. Smear some engine oil on the rubber gasket of the new filter and screw it into place (see illustration). Overtightening the filter will damage the gasket, so don't use a filter wrench. Most filter manufacturers recommend tightening the filter by hand only. Normally they should be tightened 3/4-turn after the gasket contacts the block, but be sure to follow the directions on the filter or container.
22   Remove all tools and materials from under the vehicle, being careful not to spill the oil in the drain pan, then lower the vehicle if it was raised.

All models

23   Add the specified type of new oil to the engine through the oil filler cap. Use a funnel to prevent oil from spilling onto the top of the

7.18 The oil filter is usually on very tight and in most cases, will require a special oil filter wrench to remove it - DO NOT use the wrench to tighten the new filter

engine. Add the specified amount of oil, minus one quart. Wait about 15 minutes to allow the oil to drain into the pan, then check the level on the dipstick (see Section 4 if necessary). If the oil level is in the OK range, install the filler cap.
24   Start the engine and run it for about a minute. While the engine is running, look under the vehicle and check for leaks at the oil pan drain plug and around the oil filter. If either one is leaking, stop the engine and tighten the plug or filter slightly.
25   Turn the engine off and wait a few minutes, then recheck the level on the dipstick. Add oil as necessary to bring the level near the MAX mark. Be careful not to overfill the engine.
26   Fully insert the dipstick and install the filler cap hand-tight.
27   During the first few trips after an oil change, make it a point to check frequently for leaks and proper oil level.
28   The old oil drained from the engine cannot be reused in its present state and should be disposed of. Check with your local auto parts store, disposal facility or environmental agency to see if they will accept the oil for recycling. After the oil has cooled it can be drained into a container (capped plastic jugs, topped bottles, milk cartons, etc.) for transport to one of these disposal sites. Don't dispose of the oil by pouring it on the ground or down a drain!

Oil change/oil life indicator reset

29   On the left-hand side of the steering wheel, press the right arrow button, then from the settings menu scroll to the "convenience" message. Press the right arrow button again, scrolling from the "convenience" menu until the "oil life reset" message is displayed.
30   Press and hold the OK button until the instrument cluster displays "Reset Successful". When the oil life indicator is reset the instrument cluster will display 100%.
31   If the instrument cluster displays "Not Reset or Reset Cancelled" repeat Steps 29 and 30.

8   Chassis lubrication (every 3000 miles or 3 months)

1   Refer to *Recommended lubricants and fluids* at the front of this Chapter to obtain the necessary grease, etc. You will also need a grease gun (see illustration). Occasionally plugs will be installed rather than grease fittings. If so, grease fittings will have to be purchased and installed.

2   Look under the vehicle for grease fittings or plugs on the steering, suspension, and driveline components. They are normally found on the tie-rod ends and universal joints. If there are plugs, remove them and install grease fittings, which will thread into the component. An automotive parts store will be able to supply the correct fittings. Straight, as well as angled, fittings are available.

3   For easier access under the vehicle, raise it with a jack and place jackstands under the frame. Make sure it is safely supported by the stands. If the wheels are to be removed at this interval for tire rotation or brake inspection, loosen the lug nuts slightly while the vehicle is still on the ground.

4   Before beginning, force a little grease out of the nozzle to remove any dirt from the end of the gun. Wipe the nozzle clean with a rag.

5   With the grease gun and plenty of clean rags, crawl under the vehicle and begin lubricating the components.

6   Wipe the grease fitting clean and push the nozzle firmly over it. Squeeze the trigger on the grease gun to force grease into the component. The component should be lubricated until the rubber seal is firm to the touch. Do not pump too much grease into the fittings as it could rupture the seal. For all other suspension and steering components, continue pumping grease into the fitting until it oozes out of the joint between the two components. If it escapes around the grease gun nozzle, the fitting is clogged or the nozzle is not completely seated on the fitting. Resecure the gun nozzle to the fitting and try again. If necessary, replace the fitting with a new one.

Note: *Not all models have grease fittings for the steering joints. They are factory sealed and do not need lubrication.*

7   Wipe the excess grease from the components and the grease fitting. Repeat the procedure for the remaining fittings.

8   On models equipped with an automatic transmission, lubricate the shift linkage with a little clean engine oil.

9   On 4WD models, lubricate the transfer case shift mechanism contact surfaces with clean engine oil.

10   Lubricate the driveshaft slip-joints.

Note: *It may be necessary to disassemble the driveshaft to lubricate the slip joint (see Chapter 8).*

11   Lubricate conventional universal joints until grease can be seen coming out of the contact points.

12   While you are under the vehicle, clean

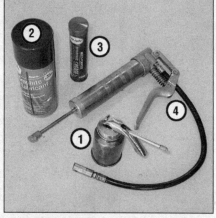

8.1 Materials required for chassis and body lubrication

1   **Engine oil** - *Light engine oil in a can like this can be used for door and hood hinges*

2   **Graphite spray** - *Used to lubricate lock cylinders*

3   **Grease** - *Grease, in a variety of types and weights, is available for use in a grease gun. Check the Specifications for your requirements*

4   **Grease gun** - *A common grease gun, shown here with a detachable hose and nozzle, is needed for chassis lubrication. After use, clean it thoroughly!*

and lubricate the parking brake cable along with the cable guides and levers. This can be done by smearing some chassis grease onto the cable and its related parts with your fingers.

13   Open the hood and smear a little chassis grease on the hood latch mechanism. Have an assistant pull the hood release lever from inside the vehicle as you lubricate the cable at the latch.

14   Lubricate all the hinges (door, hood, etc.) with engine oil to keep them in proper working order.

15   The key lock cylinders can be lubricated with spray-on graphite or silicone lubricant, which is available at auto parts stores.

16   Lubricate the door weatherstripping with silicone spray. This will reduce chafing and retard wear.

9   Battery check, maintenance and charging (every 6000 miles or 6 months)

Warning: *Certain precautions must be followed when checking and servicing the battery. Hydrogen gas, which is highly flammable, is always present in the battery cells, so keep lighted tobacco and all other open flames and sparks away from the battery. The electrolyte inside the battery is actually diluted sul-*

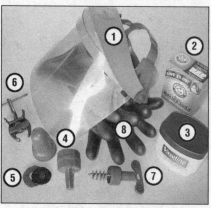

9.1 Tools and materials required for battery maintenance

1   **Face shield/safety goggles** - *When removing corrosion with a brush, the acidic particles can easily fly up into your eyes*

2   **Baking soda** - *A solution of baking soda and water can be used to neutralize corrosion*

3   **Petroleum jelly** - *A layer of this on the battery posts will help prevent corrosion*

4   **Battery post/cable cleaner** - *This wire brush cleaning tool will remove all traces of corrosion from the battery posts and cable clamps*

5   **Treated felt washers** - *Placing one of these on each post, directly under the cable clamps, will help prevent corrosion*

6   **Puller** - *Sometimes the cable clamps are very difficult to pull off the posts, even after the nut/bolt has been completely loosened. This tool pulls the clamp straight up and off the post without damage*

7   **Battery post/cable cleaner** - *Here is another cleaning tool which is a slightly different version of Number 4 above, but it does the same thing*

8   **Rubber gloves** - *Another safety item to consider when servicing the battery; remember that's acid inside the battery!*

furic acid, which will cause injury if splashed on your skin or in your eyes. It will also ruin clothes and painted surfaces. When removing the battery cables, always detach the negative cable first and hook it up last!*

1   A routine preventive maintenance program for the battery(ies) in your vehicle is the only way to ensure quick and reliable starts. But before performing any battery maintenance, make sure that you have the proper equipment necessary to work safely around the battery (see illustration).

2   There are also several precautions that should be taken whenever battery maintenance is performed. Before servicing the battery, always turn the engine and all accesso-

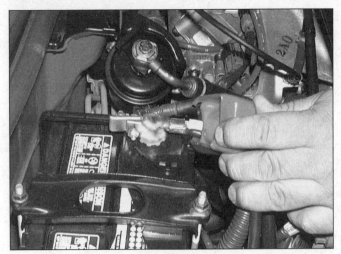

9.6a Battery terminal corrosion usually appears as light, fluffy powder

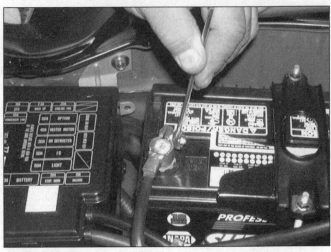

9.6b Removing the cable from a battery post with a wrench - sometimes special battery pliers are required for this procedure if corrosion has caused deterioration of the nut hex (always remove the ground cable first and hook it up last!)

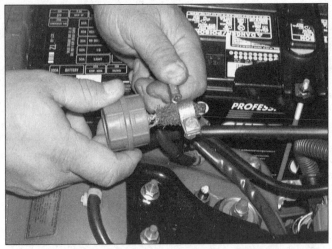

9.7a When cleaning the cable clamps, all corrosion must be removed (the inside of the clamp is tapered to match the taper on the post, so don't remove too much material)

9.7b Regardless of the type of tool used on the battery posts, a clean, shiny surface should be the result

ries off and disconnect the cable(s) from the negative terminal(s) of the battery(ies) (see Chapter 5).

3   The battery produces hydrogen gas, which is both flammable and explosive. Never create a spark, smoke or light a match around the battery. Always charge the battery in a ventilated area.

4   Electrolyte contains poisonous and corrosive sulfuric acid. Do not allow it to get in your eyes, on your skin or your clothes. Never ingest it. Wear protective safety glasses when working near the battery. Keep children away from the battery.

5   Note the external condition of the battery. If the positive terminal and cable clamp on your vehicle's battery is equipped with a rubber protector, make sure that it's not torn or damaged. It should completely cover the terminal. Look for any corroded or loose con-

nections, cracks in the case or cover or loose hold-down clamps. Also check the entire length of each cable for cracks and frayed conductors.

6   If corrosion, which looks like white, fluffy deposits (see illustration) is evident, particularly around the terminals, the battery should be removed for cleaning. Loosen the cable clamp bolts with a wrench, being careful to remove the ground cable first, and slide them off the terminals (see illustration). Then disconnect the hold-down clamp bolt and nut, remove the clamp and lift the battery from the engine compartment.

7   Clean the cable clamps thoroughly with a battery brush or a terminal cleaner and a solution of warm water and baking soda (see illustration). Wash the terminals and the top of the battery case with the same solution but make sure that the solution doesn't get into

the battery. When cleaning the cables, terminals and battery top, wear safety goggles and rubber gloves to prevent any solution from coming in contact with your eyes or hands. Wear old clothes too - even diluted, sulfuric acid splashed onto clothes will burn holes in them. If the terminals have been extensively corroded, clean them up with a terminal cleaner (see illustration). Thoroughly wash all cleaned areas with plain water.

8   Make sure that the battery tray is in good condition and the hold-down clamp bolts are tight. If the battery is removed from the tray, make sure no parts remain in the bottom of the tray when the battery is reinstalled. When reinstalling the hold-down clamp bolts, do not overtighten them.

9   Information on removing and installing the battery(ies) can be found in Chapter 5. Information on jump starting can be found at

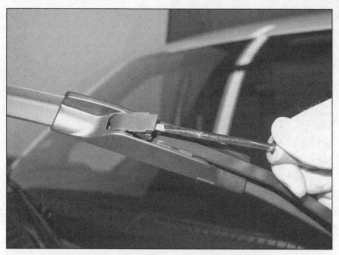

10.4 Pry the cover open to access the release lever

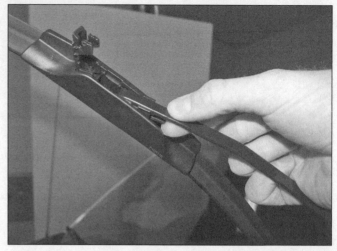

10.5 Press on the release tab and slide the blade assembly out of the hook in the arm

the front of this manual. For more detailed battery checking procedures, refer to the *Haynes Automotive Electrical Manual*.

Cleaning
10   Corrosion on the hold-down components, battery case and surrounding areas can be removed with a solution of water and baking soda. Thoroughly rinse all cleaned areas with plain water.
11   Any metal parts of the vehicle damaged by corrosion should be covered with a zinc-based primer, then painted.

Charging
Warning: *When batteries are being charged, hydrogen gas, which is very explosive and flammable, is produced. Do not smoke or allow open flames near a charging or a recently charged battery. Wear eye protection when near the battery during charging. Also, make sure the charger is unplugged before connecting or disconnecting the battery from the charger.*
12   Slow-rate charging is the best way to restore a battery that's discharged to the point where it will not start the engine. It's also a good way to maintain the battery charge in a vehicle that's only driven a few miles between starts. Maintaining the battery charge is particularly important in the winter when the battery must work harder to start the engine and electrical accessories that drain the battery are in greater use.
13   It's best to use a one or two-amp battery charger (sometimes called a "trickle" charger). They are the safest and put the least strain on the battery. They are also the least expensive. For a faster charge, you can use a higher amperage charger, but don't use one rated more than 1/10th the amp/hour rating of the battery. Rapid boost charges that claim to restore the power of the battery in one to two hours are hardest on the battery and can damage batteries not in good condition. This type of charging should only be used in emer-

gency situations.
14   The average time necessary to charge a battery should be listed in the instructions that come with the charger. As a general rule, a trickle charger will charge a battery in 12 to 16 hours.

10   Windshield wiper blade inspection and replacement (every 6000 miles or 6 months)

1   The windshield wiper and blade assembly should be inspected periodically for damage, loose components and cracked or worn blade elements.
2   Road film can build up on the wiper blades and affect their efficiency, so they should be washed regularly with a mild detergent solution.
3   If the wiper blade elements are cracked, worn or warped, or no longer clean adequately, they should be replaced with new ones.
4   Lift the arm assembly away from the glass for clearance, then use a small screwdriver to release the cover (see illustration).
5   Press on the release lever, then slide the wiper blade assembly out of the hook in the end of the arm (see illustration).
Note: *The cover on the blade might prevent the arm clearance needed for blade removal, and may have to be swiveled as necessary.*
6   Installation is the reverse of removal.

11   Tire rotation (every 6000 miles or 6 months)

Caution: *Some vehicles have different front and rear tire pressures. On models with different pressures, when the tires are rotated the tire pressures must be adjusted to the correct pressure and the tire pressure sensors must be relearned or "trained" using a*

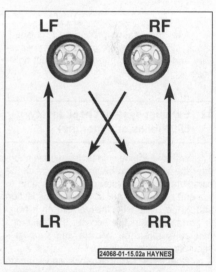

11.2 The recommended four-tire rotation pattern for non-directional tires

tire monitor activation tool. The tire light will flash and a "TRAIN LF/RF TIRE" message will be displayed on the instrument panel display. To relearn or train the sensor, a tire pressure monitor activation tool must be used. This is a procedure best performed at a dealership.
1   The tires should be rotated at the specified intervals and whenever uneven wear is noticed. Since the vehicle will be raised and the tires removed anyway, check the brakes also (see Section 18).
2   Radial tires must be rotated in a specific pattern (see illustration).
3   Refer to the information in *Jacking and towing* at the front of this manual for the proper procedure to follow when raising the vehicle and changing a tire.
4   The vehicle must be raised on a hoist or supported on jackstands to get all four wheels off the ground. Make sure the vehicle is safely supported!

12.2a Check the connections for exhaust leaks - also check that the clamp retaining nuts/bolts are securely tightened

12.2b Check the exhaust system hangers for damage and cracks

5   After the rotation procedure is finished, check and adjust the tire pressures as necessary and be sure to check the lug nut tightness.

12   Exhaust system check (every 6000 miles or 6 months)

1   With the engine cold (at least three hours after the vehicle has been driven), check the complete exhaust system from the engine to the end of the tailpipe. Ideally, the inspection should be done with the vehicle on a hoist to permit unrestricted access. If a hoist isn't available, raise the vehicle and support it securely on jackstands.
2   Check the exhaust pipes and connections for evidence of leaks, severe corrosion and damage. Make sure that all brackets and hangers are in good condition and tight (see illustrations).
3   At the same time, inspect the underside of the vehicle body for holes, corrosion, open seams, etc., which may allow exhaust gases to enter the passenger compartment. Seal all body openings with silicone or body putty.
4   Rattles and other noises can often be traced to the exhaust system, especially the mounts and hangers. Try to move the pipes, muffler and catalytic converter. If the components can come in contact with the body or suspension parts, secure the exhaust system with new mounts.
5   Check the running condition of the engine by inspecting inside the end of the tailpipe (with the engine off). The exhaust deposits here are an indication of engine state-of-tune. If the pipe is black and sooty or coated with white deposits, the engine may need a tune-up, including a thorough fuel system inspection and adjustment.

13   Seat belt check (every 6000 miles or 6 months)

1   Check seat belts, buckles, latch plates and guide loops for obvious damage and signs of wear.
2   See if the seat belt reminder light comes on when the key is turned to the Run or Start position. A chime should also sound.
3   The seat belts are designed to lock up during a sudden stop or impact, yet allow free movement during normal driving. Make sure the retractors return the belt against your chest while driving and rewind the belt fully when the buckle is unlatched.
4   If any of the above checks reveal problems with the seat belt system, replace parts as necessary.

14   Underhood hose check and replacement (every 15,000 miles or 12 months)

Warning: *Replacement of air conditioning hoses must be left to a dealer service department or air conditioning shop that has the equipment to depressurize the system safely. Never remove air conditioning components or hoses until the system has been depressurized.*

General

1   High temperatures under the hood can cause deterioration of the rubber and plastic hoses used for engine, accessory and emission systems operation. Periodic inspection should be made for cracks, loose clamps, material hardening and leaks.
2   Information specific to the cooling system hoses can be found in Section 15.
3   Most (but not all) hoses are secured to the fittings with clamps. Where clamps are used, check to be sure they haven't lost their tension, allowing the hose to leak. If clamps aren't used, make sure the hose has not expanded and/or hardened where it slips over the fitting, allowing it to leak.

PCV system hose

4   To reduce hydrocarbon emissions, crankcase blow-by gas is vented through the PCV valve in the valve cover to the intake manifold via a rubber hose (or plastic quick-connect tube) on most models. The blow-by gases mix with incoming air in the intake manifold before being burned in the combustion chambers.
5   Check the PCV hose for cracks, leaks and other damage. Disconnect it from the valve cover and the intake manifold and check the inside for obstructions. If it's clogged, clean it out with solvent.
6   For information specific to the PCV valve, see Section 27.

Vacuum hoses

7   It's quite common for vacuum hoses, especially those in the emissions system, to be color coded or identified by colored stripes molded into them. Various systems require hoses with different wall thickness, collapse resistance and temperature resistance. When replacing hoses, be sure the new ones are made of the same material.
8   Often the only effective way to check a hose is to remove it completely from the vehicle. If more than one hose is removed, be sure to label the hoses and fittings to ensure correct installation.
9   When checking vacuum hoses, be sure to include any plastic T-fittings in the check. Inspect the fittings for cracks and the hose where it fits over each fitting for distortion, which could cause leakage.
10   A small piece of vacuum hose (1/4-inch inside diameter) can be used as a stethoscope to detect vacuum leaks. Hold one end of the hose to your ear and probe around vac-

uum hoses and fittings, listening for the "hissing" sound characteristic of a vacuum leak. **Warning:** *When probing with the vacuum hose stethoscope, be careful not to come into contact with moving engine components such as drivebelts, the cooling fan, etc.*

Fuel hose

Warning: *Gasoline is flammable, so take extra precautions when you work on any part of the fuel system. Don't smoke or allow open flames or bare light bulbs near the work area, and don't work in a garage where a gas-type appliance (such as a water heater or clothes dryer) is present. Since fuel is carcinogenic, wear latex gloves when there's a possibility of being exposed to fuel, and, if you spill any fuel on your skin, rinse it off immediately with soap and water. Mop up any spills immediately and do not store fuel-soaked rags where they could ignite. The fuel system is under constant pressure, so, if any fuel lines are to be disconnected, the fuel pressure in the system must be relieved first (see Chapter 4 for more information). When you perform any kind of work on the fuel system, wear safety glasses and have a Class B type fire extinguisher on hand.*

11 The fuel lines are usually under pressure, so if any fuel lines are to be disconnected be prepared to catch spilled fuel. **Warning:** *Your vehicle is equipped with fuel injection and you must relieve the fuel system pressure before servicing the fuel lines. Refer to Chapter 4 for the fuel system pressure relief procedure.*

12 Check all flexible fuel lines for deterioration and chafing. Check especially for cracks in areas where the hose bends and just before fittings, such as where a hose attaches to the fuel pump, fuel filter and fuel injection unit.
13 When replacing a hose, use only hose that is specifically designed for your fuel injection system.
14 Spring-type clamps are sometimes used on fuel return or vapor lines. These clamps often lose their tension over a period of time, and can be "sprung" during removal. Replace all spring-type clamps with screw clamps whenever a hose is replaced. Some fuel lines use spring-lock type couplings, which require a special tool to disconnect. See Chapter 4 for more information on this type of couplings.

Metal lines

15 Sections of metal line are often used for fuel line between the fuel pump and the fuel injection unit. Check carefully to make sure the line isn't bent, crimped or cracked.
16 If a section of metal fuel line must be replaced, use seamless steel tubing only, since copper and aluminum tubing do not have the strength necessary to withstand vibration caused by the engine.
17 Check the metal brake lines where they enter the master cylinder and brake proportioning unit (if used) for cracks in the lines and loose fittings. Any sign of brake fluid leakage calls for an immediate thorough inspection of the brake system.

15 Cooling system check (every 15,000 miles or 12 months)

1 Many major engine failures can be attributed to a faulty cooling system. The cooling system also plays an important role in prolonging transmission life because it cools the fluid.
2 The engine should be cold for the cooling system check, so perform the following procedure before the vehicle is driven for the day or after it has been shut off for at least three hours.
3 Remove the cap from the expansion tank. Clean the cap thoroughly, inside and out, with clean water. Also clean the filler neck on the expansion tank. The presence of rust or corrosion in the filler neck means the coolant should be changed (see Section 23). The coolant inside the radiator should be relatively clean and transparent. If it's rust colored, drain the system and refill it with new coolant.
4 Carefully check the radiator hoses and the smaller diameter heater hoses (see illustration). Inspect each coolant hose along its entire length, replacing any hose which is cracked, swollen or deteriorated. Cracks will show up better if the hose is squeezed. Pay close attention to hose clamps that secure the hoses to cooling system components. Hose clamps can pinch and puncture hoses, resulting in coolant leaks. Some hoses are hidden from view so sometimes you'll have to trace a coolant leak.
5 Make sure that all hose connections are tight. A leak in the cooling system will usually show up as white or rust colored deposits on the area adjoining the leak. If wire-type clamps are used on the hoses, it may be a good idea to replace them with screw-type clamps.
6 Clean the front of the radiator and air conditioning condenser with compressed air, if available, or a soft brush. Remove all bugs, leaves, etc., embedded in the radiator fins. Be extremely careful not to damage the cooling fins or cut your fingers on them.
7 If the coolant level has been dropping consistently and no leaks are detectable, have the radiator cap (or expansion tank cap) and cooling system pressure checked at a service station.

16 Fuel system check (every 15,000 miles or 12 months)

Warning: *Gasoline is flammable, so take extra precautions when you work on any part of the fuel system. Don't smoke or allow open flames or bare light bulbs near the work area, and don't work in a garage where a gas-type appliance (such as a water heater or clothes dryer) is present. Since fuel is carcinogenic, wear latex gloves when there's a possibility of being exposed to fuel, and, if you spill any fuel on your skin, rinse it off immediately with soap and water. Mop up any spills immediately*

Check for a chafed area that could fail prematurely.

Check for a soft area indicating the hose has deteriorated inside.

Overtightening the clamp on a hardened hose will damage the hose and cause a leak.

Check each hose for swelling and oil-soaked ends. Cracks and breaks can be located by squeezing the hose.

15.4 Hoses, like drivebelts, have a habit of failing at the worst possible time - to prevent the inconvenience of a blown radiator or heater hose, inspect them carefully as shown here

and do not store fuel-soaked rags where they could ignite. When you perform any kind of work on the fuel system, wear safety glasses and have a Class B type fire extinguisher on hand. The fuel system is under constant pressure, so, before any lines are disconnected, the fuel system pressure must be relieved (see Chapter 4).

1 If you smell gasoline while driving or after the vehicle has been sitting in the sun, inspect the fuel system immediately.
2 Remove the fuel filler cap and inspect it for damage and corrosion. The gasket should have an unbroken sealing imprint. If the gasket is damaged or corroded, install a new cap.
3 Inspect the fuel feed and return lines for cracks. Make sure that the connections between the fuel lines and the fuel injection system and between the fuel lines and the in-

17.6 Check the shocks for leakage at the indicated area (rear shock shown)

17.9a Inspect the steering and suspension components for torn grease seals (arrows)

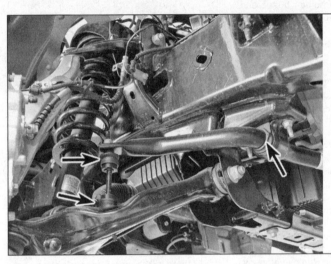

17.9b Check the stabilizer bar and link bushings for deterioration at the front and the rear of the vehicle

line fuel filter (if equipped) are tight.

Warning: *Your vehicle is fuel injected, so you must relieve the fuel system pressure before servicing fuel system components. The fuel system pressure relief procedure is outlined in Chapter 4.*

4   Since some components of the fuel system - the fuel tank and part of the fuel feed and return lines, for example - are underneath the vehicle, they can be inspected more easily with the vehicle raised on a hoist. If that's not possible, raise the vehicle and support it on jackstands.

5   With the vehicle raised and safely supported, inspect the gas tank and filler neck for punctures, cracks and other damage. The connection between the filler neck and the tank is particularly critical. Sometimes a rubber filler neck will leak because of loose clamps or deteriorated rubber. Inspect all fuel tank mounting brackets and straps to be sure that the tank is securely attached to the vehicle.

Warning: *Do not, under any circumstances, try to repair a fuel tank (except rubber components). A welding torch or any open flame*

can easily cause fuel vapors inside the tank to explode.

6   Carefully check all rubber hoses and metal lines leading away from the fuel tank. Check for loose connections, deteriorated hoses, crimped lines and other damage. Repair or replace damaged sections as necessary (see Chapter 4).

---

17   Steering and suspension check (every 15,000 miles or 12 months)

Note: *The steering linkage and suspension components should be checked periodically. Worn or damaged suspension and steering linkage components can result in excessive and abnormal tire wear, poor ride quality and vehicle handling and reduced fuel economy. For detailed illustrations of the steering and suspension components, refer to Chapter 10.*

Shock absorber check

1   Park the vehicle on level ground, turn the

engine off and set the parking brake. Check the tire pressures.

2   Push down at one corner of the vehicle, then release it while noting the movement of the body. It should stop moving and come to rest in a level position within one or two bounces.

3   If the vehicle continues to move up-and-down or if it fails to return to its original position, a worn or weak shock absorber is probably the reason.

4   Repeat the above check at each of the three remaining corners of the vehicle.

5   Raise the vehicle and support it securely on jackstands.

6   Check the shock absorbers for evidence of fluid leakage (see illustration). A light film of fluid is no cause for concern. Make sure that any fluid noted is from the shocks and not from some other source. If leakage is noted, replace the shocks as a set.

7   Check the shocks to be sure that they are securely mounted and undamaged. Check the upper mounts for damage and wear. If damage or wear is noted, replace the shocks as a set (front or rear).

8   If the shocks must be replaced, refer to Chapter 10 for the procedure.

Steering and suspension check

9   Visually inspect the steering and suspension components for damage and distortion. Look for damaged seals, boots and bushings and leaks of any kind (see illustrations).

10   Clean the lower end of the steering knuckle. Have an assistant grasp the lower edge of the tire and move the wheel in-and-out while you look for movement at the steering knuckle-to-control arm balljoint. If there is 1/32-inch or more movement the suspension balljoint(s) must be replaced.

11   Grasp each front tire at the front and rear edges, push in at the front, pull out at the rear and feel for play in the steering system com-

17.11 With the steering wheel locked and the vehicle raised, grasp the front tire as shown and try to move it back-and-forth - if any play is noted, check the tie-rod ends for looseness

18.6 You will find an inspection hole(s) like this in each caliper - placing a ruler across the hole should enable you to determine the thickness of remaining pad material for the inner (1) and outer pads (2) - the outer pad can be difficult to see

ponents. If any freeplay is noted, check the tie-rod ends for looseness (see illustration).

12 Additional steering and suspension system information and illustrations can be found in Chapter 10.

18 Brake check (every 15,000 miles or 12 months)

Warning: *The dust created by the brake system is harmful to your health. Never blow it out with compressed air and don't inhale any of it. An approved filtering mask should be worn when working on the brakes. Do not, under any circumstances, use petroleum-based solvents to clean brake parts. Use brake system cleaner only! Try to use non-asbestos replacement parts whenever possible.*

Note: *For detailed photographs of the brake system, refer to Chapter 9.*

1   In addition to the specified intervals, the brakes should be inspected every time the wheels are removed or whenever a defect is suspected.

2   Any of the following symptoms could indicate a potential brake system defect: The vehicle pulls to one side when the brake pedal is depressed; the brakes make squealing or dragging noises when applied; brake pedal travel is excessive; the pedal pulsates; brake fluid leaks, usually onto the inside of the tire or wheel.

3   Loosen the wheel lug nuts.

4   Raise the vehicle and place it securely on jackstands.

5   Remove the wheels (see Jacking and towing at the front of this book, or your owner's manual, if necessary).

Disc brakes

6   There are two pads (an outer and an inner) in each caliper. The pads are visible through inspection holes in each caliper (see

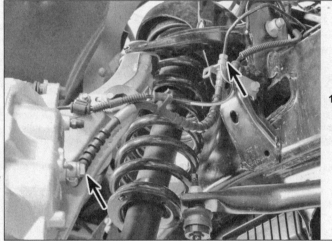

18.11 Check along the brake hoses and at each fitting for deterioration and cracks

illustration).

7   Check the pad thickness by looking at each end of the caliper and through the inspection hole in the caliper body. If the lining material is less than the thickness listed in this Chapter's Specifications, replace the pads.

Note: *Keep in mind that the lining material is riveted or bonded to a metal backing plate and the metal portion is not included in this measurement.*

8   If it is difficult to determine the exact thickness of the remaining pad material by the above method, or if you are at all concerned about the condition of the pads, remove the caliper(s), then remove the pads from the calipers for further inspection (refer to Chapter 9).

9   Once the pads are removed from the calipers, clean them with brake cleaner and re-measure them with a ruler or a vernier caliper.

10   Measure the disc thickness with a micrometer to make sure that it still has service life remaining. If any disc is thinner than the specified minimum thickness, replace it

(see Chapter 9). Even if the disc has service life remaining, check its condition. Look for scoring, gouging and burned spots. If these conditions exist, remove the disc and have it resurfaced (see Chapter 9).

11   Before installing the wheels, check all brake lines and hoses for damage, wear, deformation, cracks, corrosion, leakage, bends and twists, particularly in the vicinity of the rubber hoses at the calipers (see illustration). Check the clamps for tightness and the connections for leakage. Make sure that all hoses and lines are clear of sharp edges, moving parts and the exhaust system. If any of the above conditions are noted, repair, reroute or replace the lines and/or fittings as necessary (see Chapter 9).

Brake booster check

12   Sit in the driver's seat and perform the following sequence of tests.

13   With the brake fully depressed, start the engine - the pedal should move down a little when the engine starts.

14   With the engine running, depress the brake pedal several times - the travel distance should not change.
15   Depress the brake, stop the engine and hold the pedal in for about 30 seconds - the pedal should neither sink nor rise.
16   Restart the engine, run it for about a minute and turn it off. Then, firmly depress the brake several times - the pedal travel should decrease with each application.
17   If your brakes do not operate as described, the brake booster has failed. Refer to Chapter 9 for the replacement procedure.

Parking brake

18   One method of checking the parking brake is to park the vehicle on a steep hill with the parking brake set and the transmission in Neutral (stay in the vehicle for this check!). If the parking brake cannot prevent the vehicle from rolling, it's in need of adjustment (see Chapter 9).

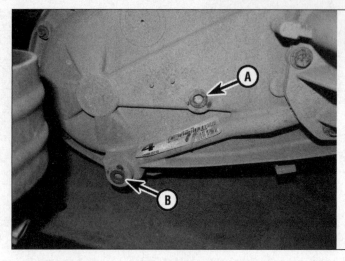

19.1 Typical transfer case check/fill plug (A) and drain plug (B) are located on the rear of the transfer case

19   Transfer case lubricant level check (4WD models) (every 15,000 miles or 12 months)

Note: *Make sure the vehicle is on level ground for the check.*
1   The lubricant level is checked by removing a plug from the side of the case (see illustration). If the vehicle is raised to gain access to the plug, be sure to support it safely on jackstands - DO NOT crawl under the vehicle when it's supported only by a jack!
2   With the engine and transfer case cold, remove the check/fill plug. If lubricant immediately starts leaking out, thread the plug back into the case - the level is correct. If it doesn't, completely remove the plug and reach inside the hole with your finger. The level should be even with the bottom of the plug hole.
3   If more lubricant is needed, use a syringe or small pump to add it through the opening.
4   Thread the plug back into the case and tighten it securely. Drive the vehicle, then check for leaks around the plug.

20   Differential lubricant level check (every 15,000 miles or 12 months)

Note: *Make sure the vehicle is on level ground for the check.*
1   The differential has a check/fill plug which must be removed to check the lubricant level. If the vehicle is raised to gain access to the plug, be sure to support it safely on jackstands - DO NOT crawl under the vehicle when it's supported only by the jack!
2   Remove the check/fill plug from the differential (see illustrations).
3   Use your finger as a dipstick to make sure the lubricant level is even with the bottom of the plug hole. If not, use a syringe to add the recommended lubricant until it just starts to run out of the opening. On some models a tag is located in the area of the plug which gives information regarding lubricant type, particularly on models equipped with a Traction Lok differential.
4   Install the plug and tighten it securely.

21   Cabin air filter replacement (every 15,000 miles or 12 months)

1   Open and fully lower the glove box door (see Chapter 11).
2   Remove the upper glove box rubber panel cover, then remove the fasteners and upper glove box panel (see Chapter 11).
3   Release the tabs on each side of the filter access cover and lift off the cover, disengaging the bottom retaining tabs (see illustration).
4   Remove the filter element from the housing (see illustration).
5   Installation is the reverse of removal. Make sure the arrow on the side of the filter element is pointing UP.

20.2 The check/fill plug is located at the right-front of the differential housing (plug locations may vary by model, but will generally be at the same height)

21.3 Release the tabs (1), then disengage the bottom tabs (2) and remove the filter access door

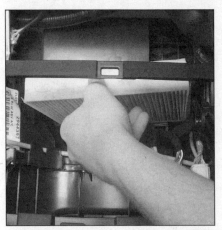

21.4 Remove the filter from the housing

22.1a Release the filter cover clamps…

22.1b … slide the cover forward until the tabs at the rear of the housing are free…

22   Air filter check and replacement (every 30,000 miles or 24 months)

1   The air filter is located inside a housing at the left (driver's) side of the engine compartment. To remove the air filter, release the housing cover clamps, then lift-off the cover and remove the air filter element (see illustrations).

2   Inspect the outer surface of the filter element. If it is dirty, replace it. If it is only moderately dusty, it can be reused by blowing it clean with compressed air, in the reverse direction of normal engine airflow. Because the factory installed filter is a pleated paper type filter, it cannot be washed or oiled. If it cannot be cleaned satisfactorily with compressed air, discard and replace it.

Caution: *Never drive the vehicle with the air filter removed. Excessive engine wear could result and backfiring could even cause a fire under the hood.*

3   Wipe out the inside of the air filter housing.

4   Place the new air filter element into the

housing, making sure it seats properly.

5   The remainder of installation is the reverse of removal.

23   Cooling system servicing (draining, flushing and refilling) (every 30,000 miles or 24 months)

Warning: *Do not allow antifreeze to come in contact with your skin or painted surfaces of the vehicle. Rinse off spills immediately with plenty of water. Antifreeze is highly toxic if ingested. Never leave antifreeze lying around in an open container or in puddles on the floor; children and pets are attracted by its sweet smell and may drink it. Check with local authorities about disposing of used antifreeze. Many communities have collection centers which will see that antifreeze is disposed of safely.*

1   Periodically, the cooling system should be drained, flushed and refilled to replenish the antifreeze mixture and prevent formation of rust and corrosion, which can impair the

performance of the cooling system and cause engine damage. When the cooling system is serviced, all hoses and the expansion tank cap should be checked and replaced if necessary.

Draining

2   Apply the parking brake and block the wheels. If the vehicle has just been driven, wait several hours to allow the engine to cool down before beginning this procedure.

3   Once the engine is completely cool, remove the expansion tank cap (see Section 4).

4   Move a large container under the radiator drain to catch the coolant. Attach a 3/8-inch diameter hose to the drain fitting, if available, to direct the coolant into the container, then open the drain fitting with a screwdriver (see illustration). Allow time for the coolant to drain completely.

5   After the coolant stops flowing out of the radiator, move the container under the engine block drain plugs (if equipped) and allow the coolant in the block to drain (see illustration).

6   While the coolant is draining, check the

22.1c … then lift-off the cover and remove the air filter element

23.4 The radiator drain fitting is located at the bottom-left corner of the radiator

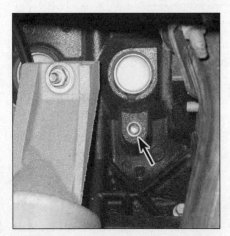

23.5 If equipped, the block drain plugs (arrow) are generally located about one to two inches above the oil pan - there is one on each side of the engine block

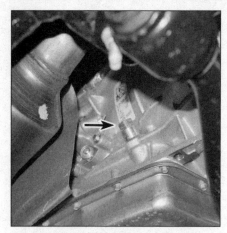

24.5 Transmission fill plug/dipstick location

24.8a Loosen the transmission pan bolts…

24.8b … then pry the pan loose and allow the transmission fluid to drain out of the front of the pan

condition of the radiator hoses, heater hoses and clamps (refer to Section 15 if necessary). Replace any damaged clamps or hoses.

7   Reinstall the block drain plugs and tighten them securely.

Flushing

8   Close the radiator drain fitting, then fill the cooling system with clean water, following the Refilling procedure (see Step 14).

9   Start the engine and allow it to reach normal operating temperature, then rev up the engine a few times.

10   Turn the engine off and allow it to cool completely, then drain the system as described earlier.

11   Repeat Steps 8 through 10 until the water being drained is free of contaminants.

12   In severe cases of contamination or clogging of the radiator, remove the radiator (see Chapter 3) and have a radiator repair facility clean and repair it if necessary.

13   Many deposits can be removed by the chemical action of a cleaner available at auto parts stores. Follow the procedure outlined in the manufacturer's instructions.

Note: *When the coolant is regularly drained and the system refilled with the correct anti-freeze/water mixture, there should be no need to use chemical cleaners or descalers.*

Refilling

Note: *Ford recommends that the climate control system is turned off during the refilling procedure.*

14   Close and tighten the radiator drain fitting.

15   Slowly add new coolant (a 50/50 mixture of water and antifreeze) to the expansion tank until the level reaches the MAX mark. See this Chapter's Specifications for the recommended coolant types.

16   Install the expansion tank cap. Start and run the engine in a well-ventilated area for about a minute, then increase the engine RPM to 3500 for 30 seconds.

17   Turn the engine off and wait one minute.

18   With the engine still sufficiently cold, slowly open the expansion tank cap and top-up the expansion tank with coolant until the level is slightly above the MIN mark.

19   Install the expansion tank cap. Start and run the engine again until it reaches normal operating temperature (the thermostat will open and the upper radiator hose will become hot).

20   Rev the engine up to 3500 RPM for 30 seconds, then bring the engine to idle for 30 seconds.

21   Turn the engine off and wait another minute.

22   Repeat Steps 20 and 21, 5 more times. This will purge any air pockets remaining in the system.

23   Turn the engine off and let it cool completely. Remove the cap and add more coolant mixture to bring the level slightly above the MIN mark with the engine cool.

24   Squeeze the upper radiator hose to expel air, then add more coolant mixture if necessary. Install the expansion tank cap.

25   Start the engine, allow it to reach normal operating temperature and check for leaks. Also, set the heater and blower controls to the maximum setting and check to see that the heater output from the air ducts is warm. This is a good indication that all air has been purged from the cooling system.

24   Automatic transmission fluid and filter change (every 30,000 miles or 24 months)

1   At the specified intervals, the transmission fluid should be drained and replaced. Since the fluid will remain hot long after driving, perform this procedure only after the engine has cooled down completely.

2   Before beginning work, purchase the transmission fluid specified in *Recommended lubricants and fluids* at the beginning of this Chapter, a new filter and filter seal (auxiliary

pump inlet tube seal), and if necessary, a new gasket. Never reuse the old filter or filter seal! **Note:** *The gasket is reusable as long as it isn't damaged.*

3   Other tools necessary for this job include jackstands to support the vehicle in a raised position, a drain pan capable of holding at least ten quarts, newspapers and clean rags.

4   Raise the front and rear of the vehicle and support it securely and evenly on jackstands. The vehicle must be supported in a level position.

Note: *The 6-speed and 10-speed transmissions covered by this manual do not have a drain plug - the fluid should be removed through the transmission fill plug using a siphon kit, if available.*

5   Remove the transmission fill plug and dipstick from the right side of the transmission (see illustration).

6   Insert a siphon hose into the fill plug hole and siphon as much fluid out as possible.

Warning: *Never start a siphon by mouth! Proper siphon kits are available at most auto parts stores.*

7   On 10-speed models, remove the transmission pan heat shield and shift linkage cover before removing the pan.

8   Place a large drain pan underneath the transmission. Loosen the transmission pan bolts, then carefully pry the front of the transmission pan loose with a screwdriver and allow the fluid to drain (see illustrations). Don't damage the pan or transmission gasket surfaces or leaks could develop.

9   Remove all the pan bolts, transmission pan and gasket. Drain out the remaining fluid from the pan into the drain container. Carefully clean the gasket surface of the transmission to remove all traces of the old gasket and sealant.

10   Remove the magnet(s) from the pan, then clean the transmission pan and gasket mating surface with solvent and dry it thoroughly. Also clean the magnets, then place them on their original locations on the pan (see illustrations).

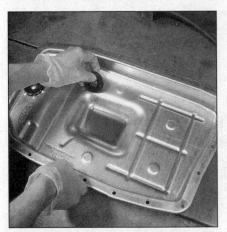

24.10a Remove the magnets from the pan…

24.10b … then clean the pan and magnets. Make sure the pan is completely clean and dried, then reinstall the magnets

24.11a Pull the filter straight down and out of the valve body (wiggling it as needed)…

11   On 6-speed models, pull the filter straight down and out of the valve body. If the filter seal or auxiliary pump inlet tube seal did not come out with the filter, remove them from the transmission, being careful not to gouge the seal bores in any way (see illustrations).
Note: *A new auxiliary pump inlet tube seal will need to be used when installing the filter*
12   On 10-speed models, remove the filter mounting bolts and the old filter from the transmission. If the filter seal did not come out with the filter, remove it from the transmission being careful not to gouge the seal bore in any way.
13   Install a new seal(s) - applying ATF to the seal(s) first - and filter. On 10-speed models, tighten the filter bolts to the torque listed in this Chapter's Specifications.
14   Make sure the gasket surface on the transmission pan is clean, then install the gasket (see illustration).
15   Put the pan in place against the transmission and install the bolts. Working around the pan in a criss-cross pattern, tighten each bolt a little at a time until the final torque figure listed in this Chapter's Specifications is reached. Don't overtighten the bolts!
16   Using a hand pump or squeeze bottle, add 3-1/2 quarts of the specified type of automatic transmission fluid through the filler plug/dipstick opening.
17   Check the transmission fluid level with the dipstick, adding more fluid as necessary, 1/2 pint at a time - until the level reaches the cross-hatched area (not the dotted area) on the dipstick (see Section 6).
18   With the transmission in Park and the parking brake set, start and run the engine at idle.
19   With your foot on the brake, move the gear selector through each range, pausing for a few seconds in between, then back to Park. Check the fluid level with the engine still idling. Add fluid as necessary to reach the correct level.
Caution: *Add fluid 1/2-pint at a time to avoid overfilling the transmission.*

24.11b … then remove the auxiliary pump inlet tube seal from the valve body if it did not come out with the filter (6-speed model shown)

24.14 Make sure the gasket surface on the pan is clean, then install a new gasket (or reinstall the old gasket if it's not damaged)

20   A more accurate fluid level check can be made with the transmission at normal operating temperature (see Section 6).
21   Check under the vehicle for leaks during the first few trips.

25 Brake fluid change (every 30,000 miles or 24 months)

Warning: *Brake fluid can harm your eyes and damage painted surfaces, so use extreme caution when handling or pouring it. Do not use brake fluid that has been standing open or is more than one year old. Brake fluid absorbs moisture from the air. Excess moisture can cause a dangerous loss of braking effectiveness.*
1   At the specified intervals, the brake fluid should be drained and replaced. Since the brake fluid may drip or splash when pouring it, place plenty of rags around the master cylinder to protect any surrounding painted surfaces.

2   Before beginning work, purchase the specified brake fluid (see Recommended lubricants and fluids at the beginning of this Chapter).
3   Remove the cap from the master cylinder reservoir.
4   Using a hand suction pump or similar device, withdraw the fluid from the master cylinder reservoir.
5   Add new fluid to the master cylinder until it rises to the base of the filler neck.
6   Bleed the brake system as described in Chapter 9 at all four brakes until new and uncontaminated fluid is expelled from the bleeder screw. Be sure to maintain the fluid level in the master cylinder as you perform the bleeding process. If you allow the master cylinder to run dry, air will enter the system.
7   Refill the master cylinder with fluid and check the operation of the brakes. The pedal should feel solid when depressed, with no sponginess.
Warning: *Do not operate the vehicle if you are in doubt about the effectiveness of the brake system.*

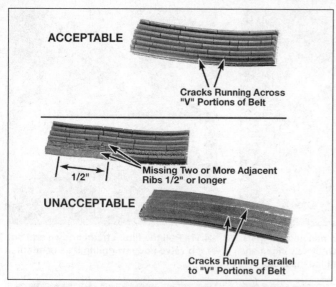

ACCEPTABLE

Cracks Running Across
"V" Portions of Belt

1/2"

Missing Two or More Adjacent
Ribs 1/2" or longer

UNACCEPTABLE

Cracks Running Parallel
to "V" Portions of Belt

26.4 Small cracks in the underside of a V-ribbed belt are acceptable - lengthwise cracks, or missing pieces that cause the belt to make noise, are cause for replacement

26.7 Rotate the tensioner arm to relieve belt tension - 2.7L V6 engine shown

26 Drivebelt check (every 3000 miles or 3 months) and replacement (every 60,000 miles or 48 months)

1   The drivebelt(s) is located at the front of the engine and plays an important role in the overall operation of the vehicle and its components. Due to its function and material make-up, the drivebelt is prone to failure after a period of time and should be inspected and replaced periodically to prevent major engine damage.

2   2.7L V6 models are equipped with a single automatically adjusted serpentine drivebelt, which is used to drive all of the accessory components such as the alternator, water pump and air conditioning compressor. 3.5L V6 models (turbo and non-turbo) are equipped with two drivebelts - a main accessory serpentine belt that drives the alternator and water pump and is automatically adjusted, and an air conditioning compressor drivebelt that doesn't use a tensioner. V8 models are equipped with two automatically adjusted serpentine drivebelts - a main belt that is used to drive the alternator and water pump, and another that drives the air conditioning compressor.

Inspection

3   With the engine off, open the hood and locate the drivebelt at the front of the engine. Using your fingers (and a flashlight, if necessary), move along the belts checking for cracks and separation of the belt plies. Also check for fraying and glazing, which gives the belt a shiny appearance. Both sides of each belt should be inspected, which means you will have to twist the belt to check the underside.

4   Check the ribs on the underside of the belt. They should all be the same depth, with none of the surface uneven (see illustration).

5   The tension of the belt is automatically adjusted by the belt tensioner and does not require any adjustments. The tensioner can be checked with the belt removed, by moving the tensioner from its release position through a full stroke and back to make sure there is no excessive sticking, grabbing or binding, and to make sure there is tension on the drivebelt tensioner spring at all times. Check the drivebelt wear (see Steps 3 and 4).

Replacement

6   Raise the vehicle and support it securely on jackstands, then remove the engine under cover, if accessing the drivebelt from below. To access the drivebelt tensioner(s) from above, remove the air intake duct and housing, or any other intake ducting that may interfere with drivebelt access, where equipped (see Chapter 4).
Note: *It is easier to access the tensioner from under the vehicle.*

Accessory drivebelt(s)

7   To replace the accessory drivebelt, rotate the tensioner to relieve the tension on the belt (see illustration), then slip the belt off of an accessible pulley. Once the belt is loose, allow the tensioner to slowly come to rest at its stopping point.On all models, place a socket with a breaker bar on the tensioner pulley center bolt. On V6 models, rotate the tensioner clockwise and on V8 models rotate the tensioner counterclockwise.

8   V8 models have a second rear (inner) air conditioning compressor drivebelt which has a square hole in the tensioner arm that will accept a 3/8-inch drive breaker bar, rotate the tensioner clockwise to relieve the tension on the belt.

9   Remove the belt from the remaining auxiliary components.

10   Route the new belt loosely over the various pulleys, then rotate the tensioner to allow the belt to be installed. Slowly release the belt tensioner when the belt is fitted onto all the pulleys. Make sure the belt fits properly into the pulley grooves - it must be completely engaged (see illustrations).
Note: *Most models have a drivebelt routing decal on the upper radiator panel to help during drivebelt installation.*

3.5L V6 model air conditioning compressor drivebelt

11   Remove the accessory drivebelt (see Steps 7 through 9).

12   Remove the engine splash shield/under cover.

13   Using a pair of diagonal cutting pliers, cut the air conditioning belt to remove it.
Note: *Some tool manufacturers make air conditioning compressor belt removal tools that can remove the belt without cutting it off. We only recommend using this type of tool if the belt if relatively new and will be reused. Always check the belt for damage after the removal process.*

14   Place one end of the new belt behind the crankshaft pulley, and the other end onto the compressor pulley, making sure the belt is fully seated in the pulley grooves.

15   Place part of the belt onto the top of the crankshaft pulley grooves, letting the rest of the belt toward the bottom of the crankshaft pulley hang/fold inward.

16   At this stage, the belt should be placed evenly onto the compressor pulley and part way onto the top of the crank pulley. While holding the belt in place at the top of the crank pulley, use a cable tie to hold the belt in place at the top crankshaft grooves.

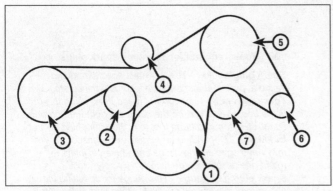

26.10a The drivebelt routing schematic for 2.7L V6 models

1 Crankshaft pulley	4 Idler pulley
2 Tensioner and pulley	5 Water pump pulley
3 Air conditioning	6 Alternator pulley
compressor	7 Idler pulley

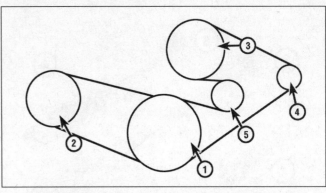

26.10b The drivebelt routing schematic for 3.5L V6 models

1 Crankshaft pulley	3 Water pump
2 Air conditioning	4 Alternator
compressor	5 Tensioner and pulley

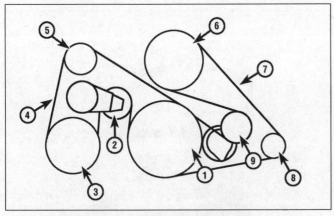

26.10c The drivebelt routing schematic for 5.0L V8 models

1 Crankshaft pulley	5 Idler pulley
2 Tensioner and pulley	6 Water pump
(rear belt)	7 Front belt
3 Air conditioning	8 Alternator
compressor	9 Tensioner and pulley
4 Rear belt	(front belt)

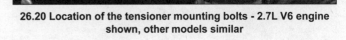

26.20 Location of the tensioner mounting bolts - 2.7L V6 engine shown, other models similar

17   Rotate the crankshaft pulley clockwise with a socket and ratchet, which should lift the belt onto the crankshaft pulley grooves. **Warning:** *DO NOT crank the engine with the starter during this process! Rotate the engine by hand only.*
18   The remainder of installation is the reverse of removal. Make sure the belt is even with the pulley grooves.

Tensioner
19   Remove the accessory drivebelt(s) (see Steps 7 through 9).
20   Remove the tensioner mounting bolt(s) (see illustration) and remove the tensioner. **Note:** *V8 models use a single mounting bolt for each tensioner and V6 models use two tensioner mounting bolts.*
21   Install the tensioner and tighten the mounting bolts to the torque listed in this Chapter's Specifications.
22   Installation is the reverse of removal.

27 Positive Crankcase Ventilation (PCV) system check and replacement (every 60,000 miles or 48 months)

Note: *To maintain efficient operation of the PCV system, clean the hoses and check the PCV valve at the intervals recommended in the maintenance schedule. For additional information on the PCV system, refer to Chapter 6.*
1   The PCV valve is located in the right-side valve cover (see illustration). **Note:** *When the PCV valve is removed, the retaining tabs on the valve are damaged and a new PCV valve must be installed.*
2   Start the engine and allow it to idle, then disconnect the PCV hose from the PCV valve and feel for vacuum at the end of the hose. If vacuum is felt, then the hose connecting to the PCV valve is not clogged. Turn off the engine.

27.1 Location of the PCV valve - 2.7L engine shown (other models similar)

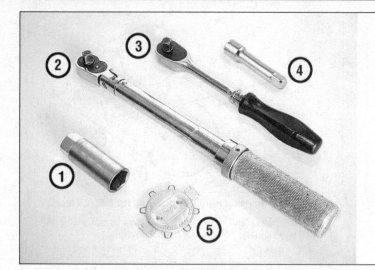

28.1 Tools required for changing spark plugs

1   **Spark plug socket** - This will have special padding inside to protect the spark plug's porcelain insulator
2   **Torque wrench** - Although not mandatory, using this tool is the best way to ensure the plugs are tightened properly
3   **Ratchet** - Standard hand tool to fit the spark plug socket
4   **Extension** - Depending on model and accessories, you may need special extensions and universal joints to reach one or more of the plugs
5   **Spark plug gap gauge** - This gauge for checking the gap comes in a variety of styles. Make sure the gap for your engine is included

28.4a Spark plug manufacturers recommend using a wire-type gauge when checking the gap - if the wire does not slide between the electrodes with a slight drag, adjustment is required

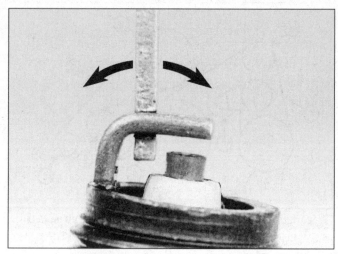

28.4b To change the gap, bend the side electrode only, as indicated by the arrows, and be very careful not to crack or chip the porcelain insulator surrounding the center electrode

3   If little or no vacuum is felt at the hose, check for a plugged or cracked hose between the PCV valve and the intake manifold.
4   If a problem is suspected at the PCV valve, remove the valve with an appropriate sized wrench, then shake the valve freely by hand. If the valve does not rattle, this indicates that it is stuck open or closed and will need to be replaced.
5   If the valve is clogged, the hose may also be plugged. Remove the hose between the valve and the intake manifold and clean it with solvent. For plastic PCV hoses, make sure the solvent is safe for application on plastic.
6   After cleaning the hose, inspect it for damage, wear and deterioration. Make sure it fits snugly on the fittings.
7   Install a new PCV valve if removed. To install the PCV valve, insert the valve into the cover and rotate the valve until the retaining tabs click into place. Connect the PCV hose to the valve and intake manifold.

28   Spark plug check and replacement (every 60,000 miles or 48 months)

1   In most cases, the tools necessary for spark plug replacement include a spark plug socket which fits onto a ratchet (spark plug sockets are padded inside to prevent damage to the porcelain insulators on the new plugs), various extensions and a gap gauge to check and adjust the gaps on the new plugs (see illustration). A torque wrench should be used to tighten the new plugs.
2   The best approach when replacing the spark plugs is to purchase the new ones in advance, adjust them to the proper gap and replace the plugs one at a time. When buying the new spark plugs, be sure to obtain the correct plug type for your particular engine. This information can be found in this Chapter's Specifications or in the owner's manual.

3   Allow the engine to cool completely before attempting to remove any of the plugs. These engines are equipped with aluminum cylinder heads, which can be damaged if the spark plugs are removed when the engine is hot. While you are waiting for the engine to cool, check the new plugs for defects and adjust the gaps.
4   The gap is checked by inserting the proper thickness gauge between the electrodes at the tip of the plug (see illustration). The gap between the electrodes should be the same as the one specified on the Emissions Control Information label. The wire should just slide between the electrodes with a slight amount of drag. If the gap is incorrect, use the adjuster on the gauge body to bend the curved side electrode slightly until the specified gap is obtained (see illustration). If the side electrode is not exactly over the center electrode, bend it with the adjuster until it is. Check for cracks in the porcelain insulator (if

28.6a The ignition coils must be removed to access the spark plugs - disconnect the harness retaining clip from the stud bolt…

28.6b … then disconnect the electrical connector (1) and remove the coil retaining bolt (2)…

28.6c … pull straight up and out to remove the coil (2.7L V6 model shown - other models similar)

28.8 Use a ratchet and spark plug socket on an extension to remove the spark plugs

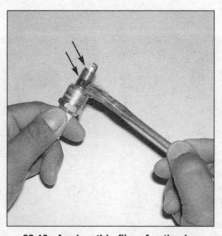

28.10a Apply a thin film of anti-seize compound to the spark plug threads

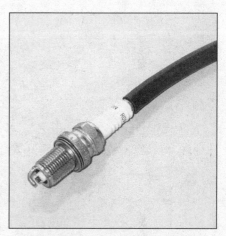

28.10b A length of rubber hose will save time and prevent damaged threads when installing the spark plugs

any are found, the plug should not be used).
Caution: *Some spark plug manufacturers recommend against checking and/or adjusting the gap on certain types of plugs - these plugs have been preset to a specified gap at the factory or contain a delicate layer of iridium that could be easily scraped off. Be sure to follow the directions provided with the plugs before checking/adjusting the gap.*

Replacement

5   These models are equipped with individual ignition coils mounted on top of the spark plugs which must be removed to access the spark plugs. On 3.5L non-turbocharged engines, the upper intake manifold must be removed to access the right-side ignition coils (see Chapter 2A).
6   To remove the spark plugs, the individual ignition coils must be removed first to access the spark plugs (see illustrations).
7   If compressed air is available, use it to blow any dirt or foreign material away from the spark plug to eliminate the possibility of

debris falling into the cylinder as the spark plug is removed.
8   Place the spark plug socket with an extension over the plug (see illustration) and remove it from the engine by turning it in a counterclockwise direction.
9   Compare each old spark plug to those shown on the inside of the back cover to get an indication of the general running condition of the engine.
10   Apply a small amount of anti-seize compound to the spark plug threads (see illustration). Install one of the new plugs into the hole until you can no longer turn it with your fingers, then tighten it with a torque wrench (if available) or the ratchet. It is a good idea to slip a short length of rubber hose over the end of the plug to use as a tool to thread it into place (see illustration). The hose will grip the plug well enough to turn it, but will start to slip if the plug begins to cross-thread in the hole - this will prevent damaged threads and the accompanying repair costs.
11   Before pushing the ignition coil onto the

end of the plug, inspect it following the procedures outlined in Section 29 .
12   Repeat the procedure for the remaining spark plugs. Installation is the reverse of removal.

29 Ignition coil check and replacement (every 60,000 miles or 48 months)

1   Clean the coils with a dampened cloth and dry them thoroughly.
2   Inspect each coil for cracks, damage and carbon tracking. Make sure the coil fits securely onto the upper spark plug and the electrical connector connects securely to each coil. If damage exists, replace the coil (see Section 28).
3   It's also a good idea to apply a small amount of dielectric compound to the opening of the coil boot (where the spark plug fits into) before installing the coil onto the plug. This will ensure a clean coil-to-plug connection.

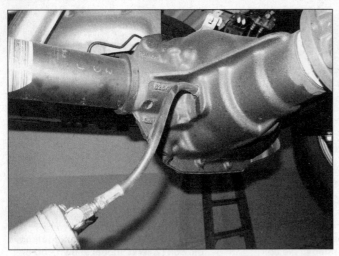

30.5 Insert the hose into the plug opening and down to the bottom of the differential housing, then suction the lubricant out

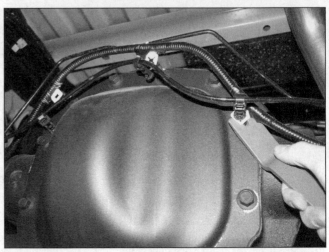

30.8 Release the harness clips from along the top of the differential cover

30.9a Remove the bolts from the lower edge of the cover...

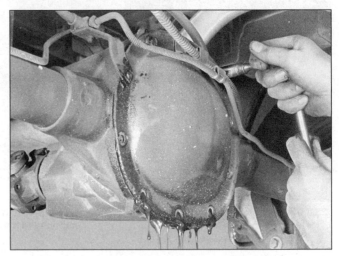

30.9b ... then loosen the top bolts and let the lubricant drain

30   Differential lubricant change (every 100,000 miles or 60 months)

Dr.ain

1   This procedure should be performed after the vehicle has been driven so the lubricant will be warm and therefore flow out of the differential more easily.

2   Raise the vehicle and support it securely on jackstands.

3   The easiest way to drain the differential(s) is to remove the lubricant through the filler plug hole with a suction pump. If the differential cover gasket is leaking, it will be necessary to remove the cover to drain the lubricant (which will also allow you to inspect the differential).

Changing the lubricant with a suction pump

4   Remove the filler plug from the differential (see Section 20).

5   Insert the suction pump flexible hose in the fill hole and down into the bottom of the differential housing (see illustration).

6   Using the pump, suction out as much lubricant as possible.

Changing rear differential lubricant by removing the cover

Note: *Vehicles equipped with 9.75 inch ring gear differentials use a metal gasket instead of RTV sealant (8.8 inch ring gear, as shown). The metal gasket on 9.75 inch differentials must be replaced with a new one if removed.*

7   Move a drain pan, rags, newspapers and wrenches under the vehicle.

8   Release the wiring harness clips from along the top of the differential cover (see illustration).

9   Remove the bolts on the lower half of the cover. Loosen the bolts on the upper half and use them to loosely retain the cover (see illustrations). Allow the oil to drain into the pan, then completely remove the cover.

10   Using a lint-free rag, clean the inside of the cover and the accessible areas of the differential housing. As this is done, check for chipped gears and metal particles in the lubricant, indicating that the differential should be more thoroughly inspected and/or repaired.

11   Thoroughly clean the gasket mating surfaces of the differential housing and the cover plate. Use a gasket scraper or putty knife to remove all traces of the old gasket (see illustration).

12   Apply a thin layer of RTV sealant to the cover flange, staying on the inside of the bolt holes.

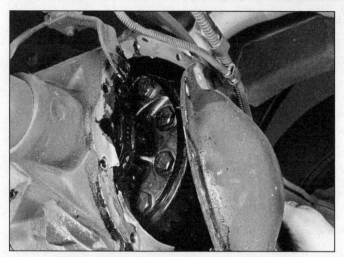

30.9c Once the lubricant has drained, remove the cover

30.11 Carefully scrape off the old material to ensure a leak-free seal

13   Within 15 minutes, carefully place the cover onto the differential and install the bolts and stud bolts in their correct locations. Tighten the cover bolts to the torque listed in this Chapter's Specifications.

Refill

14   Use a hand pump, syringe or funnel to fill the differential housing with the specified lubricant until it's level with the bottom of the filler plug hole. If RTV sealant was used, allow sufficient time for the sealant to cure before filling the differential.
15   Install the fill plug and tighten it securely.

31   Transfer case lubricant change (4WD models) (every 100,000 miles or 60 months)

1   Drive the vehicle for at least 15 minutes to warm the lubricant in the case. Perform this warm-up procedure with 4WD engaged, if possible.
2   Raise the vehicle and support it securely on jackstands.
3   Remove the drain plug from the lower part of the case and allow the old lubricant to drain completely (see illustration 19.1).
4   After the lubricant has drained com-

pletely, clean the plug and the plug opening, apply thread sealant to the plug, then reinstall the plug and tighten it securely.
5   Remove the filler plug from the case.
6   Fill the case with the specified lubricant until it is level with the lower edge of the filler hole.
7   Clean the filler plug and the plug opening, apply thread sealant to the plug, then reinstall the plug and tighten it securely.
8   Drive the vehicle for a short distance, then check the drain and fill plugs for leakage.

Notes

Chapter 2 Part A
V6 engines

Contents

	Section
Camshafts and tappets/roller followers and lash adjusters - removal, inspection and installation	11
Crankshaft pulley and crankshaft front seal - replacement	7
Cylinder heads - removal and installation	8
Driveplate - removal and installation	14
Engine front cover - removal and installation	9
Engine mounts - check and replacement	16
Exhaust manifolds - removal and installation	6
General information	1

	Section
Intake manifold(s) - removal and installation	5
Oil pan - removal and installation	12
Oil pump - removal and installation	13
Rear main oil seal - replacement	15
Repair operations possible with the engine in the vehicle	2
Timing chains and sprockets - removal and installation	10
Valve clearance (3.5L Duratec and 2016 and earlier 3.5L EcoBoost engines) - check and adjustment	3
Valve covers - removal and installation	4

Specifications

General

Displacement
2.7L engine	164 cubic inches
3.5L engine	214 cubic inches

Cylinder numbers (front-to-rear)
Left (driver's) side	4-5-6
Right side	1-2-3
Firing order	1-4-2-5-3-6

Cylinder head warpage limit
Lengthwise	0.003 inch
Widthwise	0.002 inch

36061-1-specs.B HAYNES

Cylinder locations

Camshaft

Lobe lift

2.7L engine
Intake	0.2067 inch
Exhaust	0.1870 inch
3.5L engine (intake and exhaust)	0.373 inch
3.7L engine (intake and exhaust)	0.390 inch
Lobe wear limit	0.0024 inch

Endplay
Standard	0.001 to 0.006 inch
Service limit	0.0074 inch

Journal diameter
First journal	1.535 to 1.536 inches
Intermediate journals	1.021 to 1.022 inches
Journal-to-bearing (oil) clearance	0.0029 inch
Journal runout limit	0.0015 inch

Valve clearance - 3.5L Duratec (non-turbo) and 2016 and earlier 3.5L EcoBoost engines only, (room temperature, measured with camshaft at base circle)
Intake	0.006 to 0.01 inch
Exhaust	0.0142 to 0.0181 inch

Torque specifications

Ft-lbs (unless otherwise indicated)

Note: *One foot-pound (ft-lb) of torque is equivalent to 12 inch-pounds (in-lbs) of torque. Torque values below approximately 15 foot-pounds are expressed in inch-pounds, because most foot-pound torque wrenches are not accurate at these smaller values.*

Variable Camshaft Timing (VCT) unit (camshaft sprocket) bolt (new)
  2.7L engine
    Step 1 30
    Step 2 .... Loosen one full turn
    Step 3 37
    Step 4 .... Tighten an additional 90-degrees
  3.5L engines
    Step 1 30
    Step 2 .... Loosen one full turn
    Step 3 18
    Step 4
      3.5L non-turbocharged and 2016 and earlier
        turbocharged models... Tighten an additional 180-degrees
      2017 3.5L turbocharged models... Tighten an additional 150-degrees
Camshaft cap bolts
  2.7L engine .... 89 in-lbs
  3.5L engines
    Step 1 .... 71 in-lbs
    Step 2 .... Tighten an additional 45 degrees
    Step 3 .... Loosen bolts 8 through 11
    Step 4 .... Repeat Steps 1 and 2 on bolts 8 through 11
Crankshaft pulley bolt
  2.7L engine
    Step 1 166
    Step 2 .... Loosen one turn
    Step 3 26
    Step 4 .... Tighten an additional 270-degrees
  3.5L engines
    Step 1 89
    Step 2 .... Loosen one turn
    Step 3 37
    Step 4 .... Tighten an additional 90-degrees
Crankshaft rear seal retainer
  2.7L engine and 3.5L turbocharged engine....................................... 89 in-lbs
  3.5L non-turbocharged engine
    Crankshaft rear seal retainer-to-engine block bolts..................... 89 in-lbs
    Crankshaft rear seal retainer-to-oil pan bolts
      Step 1 .... 89 in-lbs
      Step 2 .... Tighten an additional 45-degrees
Crossmember bolts 66
Cylinder head bolts (new, oiled) (in sequence - see illustration 8.22a or 8.22b)
  2.7L engine
    Step 1 .... 177 in-lbs
    Step 2 .... Loosen two turns
    Step 3 37
    Step 4 .... Tighten an additional 180-degrees
  3.5L engines
    Step 1 .... 177 in-lbs
    Step 2 26
    Step 3 .... Tighten an additional 90-degrees
    Step 4 .... Tighten an additional 90-degrees
    Step 5 .... Tighten an additional 45-degrees
    M6 bolt at front of cylinder head .... 89 in-lbs
Drivebelt tensioner pulley mounting bolt(s) 18
Exhaust manifold nuts
  Step 1 .... 168 in-lbs
  Step 2 18
Exhaust manifold studs .... 106 in-lbs
Driveplate bolts.. 59

Torque specifications (continued)

Ft-lbs (unless otherwise indicated)

Note: *One foot-pound (ft-lb) of torque is equivalent to 12 inch-pounds (in-lbs) of torque. Torque values below approximately 15 foot-pounds are expressed in inch-pounds, because most foot-pound torque wrenches are not accurate at these smaller values.*

Intake manifold bolts	
2.7L turbocharged engine	89 in-lbs
3.5L turbocharged engine	
Step 1	89 in-lbs
Step 2	Tighten an additional 45-degrees
3.5L non-turbochrged engine	
Lower intake manifold-to-cylinder heads	89 in-lbs
Upper intake manifold-to-lower intake manifold	
Step 1	89 in-lbs
Step 2	Tighten an additional 45-degrees
Oil pan-to-block bolts	9 in-lbs
Oil pump screen nuts-to-engine block nuts	89 in-lbs
Oil pump mounting bolts	89 in-lbs
Oil filter adapter bolt	
Step 1	89 in-lbs
Step 2	Tighten an additional 45 degrees
Engine front cover-to-block bolts	
2.7L engine (see illustration 9.29)	
Step 1, bolts 1 through 11	18
Step 2, bolts 12 and 13	35
Step 3, bolts 14 through 21	18
3.5L engines (see illustration 9.31)	
Step 1, bolts 1 through 21	89 in-lbs
Step 2, bolts 1 through 20	18
Step 3, bolt 21	177 in-lbs
Step 4, bolt 21	Tighten an additional 90-degrees
Step 5, bolt 22	89 in-lbs
Step 6, bolt 22	Tighten an additional 45 degrees
Oil pan-to-timing chain cover bolts	89 in-lbs
Engine mount fasteners	
Through-bolts	258
Mount bracket-to-engine block bolts	57
Mount-to-frame bolts	129
Mount nuts	111
Timing chain tensioner bolts	96 in-lbs
Turbocharger-to-exhaust manifold bolts	24
Turbocharger bracket-to-block bolts	89 in-lbs
Turbocharger bracket-to-turbocharger bolt	159 in-lbs
Valve cover bolts	89 in-lbs
Variable Camshaft Timing oil control solenoid bolts	
Step 1	71 in-lbs
Step 2	Tighten an additional 20 degrees

Note: *Refer to Part C for additional specifications.*

1   General information

1   Chapter 2A is devoted to in-vehicle repair procedures for the 2.7L turbocharged Eco-Boost V6, the 3.5L Duratec non-turbocharged V6 and the 3.5L turbocharged EcoBoost V6 engines. The 2.7L engines utilize a compacted graphite iron cylinder block, while the 3.5L engines utilize a cast-aluminum block. All have six cylinders arranged in a V-shape at a 60-degree angle between the two banks. The cylinder heads on all models are cast-aluminum and the valve actuation is via two overhead camshafts in each cylinder head with four valves per cylinder (one for each intake valve and one for each exhaust valve). The principal differences are that the 2.7L and 3.5L turbocharged engines are equipped with direct injection of fuel into the cylinders and the use of two turbochargers, while the 3.5L non-turbocharged engine does not have direct injection or turbochargers. Information concerning engine removal and installation and engine overhaul can be found in Chapter 2C. The following repair procedures are based on the assumption that the engine is installed in the vehicle. If the engine has been removed from the vehicle and mounted on a stand, many of the steps outlined in this Chapter will not apply.

2   Repair operations possible with the engine in the vehicle

1   Many major repair operations can be accomplished without removing the engine from the vehicle.
2   Clean the engine compartment and the exterior of the engine with some type of pressure washer before any work is done. It will make the job easier and help keep dirt out of the internal areas of the engine.
3   If vacuum, exhaust, oil or coolant leaks develop, indicating a need for gasket or seal replacement, the repairs can generally be made with the engine in the vehicle. The intake and exhaust manifold gaskets, timing cover gasket, oil pan gasket, crankshaft oil seals and cylinder head gaskets are all accessible with the engine in place.
4   Exterior engine components, such as the intake and exhaust manifolds, the oil pan (and the oil pump), the water pump, the starter motor, the alternator, and the fuel system components can be removed for repair with the engine in place.
5   Since the cylinder heads can be removed without pulling the engine, valve component servicing can also be accomplished with the engine in the vehicle. Replacement of the timing chain and sprockets is also possible with the engine in the vehicle.
6   In extreme cases caused by a lack of necessary equipment, repair or replacement of piston rings, pistons, connecting rods and rod bearings is possible with the engine in the vehicle. However, this practice is not recommended because of the cleaning and preparation work that must be done to the components involved.

3   Valve clearance (3.5L Duratec and 2016 and earlier 3.5L EcoBoost engines) - check and adjustment

Note: *The engine must be room temperature before checking the valve clearances.*
Note: *Checking and, if necessary, adjusting the valve clearance is only necessary after replacement of the camshaft(s) or other valve-related parts, or if the valvetrain is making excessive noise.*
1   Disconnect the cable from the negative terminal of the battery (see Chapter 5).
2   Remove the spark plugs (see Chapter 1).
3   Remove the valve covers (see Section 4).
4   Using a socket and a breaker bar on the crankshaft pulley center bolt, rotate the engine until the cam lobes on the cylinder to be checked are pointing away from the tappets.
5   Measure the clearance of the indicated valves with a feeler gauge (see illustration). Record each measurement and compare your measurements with the desired valve clearance found in this Chapter's Specifications. Note which are out of specification, as this data will be used later to determine the required replacement tappets.
6   Repeat Steps 4 and 5 until the clearances for all valves have been measured.
7   If a clearance is out of specification, the tappet must be replaced with a new tappet that has a different thickness head to correct the clearance. Refer to Section 11 and remove the camshafts to access the tappets.
8   Mark the lifters that are to be replaced, and record which valve they came from. Use a micrometer to measure the thickness of the head of the lifter, making sure the measurement is precise and on the center projection on the underside of the lifter (see illustration).
9   To calculate the correct thickness for a replacement lifter that will place the valve clearance within the specified value, use the following formula:
10   $N = R + (M1 - M2)$
11   N = thickness of new tappet
12   R = measured valve clearance
13   $M1$ = thickness of old tappet
14   $M2$ = standard valve clearance
15   Lifters are marked on the underside as to their size. A marking of 3.310 on the underside of the lifter indicates a thickness value of 3.31 mm, or 0.13 inch.
16   Mark the new lifters as to their destination, lubricate them with engine assembly lube and install them. After replacing the lifters, refer to Section 11 to reinstall the camshafts and Section 10 to reinstall the timing chains, then re-check the valve clearances.

3.5 Measure the clearance for each valve with a feeler gauge of the specified thickness - if the clearance is correct, you should feel a slight drag on the gauge as you pull it out

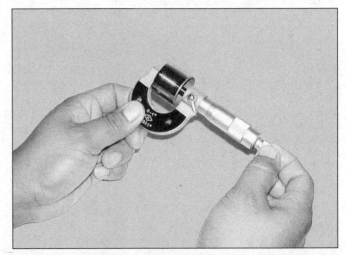

3.8 Use a micrometer to measure the thickness of the head of the tappet

4   Valve covers - removal and installation

Removal

1   If you're going to be removing the left valve cover on a 3.5L turbochaged engine, relieve the fuel system pressure (see Chapter 4).

2   Disconnect the cable from the negative battery terminal (see Chapter 5, Section 3).

3   Remove the engine cover, if equipped.

Left (driver's side) valve cover

4   Remove the air filter housing (see Chapter 4).

2.7L engine

5   Remove the charge air cooler intake pipe (see Chapter 4).

6   Remove the throttle body (see Chapter 4).

7   Disconnect the quick-connect fittings to the EVAP purge control valve then remove the purge valve from the intake manifold (see Chapter 6).

8   Disconnect the vacuum hose retainers and wire harness retainers then remove the turbocharger control solenoid bolts (see Chapter 4) and move the solenoid out of the way.

9   Remove the engine lifting bracket and charge air cooler bracket nut/bolts and brackets.

10   Remove the engine oil dipstick.

3.5L non-turbocharged engines

11   Disconnect the vent tube from the valve cover (see illustration).

12   Remove the dipstick.

3.5L turbocharged engines

13   Remove the dipstick.

14   Disconnect the quick-connectors for the PCV hose then detach the PCV hose from the valve cover and manifold.

15   Remove the nuts securing the charge air cooler bracket from the cylinder head.

16   Disconnect the quick-connectors for the two turbocharger regulator tubes and set them aside then remove the inlet and outlet tube from the turbocharger (see Chapter 4).

17   Remove the high-pressure fuel pump (see Chapter 4).

Right (passenger's side) valve cover

2.7L engines

Warning: *Wait until the engine is completely cool before beginning this procedure.*

18   Drain the cooling system (see Chapter 1).

19   Disconnect the quick-connector fittings for the PCV hose then detach the PCV hose from the valve cover and manifold.

20   Disconnect the main engine wiring harness connectors from the PCM (see Chapter 6) and move the harness out of the way.

21   Disconnect the heater hoses around the right valve cover and cap the hoses.

22   Remove the bracket fasteners and bracket from the front corner of the cylinder head.

23   Remove the coolant pipe mounting bolts and move the coolant pipe out of the way.

3.5L non-turbocharged engines

24   Detach the PCV hose from the valve cover (see illustration).

25   Remove the heater hose retaining nut and move the hose out of the way.

Both valve covers

26   Remove the ignition coils from the cover to be removed (see Chapter 5).

27   Disconnect the two electrical connectors at the valve cover for the VCT solenoids (being careful not to twist the solenoids) (see illustration) and the electrical connectors from the camshaft position sensors (CMP).

4.11 Detach the vent tube from the valve cover - 3.5L non-turbocharged model shown

4.24 Detach the PCV hose from the valve cover

4.27 Disconnect the electrical connectors from the VCT oil control solenoids in each valve cover. It's a good idea to mark one of the electrical connectors and solenoids to prevent mixing up the connectors on reassembly

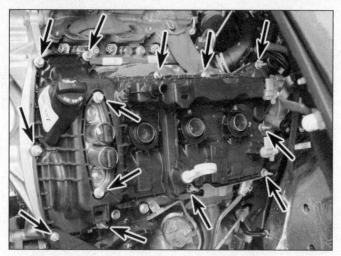

4.28a Valve cover fasteners - 2.7L turbocharged model shown

4.28b Valve cover fasteners - 3.5L non-turbocharged model shown

28   Remove the valve cover fasteners, then separate the wiring/clips and remove the valve cover from the cylinder head (see illustrations). Wiggle the valve cover by hand to detach it from the cylinder head if it's stuck. **Caution:** *Do not use a hammer to knock the cover loose. Try to slip a flexible putty knife between the cylinder head and cover to break the gasket seal. Don't pry at the cover-to-cylinder head joint or damage to the sealing surfaces may occur (leading to oil leaks in the future).*

Installation

29   The mating surfaces of each cylinder head and valve cover must be perfectly clean when the covers are installed. Remove all traces of sealant and old gasket material, then clean the mating surfaces with brake cleaner. If there's sealant or oil on the mating surfaces when the cover is installed, oil leaks may develop.
30   Inspect the spark plug seals, the seals for the VCT solenoids and the valve cover

gasket (see illustration). Do not replace them unless necessary.
31   Make sure the bolt seals are in good condition, too (see illustration).
32   Apply a bead of RTV sealant to the joints

where the engine front cover meets the cylinder head and install the valve cover within four minutes (see illustration).
33   Carefully position the cover on the cylinder head and install the bolts.

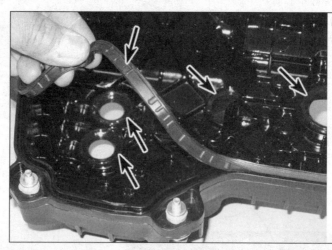

4.30 Check the spark plug tube seals, VCT solenoid seals and valve cover gasket. If they are in good condition they can be reused

4.31 Check the bolt seals - replace them if they're not in good condition

4.32 Apply RTV sealant to the seams where the front cover meets the cylinder head

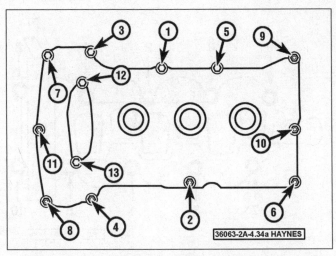

4.34a Valve cover bolt tightening sequence - 2.7L engines (left side shown, right side similar)

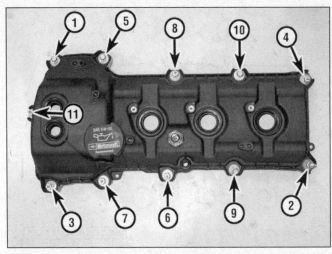

4.34b Valve cover bolt tightening sequence 3.5L engines (left side shown, right side similar)

34   Tighten the bolts a little at a time, in the proper sequence (see illustrations), to the torque listed in this Chapter's Specifications.
35   The remaining installation steps are the reverse of removal.
36   Start the engine and check carefully for oil leaks as the engine warms up.

---

5   Intake manifold(s) - removal and installation

Warning: *If you're working on a 3.5L non-turbocharged engine and are going to be removing the lower intake manifold, relieve the fuel system pressure (see Chapter 4).*

1   Disconnect the cable from the negative battery terminal (see Chapter 5, Section 3).
2   Remove the engine cover.
3   Remove the air filter housing and intake duct (see Chapter 4).

2.7L engine
Removal
4   Remove the charge air cooler pipes (see Chapter 4).
5   Disconnect the quick-connect fittings to the EVAP purge control valve then remove the purge valve from the intake manifold (see Chapter 6).
6   Disconnect the quick-connectors for the PCV hose then detach the PCV hose from the valve cover and manifold.

7   Disconnect the engine wiring harness electrical connectors, the MAP sensor electrical connector and retainers for the vacuum lines and wiring harness.
8   Disconnect the electrical connector at the throttle body and unclip the harness from the retainers.
9   Remove the coolant pipe mounting bolts and move the coolant pipe out of the way.
10   Remove the manifold mounting bolts and detach the manifold from the engine (see illustration).

Installation
11   Remove the old gaskets from the manifold (see illustration). Clean the manifold and cylinder head mating surfaces.

5.10 Carefully lift the manifold off of the engine - Do not use a hammer, and once the manifold is off, cover the intake ports of the engine with clean shop rags.

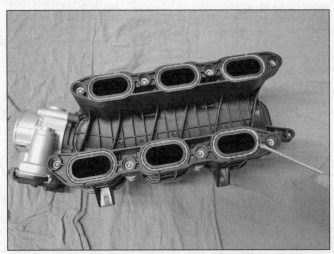

5.11 Use a small screwdriver or pick and pull the old gaskets out of the grooves in the intake manifold

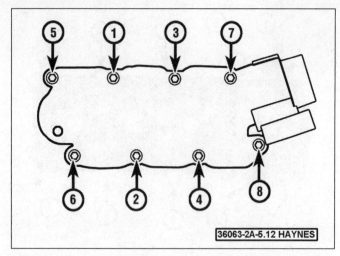

5.12 Intake manifold bolt tightening sequence - 2.7L V6 engine

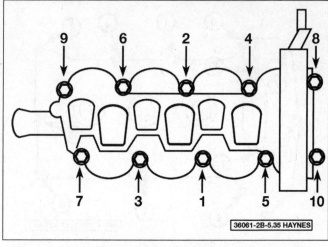

5.30 Lower intake manifold bolt tightening sequence - 3.5L non-turbocharged V6 engine

12   Install the new manifold gaskets to the grooves in the manifold. Install the manifold and bolts. Tighten the bolts in the indicated sequence to the torque listed in this Chapter's Specifications (see illustration).
13   The remainder of the installation is the reverse of removal.

3.5L non-turbocharged engine
Removal
14   If you're going to be removing the lower intake manifold, relieve the fuel system pressure (if not already done) (see Chapter 4).

Upper intake manifold
15   Remove the PCV tube from the manifold.
16   Disconnect the electrical connector from the throttle body (see Chapter 4).
17   Disconnect the EVAP tube and the EVAP canister purge valve electrical connector (see Chapter 6).
18   Disconnect the vacuum hose connector and the brake booster vacuum hose from the upper intake manifold.
19   Disconnect the PCV valve hoses from the valve covers and remove them from the engine (see Chapter 6).
20   Remove the mounting bolts from the upper intake manifold, then lift the upper manifold off of the lower manifold.
21   Cover the air intake passages with a shop towel to prevent tools or debris from falling inside the engine.

Lower intake manifold
Warning: *Wait until the engine is completely cool before beginning this procedure.*
22   Remove the upper intake manifold.
23   Drain the cooling system (see Chapter 1).
24   Cover the drivebelt with plastic wrap, then remove the thermostat housing (see Chapter 3). Disconnect the heater hose from the manifold.
25   Detach the fuel line from the fuel rail (see Chapter 4) then remove the fuel rail insulators.
26   Disconnect the electrical connectors from the injectors.

27   Loosen the intake manifold mounting bolts in 1/4-turn increments in the reverse of the tightening sequence (see illustration 5.30) until they can be removed by hand.

Installation
Lower intake manifold
28   Remove the gaskets from the grooves in the manifold. Clean the manifold and cylinder head mating surfaces.
29   Install new gaskets into the grooves in the manifold, then carefully set the manifold in place.
30   Install the bolts and tighten them to the torque listed in this Chapter's Specifications, following the recommended sequence (see illustration).
31   The remaining installation steps are the reverse of removal.
32   Refill the cooling system (see Chapter 1).
33   Start the engine and check carefully for oil or coolant leaks at the intake manifold joints.

Upper intake manifold
34   Remove the gaskets from the grooves in the manifold. Clean the mating surfaces of the upper and lower manifolds.

35   Install new gaskets into the grooves in the manifold, then carefully set the manifold in place.
36   Install the bolts and tighten them to the torque listed in this Chapter's Specifications, following the recommended sequence (see illustration).
37   The remaining installation steps are the reverse of removal.

3.5L turbocharged engines
Removal
38   Remove the three bolts and the engine cover bracket from the intake manifold.
39   Loosen the large hose clamp securing the hose to the charge air controller and remove the hose from the throttle body.
40   Disconnect the electrical connector at the throttle body.
41   Disconnect the PCV electrical connector.
42   Disconnect the brake booster vacuum hose from the intake manifold, then disconnect the MAP sensor and the EVAP canister purge valve connectors.
43   Disconnect the turbocharger vacuum regulator hose from the intake manifold, then release the pushpin securing the turbocharger

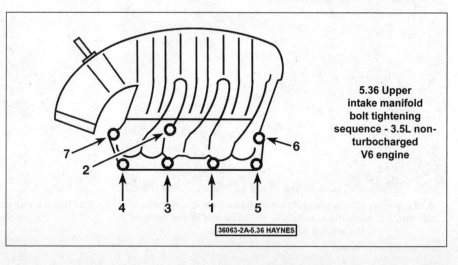

5.36 Upper intake manifold bolt tightening sequence - 3.5L non-turbocharged V6 engine

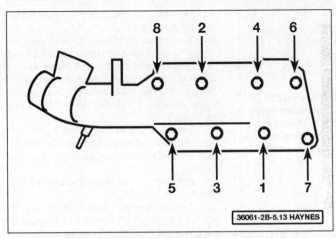

5.46 Intake manifold bolt tightening sequence - 3.5L V6 turbocharged engine

6.7 From below, remove the two catalytic converter-to-exhaust manifolds (left side shown, right side similar)

vacuum regulator to the intake manifold.
44   Remove the manifold mounting bolts and detach the manifold from the engine.
Note: *Do not use a hammer, and once the manifold is off, cover the intake ports of the engine with clean shop rags.*

Installation
45   Remove the old gaskets from the manifold. Clean the manifold and cylinder head mating surfaces.
46   Install the new manifold gaskets to the grooves in the manifold. Install the manifold and bolts. Tighten the bolts in the indicated sequence to the torque listed in this Chapter's Specifications (see illustration).
47   The remainder of the installation is the reverse of removal.

6   Exhaust manifolds - removal and installation

Removal
Note: *On 2.7L engines, the exhaust manifold is integrated into the cylinder head and and the turbochargers bolt directly to the cylinder heads.*
1   Disconnect the cable from the negative battery terminal (see Chapter 5, Section 3)
2   Loosen the lug nuts on the manifold side you're working on. Raise the vehicle and support it securely on jackstands then remove the wheel.
3   Also remove the inner fender splash shield (see Chapter 11).
4   On 3.5L turbocharged engines, remove the turbocharger from the manifold you're working on (see Chapter 4).
5   As a precaution, disconnect the oxygen sensor electrical connectors (see Chapter 6).
6   On 3.5L non-turbocharged engines, working under the vehicle, apply penetrating oil to the exhaust Y-pipe-to-manifold studs and nuts (they're usually rusty).
7   On 3.5L non-turbocharged engines, remove the nuts holding the catalytic converter-to-exhaust manifolds (see illustration).
8   On 3.7L engines, remove the two bolts and remove the exhaust manifold heat shield.
9   Remove the manifold mounting nuts and detach the manifold from the cylinder head.
10   Remove the exhaust gaskets and clean the gasket surfaces on the manifold and cylinder heads.

Installation
Note: *The manufacturer recommends remov-*
ing the exhaust mounting studs from the cylinder heads and installing new studs.
11   Check the exhaust manifold for cracks and make sure all the stud threads are clean and undamaged. The exhaust manifold and cylinder head mating surfaces must be clean before the manifolds are reinstalled.
12   Position the exhaust manifold and new gasket over the studs on the cylinder head and install the mounting nuts.
13   Tighten the nuts in sequence (see illustrations) to the torque listed in this Chapter's Specifications is reached.
14   The remaining installation steps are the reverse of removal.
15   Start the engine and check for exhaust leaks.

7   Crankshaft pulley and crankshaft front seal - replacement

Replacement with timing chain cover in place
1   Disconnect the cable from the negative battery terminal (see Chapter 5, Section 3)
2   Remove the drivebelt(s) (see Chapter 1).

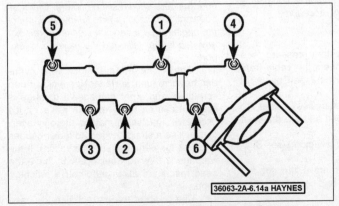

6.13a 3.5L non-turbocharged engine manifold tightening sequence

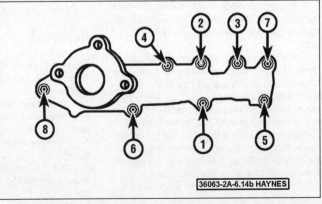

6.13b 3.5L turbocharged engine manifold tightening sequence

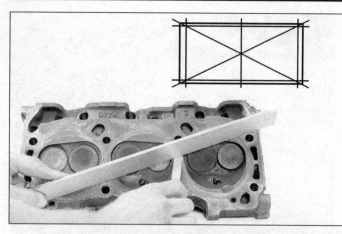

8.17 Check the cylinder head and block surfaces for flatness with a straightedge

3   Secure the crankshaft from rotating with a strap or chain wrench (wrap a length of rag or old drivebelt around the pulley to protect it). Remove the bolt from the front of the crankshaft, then use a three-jaw puller to detach the crankshaft pulley. Clean the crankshaft nose and the seal contact surface on the pulley with RTV remover. Leave the Woodruff key in place in the crankshaft keyway.
Caution: *Be sure to use an adapter between the puller screw and the nose of the crankshaft so as not to damage the threads in the crankshaft. Also, don't use a puller with jaws that grip the outer edge of the damper. The puller must be the type that applies force to the damper hub only.*
4   Carefully remove the seal from the timing chain cover with a screwdriver or seal removal tool. Be careful not to damage the cover or scratch the wall of the seal bore. If the engine has accumulated a lot of miles, apply penetrating oil to the seal-to-cover joint and allow it to soak in before attempting to remove the seal.
5   Check the seal bore and crankshaft, as well as the seal contact surface on the pulley for nicks and burrs. Position the new seal in the bore with the open end of the seal facing IN. A film of engine oil applied to the outer edge of the new seal will make installation easier.
6   Drive the seal into the bore with a seal driver or a large socket and hammer until it's completely seated. If you're using a socket, select one that's the same outside diameter as the seal.
7   Apply clean engine oil to the seal contact surface of the crankshaft pulley and coat the keyway (groove) with a thin layer of RTV sealant.
8   Install the pulley on the end of the crankshaft. The keyway in the pulley bore must be aligned with the Woodruff key in the crankshaft nose. If the pulley can't be seated by hand, tap it into place with a soft-face hammer or slip a large washer over the bolt, install the bolt and tighten it to press the pulley into place. Remove the large washer, then install the bolt and tighten it in Steps to the torque listed in this Chapter's Specifications.
9   Install the remaining parts removed for access to the seal.
10   Start the engine and check for leaks.

Replacement with engine front cover removed

11   Remove the engine front cover (see Section 9).
12   Use a punch or screwdriver and hammer to drive the seal out of the cover from the back side. Support the cover as close to the seal bore as possible, using blocks of wood. Be careful not to distort the cover or scratch the wall of the seal bore. If the engine has accumulated a lot of miles, apply penetrating oil to the seal-to-cover joint on each side and allow it to soak in before attempting to drive the seal out.
13   Clean the bore to remove any old seal material and corrosion. Support the cover on blocks of wood and position the new seal in the bore with the open end of the seal facing IN. A film of oil applied to the outer edge of the new seal will make installation easier.
14   Drive the seal into the bore with a seal driver or a large socket and hammer until it's completely seated. If you're using a socket, select one that's the same outside diameter as the seal.
15   Reinstall the engine front cover (see Section 9) and crankshaft pulley (see Step 8).
16   Start the engine and check for leaks.

8   Cylinder heads - removal and installation

Warning: *Wait until the engine is completely cool before beginning this procedure.*

Removal

1   Relieve the fuel system pressure (see Chapter 4), then disconnect the cable from the negative battery terminal (see Chapter 5, Section 3).
2   Drain the cooling system (see Chapter 1).
3   Remove the drivebelt and the drivebelt tensioner (see Chapter 1).
4   Remove the intake manifold(s) (see Section 5).
5   On 3.5L models, remove the coolant crossover manifold bolts and crossover manifold.
6   Remove the exhaust manifold (see Section 6).

7   Remove the turbocharger(s) (see Chapter 4), if equipped.
8   On turbocharged models, disconnect the high-pressure fuel line(s) from the fuel rail and high-pressure fuel pump (see Chapter 4).
Caution: *The manufacturer requires the fuel line from the fuel rail to the high-pressure fuel pump always be replaced once it has been removed.*
9   Remove the valve covers (see Section 4).
10   Remove the front cover (see Section 9), timing chains and timing chain guides (see Section 10).
11   Remove the camshafts and tappets (see Section 11).
12   On 3.5L engines, remove the two Camshaft Position (CMP) sensors at the rear of each cylinder head. On all models, disconnect any other electrical connectors from the cylinder head and mark them with tape for correct reassembly.
13   Loosen the cylinder head bolts in 1/4-turn increments until they can be removed by hand. Work from bolt-to-bolt in a pattern that's the reverse of the tightening sequence (see illustration 8.22a or 8.22b).
Caution: *Remove the bolts and discard them - new bolts must be used when installing the cylinder head(s).*
14   Lift the cylinder head(s) off the engine. If resistance is felt, DO NOT pry between the cylinder head and engine block as damage to the mating surfaces will result. To dislodge the cylinder head, place a wood block against the end of it and strike the wood block with a hammer or pry against a casting protrusion. Store the cylinder heads on blocks of wood to prevent damage to the gasket sealing surfaces.
15   Cylinder head disassembly and inspection procedures should be performed by a qualified automotive machine shop.

Installation

16   The mating surfaces of the cylinder heads and engine block must be perfectly clean when the cylinder heads are installed.
Caution: *Do not use a scraper of any kind or abrasive discs to remove old gasket material, as the block, heads and intake manifold(s) are aluminum (except for on the 2.7L engine; the block is constructed of compacted graphite iron, but care should still be taken). Cover all openings with shop rags to keep debris out of the engine. Use a vacuum cleaner to remove any debris that falls into the valley or intake ports.*
17   Check the engine block and cylinder head mating surfaces for nicks, deep scratches and other damage. If damage is slight, it can be removed with a file - if it's excessive, machining may be the only alternative. Use a straightedge and feeler gauges to check for warpage (see illustration). If the warpage is beyond Specifications, have the head machined at an automotive machine shop.
18   Use a tap of the correct size to chase the threads in the block head bolt holes. Dirt,

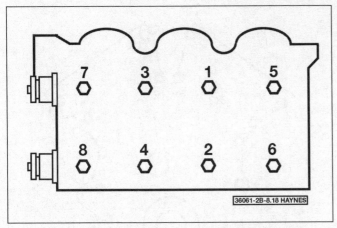

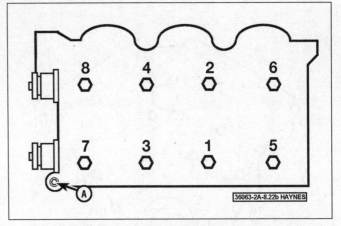

8.22a Cylinder head bolt tightening sequence - 2.7L engine

8.22b Cylinder head bolt tightening sequence - 3.5L engines

corrosion, sealant and damaged threads will affect torque readings.

19 Position the new gasket(s) over the dowel pins in the engine block. Make sure it's facing the right way. If the cylinder head is to be replaced, a new secondary timing chain tensioner will be required.

20 Carefully position the cylinder head(s) on the engine block without disturbing the gasket(s).

21 Before installing the new cylinder head bolts, lightly oil the threads.

22 Install the bolts and tighten them finger-tight. Tighten the bolts, in the recommended sequence, to the torque listed in this Chapter's Specifications (see illustrations).

23 On 3.5L engines, install and tighten the M6 bolt at the front of the cylinder head (see illustration 8.22b)to the torque listed in this Chapter's Specifications.

24 The remaining installation steps are the reverse of removal.

25 Change the engine oil and filter and refill the cooling system (see Chapter 1), then start the engine and check carefully for oil and coolant leaks.

9 Engine front cover - removal and installation

Warning: *The engine must be completely cool before beginning this procedure.*

Removal

1 Relieve the fuel system pressure (see Chapter 4), then disconnect the cable from the negative terminal of the battery (see Chapter 5).

2 Drain the cooling system and engine oil, and remove the oil filter (see Chapter 1).

3 Remove the transmission housing cover, if equipped.

4 Remove the expansion tank (see Chapter 3).

5 Remove the air cleaner housing and inlet and outlet ducts (see Chapter 4).

6 Disconnect the upper and lower radiator hoses from the engine, then secure the hoses out of the way.

7 On turbocharged models, remove the charge air cooler inlet and outlet pipes (see Chapter 4).

8 On 2.7L engines, rotate the turbocharger bypass hose retaining ring counterclockwise 180-degrees and disconnect the lower end of the hose.

9 On 3.5L turbocharged engines, remove the turbocharger inlet and outlet tube (see Chapter 4).

10 Remove the engine oil cooler (see Chapter 3).

11 If you're working on a 3.5L turbocharged engine, remove the intake manifold (see Section 5).

12 If you're working on 3.5L non-turbocharged engine, remove the upper intake manifold support bracket.

13 Remove the valve covers (see Section 4).

14 Remove the crankshaft pulley and crankshaft front oil seal (see Section 7).

15 Remove the drivebelt tensioner (see Chapter 1) and remove all accessory brackets attached to the timing chain cover (see illustration).

16 Remove drivebelt idler pulley bolt and pulley.

17 Remove the alternator bolt and swing the alternator out of the way.

18 On 2.7L models, remove the cabin heater coolant pump (see Chapter 3).

19 Remove the water pump (see Chapter 3).

20 Remove the air conditioning compressor mounting bolts without disconnecting the refrigerant lines (see Chapter 3).

21 Disconnect the oil control solenoid electrical connector then detach the wiring harness retainers and move the harness out of the way.

22 On 2.7L models, remove the oil pan.

23 Remove the front cover bolts and separate the cover from the engine block.

Caution: *DO NOT use excessive force or you may crack the cover. If the cover is difficult to remove, double check to make sure all of the*

bolts have been removed.

Note: *There are seven pry spots around the front cover. Work gently at each one until the cover comes off.*

Installation

24 Clean the gasket mating surfaces with brake system cleaner.

25 While the cover is off the engine, it's a good idea to install a new crankshaft front seal (see Section 7). There is also a radial seal in the center of the front cover, a radial seal at the bottom of the front cover (3.5L EcoBoost engine), an oil gallery seal on the front of the engine block (2.7L engine) and an O-ring type seal at the lower corner of the front cover (2.7L engine). Install new seals before mounting the front cover.

26 Apply a 1/8-inch bead of High Performance RTV sealant to the mating surface of the cover. Be sure to also apply the sealant to the bosses on the interior of the cover where the bolts go through.

27 Apply a 3/16-inch bead of High Performance RTV sealant to the areas where the

9.15 Remove the drivebelt, the idler pulley (indicated), alternator and crankshaft pulley

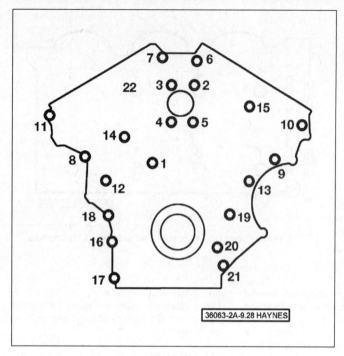

9.29 2.7L engine front cover bolt tightening sequence

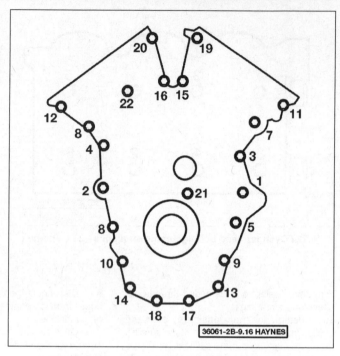

9.31 3.5L engine front cover bolt tightening sequence

oil pan and cylinder heads meet the engine block.

28 Slide the front cover onto the engine. The dowel pins will position it correctly.

29 On 2.7L models, follow the correct sequence (see illustration), tighten the bolts to the torque listed in this Chapter's Specifications. All the bolts must be tightened within 35 minutes.

Caution: *The front cover must be installed within 10 minutes of applying the RTV sealant or oil leaks may occur.*

30 On 3.5L engine models, install all the bolts finger-tight within four minutes of applying the High performance RTV.

31 On 3.5L engine models, follow the correct sequence (see illustration), tighten the bolts to the torque listed in this Chapter's Specifications. All the bolts must be tightened within 35 minutes.

32 Install the remaining parts in the reverse order of removal.

33 Install a new oil filter, then add engine oil and coolant (see Chapter 1).

34 Run the engine and check for leaks.

10 Timing chains and sprockets - removal and installation

Caution: *These engines are difficult to work on and require some special tools. On any procedure involving the timing chains, the Steps must be read carefully and disassembly must proceed using the special tools, otherwise damage to the engine will result.*

Caution: *Because this is an "interference" engine design, if the timing chain has broken, there will be damage to the valves (and pos-*

sibly the pistons) and will require removal of the cylinder heads.

Caution: *The timing system is complex. Severe engine damage will occur if you make any mistakes. Do not attempt this procedure unless you are highly experienced with this type of repair. If you are at all unsure of your abilities, consult an expert. Double-check all your work and be sure everything is correct before you attempt to start the engine.*

Removal

1 If you're working on a 3.5L turbocharged engine, disconnect the cable from the negative battery terminal (see Chapter 5, Section 3)

2 Remove the valve covers (see Section 4).

3 Remove the engine front cover (see Section 9).

2.7L engines

4 Starting with the right-side chain, reinstall the crankshaft pulley bolt then rotate the engine until the keyway on the crankshaft is at 11 o'clock position.

5 Verify the triangle timing marks on the VCT units are at the 2 o'clock (intake unit) and 11 o'clock (exhaust unit) positions. If the circle timing marks are at these positions, the crankshaft must be turned clockwise one revolution (360 degrees).

6 Remove the right side tensioner mounting bolts and tensioner.

7 Slide the right side tensioner arm/guide off the pivot and remove the arm.

8 Remove the timing chain guide bolts and guide.

9 Lift the timing chain up and off of the VCT units then off of the crankshaft sprocket.

10 Remove the crankshaft pulley bolt and

slide the crankshaft outer sprocket off of the crankshaft.

11 Starting with the left-side chain, reinstall the crankshaft pulley bolt, then rotate the engine 360-degrees until the keyway on the crankshaft is at 11 o'clock position.

12 Verify the circle timing marks on the VCT units are at the 10 o'clock (intake unit) and 12:30 (exhaust unit) positions. If the triangle timing marks are at these positions the crankshaft must be turned clockwise one revolution (360 degrees).

13 Remove the crankshaft pulley bolt then pull the oil pump chain tensioner back until a drill bit or Allen wrench can be inserted through the holes in the tensioner. With the tensioner in this position, remove the mounting bolt and tensioner.

14 Remove the oil pump chain guide bolts and guide.

15 Lift the oil pump chain up and off of the crankshaft sprocket, then down and out of the oil pump sprocket.

16 Remove the left side tensioner mounting bolts and tensioner.

17 Slide the left side tensioner arm/guide off the pivot and remove the arm.

18 Remove the timing chain guide bolts and guide.

19 Lift the timing chain up and off of the VCT units then off of the crankshaft sprocket.

20 Slide the crankshaft inner sprocket off of the crankshaft.

VCT unit removal

Note: *If the right-side VCT units are being removed at the same time as the left-side VCT units, remove the right side VCT units first.*

21 Remove the timing chain(s).

10.25 Remove three of the camshaft cap bolts to remove the valvetrain oil tubes

10.30 Remove the VCT oil control solenoid mounting bolts (A and B) - (C) is the exhaust VCT unit and (D) is the intake VCT unit

22 Install special tool 303-1248 over the camshafts to lock them into place.
23 Remove the VCT unit center bolts and slide the VCT units off of the camshafts. Always replace the VCT unit center mounting bolt.

3.5L non-turbocharged engines and 2016 and earlier turbocharged 3.5L engines

24 Turn the engine clockwise until the VCT units (camshaft sprockets) on each intake camshaft are positioned at 90-degrees (12 o'clock) in relation to the top surface of the cylinder heads.
25 Remove the bolts that secure the valvetrain oil tubes to each cylinder head (see illustration).
26 Install the special camshaft locking tools (303-1248), with the tools holding the flats on each camshaft.
27 If you can't see the timing marks on the timing chain, add a paint dot to align with the marks on the VCT units and the crankshaft timing sprocket.
28 Remove the two bolts and the primary timing chain tensioner arm, then unbolt and remove the two tensioners.
29 Remove the mounting bolts and the lower-left chain guide, then the lower right chain guide.
30 Remove the bolts securing the VCT solenoids to the cylinder heads (see illustration). You may have to twist or wiggle the solenoids to disengage them.
Note: *The intake solenoids are white, the exhaust solenoids are black.*
31 Keep the VCT solenoids in clean plastic sandwich bags, marked with their destination.
32 Remove the primary timing chain.
33 The two camshafts on each cylinder head are jointly driven by a smaller secondary timing chain.
34 Depress and lock the secondary chain tensioner on each bank, using the factory

tool (303-1530) inserted in the large hole at the camshaft first bearing cap, or a length of threaded rod and nuts to hold the tensioner down, by pushing from the camshaft bearing cap.
35 With the camshafts still locked at TDC, remove the mounting bolts from the VCT units (camshaft sprockets), and remove the sprockets and secondary timing chains from the camshafts.
36 If the primary timing chain sprocket (at the center of the front of the block) is to be replaced, remove the nine bolts securing the plate that mounts the gear to the front of the block.

2017 3.5L turbocharged engines

37 Starting with the right-side chain, reinstall the crankshaft pulley bolt, then rotate the engine 360-degrees until the keyway on the crankshaft is at 11 o'clock position.
38 Verify the timing marks on the VCT units are at the 12:30 (intake unit) and 11 o'clock (exhaust unit) positions.
39 Install special tool 303-1655 over the camshafts to lock them into place.
40 Remove the bolts from the right-side chain tensioner and remove the tensioner. It may be necessary to rotate the crankshaft slightly to take the pressure off of the tensioner before it can be removed.
41 Slide the right-side timing chain tensioner arm off of the pivot and remove the arm.
42 Remove the right-side timing chain guide bolts and guide.
43 Remove the right-hand primary chain.
44 Remove the crankshaft pulley bolt.
45 Starting with the left-side chain, verify the timing marks on the VCT units are at the 11:30 (intake unit) and 1 o'clock (exhaust unit) positions.
46 Install special tool 303-1655 over the camshafts to lock them into place.
47 Remove the stud-bolt and bolts from the left-side chain tensioner and remove the tensioner. It may be necessary to rotate the

crankshaft slightly to take the pressure off of the tensioner before it can be removed.
48 Slide the left-side timing chain tensioner arm off of the pivot then remove the left-side chain guide bolt and guide.
49 Remove the left-side timing chain guide bolts and guide.
50 Remove the left-side chain.
51 Remove the crankshaft pulley bolt and slide the crankshaft sprocket off of the crankshaft.
52 Remove the bolts that secure the valvetrain oil tubes to each cylinder head (see illustration).

VCT unit removal
Note: *If the right side VCT units are being remove at the same time as the left side VCT units, remove the right side VCT units first.*
53 Remove the timing chain(s).
54 Install special tool 303-1655 over the camshafts to lock them into place.
55 Remove the VCT unit center bolts and slide the VCT units off of the camshafts. Always replace the VCT unit center mounting bolt.

Installation

2.7L engines
Note: *The VCT units have two timing marks on them, a triangle and a circle. When removing and installing the left-side VCT, use the circle marks.*
56 Starting with the left-side chain, install the left-side VCT units on to the camshafts with the circle timing marks at the 10 o'clock (intake) and 12:30 (exhaust) positions.
57 Install new VCT unit center bolts and tighten the bolts to the torque listed in this Chapter's Specifications.
58 Slide the inner crankshaft sprocket over the end of the crankshaft.
59 Place the left-side timing chain over the VCT units with the single colored links aligned with the circle timing marks on the VCT units

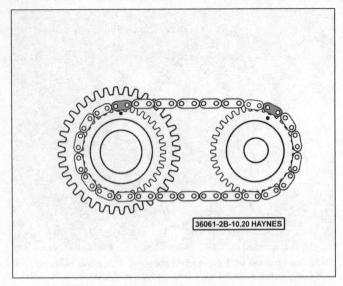

10.85 Align the colored links of the secondary timing chain with the marks on the back of the sprockets (VCT units)

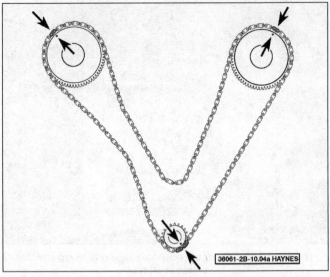

10.87 Align the colored links on the primary timing chain with the marks on the crankshaft and camshaft sprockets (VCT units)

at the 10 o'clock and 12:30 positions then align the double colored links on the chain so the timing mark on the crankshaft sprocket is in between both links.

60 Install the chain guide and bolts and tighten the guide bolts to the torque listed in this Chapter's Specifications.

61 Slide the left-side timing chain tensioner arm on to the pivot.

62 Slide the tensioner piston out of the tensioner body.

63 Using a vise, cover the vise jaws with covers or towels to prevent damage to the tensioner piston then mount the piston vertically in the vise. Using a flat-blade screwdriver, push the ratchet mechanism down inside the tensioner piston then rotate the screwdriver clockwise, one full turn until a click is heard. **Note:** *If an audible click is not heard, the ratcheting mechanism is not locked in place.*

64 Remove the tensioner piston from the vise and insert the piston into the tensioner body until a retaining pin can be inserted through the hole in the tensioner body to lock the piston in the retracted position.

65 Install the left-side tensioner and tighten the bolts to the torque listed in this Chapter's Specifications, make sure the end of the tensioner is properly engaged with the tensioner arm.

66 With the tensioner piston properly engaged with the tensioner arm remove the retaining pin.

67 Install the oil pump chain over the crankshaft and oil pump drive sprockets.

68 Install the oil pump chain guide and bolts, then tighten the bolts to the torque listed in this Chapter's Specifications.

69 Install the oil pump chain tensioner and bolt, then tighten the bolt to the torque listed in this Chapter's Specifications, then remove the retaining pin.

70 Install the crankshaft mounting bolt,

then rotate the crankshaft one full turn (360-degrees) until the keyway on the crankshaft is at the 11 o'clock position.

71 Remove the crankshaft bolt and replace it with a new one then side the crankshaft sprocket onto the end of the crankshaft.

72 Install the right-side VCT units on to the camshafts with the triangle timing marks at the 2 o'clock (intake) and 11 o'clock (exhaust) positions.

73 Install new VCT unit center bolts and tighten the bolts to the torque listed in this Chapter's Specifications.

74 Place the left-side timing chain over the VCT units with the single colored links aligned with the triangle timing marks on the VCT units at the 2 o'clock and 11 o'clock positions, then align the double colored links on the chain so the timing mark on the crankshaft sprocket is in between both links.

75 Install the chain guide and bolts and tighten the guide bolts to the torque listed in this Chapter's Specifications.

76 Slide the right-side timing chain tensioner arm on to the pivot.

77 Slide the tensioner piston out of the tensioner body.

78 Using a vise, cover the vise jaws with covers or towels to prevent damage to the tensioner piston, then mount the piston vertically in the vise. Using a flat-blade screwdriver, push the ratchet mechanism down inside the tensioner piston then rotate the screwdriver clockwise, one full turn until a click is heard. **Note:** *If an audible click is not heard the ratcheting mechanism is not locked in place.*

79 Remove the tensioner piston from the vise and insert the piston into the tensioner body until a retaining pin can be inserted through the hole in the tensioner body to lock the piston in the retracted position.

80 Install the right-side tensioner and tighten the bolts to the torque listed in this

Chapter's Specifications , make sure the end of the tensioner is properly engaged with the tensioner arm.

81 With the tensioner piston properly engaged with the tensioner arm remove the retaining pin.

3.5L non-turbocharged engines and 2016 and earlier turbocharged 3.5L engines

82 If the primary chain gear and its plate were removed, clean the mounting surface and the block and install the sprocket and plate with a new gasket. Prepare the primary chain tensioners by pushing in the release button and compressing the plunger until a nail or large paper clip can be inserted to hold the plunger.

83 If the secondary timing chain tensioners were removed, they cannot be reused. New tensioners must be installed. **Caution:** *Do not remove the plastic clip that is keeping the new tensioner compressed.*

84 The tensioner is installed to the correct depth when you hear a "snap" sound. Install the tensioner shoe. The plastic clip can now be removed with pliers.

85 Align the colored links with the marks on the VCT units and install the chain on the backside of the VCT units (see illustration). Align the two VCT units with the dowel pins on the front of the camshafts.

86 New bolts must be used to install the VCT units. Tighten the bolts to the torque listed in this Chapter's Specifications.

87 When the secondary chains and VCT units are installed and aligned, install the primary timing chain, aligning the colored links with the marks on the sprockets (see illustration). When all components are installed and aligned, pull the pins holding back the two primary chain tensioners.

2017 3.5L turbocharged engines

Note: *The VCT units have two timing marks on them: a triangle and a circle. When removing and installing the left-side VCT, use the circle marks.*

88 Starting with the left-side chain, install the left-side VCT units on to the camshafts with the circle timing marks at the 11:30 (intake) and 1 o'clock (exhaust) positions.

89 Install new VCT unit center bolts and tighten the bolts to the torque listed in this Chapter's Specifications.

90 Slide the crankshaft sprocket over the end of the crankshaft.

91 Place the left-side timing chain over the VCT units with the single colored links aligned with the timing marks on the VCT units at the 11:30 and 1 o'clock positions, then align the double colored links on the chain so the timing mark on the crankshaft sprocket is in between both links.

92 Install the chain guide and bolts and tighten the guide bolts to the torque listed in this Chapter's Specifications.

93 Slide the left-side timing chain tensioner arm on to the pivot.

94 Place the tensioner into a soft-jawed vise, using a pair of needle nose pliers to compress the ratchet wire clip ends together, then compress the plunger while holding the ratchet wire together until a locking pin can be inserted through the body of the tensioner to hold the plunger in the compressed position.

95 Remove the tensioner from the vise and install the left-side tensioner. Tighten the bolts to the torque listed in this Chapter's Specifications. Make sure the end of the tensioner is properly engaged with the tensioner arm.

96 With the tensioner piston properly engaged with the tensioner arm, remove the retaining pin.

97 Remove the special service tool 303-1655 from the camshafts.

98 Place the right-side timing chain over the VCT units with the single colored links aligned with the timing marks on the VCT units at the 12:30 and 11 o'clock positions, then align the double colored links on the chain so the timing mark on the crankshaft sprocket is in between both links.

99 Install the crankshaft pulley bolt and rotate the crankshaft one full turn (360-degrees) until the keyway on the crankshaft is at the 11 o'clock position.

100 Remove the crankshaft bolt and replace it with a new one.

101 Install new VCT unit center bolts and tighten the bolts to the torque listed in this Chapter's Specifications.

102 Install the chain guide and bolts and tighten the guide bolts to the torque listed in this Chapter's Specifications.

103 Slide the right-side timing chain tensioner arm on to the pivot.

104 Compress the right-side tensioner (see Steps 94 and 95).

105 Install the right-side tensioner and tighten the bolts to the torque listed in this Chapter's Specifications, make sure the end of the tensioner is properly engaged with the tensioner arm.

106 With the tensioner piston properly engaged with the tensioner arm remove the retaining pin.

All models

107 Reinstall the remaining parts in the reverse order of removal.

108 Carefully rotate the crankshaft by hand through at least two full revolutions (use a socket and breaker bar on the crankshaft pulley center bolt).

Caution: *If you feel any resistance, STOP! There is something wrong -most likely, valves are contacting the pistons. You must find the problem before proceeding.*

109 Install a new oil filter, then add engine oil and coolant (see Chapter 1).

110 Run the engine and check for leaks.

11 Camshafts and tappets/roller followers and lash adjusters - removal, inspection and installation

Caution: *These engines are difficult to work on and require some special tools. On any procedure involving the timing chains, the Steps must be read carefully and disassembly must proceed using the special tools, otherwise damage to the engine will result.*

Caution: *Because this is an "interference" engine design, if the timing chain has broken, there will be damage to the valves (and possibly the pistons) and will require removal of the cylinder heads.*

Caution: *The timing system is complex. Severe engine damage will occur if you make any mistakes. Do not attempt this procedure unless you are highly experienced with this type of repair. If you are at all unsure of your abilities, consult an expert. Double-check all your work and be sure everything is correct before you attempt to start the engine.*

Caution: *2.7L and 3.5L turbocharged models are equipped with Direct Injection (DI) and a high-pressure fuel pump. Fuel pressure in the high-pressure system on Direct Injection (DI) systems is under extremely high pressure. Be sure to correctly perform the fuel pressure relief procedure prior to servicing any of the high-pressure fuel system components to prevent injury (see Chapter 4, Section 4).*

Note: *3.5L Duratec and 2016 and earlier 3.5L EcoBoost engines use solid tappets (cam followers). 2.7L and 2017 3.5L EcoBoost engines use roller followers and hydraulic lash adjusters.*

Removal

Note: *If you're removing the camshafts from both sides, remove the right (passenger's) side first.*

2.7L engines and 2017 3.5L turbocharged engines

1 Raise the vehicle and support it securely on jackstands.

2 Relieve the fuel pressure (see Chapter 4).

3 Disconnect the cable from the negative battery terminal (see Chapter 5)

4 Remove the high-pressure fuel pump drive (see Chapter 4) when removing the right-side camshafts or the brake vacuum pump (see Chapter 9) when removing the left-side camshafts.

5 Refer to Section 10 and remove the timing chain(s) and camshaft VCT units.

6 Loosen then remove the front "mega-cap" mounting bolts and mega-cap first.

Caution: *The front camshaft mega-cap must be removed first then the remaining camshaft bearing caps or possible engine damage may occur.*

7 Loosen the camshaft caps mounting bolts and remove the caps.

Caution: *Keep the caps in order and don't mix them up.*

8 Remove the camshafts from the cylinder head(s).

9 Remove the roller followers and lash adjusters as assemblies. Keep the followers and lash adjusters in order and don't mix them up.

10 Remove the spring clips on the camshaft roller followers and separate the lash adjusters from the rockers.

Caution: *If the original components are to be reinstalled, they must be installed in their original locations*

2016 and earlier 3.5L turbocharged engines and all 3.5L non-turbocharged engines

11 Before removing the camshafts, check the valve clearances (see Section 3).

12 Refer to Section 10 and remove the timings chain and camshaft VCT units also the tensioner holding tool and camshaft holding tools.

13 Loosen the camshaft caps and "mega-cap" mounting bolts and remove the caps.

Caution: *Keep the caps in order and don't mix them up. Remove the camshafts from the cylinder head.*

14 When removing the right-side camshafts on 3.5L turbocharged models, remove the brake vacuum pump (see Chapter 9).

15 With the camshafts removed, the tappets can be removed using a magnet.

Caution: *They must be stored in an egg carton or other divided and marked container, so they can be restored to their original locations during reassembly.*

Inspection

16 After the camshafts have been removed, clean them with solvent, then inspect the bearing journals for uneven wear and pitting. If the journals are damaged, the bearing saddles in the cylinder heads and caps are probably damaged as well. The head and camshaft caps will have to be replaced.

17 Measure the bearing journals with a micrometer and compare to the Specifications in this Chapter to determine whether they are

11.18a Lobe lift can be obtained by measuring camshaft lobe height . . .

11.18b . . . and by measuring the camshaft base circle - the difference between the two measurements equals lobe lift

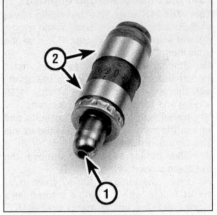

11.20a Inspect the lash adjuster for signs of excessive wear or damage, such as pitting, scoring or signs of overheating (bluing or discoloration) - the areas of wear are the rocker arm pivot point (1) and the side surfaces where the lifter body contacts the cylinder head bore (2)

excessively worn or out-of-round.

18   Measure the camshaft lobe height and the base circle (see illustrations). The difference between the two measurements is the lobe lift (lobe height - base circle = lobe lift). Record this figure for future reference and repeat the check on the remaining camshaft lobes. Compare the results to the values listed in this Chapter's Specifications.

19   Inspect the camshaft lobes for heat discoloration, score marks, chipped areas, pitting and uneven wear. If the lobes are in good condition and if the lobe lift measurements are as specified, you can reuse the camshafts.

20   On 2.7L engines and 2017 3.5L turbocharged engines, check the lash adjusters and roller followers for wear (see illustrations).

Installation

2.7L engines and 2017 3.5L turbocharged engines

21   On 2.7L engines, insert the lash adjuster onto the spring clips on the camshaft roller fol-

lowers, then lubricate them with oil and install them into their original locations. On 3.5L turbocharged engines, lubricate the lash adjusters with oil and install them into their original locations.

Caution: *On 2017 3.5L turbocharged engines, do not install the camshaft roller followers at this time. They will be installed later (see Steps 28 through 31). If the followers are installed before the camshafts caps are tightened, the camshaft caps can become distorted when the camshafts are tightened and cause severe damage to the engine.*

22   Lubricate the camshaft bearing journals and cam lobes with moly-based grease or camshaft installation lubricant.

23   Position the camshafts in the cylinder head in their neutral positions (see illustrations).

24   Apply a small 1 mm bead of RTV to the rear camshaft cap at the inner corners, then install the camshaft cap and remaining camshaft caps with bolts, loosely tightening the cap bolts at this time.

25   Install the front "mega-cap" and bolts and loosely tighten the mega-cap bolts, at

this time.

26   Tighten all the camshaft bolts, in sequence, to the torque listed in this Chapter's Specifications (see illustrations).

3.5L turbocharged engines

27   Install the camshaft holding tools to the left camshafts then install the VCT units (see Section 10).

28   Install the timing chains (see Section 10) but on 3.5L turbocharged models do not install the valve covers.

2017 3.5L turbocharged engine

29   Starting with the front cylinder, rotate the crankshaft pulley clockwise until the cylinder camshaft lobes are pointing upwards.

30   Install special service tool 303-1633 and 303-1633-01 over the camshaft and on to the top of the valve springs. Tighten the knob on the tool clockwise, to depress the valve and spring.

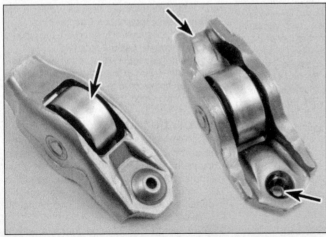

11.20b Check the rocker arm roller, the valve stem contact point and lash adjuster contact point

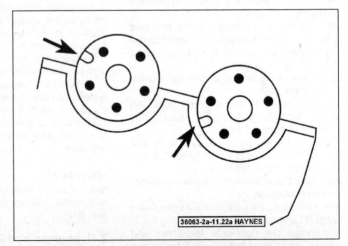

11.23a When installing the left (driver's) side cylinder head camshafts, position the D-slots pins like this - 2.7L engines

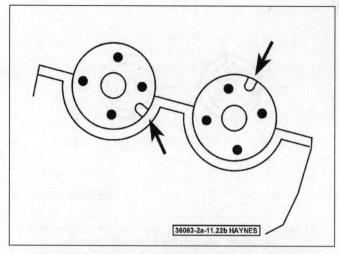

11.23b When installing the left (driver's) side cylinder head camshafts, position the D-slots pins like this - 2017 3.5L turbocharged engines

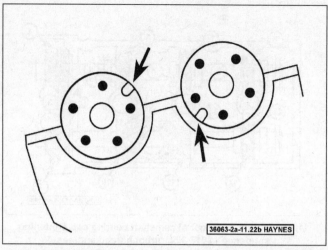

11.23c When installing the right (passenger's) side cylinder head camshafts, position the D-slots pins like this - 2.7L engines

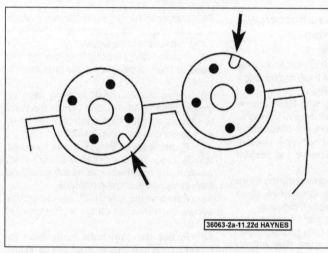

11.23d When installing the right (passenger's) side cylinder head camshafts, position the D-slots pins like this - 2017 3.5L turbocharged engines

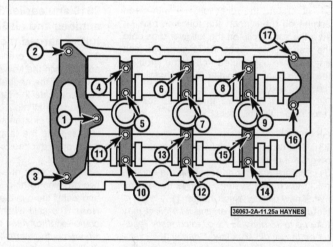

11.26a Left (driver's) camshaft bearing cap tightening sequence - 2.7L engine

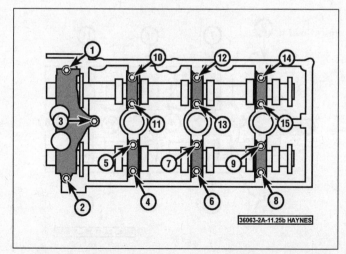

11.26b Left (driver's) camshaft bearing cap tightening sequence - 2017 3.5L turbocharged engines

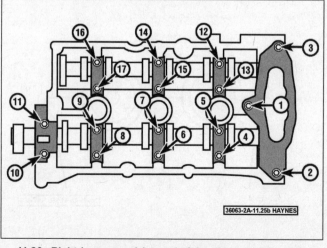

11.26c Right (passenger's) camshaft bearing cap tightening sequence - 2.7L engine

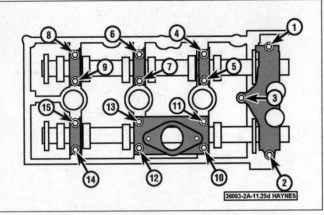

11.26d Right (passenger's) camshaft bearing cap tightening sequence - 2017 3.5L turbocharged engines

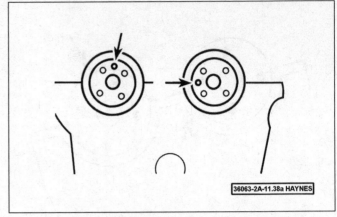

11.39a When installing the left (driver's) side cylinder head camshafts, position the dowel pins like this

31   Lubricate the roller follower with clean engine oil then insert the follower, making sure the spring clip on the follower clips onto the lash adjuster. Once the follower and lash adjuster are assembled, rotate the knob on the tool counterclockwise to slowly release the valve and spring.

32   Repeat Steps 28 through 30 for the remaining roller followers.

All models

33   The remaining installation steps are the reverse of removal.

34   Before starting and running the engine, refill the cooling system, change the oil and install new oil filter (see Chapter 1).

Note: *After filling the engine with oil, it may take up to 15 minutes for oil to correctly register on the oil dip stick (see Chapter 1).*

2016 and earlier 3.5L turbocharged engines and all 3.5L non-turbocharged models

35   Rotate the crankshaft counterclockwise and position the keyway in the 9 o'clock position (this is the neutral position).

36   Lubricate the tappets with clean engine oil and reinstall them in their original locations. If any valve clearances were out-of-specification, replace the tappet(s) with new ones of the proper thickness to achieve the desired clearance.

37   At the front of each camshaft, there are two grooves to hold seals. Obtain new seals and install them in the camshaft grooves.

Note: *The split where the ends of each seal come together must face UP (12 o'clock position) on the camshafts when they are installed.*

38   Lubricate the camshaft bearing journals and cam lobes with moly-based grease or camshaft installation lubricant.

39   Position the camshafts in the cylinder head in their neutral positions (see illustrations).

40   Install the camshaft bearing caps (in their original locations), and tighten the bolts, in sequence, to the torque listed in this Chapter's Specifications (see illustration).

41   Recheck the valve clearances (see Section 3). Since the crankshaft is in the neutral position, the camshafts can be turned without the valves contacting the pistons.

42   Remove the camshaft cap bolts that secure the valvetrain oil tubes. Remove the oil tubes.

43   Rotate the camshafts to position the dowel pins in their proper positions for installing the VCT units and timing chains (see illus-

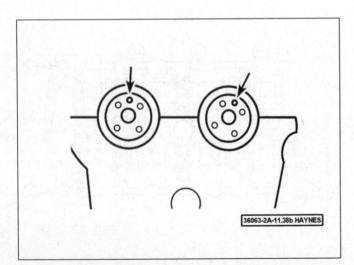

11.39b When installing the right (passenger's) side cylinder head camshafts, position the dowel pins like this

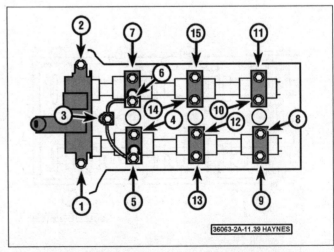

11.40 Camshaft bearing cap tightening sequence

trations). Install the camshaft holding tools.

44   Rotate the crankshaft clockwise to position the keyway in the 11 o'clock position.

45   Install the VCT units (see Section 10).

46   Install the timing chains (see Section 10).

47   Reinstall the valvetrain oil tubes and tighten the bearing cap bolts to the torque listed in this Chapter's Specifications.

48   The remaining installation steps are the reverse of removal.

49   Before starting and running the engine, refill the cooling system, change the oil and install new oil filter (see Chapter 1).

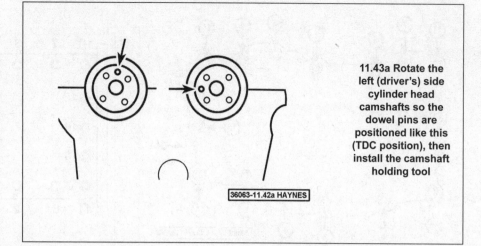

11.43a Rotate the left (driver's) side cylinder head camshafts so the dowel pins are positioned like this (TDC position), then install the camshaft holding tool

---

12   Oil pan - removal and installation

Note: *The manufacturer states that the oil pan is not re-useable on 2.7L engines. If removed, a new one must be installed.*

Removal

1   Disconnect the cable from the negative battery terminal (see Chapter 5, Section 3).

2   Remove the oil dipstick.

3   Drain the engine oil and remove the oil filter (see Chapter 1).

4   Raise the vehicle and support it securely on jackstands. On 4WD models, strap the front differential to a sturdy jack, remove the bushing bolts and lower the front axle enough to allow clearance for oil pan removal (see Chapter 8).

5   Remove the transmission cooler bracket fasteners then disconnect the transmission cooler from the transmission (see Chapter 7A).

6   Disconnect the oxygen-sensor harness clips and the starter motor harness clips from the oil pan. Position the harness out of the way.

7   Disconnect the alternator harness from the engine front cover.

8   Remove the under-vehicle splash shield

by twisting the quarter-turn fasteners counterclockwise.

9   On models with an air dam below the radiator, remove the two bolts and the air dam.

10   On models with a skid-plate, remove the mounting bolts and the skid-plate.

11   Remove the nuts/bolts securing the crossmember below the oil pan, and remove the crossmember (see illustration).

12   On 2.7L engines, remove oil pan-to-engine bolts.

13   On 3.5L engines, remove the front cover-to-oil pan bolts, the oil pan-to-transmission bolts and the oil pan-to-engine block bolts.

14   On 3.5L engines, loosen the following bolts 3/16-inch: the four upper bellhousing bolts, the bellhousing bolt above the starter motor, the two mounting bolts on the left side of the bellhousing, and the two nuts in the center of the transmission crossmember. Move the transmission rearward as allowed by the loosened fasteners.

15   There are two notches at the top rear corners of the oil pan where a large screwdriver

can safely be used to pry the pan loose.

Installation

Caution: *Do not use abrasive discs or scrapers on either the engine or the pan mounting surfaces. The aluminum and plastic components can easily be gouged, leading to oil leakage.*

16   Clean the surfaces of the pan, the engine, front cover and transmission of all traces of RTV sealant.

17   On 2.7L engines, install a new pan-to-oil pump seal.

18   Apply a 7/32-inch (5.5 mm) bead of High Performance RTV sealant at the junctures of the rear main seal housing and the block, and also where the pan meets the front cover.

19   Apply a 1/8-inch (3 mm) bead of High Performance RTV sealant around the inner perimeter of the oil pan's mounting surface and install the oil pan. Install the four corner bolts within four minutes of applying the RTV sealant. Install and tighten the remaining bolts within an hour.

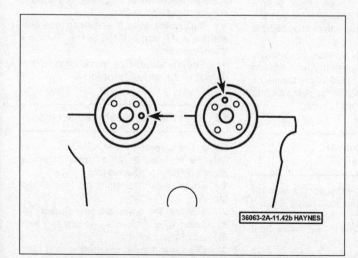

11.43b Rotate the right (passenger's) side cylinder head camshafts so the dowel pins are positioned like this (TDC position), then install the camshaft holding tool

12.11 Remove the crossmember mounting fasteners

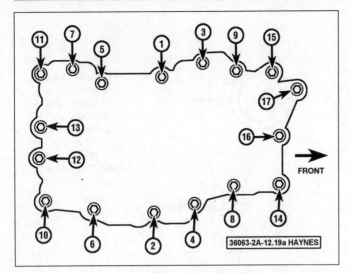

12.20a Oil pan-to-engine bolt tightening sequence - 2.7L engines

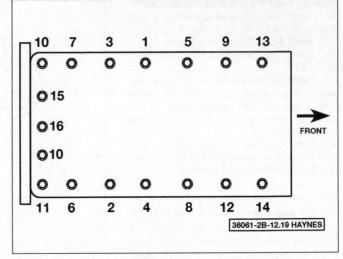

12.20b Oil pan-to-engine bolt tightening sequence - 3.5L engines

20   When all of the pan-to-engine bolts are started, tighten the bolts, in sequence, to the torque listed in this Chapter's Specifications (see illustrations). On 3.5L engines, after the pan-to-engine bolts are tightened, install and tighten the pan-to-transmission bolts, and all fasteners loosened in Steps 13 and 14.
Caution: *You must work fast to secure the oil pan to the engine within 10 minutes of applying the RTV.*
Note: *All bolts must be fully tightened within 60 minutes of applying the the High Performance RTV or oil leaks can occur.*
21   The remaining steps are the reverse of removal.
Caution: *Don't forget to add engine oil and install a new oil filter (see Chapter 1), but wait at least 90 minutes before doing so.*
22   Start the engine and check carefully for oil leaks at the oil pan.

13   Oil pump - removal and installation

1   Drain the oil and remove the oil filter (see Chapter 1).
2   Remove the oil pan (see Section 12).

2.7L engines

3   Slowly rotate the oil pump drive chain tensioner counterclockwise until a small drill bit or Allen wrench can be inserted through both holes in the tensioner, locking the tensioner against the spring.
4   Remove the four oil pump mounting bolts while supporting the rear of the pump.
5   Slowly lower the rear of the oil pump until the oil pump sprocket can be lifted out of the chain and from the vehicle.
6   Before installing the oil pump, pour a couple of tablespoons of engine oil into the pump the rotate the pump sprocket by hand to

prime the pump.
7   Place the sprocket on the pump back into the chain then raise the rear of the pump and install the mounting bolts. Tighten the bolts evenly to the torque listed in this Chapter's Specifications.
8   Remaining installation is the reverse of removal.

3.5L engines

9   Remove the engine front cover (see Section 9).
10   Remove the primary timing chain (see Section 10).
11   Slide the crankshaft sprocket from the crankshaft.
12   Remove the three fasteners and the oil pump pickup and screen assembly.
13   Remove the three oil pump mounting bolts and remove the oil pump.
14   Before installing the oil pump, pour a couple of tablespoons of engine oil into the pump the rotate the pump sprocket by hand to prime the pump.
15   Installation is the reverse of removal. After bolting the oil pump in place tighten the bolts to the torque listed in this Chapter's Specifications, reinstall the oil pump pickup tube and screen with a new O-ring.

14   Driveplate - removal and installation

1   Raise the vehicle and support it securely on jackstands, then refer to Chapter 7A and remove the transmission. If it's leaking, now would be a very good time to replace the front pump seal/O-ring.
2   Look for factory paint marks that indicate driveplate-to-crankshaft alignment. If they aren't there, use a center-punch or paint to make alignment marks on the driveplate and

crankshaft to ensure correct alignment during reinstallation.
3   Remove the bolts that secure the driveplate to the crankshaft. If the crankshaft turns, use a flywheel holding tool or wedge a screwdriver in the ring gear teeth to jam the driveplate.
4   Remove the driveplate from the crankshaft.
5   Check for cracked and broken ring gear teeth.
6   Clean and inspect the mating surfaces of the driveplate and the crankshaft. If the crankshaft rear seal is leaking, replace it before reinstalling the driveplate (see Section 15).
7   Position the driveplate against the crankshaft, but make sure the crankshaft sensor ring is positioned between the driveplate and the engine. Be sure to align the marks made during removal. Note that some engines have an alignment dowel or staggered bolt holes to ensure correct installation.
8   Tighten the bolts, in sequence (see illustration) to the torque listed in this Chapter's Specifications.
9   The remainder of installation is the reverse of the removal procedure.

15   Rear main oil seal - replacement

Note: *The crankshaft rear seal and retainer must be replaced as an assembly, the seal cannot be replaced separately.*
1   Remove the transmission (see Chapter 7A).
2   Remove the driveplate (see Section 14) then remove the crankshaft sensor ring from the end of the crankshaft.
3   Disconnect the crankshaft sensor electrical connector, then remove the crankshaft sensor mounting bolts and the sensor from the seal housing (see Chapter 6).

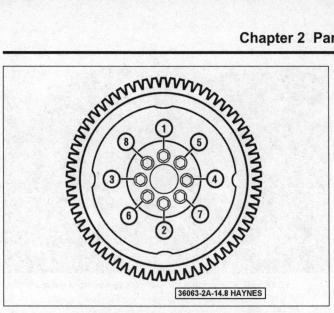

14.8 Driveplate bolt tightening sequence

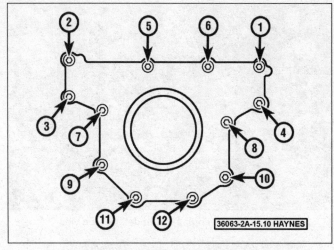

15.10 2.7L engine, rear crankshaft seal retainer tightening sequence

4 Remove the oil pan-to-seal housing bolts.

5 Remove the seal retainer mounting bolts and the retainer from the rear of the engine.

6 Use only a plastic gasket scraper or putty knife to remove all traces of old gasket material and sealant from the pan and engine block.

Caution: *To prevent an oil leak after the new seal is installed, be very careful not to scratch or otherwise damage the crankshaft sealing surface or the engine block.*

7 Remove all traces of RTV sealant. Apply a 3/16-inch bead of high performance RTV along the sealing surfaces of the retainer where the block and oil pan flanges meet.

8 Apply a film of clean engine oil to the lips of the new seal and around the crankshaft where the seal makes contact.

9 Install the retainer assembly to the engine at an angle, with the bottom of the retainer touching the oil pan, tilt the retainer up and onto the rear of the cylinder block then install all the bolts within 10 minutes of applying the sealant.

10 On 2.7L turbocharged engines, tighten the bolts in sequence (see illustration), to the torque listed in this Chapter's Specifications.

11 On 3.5L engines, install the seal retainer-to-engine block bolts first, then tighten the bolts, in sequence (see illustration) to the torque listed in this Chapter's Specifications, then install the oil pan-to-seal retainer bolts and tighten the bolts to the torque listed in this Chapter's Specifications.

12 Reinstall the crankshaft sensor (see Chapter 6), the crankshaft sensor ring and the driveplate, making sure the crankshaft sensor ring is between the crankshaft and the driveplate.

13 Reinstall the transmission (see Chapter 7A).

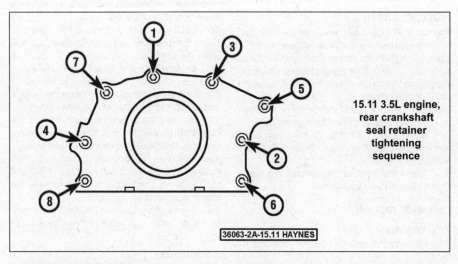

15.11 3.5L engine, rear crankshaft seal retainer tightening sequence

16 Engine mounts - check and replacement

Note: *The tightening torque required for installing the engine mount through-bolts is considerable. Make sure you have access to a high-torque torque wrench before beginning.*

Note: *The following is the factory-recommended procedure, using an engine support fixture from above. With some creativity and depending on tool selection, it may be possible to replace the engine mounts without performing some of the steps listed here.*

1 There are three powertrain mounts on the vehicles covered by this manual; left and right engine mounts attached to the engine block and the frame, and a rear mount attached to the transmission and the transmission crossmember. The rear transmission mount is covered in Chapter 7A. Engine mounts seldom require attention, but broken or deteriorated mounts should be replaced immediately or the added strain placed on the driveline components may cause damage or wear.

Check

2 During the check, the engine must be raised slightly to remove the weight from the mounts.

3 Raise the vehicle and support it securely on jackstands.

4 Position a jack under the engine oil pan. Place a large wood block between the jack head and the oil pan, then carefully raise the engine just enough to take the weight off the mounts.

Warning: *DO NOT place any part of your body under the engine when it's supported only by a jack!*

5 Check for relative movement between the inner and outer portions of the mount (use a large screwdriver or prybar to attempt to move the mounts). If movement is noted, lower the engine and tighten the mount fasteners.

6 Check the mounts to see if the rubber

16.17 Left side engine mount details - top view

1   Mount-to-frame bolts   2   Through-bolt

16.18 Left side engine mount details - bottom view

1   Mount nuts   2   Through bolt

is cracked, hardened or separated from the metal casing which would indicate a need for replacement.

Replacement

Warning: *A high amount of torque must be employed to remove/install the engine mounts. Unless you have the proper tools, you may not be able to fully tighten the fasteners, which is an unsafe condition. Have the job done at a shop or dealership.*

Caution: *Use only hand tools to either remove or install the engine mount through-bolts.*

7   Disconnect the cable from the negative terminal of the battery (see Chapter 5, Section 3).

8   Raise the front of the vehicle and support it securely on jackstands.

Left-side mount

2.7L engines

9   Remove the air filter housing (see Chapter 4).

10   Remove the charge air cooler intake and outlet pipes (see Chapter 4).

11   Remove the under-vehicle splash shield and skid plate if equipped.

12   Remove the front exhaust Y pipe bolts from all three ends and lower the pipe.

13   On 4WD models, remove the front driveshaft (see Chapter 8).

16.40 Remove the wiring harness plastic push-pin (1) and ground wire bolt (2)

14   On 4WD models, support the front axle housing with a floor jack, then remove the three housing mounting bolts (see Chapter 8) and lower the housing down enough to allow the mount to be removed.

15   On 2WD models, remove the front stabilizer bar bracket nuts (see Chapter 10) and allow the bar to swing down.

16   Using a floor jack, place a block of wood onto the jack, then place the jack at the rear of the engine-transmission and raise the engine just enough to take the weight off the mount.

17   Remove the engine mount-to-frame bolts (see illustration). Use only hand tools - do not use impact tools to remove the mount bolts.

18   Remove the engine mount nuts and through-bolt (see illustration). Use only hand tools - do not use impact tools to remove the mount nuts/bolts.

19   If necessary, remove the mount bracket-to-engine bolts and bracket from the side of the engine.

3.5L engines

20   Remove the hood (see Chapter 11).

21   Remove the air filter housing (see Chapter 4).

22   On turbocharged models, remove the charge air cooler intake and outlet pipes (see Chapter 4).

23   Remove the intake manifold (see Section 6).

24   Remove the right rear ignition coil (see Chapter 5).

25   Attach lifting eyes at the right-front and left-rear of the engine. Support the engine with a hoist or a lifting device such as an engine support fixture.

Caution: *Raise the engine just enough to take the weight off the engine mounts.*

26   Remove the under-vehicle splash shield.

27   Remove the skid plate, if equipped.

28   Remove the front exhaust Y pipe bolts from all three ends and lower the pipe.

29   Loosen, but don't remove, the nuts on the transmission mount crossmember (see Chapter 7A).

30   Remove the under-vehicle splash shield.

31   Loosen, but don't remove, the nuts on the transmission mount crossmember (see Chapter 7A).

32   On 4WD models, place a floor jack under the front differential and chain or otherwise securely retain the differential to the jack. Raise the front axle slightly, and remove the differential mounting bushing bolts, then lower the differential for room to access the engine mounts. Remove the front driveshaft (see Chapter 8).

33   Remove the engine mount through-bolt (see illustrations 16.17 and 16.18). use only hand tools do not use impact tools to remove the mount nuts/bolts.

34   Remove the bracket-to-engine block bolts, then remove the bracket.

35   Remove the three bolts securing the mount insulator to the frame rail.

Right-side mount

2.7L engines

36   Remove the air filter housing (see Chapter 4).

37   Remove the charge air cooler intake and outlet pipes (see Chapter 4).

38   Remove the under-vehicle splash shield and skid plate if equipped.

39   Remove the starter (see Chapter 5).

40   Remove the harness plastic push-pin fastener and the ground wire bolt (see illustration).

41 Remove the drivebelt (see Chapter 1).
42 Remove the right front tire and right front splash shield (see Chapter 11).
43 Remove the air conditioning compressor mounting bolts and secure the compressor out of the way without disconnecting the compressor lines (see Chapter 3).
44 Remove the front exhaust Y pipe bolts from all three ends and lower the pipe.
45 On 4WD models, remove the front drive shaft (see Chapter 8).
46 On 2WD models, remove the front stabilizer bar bracket nuts (see Chapter 10) and allow the bar to swing down.
47 Using a floor jack, place a block of wood onto the jack, then place the jack at the rear of the engine-transmission and raise the engine just enough to take the weight off the mount.
48 Remove the engine mount-to-frame bolts (see illustration 16.17), use only hand tools. Do not use impact tools to remove the mount bolts.
49 Remove the engine mount nuts and through bolt (see illustration 16.18). Use only hand tools; do not use impact tools to remove the mount nuts/bolts.
50 If necessary remove the mount bracket-to-engine bolts and bracket from the side of the engine.

3.5L engines

51 Remove the hood (see Chapter 11).
52 Remove the air filter housing (see Chapter 4).
53 On turbocharged models, remove the charge air cooler intake and outlet pipes (see Chapter 4).
54 Remove the intake manifold (see Section 6).
55 Remove the right rear ignition coil (see Chapter 5).
56 Attach lifting eyes at the right-front and left-rear of the engine. Support the engine with a crane or a lifting device such as an engine support fixture.
Caution: *Raise the engine just enough to take the weight off the engine mounts.*
57 Remove the under-vehicle splash shield and skid plate, if equipped.
58 Remove the starter (see Chapter 5).
59 Remove the drivebelt (see Chapter 1).
60 Disconnect the electrical connector to the coolant pump, then remove the coolant pump mounting bolts, without disconnecting the coolant hoses (see Chapter 3, Section 13).
61 Disconnect the electrical connectors to the air conditioning compressor then remove the air conditioning compressor mounting bolts and secure the compressor out of the way without disconnecting the compressor lines (see Chapter 3).
62 Remove the front exhaust Y pipe bolts from all three ends and lower the pipe.
63 Loosen, but don't remove, the nuts on the transmission mount crossmember (see Chapter 7A).
64 Remove the under-vehicle splash shield.
65 Loosen, but don't remove, the nuts on the transmission mount crossmember (see Chapter 7A).
66 On 4WD models, place a floor jack under the front differential and chain or otherwise securely retain the differential to the jack. Raise the front axle slightly, and remove the differential mounting bushing bolts, then lower the differential for room to access the engine mounts. Remove the front driveshaft (see Chapter 8).
67 Remove the engine mount through-bolt (see illustrations 16.17 and 16.18). Use only hand tools - do not use impact tools to remove the mount nuts/bolts.
Note: *It may be necessary to remove the mount-to-engine bracket to allow the mount to be removed.*
68 Remove the bracket-to-engine block bolts, then remove the bracket.
69 Remove the three bolts securing the mount insulator to the frame rail.

All models

70 Install the new engine mount, tightening the bolts to the torque listed in this Chapter's Specifications.
71 Install the engine mount onto the engine support bracket and tighten the bolts securely. Then install the mount through-bolts, using thread locking compound on the threads.
72 The remainder of the installation is the reverse of removal. Remove the engine hoist and the jackstands and lower the vehicle.
Caution: *Be sure to tighten the nuts at the transmission crossmember.*

Notes

Chapter 2 Part B
V8 engine

Contents

	Section		Section
Camshaft(s) - removal, inspection and installation	12	Rear main oil seal - replacement	17
Crankshaft pulley and front oil seal - removal and installation	7	Repair operations possible with the engine in the vehicle	2
Cylinder heads - removal and installation	13	Roller followers and valve lash adjusters - removal,	
Engine mounts - check and replacement	18	inspection and installation	10
Exhaust manifolds - removal and installation	6	Timing chain cover - removal and installation	8
Flywheel/driveplate - removal and installation	16	Timing chains, tensioners and sprockets - removal,	
General information	1	inspection and installation	9
Intake manifold - removal and installation	5	Top Dead Center (TDC) for number one piston - locating	3
Oil pan - removal and installation	14	Valve covers - removal and installation	4
Oil pump - removal and installation	15	Variable Camshaft Timing (VCT) system - general information	11

Specifications

General

Displacement	5.0 liters (302 cubic inches)
Cylinder numbers (front to rear)	
Right side	1-2-3-4
Left (driver's) side	5-6-7-8
Firing order	1-3-7-2-6-5-4-8

Camshaft

Lobe lift	
Intake	0.2347 inch
Exhaust	0.2161 inch
Allowable lobe lift loss	Not available
Endplay	0.0014 to 0.0067 inch
Runout	0.0016 inch
Journal diameter	1.1268 inches
Bearing inside diameter	1.1282 to 1.1292 inches
Journal-to-bearing (oil) clearance	0.001 to 0.003 inch

5.0L V8 ENGINE
1-3-7-2-6-5-4-8

36063-02B-00.00a HAYNES

Cylinder locations

Torque specifications   **Ft-lbs** (unless otherwise indicated)

Note: *One foot-pound (ft-lb) of torque is equivalent to 12 inch-pounds (in-lbs) of torque. Torque values below approximately 15 foot-pounds are expressed in inch-pounds, because most foot-pound torque wrenches are not accurate at these smaller values.*

Air conditioning compressor drivebelt tensioner mounting bolt	18
Camshaft sprocket/Variable Camshaft Timing (VCT) unit bolt*	
Step 1	133 in-lbs
Step 2	Tighten an additional 90-degrees
Camshaft cap bolts	
Step 1	53 in-lbs
Step 2	Tighten an additional 45-degrees
Coolant crossover assembly bolts	89 in-lbs
Cylinder head bolts*	
Step 1	18
Step 2	55
Step 3	Loosen all bolts 180-degrees
Step 4	18
Step 5	26
Step 6	Tighten an additional 90-degrees
Step 7	Tighten an additional 90-degrees
Crankshaft pulley-to-crankshaft bolt	
Step 1	103
Step 2	Loosen one full turn
Step 3	74
Step 4	Tighten an additional 90-degrees
Crossmember mounting bolts	66
Engine mount bracket-to-engine block bolts	46
Engine mount-to-engine bracket bolts	129
Engine mount through-bolt	258
Engine mount stud bolts (right side)	30
Engine mount stud nuts (right side)	111
Main drivebelt tensioner bolt	35
Exhaust manifold studs	
Cylinder head studs	18
Exhaust pipe studs	30
Exhaust manifold-to-cylinder head nuts	
Step 1	18
Step 2	24
Exhaust pipe-to-exhaust manifold nuts	30
Exhaust pipe Torca-clamp	41
Catalytic converter-to-exhaust manifold bolts	30
Driveplate bolts	
Step 1	177 in-lbs
Step 2	Tighten an additional 60-degrees
Intake manifold-to-cylinder head bolts	
Step 1 (manifold bolts)	106 in-lbs
Step 2 (manifold bolts)	Tighten an additional 35-degrees
Step 3 (fuel rail bolts)	89 in-lbs
Step 4 (fuel rail bolts)	Tighten an additional 90-degrees
Oil pan-to-engine block bolts	
Step 1	18 in-lbs
Step 2	89 in-lbs
Step 3	Tighten an additional 45-degrees
Oil pan-to-rear main seal retainer bolts	15
Oil filter adapter bolts	18
Oil pump-to-engine block mounting bolts	
Step 1, in the following sequence:	
Lower bolt	89 in-lbs
Upper stud bolt	18
Upper bolt	89 in-lbs
Lower stud bolt	177 in-lbs
Step 2, in the following sequence:	
Lower bolt	Tighten an additional 45-degrees
Upper stud bolt	Tighten an additional 75-degrees
Upper bolt	Tighten an additional 45-degrees
Lower stud bolt	Tighten an additional 60-degrees
Oil pick-up screen-to-engine block bolt	18
Oil pick-up tube-to-oil pump bolts	
Step 1	89 in-lbs
Step 2	Tighten an additional 45-degrees

Torque specifications
Ft-lbs (unless otherwise indicated)

Note: *One foot-pound (ft-lb) of torque is equivalent to 12 inch-pounds (in-lbs) of torque. Torque values below approximately 15 foot-pounds are expressed in inch-pounds, because most foot-pound torque wrenches are not accurate at these smaller values.*

Rear main seal retainer-to-engine block bolts
    Step 1 .... 89 in-lbs
    Step 2 .... Tighten an additional 45-degrees
Timing chain cover bolts (in sequence, see illustration)
    Step 1, bolts 1-15 (cover-to-cylinder head and block)....................... 18
    Step 2, bolts 16-19 (cover-to-oil pan).................... 89 in-lbs
    Step 3, bolts 1-15 (cover-to-cylinder head and block)....................... Tighten an additional 60-degrees
    Step 4, bolts 16-19 (cover-to-oil pan)................... Tighten an additional 45-degrees
Timing chain cover-to-oil filter adapter bolt
    Step 1 18
    Step 2 .... Tighten an additional 60-degrees
Timing chain cover-to-oil filter adapter jack screw (10 mm Hex)............. 44 in-lbs
Timing chain stationary guide bolts .... 89 in-lbs
Timing chain tensioner bolts... 89 in-lbs
Valve cover bolts .... 89 in-lbs
Use new bolts

1 General information

1   This Part of Chapter 2 is devoted to in-vehicle repair procedures for the 5.0L Dual Overhead Camshaft (DOHC) engine. The 5.0L (four-cam) engine has an aluminum block and heads and four valves per cylinder. Information concerning engine removal and installation can be found in Chapter 2C.

2   These engines are an interference design. In the event the timing chain breaks, the pistons will contact the valves and cause damage.

2 Repair operations possible with the engine in the vehicle

1   Many major repair operations can be accomplished without removing the engine from the vehicle.

2   If possible, clean the engine compartment and the exterior of the engine with some type of pressure washer before any work is started. It will make the job easier and help keep dirt out of the internal areas of the engine.

3   If vacuum, exhaust, oil or coolant leaks develop, indicating a need for gasket or seal replacement, the repairs can generally be made with the engine in the vehicle. The intake and exhaust manifold gaskets, timing cover gasket, oil pan gasket, crankshaft oil seals and cylinder head gaskets are all accessible with the engine in place.

4   Exterior engine components, such as the intake and exhaust manifolds, the oil pan, the water pump, the starter motor, the alternator and the fuel system components can be removed for repair with the engine in place.

5   Since the cylinder heads can be removed without pulling the engine, valve component servicing can also be accomplished with the engine in the vehicle. Replacement of the timing chain and sprockets is also possible with the engine in the vehicle.

3 Top Dead Center (TDC) for number one piston - locating

1   Refer to Chapter 2A, for the TDC locating procedure, but use the illustration provided with this Section for the appropriate reference marks and the following exceptions:
Remove the ignition coils (see Chapter 5).

A) *Remove the spark plugs and install a compression gauge in the number one cylinder. Turn the crankshaft clockwise with a socket and breaker bar.*

b) *When the piston approaches TDC, compression will be noted on the compression gauge. Continue turning the crankshaft until the notch in the crankshaft pulley is aligned with the TDC mark on the front cover. At this point, number one cylinder is at TDC on the compression stroke.*

c) *On engines without TDC marks, remove the right-side valve cover and rotate the engine until the valves of Number 1 cylinder are closed. This is approximately TDC.*

d) *After the number one piston has been positioned at TDC on the compression stroke, TDC for any of the remaining cylinders can be located by turning the crankshaft in 90-degree increments and following the firing order (refer to the Specifications). Divide the crankshaft pulley into four equal sections with chalk marks at four points, each indicating 90-degrees of crankshaft rotation.*

4 Valve covers - removal and installation

Warning: *If you are removing the right-side valve cover, wait until the engine is completely cool before beginning this procedure.*

Removal

1   Disconnect the cable from the negative battery terminal (see Chapter 5).

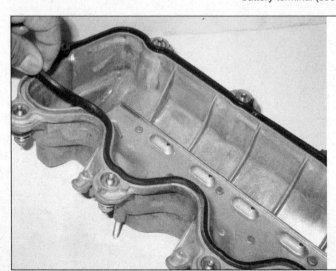

4.14 Make sure the gasket is pushed all the way into the groove in the valve cover

2   If you're removing the left valve cover, remove the air intake duct and the air filter housing (see Chapter 4).

3   If you're removing the right valve cover, drain the cooling system (see Chapter 1).

4   If a PCV hose or tube is connected to the valve cover that you're removing, disconnect it (see Chapter 6). If the PCV valve is electrically heated, disconnect the electrical connector from the PCV valve.

5   Remove the ignition coils from the valve cover that you're removing (see Chapter 5).

6   If you're removing the right valve cover, disconnect the heater hose quick-connect fittings and remove the hoses above the cover.

7   Remove the nut and the ground wire to the corner of the cover(s).

8   If a wiring harness is routed across a valve cover, disconnect the harness electrical connectors. Detach the pin-type wiring harness retainers from the valve cover studs and harness brackets, and set the harness aside. Disconnect the fuel injector harness from the injectors and position the harness off to the side (see Chapter 4). If your're removing the right valve cover, disconnect the left harness connector to the PCM (see Chapter 6) and the main harness connector next to the PCM.

9   If you're removing the left valve cover, remove the engine oil dipstick, depress the tabs then rotate the tube counterclockwise and pull the dipstick tube from the valve cover.

10   Disconnect the electrical connectors from the Variable Camshaft Timing (VCT) oil control solenoid(s).

11   Remove the valve cover bolts, following the reverse of the tightening sequence (see illustrations 4.17a or 4.17b), then remove the valve cover.

Installation

12   The mating surfaces of each cylinder head and valve cover must be perfectly clean when the valve covers are installed. Remove all traces of sealant. If there's old sealant or oil on the mating surfaces when the valve cover is installed, oil leaks may develop.

13   Inspect the solenoid valve seals and spark plug tube seals. If they need to be replaced, pry the seal(s) out of the cover then use a socket that matches the diameter of the seal and drive a new seal into place on the cover.

14   Install a new valve cover gasket in the cover's groove. Make sure the gasket is pushed all the way into the groove in the valve cover (see illustration). The use of sealant in the groove will help hold the gasket in place.

15   At the mating joint (two spots per cylinder head) between the timing chain cover and cylinder head, apply a dab of RTV sealant before installing the valve cover.

16   Carefully position the valve cover on the cylinder head and install the studs and bolts.
Note: *Install the covers within five minutes of applying the RTV sealant.*

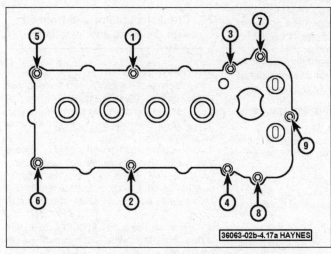

4.17a Right-side valve cover bolt tightening sequence

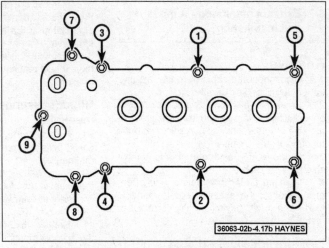

4.17b Left-side valve cover bolt tightening sequence

17 Tighten the fasteners, in sequence, to the torque listed in this Chapter's Specifications (see illustrations).

18 The remainder of installation is the reverse of removal.

19 If the right-side valve cover was removed, refill the cooling system (see Chapter 1).

20 Start the engine and check for oil leaks as the engine warms up.

5 Intake manifold - removal and installation

Warning: *Wait until the engine is completely cool before beginning this procedure.*

Removal

1 Relieve the fuel system pressure (see Chapter 4).

2 Disconnect the cable from the negative battery terminal (see Chapter 5).

3 Remove the air intake duct and the air filter housing (see Chapter 4).

4 Disconnect the electrical connectors from the throttle body and the fuel injectors (see Chapter 4).

5 Label and disconnect the brake booster vacuum line and any other vacuum lines connected to the intake manifold.

6 Disconnect the quick-connect coupling from the PCV tubes.

7 Disconnect the quick-connect coupling from the brake booster (see Chapter 9) and the EVAP canister purge valve (see Chapter 6).

8 Disconnect the fuel supply line from the fuel rail (see Chapter 4).

9 Remove the throttle body (see Chapter 4).

10 Detach the electrical harness where it attaches to the valve covers or intake manifold, then disconnect the electrical connectors at the ignition coils.

11 Disconnect the EVAP tube (quick-connect) and the PCV hose.

12 Remove the fuel injector insulators and

disconnect the purge valve electrical connector. Disconnect the fuel injector connectors and the wiring harness at the rear of the intake manifold.

13 Remove the four fuel rail bolts and six intake manifold bolts.

14 Lift the manifold from the cylinder heads. If it is stuck, it shouldn't take more than a little bit of force to jar it loose.

15 Remove the intake manifold O-ring gaskets and clean all traces of dirt and gasket or sealant material from the sealing surfaces of the cylinder heads and intake manifold.

Caution: *The mating surfaces of the cylinder heads and intake manifold must be perfectly clean. Do not use metal scrapers, wire brushes, power abrasive discs or other abrasive means to clean sealing surfaces; these tools can scratch and gouge gasket surfaces, which creates leak paths. While the manifold is removed, cover the open engine areas with shop rags to keep debris out of the engine.*

Use a vacuum cleaner to remove any debris that falls into the intake ports in the cylinder heads.

Installation

16 If you are replacing the manifold, transfer all components to the new unit.

17 Install new O-ring type intake manifold gaskets into their grooves in the manifold.

18 Carefully set the intake manifold in place.

19 Install the intake manifold bolts first and, following the recommended tightening sequence (see illustration), tighten them to the torque listed in this Chapter's Specifications. Install the fuel rail bolts second and following the recommended sequence, tighten them to the torque listed in this Chapter's Specifications.

20 The remainder of installation is the reverse of removal.

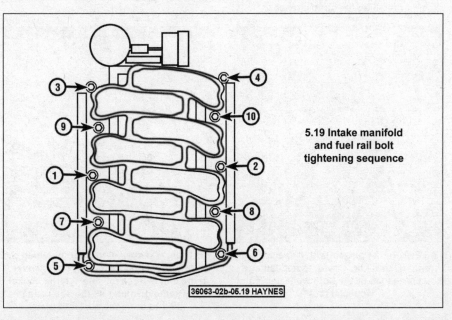

5.19 Intake manifold and fuel rail bolt tightening sequence

6   Exhaust manifolds - removal and installation

Removal

1   Disconnect the cable from the negative battery terminal (see Chapter 5).
2   Raise the vehicle and support it securely on jackstands. Remove tire from the appropriate side then the inner splash shield from the fenderwell (see Chapter 11).
3   Remove the skid plates and splash shields, if equipped.
4   Working under the vehicle, apply penetrating oil to the exhaust pipe-to-manifold studs and nuts (they're usually corroded or rusty).

Left (driver's side) exhaust manifold

5   Remove the air intake duct and the air filter housing cover (see Chapter 4).
6   Remove the exhaust manifold heat shield bolts and remove the heat shield from the manifold.

7.4 Wrap a shop rag or a piece of drivebelt material around the pulley before installing the strap wrench

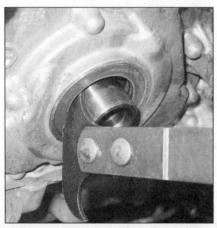

7.6 Pry out the oil seal with a special seal removal tool - be careful to not damage the crankshaft or the bore while using the special tool

7   Remove the catalytic converter nuts from the exhaust manifold, loosen the converter pipe clamp at the exhaust pipe, then detach the converter from the manifold.
8   Remove the eight mounting nuts from the exhaust manifold and remove the exhaust manifold.

Right (passenger's side) exhaust manifold

9   Remove the exhaust manifold heat shield bolts and remove the heat shield from the manifold.
10   Remove the catalytic converter nuts from the exhaust manifolds and move the catalytic converter assemblies to the rear of the vehicle (see Chapter 6).
11   Remove the eight mounting nuts from the exhaust manifold and remove the exhaust manifold.

Installation

12   The manufacturer recommends that, when an exhaust manifold is removed, all exhaust manifold studs be removed and discarded and replaced with new studs and new nuts. Use a little anti-seize on the studs, and tighten the new studs to the torque listed in this Chapter's Specifications.
13   Inspect the exhaust manifolds for cracks. If you're using the old exhaust manifold studs, make sure the stud threads are clean and undamaged. The exhaust manifold and cylinder head mating surfaces must be clean before the exhaust manifolds are reinstalled - use a gasket scraper to remove all carbon deposits.
14   Position a new gasket in place and slip the exhaust manifold over the studs on the cylinder head. Install the mounting nuts. When tightening the mounting nuts, work from the center outwards, alternating between top and bottom rows. Tighten the bolts in two steps to the torque values listed in this Chapter's Specifications.
15   The remainder of installation is the reverse of removal.

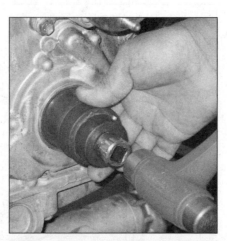

7.8 There is a special tool for installing the front oil seal into the timing chain cover - if the tool is not available, a large socket (the same diameter as the seal) can be used to drive the seal into place

7   Crankshaft pulley and front oil seal - removal and installation

Removal

1   Disconnect the cable from the negative battery terminal (see Chapter 5).
2   Remove the drivebelts (see Chapter 1).
3   Raise the vehicle and support it securely on jackstands.
4   Use a breaker bar and socket to remove the crankshaft pulley center bolt (see illustration). It will be necessary to lock the pulley in position using a strap or chain wrench. Discard the bolt and obtain a new one for installation.
5   Remove the pulley from the crankshaft with a three-jaw puller that grabs the inner portion of the hub.
Caution: *An adapter should be used between the puller bolt and the crankshaft (to prevent damage to the bore and threads in the end of the crankshaft).*
6   Use a seal puller to remove the crankshaft front oil seal (see illustration).
7   Clean the seal bore and check it for nicks or gouges. Also, examine the area of the hub that rides in the seal for signs of abnormal wear or scoring.

Installation

Caution: *A new bolt must be used when reinstalling the crankshaft pulley.*
8   Coat the lip of the new seal with clean engine oil and drive it into the bore with a seal driver or a large socket slightly smaller in diameter than the seal (see illustration). The open side of the seal faces into the engine.
9   Lubricate the oil seal contact surface of the crankshaft pulley hub (see illustration) with multi-purpose grease or clean engine oil. Apply a dab of RTV sealant to the front end and center of the keyway in the crankshaft pulley before installation.
10   Install the crankshaft pulley with a spe-

7.9 Inspect the crankshaft pulley for signs of damage or excessive wear

1   *Oil seal surface*
2   *Woodruff keyway*

cial installation tool, available at most auto parts stores. Do not use a hammer to install the pulley. Install the new crankshaft pulley bolt and tighten it to the torque listed in this Chapter's Specifications.

11   The remainder of installation is the reverse of removal.

8   Timing chain cover - removal and installation

Warning: *Wait until the engine is completely cool before beginning this procedure.*
Note: *The timing chain cover is also referred to as the engine front cover.*

Removal

1   Disconnect the cable from the negative battery terminal (see Chapter 5).
2   Raise the vehicle and support it securely on jackstands, then remove the skid plates and splash shields, if equipped.
3   Drain the engine oil and remove the oil filter (see Chapter 1).
4   Drain the cooling system (see Chapter 1).
5   Remove the expansion tank (see Chapter 3).
6   Remove the drivebelts (see Chapter 1), the drivebelt idler pulleys from the timing chain cover and the water pump pulley (see Chapter 3).
7   Remove the crankshaft pulley and front oil seal (see Section 7).
8   Remove both valve covers (see Section 4).
9   Remove the fasteners for the transmission cooler line brackets and secure the cooler lines out of the way.
10   Disconnect the EVAP canister purge valve electrical connector (see Chapter 6). Remove the nut from the ground strap stud and disconnect the ground strap, then remove the harness retainers along the perimeter of the cover and secure the harness out of the way.

11   Remove the alternator (see Chapter 5).
12   Remove the thermostat housing and water pump (see Chapter 3).
13   Remove the throttle body (see Chapter 4).
14   Disconnect the wiring harness retainers attached to the oil pan rail and move the harnesses out of the way.
15   Remove the four oil pan-to-timing chain cover bolts (see Section 14).
Note: *Two of the fasteners are stud bolts; be sure to note their locations.*
16   Remove the engine oil filter adapter bolt from the front cover ("A" in illustration 8.26). With the adapter bolt removed, use a 10 mm hex bit and remove the oil filter jack screw from the same hole location.
17   Remove the timing chain cover-to-engine block bolts. Note the locations of studs and different-length bolts so they can be reinstalled in their original locations.
18   Separate the timing chain cover from the engine block (see illustration). If it's stuck, tap it gently with a soft-face hammer to break the gasket bond.
Caution: *DO NOT use excessive force or you*

may crack the cover. If the cover is difficult to remove, make sure all of the bolts and studs have been removed.
19   Remove the timing chain cover-to-cylinder block dowels.

Installation

20   Clean the mating surfaces of the timing chain cover, engine block and cylinder heads to remove all traces of old gasket material, oil and dirt.
Caution: *Be careful when cleaning any of the aluminum components. Use of a metal scraper could cause scratches or gouges that could lead to an oil leak later.*
21   Insert the front cover dowels into the cylinder block.
22   Install new gaskets into the grooves of the timing chain cover (see illustration).
23   Apply a 1/8-inch bead of RTV sealant to the junctions of the oil pan-to-engine block and the cylinder head-to-engine block (see illustration). Apply a small dab of RTV where the timing chain cover and engine block meet, and where the timing chain cover and cylinder heads meet at the valve cover surfaces.

8.18 Separate the timing chain cover from the engine, using a soft-faced hammer if necessary to break the gasket seal

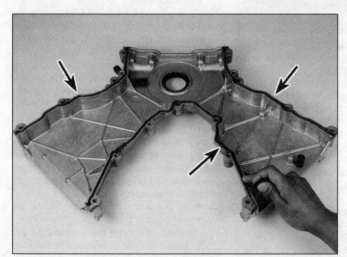

8.22 Install the new gaskets into the grooves in the back of the timing chain cover

8.23 Apply a bead of RTV sealant to the mating junctions of the oil pan-to-engine block and cylinder head-to-engine block

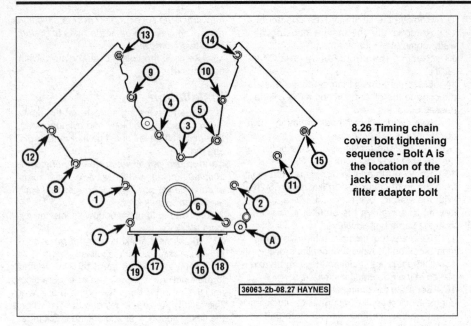

8.26 Timing chain cover bolt tightening sequence - Bolt A is the location of the jack screw and oil filter adapter bolt

36063-2b-08.27 HAYNES

9.4 Use the special tool (303-448) to rotate the crankshaft

24   Lubricate the timing chains and the lip of the crankshaft front oil seal with clean engine oil.

25   From the back side of the cover, locate the VCT pins and depress them until they are flush with the cover.

Warning: *The VCT variable force solenoid pins must be fully depressed to avoid interference with the VCT valve tips. If the tips are not depressed, severe engine damage can occur.*

26   Install the timing chain cover on the engine, within five minutes of applying the RTV sealant. Position the bottom/front edge of the timing chain cover flush with the front edge of the oil pan and tilt the top of the cover into place against the engine. Do not press the cover straight in against the engine or the sealant may be scraped off the front of the oil pan and cause a leak. Tighten the timing chain cover-to-engine block bolts and cover-to-oil pan bolts in the recommended sequence (see illustration) to the torque listed in this Chapter's Specifications.

27   Install the remaining parts in the reverse order of removal.

28   Add the proper type and quantity of engine oil and refill the cooling system (see Chapter 1). Run the engine and check for leaks.

---

9   Timing chains, tensioners and sprockets - removal, inspection and installation

---

Caution: *These engines are difficult to work on and require special tools. On any procedure involving timing chain, camshaft(s) or cylinder head removal, the steps must be read carefully and disassembly must proceed using the special tools, otherwise damage to the engine could result.*

Caution: *The timing system is complex. Severe engine damage will occur if you make any mistakes. Do not attempt this procedure*

unless you are highly experienced with this type of repair. If you are at all unsure of your abilities, consult an expert. Double-check all your work and be sure everything is correct before you attempt to start the engine.

Caution: *Because this is an interference engine design; if one of the chains has broken, there will be damage to the valves (and possibly the pistons), and removal of the cylinder head(s) will be required.*

Note: *A special crankshaft holding/rotating tool (Rotunda part no. 303-448) is required for this procedure.*

Note: *If you are removing the left-side timing chain (for access to the left cylinder head, for example), the right-side timing chain must be removed first.*

Removal

1   Disconnect the cable from the negative battery terminal (see Chapter 5).

2   Remove the spark plugs (see Chapter 1) and position the number one cylinder on TDC (see Section 3).

3   Remove the valve covers (see Section 4) and the timing chain cover (see Section 8). Two long timing chains connect the crankshaft to the camshafts.

4   Starting with the right (passenger's side) primary chain, use the special tool (303-448) to rotate the crankshaft during this procedure (see illustration). Slide the tool over the end of the crankshaft snout, then rotate the crankshaft until the keyway on the crankshaft is at the 7:30 position.

Caution: *Check the right-side VCT unit (timing chain sprocket) on the exhaust camshaft; the RH mark must be at the top. If it is not, rotate the crankshaft one complete revolution and return the keyway to the 7:30 position.*

5   Push in on the right (paassenger's side) primary chain tensioner arm to compress the plunger in the tensioner. Keep it depressed until you can insert a paper clip or drill bit into the hole in the tensioner to keep it retracted.

6   Turn the crankshaft just a little, if necessary, to provide some slack in the timing chain.

7   Remove the right-side tensioner, then the tensioner arm and the stationary chain guide bolt and guide.

8   Remove the right-side primary timing chain.

Caution: *If it was turned slightly, return the crankshaft keyway back to the 7:30 position.*

9   Remove the three bolts securing each VCT (sprocket) assembly to the right-side intake and exhaust camshafts.

Caution: *Don't allow the shafts to turn as this is done. Place a large wrench on the flats of the camshaft while using a ratchet and socket to remove the VCT assembly mounting bolts.*

10   Slide the VCT units forward 5/64-inch (2 mm).

11   Push down on the right-side secondary chain tensioner while twisting the plastic guide on the top of the tensioner until it is positioned 90-degrees to the timing chain. The VCT assemblies and secondary chain can now be removed.

Caution: *Don't mix up the VCT units; they are not interchangeable.*

12   Using special tool 303-448, rotate the crankshaft clockwise 360 degrees (one complete revolution). Continue to turn the crankshaft until the keyway is in the 3:30 position.

13   Push in on the left (driver's side) primary chain tensioner arm to compress the plunger in the tensioner. Keep it depressed until you can insert a large paper clip or drill bit in the hole in the tensioner.

14   Turn the crankshaft just a little, if necessary, to provide some slack in the timing chain. Remove the left-side tensioner, then the tensioner arm and the stationary chain guide bolt and guide. Remove the left-side primary timing chain.

Caution: *If it was turned slightly, return the crankshaft keyway back to the 3:30 position.*

15   Remove the three bolts securing each VCT (sprocket) assembly to the left-side intake and exhaust camshafts.

Caution: *Don't allow the shafts to turn as this is done. Place a large wrench on the flats of*

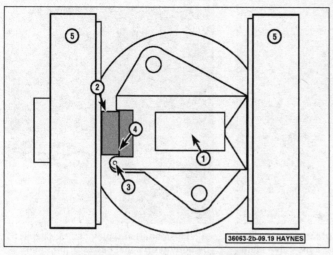

9.19a Timing chain tensioner details

1 Tensioner body
2 Tensioner piston
3 Lock pin hole
4 Tensioner piston shoulder
5 Vise jaws

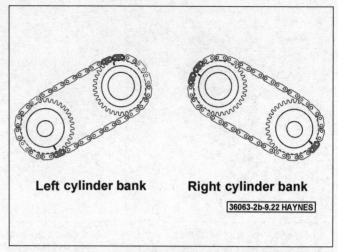

9.22 Secondary timing chain alignment marks (as viewed from the back side of the VCT units)

the camshaft while using a ratchet and socket to remove the VCT assembly mounting bolts.

16 Slide the VCT units forward 5/64-inch (2 mm). Push down on the left-side secondary chain tensioner while twisting the plastic guide on the top of the tensioner until it is positioned 90-degrees to the timing chain. The VCT assemblies and secondary chain can now be removed.

Caution: *Don't mix up the VCT units; they are not interchangeable.*

Inspection

17 Inspect the individual sprocket teeth and keyways for wear and damage.

18 Check the chain for cracked plates, and pitted or worn rollers. Check the wear surface of the chain guides for wear and damage. Replace any worn or defective parts with new ones.

Caution: *If excessive plastic material is missing from the chain guides, the oil pan should be removed and cleaned of all debris (see Section 13). Check the oil pick-up tube screen, too.*

19 Check the timing chain tensioners:

a) *Check the condition of the tensioner seal. Make sure the seal is intact and not broken, chipped or damaged.*

b) *Check the condition of the plunger. Depress the plunger to make sure it moves freely.*

c) *Remove the plastic oil filter in the center hole of the VCT assemblies. Install new filters with the wide end out.*

d) *The tensioners can be kept in the retracted position with a drill bit or paper clip.*

e) *Compress the tensioner in a vise until the shoulder on the piston is compressed past the lock pin hole and place the drill bit or paper clip into the lock pin hole to hold it in the compressed position (see illustration).*

Installation

Caution: *Before starting the engine, carefully rotate the crankshaft by hand through at least two full revolutions (use a socket and breaker bar on the crankshaft pulley center bolt). If you feel any resistance, STOP! There is something wrong - most likely, valves are contacting the pistons. You must find the problem before proceeding.*

20 Install the timing chain stationary guides for both sides, then tighten the bolts to the torque listed in this Chapter's Specifications.

21 Install the crankshaft sprocket on the crankshaft with the timing marks facing forward.

22 Align the marks on the back sides of the intake and exhaust VCT assemblies with the marks on the secondary chains (see illustration). The intake VCT mark must line up between two colored links, while the exhaust VCT mark must align directly with its colored link. Position the VCT assemblies aligned with their camshafts, but not engaged fully (5/64-inch [2 mm] from fully engaged). The exhaust VCT unit on the right cylinder bank must be positioned with its timing mark for the primary chain in approximately the 10 o'clock position, while the exhaust VCT unit on the left cylinder bank must be in approximately the 3 o'clock position; if necessary, turn the camshaft(s) slightly to allow engagement of the VCT units.

23 Rotate the secondary chain tensioner back 1/4-turn, then push the VCT units so they are completely seated on the camshafts.

24 Hold the camshafts from turning by placing a wrench on their flats, then install and tighten the new VCT bolts to the torque listed in this Chapter's Specifications.

25 Install the left-side primary timing chain with its colored link aligning with the mark on the VCT assembly and the crankshaft sprocket.

26 Install the secondary chain guide, tensioner arm and tensioner.

27 Remove the pin holding the tensioner in the retracted position.

28 Using the special tool (see illustration 9.4), turn the crankshaft clockwise until the keyway is in the 7:30 position.

29 Align the marks on the back sides of the intake and exhaust VCT assemblies with the marks on the secondary chains (see illustration 9.22). The intake VCT mark must line up between two colored links, while the exhaust VCT mark must align directly with its colored link. Position the VCT assemblies aligned with their camshafts, but not engaged fully (5/64-inch [2 mm] from fully engaged). The exhaust VCT unit should be positioned with its timing mark for the primary chain in approximately the 10 o'clock position; if necessary, turn the camshaft(s) slightly to allow engagement of the VCT units.

30 Rotate the secondary chain tensioner back 1/4-turn, then push the VCT units so they are completely seated on the camshafts.

31 Hold the camshafts from turning by placing a wrench on their flats, then install and tighten the new VCT bolts to the torque listed in this Chapter's Specifications.

32 Install the right-side primary timing chain with its colored link aligning with the mark on the VCT assembly and the crankshaft sprocket. Install the secondary chain guide, tensioner arm and tensioner.

33 Remove the pin holding the tensioner in the retracted position.

34 Slowly rotate the crankshaft in the normal direction of rotation (clockwise) at least two revolutions and again bring the engine to TDC. If you feel any resistance, stop and find out why.

35 The remainder of installation is the reverse of removal.

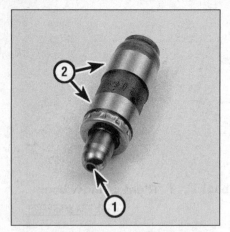

10.4 Inspect the lash adjuster for signs of excessive wear or damage, such as pitting, scoring or signs of overheating (bluing or discoloration), where the tip contacts the camshaft follower (1) and the side surfaces that contact the lifter bore in the cylinder head (2)

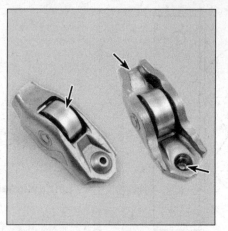

10.6 Check the roller surface of the rocker arms and the areas where the valve stem and lash adjuster contact the rocker

12.3 Camshaft end play can be checked by setting up a dial indicator off the front of the camshaft and prying the camshaft gently forward and back

10 Roller followers and valve lash adjusters - removal, inspection and installation

Caution: *These engines are difficult to work on and require special tools for many procedures. On any procedure involving timing chain, camshaft or cylinder head removal, the steps must be read carefully and disassembly must proceed using the special tools, otherwise damage to the engine could result.*

Removal

1   Remove the valve cover(s) (see Section 4).
2   Remove the camshaft that operates the roller followers being serviced (see Section 12).
3   Separate the hydraulic lash adjusters from the clips that secure them to the roller followers.
Note: *Store the parts so that each lash adjuster is with its original roller follower.*

Inspection

4   Inspect each adjuster carefully for signs of wear or damage. The areas of possible wear are the ball tip that contacts the roller follower and the sides of the adjuster that contact the bore in the cylinder head (see illustration). Since the lash adjusters can become clogged as mileage increases, we recommend replacing them if you're concerned about their condition or if the engine is exhibiting valve tapping noises.
5   A thin wire or paper clip can be placed in the oil hole to move the plunger and make sure it's not stuck. It's recommended that if replacement of any of the adjusters is necessary, that the entire set be replaced. This will avoid the need to repeat the repair procedure as the others require replacement in the future.

Note: *The lash adjuster must have no more than 1/16-inch of total plunger travel.*
6   Inspect the roller lifters for signs of wear or damage. The areas of wear are the ball socket that contacts the lash adjuster and the roller where the follower contacts the camshaft (see illustration).

Installation

Note: *When re-starting the engine after replacing the adjusters, the adjusters will normally make some tapping noises, until all the air is bled from them. After the engine is warmed-up, raise the speed from idle to 3,000 rpm for one minute. Stop the engine and let it cool down. All of the noise should be gone when it is restarted.*
7   Before installing the lash adjusters, bleed as much air as possible out of them. Stand the adjusters upright in a container of oil. Use a thin wire or paper clip to work the plunger up and down. This primes the adjuster and removes most of the air. Leave the adjusters in the oil until ready to install (just be sure not to mix them up).
8   Lubricate the valve stem tip, rocker arm, and lash adjuster bore with clean engine oil.
9   Install the lash adjusters and roller followers.
10   Install the camshaft(s) for the lifter(s) being serviced (see Section 12).
11   The remainder of installation is the reverse of removal.

11 Variable Camshaft Timing (VCT) system - general information

1   The Variable Camshaft Timing (VCT) system consists of a VCT solenoid (or a pair of VCT solenoids on DOHC engines) mounted on the front of each cylinder head over the camshaft(s), a Camshaft Position (CMP) sensor with a trigger wheel and a variable camshaft timing sprocket mounted on each

camshaft. When oil flow is sent to the timing sprockets by way of the VCT solenoids, the phasing of the camshafts is altered, thereby advancing or retarding the actuation of the valves. The Variable Camshaft Timing (VCT) system oil control solenoid replacement procedure is in Chapter 6. The VCT units, sometimes called camshaft phasers, are removed and installed in Section 9 of this Chapter.
2   The Variable Camshaft Timing (VCT) system should be diagnosed by a dealer service department or other qualified automotive repair facility. The VCT system is controlled and monitored by the Powertrain Control Module (PCM), thereby requiring a specialized scan tool for diagnostics.

12 Camshaft(s) - removal, inspection and installation

Caution: *These engines are difficult to work on and require special tools for many procedures. On any procedure involving timing chain, camshaft or cylinder head removal, the steps must be read carefully and disassembly must proceed using the special tools, otherwise damage to the engine could result.*

Removal

1   Remove the valve covers (see Section 4), and the timing chain cover (see Section 8).
2   Remove the timing chains (see Section 9).
3   Measure the thrust clearance (endplay) of the camshaft(s) with a dial indicator (see illustration). If the clearance is greater than the value listed in this Chapter's Specifications, replace the camshaft and/or the cylinder head.
4   Hold the flats of the camshaft with a wrench while using a ratchet and socket to remove the VCT mounting bolts (see Section 9).
Note: *If the VCT units are being removed from both cylinder banks, remove the right hand VCT units first.*

12.12 Areas to look for excessive wear or damage on the camshafts are the bearing surfaces and the camshaft lobes

12.13a Measure the camshaft bearing journal diameter

12.13b Measure the camshaft lobe at its greatest dimension

5   Remove the VCT oil filter screens from the front of each camshaft. The filters must be replaced each time the VCT assembly has been removed.

6   Slide the VCT assemblies and secondary chain forward about 5/64-inch (2 mm).

7   Push down on the secondary timing chain tensioner until slack in the chain is felt then rotate the tensioner 90-degrees counterclockwise.

8   Slide the VCT assemblies and chain off of the camshafts as a unit.

9   Remove the larger camshaft cap (megacap) at the front first. Loosen and remove the remainder of the bearing cap bolts, 1/4-turn at a time, in the reverse of the tightening sequence (see illustration 12.20c), and remove the caps.

10   Lift the camshafts out of their bearing saddles and set the cams aside.

11   Keep the camshafts clean and mark them with paint to indicate left or right and intake or exhaust.

Inspection

12   Visually examine the cam lobes and bearing journals for score marks, pitting, galling and evidence of overheating (blue, discolored areas). Look for flaking of the hardened surface of each lobe (see illustration). Inspect the bearing surfaces of the camshaft bearing caps for signs of excessive wear, damage or overheating.

13   Using a micrometer, measure the diameter of each camshaft journal and the lift of each camshaft lobe (see illustrations). Compare your measurements with the Specifications listed at the front of this Chapter, and if the diameter of any one of these is less than specified, replace the camshaft.

14   Check the oil clearance for each camshaft journal as follows:

a) Clean the bearing surfaces and the camshaft journals with lacquer thinner or acetone.

b) Carefully lay the camshaft(s) in place in the cylinder head. Don't install the rocker arms or lash adjusters and don't use any lubrication.

c) Lay a strip of Plastigage on each journal (see illustration).

d) Install the camshaft bearing caps.

e) Tighten the cap bolts, a little at a time, to the torque listed in this Chapter's Specifications. **Note:** Don't turn the camshaft while the Plastigage is in place.

f) Remove the bolts and detach the caps.

g) Compare the width of the crushed Plastigage (at its widest point) to the scale on the Plastigage envelope (see illustration).

h) If the clearance is greater than specified, and the diameter of any journal is less than specified, replace the camshaft. If the journal diameters are within specifications but the oil clearance is too great, the cylinder head is worn and must be replaced.

12.13c Subtract the camshaft lobe diameter at its smallest dimension to obtain the lobe lift specification

12.14a Lay a strip of Plastigage on each of the camshaft journals

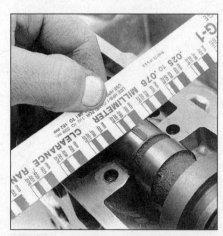

12.14b Compare the width of the crushed Plastigage to the scale on the envelope to determine the oil clearance

15   Scrape off the Plastigage with your fingernail or the edge of a credit card - don't scratch or nick the journals or bearing surfaces.

Installation

16   If the lash adjusters and/or camshaft followers have been removed, install them in their original locations (see Section 10).

17   Apply moly-base grease or camshaft installation lube to the camshaft lobes and bearing journals, then install the camshaft(s).

18   Install the camshaft caps in the correct locations, and loosely install all the bolts.

19   Align the VCT assemblies and chains (see Section 9).

20   Rotate the camshafts to their Neutral position before proceeding with installation of the VCT assemblies and timing chains (see illustrations). Follow the bolt-tightening sequence (see illustration), and tighten the bolts to the torque listed in this Chapter's Specifications.

21   Install the VCT assemblies and chains and timing chain(s) (see Section 9).

22   The remainder of installation is the reverse of removal.

13   Cylinder heads - removal and installation

Warning: *Wait until the engine is completely cool before beginning this procedure.*

Caution: *These engines are difficult to work on and require special tools for many procedures. On any procedure involving timing chains, the steps must be read carefully and disassembly must proceed using the special tools, otherwise damage to the engine could result.*

Caution: *The engine must be completely cool when the cylinder heads are removed. Failure to allow the engine to cool off could result in cylinder head warpage.*

Removal

1   Relieve the fuel system pressure (see Chapter 4)

2   Disconnect the cable from the negative battery terminal (see Chapter 5).

3   Drain the cooling system (see Chapter 3).

4   Remove the valve covers (see Section 4).

5   Remove the intake manifold (see Section 5).

6   Remove the exhaust manifolds (see Section 6).

7   Remove the timing chains, tensioners and sprockets (see Section 9).

8   Remove the camshafts (see Section 12).

9   Following the reverse of the tightening sequence (see illustration 13.19a or 13.19b), use a breaker bar to remove the cylinder head bolts. Loosen the bolts in sequence 1/4-turn at a time. Discard the bolts and obtain new ones for reassembly.

10   Lift the cylinder head(s) off the engine. If resistance is felt, place a wood block against the end and strike the wood block with a hammer.

Caution: *The cylinder heads are aluminum; store them on wood blocks to prevent damage to the gasket sealing surfaces.*

11   If the head sticks, use a prybar at the corners of the cylinder head-to-engine block mating surface to break the cylinder head gasket seal. Do not pry between the cylinder head and engine block in the gasket sealing area.

12   Remove the cylinder head gasket(s). Before removing, note which gasket goes on which side (they are different and cannot be interchanged).

Installation

Caution: *New cylinder head bolts must be used for reassembly. Failure to use new bolts may result in cylinder head gasket leakage and engine damage.*

13   The mating surfaces of the cylinder heads and engine block must be perfectly clean when the cylinder heads are installed. Use a gasket scraper to remove all traces of carbon and old gasket material, then clean the mating surfaces with silicone gasket remover and a plastic scraper. If there's oil on the mating surfaces when the cylinder heads are installed, the gaskets may not seal correctly and leaks may develop. When working on the engine block, cover the open areas of the engine with shop rags to keep debris out during repair and reassembly. Use a vacuum cleaner to remove any

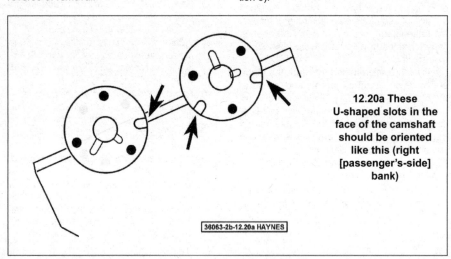

12.20a These U-shaped slots in the face of the camshaft should be oriented like this (right [passenger's-side] bank)

36063-2b-12.20a HAYNES

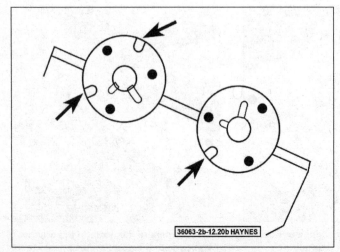

12.20b These U-shaped slots in the face of the camshaft should be oriented like this (left [driver's-side] bank)

36063-2b-12.20b HAYNES

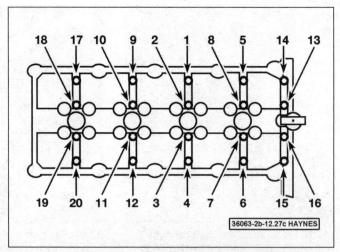

36063-2b-12.27c HAYNES

12.20c Camshaft cap bolt tightening sequence

13.17 Position the gaskets on the correct cylinder banks, then push them down over the alignment dowels

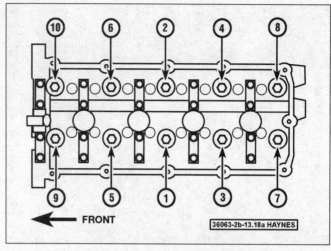

13.18a Cylinder head bolt-tightening sequence

debris that falls into the cylinders.

Caution: *Do not use abrasive wheels or metal scrapers on the heads or block surface; use a plastic scraper and chemical gasket remover, or the head gasket surfaces could have future leaks.*

14   Check the engine block and cylinder head mating surfaces for nicks, deep scratches and other damage.

15   Use a tap of the correct size to chase the threads in the cylinder head bolt holes. Dirt, corrosion, sealant and damaged threads will affect torque readings.

16   Make sure the new gaskets are installed on the correct cylinder banks. They are not interchangeable.

17   Position the new gasket(s) over the alignment dowels (see illustration) in the engine block.

Caution: *The method used for the cylinder head bolt tightening procedure is referred to*

as "torque-angle" or "torque-to-yield" method. Follow the procedure exactly.

18   Carefully position the cylinder heads on the engine block without disturbing the gaskets. Install the NEW cylinder head bolts (the cylinder head bolts are of a torque-to-yield design and they cannot be reused). Following the recommended sequence (see illustrations), tighten the cylinder head bolts, in stages, to the torque and angle of rotation listed in this Chapter's Specifications. If the adapter is not available, mark each bolt with a paint stripe to aid in the torque angle process.

19   The remainder of installation is the reverse of removal.

20   Change the engine oil and filter and refill the cooling system (see Chapter 1), then start the engine and check carefully for oil and coolant leaks.

14   Oil pan - removal and installation

Removal

1   Disconnect the cable from the negative battery terminal (see Chapter 5).

2   Raise the vehicle and support it securely on jackstands.

3   Drain the engine oil and remove the oil filter (see Chapter 1).

4   Remove the oil dip stick from the tube.

5   Remove the skid plates and splash shields, if equipped.

6   Remove the front crossmember (see illustration).

7   On 4WD models, support the front differential with a floor jack and chain the differential to the jack, then remove the front axle support bushing bolts and lower the front axle. Make sure that no vacuum lines or wir-

13.18b Mark each cylinder head bolt with a paint stripe and, using a breaker bar and socket, tighten the bolts in sequence to the correct torque angle

14.6 Crossmember through bolt/nut locations

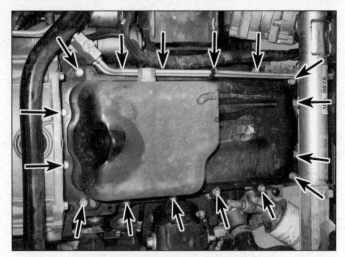

14.10 Remove the bolts from around the perimeter of the oil pan

14.14 Apply a bead of RTV sealant at the junctions of the front cover-to-engine block and the rear seal retainer-to-engine block before installing the oil pan

ing are stretched while lowering or raising the front axle.

8   Remove the fasteners for the transmission cooler line brackets and secure the cooler lines out of the way.

9   Disconnect the wiring harness retainers attached to the oil pan rail and move the harnesses out of the way.

10   Remove the oil pan mounting bolts (see illustration).

11   Carefully separate the oil pan from the engine block. Don't pry between the engine block and oil pan or damage to the sealing surfaces may result and oil leaks could develop. Instead, dislodge the oil pan with a large rubber mallet or a wood block and a hammer.

Installation

12   Use only a plastic gasket scraper or putty knife to remove all traces of old gasket material and sealant from the pan and engine block.
Caution: *Be careful not to gouge the oil pan or block, or oil leaks could develop later.*

13   Clean the mating surfaces with RTV gasket remover. Make sure the bolt holes in the engine block are clean.

14   Apply a bead of RTV sealant to the four corner seams where the rear seal retainer meets the engine block, and where the front cover meets the engine block (see illustration).
Caution: *You must work fast to secure the oil pan to the engine within 5 minutes of applying the RTV.*

15   Carefully position the oil pan against the engine block and install the bolts finger-tight. Make sure the gaskets haven't shifted, then tighten the bolts in sequence (see illustration) to the torque listed in this Chapter's Specifications. Start at the center of the oil pan and work out toward the ends in a spiral pattern.

16   The remainder of installation is the reverse of removal.
Caution: *Allow at least 90 minutes for the RTV to dry, then refill the engine with oil before starting it (see Chapter 1).*

17   Start the engine and check carefully for

oil leaks at the oil pan. Drive the vehicle and check again.

15 Oil pump - removal and installation

Warning: *The engine must be completely cool before beginning this procedure.*
Note: *The oil pump is available as a complete replacement unit only. No service parts or specifications are available from the manufacturer.*

Removal

1   Raise the vehicle and support it securely on jackstands.

2   Drain the engine oil (see Chapter 1).

3   Remove the oil pan (see Section 14). Remove the two bolts that attach the oil pump pick-up tube to the oil pump (see illustration).

4   Remove the timing chain cover, timing chains, chain guides and crankshaft sprocket (see Section 9).

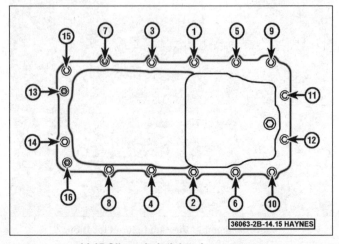

14.15 Oil pan bolt tightening sequence

15.3 Remove the two bolts retaining the pickup tube to the oil pump

Chapter 2B V8 engine

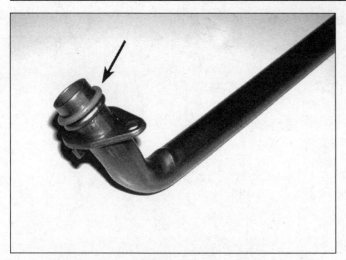

15.6 Before bolting the pickup tube back into the oil pump, inspect the O-ring and replace it if necessary

17.7 Inspect the seal contact surface on the crankshaft for signs of excessive wear or grooves (seal retainer removed for clarity - typical engine shown)

5   Remove the oil pump mounting fasteners and separate the pump from the engine block. The oil pump is mounted with four fasteners: two bolts and two stud-bolts. Note the location of the studs.

Installation

6   Inspect the O-ring gasket on the pick-up tube (see illustration). If it's damaged, replace it.

7   Install the oil pump to the engine and tighten the bolts to the torque listed in this Chapter's Specifications.

Note: *Prime the oil pump prior to installation. Pour clean oil into the pick-up port and turn the pump by hand.*

8   The remainder of installation is the reverse of removal.

9   Fill the engine with the correct type and quantity of oil. Start the engine and check for leaks.

16   Flywheel/driveplate - removal and installation

1   This procedure is essentially the same as for the V6 engine. Refer to Part A of this Chapter and follow the procedure outlined there. However, use the bolt torque value listed in this Chapter's Specifications.

17   Rear main oil seal - replacement

Note: *Rear main oil seal replacement is a time-consuming job requiring several special tools; read through the procedure and obtain the necessary tools before beginning.*

1   Disconnect the cable from the negative battery terminal (see Chapter 5).

2   Raise the vehicle and support it securely on jackstands.

3   Remove the transmission (see Chapter 7A).

4   Remove the flywheel/driveplate (see Section 16).

5   Remove the toothed-wheel (used by the CKP sensor) between the crankshaft and driveplate.

6   Use a special tool and remove the rear main oil seal from the retainer.

Caution: *To prevent an oil leak after the new seal is installed, be very careful not to scratch or otherwise damage the crankshaft sealing surface or the bore in the engine block.*

7   Clean the crankshaft and seal bore in the retainer thoroughly and de-grease these areas with brake system cleaner. Check the seal contact surface on the crankshaft very carefully for scratches or nicks that could damage the new seal lip and cause oil leaks (see illustration). Lubricate the lip of the new seal and the outer diameter of the crankshaft with engine oil. Make sure the edges of the new oil seal are not rolled over.

8   Position the new seal onto the crankshaft. Use a special rear main oil seal installation tool to drive the seal in place. Make sure the seal is not off-set; it must be flush along the entire circumference of the seal retainer. An alternative method is to remove the seal retainer plate, and replace the seal on the bench, then apply a new gasket and RTV to the seal retainer plate and install it within five minutes of applying the RTV.

Caution: *When installing the new seal, if so marked, the words THIS SIDE OUT on the seal must face out, toward the rear of the engine.*

9   Use a special tool and install the crankshaft rear oil slinger.

10   The remainder of installation is the reverse of removal.

18   Engine mounts - check and replacement

1   This procedure is essentially the same as for the V6 engine. Refer to Part A and follow the procedure outlined there, but use the torque values listed in this Chapter's Specifications.

Note: *The amount of bolt installation torque applied to engine mounts in the covered trucks is substantial. Before beginning, make sure you have the proper tools and torque wrench that can tighten to the correct Specifications.*

Notes

Notes

Notes

Chapter 2 Part C
General engine overhaul procedures

Contents

	Section
Crankshaft - removal and installation	10
Cylinder compression check	3
Engine - removal and installation	7
Engine overhaul - disassembly sequence	8
Engine overhaul - reassembly sequence	11
Engine rebuilding alternatives	5
Engine removal - methods and precautions	6
General information - engine overhaul	1
Initial start-up and break-in after overhaul	12
Oil pressure check	2
Pistons and connecting rods - removal and installation	9
Vacuum gauge diagnostic checks	4

Specifications

General

Displacement
- 2.7L EcoBoost V6 engine .... 164 cubic inches
- 3.5L Duratec V6 engine .... 214 cubic inches
- 3.5L EcoBoost V6 engine .... 214 cubic inches
- 5.0L V8 engine .... 302 cubic inches

Bore and stroke
- 2.7L EcoBoost V6 engine .... 3.268 X 3.268 inches
- 3.5L Duratec V6 engine .... 3.641 X 3.413 inches
- 3.5L EcoBoost V6 engine .... 3.641 X 3.413 inches
- 5.0L V8 engine .... 3.629 X 3.649 inches

Compression ratio
- 2.7L EcoBoost V6 engine 10:1
- 3.5L Duratec V6 engine 10.8:1
- 3.5L EcoBoost V6 engine 10:1
- 5.0L V8 engine 10.5:1

Cylinder compression .... Lowest cylinder must be within 75 percent of highest cylinder

Oil pressure (engine at operating temperature)
- 2.7L V6 engines .... 21 psi @ 2,000 rpm
- 3.5L V6 engines (all) .... 30 psi @ 1,500 rpm
- 5.0L V8 engine
  - at Idle .... 10 to 15 psi
  - at 2,000 rpm .... 30 to 40 psi

Torque specifications

Ft-lbs (unless otherwise indicated)

Note: *One foot-pound (ft-lb) of torque is equivalent to 12 inch-pounds (in-lbs) of torque. Torque values below approximately 15 foot-pounds are expressed in inch-pounds, because most foot-pound torque wrenches are not accurate at these smaller values.*

Flywheel/driveplate mounting bolts	See Chapter 2A or Chapter 2B
Torque converter nuts	30
Connecting rod bearing cap bolts*	
2.7L V6 engines	
Step 1	24
Step 2	Loosen bolts 180-degrees
Step 3	24
Step 4	Tighten an additional 90-degrees
3.5L V6 engine	
Step 1	17
Step 2	32
Step 3	Tighten an additional 90-degrees
5.0L V8 engine	
Step 1	177 in-lbs
Step 2	28
Step 3	Tighten an additional 105-degrees
Main bearing cap bolts* (tighten the bolts in the order listed here)	
2.7L V6 engines	
Vertical cap bolts	
Step 1	30
Step 2	Loosen bolts 360-degrees
Step 3	26
Step 4	Tighten an additional 180-degrees
Engine block skirt stiffener	
Step 1, Bolt A and B (see illustration 10.36)	35 in-lbs
Step 1, Bolt A and B	Loosen bolts 360-degrees
Step 3	Alignment verification (see Section 10, Step 36)
Step 4 (see illustration 10.37)	35 in-lbs
Step 5	18
3.5L V6 engines	
Vertical cap bolts	
Step 1	24
Step 2	Tighten an additional 135-degrees
Side bolts	
Step 1, side bolts (new)	33
Step 2, side bolts	Tighten an additional 90-degrees
Main bearing cap support brace bolts*	
Step 1	18
Step 2	Tighten an additional 180-degrees
5.0L V8 engine	
Vertical bolts	
Step 1, bolts 1 through 20	177 in-lbs
Step 2, bolts 1 through 10	30
Step 3, bolts 11 through 20	48
Step 4, bolts 1 through 20	Tighten an additional 90-degrees
Side bolts (new)	
Step 1	89 in-lbs
Step 2	22
Step 3	Tighten an additional 60-degrees

* Use new bolts

1.10a An engine block being bored. An engine rebuilder will use special machinery to recondition the cylinder bores

1.10b If the cylinders are bored, the machine shop will normally hone the engine on a machine like this

1 General information - engine overhaul

1 Included in Chapter 2C are general information and diagnostic testing procedures for determining the overall mechanical condition of your engine.

2 The information ranges from advice concerning preparation for an overhaul and the purchase of replacement parts and/or components to detailed, step-by-step procedures covering removal and installation.

3 The following Sections have been written to help you determine whether your engine needs to be overhauled and how to remove and install it once you've determined it needs to be rebuilt. For information concerning in-vehicle engine repair, see Chapter 2A or Chapter 2B.

4 The Specifications included in this Part are general in nature and include only those necessary for testing the oil pressure and checking the engine compression. Refer to Chapter 2A or Chapter 2B for additional engine Specifications.

5 It's not always easy to determine when, or if, an engine should be completely overhauled, because a number of factors must be considered.

6 High mileage is not necessarily an indication that an overhaul is needed, while low mileage doesn't preclude the need for an overhaul. Frequency of servicing is probably the most important consideration. An engine that's had regular and frequent oil and filter changes, as well as other required maintenance, will most likely give many thousands of miles of reliable service. Conversely, a neglected engine may require an overhaul very early in its service life.

7 Excessive oil consumption is an indication that piston rings, valve seals and/or valve guides are in need of attention. Make sure that oil leaks aren't responsible before deciding that the rings and/or guides are bad. Perform a cylinder compression check to determine the extent of the work required (see

Section 3). Also check the vacuum readings under various conditions (see Section 4).

8 Check the oil pressure with a gauge installed in place of the oil pressure sending unit and compare it to this Chapter's Specifications (see Section 2). If it's extremely low, the bearings and/or oil pump are probably worn out.

9 Loss of power, rough running, knocking or metallic engine noises, excessive valve train noise and high fuel consumption rates may also point to the need for an overhaul, especially if they're all present at the same time. If a complete tune-up doesn't remedy the situation, major mechanical work is the only solution.

10 An engine overhaul involves restoring the internal parts to the specifications of a new engine. During an overhaul, the piston rings are replaced and the cylinder walls are reconditioned (rebored and/or honed) (see illustrations 1.10a and 1.10b). If a rebore is done by an automotive machine shop, new oversize pistons will also be installed. The main bearings, connecting rod bearings and camshaft bearings are generally replaced with new ones and, if necessary, the crankshaft may be

reground to restore the journals (see illustration 1.10c). Generally, the valves are serviced as well, since they're usually in less-than-perfect condition at this point. While the engine is being overhauled, other components, such as the distributor, starter and alternator, can be rebuilt as well. The end result should be similar to a new engine that will give many trouble free miles.

Note: *Critical cooling system components such as the hoses, drivebelts, thermostat and water pump should be replaced with new parts when an engine is overhauled. The radiator should be checked carefully to ensure that it isn't clogged or leaking (see Chapter 1). If you purchase a rebuilt engine or short block, some rebuilders will not warranty their engines unless the radiator has been professionally flushed. Also, we don't recommend overhauling the oil pump - always install a new one when an engine is rebuilt.*

11 Overhauling the internal components on today's engines is a difficult and time-consuming task which requires a significant amount of specialty tools and is best left to a professional engine rebuilder (see illustrations 1.11a, 1.11b and 1.11c). A competent engine

1.10c A crankshaft having a main bearing journal ground

1.11a A machinist checks for a bent connecting rod, using specialized equipment

rebuilder will handle the inspection of your old parts and offer advice concerning the reconditioning or replacement of the original engine, never purchase parts or have machine work done on other components until the block has been thoroughly inspected by a professional machine shop. As a general rule, time is the primary cost of an overhaul, especially since the vehicle may be tied up for a minimum of two weeks or more. Be aware that some engine builders only have the capability to rebuild the engine you bring them while other rebuilders have a large inventory of rebuilt exchange engines in stock. Also be aware that many machine shops could take as much as two weeks time to completely rebuild your engine depending on shop workload. Sometimes it makes more sense to simply exchange your engine for another engine that's already rebuilt to save time.

1.11b A bore gauge being used to check the main bearing bore

1.11c Uneven piston wear like this indicates a bent connecting rod

2   Oil pressure check

1   Low engine oil pressure can be a sign of an engine in need of rebuilding. A "low oil pressure" indicator (often called an "idiot light") is not a test of the oiling system. Such indicators only come on when the oil pressure is dangerously low. Even a factory oil pressure gauge in the instrument panel is only a relative indication, although much better for driver information than a warning light. A better test is with a mechanical (not electrical) oil pressure gauge.

2   Locate the oil pressure sending unit:

a)   *On 2.7L V6 engines, the oil pressure sending unit is located on the passenger's side cylinder head, near the turbocharger (see illustration).*

b)   *On 3.5L V6 engines, the oil pressure sending unit is located near the lower left side of the engine on the oil filter adapter behind the alternator.*

c)   *On 5.0L V8 engines, the oil pressure sending unit is located near the lower left side of the engine on the oil filter adapter.*

3   Unscrew and remove the oil pressure sending unit and screw in the hose for your oil pressure gauge. If necessary, install an adapter fitting. Use Teflon tape or thread sealant on the threads of the adapter and/or the fitting on the end of your gauge's hose.

4   Connect an accurate tachometer to the engine, according to the tachometer manufacturer's instructions.

5   Check the oil pressure with the engine running (normal operating temperature) at the specified engine speed, and compare it to this Chapter's Specifications. If it's extremely low, the bearings and/or oil pump are probably worn out.

3   Cylinder compression check

1   A compression check will tell you what mechanical condition the upper end of your engine (pistons, rings, valves, head gaskets) is in. Specifically, it can tell you if the compression is down due to leakage caused by worn piston rings, defective valves and seats or a blown head gasket.

Note: *The engine must be at normal operating temperature and the battery must be fully charged for this check.*

2   Begin by cleaning the area around the spark plugs before you remove them (compressed air should be used, if available). The idea is to prevent dirt from getting into the cylinders as the compression check is being done.

3   Disable the fuel pump by disconnecting the electrical connector from the FPDM (see Chapter 4, Section 4).

4   Remove the ignition coils (see Chapter 5) then remove all of the spark plugs from the engine (see Chapter 1).

Note: *On 3.5L Duratec (non-turbocharged) the upper intake manifold must be removed to access the ignition coils and spark plugs (see Chapter 2A).*

5   Install a compression gauge in the spark plug hole (see illustration).

2.2 Oil pressure sending unit location - 2.7L V6 engine shown, other engines similar

3.5 Use a compression gauge with a threaded fitting for the spark plug hole, not the type that requires hand pressure to maintain the seal - typical installation shown

4.4 A simple vacuum gauge can be handy in diagnosing engine condition and performance

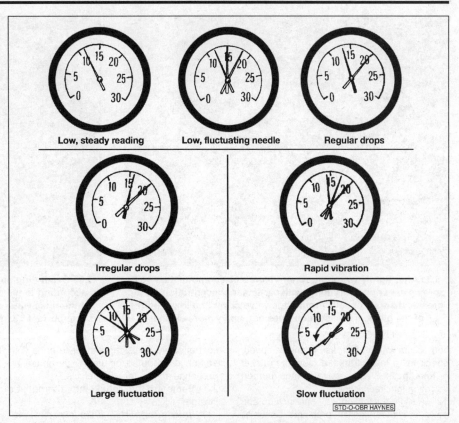

Low, steady reading   Low, fluctuating needle   Regular drops

Irregular drops   Rapid vibration

Large fluctuation   Slow fluctuation

STD-O-OBR HAYNES

4.6 Typical vacuum gauge readings

6   Have an assistant depress the accelerator pedal to the floor and crank the engine over at least seven compression strokes, while you watch the gauge. The compression should build up quickly in a healthy engine. Low compression on the first stroke, followed by gradually increasing pressure on successive strokes, indicates worn piston rings. A low compression reading on the first stroke, which doesn't build up during successive strokes, indicates leaking valves or a blown head gasket (a cracked head could also be the cause). Deposits on the undersides of the valve heads can also cause low compression. Record the highest gauge reading obtained.

7   Repeat the procedure for the remaining cylinders and compare the results to this Chapter's Specifications.

8   Add some engine oil (about three squirts from a plunger-type oil can) to each cylinder, through the spark plug hole, and repeat the test.

9   If the compression increases after the oil is added, the piston rings are definitely worn. If the compression doesn't increase significantly, the leakage is occurring at the valves or head gasket. Leakage past the valves may be caused by burned valve seats and/or faces or warped, cracked or bent valves.

10   If two adjacent cylinders have equally low compression, there's a strong possibility that the head gasket between them is blown. The appearance of coolant in the combustion chambers or the crankcase would verify this condition.

11   If one cylinder is slightly lower than the others, and the engine has a slightly rough idle, a worn lobe on the camshaft could be the cause.

12   If the compression is unusually high, the combustion chambers are probably coated with carbon deposits. If that's the case, the cylinder head(s) should be removed and decarbonized.

13   If compression is way down or varies greatly between cylinders, it would be a good idea to have a leak-down test performed by an automotive repair shop. This test will pinpoint exactly where the leakage is occurring and how severe it is.

4   Vacuum gauge diagnostic checks

1   A vacuum gauge provides inexpensive but valuable information about what is going on in the engine. You can check for worn rings or cylinder walls, leaking head or intake manifold gaskets, incorrect carburetor adjustments, restricted exhaust, stuck or burned valves, weak valve springs, improper ignition or valve timing and ignition problems.

2   Unfortunately, vacuum gauge readings are easy to misinterpret, so they should be used in conjunction with other tests to confirm the diagnosis.

3   Both the absolute readings and the rate of needle movement are important for accurate interpretation. Most gauges measure vacuum in inches of mercury (in-Hg). The following references to vacuum assume the diagnosis is being performed at sea level. As elevation increases (or atmospheric pressure decreases), the reading will decrease. For every 1,000 foot increase in elevation above approximately 2,000 feet, the gauge readings will decrease about one inch of mercury.

4   Connect the vacuum gauge directly to the intake manifold vacuum, not to ported (throttle body) vacuum (see illustration). Be sure no hoses are left disconnected during the test or false readings will result.

5   Before you begin the test, allow the engine to warm up completely. Block the wheels and set the parking brake. With the transmission in Park, start the engine and

allow it to run at normal idle speed.
Warning: *Keep your hands and the vacuum gauge clear of the fans.*

6   Read the vacuum gauge; an average, healthy engine should normally produce about 17 to 22 in-Hg with a fairly steady needle (see illustration). Refer to the following vacuum gauge readings and what they indicate about the engine's condition:

7   A low steady reading usually indicates a leaking gasket between the intake manifold and cylinder head(s) or throttle body, a leaky vacuum hose, late ignition timing or incorrect camshaft timing. Check ignition timing with a timing light and eliminate all other possible causes, utilizing the tests provided in this Chapter before you remove the timing chain cover to check the timing marks.

8   If the reading is three to eight inches below normal and it fluctuates at that low reading, suspect an intake manifold gasket leak at an intake port or a faulty fuel injector.

9   If the needle has regular drops of about two-to-four inches at a steady rate, the valves are probably leaking. Perform a compression check or leak-down test to confirm this.

10   An irregular drop or down-flick of the needle can be caused by a sticking valve or an ignition misfire. Perform a compression check or leak-down test and read the spark plugs.

11   A rapid vibration of about four in-Hg vibration at idle combined with exhaust smoke indicates worn valve guides. Perform a leak-down test to confirm this. If the rapid vibra-

6.3a After tightly wrapping water-vulnerable components, use a spray cleaner on everything, with particular concentration on the greasiest areas, usually around the valve cover and lower edges of the block. If one section dries out, apply more cleaner

6.3b Depending on how dirty the engine is, let the cleaner soak in according to the directions and hose off the grime and cleaner. Get the rinse water down into every area you can get at; then dry important components with a hair dryer or paper towels

tion occurs with an increase in engine speed, check for a leaking intake manifold gasket or head gasket, weak valve springs, burned valves or ignition misfire.

12   A slight fluctuation, say one inch up and down, may mean ignition problems. Check all the usual tune-up items and, if necessary, run the engine on an ignition analyzer.

13   If there is a large fluctuation, perform a compression or leak-down test to look for a weak or dead cylinder or a blown head gasket.

14   If the needle moves slowly through a wide range, check for a clogged PCV system, incorrect idle fuel mixture, throttle body or intake manifold gasket leaks.

15   Check for a slow return after revving the engine by quickly snapping the throttle open until the engine reaches about 2,500 rpm and let it shut. Normally the reading should drop to near zero, rise above normal idle reading (about 5 in-Hg over) and return to the previous idle reading. If the vacuum returns slowly and doesn't peak when the throttle is snapped shut, the rings may be worn. If there is a long delay, look for a restricted exhaust system (often the muffler or catalytic converter). An easy way to check this is to temporarily disconnect the exhaust ahead of the suspected part and redo the test.

5   Engine rebuilding alternatives

1   The do-it-yourselfer is faced with a number of options when purchasing a rebuilt engine. The major considerations are cost, warranty, parts availability and the time required for the rebuilder to complete the project. The decision to replace the engine block, piston/connecting rod assemblies and crankshaft depends on the final inspection results of your engine. Only then can you make a

cost effective decision whether to have your engine overhauled or simply purchase an exchange engine for your vehicle.

2   Some of the rebuilding alternatives include:

a)   *Individual parts - If the inspection procedures reveal that the engine block and most engine components are in reusable condition, purchasing individual parts and having a rebuilder rebuild your engine may be the most economical alternative. The block, crankshaft and piston/connecting rod assemblies should all be inspected carefully by a machine shop first.*

b)   *Short block - A short block consists of an engine block with a crankshaft and piston/connecting rod assemblies already installed. All new bearings are incorporated and all clearances will be correct. The existing camshafts, valve train components, cylinder head and external parts can be bolted to the short block with little or no machine shop work necessary.*

c)   *Long block - A long block consists of a short block plus an oil pump, oil pan, cylinder head, valve cover, camshaft and valve train components, timing sprockets and chain or gears and timing cover. All components are installed with new bearings, seals and gaskets incorporated throughout. The installation of manifolds and external parts is all that's necessary.*

d)   *Low mileage used engines - Some companies now offer low mileage used engines which is a very cost effective way to get your vehicle up and running again. These engines often come from vehicles which have been in totaled in accidents or come from other countries which have a higher vehicle turn over rate. A low mileage used engine also usually has a similar warranty like the newly remanufactured engines.*

3   Give careful thought to which alternative is best for you and discuss the situation with local automotive machine shops, auto parts dealers and experienced rebuilders before ordering or purchasing replacement parts.

6   Engine removal - methods and precautions

1   If you've decided that an engine must be removed for overhaul or major repair work, several preliminary steps should be taken. Read all removal and installation procedures carefully prior to committing to this job.

2   Locating a suitable place to work is extremely important. Adequate work space, along with storage space for the vehicle, will be needed. If a shop or garage isn't available, at the very least a flat, level, clean work surface made of concrete or asphalt is required.

3   Cleaning the engine compartment and engine before beginning the removal procedure will help keep tools clean and organized (see illustrations 6.3a and 6.3b).

4   An engine hoist will also be necessary. Make sure the hoist is rated in excess of the combined weight of the engine and transmission. Safety is of primary importance, considering the potential hazards involved in removing the engine from the vehicle.

5   If you're a novice at engine removal, get at least one helper. One person cannot easily do all the things you need to do to remove a big heavy engine and transmission assembly from the engine compartment. Also helpful is to seek advice and assistance from someone who's experienced in engine removal.

6   Plan the operation ahead of time. Arrange for or obtain all of the tools and equipment you'll need prior to beginning the

job (see illustrations 6.6a and 6.6b). Some of the equipment necessary to perform engine removal and installation safely and with relative ease are (in addition to a vehicle hoist and an engine hoist) a heavy duty floor jack (preferably fitted with a transmission jack head adapter), complete sets of wrenches and sockets as described in the front of this manual, wooden blocks, plenty of rags and cleaning solvent for mopping up spilled oil, coolant and gasoline.

7   Plan for the vehicle to be out of use for quite a while. A machine shop can do the work that is beyond the scope of the home mechanic. Machine shops often have a busy schedule, so before removing the engine, consult the shop for an estimate of how long it will take to rebuild or repair the components that may need work.

7   Engine - removal and installation

Warning: *Gasoline is extremely flammable, so take extra precautions when you work on any part of the fuel system. Don't smoke or allow open flames or bare light bulbs near the work area, and don't work in a garage where a gas-type appliance (such as a water heater or clothes dryer) is present. Since gasoline is carcinogenic, wear fuel-resistant gloves when there's a possibility of being exposed to fuel, and, if you spill any fuel on your skin, rinse it off immediately with soap and water. Mop up any spills immediately and do not store fuel-soaked rags where they could ignite. The fuel system is under constant pressure, so, if any fuel lines are to be disconnected, the fuel pressure in the system must be relieved first (see Chapter 4 for more information). When you perform any kind of work on the fuel system, wear safety glasses and have a Class B type fire extinguisher on hand.*

Warning: *The air conditioning system is under high pressure. DO NOT loosen any fittings or remove any components until after the system has been discharged. Air conditioning refrigerant should be properly discharged into an*

6.6a Get an engine stand sturdy enough to firmly support the engine while you're working on it. Stay away from three-wheeled models: they have a tendency to tip over more easily, so get a four-wheeled unit.

6.6b Since many of the fasteners on these engines are tightened using the angle torque method, a torque angle gauge is essential for proper assembly

EPA-approved container at a dealer service department or an automotive air conditioning repair facility. Always wear eye protection when disconnecting air conditioning system fittings.

Warning: *The engine must be completely cool before beginning this procedure.*

Removal

1   Have the air conditioning system discharged by a licensed automotive air conditioning technician.
2   Relieve the fuel system pressure (see Chapter 4).
3   Disconnect the cable from the negative battery terminal (see Chapter 5).
4   Raise the vehicle and support it securely on jackstands.
5   Remove the skid plates and splash shields, if equipped.
6   Remove the front crossmember (see illustration).
7   Remove the fender splash shields and the hood (see Chapter 11). Cover the fenders

using special pads. An old bedspread or blanket will also work.
8   Remove the intake ducts and the air filter housing (see Chapter 4).
9   Disconnect the quick-release connectors to the EVAP tubes (see Chapter 6) and the vacuum lines.
10   Remove the charge air cooler, cooler intake pipe and outlet pipe (see Chapter 4).
11   On 2.7L models, remove the high-pressure fuel pump noise insulator, then disconnect the fuel feed line quick-connect coupling (see Chapter 4).
12   Disconnect the electrical connectors from the Powertrain Control Module (PCM) (see Chapter 6).
13   Clearly label and disconnect all vacuum lines, emissions hoses, wiring harness connectors, ground straps and fuel lines between the engine and the chassis. Masking tape and/or a touch up paint applicator work well for marking items (see illustration). Take instant photos or sketch the locations of components and brackets.

7.6 Crossmember mounting bolts

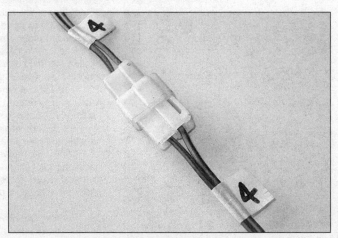

7.13 Label both ends of each wire and hose before disconnecting it

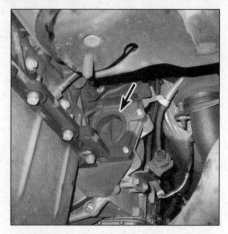

7.29 Remove the round opening cover...

7.30 . . . for access to the torque converter nuts

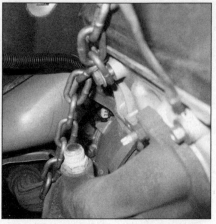

7.32a Attach the chain to a threaded boss or stud on the cylinder head

14   Remove the drivebelt (see Chapter 1).
15   Remove the alternator (see Chapter 5).
16   Remove the air conditioning lines from the condenser and the manifold and tube assembly at the rear of the engine compartment (see Chapter 3). Remove the air conditioning manifold and tube bracket.
17   Drain the cooling system (see Chapter 1).
18   Drain the engine oil and remove the oil filter (see Chapter 1).
19   Remove the cooling fan(s) and shroud(s) (see Chapter 3).
20   Detach the lower radiator hose from the engine (see Chapter 3).
21   Remove the expansion tank and radiator (see Chapter 3).
22   Detach the heater hoses at the firewall (see Chapter 3). Also, remove the upper radiator hose.
23   If you're working on a turbocharged model, remove the turbocharger intake and outlet tubes.
24   Remove the air conditioning compressor (see Chapter 3). Plug the openings to prevent contamination.
25   Remove the condenser and evaporator core line nuts (see Chapter 3), then disconnect the lines and plug the openings to pre-

vent contamination.
26   On 3.5L Duratec V6 models, remove the upper intake manifold.
27   Unplug the upstream oxygen sensor electrical connector(s). Detach the heat shields, exhaust brackets and the exhaust pipes from the exhaust manifolds (see Chapter 2A or 2B).
28   On V6 models, remove the inspection cover fasteners and cover from the side of the transmission bellhousing.
29   On V8 models, remove the block opening cover (see illustration).
30   Remove the torque converter nuts (see illustration). Turn the crankshaft with a wrench to bring each nut into view.
31   Remove the starter motor (see Chapter 5).
32   Roll the engine hoist into position and attach the chain or sling to the engine (see illustrations). Take up the slack in the sling or chain, but don't lift the engine.
Warning: *DO NOT place any part of your body under the engine when it's supported only by a hoist or other lifting device.*
33   Remove the engine mount through-bolts (see Chapter 2A or Chapter 2B).
34   Loosen the transmission mount at the rear of the transmission.
35   Support the transmission with a floor jack. Be sure to place a piece of wood on the jack head to protect the transmission.
36   Recheck to be sure nothing is still connecting the engine to the vehicle. Disconnect anything still remaining.
37   Raise the engine slightly and inspect it thoroughly once more to make sure that nothing is still attached, then slowly raise the engine out of the engine compartment. Check carefully to make sure nothing is hanging up.
38   It may be necessary to tilt or turn the engine as it is being raised.
Warning: *Don't place any part of your body under the engine or between the engine and the vehicle.*
39   Remove the driveplate (see Chapter 2A or Chapter 2B) and mount the engine on an engine stand.
40   Inspect the engine mounts (see Chapter

2A or Chapter 2B) and transmission mount (see Chapter 7A). If they're worn or damaged, replace them.

Installation

41   Install the driveplate (see Chapter 2A or Chapter 2B).
42   Lubricate the torque converter hub with multi-purpose grease.
43   Carefully lower the engine into the engine compartment and engage it with the engine mounts and the transmission.
44   Install the transmission-to-engine bolts and tighten them securely.
Caution: *DO NOT use the bolts to force the transmission and engine together!*
45   Reinstall the remaining components in the reverse order of removal.
46   Add coolant, oil and transmission fluid as needed (see Chapter 1).
47   Reconnect the battery, run the engine and check for leaks and proper operation of all accessories, then install the hood and test drive the vehicle. The Powertrain Control Module (PCM) must relearn its idle and fuel trim strategy for optimum driveability and performance, which may take a few trips.
48   Have the air conditioning system recharged by the shop that discharged it.

8   Engine overhaul - disassembly sequence

1   It's much easier to remove the external components if it's mounted on a portable engine stand. A stand can often be rented quite cheaply from an equipment rental yard. Before the engine is mounted on a stand, the flywheel/driveplate should be removed from the engine.
2   If a stand isn't available, it's possible to remove the external engine components with it blocked up on the floor. Be extra careful not to tip or drop the engine when working without a stand.
3   If you're going to obtain a rebuilt engine, all external components must come off first,

7.32b Attach the chain or load leveling device to the hoist and take up the slack

9.1 Before you try to remove the pistons, use a ridge reamer to remove the raised material (ridge) from the top of the cylinders

9.3 Checking the connecting rod endplay (side clearance)

to be transferred to the replacement engine. These components include:

 Driveplate
 Ignition coils
 Emissions-related components
 Engine mounts and mount brackets
 Engine rear cover (spacer plate between
  driveplate and engine block)
 Intake/exhaust manifolds
 Valve covers
 Fuel injection components
 Oil filter
 Spark plugs
 Thermostat and housing assembly
 Water pump

Note: *When removing the external components from the engine, pay close attention to details that may be helpful or important during installation. Note the installed position of gaskets, seals, spacers, pins, brackets, washers, bolts and other small items.*

4 If you're going to obtain a short block (assembled engine block, crankshaft, pistons and connecting rods), then remove the timing chain, cylinder head, oil pan, oil pump pick-up tube, oil pump and water pump from your engine so that you can turn in your old short block to the rebuilder as a core. See *Engine rebuilding alternatives* for additional information regarding the different possibilities to be considered.

9 Pistons and connecting rods - removal and installation

Removal

Note: *Prior to removing the piston/connecting rod assemblies, remove the cylinder head and oil pan(see Chapter 2A or Chapter 2B).*

1 Use your fingernail to feel if a ridge has formed at the upper limit of ring travel (about 1/4-inch down from the top of each cylinder). If carbon deposits or cylinder wear have produced ridges, they must be completely removed with a special tool (see illustration). Follow the manufacturer's instructions

provided with the tool. Failure to remove the ridges before attempting to remove the piston/connecting rod assemblies may result in piston breakage.

2 After the cylinder ridges have been removed, turn the engine so the crankshaft is facing up.

Note: *To access the main bearing caps and piston rod caps, remove the the engine block skirt stiffener. On 2.7L engines and on 3.5L engines remove the main bearing cap support brace (see Section 10).*

3 Before the main bearing cap assembly and connecting rods are removed, check the connecting rod endplay with feeler gauges. Slide them between the first connecting rod and the crankshaft throw until the play is removed (see illustration). Repeat this procedure for each connecting rod. The endplay is equal to the thickness of the feeler gauge(s). Check with an automotive machine shop for the endplay service limit (a typical endplay limit should measure between 0.005 to 0.015 inch [0.127 to 0.381 mm]). If the play exceeds the service limit, new connecting rods will be required. If new rods (or a new crankshaft) are installed, the endplay may fall under the minimum allowable. If it does, the rods will have to be machined to restore it. If necessary, consult an automotive machine shop for advice.

4 Check the connecting rods and caps for identification marks. If they aren't plainly marked, use paint or marker to clearly identify each rod and cap (1, 2, 3, etc., depending on the cylinder they're associated with) (see illustration).

5 Remove the connecting rod cap bolts evenly.

Note: *Obtain new bolts for final installation, but save the old bolts for the oil clearance check that will be performed later.*

6 Remove the number one connecting rod cap and bearing insert. Don't drop the bearing insert out of the cap.

7 Remove the bearing insert and push the connecting rod/piston assembly out through the top of the engine. Use a wooden or plastic hammer handle to push on the upper bearing

9.4 If the connecting rods and caps are not marked, mark the caps to the rods by cylinder number (for example, this would be the No. 4 connecting rod)

surface in the connecting rod. If resistance is felt, double-check to make sure that all of the ridge was removed from the cylinder.

8 Repeat the procedure for the remaining cylinders.

9 After removal, reassemble the connecting rod caps and bearing inserts in their respective connecting rods and install the cap bolts finger-tight. Leaving the old bearing inserts in place until reassembly will help prevent the connecting rod bearing surfaces from being accidentally nicked or gouged.

10 The pistons and connecting rods are now ready for inspection and overhaul at an automotive machine shop.

Piston ring installation

11 Before installing the new piston rings, the ring end gaps must be checked. It's assumed that the piston ring side clearance has been checked and verified correct.

12 Lay out the piston/connecting rod assemblies and the new ring sets so the ring sets will be matched with the same piston and cylinder during the end gap measurement and engine assembly.

13 Insert the top (number one) ring into the first cylinder and square it up with the cylinder

9.13 Install the piston ring into the cylinder then push it down into position using a piston so the ring will be square in the cylinder

9.14 With the ring square in the cylinder, measure the ring end gap with a feeler gauge

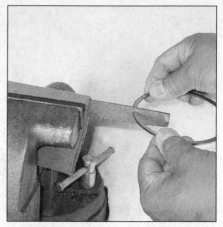

9.15 If the ring end gap is too small, clamp a file in a vise as shown and file the piston ring ends - be sure to remove all raised material

9.19a Installing the oil ring spacer in the piston oil ring groove

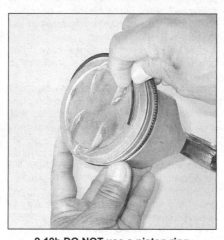

9.19b DO NOT use a piston ring installation tool when installing the oil control side rails (oil rings)

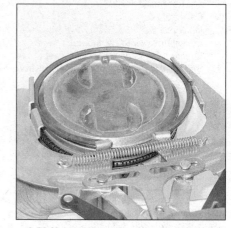

9.22 Use a piston ring installation tool to install the number 2 and the number 1 (top) compression rings - be sure the directional mark on the piston ring(s) is facing toward the top of the piston

walls by pushing it in with the top of the piston (see illustration). The ring should be near the bottom of the cylinder, at the lower limit of ring travel.

14   To measure the end gap, slip feeler gauges between the ends of the ring until a gauge equal to the gap width is found (see illustration). The feeler gauge should slide between the ring ends with a slight amount of drag. A typical ring gap should fall between 0.010 and 0.020 inch [0.25 to 0.50 mm] for compression rings and up to 0.030 inch [0.76 mm] for the oil ring steel rails. If the gap is larger or smaller than specified, double-check to make sure you have the correct rings before proceeding.

15   If the gap is too small, it must be enlarged or the ring ends may come in contact with each other during engine operation, which can cause serious damage to the engine. If necessary, increase the end gaps by filing the ring ends very carefully with a fine file. Mount the file in a vise equipped with soft jaws, slip the ring over the file with the ends contacting the file face and slowly move the ring to

remove material from the ends. When performing this operation, file only by pushing the ring from the outside end of the file towards the vise (see illustration).

16   Excess end gap isn't critical unless it's greater than 0.040 inch (1.01 mm). Again, double-check to make sure you have the correct ring type.

17   Repeat the procedure for each ring that will be installed in the first cylinder and for each ring in the remaining cylinders. Remember to keep rings, pistons and cylinders matched up.

18   Once the ring end gaps have been checked/corrected, the rings can be installed on the pistons.

19   The oil control ring (lowest one on the piston) is usually installed first. It's composed of three separate components. Slip the spacer/expander into the groove (see illustration). If an anti-rotation tang is used, make sure it's inserted into the drilled hole in the ring groove. Next, install the upper side rail in the same manner (see illustration). Don't use a piston ring installation tool on the oil ring

side rails, as they may be damaged. Instead, place one end of the side rail into the groove between the spacer/expander and the ring land, hold it firmly in place and slide a finger around the piston while pushing the rail into the groove. Finally, install the lower side rail.

20   After the three oil ring components have been installed, check to make sure that both the upper and lower side rails can be rotated smoothly inside the ring grooves.

21   The number two (middle) ring is installed next. It's usually stamped with a mark which must face up, toward the top of the piston. Do not mix up the top and middle rings, as they have different cross-sections.

Note: *Always follow the instructions printed on the ring package or box - different manufacturers may require different approaches.*

22   Use a piston ring installation tool and make sure the identification mark is facing the top of the piston, then slip the ring into the middle groove on the piston (see illustration). Don't expand the ring any more than necessary to slide it over the piston.

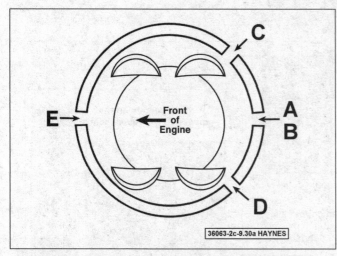

9.30a Position the piston ring end gaps as shown here before installing the piston/connecting rod assemblies into the engine - V6 engines

A   Center line of the piston, parallel to the wrist pin bore of the piston
B   Top compression ring gap
C   Upper oil ring gap
D   Lower oil ring gap
E   Second compression ring and oil ring spacer gap

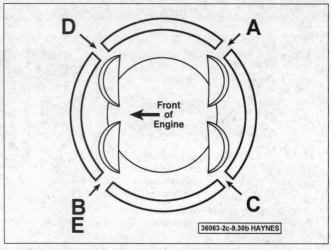

9.30b Position the piston ring end gaps as shown here before installing the piston/connecting rod assemblies into the engine - V8 engines

A   Top compression ring gap
B   Second compression ring
C   Upper oil ring gap
D   Lower oil ring gap
E   Oil ring spacer gap

23   Install the number one (top) ring in the same manner. Make sure the mark is facing up. Be careful not to confuse the number one and number two rings.
24   Repeat the procedure for the remaining pistons and rings.

Installation

25   Before installing the piston/connecting rod assemblies, the cylinder walls must be perfectly clean, the top edge of each cylinder bore must be chamfered, and the crankshaft must be in place.
26   Remove the cap from the end of the number one connecting rod (refer to the marks made during removal). Remove the original bearing inserts and wipe the bearing surfaces of the connecting rod and cap with a clean, lint-free cloth. They must be kept spotlessly clean.

Connecting rod bearing oil clearance check

27   Clean the back side of the new upper bearing insert, then lay it in place in the connecting rod.
28   Make sure the tab on the bearing fits into the recess in the rod. Don't hammer the bearing insert into place and be very careful not to nick or gouge the bearing face. Don't lubricate the bearing at this time.
29   Clean the back side of the other bearing insert and install it in the rod cap. Again, make sure the tab on the bearing fits into the recess in the cap, and don't apply any lubricant. It's critically important that the mating surfaces of the bearing and connecting rod are perfectly clean and oil free when they're assembled.
30   Position the piston ring gaps at intervals

around the piston as shown (see illustrations).
31   Lubricate the piston and rings with clean engine oil and attach a piston ring compressor to the piston. Leave the skirt protruding about 1/4-inch to guide the piston into the cylinder. The rings must be compressed until they're flush with the piston.
32   Rotate the crankshaft until the number one connecting rod journal is at BDC (bottom dead center) and apply a liberal coat of engine oil to the cylinder walls.
33   With the weight designation mark on top of the piston facing the front (timing chain end) of the engine, gently insert the piston/connecting rod assembly into the number one cylinder bore and rest the bottom edge of the ring compressor on the engine block. Install the pistons with the cavity mark(s) facing toward the timing chain.

34   Tap the top edge of the ring compressor to make sure it's contacting the block around its entire circumference.
35   Gently tap on the top of the piston with the end of a wooden or plastic hammer handle (see illustration) while guiding the end of the connecting rod into place on the crankshaft journal. The piston rings may try to pop out of the ring compressor just before entering the cylinder bore, so keep some downward pressure on the ring compressor. Work slowly, and if any resistance is felt as the piston enters the cylinder, stop immediately. Find out what's hanging up and fix it before proceeding. Do not, for any reason, force the piston into the cylinder - you might break a ring and/or the piston.
36   Once the piston/connecting rod assembly is installed, the connecting rod bearing oil

9.35 Use a plastic or wooden hammer handle to push the piston into the cylinder

ENGINE BEARING ANALYSIS

Debris

Aluminum bearing embedded with glass beads

Babbitt bearing embedded with debris from machinings

Microscopic detail of debris

Microscopic detail of gouges

Overplated copper alloy bearing gouged by cast iron debris

Damaged lining caused by dirt left on the bearing back

Microscopic detail of glass beads

Misassembly

Result of a lower half assembled as an upper - blocking the oil flow

Excessive oil clearance is indicated by a short contact arc

Polished and oil-stained backs are a result of a poor fit in the housing bore

Result of a wrong, reversed, or shifted cap

Overloading

Damage from excessive idling which resulted in an oil film unable to support the load imposed

Damaged upper connecting rod bearings caused by engine lugging; the lower main bearings (not shown) were similarly affected

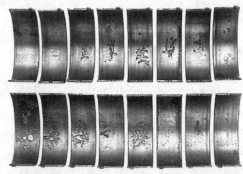

The damage shown in these upper and lower connecting rod bearings was caused by engine operation at a higher-than-rated speed under load

Misalignment

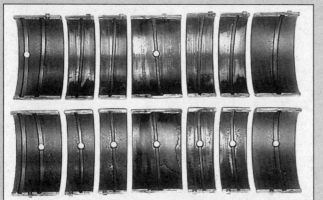

A warped crankshaft caused this pattern of severe wear in the center, diminishing toward the ends

A poorly finished crankshaft caused the equally spaced scoring shown

A tapered housing bore caused the damage along one edge of this pair

A bent connecting rod led to the damage in the "V" pattern

Lubrication

Result of dry start: The bearings on the left, farthest from the oil pump, show more damage

Result of a low oil supply or oil starvation

Severe wear as a result of inadequate oil clearance

Corrosion

Microscopic detail of corrosion

Corrosion is an acid attack on the bearing lining generally caused by inadequate maintenance, extremely hot or cold operation, or inferior oils or fuels

Microscopic detail of cavitation

Example of cavitation - a surface erosion caused by pressure changes in the oil film

Damage from excessive thrust or insufficient axial clearance

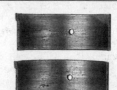

Bearing affected by oil dilution caused by excessive blow-by or a rich mixture

9.37 Place Plastigage on each connecting rod bearing journal parallel to the crankshaft centerline

9.41 Use the scale on the Plastigage package to determine the bearing oil clearance - be sure to measure the widest part of the Plastigage and use the correct scale; it comes with both standard and metric scales

clearance must be checked before the rod cap is permanently installed.

37   Cut a piece of the appropriate size Plastigage slightly shorter than the width of the connecting rod bearing and lay it in place on the number one connecting rod journal, parallel with the journal axis (see illustration).

38   Clean the connecting rod cap bearing face and install the rod cap. Make sure the mating mark on the cap is on the same side as the mark on the connecting rod (see illustration 9.4).

39   Install the old rod bolts, at this time, and tighten them to the torque listed in this Chapter's Specifications.

Note: *Use a thin-wall socket to avoid erroneous torque readings that can result if the socket is wedged between the rod cap and the bolt. If the socket tends to wedge itself between the fastener and the cap, lift up on it slightly until it no longer contacts the cap. DO NOT rotate the crankshaft at any time during this operation.*

40   Remove the fasteners and detach the rod cap, being very careful not to disturb the Plastigage. Discard the cap bolts at this time as they cannot be reused.

Note: *You MUST use new connecting rod bolts.*

41   Compare the width of the crushed Plastigage to the scale printed on the Plastigage envelope to obtain the oil clearance (see illustration). The connecting rod oil clearance is usually about 0.001 to 0.002 inch. Consult an automotive machine shop for the clearance specified for the rod bearings on your engine.

42   If the clearance is not as specified, the bearing inserts may be the wrong size (which means different ones will be required). Before deciding that different inserts are needed, make sure that no dirt or oil was between the bearing inserts and the connecting rod or cap when the clearance was measured. Also, recheck the journal diameter. If the Plastigage was wider at one end than the other, the journal may be

tapered. If the clearance still exceeds the limit specified, the bearing will have to be replaced with an undersize bearing.

Caution: *When installing a new crankshaft always use a standard size bearing.*

Final installation

43   Carefully scrape all traces of the Plastigage material off the rod journal and/or bearing face. Be very careful not to scratch the bearing - use your fingernail or the edge of a plastic card.

44   Make sure the bearing faces are perfectly clean, then apply a uniform layer of clean moly-base grease or engine assembly lube to both of them. You'll have to push the piston into the cylinder to expose the face of the bearing insert in the connecting rod.

45   Slide the connecting rod back into place on the journal, install the rod cap, install the new bolts and tighten them to the torque listed in this Chapter's Specifications.

Caution: *Install new connecting rod cap bolts. Do NOT reuse old bolts - they have stretched and cannot be reused (see Step 5).*

46   Repeat the entire procedure for the remaining pistons/connecting rods.

47   The important points to remember are:

a) *Keep the back sides of the bearing inserts and the insides of the connecting rods and caps perfectly clean when assembling them.*

b) *Make sure you have the correct piston/ rod assembly for each cylinder.*

c) *The mark on the piston must face the front (timing chain end) of the engine.*

d) *Lubricate the cylinder walls liberally with clean oil.*

e) *Lubricate the bearing faces when installing the rod caps after the oil clearance has been checked.*

48   After all the piston/connecting rod assemblies have been correctly installed, rotate the crankshaft a number of times by

hand to check for any obvious binding.

49   As a final step, check the connecting rod endplay, as described in Step 3. If it was correct before disassembly and the original crankshaft and rods were reinstalled, it should still be correct. If new rods or a new crankshaft were installed, the endplay may be inadequate. If so, the rods will have to be removed and taken to an automotive machine shop for resizing.

50   On 2.7L engines, install the engine block skirt stiffener and on 3.5L engines install the main bearing cap support brace (see Section 10).

10   Crankshaft - removal and installation

Removal

Note: *The crankshaft can be removed only after the engine has been removed from the vehicle. It's assumed that the driveplate, crankshaft pulley, timing chains, oil pan, oil pump body, oil pump drive chain (2.7L engines), crankshaft sensor ring, oil filter, engine block skirt stiffener (2.7L engines), main cap support brace (3.5L engines) and piston/connecting rod assemblies have already been removed. The rear main oil seal retainer must be unbolted and separated from the block before proceeding with crankshaft removal.*

1   Before the crankshaft is removed, measure the endplay. Mount a dial indicator with the indicator in line with the crankshaft and just touching the end of the crankshaft as shown (see illustration).

2   Pry the crankshaft all the way to the rear and zero the dial indicator. Next, pry the crankshaft to the front as far as possible and check the reading on the dial indicator. The distance traveled is the endplay. A typical crankshaft

10.1 Checking crankshaft endplay with a dial indicator

10.3 Checking the crankshaft endplay with feeler gauges at the thrust bearing journal

endplay will fall between 0.003 to 0.010 inch (0.076 to 0.254 mm). If it is greater than that, check the crankshaft thrust surfaces for wear after it's removed. If no wear is evident, new main bearings should correct the endplay.

a) On 2.7L and 3.5L V6 engines, the thrust bearings are installed at the number 4 crankshaft saddle and bearing cap.

b) On 5.0L V8 engines, the thrust bearings are installed at number 5 crankshaft saddle and bearing cap.

Note: *When installing thrust washers, make sure the grooves in the washer face the crankshaft.*

3   If a dial indicator isn't available, feeler gauges can be used. Gently pry the crankshaft all the way to the front of the engine. Slip feeler gauges between the crankshaft and the front face of the thrust bearing or washer to determine the clearance (see illustration).

4   On 2.7L engines, remove the engine block stiffener bolts, then insert a small pry bar between the four pry pads on the block and stiffener and pry the stiffener up to break the seal. Remove the stiffener then remove the stiffener-to-block seal from the stiffener.

5   On 3.5L engines, remove the main bearing cap support brace bolts, in reverse order of installation sequence (see illustration 10.38) and remove the support brace.

6   Loosen the main bearing cap bolts 1/4-turn at a time each, until they can be removed by hand. On V8 models, follow the reverse of the tightening sequence (see illustrations 10.21d and 10.21e).

7   Remove the main bearing caps. Gently tap the main bearing cap with a soft-face hammer. Pull the main bearing cap straight up and off the cylinder block. Try not to drop the bearing inserts if they come out with the assembly.

8   Carefully lift the crankshaft out of the engine. It may be a good idea to have an assistant available, since the crankshaft is quite heavy and awkward to handle. With the

bearing inserts in place inside the engine block and main bearing caps, reinstall the main bearing cap assembly onto the engine block and tighten the bolts finger-tight. Make sure the caps are in the exact order they were removed with the arrow pointing toward the front (timing chain and front cover) of the engine.

Installation

9   Crankshaft installation is the first step in engine reassembly. It's assumed at this point that the engine block and crankshaft have been cleaned, inspected and repaired or reconditioned.

10   Position the engine block with the bottom facing up.

11   Remove the mounting bolts and lift off the main bearing caps.

12   If they're still in place, remove the original bearing inserts from the block and from the main bearing cap assembly. Wipe the bearing surfaces of the block and main bearing cap assembly with a clean, lint-free cloth. They must be kept spotlessly clean. This is critical for determining the correct bearing oil clearance.

Main bearing oil clearance check

13   Without mixing them up, clean the back sides of the new upper main bearing inserts (with grooves and oil holes) and lay one in each main bearing saddle in the engine block. Each upper bearing (engine block) has an oil groove and oil hole in it. The thrust washer or thrust bearing insert must be installed in the correct location. Clean the back sides of the lower main bearing inserts and lay them in the corresponding location in the main bearing cap assembly. Make sure the tab on the bearing insert fits into the recess in the block or main bearing cap assembly.

Caution: *The oil holes in the block must line up with the oil holes in the engine block inserts.*

Note: *The oil grooves in the thrust washers must face toward the front of the engine.*

Caution: *Do not hammer the bearing insert into place and don't nick or gouge the bearing faces. DO NOT apply any lubrication at this time.*

14   Clean the faces of the bearing inserts in the block and the crankshaft main bearing journals with a clean, lint-free cloth.

15   Check or clean the oil holes in the crankshaft, as any dirt here can go only one way - straight through the new bearings.

16   Once you're certain the crankshaft is clean, carefully lay it in position in the cylinder block.

17   Before the crankshaft can be permanently installed, the main bearing oil clearance must be checked.

18   Cut several strips of the appropriate size of Plastigage. They must be slightly shorter than the width of the main bearing journal.

19   Place one piece on each crankshaft main bearing journal, parallel with the journal axis as shown (see illustration).

10.19 Place the Plastigage onto the crankshaft bearing journal as shown

20   Clean the faces of the bearing inserts in the main bearing cap assembly. Hold the bearing inserts in place and install the assembly onto the crankshaft and cylinder block. DO NOT disturb the Plastigage.

21   Apply clean engine oil to all bolt threads prior to installation, then install all bolts finger-tight. Tighten the bearing cap assembly bolts in the sequence shown (see illustrations) progressing in steps, to the torque listed in this Chapter's Specifications. DO NOT rotate the crankshaft at any time during this operation.

Note: *V8 engines and 3.5L V6 engines are equipped with side bolts, the 2.7L engine is equipped with a block skirt stiffener and the 3.5L engine is equipped with a main cap support brace, but it isn't necessary to install them for the oil clearance check.*

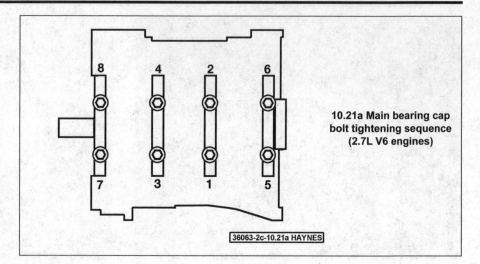

10.21a Main bearing cap bolt tightening sequence (2.7L V6 engines)

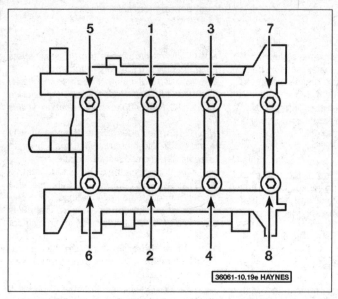

10.21b Main cap bolt tightening sequence - 3.5L V6 engines

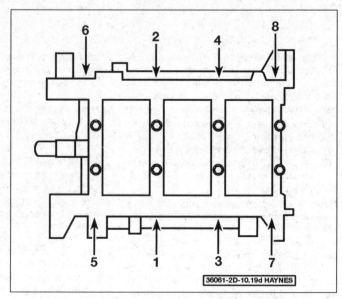

10.21c Side bolt tightening sequence - 3.5L V6 engines

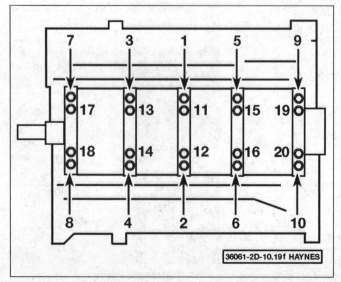

10.21d Main cap bolt tightening sequence - 5.0L V8 engines

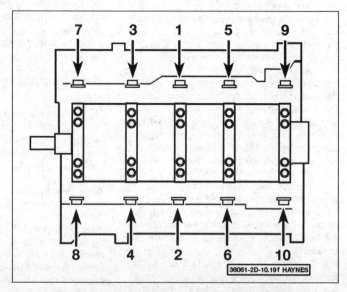

10.21e Side bolt tightening sequence - 5.0L V8 engines

10.23 Use the scale on the Plastigage package to determine the bearing oil clearance - be sure to measure the widest part of the Plastigage and use the correct scale; it comes with both standard and metric scales

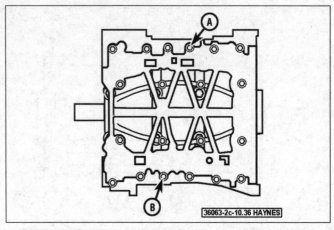

10.36 Tighten bolts A and B then align the engine block stiffener to the engine block

22   Remove the bolts in the reverse order of the tightening sequence and carefully lift the main bearing caps straight up and off the block. Do not disturb the Plastigage or rotate the crankshaft. If the main bearing cap assembly is difficult to remove, tap it gently from side-to-side with a soft-face hammer to loosen it.

23   Compare the width of the crushed Plastigage on each journal to the scale printed on the Plastigage envelope to determine the main bearing oil clearance (see illustration). Check with an automotive machine shop for the crankshaft endplay service limits.

24   If the clearance is not as specified, the bearing inserts may be the wrong size (which means different ones will be required). Before deciding if different inserts are needed, make sure that no dirt or oil was between the bearing inserts and the cap assembly or block when the clearance was measured. If the Plastigage was wider at one end than the other, the crankshaft journal may be tapered. If the clearance still exceeds the limit specified, the bearing insert(s) will have to be replaced with an undersize bearing insert(s).

Caution: *When installing a new crankshaft always install a standard bearing insert set.*

25   Carefully scrape all traces of the Plastigage material off the main bearing journals and/or the bearing insert faces. Be sure to remove all residue from the oil holes. Use your fingernail or the edge of a plastic card - don't nick or scratch the bearing faces.

Final installation

26   Carefully lift the crankshaft out of the cylinder block.

27   Clean the bearing insert faces in the cylinder block, then apply a thin, uniform layer of moly-base grease or engine assembly lube to each of the bearing surfaces. Be sure to coat the thrust faces as well as the journal face of the thrust bearing.

28   Make sure the crankshaft journals are clean, then lay the crankshaft back in place in the cylinder block.

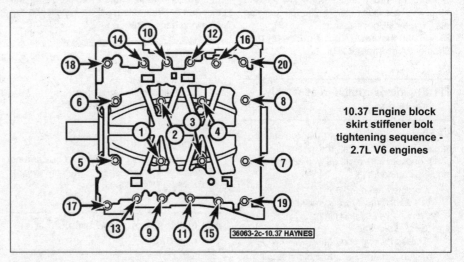

10.37 Engine block skirt stiffener bolt tightening sequence - 2.7L V6 engines

29   Clean the bearing insert faces and apply the same lubricant to them. Clean the engine block and the main bearing caps thoroughly. The surfaces must be free of oil residue.

30   On V6 engines, apply a bead of RTV sealant to the engine block on the rear main bearing cap parting line. Be sure the main bearing cap is installed within four minutes after the RTV sealant is applied.

31   Prior to installation, apply clean engine oil to all bolt threads wiping off any excess, then install all bolts finger-tight.

32   Tighten the main bearing caps following the correct torque sequence (see illustrations 10.21a through 10.21e). Tighten the bolts to the torque listed in this Chapter's Specifications.

33   Recheck the crankshaft endplay with a feeler gauge or a dial indicator. The endplay should be correct if the crankshaft thrust faces aren't worn or damaged and if new bearings have been installed.

34   Rotate the crankshaft a number of times by hand to check for any obvious binding. It should rotate with a running torque of 50 in-lbs or less. If the running torque is too high, correct the problem at this time.

35   On 2.7L engines, clean the engine block stiffener mounting surface then install a new oil seal. Apply a 3/16-inch bead of RTV sealant to the engine block skirt stiffener seal surfaces and install the stiffener over the crankshaft assembly and on to the block.

36   On 2.7L engines, install the stiffener mounting bolts hand tight, then tighten bolts A and B (see illustration) to the torque listed this Chapter's Specifications. Use a straightedge and align the rear face of the engine block skirt stiffener with the rear face of the engine block. It must be flush or up to 0.01 inch behind the face of the engine block. Use the straightedge and align the machined left side face of the engine block skirt stiffener with the machined left side faces of the engine block. It must be flush or up to 0.011 inch behind the machined left side face on the side of the engine block.

37   On 2.7L engines, once the alignment is within specifications, tighten the bolts in sequence (see illustration) to the torque listed this Chapter's Specifications.

Caution: *The engine block stiffener must be installed and tightened to the minimum specifications within 10 minutes or the stiffener must be removed and the RTV sealant cleaned off and new sealant applied.*

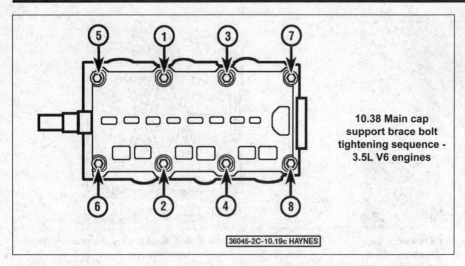

10.38 Main cap support brace bolt tightening sequence - 3.5L V6 engines

36045-2C-10.19c HAYNES

38   On 3.5L engines, install the main cap support brace and tighten the bolts in sequence (see illustration) to the torque listed this Chapter's Specifications.

39   Install the new rear main oil seal (see Chapter 2A or Chapter 2B).

11   Engine overhaul - reassembly sequence

1   Before beginning engine reassembly, make sure you have all the necessary new parts, gaskets and seals as well as the following items on hand:

Common hand tools
A 1/2-inch drive torque wrench
New engine oil and filter
Gasket sealant
Thread locking compound

3   If you obtained a short block it will be necessary to install the cylinder head, the oil pump and pick-up tube, the oil pan, the water pump, the timing chain and cover, and the valve covers (see Chapter 2A or Chapter 2B). In order to save time and avoid problems, the external components must be installed in the following general order:

Water pump
Exhaust manifolds
*Intake manifold(s)**
Valve covers
Fuel injection components
Emission control components
Oil filter
Engine mounts
Driveplate

* *The upper intake manifold on 3.5L Duratec V6 engines will be installed after the engine is installed.*

12   Initial start-up and break-in after overhaul

Warning: *Have a fire extinguisher handy when starting the engine for the first time.*

1   Once the engine has been installed in the vehicle, double-check the engine oil and coolant levels.

2   Disconnect the electrical connector from the Fuel Pump Driver Module (FPDM) (see Chapter 4, Section 4).

3   With the spark plugs out of the engine and the ignition system and fuel pump disabled, crank the engine until oil pressure registers on the gauge or the light goes out.

4   Install the spark plugs and ignition coils and reconnect the electrical connector to the FPDM.

5   Start the engine. It may take a few moments for the fuel system to build up pressure, but the engine should start without a great deal of effort.

6   After the engine starts, it should be allowed to warm up to normal operating temperature. While the engine is warming up, make a thorough check for fuel, oil and coolant leaks.

7   Shut the engine off and recheck the engine oil and coolant levels.

8   Drive the vehicle to an area with minimum traffic, accelerate from 30 to 50 mph, then allow the vehicle to slow to 30 mph with the throttle closed. Repeat the procedure 10 or 12 times. This will load the piston rings and cause them to seat properly against the cylinder walls. Check again for oil and coolant leaks.

9   Drive the vehicle gently for the first 500 miles (no sustained high speeds) and keep a constant check on the oil level. It is not unusual for an engine to use oil during the break-in period.

10   At approximately 500 to 600 miles, change the oil and filter.

11   For the next few hundred miles, drive the vehicle normally. Do not pamper it or abuse it.

12   After 2,000 miles, change the oil and filter again and consider the engine broken in.

COMMON ENGINE OVERHAUL TERMS

B

Backlash - The amount of play between two parts. Usually refers to how much one gear can be moved back and forth without moving the gear with which it's meshed.

Bearing Caps - The caps held in place by nuts or bolts which, in turn, hold the bearing surface. This space is for lubricating oil to enter.

Bearing clearance - The amount of space left between shaft and bearing surface. This space is for lubricating oil to enter.

Bearing crush - The additional height which is purposely manufactured into each bearing half to ensure complete contact of the bearing back with the housing bore when the engine is assembled.

Bearing knock - The noise created by movement of a part in a loose or worn bearing.

Blueprinting - Dismantling an engine and reassembling it to EXACT specifications.

Bore - An engine cylinder, or any cylindrical hole; also used to describe the process of enlarging or accurately refinishing a hole with a cutting tool, as to bore an engine cylinder. The bore size is the diameter of the hole.

Boring - Renewing the cylinders by cutting them out to a specified size. A boring bar is used to make the cut.

Bottom end - A term which refers collectively to the engine block, crankshaft, main bearings and the big ends of the connecting rods.

Break-in - The period of operation between installation of new or rebuilt parts and time in which parts are worn to the correct fit. Driving at reduced and varying speed for a specified mileage to permit parts to wear to the correct fit.

Bushing - A one-piece sleeve placed in a bore to serve as a bearing surface for shaft, piston pin, etc. Usually replaceable.

C

Camshaft - The shaft in the engine, on which a series of lobes are located for operating the valve mechanisms. The camshaft is driven by gears or sprockets and a timing chain. Usually referred to simply as the cam.

Carbon - Hard, or soft, black deposits found in combustion chamber, on plugs, under rings, on and under valve heads.

Cast iron - An alloy of iron and more than two percent carbon, used for engine blocks and heads because it's relatively inexpensive and easy to mold into complex shapes.

Chamfer - To bevel across (or a bevel on) the sharp edge of an object.

Chase - To repair damaged threads with a tap or die.

Combustion chamber - The space between the piston and the cylinder head, with the piston at top dead center, in which air-fuel mixture is burned.

Compression ratio - The relationship between cylinder volume (clearance volume) when the piston is at top dead center and cylinder volume when the piston is at bottom dead center.

Connecting rod - The rod that connects the crank on the crankshaft with the piston. Sometimes called a con rod.

Connecting rod cap - The part of the connecting rod assembly that attaches the rod to the crankpin.

Core plug - Soft metal plug used to plug the casting holes for the coolant passages in the block.

Crankcase - The lower part of the engine in which the crankshaft rotates; includes the lower section of the cylinder block and the oil pan.

Crank kit - A reground or reconditioned crankshaft and new main and connecting rod bearings.

Crankpin - The part of a crankshaft to which a connecting rod is attached.

Crankshaft - The main rotating member, or shaft, running the length of the crankcase, with offset throws to which the connecting rods are attached; changes the reciprocating motion of the pistons into rotating motion.

Cylinder sleeve - A replaceable sleeve, or liner, pressed into the cylinder block to form the cylinder bore.

D

Deburring - Removing the burrs (rough edges or areas) from a bearing.

Deglazer - A tool, rotated by an electric motor, used to remove glaze from cylinder walls so a new set of rings will seat.

E

Endplay - The amount of lengthwise movement between two parts. As applied to a crankshaft, the distance that the crankshaft can move forward and back in the cylinder block.

F

Face - A machinist's term that refers to removing metal from the end of a shaft or the face of a larger part, such as a flywheel.

Fatigue - A breakdown of material through a large number of loading and unloading cycles. The first signs are cracks followed shortly by breaks.

Feeler gauge - A thin strip of hardened steel, ground to an exact thickness, used to check clearances between parts.

Free height - The unloaded length or height of a spring.

Freeplay - The looseness in a linkage, or an assembly of parts, between the initial application of force and actual movement. Usually perceived as slop or slight delay.

Freeze plug - See Core plug.

G

Gallery - A large passage in the block that forms a reservoir for engine oil pressure.

Glaze - The very smooth, glassy finish that develops on cylinder walls while an engine is in service.

H

Heli-Coil - A rethreading device used when threads are worn or damaged. The device is installed in a retapped hole to reduce the thread size to the original size.

I

Installed height - The spring's measured length or height, as installed on the cylinder head. Installed height is measured from the spring seat to the underside of the spring retainer.

J

Journal - The surface of a rotating shaft which turns in a bearing.

K

Keeper - The split lock that holds the valve spring retainer in position on the valve stem.

Key - A small piece of metal inserted into matching grooves machined into two parts fitted together - such as a gear pressed onto a shaft - which prevents slippage between the two parts.

Knock - The heavy metallic engine sound, produced in the combustion chamber as a result of abnormal combustion - usually detonation. Knock is usually caused by a loose or worn bearing. Also referred to as detonation, pinging and spark knock. Connecting rod or main bearing knocks are created by too much oil clearance or insufficient lubrication.

L

Lands - The portions of metal between the piston ring grooves.

Lapping the valves - Grinding a valve face and its seat together with lapping compound.

Lash - The amount of free motion in a gear train, between gears, or in a mechanical assembly, that occurs before movement can begin. Usually refers to the lash in a valve train.

Lifter - The part that rides against the cam to transfer motion to the rest of the valve train.

M

Machining - The process of using a machine to remove metal from a metal part.

Main bearings - The plain, or babbit, bearings that support the crankshaft.

Main bearing caps - The cast iron caps, bolted to the bottom of the block, that support the main bearings.

O

O.D. - Outside diameter.

Oil gallery - A pipe or drilled passageway in the engine used to carry engine oil from one area to another.

Oil ring - The lower ring, or rings, of a piston; designed to prevent excessive amounts of oil from working up the cylinder walls and into the combustion chamber. Also called an oil-control ring.

Oil seal - A seal which keeps oil from leaking out of a compartment. Usually refers to a dynamic seal around a rotating shaft or other moving part.

O-ring - A type of sealing ring made of a special rubberlike material; in use, the O-ring is compressed into a groove to provide the sealing action.

Overhaul - To completely disassemble a unit, clean and inspect all parts, reassemble it with the original or new parts and make all adjustments necessary for proper operation.

P

Pilot bearing - A small bearing installed in the center of the flywheel (or the rear end of the crankshaft) to support the front end of the input shaft of the transmission.

Pip mark - A little dot or indentation which indicates the top side of a compression ring.

Piston - The cylindrical part, attached to the connecting rod, that moves up and down in the cylinder as the crankshaft rotates. When the fuel charge is fired, the piston transfers the force of the explosion to the connecting rod, then to the crankshaft.

Piston pin (or wrist pin) - The cylindrical and usually hollow steel pin that passes through the piston. The piston pin fastens the piston to the upper end of the connecting rod.

Piston ring - The split ring fitted to the groove in a piston. The ring contacts the sides of the ring groove and also rubs against the cylinder wall, thus sealing space between piston and wall. There are two types of rings: Compression rings seal the compression pressure in the combustion chamber; oil rings scrape excessive oil off the cylinder wall.

Piston ring groove - The slots or grooves cut in piston heads to hold piston rings in position.

Piston skirt - The portion of the piston below the rings and the piston pin hole.

Plastigage - A thin strip of plastic thread, available in different sizes, used for measuring clearances. For example, a strip of plastigage is laid across a bearing journal and mashed as parts are assembled. Then parts are disassembled and the width of the strip is measured to determine clearance between journal and bearing. Commonly used to measure crankshaft main-bearing and connecting rod bearing clearances.

Press-fit - A tight fit between two parts that requires pressure to force the parts together. Also referred to as drive, or force, fit.

Prussian blue - A blue pigment; in solution, useful in determining the area of contact between two surfaces. Prussian blue is commonly used to determine the width and location of the contact area between the valve face and the valve seat.

R

Race (bearing) - The inner or outer ring that provides a contact surface for balls or rollers in bearing.

Ream - To size, enlarge or smooth a hole by using a round cutting tool with fluted edges.

Ring job - The process of reconditioning the cylinders and installing new rings.

Runout - Wobble. The amount a shaft rotates out-of-true.

S

Saddle - The upper main bearing seat.

Scored - Scratched or grooved, as a cylinder wall may be scored by abrasive particles moved up and down by the piston rings.

Scuffing - A type of wear in which there's a transfer of material between parts moving against each other; shows up as pits or grooves in the mating surfaces.

Seat - The surface upon which another part rests or seats. For example, the valve seat is the matched surface upon which the valve face rests. Also used to refer to wearing into a good fit; for example, piston rings seat after a few miles of driving.

Short block - An engine block complete with crankshaft and piston and, usually, camshaft assemblies.

Static balance - The balance of an object while it's stationary.

Step - The wear on the lower portion of a ring land caused by excessive side and back-clearance. The height of the step indicates the ring's extra side clearance and the length of the step projecting from the back wall of the groove represents the ring's back clearance.

Stroke - The distance the piston moves when traveling from top dead center to bottom dead center, or from bottom dead center to top dead center.

Stud - A metal rod with threads on both ends.

T

Tang - A lip on the end of a plain bearing used to align the bearing during assembly.

Tap - To cut threads in a hole. Also refers to the fluted tool used to cut threads.

Taper - A gradual reduction in the width of a shaft or hole; in an engine cylinder, taper usually takes the form of uneven wear, more pronounced at the top than at the bottom.

Throws - The offset portions of the crankshaft to which the connecting rods are affixed.

Thrust bearing - The main bearing that has thrust faces to prevent excessive endplay, or forward and backward movement of the crankshaft.

Thrust washer - A bronze or hardened steel washer placed between two moving parts. The washer prevents longitudinal movement and provides a bearing surface for thrust surfaces of parts.

Tolerance - The amount of variation permitted from an exact size of measurement. Actual amount from smallest acceptable dimension to largest acceptable dimension.

U

Umbrella - An oil deflector placed near the valve tip to throw oil from the valve stem area.

Undercut - A machined groove below the normal surface.

Undersize bearings - Smaller diameter bearings used with re-ground crankshaft journals.

V

Valve grinding - Refacing a valve in a valve-refacing machine.

Valve train - The valve-operating mechanism of an engine; includes all components from the camshaft to the valve.

Vibration damper - A cylindrical weight attached to the front of the crankshaft to minimize torsional vibration (the twist-untwist actions of the crankshaft caused by the cylinder firing impulses). Also called a harmonic balancer.

W

Water jacket - The spaces around the cylinders, between the inner and outer shells of the cylinder block or head, through which coolant circulates.

Web - A supporting structure across a cavity.

Woodruff key - A key with a radiused backside (viewed from the side).

Notes

Notes

Chapter 3
Cooling, heating and air conditioning systems

Contents

	Section
Air conditioning and heater blower/control module - replacement	11
Air conditioning and heater control module - removal and installation	14
Air conditioning and heating system - check and maintenance	3
Air conditioning compressor - removal and installation	16
Air conditioning condenser - removal and installation	17
Air conditioning evaporator core - removal and installation	18
Air conditioning pressure cycling switch - replacement	19
Air conditioning receiver-drier (desiccant bag) - removal and installation	15
Air conditioning thermostatic expansion valve (TXV) - general information	20
Block heater - replacement	22

	Section
Coolant temperature sending unit - general information	10
Cooling fan and shroud - removal and installation	6
Cooling module - removal and installation	8
Expansion tank - removal and installation	5
General information	1
Heater core - removal and installation	12
Interior cabin heater coolant pump - removal and installation	13
Oil cooler - removal and installation	21
Radiator - removal and installation	7
Thermostat - replacement	4
Troubleshooting	2
Water pump - removal and installation	9

Specifications

Refrigerant type	R-134a

Torque specifications

Ft-lbs (unless otherwise indicated)

Note: *One foot-pound (ft-lb) of torque is equivalent to 12 inch-pounds (in-lbs) of torque. Torque values below approximately 15 foot-pounds are expressed in inch-pounds, because most foot-pound torque wrenches are not accurate at these smaller values.*

Air conditioning compressor bolts	18
Air conditioning condenser bolts	62 in-lbs
Refrigerant line manifold-to-thermostatic expansion valve nut	80 in-lbs
Cooling fan shroud bolts	62-in-lbs
Cooling module	22
Refrigerant line-to-compressor inlet and outlet nuts	133 in-lbs
Refrigerant line-to-condenser inlet (top) nut	71 in-lbs
Refrigerant line-to-condenser outlet (bottom) nut	133 in-lbs
Thermostatic expansion valve bolts	71 in-lbs
Expansion tank bolts	62 in-lbs
Radiator mounting bolts	133 in-lbs
Auxiliary cooler-to-radiator bolts	62 in-lbs
Thermostat housing cover bolts	89 in-lbs
Thermostat housing bolts	
Step 1	71 in-lbs
Step 2	Tighten an additional 45-degrees

Torque specifications (continued)

Note: *One foot-pound (ft-lb) of torque is equivalent to 12 inch-pounds (in-lbs) of torque. Torque values below approximately 15 foot-pounds are expressed in inch-pounds, because most foot-pound torque wrenches are not accurate at these smaller values.*

Water pump bolts
     2.7L engine (see illustration 9.17)
         Step 1 all bolts.. Hand tighten
         Step 2, bolts 1-7... 89 in-lbs
         Step 3, bolts 1-7... Tighten an additional 45-degrees
         Step 4, bolt 8.. 18
     3.5L engines
         Step 1 .... Hand tighten
         Step 2 .... 89 in-lbs
         Step 3 .... Tighten an additional 45-degrees
     5.0L engine
         Step 1 .... Hand tighten
         Step 2 .... 177 in-lbs
         Step 3 .... Tighten an additional 60-degrees
Water pump pulley bolts
     2.7L engine .... 89 in-lbs
     3.5L and 5.0L engines.. 18
Cabin heater coolant pump bolts... 62 in-lbs
Oil cooler
     2.7L V6 engine (bolts) .... 89 in-lbs
     3.5L V6 and 5.0L V8 engines (threaded insert)...................... 43
Block heater.. 30

---

1   General information

Engine cooling system

1   The cooling system consists of a radiator, an expansion tank, a pressure cap (located on the expansion tank), a single thermostat, cooling fans and a belt-driven water pump.

2   The expansion tank (referred to by the manufacturer as a "degas bottle") functions somewhat differently than a conventional recovery tank. Designed to separate any trapped air in the coolant, it is pressurized by the radiator and has a pressure cap on top. The radiator on these models does not have a pressure cap. When the thermostat is closed, no coolant flows in the expansion tank, but when the engine is fully warmed up, coolant flows from the top of the radiator through a small hose that enters the top of the expansion tank, where the air separates and the coolant falls into a coolant reservoir in the bottom of the tank, which is fed to the cooling system through a larger hose connected to the lower radiator hose.

Warning: *Unlike a conventional coolant recovery tank, the pressure cap on the expansion tank should never be opened after the engine has warmed up, because of the danger of severe burns caused by steam or scalding coolant.*

3   Coolant in the left side of the radiator circulates through the lower radiator hose to the water pump, where it is forced through coolant passages in the cylinder block. The coolant then travels up into the cylinder head, circulates around the combustion chambers and valve seats, travels out of the cylinder head past the open thermostat into the upper radiator hose and back into the radiator.

4   When the engine is cold, the thermostat restricts the circulation of coolant to the engine. When the minimum operating temperature is reached, the thermostat begins to open, allowing coolant to return to the radiator.

Transmission cooling systems

5   Vehicles with an automatic transmission are equipped with a external transmission cooler. The cooler is located in front of the radiator and is connected to the cooler by two hoses: one delivers hot transmission fluid to the radiator and the other brings the cooled fluid back to the transmission.

Engine oil cooling system

6   Besides the engine and transmission cooling systems described above, engine heat is also dissipated through an external oil cooler that's integrated into the lubrication system. The oil cooler helps keep engine oil temperatures within design limits under extreme load conditions.

7   The oil cooling system consists of a cooler housing mounted between the oil filter and the filter adapter (3.5L V6 and V8 models) or a cooler mounted on the front cover at the front of the right cylinder head (2.7L V6 models) and a pair of hoses that circulate coolant through the cooler.

Heating system

8   The heating system consists of the heater controls, the heater core, the heater blower assembly (which houses the blower motor and the blower motor resistor), and the hoses connecting the heater core to the engine cooling system. Hot engine coolant is circulated through the heater core. When the heater mode is activated, a flap door opens to expose the heater box to the passenger compartment. A fan switch on the heater controls activates the blower motor, which forces air through the core, heating the air.

Air conditioning system

9   The air conditioning system consists of the condenser, which is mounted in front of the radiator, the evaporator case assembly under the dash, a compressor mounted on the engine, and the plumbing connecting all of the above components.

10   A blower fan forces the warmer air of the passenger compartment through the evaporator core (sort of a radiator-in-reverse), transferring the heat from the air to the refrigerant. The liquid refrigerant boils off into low pressure vapor, taking the heat with it when it leaves the evaporator.

2.2 The cooling system pressure tester is connected in place of the pressure cap on the coolant expansion tank, then pumped up to pressurize the system

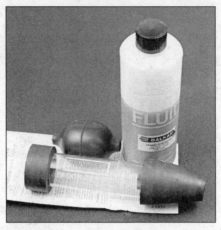

2.5a The combustion leak detector consists of a bulb, syringe and test fluid

2.5b Place the tester over the cooling system filler neck and use the bulb to draw a sample into the tester

2   Troubleshooting

Coolant leaks

1   A coolant leak can develop anywhere in the cooling system, but the most common causes are:

a) A loose or weak hose clamp
b) A defective hose
c) A faulty pressure cap
d) A damaged radiator
e) A bad heater core
f) A faulty water pump
g) A leaking gasket at any joint that carries coolant

2   Coolant leaks aren't always easy to find. Sometimes they can only be detected when the cooling system is under pressure. Here's where a cooling system pressure tester comes in handy. After the engine has cooled completely, the tester is attached in place of the pressure cap on the expansion tank, then pumped up to the pressure value equal to that of the pressure cap rating (see illustration). Now, leaks that only exist when the engine is fully warmed up will become apparent. The tester can be left connected to locate a nagging slow leak.

Coolant level drops, but no external leaks

3   If you find it necessary to keep adding coolant, but there are no external leaks, the probable causes include:

a) A blown head gasket
b) A leaking intake manifold gasket (only on engines that have coolant passages in the manifold) cracked cylinder head or cylinder block

4   Any of the above problems will also usually result in contamination of the engine oil, which will cause it to take on a milkshake-like appearance. A bad head gasket or cracked head or block can also result in engine oil contaminating the cooling system.

5   Combustion leak detectors (also known as block testers) are available at most auto parts stores. These work by detecting exhaust gases in the cooling system, which indicate a compression leak from a cylinder into the coolant. The tester consists of a large bulb-type syringe and bottle of test fluid (see illustration). A measured amount of the fluid is added to the syringe. The syringe is placed over the cooling system filler neck and, with the engine running, the bulb is squeezed and a sample of the gases present in the cooling system are drawn up through the test fluid (see illustration). If any combustion gases are present in the sample taken, the test fluid will change color.

6   If the test indicates combustion gas is present in the cooling system, you can be sure that the engine has a blown head gasket or a crack in the cylinder head or block, and will require disassembly to repair.

Pressure cap

Warning: *Wait until the engine is completely cool before beginning this check.*

7   The cooling system is sealed by a spring-loaded cap, which raises the boiling point of the coolant. If the cap's seal or spring are worn out, the coolant can boil and escape past the cap. With the engine completely cool, remove the cap and check the seal; if it's cracked, hardened or deteriorated in any way, replace it with a new one.

8   Even if the seal is good, the spring might not be; this can be checked with a cooling system pressure tester (see illustration). If the cap can't hold a pressure within approximately 1-1/2 lbs of its rated pressure (which is marked on the cap), replace it with a new one.

9   The cap is also equipped with a vacuum relief spring. When the engine cools off, a vacuum is created in the cooling system. The vacuum relief spring allows air back into the system, which will equalize the pressure and prevent damage to the radiator (the radiator

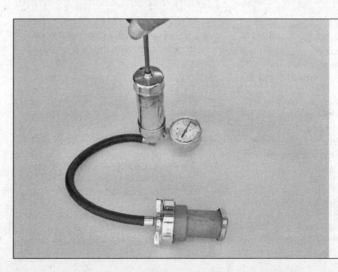

2.8 Checking a cooling system pressure cap with a cooling system pressure tester

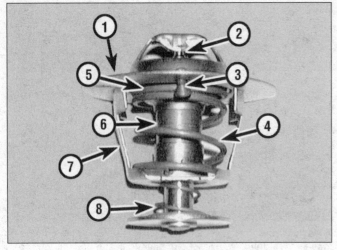

2.10 Typical thermostat:

1	Flange	5	Valve seat
2	Piston	6	Valve
3	Jiggle valve	7	Frame
4	Main coil spring	8	Secondary coil spring

2.24 The water pump weep hole is generally located on the underside of the pump

tanks could collapse if the vacuum is great enough). If, after turning the engine off and allowing it to cool down you notice any of the cooling system hoses collapsing, replace the pressure cap with a new one.

Thermostat

10   Before assuming the thermostat (see illustration) is responsible for a cooling system problem, check the coolant level (see Chapter 1), drivebelt tension (see Chapter 1) and temperature gauge (or light) operation.

11   If the engine takes a long time to warm up (as indicated by the temperature gauge or heater operation), the thermostat is probably stuck open. Replace the thermostat with a new one.

12   If the engine runs hot or overheats, a thorough test of the thermostat should be performed.

13   Definitive testing of the thermostat can only be made when it is removed from the vehicle. If the thermostat is stuck in the open position at room temperature, it is faulty and must be replaced.

Caution: *Do not drive the vehicle without a thermostat. The computer may stay in open loop and emissions and fuel economy will suffer.*

14   To test a thermostat, suspend the (closed) thermostat on a length of string or wire in a pot of cold water.

15   Heat the water on a stove while observing the thermostat. The thermostat should fully open before the water boils.

16   If the thermostat doesn't open and close as specified, or sticks in any position, replace it.

Cooling fan

Electric cooling fan

17   If the engine is overheating and the cooling fan is not coming on when the engine tem-

perature rises to an excessive level, unplug the fan motor electrical connector(s) and connect the motor directly to the battery with fused jumper wires. If the fan motor doesn't come on, replace the motor.

18   If the radiator fan motor is okay, but it isn't coming on when the engine gets hot, the fan relay might be defective. A relay is used to control a circuit by turning it on and off in response to a control decision by the Powertrain Control Module (PCM). These control circuits are fairly complex, and checking them should be left to a qualified automotive technician. Sometimes, the control system can be fixed by simply identifying and replacing a bad relay.

19   Locate the fan relays in the engine compartment fuse/relay box.

20   Test the relay (see Chapter 12).

21   If the relay is okay, check all wiring and connections to the fan motor. Refer to the wiring diagrams at the end of Chapter 12. If no obvious problems are found, the problem could be the Engine Coolant Temperature (ECT) sensor or the Powertrain Control Module (PCM). Have the cooling fan system and circuit diagnosed by a dealer service department or repair shop with the proper diagnostic equipment.

Water pump

22   A failure in the water pump can cause serious engine damage due to overheating.

Drivebelt-driven water pump

23   There are two ways to check the operation of the water pump while it's installed on the engine. If the pump is found to be defective, it should be replaced with a new or rebuilt unit.

24   Water pumps are equipped with weep (or vent) holes (see illustration). If a failure occurs in the pump seal, coolant will leak from

the hole.

25   If the water pump shaft bearings fail, there may be a howling sound at the pump while it's running. Shaft wear can be felt with the drivebelt removed if the water pump pulley is rocked up and down (with the engine off).

Timing chain or timing belt-driven water pump

26   Water pumps driven by the timing chain or timing belt are located underneath the timing chain or timing belt cover.

27   Checking the water pump is limited because of where it is located. However, some basic checks can be made before deciding to remove the water pump. If the pump is found to be defective, it should be replaced with a new or rebuilt unit.

28   One sign that the water pump may be failing is that the heater (climate control) may not work well. Warm the engine to normal operating temperature, confirm that the coolant level is correct, then run the heater and check for hot air coming from the ducts.

29   Check for noises coming from the water pump area. If the water pump impeller shaft or bearings are failing, there may be a howling sound at the pump while the engine is running.

Note: *Be careful not to mistake drivebelt noise (squealing) for water pump bearing or shaft failure.*

30   If you suspect water pump failure due to noise, wear can be confirmed by feeling for play at the pump shaft. This can be done by rocking the drive sprocket on the pump shaft up and down. To do this you will need to remove the tension on the timing chain or belt as well as access the water pump.

All water pumps

31   In rare cases or on high-mileage vehicles, another sign of water pump failure may

be the presence of coolant in the engine oil. This condition will adversely affect the engine in varying degrees.

Note: *Finding coolant in the engine oil could indicate other serious issues besides a failed water pump, such as a blown head gasket or a cracked cylinder head or block.*

32   Even a pump that exhibits no outward signs of a problem, such as noise or leakage, can still be due for replacement. Removal for close examination is the only sure way to tell. Sometimes the fins on the back of the impeller can corrode to the point that cooling efficiency is diminished significantly.

Heater system

33   Little can go wrong with a heater. If the fan motor will run at all speeds, the electrical part of the system is okay. The three basic heater problems fall into the following general categories:

a) *Not enough heat*
b) *Heat all the time*
c) *No heat*

34   If there's not enough heat, the control valve or door is stuck in a partially open position, the coolant coming from the engine isn't hot enough, or the heater core is restricted. If the coolant isn't hot enough, the thermostat in the engine cooling system is stuck open, allowing coolant to pass through the engine so rapidly that it doesn't heat up quickly enough. If the vehicle is equipped with a temperature gauge instead of a warning light, watch to see if the engine temperature rises to the normal operating range after driving for a reasonable distance.

35   If there's heat all the time, the control valve or the door is stuck wide open.

36   If there's no heat, coolant is probably not reaching the heater core, or the heater core is plugged. The likely cause is a collapsed or plugged hose, core, or a frozen heater control valve. If the heater is the type that flows coolant all the time, the cause is a stuck door or a broken or kinked control cable.

Air conditioning system

37   If the cool air output is inadequate: Inspect the condenser coils and fins to make sure they're clear.

a) *Check the compressor clutch for slippage.*
b) *Check the blower motor for proper operation.*
c) *Inspect the blower discharge passage for obstructions.*
d) *Check the system air intake filter for clogging.*

38   If the system provides intermittent cooling air:

a) *Check the circuit breaker, blower switch and blower motor for a malfunction.*
b) *Make sure the compressor clutch isn't slipping.*
c) *Inspect the plenum door to make sure it's operating properly.*

d) *Inspect the evaporator to make sure it isn't clogged.*
e) *If the unit is icing up, it may be caused by excessive moisture in the system, incorrect super heat switch adjustment or low thermostat adjustment.*

39   If the system provides no cooling air:

a) *Inspect the compressor drivebelt. Make sure it's not loose or broken.*
b) *Make sure the compressor clutch engages. If it doesn't, check for a blown fuse.*
c) *Inspect the wire harness for broken or disconnected wires.*
d) *If the compressor clutch doesn't engage, bridge the terminals of the air conditioning pressure switch(es) with a jumper wire; if the clutch now engages, and the system is properly charged, the pressure switch is bad.*
e) *Make sure the blower motor is not disconnected or burned out.*
f) *Make sure the compressor isn't partially or completely seized.*
g) *Inspect the refrigerant lines for leaks.*
h) *Check the components for leaks.*
i) *Inspect the receiver-drier/accumulator or expansion valve/tube for clogged screens.*

40   If the system is noisy:

a) *Look for loose panels in the passenger compartment.*
b) *Inspect the compressor drivebelt. It may be loose or worn.*
c) *Check the compressor mounting bolts. They should be tight.*
d) *Listen carefully to the compressor. It may be worn out.*
e) *Listen to the idler pulley and bearing and the clutch. Either may be defective.*
f) *The winding in the compressor clutch coil or solenoid may be defective.*
g) *The compressor oil level may be low.*
h) *The blower motor fan bushing or the motor itself may be worn out.*
i) *If there is an excessive charge in the system, you'll hear a rumbling noise in the high pressure line, a thumping noise in the compressor, or see bubbles or cloudiness in the sight glass.*
j) *If there's a low charge in the system, you might hear hissing in the evaporator case at the expansion valve, or see bubbles or cloudiness in the sight glass.*

---

3   Air conditioning and heating system - check and maintenance

Air conditioning system

Warning: *The air conditioning system is under high pressure. Do not loosen any hose fittings or remove any components until after the system has been discharged. Air conditioning refrigerant should be properly discharged into an EPA-approved recovery/recycling unit at a dealer service department or an automotive air conditioning repair facility. Always wear eye*

protection when disconnecting air conditioning system fittings.

Caution: *All models covered by this manual use environmentally friendly R-134a. This refrigerant (and its appropriate refrigerant oils) are not compatible with R-12 refrigerant system components and must never be mixed or the components will be damaged.*

Caution: *When replacing entire components, additional refrigerant oil should be added equal to the amount that is removed with the component being replaced. Read the can before adding any oil to the system, to make sure it is compatible with the R-134a system.*

1   The following maintenance checks should be performed on a regular basis to ensure that the air conditioning continues to operate at peak efficiency.

a) *Inspect the condition of the compressor drivebelt. If it is worn or deteriorated, replace it (see Chapter 1).*
b) *Check the drivebelt tension (see Chapter 1).*
c) *Inspect the system hoses. Look for cracks, bubbles, hardening and deterioration. Inspect the hoses and all fittings for oil bubbles or seepage. If there is any evidence of wear, damage or leakage, replace the hose(s).*
d) *Inspect the condenser fins for leaves, bugs and any other foreign material that may have embedded itself in the fins. Use a fin comb or compressed air to remove debris from the condenser.*
e) *Make sure the system has the correct refrigerant charge.*
f) *If you hear water sloshing around in the dash area or have water dripping on the carpet, check the evaporator housing drain tube and insert a piece of wire into the opening to check for blockage (see illustration 3.24).*

2   It's a good idea to operate the system for about ten minutes at least once a month. This is particularly important during the winter months because long term non-use can cause hardening, and subsequent failure, of the seals. Note that using the Defrost function operates the compressor.

3   If the air conditioning system is not working properly, proceed to Step 6 and perform the general checks outlined below.

4   Because of the complexity of the air conditioning system and the special equipment necessary to service it, in-depth troubleshooting and repairs beyond checking the refrigerant charge and the compressor clutch operation are not included in this manual. However, simple checks and component replacement procedures are provided in this chapter. For more complete information on the air conditioning system, refer to the *Haynes Automotive Heating and Air Conditioning Manual.*

5   The most common cause of poor cooling is simply a low system refrigerant charge. If a noticeable drop in system cooling ability occurs, one of the following quick checks will help you determine if the refrigerant level is low.

3.8 Insert a thermometer in a vent, turn on the air conditioning system and wait for it to cool down; depending on the humidity, the output air should be 35 to 40 degrees cooler than the ambient air temperature

3.10 R-134a automotive air conditioning charging kit

3.12 Location of the low-side charging port

Checking the refrigerant charge

6   Warm the engine up to normal operating temperature.

7   Place the air conditioning temperature selector at the coldest setting and put the blower at the highest setting.

8   Insert a thermometer in the center air distribution duct (see illustration) while operating the air conditioning system at its maximum setting - the temperature of the output air should be 35 to 40 degrees F below the ambient air temperature (down to approximately 40 degrees F). If the ambient (outside) air temperature is very high, say 110 degrees F, the duct air temperature may be as high as 60 degrees F, but generally the air conditioning is 35 to 40 degrees F cooler than the ambient air.

9   Further inspection or testing of the system requires special tools and techniques and is beyond the scope of the home mechanic.

Adding refrigerant

Caution: *Make sure any refrigerant, refrigerant oil or replacement component you purchase is designated as compatible with R-134a systems.*

10   Purchase an R-134a automotive charging kit at an auto parts store (see illustration). A charging kit includes a can of refrigerant, a tap valve and a short section of hose that can be attached between the tap valve and the system low side service valve.

Caution: *Never add more than one can of refrigerant to the system. If more refrigerant than that is required, the system should be evacuated and leak tested.*

11   Back off the valve handle on the charging kit and screw the kit onto the refrigerant can, making sure first that the O-ring or rubber seal inside the threaded portion of the kit is in place.

Warning: *Wear protective eyewear when dealing with pressurized refrigerant cans.*

12   Remove the dust cap from the low-side

charging port and attach the hose's quick-connect fitting to the port (see illustration). The fittings on the charging kit are designed to fit only on the low side of the system.

Warning: *DO NOT hook the charging kit hose to the system high side!*

13   Warm up the engine and turn on the air conditioning. Keep the charging kit hose away from the fan and other moving parts.

Note: *The charging process requires the compressor to be running. If the clutch cycles off, you can put the air conditioning switch on High and leave the car doors open to keep the clutch on and compressor working. The compressor can be kept on during the charging by removing the connector from the pressure switch and bridging it with a paper clip or jumper wire during the procedure.*

14   Turn the valve handle on the kit until the stem pierces the can, then back the handle out to release the refrigerant. You should be able to hear the rush of gas. Keep the can upright at all times, but shake it occasionally. Allow stabilization time between each addition.

Note: *The charging process will go faster if you wrap the can with a hot-water-soaked rag to keep the can from freezing up.*

15   If you have an accurate thermometer, you can place it in the center air conditioning duct inside the vehicle and keep track of the output air temperature. A charged system that is working properly should cool down to approximately 40 degrees F. If the ambient (outside) air temperature is very high, say 110 degrees F, the duct air temperature may be as high as 60 degrees F, but generally the air conditioning is 35 to 40 degrees F cooler than the ambient air.

16   When the can is empty, turn the valve handle to the closed position and release the connection from the low-side port. Reinstall the dust cap.

17   Remove the charging kit from the can and store the kit for future use with the piercing valve in the UP position, to prevent inadvertently piercing the can on the next use.

Heating systems

18   If the carpet under the heater core is damp, or if antifreeze vapor or steam is coming through the vents, the heater core is leaking. Remove it (see Section 12) and install a new unit (most radiator shops will not repair a leaking heater core).

19   If the air coming out of the heater vents isn't hot, the problem could stem from any of the following causes:

a) *The thermostat is stuck open, preventing the engine coolant from warming up enough to carry heat to the heater core. Replace the thermostat (see Section 4).*

b) *There is a blockage in the system, preventing the flow of coolant through the heater core.*

c) *Feel both heater hoses at the firewall. They should be hot. If one of them is cold, there is an obstruction in one of the hoses or in the heater core, or the heater control valve is shut.*

d) *Detach the hoses and back flush the heater core with a water hose. If the heater core is clear but circulation is impeded, remove the two hoses and flush them out with a water hose.*

e) *If flushing fails to remove the blockage from the heater core, the core must be replaced (see Section 12).*

Eliminating air conditioning odors

20   Unpleasant odors that often develop in air conditioning systems are caused by the growth of a fungus, usually on the surface of the evaporator core. The warm, humid environment there is a perfect breeding ground for mildew to develop.

21   The evaporator core on most vehicles is difficult to access, and factory dealerships have a lengthy, expensive process for eliminating the fungus by opening up the evaporator case and using a powerful disinfectant and

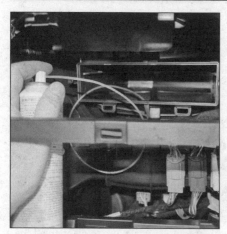

3.23 Remove the cabin air filter (see Chapter 1) and insert the nozzle of the disinfectant can into the housing

3.24 The evaporator drain hose protrudes through a grommet located on the passenger's side of the firewall

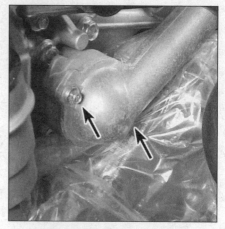

4.5 Remove the thermostat cover mounting bolts - 2.7L engine shown

rinse on the core until the fungus is gone. You can service your own system at home, but it takes something much stronger than basic household germ-killers or deodorizers.

22 Aerosol disinfectants for automotive air conditioning systems are available in most auto parts stores, but remember when shopping for them that the most effective treatments are also the most expensive. The basic procedure for using these sprays is to start by running the system in the RECIRC mode for ten minutes with the blower on its highest speed. Use the highest heat mode to dry out the system and keep the compressor from engaging by disconnecting the wiring connector at the compressor.

23 The disinfectant can usually comes with a long spray hose (see illustration). Insert the nozzle into the vents closest to the evaporator core, and spray according to the manufacturer's recommendations. Try to cover the whole surface of the evaporator core, by aiming the spray up, down and sideways. Follow the manufacturer's recommendations for the length of spray and waiting time between applications.

24 Once the evaporator has been cleaned, the best way to prevent the mildew from coming back again is to make sure your evaporator housing drain tube is clear (see illustration).

Automatic heating and air conditioning systems

25 Some vehicles are equipped with an optional automatic climate control system. This system has its own computer that receives input from various sensors in the heating and air conditioning system. This computer, like the PCM, has self-diagnostic capabilities to help pinpoint problems or faults within the system. Vehicles equipped with automatic heating and air conditioning systems are very complex and considered beyond the scope of the home mechanic.

Vehicles equipped with automatic heating and air conditioning systems should be taken to a dealer service department or other qualified facility for repair.

4 Thermostat - replacement

Warning: *Wait until the engine is completely cool before beginning this procedure.*
Note: *Cover the drivebelts with kitchen plastic-wrap. If coolant gets on the belts it can ruin them.*
1   Disconnect the cable from the negative battery terminal (see Chapter 5, Section 3).
2   Drain the cooling system (see Chapter 1). If the coolant is relatively new and still in good condition, save it and reuse it.
3   Remove the air duct between the air filter housing and the throttle body if necessary (see Chapter 4).
4   Follow the lower radiator hose to the thermostat housing. It's a good idea to cover the drivebelt and components under the thermostat with plastic.

5   Remove the fasteners and detach the thermostat cover (see illustration). If the cover is stuck, tap it with a soft-face hammer to jar it loose. Be prepared for some coolant to spill as the gasket seal is broken.
Note: *The radiator hose can remain attached to the thermostat housing cover.*
6   Note how the thermostat is installed with emphasis on the position of the small jiggle valve (see illustration), which should be at the 12 o'clock position, then remove the thermostat O-ring and thermostat.
7   Clean the housing and cover of all dirt and scale.
8   Position the thermostat into the housing with the jiggle valve at the top. Place a new O-ring gasket against the thermostat, then install the housing cover and tighten the bolts to the torque listed in this Chapter's Specifications.
9   Refill the cooling system (see Chapter 1) and reconnect the battery (see Chapter 5, Section 3).
10   Start the engine and allow it to reach normal operating temperature, then check for leaks and proper thermostat operation.

4.6 Note the locations of the jiggle valve; it should be at the top (12 o'clock position)

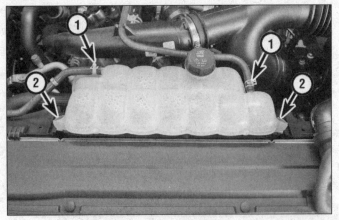

5.2 Expansion tank details

1   *Upper hose clamps*   2   *Mounting bolts*

5.3 Use a small screwdriver to pull the clip out to disconnect the quick-connect hose

6.6 Disconnect the two electrical connectors to the cooling fans

5   Expansion tank - removal and installation

Warning: *The engine must be completely cool before beginning this procedure.*

1   Drain the cooling system (see Chapter 1) below the level of the expansion tank.
2   Using hose clamp pliers, disconnect the clamps and remove the hoses from the ends of the expansion tank (see illustration).
3   Remove the lower hose retaining clip (see illustration) and disconnect the quick-connect hose from the bottom of the expansion tank.
4   Unscrew the expansion tank mounting bolts and remove the expansion tank.
5   Installation is the reverse of removal.
6   Refill the cooling system (see Chapter 1).

6   Cooling fan and shroud - removal and installation

Warning: *Wait until the engine is completely cool before beginning this procedure.*

Removal

1   Disconnect the cable from the negative terminal of the battery (see Chapter 5).
2   Remove the air inlet duct, air filter housing and the air duct between the air filter housing and the throttle body (see Chapter 4).
3   On turbocharged models, remove the charge air cooler outlet pipe (see Chapter 4).
4   On 3.5L non-turbocharged and 5.0L models, remove the upper radiator air deflector plastic push-pin type retainers and deflector.
5   Remove the expansion tank mounting bolts and move the tank out of the way without disconnecting the hoses (see Section 5).
6   Disconnect the electrical connectors to the cooling fans (see illustration).
7   Detach the wiring harness plastic push-pin retainers around the fan shroud and remove the harness from the shroud (see illustration).
8   Remove the two shroud mounting bolts (see illustration) then lift the shroud up a few inches and place a block of wood under the shroud. Working from below, disconnect the lower radiator shield from the shroud by removing the four plastic push-pin retainers

6.7 Use a trim tool to detach the wiring harness plastic push-pin retainers

6.8a Shroud mounting bolt locations

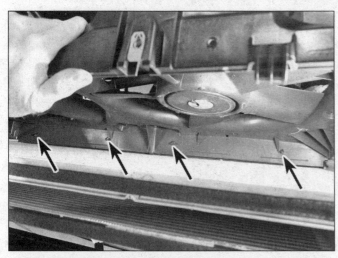

6.8b With the fan shroud pushed back you can see the four retainers that must be removed from below

6.9 Carefully lift the shroud up and out of the vehicle

(see illustration) then remove the shroud.
9   Remove the fan and shroud assembly from the engine compartment (see illustration).
10   Installation is the reverse of removal, making sure to replace any broken plastic retainers.

7   Radiator - removal and installation

Warning: *The air conditioning system is under high pressure. DO NOT loosen any fittings or remove any components until after the system has been discharged. Air conditioning refrigerant should be properly discharged into an EPA-approved container at a dealer service department or an automotive air conditioning repair facility. Always wear eye protection when disconnecting air conditioning system fittings.*

Warning: *The engine must be completely cool when this procedure is performed.*
1   Drain the cooling system (see Chapter 1).
2   Remove the cooling fan and shroud (see Section 6).
3   Disconnect the upper radiator hose and the expansion tank hose from the radiator (see illustration).
4   Remove the lower radiator hose retaining clip (see illustration) and disconnect the quick-connect hose from the bottom of the radiator.
5   Remove the radiator grille (see Chapter 11).
6   Remove the left and right side air deflector push-pin retainers (see illustration) and move the deflectors out of the way.
7   On models without an auxiliary transmission cooler, disconnect the transmission cooler lines from the radiator and plug the openings.

7.3 Disconnect the upper radiator hose and the expansion tank hose clamps, then detach the hoses

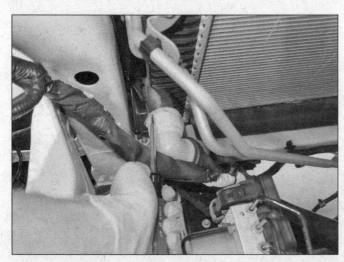

7.4 Use a screwdriver to pull the clip out to disconnect the quick-connect hose

7.6 Locations of the left and right side air deflector push-pin retainers

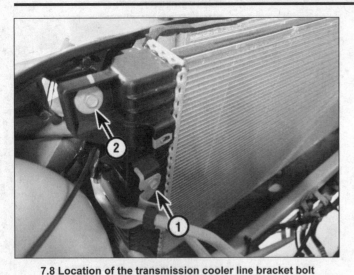

7.8 Location of the transmission cooler line bracket bolt

1   *Transmission cooler line bracket bolt*
2   *Left-side radiator mounting bolt*

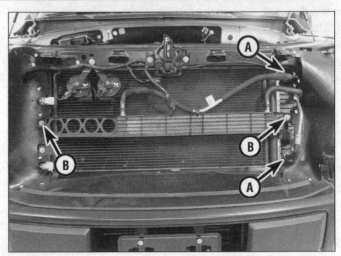

7.9 Disconnect the auxiliary cooler lines (A) then remove the cooler mounting bolts (B)

7.11a Condenser right-side lower mounting bolt location

8   Remove the transmission cooler line bracket bolt (see illustration).
9   On models with an auxiliary transmission cooler, disconnect the transmission cooler lines from the radiator and plug the openings, then remove the auxiliary cooler mounting bolts (see illustration) and secure the cooler out of the way.
10   Remove the radiator mounting bolts and tilt the radiator backwards.
11   Remove the condenser mounting bolts (see illustrations).
12   Depress the condenser retaining tabs then lift the condenser up to separate it from the radiator (see illustration).
13   Lift the radiator up and out of the vehicle, taking care not to damage the fins on the radiator or the condenser.
14   Installation is the reverse of removal, making sure the condenser clips into its brackets on the radiator and the radiator is

seated in the lower grommets (see illustration). Tighten the mounting bolts to the torque listed in this Chapter's Specifications.
15   Fill the cooling system with the proper mixture of antifreeze, and also check the automatic transmission and power steering fluid levels.
16   Start the engine and allow it to reach normal operating temperature, then check for leaks.

8   Cooling module - removal and installation

Warning: *The air conditioning system is under high pressure. DO NOT loosen any fittings or remove any components until after the system has been discharged. Air conditioning refrigerant should be properly discharged into an EPA-*

7.11b Condenser right-side upper mounting bolt location

7.12 Depress the locking tabs inward and lift the condenser up and out of its mounts on the radiator

7.14 Make sure the radiator is seated properly into the grommets

8.16 Cooling module mounting bolt locations (left-side shown, right side identical)

9.5 Water pump pulley mounting bolts

9.9 Squeeze the clamp and slide it back on the hose, then detach the hose from the water pump

approved container at a dealer service department or an automotive air conditioning repair facility. Always wear eye protection when disconnecting air conditioning system fittings.
Warning: *The engine must be completely cool when this procedure is performed.*
Note: *The cooling module consists of the radiator, air conditioning condenser and transmission fluid cooler. These components can all be removed as a unit for certain procedures where improved access to the front of the engine is required.*

1   Have the air conditioning system discharged by a licensed air conditioning technician.
2   Drain the cooling system (see Chapter 1).
3   Remove the air filter housing and outlet pipe.
4   Remove the expansion tank mounting bolts and move the tank out of the way without disconnecting the hoses.
5   Disconnect the electrical connectors to the fan motors and the wiring harness retainers from the shroud.
6   Remove both headlight housings (see Chapter 12).
7   Remove the grille (see Chapter 11).
8   Remove the hood latch and cable (see Chapter 11).
9   Remove the side air deflector push-pins and remove the side air deflectors (see Section 7).
10   Remove the lower air deflector push-pins and remove the air deflector from the front bumper.
11   Disconnect the electrical connector and remove the connector bracket bolt from the frame. Then disconnect the electrical connector horn and impact sensors and move the harness out of the way.
12   Disconnect the lines to the condenser (see Section 17).
13   Disconnect the hoses to the radiator (see Section 7).
14   Disconnect the transmission cooler line brackets and quick-connect couplings (V6 models) or standard spring clamps (V8 models) then separate the lines (see Chapter 7A).

15   Disconnect the electrical connectors at the shroud, to the charge air cooler (CAC) (see Chapter 4) and impact sensors (see Chapter 12).
16   Remove the cooling module nuts and bolts (see illustration).
17   With the help of an assistant, remove the cooling module.
18   Installation is the reverse of removal. When installing the module, tighten the fasteners to the torque listed in this Chapter's Specifications.
19   Fill the system with the proper mixture of antifreeze, and also check the automatic transmission and power steering fluid levels.
20   Start the engine and allow it to reach normal operating temperature, then check for leaks.
21   Have the air conditioning system recharged by the shop that discharged it.

9   Water pump - removal and installation

Removal

Warning: *Wait until the engine is completely cool before beginning this procedure.*
1   Disconnect the cable from the negative battery terminal (see Chapter 5).

2   Drain the cooling system (see Chapter 1).
3   Remove the air filter housing and inlet and outlet ducts (see Chapter 4).

2.7L engine
4   Remove the charge air cooler outlet pipe (see Chapter 4).
5   Loosen the water pump pulley bolts (see illustration).
6   Remove the drivebelt (see Chapter 1).
7   Remove the water pump pulley bolts and pulley.
8   Remove the thermostat (see Section 4).
9   Disconnect the hose from the water pump (see illustration).
10   Remove the water pump mounting bolts (see illustration), then pull the water pump forward to disconnect the coolant inlet pipe grommet on the backside of the water pump. Take note of the installed positions of the various bolts.
Note: *If the water pump sticks, dislodge it with a soft-face hammer or a hammer and a block of wood, then pull the pump forward.*
11   Remove the grommet from the coolant intake pipe or back of the water pump.
12   Before installation, remove and clean the mating surface on the front cover (and water pump, if the same pump is to be installed).
13   Inspect the grommet and sealing surface of water pump housing, the front cover and the coolant intake pipe for dirt and/or debris.

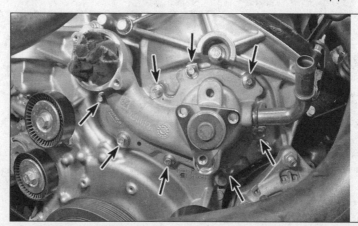

9.10 Water pump mounting bolts

Clean them thoroughly before reassembly.

14   Lubricate the inside and outside of a new grommet with clean antifreeze, then press the grommet (see illustration) into the back side of the pump until the edge is flush with the pump housing.

15   Lubricate the new O-ring gasket with clean antifreeze, then install it into the groove along the front cover sealing surface (see illustration).

16   Verify the dowel pins are still remaining in the front cover.

17   Install the water pump (see illustration) and tighten the bolts by hand evenly, then tighten the bolts to the torque listed in this Chapter's Specifications.

18   Remove the expansion tank mounting bolts and move the tank out of the way without disconnecting the hoses.

19   Disconnect the four hoses to the thermostat housing, then remove the housing bolts and housing from the front cover.

20   If the water pump pulley bolts aren't too tight, you might be able to loosen them now, using the drivebelt to hold the pulley. If that doesn't work, you'll have to hold the pulley with a strap wrench after you remove the drivebelt.

21   Remove the drivebelt (see Chapter 1).

Note: *Cover the air conditioning compressor drivebelt with kitchen plastic wrap. If coolant gets on the belt it can ruin it.*

22   Remove the pulley bolts and remove the pulley. If you were unable to loosen the water pump pulley bolts with the drivebelt installed, use a strap wrench to hold the pulley as you loosen the bolts.

23   Remove the hose retaining clip and disconnect the quick-connect hose from the bottom of the expansion tank and heater hose at the engine.

24   Remove the water pump retaining bolts and remove the water pump. Take note of the installed positions of the various bolts.

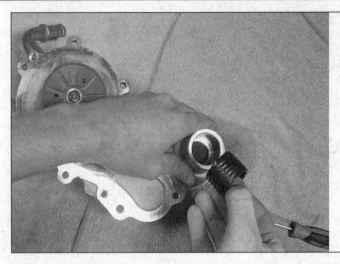

9.14 Install the new grommet into the back of the pump (even if it had stuck on the coolant pipe)

Note: *If the water pump sticks, dislodge it with a soft-face hammer or a hammer and a block of wood.*

25   Before installation, remove and clean the mating surface on the front cover (and water pump, if the same pump is to be installed).

26   Lubricate a new O-ring seal with clean antifreeze and install it to the water pump. On 3.5L V6 models also install a new gasket.

27   Install the water pump or water pump and tighten the bolts by hand evenly, then tighten the bolts to the torque listed in this Chapter's Specifications.

All engines

28   The remainder of installation is the reverse of removal.

29   Refill the cooling system (see Chapter 1).

30   Start the engine and make sure there are no leaks. Check the level frequently during the first few weeks of operation to ensure there are no leaks and that the coolant level is stable.

10   Coolant temperature sending unit - general information

1   The coolant temperature indicator system consists of a temperature gauge/indicator mounted in the dash and a Cylinder Head Temperature (CHT) sensor or an Engine Coolant Temperature (ECT) sensor (2.7L models) (see Chapter 6).

Note: *2.7L engine models, use both a Cylinder Head Temperature (CHT) sensor and a Engine Coolant Temperature (ECT) sensor.*

2   These sensors also serve as the sensor(s) for the Powertrain Control Module (PCM).

3   If an overheating indication occurs, check the coolant level in the system. Make sure that the wiring between the gauge and the sensor(s) is secure and all fuses are intact.

9.15 Make sure the new O-ring gasket seats properly in the front cover groove

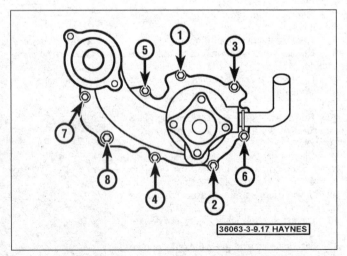

9.17 2.7L engine water pump bolt tightening sequence 3.5L V6 and 5.0L V8 engines

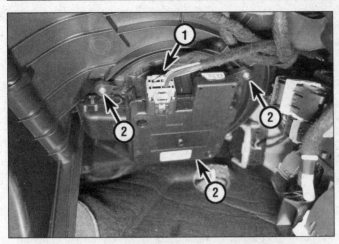

11.5 Disconnect the electrical connector from the blower motor control module (1), then remove the mounting screws (2)

12.3 Press the plastic tabs on the heater hose fittings to release the heater hoses

11 Air conditioning and heater blower/control module - replacement

Note: *The blower motor and the blower motor speed control module have been combined into one assembly called the blower motor control module.*

1 Disconnect the cable from the negative battery terminal (see Chapter 5).
2 Remove the passenger's side lower trim panel plastic push-pins and panel.
3 Remove the passenger's side kick-panel (see Chapter 11).
4 On 4WD models, remove the transfer case control module (TCCM) (see Chapter 7B).
5 Disconnect the electrical connector from the blower motor module (see illustration).
6 Remove the blower motor/control module screws and separate the module from the housing.
7 Installation is the reverse of removal.

12 Heater core - removal and installation

Warning: *The vehicles covered by this manual are equipped with a Supplemental Restraint System (SRS), more commonly known as airbags. Always disable the airbag system before working in the vicinity of any airbag system components to avoid the possibility of accidental deployment of the airbag, which could cause personal injury (see Chapter 12).*

Note: *The heater and evaporator cores are mounted in a large housing under the instrument panel. The instrument panel must be removed for access to the housing, and this is a difficult procedure for the home mechanic, involving many hard-to-find/reach fasteners and electrical connectors.*

Removal

1 Have the air conditioning system discharged by a licensed air conditioning technician.
2 Drain the cooling system (see Chapter 1).
3 Detach the heater hoses from the heater

core pipes on the engine compartment side of the firewall (see illustration). Plug the heater core pipes to prevent leakage when the HVAC housing is removed.
4 Remove the nut and detach the refrigerant lines from the Thermostatic Expansion Valve (TXV) at the firewall (see illustration). Plug the lines and ports. Also remove the HVAC housing nut accessible from the engine compartment side of the firewall.
5 Remove the instrument panel (see Chapter 11).
6 Detach all electrical connectors and wiring harness clips from the HVAC housing.
7 Unscrew the nuts securing the HVAC housing to the firewall and remove the HVAC housing from the passenger compartment (see illustration).

Note: *It's a good idea to cover the floor with plastic sheeting in case some coolant leaks out of the heater core when the HVAC housing is removed.*

Note: *On models with a duct that leads to the rear seating area, detach the HVAC housing from the firewall and tilt the top to the rear do detach it from the duct.*

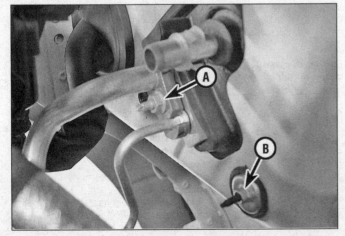

12.4 Refrigerant line manifold nut at the TXV (A) and HVAC housing mounting nut (B)

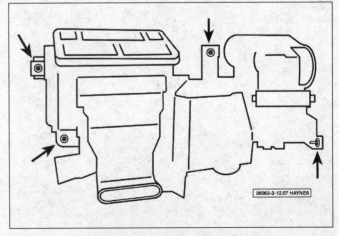

12.7 HVAC housing-to-firewall nut locations

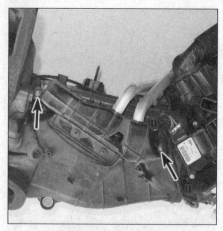

12.8a Remove the heater core cover screws. . .

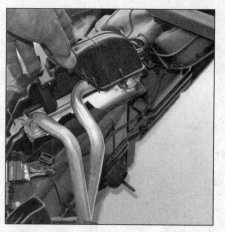

12.8b. . . then separate the cover from the case - heater/evaporator case removed for clarity

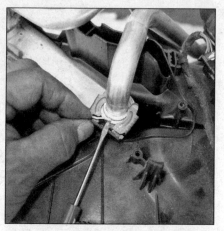

12.9a Use a small screwdriver to pry up the clip lock, then remove the clip…

12.9b … and separate the tubes from the heater core

12.10 Lift the heater core out of the case and replace the O-rings on the heater core tubes

8   Remove the heater core cover screws and cover (see illustrations).
9   Disconnect the heater core tube clips at the heater core and disconnect the tubes from the heater core (see illustrations). Always replace the O-ring and clips with new ones.
10   Remove the heater core from the case (see illustration).

Installation

11   Installation is the reverse of removal, noting for the following:
  a) Replace the heater core tube O-rings and the tube clips with new ones.
  b) Fill the cooling system with the correct type and amount of coolant (see Chapter 1).
  c) Start the engine and check for leaks.
  d) Have the air conditioning system recharged by the shop that discharged it.

13   Interior cabin heater coolant pump - removal and installation

Note: The cabin heater coolant pump is located directly above the thermostat housing. Only 2.7L and 3.5L turbocharged models are equipped with a cabin heater coolant pump.

Removal

Warning: Wait until the engine is completely cool before beginning this procedure.
1   Disconnect the cable from the negative battery terminal (see Chapter 5).
2   Drain the cooling system (see Chapter 1).
3   Disconnect and remove the air filter housing outlet hose (see Chapter 4).
4   Disconnect the electrical connector from the coolant pump.
5   Disconnect the hoses from the coolant pump (see illustration).
6   Remove the cabin heater coolant pump mounting bolts and remove the pump.
7   Install the cabin heater coolant pump bolts by hand, then tighten the bolts to the torque listed in this Chapter's Specifications.

13.5 Interior cabin heater coolant pump details

1 Hose clamp and hoses
2 Pump motor electrical connector
3 Pump bracket mounting bolts - 1 of 2 shown

15.3 Unscrew the cap to access the snap-ring and inner receiver-drier plug

16.8 Unplug the electrical connector from the compressor clutch field coil

16.9 To disconnect the inlet and outlet lines from the compressor, remove the manifold nuts; be sure to replace the manifold O-rings before reattaching them

8   The remainder of installation is the reverse of removal.
9   Refill the cooling system (see Chapter 1).
10   Start the engine and make sure there are no leaks. Check the level frequently during the first few weeks of operation to ensure there are no leaks and that the coolant level is stable.

14 Air conditioning and heater control module - removal and installation

Warning: *The vehicles covered by this manual are equipped with a Supplemental Restraint System (SRS), more commonly known as airbags. Always disable the airbag system before working in the vicinity of any airbag system components to avoid the possibility of accidental deployment of the airbag, which could cause personal injury (see Chapter 12).*
Note: *The air conditioning heater control module is integrated into the Front Controls Interface Module (FCIM) and is serviceable only as part of the FCIM (see Chapter 12, Section 13).*
Warning: *If you are replacing the FCIM (Front Control Interface Module) upload the FCIM configuration into a scan tool so that it can be reloaded into the replacement unit. This will have to be done by the appropriately equipped repair facility.*

15 Air conditioning receiver-drier (desiccant bag) - removal and installation

Warning: *The air conditioning system is under high pressure. DO NOT loosen any fittings or remove any components until after the system has been discharged. Air conditioning refrigerant should be properly discharged into an EPA-approved container at a dealer service department or an automotive air condition-*

ing repair facility. Always wear eye protection when disconnecting air conditioning system fittings.
Note: *These vehicles are not equipped with a traditional receiver-drier. Instead, a desiccant bag (cartridge) is built into the left side of the condenser. It should be replaced whenever the compressor is replaced or whenever a component has been replaced because of a leak in the system.*
1   Have the air conditioning system discharged by a licensed air conditioning technician.
2   Remove the condenser (see Section 17).
3   Remove the plastic receiver-drier cap (see illustration).
4   Once the cap is removed, depress the receiver drier plug slightly and use a small screwdriver to remove the snap-ring.
5   Screw a M5 mm bolt into the drier plug and pull the receiver/drier cartridge out of the condenser. Cap the opening.
6   Installation is the reverse of removal.
7   Take the vehicle to the shop that discharged it and have the system evacuated and recharged.

16 Air conditioning compressor - removal and installation

Removal
Warning: *The air conditioning system is under high pressure. DO NOT loosen any fittings or remove any components until after the system has been discharged. Air conditioning refrigerant should be properly discharged into an EPA-approved container at a dealer service department or an automotive air conditioning repair facility. Always wear eye protection when disconnecting air conditioning system fittings.*
1   Have the air conditioning system discharged by a licensed air conditioning technician.

16.10 Air conditioning compressor mounting bolts

2   Disconnect the cable from the negative battery terminal, (see Chapter 5).
3   Remove the drivebelt(s) (see Chapter 1).
4   Loosen the right-front wheel lug nuts, then raise the front of the vehicle and support it securely it on jackstands. Remove the wheel.
5   On 5.0L models, remove the skid plates and splash shields, if equipped.
6   Remove the right-side inner fender splash shield (see Chapter 11).
7   On 3.5L turbocharged engines, remove the turbocharger inlet tube (see Chapter 4).
8   Disconnect the electrical connector from the compressor clutch field coil (see illustration).
9   Disconnect the compressor inlet and outlet lines from the compressor (see illustration). Remove and discard the old O-rings.
10   Remove the compressor mounting bolts (see illustration) and remove the compressor.

Installation
11   If a new compressor is being installed, follow the directions with the compressor

17.6 To disconnect the refrigerant inlet and outlet lines from the condenser, remove these nuts

17.8a Condenser lower mounting bolt location…

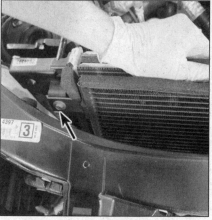

17.8b … and upper mounting bolt location

regarding the draining of excess oil prior to installation.

12   The clutch may have to be transferred from the original to the new compressor.

13   Before reconnecting the inlet and outlet lines to the compressor, replace all manifold O-rings and lubricate them with refrigerant oil.

14   Have the system evacuated, recharged and leak tested by the shop that discharged it.

15   Installation is otherwise the reverse of removal.

17   Air conditioning condenser - removal and installation

Warning: *The air conditioning system is under high pressure. DO NOT loosen any fittings or remove any components until after the system has been discharged. Air conditioning refrigerant should be properly discharged into an EPA-approved container at a dealer service department or an automotive air conditioning repair facility. Always wear eye protection when disconnecting air conditioning system fittings.*

Warning: *Wait until the engine is completely cool before beginning this procedure.*

1   Have the air conditioning system discharged by a licensed air conditioning technician.

2   Remove the grille (see Chapter 11).

3   Remove the air filter housing and inlet and outlet ducts (see Chapter 4).

4   Remove the air deflector push-pin retainers (see illustration 7.6) and move the deflectors out of the way.

5   Remove the transmission auxiliary cooler mounting bolts (see illustration 7.9) and secure the cooler out of the way. It is not necessary to disconnect the lines from the cooler.

6   Disconnect the refrigerant inlet and outlet line nuts, then detach the lines from the condenser (see illustration). Remove and discard the old O-rings.

7   Remove the radiator fasteners and tilt the cooling module backwards.

8   Remove the condenser mounting bolts (see illustrations).

9   Depress the condenser retaining tabs (see illustration) then lift the condenser up and

out of the vehicle, taking care not to damage the fins on the radiator or condenser. If you're going to reinstall the same condenser, store it with the line fittings facing up to prevent oil from draining out.

10   If you're going to install a new condenser, pour one ounce of refrigerant oil of the correct type into it prior to installation.

11   Before reconnecting the refrigerant lines to the condenser, be sure to coat a pair of new O-rings with refrigerant oil, install them in the refrigerant line fittings and then tighten the condenser inlet and outlet nuts to the torque listed in this Chapter's Specifications.

12   Installation is otherwise the reverse of removal, making sure the tabs on the condenser lock into the brackets on the radiator (see illustration).

13   Have the system evacuated, recharged and leak tested by the shop that discharged it.

18   Air conditioning evaporator core - removal and installation

Note: *At the time of writing, the manufacturer stated that the evaporator is not removable from the Heating, Ventilation and Air Conditioning (HVAC) housing and must be replaced as a unit with the housing. Refer to Section 12 for HVAC housing and heater core removal and installation procedure.*

19   Air conditioning pressure cycling switch - replacement

Warning: *A Schrader valve prevents refrigerant loss during pressure cycling switch replacement. Wear protective eyewear when removing the switch as a precaution, however.*
Note: *The pressure cycling switch threaded into a fitting on the compressor-to-condenser discharge line at the right side of the engine compartment, next to the battery box.*

17.9 Depress the locking tab inwards and lift the condenser up and out

17.12 Make sure the tabs on the condenser are seated into the bracket on the radiator (lower tab shown)

19.1 To remove the air conditioning pressure cycling switch, unplug the electrical connector and unscrew the switch from the refrigerant line

20.2 The Thermostatic Expansion Valve is located on the firewall - heater hoses removed for clarity

21.4 Disconnect the two coolant hoses - 2.7L model shown, other models similar

1   Unplug the electrical connector from the pressure cycling switch (see illustration).
Caution: *Hold the boss on the refrigerant line with a wrench when unscrewing the switch to prevent damage to the refrigerant line.*
2   Unscrew the pressure cycling switch from the refrigerant line.
3   Lubricate the switch O-ring with clean refrigerant oil of the correct type.
4   Screw the new switch onto the refrigerant line fitting until hand tight, then tighten it securely.
5   Reconnect the electrical connector.

20 Air conditioning thermostatic expansion valve (TXV) - general information

Warning: *The air conditioning system is under high pressure. DO NOT loosen any hose fittings or remove any components until the system has been discharged. Air conditioning refrigerant must be properly discharged into an EPA-approved recovery/recycling unit by a dealer service department or an automotive*

air conditioning repair facility. Always wear eye protection when disconnecting air conditioning system fittings.
1   There are several ways that air conditioning systems convert the high-pressure liquid refrigerant from the compressor to lower-pressure vapor. The conversion takes place at the air conditioning evaporator; the evaporator is chilled as the refrigerant passes through, cooling the airflow through the evaporator for delivery to the vents. The conversion is usually accomplished by a sudden change in the tubing size. Many vehicles have a removable controlled orifice in one of the refrigerant lines at the firewall.
2   The models covered by this manual use a Thermostatic Expansion Valve (TXV) that accomplishes the same thing as a controlled orifice (see illustration).
3   Have the air conditioning system discharged by a licensed air conditioning technician.
4   Loosen the right-front wheel lug nuts, then raise the vehicle and support it securely on jackstands. Remove the wheel.
5   Remove the right-side inner fender splash shield (see Chapter 11).

6   Remove the refrigerant manifold line bracket fastener below the battery.
7   Remove the refrigerant line manifold mounting nut, disconnect the refrigerant line manifold from the TXV at the firewall and remove the O-rings.
8   Remove the TXV valve Allen head bolts, separate the TXV valve from the evaporator and remove the O-rings.
9   Installation is the reverse of removal, making sure to use new O-rings.
10   Have the system evacuated, recharged and leak tested by the shop that discharged it.

21 Oil cooler - removal and installation

Warning: *Wait until the engine is completely cool before beginning this procedure.*
Note: *On 2.7L engines the oil cooler is located on the front cover, at the front of the right-side cylinder head. On all other models it is located at the lower left front of the engine.*
1   Raise the vehicle and support it securely on jackstands.
2   Drain the engine coolant (see Chapter 1).
3   Remove the oil filter (see Chapter 1).
4   Disconnect the two coolant hoses from the oil cooler (see illustration).

2.7L V6 engines
5   Remove the oil cooler mounting bolts (see illustration) and remove the oil cooler from the front cover.
6   Remove the seal from the front cover.
7   Install a new seal into the front cover.
8   Install the oil cooler and mounting bolts then tighten the bolts to the torque listed this Chapter's Specifications.
9   Remaining installation is the reverse of removal, refill the cooling system and check the engine oil level (see Chapter 1).

21.5 Oil cooler mounting bolt locations

3.5L V6 and 5.0L V8 engines

10 The oil cooler is attached to the engine by the same large threaded tube that the oil filter is screwed onto. Remove the oil cooler threaded tube and remove the oil cooler assembly.

11 Installation is the reverse of removal. Be sure to use a new O-ring gasket between the oil cooler and the engine.

12 Refill the cooling system and check the engine oil level (see Chapter 1).

22 Block heater - replacement

Warning: *The engine must be completely cool before beginning this procedure.*

Note: *The block heater is located on the left side of the engine block (on models so equipped).*

1 Loosen the left-front wheel lug nuts, then raise the front of the vehicle and support it securely on jackstands. Remove the wheel and the inner fender splash shield (see Chapter 11).

Note: *It is not necessary to remove the wheel on V8 models.*

22.6 Location of the block heater. Not all models are equipped with a block heater, such as this one; a plug is installed in its place (2.7L engine shown, others similar)

2 Drain the cooling system (see Chapter 1).

3 Turbocharged models: Remove the air filter housing and outlet pipe, and the left-side turbocharger inlet duct (see Chapter 4).

4 V8 models: Remove the under-vehicle splash shields and skid plates, if equipped.

5 4WD V8 models: Remove the alternator (see Chapter 5).

6 Disconnect the electrical connector from the block heater, then unscrew the block heater from the cylinder block (see illustration).

7 Installation is the reverse of the removal procedure. Tighten the block heater to the torque listed in this Chapter's Specifications.

8 Refill the cooling system (see Chapter 1).

Notes

Notes

Chapter 4
Fuel and exhaust systems

Contents

	Section
Accelerator Pedal Position (APP) sensor - replacement and adjustment	3
Air bypass valve - removal and installation	18
Air filter housing - removal and installation	14
Exhaust system servicing - general information	21
Fuel level sending unit - replacement	13
Fuel lines and fittings - general information and disconnection	6
Fuel pressure regulator - removal and installation	12
Fuel pressure relief procedure	4
Fuel Pump Driver Module (FPDM) - replacement	11
Fuel pump/fuel pressure - check	5

	Section
Fuel pump/fuel pump module - removal and installation	9
Fuel rails and injectors - removal and installation	16
Fuel tank - cleaning and repair	8
Fuel tank - removal and installation	7
General information and precautions	1
High-pressure fuel pump - removal and installation	10
Intercooler - removal and installation	20
Throttle body - removal and installation	15
Troubleshooting	2
Turbocharger(s) - removal and installation	17
Wastegate control actuator - replacement and adjustment	19

Specifications

Fuel system

Fuel system pressure (engine running at idle)
- 2.7L and 3.5L turbocharged models ... 51 to 87 psi (low pressure system)*
- 3.5L non-turbo and 5.0L models ... 51 to 67 psi
- Injector resistance (approximate) ... Unspecified**

*NEVER attempt to check fuel pressure on the high-pressure side of direct-injected systems.
**Although unspecified, testing can be done for comparison purposes and to check for an open or shorted coil.

Torque specifications

Ft-lbs (unless otherwise indicated)

Note: *One foot-pound (ft-lb) of torque is equivalent to 12 inch-pounds (in-lbs) of torque. Torque values below approximately 15 foot-pounds are expressed in inch-pounds, because most foot-pound torque wrenches are not accurate at these smaller values.*

Throttle body bolts
  2.7L engine .... 89 in-lbs
  3.5L engines
    Step 1 .... 89 in-lbs
    Step 2 .... Tighten an additional 90 degrees
  5.0L engine
    Step 1 .... 62 in-lbs
    Step 2 .... Tighten an additional 60 degrees
Fuel rail mounting bolts
  2.7L engine 18
  3.5L non-turbo engine .... 89 in-lbs
  3.5L turbocharged engine
    DI injection fuel rail
      Step 1 .... 89 in-lbs
      Step 2 .... Tighten an additional 45 degrees
    Port injection fuel rail .... 89 in-lbs
  5.0L engine
    Step 1 .... 89 in-lbs
    Step 2 .... Tighten an additional 90 degrees
Fuel rail pressure/temperature sensors
  2.7L engine
    Step 1 .... 44 in-lbs
    Step 2 .... Tighten an additional 19 degrees
  3.5L engine 24
Fuel tank strap bolts 30
High-pressure fuel pump nuts
  2.7L engine
    Step 1 .... 177 in-lbs
    Step 2 .... Tighten an additional 45 degrees
  3.5L turbocharged engine
    Step 1 .... 89 in-lbs
    Step 2 .... Tighten an additional 45 degrees
High-pressure fuel pump mounting plate bolt (3.5L turbocharged engine)   89 in-lbs
High-pressure fuel feed lines
  Fittings
    Step 1 .... 62 in-lbs
    Step 2 .... 89 in-lbs
    Step 3 .... Tighten an additional 25 to 30 degrees
  Mounting bolts (3.5L turbocharged engine)
    Step 1 .... 89 in-lbs
    Step 2 .... Tighten an additional 45 degrees
Turbocharger mounting flange bolts/nuts
  2.7L engine
    Step 1 - Bolt 44
    Step 2 - Front Nut 44
    Step 3 - Rear Nut 27
    Step 4 - Bolt 44
    Step 5 - Front Nut 44
    Step 6 - Rear Nut 27
  3.5L turbocharged engine
    2016 and earlier 24
    2017 and later
      Step 1 .... 177 in-lbs
      Step 2 24
Turbocharger exhaust flange nuts 30

1 General information and precautions

Fuel system warnings

Warning: *Gasoline is extremely flammable and repairing fuel system components can be dangerous. Consider your automotive repair knowledge and experience before attempting repairs, which may be better suited for a professional mechanic.*

- Don't smoke or allow open flames or bare light bulbs near the work area
- Don't work in a garage with a gas-type appliance (water heater, clothes dryer)
- Use fuel-resistant gloves. If any fuel spills on your skin, wash it off immediately with soap and water
- Clean up spills immediately
- Do not store fuel-soaked rags where they could ignite
- Prior to disconnecting any fuel line, you must relieve the fuel pressure (see Section 4)
- Wear safety glasses
- Have a proper fire extinguisher on hand

Fuel system

1 This Chapter covers the removal and installation procedures for the important parts of the air intake, fuel and exhaust systems. Because emission control systems are integral parts of the engine management system, there are many cross-references to Chapter 6. Information on the engine management system, information sensors and output actuators is also in Chapter 6.

2 The air intake system consists of the air filter housing, the air intake duct, the throttle body, and the intake manifold. Incoming air passes through the air filter element, the air intake duct, the throttle body, the intake manifold plenum and the intake manifold runners before being mixed with fuel sprayed into the intake ports by the fuel injectors.

3 The Sequential Fuel Injection (SFI) system consists of the fuel tank, a 2-speed electric fuel pump/fuel level sending unit module mounted inside the tank, the fuel pressure regulator (integral with the fuel pump module), a fuel pump flow control module, the fuel rail, the fuel injectors, and the metal and flexible fuel lines that connect the various components of the SFI system. 3.5L non-turbo and 5.0L models are equipped with the SFI system.

4 The Direct Injection (DI) system consists of the fuel tank, a 2-speed electric fuel pump/fuel level sending unit module mounted inside the tank, the fuel pressure regulator (integral with the fuel pump module), a fuel pump flow control module, the hi-pressure fuel pump, the fuel rail, the fuel injectors, and the metal and flexible fuel lines that connect the various components of the DI system. 2.7L and 3.5L turbocharged models are equipped with the DI system.

5 The lifetime fuel filter is part of the fuel pump module and is not serviceable.

6 Fuel is circulated from the fuel pump to the fuel rail through fuel lines running along the underside of the vehicle. Various sections of the fuel line are either rigid metal or nylon, or flexible fuel hose. The various sections of the fuel hose are connected either by quick-connect fittings or threaded metal fittings.

Exhaust system

7 The exhaust system consists of the exhaust manifold, catalytic converter, muffler, tailpipe and all connecting pipes, flanges and clamps. The catalytic converter is an emission control device added to the exhaust system to reduce pollutants.

2 Troubleshooting

Fuel pump

1 The fuel pump is located inside the fuel tank. Sit inside the vehicle with the windows closed, turn the ignition key to On (not Start) and listen for the sound of the fuel pump as it's briefly activated. You will only hear the sound for a second or two, but that sound tells you that the pump is working. Alternatively, have an assistant listen at the fuel filler cap.

2 If the pump does not come on, check the fuel pump fuse(s) and fuel pump relay (see illustration). If the fuse(s) and relay are okay, check the wiring back to the Fuel Pump Driver Module (FPDM - see Section 11) and fuel pump. If the fuses, relay and wiring are okay, the fuel pump is probably defective. If the pump runs continuously with the ignition key in the On position, the Powertrain Control Module (PCM) is probably defective. Have the PCM checked by a professional mechanic.

Fuel injection system

Caution: *The following procedure applies to the complete SFI system and the fuel system before the high-pressure pump on DI systems. DI systems operate under very high pressures and require special tools to diagnose correctly.*

Note: *The following procedure is based on the assumption that the fuel pump is working and the fuel pressure is adequate (see Section 5).*

3 Check all electrical connectors that are related to the system. Check the ground wire connections for tightness.

4 Verify that the battery is fully charged (see Chapter 5).

5 Inspect the air filter element (see Chapter 1).

6 Check all fuses related to the fuel system (see Chapter 12).

7 Check the air induction system between the throttle body and the intake manifold for air leaks. Also inspect the condition of all vacuum hoses connected to the intake manifold and to the throttle body.

8 Remove the air intake duct from the throttle body and look for dirt, carbon, varnish, or other residue in the throttle body, particularly around the throttle plate. If it's dirty, clean it with carb cleaner, a toothbrush and a clean

2.2 Fuel system related underhood fuse/ relay box details

1 *Fuel pump relay 51 (supplies power to the Fuel Pump Control Module)*
2 *Fuel pump relay fuse F56 (20 amp; always hot)*
3 *Fuel pump fuse F9 (30 amp; not all models)*

2.9 An automotive stethoscope is used to listen to the fuel injectors in operation

shop towel.

9 With the engine running, place an automotive stethoscope against each injector, one at a time, and listen for a clicking sound that indicates operation (see illustration).

Warning: *Stay clear of the drivebelt and any rotating or hot components.*

Note: *This check can only be performed on the V8 engine (on the V6 engines the injectors are concealed).*

10 If you can hear the injectors operating, but the engine is misfiring, the electrical circuits are functioning correctly, but the injectors might be dirty or clogged. Try a commercial injector cleaning product (available at auto parts stores). If cleaning the injectors doesn't help, replace the injector(s).

11 If an injector is not operating (it makes no sound), disconnect the injector electrical

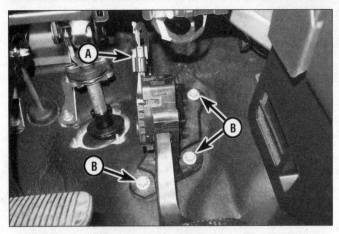

3.4 Slide the connector lock up then depress the tab (A) and disconnect the electrical connector, then remove the APP sensor mounting fasteners (B)

4.1 The FPDM is located on the frame crossmember, forward of the rear axle and above the fuel tank

connector and measure the resistance across the injector terminals with an ohmmeter. Compare this measurement to the other injectors. If the resistance of the non-operational injector is quite different from the other injectors, replace it.

12   If the injector is not operating, but the resistance reading is within the range of resistance of the other injectors, the PCM or the circuit between the PCM and the injector might be faulty.

3   Accelerator Pedal Position (APP) sensor - replacement and adjustment

Note: *All models are "drive-by-wire" and do not have an accelerator cable. The APP sensor communicates the desired pedal position to the PCM, the PCM then actuates the throttle body to the desired throttle angle.*

Note: *On models with adjustable pedals, after removing and installing or replacing the APP sensor, the cable between the brake pedal and accelerator pedal requires adjustment.*

1   The APP sensor is used to monitor the driver's demand for power. The PCM adjusts the amount of fuel injected into the cylinders according to the position of the pedal. A problem in the APP sensor circuit will set a diagnostic trouble code (see Chapter 6).

2   Disconnect the APP sensor electrical connector. On models with adjustable pedals, disconnect both connectors.

3   On models with adjustable pedals, disconnect the cable running between the brake pedal and the accelerator pedal, at the brake pedal.

4   On all models, remove the mounting fasteners and remove the APP sensor and accelerator pedal (see illustration).

5   Installation is reverse of removal.

6   On models with adjustable pedals, perform the cable adjustment procedure (see Chapter 9, Section 13).

4   Fuel pressure relief procedure

Warning: *Gasoline is extremely flammable, so take extra precautions when you work on any part of the fuel system. Don't smoke or allow open flames or bare light bulbs near the work area, and don't work in a garage where a gas-type appliance (such as a water heater or a clothes dryer) is present. Since gasoline is carcinogenic, wear fuel-resistant gloves when there's a possibility of being exposed to fuel, and, if you spill any fuel on your skin, rinse it off immediately with soap and water. Mop up any spills immediately and do not store fuel-soaked rags where they could ignite. The fuel system is under constant pressure, so, if any fuel lines are to be disconnected, the fuel pressure in the system must be relieved first. When you perform any kind of work on the fuel system, wear safety glasses and have a Class B type fire extinguisher on hand.*

Note: *After the fuel pressure has been relieved, it's a good idea to lay a shop towel over any fuel connection to be disassembled, to absorb the residual fuel that may leak out when servicing the fuel system.*

1   Unplug the Fuel Pump Driver Module (FPDM) electrical connector (see illustration).

2   Start the engine and allow it to run until it stops. This should take only a few seconds.

Warning: *On turbocharged models, the fuel pressure is relieved on the low-pressure side of the system, but pressure will still remain in the high-pressure side of the system. Before loosening any connections on the high-pressure side of the system, wait at least two hours.*

3   The fuel system pressure is now relieved. Disconnect the cable from the negative terminal of the battery before performing any work on the fuel system.

4   When you're finished working on the fuel system, simply reconnect the electrical connector to the FPDM.

5   Fuel pump/fuel pressure - check

Warning: *Gasoline is extremely flammable, so take extra precautions when you work on any part of the fuel system. See the Warning in Section 4.*

Note: *After the fuel pressure has been relieved, it's a good idea to lay a shop towel over any fuel connection to be disassembled, to absorb the residual fuel that may leak out when servicing the fuel system.*

General checks

Note: *The fuel pump relay is equipped with a primary and secondary voltage circuit. The primary circuit is controlled by the PCM and the secondary circuit is linked directly to battery voltage from the ignition switch. With the ignition switch On (engine not running), the PCM will ground the relay for one second. During cranking, the PCM grounds the fuel pump relay as long as the reference signal from the ignition system is received. If there are no reference pulses, the fuel pump will shut off after two or three seconds.*

1   If you suspect insufficient fuel delivery, check the following items first:

   a) *Check the battery and make sure it's fully charged (see Chapter 5).*
   b) *Check the fuel pump fuse.*
   c) *Check the fuel filter for restriction.*
   d) *Inspect all fuel lines to ensure that the problem is not simply a leak in a line.*

2   Verify the fuel pump actually runs. Place the transmission in Park (automatic) or Neutral (manual) and apply the parking brake. Have an assistant turn the ignition switch to On - you should hear a brief whirring noise as the pump comes on and pressurizes the system. If there is no response from the fuel pump (makes no sound), check the fuel pump electrical circuit. If the fuel pump runs, but a fuel system problem is suspected, continue with the fuel pump pressure check.

Note: *The fuel pump is easily heard through the gas tank filler neck.*

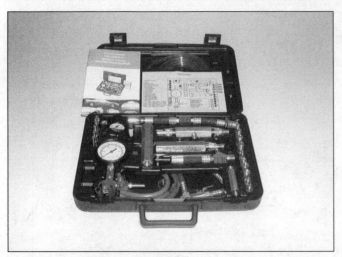

5.6 This fuel pressure testing kit contains all the necessary fittings and adapters, along with the fuel pressure gauge, to test most automotive systems

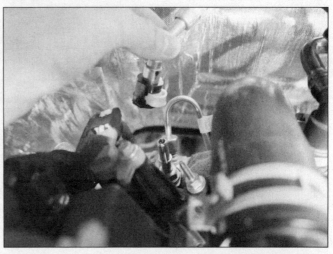

5.8 Location of the fuel line quick-connect fitting on the high-pressure fuel pump at the rear of the right-side cylinder head (2.7L model shown)

3   If the pump does not turn on (makes no sound) with the ignition switch in the On position, check the ignition fuse located in the engine compartment fuse center. Also, check the fuel pump relay. Refer to Chapter 12 for testing relays.

Note: *The fuel pump relay is located in the fuse/relay center in the engine compartment (see Section 2).*

4   If the relays are good and the fuel pump does not operate, check the fuel pump circuit. If the wiring and the connectors are good, either the FPCM (see Section 11) or the fuel pump (see Section 9) is faulty.

Note: *The PCM commands the fuel pump control module (FPCM), which in turn operates the fuel pump at either 8 or 12 volts. If you suspect that the fuel pump control module is faulty, have the system diagnosed at a dealer or a qualified repair shop. Refer to Chapter 6 for information on replacement of this component.*

Fuel pump pressure check

Note: *The following procedure applies to the complete Sequential Fuel Injection (SFI) system (also know as multi-port fuel injection) and the fuel system before the high-pressure pump on Direct Injection (DI) systems. DI systems operate under very high pressures and require special tools to diagnose correctly.*

Note: *Before proceeding, obtain a fuel pressure gauge capable of measuring fuel pressure well above the specified operating range of the fuel system you're going to test, and you'll also need fittings suitable for tee-ing the gauge into the fuel system between the fuel delivery line and the fuel rail.*

5   Relieve the fuel system pressure (see Section 4).

6   In addition to a fuel pressure gauge capable of reading fuel pressure up to 100 psi, you'll need a hose and an adapter suitable for tee-ing into the fuel system at the quick-connect fitting between the fuel delivery

hose and the fuel rail (see illustration).

7   On SFI systems, disconnect the quick-connect fitting at the connection between the fuel delivery hose and the fuel rail (if you're unfamiliar with quick-connect fittings, refer to Section 6). Tee in the fuel pressure gauge between the fuel delivery hose and the fuel rail.

8   On DI systems, disconnect the quick-connect fitting at the connection between the fuel delivery hose and the high-pressure fuel pump. Tee in the fuel pressure gauge between the fuel delivery hose and the high-pressure fuel pump (see illustration).

9   Turn the Key On, Engine Off (KOEO) and check for fuel leaks from the fuel pressure test adapter fittings.

10   Turn off all the accessories, then start the engine and let it idle. The fuel pressure should be within the operating range listed in this Chapter's Specifications. If the pressure reading is within the specified range, the system is operating correctly.

11   If the fuel pressure is higher than specified, then the pump, the Fuel Pump Driver Module (FPDM), the Powertrain Control Module (PCM) or the circuit connecting these components is probably defective. But checking this circuit is beyond the scope of the home mechanic, so have the circuit checked by a professional.

12   If the fuel pressure is lower than specified, inspect the fuel delivery lines and hoses for an obstruction or a kink. Also inspect all fuel delivery line and hose quick-connect fittings for leaks. If the lines, hoses, and connections are all in good shape, remove the fuel pump/fuel level sensor assembly (see Section 9) and inspect the fuel pump inlet strainer for restrictions. If everything else is okay, replace the fuel pump.

13   Turn the ignition switch to Off, wait five minutes and recheck the pressure on the gauge. Compare the reading with the hold pressure listed in this Chapter's Specifications.

If the hold pressure is less than specified:

 a) *The fuel delivery line or a quick-connect fitting might be leaking.*

 b) *A fuel injector (or injectors) may be leaking.*

 c) *The fuel pump might be defective.*

14   After the testing is complete, relieve the fuel pressure (see Section 4), remove the fuel pressure gauge and reconnect the fuel delivery line to the fuel rail.

---

6   Fuel lines and fittings - general information and disconnection

---

Warning: *Gasoline is extremely flammable. See Fuel system warnings in Section 1.*

1   Relieve the fuel pressure before servicing fuel lines or fittings (see Section 4), then disconnect the cable from the negative battery terminal (see Chapter 1) before proceeding.

2   The fuel supply line connects the fuel pump in the fuel tank to the fuel rail on the engine. The Evaporative Emission (EVAP) system lines connect the fuel tank to the EVAP canister and connect the canister to the intake manifold.

3   Whenever you're working under the vehicle, be sure to inspect all fuel and evaporative emission lines for leaks, kinks, dents and other damage. Always replace a damaged fuel or EVAP line immediately.

4   If you find signs of dirt in the lines during disassembly, disconnect all lines and blow them out with compressed air. Inspect the fuel strainer on the fuel pump pick-up unit for damage and deterioration.

Steel tubing

5   It is critical that the fuel lines be replaced with lines of equivalent type and specification.

6   Some steel fuel lines have threaded fittings. When loosening these fittings, hold the stationary fitting with a wrench while turning the tube nut.

Disconnecting Fuel Line Fittings

Two-tab type fitting; depress both tabs with your fingers, then pull the fuel line and the fitting apart

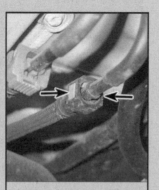

On this type of fitting, depress the two buttons on opposite sides of the fitting, then pull it off the fuel line

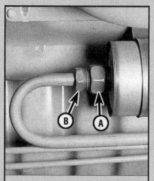

Threaded fuel line fitting; hold the stationary portion of the line or component (A) while loosening the tube nut (B) with a flare-nut wrench

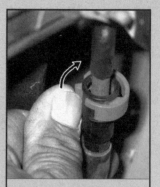

Plastic collar-type fitting; rotate the outer part of the fitting

Metal collar quick-connect fitting; pull the end of the retainer off the fuel line and disengage the other end from the female side of the fitting . . .

. . . insert a fuel line separator tool into the female side of the fitting, push it into the fitting and pull the fuel line off the pipe

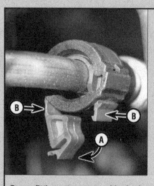

Some fittings are secured by lock tabs. Release the lock tab (A) and rotate it to the fully-opened position, squeeze the two smaller lock tabs (B) . . .

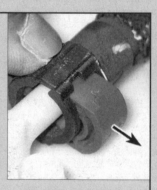

. . . then push the retainer out and pull the fuel line off the pipe

Spring-lock coupling; remove the safety cover, install a coupling release tool and close the tool around the coupling . . .

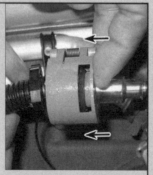

. . . push the tool into the fitting, then pull the two lines apart

Hairpin clip type fitting: push the legs of the retainer clip together, then push the clip down all the way until it stops and pull the fuel line off the pipe

7.6 Fuel tank shield

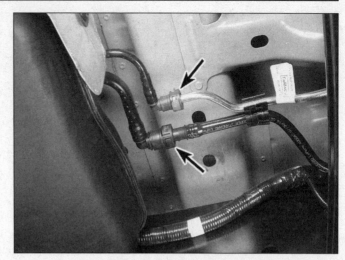

7.7 Disconnect the lines at the front of the tank

Plastic tubing

7   When replacing fuel system plastic tubing, use only original equipment replacement
plastic tubing.
Caution: *When removing or installing plastic
fuel line tubing, be careful not to bend or twist
it too much, which can damage it. Also, plastic
fuel tubing is NOT heat resistant, so keep it
away from excessive heat.*

Flexible hoses

8   When replacing fuel system flexible
hoses, use only original equipment replace-
ments.
9   Don't route fuel hoses (or metal lines)
within four inches of the exhaust system or
within ten inches of the catalytic converter.
Make sure that no rubber hoses are installed
directly against the vehicle, particularly in
places where there is any vibration. If allowed
to touch some vibrating part of the vehicle, a
hose can easily become chafed and it might
start leaking. A good rule of thumb is to maintain a minimum of 1/4-inch clearance around

a hose (or metal line) to prevent contact with
the vehicle underbody.

7   Fuel tank - removal and installation

Warning: *Gasoline is extremely flammable,
so take extra precautions when you work on
any part of the fuel system. See the Warning
in Section 4.*
Note: *Don't begin this procedure until the
gauge indicates that the tank is empty or nearly empty. If the tank must be removed when
it's full (for example, if the fuel pump malfunctions), siphon any remaining fuel from the tank
prior to removal.*

Removal

1   Relieve the fuel system pressure (see
Section 4).
2   Remove the fuel filler cap to relieve fuel
tank pressure.
3   Disconnect the cable from the negative

terminal of the battery (see Chapter 5, Section 3).
4   If the tank is full or nearly full, siphon
the fuel into an approved container using
a siphoning kit available at most auto parts
stores.
Warning: *DO NOT start the siphoning action
by mouth! Use a siphoning kit (available at
most auto parts stores).*
5   Raise the vehicle and support it securely
on jackstands.
6   if equipped, remove the fuel tank shield
(see illustration).
7   Disconnect the fuel line and EVAP vapor
line quick-connect fittings at the front of the
tank (see illustration).
8   Disconnect the fuel tank filler hose vent
tube quick-connect fitting from the top of the
fuel pump module (see illustration).
9   Disconnect the electrical connectors
from the fuel pump module and EVAP sensors.
10   Loosen the clamp and disconnect the
the fuel tank filler hose from the filler pipe (see
illustration).

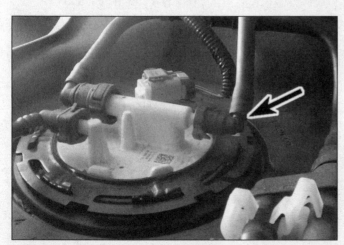

7.8 Disconnect the fuel tank filler hose vent tube from the fuel pump module

7.10 Loosening the fuel filler hose clamp

7.12a Remove the fuel tank strap bolts…

7.12b … then swing the straps down (the straps can be turned 90 degrees and detached from the frame)

11   Place a jack under the tank, then raise the jack until it's supporting the tank.

12   Remove the bolts that retain the fuel tank straps, then swing the straps down (see illustrations).

13   Lower the tank far enough to unplug any vapor lines or wire harness brackets that may be difficult to reach when the fuel tank is in the vehicle.

14   Slowly lower the jack while steadying the tank. Remove the tank from the vehicle.

15   If you're replacing the tank, or having it cleaned or repaired, refer to Section 8.

16   Refer to Section 9 to remove and install the fuel pump (gasoline) or sending unit (diesel).

Installation

17   Installation is the reverse of removal. Clean engine oil can be used as an assembly aid when pushing the fuel filler neck back into the tank.

18   Carefully angle the fuel tank filler neck into the filler pipe assembly and lift the tank into place. Torque the tank straps to the specifications in this Chapter's Specifications.

19   Install the shield to the tank.

20   Turn the ignition on and check for leaks.

8   Fuel tank - cleaning and repair

1   There may be two different types of fuel tanks available on these models: steel and plastic.

2   Fuel tanks may be steam-cleaned to remove sediment or rust in the bottom of the tank. Remove the fuel tank sending unit/fuel pump and vapor valve prior to cleaning. Allow plenty of time for the tank to air dry before returning it to service.

3   Repairs to the steel fuel tank or filler pipe should be performed by a professional with

the proper training to carry out this critical and potentially dangerous job. Even after cleaning and flushing, explosive fumes can remain and could explode during repair of the tank.

4   The plastic (polyethylene) fuel tank cannot be repaired. No reliable repair procedures are available to correct leaks or damage. Fuel tank replacement is the only approved service.

5   If the fuel tank is removed from the vehicle, it should not be placed in an area where sparks or open flames could ignite the fumes coming out of the tank. Be especially careful inside garages where a gas-type appliance is located, because the appliance could cause an explosion.

6   Whenever the fuel tank is steam-cleaned or otherwise serviced, the vapor valve assembly should be replaced. All grommets and seals must be replaced to prevent possible leakage.

9   Fuel pump/fuel pump module - removal and installation

Warning: *Gasoline is extremely flammable, so take extra precautions when you work on any part of the fuel system. See the* **Warning** *in Section 4.*

1   Remove the fuel tank (refer to Section 7).

2   Remove the fuel pump assembly from the fuel tank by turning the retaining ring counterclockwise, until it's loose (see illustration). A special tool designed for this purpose is available, but a pair of large pliers or hammer and brass punch will work. **Warning:** *If a punch is used, use only a brass punch to avoid creating sparks.*

3   Remove the retaining ring.

4   Separate the fuel pump from the assembly but do not remove.

5   Lift the fuel pump module up enough to disconnect the vent line quick-connect fitting (see illustration).

9.2 Loosen the fuel pump module lock ring using large pliers

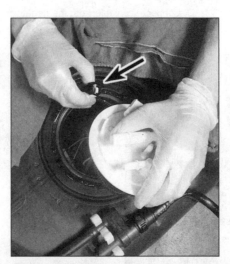

9.5 Lift the module up and disconnect the vent line

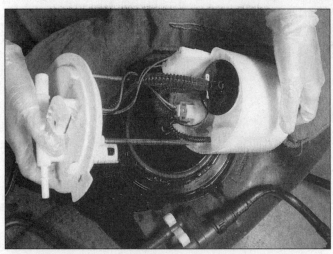

9.6 Remove the fuel pump module, tilting to prevent damage to the float arm

9.7 Remove and discard the fuel pump O-ring

6   Remove the fuel pump module from the tank, tilting as necessary for the float arm to not be damaged (see illustration).
7   Remove the fuel pump O-ring and discard (see illustration).
8   Clean the fuel pump mounting flange, the tank mounting surface and O-ring groove.
9   Installation is the reverse of removal. Apply a thin coat of heavy grease to the new O-ring to hold it in place during assembly.
10   Use care when inserting the fuel pump module into the tank. Connect the vent line quick-connect fitting.
11   Align the marks on the module and tank before tightening the retaining ring.
12   After installation, turn the ignition on and check for leaks.

10   High-pressure fuel pump - removal and installatrion

Caution: *Only 2.7L and 3.5L turbocharged models are equipped with Direct Injection (DI) and a high-pressure fuel pump.*
Warning: *Fuel pressure in the high-pressure system on Direct Injection (DI) systems is under extremely high pressure. Be sure to correctly perform the fuel pressure release procedure prior to servicing any of the high-pressure fuel system components to prevent injury (see Section 4).*
Warning: *The fuel delivery system is made up of a low-pressure system and a high-pressure system. Once the pressure on the low-pressure side of the system has been relieved, wait at least two hours before loosening any fuel line fittings in the engine compartment.*
Note: *On 2.7L models, the high-pressure fuel pump is located on the rear of the passenger (right) cylinder head. On 3.5L turbocharged models, the high-pressure fuel pump is located on the top of the passenger (right) side valve cover.*

Removal
1   Remove the two nuts at the front of the engine cover. Lift up at the front and unhook the retainers at the rear of the cover to remove.
2   Release the fuel pressure (see Section 4).
3   Disconnect the cable from the negative terminal of the battery (see Chapter 5, Section 3).
4   Remove the intake manifold (see Chapter 2A, Section 5).
5   2.7L models: Loosen the right-front wheel lug nuts, then raise the vehicle and support it securely on jackstands. Remove the inner fender splash shield (see Chapter 11).
Note: *Raising the vehicle and working through the fenderwell makes access to certain parts of this procedure easier.*
6   Locate the high-pressure fuel pump and disconnect the electrical connector.
7   Disconnect the fuel supply hose quick-connect fitting at the high-pressure fuel pump (see illustration 5.8).
8   On 2.7L and 2017 and later 3.5L turbocharged models, remove and discard the

fuel feed line between the high-pressure fuel pump and fuel rail. The feed line is not be re-used; obtain a NEW feed line for installation.
9   On 2016 and earlier 3.5L turbocharged models, remove the bolt attaching the fuel feed pipe to the intake manifold. Loosen the fuel feed line fitting at the high-pressure fuel pump. In this case, the fuel feed pipe can be reconnected and does not require replacement.
10   On 3.5L turbocharged models, disconnect the hose retainer from the high-pressure fuel pump.
11   On all models, alternately loosen two nuts attaching the high-pressure fuel pump to the cylinder head, one complete turn at a time, until removed (see illustration).
12   Carefully pull the high-pressure fuel pump out of the cylinder head.
13   If necessary, remove the high-pressure fuel pump tappet (note installation orientation during removal).
Note: *Note the notch on the high-pressure fuel pump tappet and the groove in the high-pressure fuel pump bore.*

10.11 High-pressure fuel pump retaining nuts (2.7L shown)

11.1 The FPDM is located on top of the frame crossmember

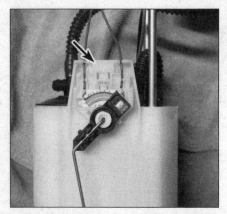

13.3 Depress the tab and slide the fuel level sending unit off

14.3 Loosen the intake tube clamp (2.7L model shown)

Installation

14   Installation is reverse of removal noting the following points:

a) *Rotate the engine CLOCKWISE ONLY until the until the high-pressure fuel pump drive lobe is at its lowest point.*

b) *Coat the bore with clean engine oil and align the notch on the high-pressure fuel pump tappet with the groove in the high-pressure fuel pump bore during installation.*

c) *Use a new O-ring on the high-pressure fuel pump. Coat the O-ring in clean engine oil.*

d) *Alternately tighten each of the high-pressure fuel pump nuts one complete turn until seated, then tighten them to the torque listed in this Chapter's Specifications.*

e) *Install a new fuel feed pipe.*

f) *Tighten all fasteners to the torque values listed in this Chapter's Specifications.*

g) *Turn the ignition ON and check for leaks before starting the engine.*

11   Fuel Pump Driver Module (FPDM) - replacement

Note: *The FPDM is located on the top of the frame crossmember above the fuel tank and forward of the rear differential.*

14.4 Remove the insulator bolt (A) and the intake scoop retainers (B)

1   Locate the FPDM and disconnect the electrical connector (see illustration).

2   Remove the FPDM mounting bolts and detach the FPDM from the frame.

3   Installation is reverse of removal. No programming is necessary.

12   Fuel pressure regulator - removal and installation

Note: *All models are equipped with a returnless fuel system. The fuel pressure regulator is part of the fuel pump module. If the fuel pressure regulator is diagnosed as faulty, the fuel pump module will need to be replaced. Refer to Section 9 for more information.*

13   Fuel level sending unit - replacement

Warning: *Gasoline is extremely flammable, so take extra precautions when you work on any part of the fuel system. See the Warning in Section 4.*

1   Remove the fuel pump module (see Section 9).

2   Remove the electrical connectors for the fuel level sending unit.

3   Press the tab to release the fuel level sending unit from the fuel pump module (see illustration).

4   Installation is the reverse of removal. Be sure to install a new rubber gasket on the fuel pump module.

5   Turn the ignition on and check for leaks.

14   Air filter housing - removal and installation

Warning: *Wait until the engine is completely cool before beginning this procedure.*

Note: *The air filter housing base and coolant reservoir are one unit.*

1   On 3.5L turbocharged models, disconnect the brake vacuum reservoir electrical connector. Remove the vacuum reservoir from the bracket and position aside.

2   On 2.7L and 3.5L turbocharged models, disconnect the two harness fasteners from the air filter housing.

3   Loosen the air intake tube clamp and disconnect the air intake tube (see illustration).

4   Remove the bolt attaching the insulator to the fender and the two plastic retainers for the intake scoop (see illustration).

5   Pull upward firmly to disengage the bottom rubber retainers and remove the air filter housing.

6   Installation is the reverse of removal.

15   Throttle body - removal and installation

Note: *All models are "drive-by-wire" and do not have an accelerator cable. The APP sensor communicates the desired pedal position to the PCM, the PCM then actuates the throttle body to the desired throttle angle.*

Removal

1   Remove the engine cover if equipped.

2   On 2.7L and 3.5L turbocharged models, disconnect the charge air cooler outlet pipe from the throttle body.

3   On 3.5L non-turbo and 5.0L models, remove the air intake tube (see Section 14).

4   On 3.5L non-turbo models, detach the hose retainer.

5   On all models, unlock the red locking tab and disconnect the Electronic Throttle Control (ETC) electrical connector from the throttle body (see illustration).

6   Remove the four throttle body mounting bolts and remove the throttle body.

7   Discard the O-ring gasket (see illustration).

8   Clean the sealing surfaces. If scraping is necessary, be careful not to damage the sealing surfaces or allow material to drop into the intake manifold. Install a new O-ring gasket.

Installation

9   Installation is the reverse of removal. Be sure to tighten the throttle body mounting nuts to the torque listed in this Chapter's Specifications.

16 Fuel rails and injectors - removal and installation

Warning: *Gasoline is extremely flammable, so take extra precautions when you work on any part of the fuel system. See the Warning in Section 4.*

Warning: *The fuel delivery system on 2.7L and 3.5L turbocharged models is made up of a low-pressure system and a high-pressure system. Once the pressure on the low-pressure side of the system has been relieved, wait at least two hours before loosening any fuel line fittings in the engine compartment.*

Warning: *Wait until the engine is completely cool before beginning this procedure.*

Fuel Rail

1   Relieve the fuel pressure (see Section 4).

2   Disconnect the cable from the negative terminal of the battery (see Chapter 5, Section 3).

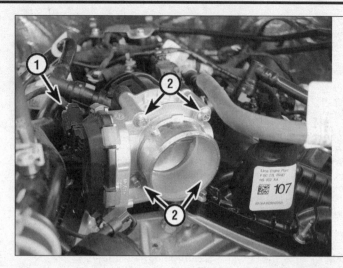

15.5 Disconnect the electrical connector (1) then remove the bolts (2) (2.7L model shown)

Removal

2.7L models

3   Remove the intake manifold (see Chapter 2A, Section 5).

4   Use compressed air to clean the area around the fuel injectors and fuel rails to prevent debris from entering the fuel system or engine.

5   Remove the high-pressure fuel pump cover on the rear of the passenger's (right) cylinder head.

6   If removing the passenger's (right) fuel rail, remove and discard the fuel feed pipe between the high-pressure fuel pump and the fuel rail (see Section 10).

7   If removing the driver's (left) fuel rail, remove and discard the high-pressure fuel pipe between the rear of the two fuel rails (see illustration).

8   Disconnect the fuel injector harness electrical connectors at the rear of the engine.

9   Remove the fuel rail mounting bolts (see illustration 16.7).

10   Carefully pull the fuel rail with the fuel injectors out of the intake manifold at the same angle as the fuel injectors. Use a slight

wiggle motion to assist in breaking the fuel injectors free from the cylinder head.

Caution: *Any injectors that remain stuck in the cylinder head must be removed using a special injector removal tool that uses a slide-hammer type procedure to remove any stuck injectors.*

Note: *If the isolator on the bottom of the fuel injector falls off during removal, replace the fuel injector*

11   If the injectors are to be serviced, disconnect the fuel injector connectors, remove and discard the injector clips and pull the injectors from the fuel rail. See the *Fuel injector seals - replacement* information in this section.

3.5L non-turbo and 5.0L models

12   On 3.5L non-turbo models, remove the upper intake manifold from the engine (see Chapter 2A, Section 5).

13   On 5.0L models, remove the engine cover.

14   On all models, disconnect the fuel rail supply hose quick-connect fitting.

15   Remove the left and right insulators covering the fuel rails.

16   Cover the disconnected fuel feed hose

15.7 Remove and discard the O-ring (2.7L model shown with intake manifold removed)

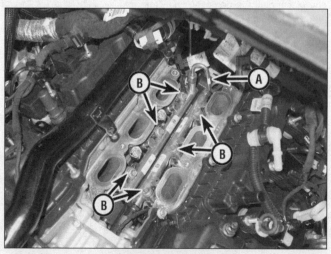

16.7 High-pressure fuel pipe (A) and fuel rail mounting bolts (B) (2.7L model shown)

and fuel rail fitting and use compressed air to clean the area around the fuel injectors and fuel rails to prevent debris from entering the fuel system or engine.

17   Disconnect the fuel injector harness connectors.

18   Remove the four fuel rail mounting bolts securing the fuel rails to the lower intake manifold.

19   Carefully pull the fuel rail with the fuel injectors out of the intake manifold. Use a slight wiggle motion to assist in breaking the fuel injectors free from the intake manifold.

20   If the injectors are to be serviced, remove and discard the injector clips and pull the injectors from the fuel rail. See the *Fuel injector seals - replacement* information in this section.

3.5L turbocharged models - 2016 and earlier

21   Remove the engine cover and high-pressure fuel pump cover.

22   Remove the intake manifold (see Chapter 2A, Section 5).

23   Use compressed air to clean the area around the fuel injectors and fuel rails to prevent debris from entering the fuel system or engine.

24   Drain the cooling system (see Chapter 1, Section 23).

25   Remove the three bolts and position the coolant crossover out of the way. Discard the O-rings for the crossover and install new ones during installation.

26   Remove the coolant pipe running down the lifter valley by firmly pulling the pipe towards the rear of the engine to disengage the front coupling. Discard the O-rings for the coolant pipe ends and install new ones during installation.

27   Remove and discard the fuel feed line between the high-pressure fuel pump and the fuel rails. Remove the bolt attaching the fuel feed pipe to the intake manifold. The feed line is not to be re-used; obtain a NEW feed line for installation.

28   Detach the harness from the fuel rails and disconnect the harness connectors and fuel rail pressure sensor connector from the rear of the engine.

29   Remove the fuel rail mounting bolts.

30   Carefully pull the fuel rail with the fuel injectors out of the intake manifold at the same angle as the fuel injectors. Use a slight wiggle motion to assist in breaking the fuel injectors free from the cylinder head.

Caution: *Any injectors that remain stuck in the cylinder head must be removed using a special injector removal tool that uses a slide-hammer type procedure to remove any stuck injectors.*

Note: *If the isolator on the bottom of the fuel injector falls off during removal, replace the fuel injector.*

31   If the injectors are to be serviced, disconnect the fuel injector connectors, remove and discard the injector clips and pull the injectors from the fuel rail. See the *Fuel injector seals - replacement* information in this section.

3.5L turbocharged models - 2017 and later

Caution: *2017 and later 3.5L turbocharged models are equipped with both DI and port injection systems.*

32   Remove the intake manifold (see Chapter 2A Section 5).

33   Remove the port injection fuel rail insulator.

34   Use compressed air to clean the area around the fuel injectors and fuel rails to prevent debris from entering the fuel system or engine.

35   Disconnect and remove the fuel line between the left and right port injection fuel rails (see Section 6).

36   Disconnect the port injection fuel rail electrical connectors at the rear of the fuel rails.

37   Remove the fuel rail mounting bolts securing the fuel rails to the engine.

38   Carefully pull the fuel rail with the fuel injectors out of the cylinder head. Use a slight wiggle motion to assist in breaking the fuel injectors free from the head.

39   If the port fuel injectors are to be serviced, disconnect the fuel injector connectors, remove and discard the injector clips and pull the injectors from the fuel rail. See the *Fuel injector seals - replacement* information in this section.

40   When removing the passenger (right) fuel rail, remove and discard the fuel feed line

between the high-pressure fuel pump and the right direct injection fuel rail.

41   When removing the driver (left) fuel rail, remove and discard the fuel feed line between the left and right direct injection fuel rails.

42   Disconnect the direct injection fuel rail electrical connectors at the rear of the fuel rails.

43   Remove the fuel rail mounting bolts.

44   Carefully pull the fuel rail with the fuel injectors out of the intake manifold at the same angle as the fuel injectors. Use a slight wiggle motion to assist in breaking the fuel injectors free from the cylinder head.

Caution: *Any injectors that remain stuck in the cylinder head must be removed using a special injector removal tool that uses a slide-hammer type procedure to remove any stuck injectors.*

Note: *If the isolator on the bottom of the fuel injector falls off during removal, replace the fuel injector.*

45   If the direct injection fuel injectors are to be serviced, disconnect the fuel injector connectors, remove and discard the injector clips and pull the injectors from the fuel rail. See the *Fuel injector seals - replacement* information in this section.

Installation

46   Installation is reverse of removal, noting the following points:

a) *Coat the injector O-rings with clean motor oil prior to installation into the fuel rail.*

b) *Install the fuel injectors to the fuel rail using new injector clips.*

c) *On 3.5L non- turbo, 2017 and later 3.5L turbocharged port injection system and 5.0L models, coat the injector O-rings with clean motor oil prior to installation into the manifold.*

d) *On 2.7L and 3.5L turbocharged models, DO NOT lubricate the injector teflon seals before installing the fuel rail and injectors to the engine.*

e) *On all models, press firmly to seat the injectors when installing the fuel rail to the engine.*

f) *On 2.7L and 3.5L turbocharged models, use NEW high-pressure fuel feed pipes.*

g) *Secure the fuel rail assembly with the retaining bolts, install the fuel feed pipes and tighten to the torque listed in this Chapter's Specifications.*

h) *On 2016 and earlier 3.5L turbocharged models, refill the cooling system (see Chapter 1).*

i) *Turn the ignition on and check for leaks.*

Fuel rail pressure/temperature sensor - replacement

Caution: *If the fuel rail pressure/temperature sensor is removed, it cannot be reused and must be replaced with a new one.*

47   On 2.7L models, the fuel rail pressure sensor is located on the rear of the driver's (left) fuel rail (see illustration). Remove the driver's (left) fuel rail and unscrew the fuel rail pressure sensor.

16.47 Location of the fuel rail pressure sensor (2.7L models)

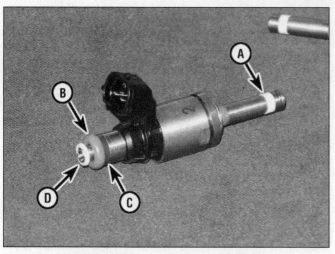

16.52 Identifying DI injector components

A   Teflon ring   C   Support ring
B   Inlet O-ring   D   Fuel inlet cap

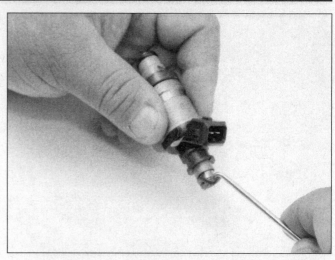

16.56 Remove the O-rings from the top and bottom of each injector

48   On 2016 and earlier 3.5L turbocharged models, the fuel rail pressure sensor is located on the front of the driver's side (left) fuel rail. Remove the intake manifold to access the sensor (see Chapter 2A, Section 5).
49   2017 and later 3.5L turbocharged models are equipped with 2 sensors; a fuel rail pressure sensor for the DI system, and a fuel rail pressure and temperature sensor on the port injection system. Both are located on the front of the driver's (left) fuel rails. Remove the intake manifold to access the sensors (see Chapter 2A, Section 5).
50   Installation is the reverse of removal.
51   Coat the O-ring with clean engine oil prior to installation. Tighten the sensor to the torque listed in this Chapter's Specifications.

Fuel injector seals - replacement

Note: *Even if you only removed the fuel rail assembly to replace a single injector or a leaking O-ring, it's a good idea to remove all of the injectors from the fuel rail and replace all of the O-rings at the same time.*
Caution: *Use care not to gouge or damage the injector surface when replacing the O-rings and seals.*

2.7L and 3.5L turbocharged models

Note: *The following information applies to Direct Injection (DI) fuel injectors.*
Note: *2017 and later 3.5L turbocharged models are equipped with both DI and port injection systems.*
52   Inspect the Teflon ring at the bottom of the injector. If replacement is required, pull the ring away from the injector body as far as possible (to prevent damage to the injector body) and cut the old Teflon ring from the injector. A special tool is used to install the new Teflon ring (see illustration).
53   Inspect the inlet O-ring and support ring. If replacement is required, note the installed position of the support ring as one side is dif-

ferent and has a bevel (the bevel faces the injector body) (see illustration).
54   Inspect the fuel inlet caps (see illustration). Remove any debris clogging the cap. If the cap is deteriorated or comes off, it is OK to discard as it is not needed for proper operation of the fuel injector. If the cap is missing, check that it is not in the fuel rail and remove as necessary.

3.5L non-turbo, 2017 and later 3.5L turbocharged port injection system and 5.0L models

55   Remove the injector clips and pull the injectors from the fuel rail.
56   Remove the injector O-rings and install new ones (see illustration).
57   Lubricate the O-rings with clean engine oil.
58   Ensure that the injector caps are clean and free of contamination.
59   Install the injectors to the fuel rail. Ensure the injector clips retain the injectors securely.

---

17   Turbocharger(s) - removal and installation

Warning: *Wait until the engine is completely cool before beginning this procedure.*
Note: *The turbochargers must be handled with care and extreme cleanliness when they are removed, as they are precision high-speed components. When parts are disconnected from the turbochargers, the openings on the turbocharger must be protected from entry of dirt or chemicals. Use high-strength tape to cover them as components are detached.*
Note: *The procedure is virtually the same for either the left or right turbocharger.*
Note: *Some turbos are equipped with heat shields, some are not. Some replacement turbos do not have provisions for heat shields as the manufacturer stopped installing them during production.*

Removal

1   The engine must be cold before removing the turbocharger(s). Before disconnecting any hoses, pipes or connections from the turbocharger, remove the heat insulation material.
2   Remove the engine cover
3   Loosen the wheel lug nuts, then raise and support the front of the vehicle on jackstands. Remove the wheel.
4   Drain the cooling system (see Chapter 1).
5   Remove the inner fender splash shield (see Chapter 11).
6   Remove the under-vehicle splash shield and transmission cover and/or skid plate (as equipped).
7   Loosen the clamps and remove the tube between the air intake tube to the air filter housing and the turbocharger inlet for the turbo to be serviced (see illustrations).
8   Loosen the clamps and remove the tube between the intercooler and turbocharger outlet for the turbo to be serviced.
9   Tape off the openings on the turbo-

17.7a Remove the air intake tube (2.7L model shown)...

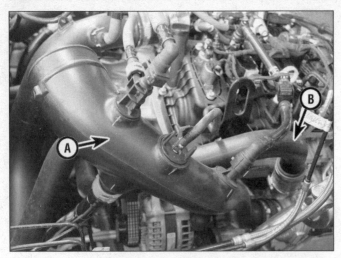

17.7b ... and the turbocharger inlet (A) and outlet (B) tubes

17.11 Remove the exhaust flange nuts (RH turbo on 2.7L model shown)

charger assembly.

10   On 2.7L or 2016 and earlier 3.5L turbocharged models, if servicing the passenger (right) turbocharger, remove the drivebelt (see Chapter 1, Section 26). Remove the three air conditioning compressor mounting bolts and position the AC compressor aside (see Chapter 3).

Warning: *Do not disconnect the refrigerant lines!*

2.7L models

11   Remove the nuts attaching the exhaust flange to the turbocharger (see illustration). The studs should not be reused.

12   Remove the fastener at the turbo and the clamp at the cylinder head to remove the coolant return line (see illustration). Discard the O-ring and use a new one.

13   Disconnect the vacuum line at the waste gate and secure out of the way.

14   If servicing the driver (left) turbocharger, remove the nut from the upper front of the turbo mounting flange. The stud should not be reused.

15   Remove the fasteners at the top of the

turbo and the front of the engine block and remove the oil supply line. Discard the O-rings and use new ones.

16   Remove the fasteners at the bottom of the turbo and the side of the engine block and remove the oil return line. Discard the O-rings and use new ones.

17   Remove the bolt securing the coolant supply line to the front of the engine block and disconnect the fitting from the block. Discard the O-ring and use a new one.

18   Remove the nut(s) and bolt attaching the turbocharger mounting flange to the cylinder head and remove the turbocharger assembly. The coolant supply line will come out with the turbocharger so use care not to damage the line.

19   Remove the bolt securing the coolant supply line to the turbo. Discard the O-ring and use a new one.

3.5L turbocharged models (2016 and earlier)

20   Remove the nuts and position the intercooler hose bracket aside to allow access to the AC compressor bolts.

21   Remove the nuts attaching the exhaust flange to the turbocharger. The studs should not be reused.

22   Disconnect the quick-connect fittings at the turbo and disconnect the coolant return line from the turbocharger.

23   Disconnect the vacuum line at the waste gate and secure out of the way.

24   Remove the bolt for the coolant and oil supply lines bracket on the side of the block.

25   Remove the bolts and disconnect the oil lines from the bottom of the turbocharger.

26   Disconnect the quick-connect fitting at the engine block for the coolant supply line.

27   Remove the bolts attaching the turbocharger mounting flange to the cylinder head and remove the turbocharger assembly. The coolant supply line will come out with the turbocharger so use care not to damage the line.

28   Disconnect the quick-connect fitting at the turbo to remove the coolant supply line.

3.5L turbocharged models (2017 and later)

29   Remove the fasteners at the side of the turbo and the front of the engine block and remove the oil supply line. Discard the O-rings and use new ones. It is recommended to discard the oil supply line and install a new one.

30   Unscrew and discard the oil supply line fitting and filter from the engine block. Use a new one at installation.

31   Remove the fasteners at the bottom of the turbo and the side of the engine block and remove the oil return line. Discard the O-rings and use new ones.

32   Disconnect the wastegate electrical connector.

33   Remove and discard the nuts attaching the exhaust flange to the turbocharger. The nuts should not be reused.

34   Remove the bolts and disconnect the coolant supply and return line fittings from the engine block. Discard the O-rings and use new ones.

17.12 Identifying turbocharger components (RH turbo on 2.7L model shown)

1   *Coolant return line*
2   *Wastegate actuator*
3   *Oil supply line*
4   *Oil return line*
5   *Coolant supply line*

35   Remove the Torx bolts attaching the turbocharger mounting flange to the exhaust manifold and remove the turbocharger assembly. The coolant supply and return lines come out with the turbocharger so use care not to damage the lines.

36   Remove the fasteners securing the coolant supply and return lines to the turbo. Discard the O-rings and use a new ones.

Installation (all models)

37   Installation is the reverse of removal, noting the following:

a) *Use new gaskets at the turbo-to-exhaust junction on each side, and new gaskets and O-rings where the oil and coolant supply and return lines connect to the turbocharger housing and engine block.*

b) *Replace the filter on the engine block end of the oil supply line.*

c) *Lubricate the oil line O-rings with clean engine oil. Lubricate the coolant line O-rings with coolant.*

d) *It is recommended to use new studs, nuts and bolts for all exhaust-side components.*

e) *Install the coolant supply line to the turbo before installing the turbo to the cylinder head.*

f) *When installing the turbocharger and coolant line, install the turbo mounting flange nuts and bolt loosely and connect the coolant supply line to the block, then tighten the flange nuts and bolt.*

g) *Use anti-seize compound on the new turbocharger-to-exhaust nuts/bolts.*

h) *Tighten all fasteners to the torque listed in this Chapter's Specifications.*

i) *Refill and bleed the cooling system and install a new oil filter and fresh engine oil.*

18   Air bypass valve - removal and installation

1   See Chapter 6, Section 16.

19   Wastegate control actuator - replacement and adjustment

Note: *Only 2017 and later 3.5L turbocharged models are equipped with electronic wastegate control actuators. All other turbocharged models use vacuum-controlled actuators.*

Replacement

1   Loosen the front wheel lug nuts, then raise the front of the vehicle and support it securely on jackstands. Remove the wheel.

2   Remove the inner fender splash shield (see Chapter 11).

3   Loosen the clamps and remove the tube between the air intake tube to the air filter housing and the turbocharger inlet for the wastegate to be serviced.

4   Loosen the clamps and remove the tube

19.7 Wastegate components (2.7L model shown)

1   *Jam nuts*
2   *Vacuum line*
3   *Mounting fasteners*

between the intercooler and turbocharger outlet for the wastegate to be serviced.

5   For the passenger's (right) side, remove the intercooler tube bracket nuts and position the hoses and bracket aside.

6   Tape off any openings on the turbocharger assembly.

7   Remove the wastegate actuator lower jam nut and disconnect the linkage.

8   Disconnect the wastegate actuator vacuum line.

9   Remove the fasteners and remove the wastegate actuator from the turbocharger.

10   Installation is reverse of removal. Install the lower jam nut loosely and do not tighten until instructed during the adjustment procedure.

Adjustment

11   With the wastegate installed and the lower jam nut installed finger-tight, push the linkage to the closed position (towards the actuator).

12   While holding the linkage closed, finger-tighten the lower jam nut.

13   While still holding the linkage closed, using a wrench, tighten the upper jam nut.

14   Release the linkage.

15   Now, pull the linkage to the open position (away from the actuator).

16   While holding the linkage open, loosen

the upper jam nut 4.5 turns exactly.

17   While holding the linkage open, hold the upper jam nut with a wrench and tighten the lower jam nut.

18   A scan tool will be necessary to clear PCM DTCs and reset the Keep Alive Memory (KAM) and monitor the PCM PID WGATE_A_V (right side) WGATE_B_V (left side).

19   While monitoring the correct PID, press the accelerator pedal to the floor for 3 seconds and slowly release. Note the minimum voltage of the PID after the pedal is fully released. It should be 1.1V to 1.3V.

20   If it is not within range, the actuator linkage require adjustment again.

20   Intercooler - removal and installation

Note: *The intercooler is located below the radiator under the front of the vehicle.*

1   Raise and support the front of the vehicle on jack stands.

2   Remove the under vehicle cover and/or skid plate (as equipped).

3   Loosen the clamps and disconnect the two intercooler inlet pipes from the passenger's (right) side of the intercooler (see illustration).

20.3 Disconnect the intercooler hoses on the passenger's side (2.7L model shown)

20.4 Release the clip for the driver's side pipe (2.7L model shown)

20.6 Intercooler mounting bolts

4   Release the clip and disconnect the intercooler outlet pipe from the driver's (left) side of the intercooler (see illustration).
5   Disconnect the turbocharger bypass valve electrical connector and quick-connect fitting from the intercooler.
6   Remove the two bolts attaching the intercooler bracket to the frame and remove the intercooler from the vehicle (see illustration).
7   Separate the intercooler from the bracket and remove the turbocharger bypass valve if necessary (see Chapter 6, Section 16).
8   Installation is reverse of removal.

21   Exhaust system servicing - general information

Warning: *Inspection and repair of exhaust system components should be done only after enough time has elapsed after driving the vehicle to allow the system components to cool completely. Also, when working under the vehicle, make sure it is securely supported on jackstands.*

1   The exhaust system consists of the exhaust manifold, the catalytic converter, the resonator, exhaust pipe, muffler and all brackets, hangers and clamps. The exhaust system is attached to the body with mounting brackets and rubber hangers (see illustrations). If any of the parts are damaged or deteriorated, excessive noise and vibration will be transmitted to the body.
2   Conducting regular inspections of the exhaust system will keep it safe and quiet. Look for any damaged or bent parts, open seams, holes, loose connections, excessive corrosion or other defects which could allow exhaust fumes to enter the vehicle. Also check the catalytic converter when you inspect the

exhaust system (see Chapter 6). Deteriorated exhaust system components should not be repaired; they should be replaced with new parts.
3   If the exhaust system components are extremely corroded or rusted together, they will probably have to be cut from the exhaust system. The convenient way to accomplish this is to have a muffler repair shop remove the corroded sections with a cutting torch. If, however, you want to save money by doing it yourself (and you don't have a welding outfit with a cutting torch), simply cut off the old components with a hacksaw. If you have compressed air, special pneumatic cutting chisels can also be used. If you decide to tackle the job at home, be sure to wear safety goggles to protect your eyes from metal chips and work gloves to protect your hands.
4   Here are some simple guidelines to follow when repairing the exhaust system:

21.1a Be sure to apply penetrating fluid to the exhaust flange nuts before attempting to remove them

21.1b Check the condition of the rubber hangers that support the exhaust system

Work from the back to the front when removing exhaust system components.

a) Apply penetrating oil to the exhaust system component fasteners to make them easier to remove.

b) Use new gaskets, hangers and clamps when installing exhaust systems components.

c) Apply anti-seize compound to the threads of all exhaust system fasteners at reassembly.

d) Be sure to allow sufficient clearance between newly installed parts and all points on the underbody to avoid overheating the floor pan and possibly damaging the interior carpet and insulation. Pay particularly close attention to the catalytic converter and heat shield.

Notes

Chapter 5
Engine electrical systems

Contents

	Section		Section
Alternator - removal and installation	7	General information and precautions	1
Battery - disconnection and reconnection	3	Ignition coils - removal and installation	6
Battery and battery tray - removal and installation	4	Starter motor - removal and installation	8
Battery cables and sensors - replacement	5	Troubleshooting	2

Specifications

Charging system
Charging voltage .... 13.5 to 15.0 volts

Torque specifications

Note: *One foot-pound (ft-lb) of torque is equivalent to 12 inch-pounds (in-lbs) of torque. Torque values below approximately 15 foot-pounds are expressed in inch-pounds, because most foot-pound torque wrenches are not accurate at these smaller values.*

	Ft-lbs (unless otherwise indicated)	Nm
Starter motor mounting bolts		
2.7L and 3.5L engines	35	48
5.0L engine	18	25
Alternator mounting bolts/nuts	35	47
Drivebelt tensioner bolt (5.0L engine)	35	47
Ignition coil fasteners		
2.7L engine	53 in-lbs	6
3.5L and 5.0L engines		
Step 1	62 in-lbs	7
Step 2	Tighten an additional 45 to 50 degrees	

1   General information and precautions

General information

Ignition system

1   The ignition system consists of ignition coils, spark plugs, the Camshaft Position (CMP) sensor, the Crankshaft Position (CKP) sensor, the knock sensor, and the Powertrain Control Module (PCM).

2   The CKP, CMP and knock sensors are information sensors used by the PCM to control ignition timing and other engine operating parameters. The PCM also uses a number of other information sensors to make decisions regarding the correct ignition timing. These other sensors include the Throttle Position (TP) sensor, the Engine Coolant Temperature (ECT) sensor, the Mass Air Flow (MAF) sensor, the Intake Air Temperature (IAT) sensor, the Vehicle Speed Sensor (VSS) and the transmission gear position sensor or Transmission Range (TR) switch. For more information on these and other sensors, refer to Chapter 6.

Charging system

3   The charging system includes the alternator (with an integral voltage regulator), the Powertrain Control Module (PCM), the Body Control Module (BCM), a charge indicator light on the dash, the battery, a fuse or fusible link and the wiring connecting all of these components. The charging system supplies electrical power for the ignition system, the lights, the radio, etc. The alternator is driven by a drivebelt.

Starting system

4   The starting system consists of the battery, the ignition switch, the starter relay, the Powertrain Control Module (PCM), the Body Control Module (BCM), the Transmission Range (TR) switch, the starter motor and solenoid assembly, and the wiring connecting all of these components.

Precautions

5   Always observe the following precautions when working on the electrical system:

a) *Be extremely careful when servicing engine electrical components. They are easily damaged if checked, connected or handled improperly.*

b) *Never leave the ignition switched on for long periods of time when the engine is not running.*

c) *Never disconnect the battery cables while the engine is running.*

d) *Maintain correct polarity when connecting battery cables from another vehicle during jump starting - see the* Booster battery (jump) starting *section at the front of this manual.*

e) *Always disconnect the cable from the negative battery terminal before working on the electrical system, but read the battery disconnection procedure first (see Section 3).*

6   It's also a good idea to review the safety-related information regarding the engine electrical systems located in the *Safety first!* section at the front of this manual before beginning any operation included in this chapter.

2   Troubleshooting

Ignition system

1   If a malfunction occurs in the ignition system, do not immediately assume that any particular part is causing the problem. First, check the following items:

a) *Make sure that the cable clamps at the battery terminals are clean and tight.*

b) *Check for any stored Diagnostic Trouble Codes (DTCs) related to the ignition system using a scan tool (see Chapter 6 Section 3).*

c) *Test the condition of the battery (see Steps 19 through 22). If it doesn't pass all the tests, replace it.*

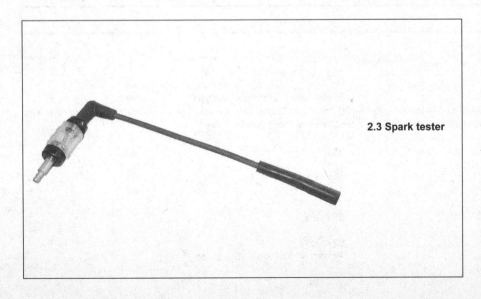

2.3 Spark tester

d) *Check the ignition coil or coil pack connections.*

e) *Check any relevant fuses in the engine compartment fuse and relay box (see Chapter 12). If they're burned, determine the cause and repair the circuit.*

Check

Warning: *Because of the high voltage generated by the ignition system, use extreme care when performing a procedure involving ignition components.*

Note: *The ignition system components on these vehicles are difficult to diagnose. In the event of ignition system failure that you can't diagnose, have the vehicle tested at a dealer service department or other qualified auto repair facility.*

Note: *For the following test, you'll need a spark tester (available at auto parts stores).*

2   If the engine turns over but won't start, verify that there is sufficient secondary ignition voltage to fire the spark plug as follows:

3   Remove a coil from a spark plug and install the tester (see illustration) between the coil boot and the spark plug.

4   Crank the engine while watching the tester. If the tester flashes, sufficient voltage is reaching the spark plug to fire it.

Caution: *Do NOT crank the engine or allow it to run for more than five seconds; running the engine for more than five seconds may set a Diagnostic Trouble Code (DTC) for a cylinder misfire.*

5   Repeat this test on the remaining cylinders.

6   Proceed on this basis until you have verified that there's a good spark from each coil. If there is, then you have verified that the coils are functioning correctly.

7   If there is no spark, then either the coil is bad or the computer may not be firing the coil.

8   Also inspect the coil electrical connector. Make sure that it's clean, tight and in good condition.

9   If all the coils are firing correctly, but the engine misfires when the coils are installed, then one or more of the plugs might be fouled. Remove and check the spark plugs or install new ones (see Chapter 1).

10   Also inspect the ignition coil boots carefully for corrosion (high resistance) or deterioration of the insulation (low resistance). If any of the boots look damaged or deteriorated, replace them as a set.

Note: *The boots may not be serviceable separately from the coils and may require coil replacement to replace the boot. It is always a good idea to replace ignition components (coils, plugs, etc) as a set.*

11   No further testing of the ignition system is possible without special tools. If the problem persists, have the ignition system tested by a dealer service department or other qualified repair shop.

Charging system

12   If a malfunction occurs in the charging system, do not automatically assume the

2.19 To test the open circuit voltage of the battery, touch the black probe of the voltmeter to the negative terminal and the red probe to the positive terminal of the battery; a fully charged battery should be at least 12.6 volts

2.21 Connect a battery load tester to the battery and check the battery condition under load following the tool manufacturer's instructions

alternator is causing the problem. First check the following items:

a) *Check the drivebelt tension and condition, as described in Chapter 1. Replace it if it's worn or deteriorated.*

b) *Make sure the alternator mounting bolts are tight.*

c) *Inspect the alternator wiring harness and the connectors at the alternator and voltage regulator. They must be in good condition, tight and have no corrosion.*

d) *Check the fuses in the underhood fuse/relay box. If any are burned, determine the cause, repair the circuit and replace the fuse (the vehicle will not start and/or the accessories will not work if the main fuse is blown).*

e) *Start the engine and check the alternator for abnormal noises (a shrieking or squealing sound indicates a bad bearing).*

f) *Check the battery. Make sure it's fully charged and in good condition (one bad cell in a battery can cause overcharging by the alternator).*

g) *Disconnect the battery cables (negative first, then positive). Inspect the battery posts and the cable clamps for corrosion. Clean them thoroughly if necessary (see Chapter 1). Reconnect the cables (positive first, negative last).*

Alternator - check

13   Use a voltmeter to check the battery voltage with the engine off. It should be at least 12.6 volts (see illustration 2.19).

14   Start the engine and check the battery voltage again. It should now be approximately 13.5 to 15 volts.

15   If the voltage reading is more or less than the specified charging voltage, the voltage regulator is probably defective, which will require replacement of the alternator (the voltage regulator is not replaceable separately). Remove the alternator and have it bench tested (most auto parts stores will do this for you).

16   The charging system (battery) light on the instrument cluster lights up when the ignition key is turned to On, but it should go out

when the engine starts.

17   If the charging system light stays on after the engine has been started, there is a problem with the charging system. Before replacing the alternator, check the battery condition, alternator belt tension and electrical cable connections.

18   If replacing the alternator doesn't restore voltage to the specified range, have the charging system tested by a dealer service department or other qualified repair shop.

Battery - check

19   Check the battery state of charge. Visually inspect the indicator eye on the top of the battery (if equipped with one); if the indicator eye is black in color, charge the battery as described in Chapter 1. Next perform an open circuit voltage test using a digital voltmeter. With the engine and all accessories Off, touch the negative probe of the voltmeter to the negative terminal of the battery and the positive probe to the positive terminal of the battery (see illustration). The battery voltage should be 12.6 volts or slightly above. If the battery is less than the specified voltage, charge the battery before proceeding to the next test. Do not proceed with the battery load test unless the battery charge is correct.

Note: *The battery's surface charge must be removed before accurate voltage measurements can be made. Turn on the high beams for ten seconds, then turn them off and let the vehicle stand for two minutes.*

20   Disconnect the negative battery cable, then the positive cable from the battery.

21   Perform a battery load test. An accurate check of the battery condition can only be performed with a load tester (see illustration). This test evaluates the ability of the battery to operate the starter and other accessories during periods of high current draw. Connect the load tester to the battery terminals. Load test the battery according to the tool manufacturer's instructions. This tool increases the load demand (current draw) on the battery.

22   Maintain the load on the battery for 15 seconds and observe that the battery voltage does not drop below 9.6 volts. If the battery

condition is weak or defective, the tool will indicate this condition immediately.

Note: *Cold temperatures will cause the minimum voltage reading to drop slightly. Follow the chart given in the manufacturer's instructions to compensate for cold climates. Minimum load voltage for freezing temperatures (32 degrees F) should be approximately 9.1 volts.*

Starting system

The starter rotates, but the engine doesn't

23   Remove the starter (see Section 8). Check the overrunning clutch and bench test the starter to make sure the drive mechanism extends fully for proper engagement with the flywheel ring gear. If it doesn't, replace the starter.

24   Check the flywheel ring gear for missing teeth and other damage. With the ignition turned off, rotate the flywheel so you can check the entire ring gear.

The starter is noisy

25   If the solenoid is making a chattering noise, first check the battery (see Steps 19 through 22). If the battery is okay, check the cables and connections.

26   If you hear a grinding, crashing metallic sound when you turn the key to Start, check for loose starter mounting bolts. If they're tight, remove the starter and inspect the teeth on the starter pinion gear and flywheel ring gear. Look for missing or damaged teeth.

27   If the starter sounds fine when you first turn the key to Start, but then stops rotating the engine and emits a zinging sound, the problem is probably a defective starter drive that's not staying engaged with the ring gear. Replace the starter.

The starter rotates slowly

28   Check the battery (see Steps 19 through 22).

29   If the battery is okay, verify all connections (at the battery, the starter solenoid and motor) are clean, corrosion-free and tight. Make sure the cables aren't frayed or damaged.

30   Check that the starter mounting bolts are tight so it grounds properly. Also check the pinion gear and flywheel ring gear for evidence of a mechanical bind (galling, deformed gear teeth or other damage).

The starter does not rotate at all

31   Check the battery (see Steps 19 through 22).

32   If the battery is okay, verify all connections (at the battery, the starter solenoid and motor) are clean, corrosion-free and tight. Make sure the cables aren't frayed or damaged.

33   Check all of the fuses in the underhood fuse/relay box.

34   Check that the starter mounting bolts are tight so it is grounded properly.

35   Check for voltage at the starter solenoid "S" terminal when the ignition key is turned to the start position. If voltage is present, replace the starter/solenoid assembly. If no voltage is present, the problem could be the starter relay, the Transmission Range (TR) sensor (see Chapter 7A), or with an electrical connector somewhere in the circuit (see the wiring diagrams). Also, on many modern vehicles, the Powertrain Control Module (PCM) and the Body Control Module (BCM) control the voltage signal to the starter solenoid; on such vehicles a special scan tool is required for diagnosis.

3   Battery - disconnection and reconnection

Note: *To disconnect the battery for service procedures requiring power to be cut from the vehicle, first open the driver's door to disable Retained Accessory Power (RAP), then loosen the cable end nut and disconnect the cable from the negative battery terminal. Isolate the cable end to prevent it from coming into accidental contact with the battery terminal.*

1   The battery is located in the right side of the engine compartment on all vehicles covered by this manual. To disconnect the battery for service procedures that require battery disconnection, simply disconnect the cable from the negative battery terminal (see Section 4). Make sure that you isolate the cable to prevent it from coming into contact with the battery negative terminal.

Warning: *Always disconnect the negative battery cable first, then the positive battery cable second. When reconnecting the battery cables, always connect the positive battery cable first, then the negative battery cable second.*

2   Some vehicle systems (radio, alarm system, power door locks, etc.) require battery power all the time, either to enable their operation or to maintain control unit memory (Powertrain Control Module, automatic transaxle control module, etc.), which would be lost if the battery were to be disconnected. So before you disconnect the battery, note the following points:

a) *Before connecting or disconnecting the cable from the negative battery terminal, make sure that you turn the ignition key and the lighting switch to their Off positions. Failure to do so could damage semiconductor components.*

b) *On a vehicle with power door locks, it is a wise precaution to remove the key from the ignition and to keep it with you, so that it does not get locked inside if the power door locks should engage accidentally when the battery is reconnected!*

c) *After the battery has been disconnected, then reconnected (or a new battery has been installed) on vehicles with an automatic transmission, the Transmission Control Module (TCM) will need some time to relearn its adaptive strategy. As a result, shifting might feel firmer than usual. This is a normal condition and will not adversely affect the operation or service life of the transaxle. Eventually, the TCM will complete its adaptive learning process and the shift feel of the transaxle will return to normal.*

d) *The engine management system's PCM has some learning capabilities that allow it to adapt or make corrections in response to minor variations in the fuel system in order to optimize drivability and idle characteristics. However, the PCM might lose some or all of this information when the battery is disconnected. The PCM must go through a relearning process before it can regain its former drivability and performance characteristics. Until it relearns this lost data, you might notice a difference in drivability, idle and/or (if you have an automatic) shift "feel." To facilitate this relearning process, refer to "Enabling the PCM to relearn" below.*

4.1 Battery details

1   *Negative cable clamp*
2   *Positive cable clamp*
3   *Battery hold-down clamp*
4   *Battery cover*

Memory savers

3   Devices known as memory savers (typically, small 9-volt batteries) can be used to avoid some of the above problems. A memory saver is usually plugged into the cigarette lighter, and then you can disconnect the vehicle battery from the electrical system. The memory saver will deliver sufficient current to maintain security alarm codes and - maybe, but don't count on it! - PCM memory. It will also run unswitched (always on) circuits such as the clock and radio memory, while isolating the car battery in the event that a short circuit occurs while the vehicle is being serviced.

Warning: *If you're going to work around any airbag system components, disconnect the battery and do not use a memory saver. If you do, the airbag could accidentally deploy and cause personal injury.*

Caution: *Because memory savers deliver current to operate unswitched circuits when the battery is disconnected, make sure that the circuit that you're going to service is actually open before working on it!*

Enabling the PCM to relearn

4   After the battery has been reconnected, perform the following procedure in order to facilitate PCM relearning:

a) *Start the engine and allow it to warm up to its normal operating temperature.*

b) *Drive the vehicle at part-throttle, under moderate acceleration and idle conditions, until normal performance returns.*

c) *Park the vehicle and apply the parking brake with the engine running.*

d) *Depress the brake pedal and put the shift lever in Drive.*

e) *Allow the engine to idle for about two minutes, or until the idle stabilizes. Make sure that the engine is at its normal operating temperature.*

4   Battery and battery tray - removal and installation

Note: *Battery straps and handlers are available at most auto parts stores for reasonable prices. They make it easier to remove and carry the battery.*

Removal

Battery

1   Disconnect the cable from the negative terminal of the battery (see illustration).

2   Disconnect the cable from the positive terminal of the battery for the battery being removed.

3   Remove the battery hold-down bracket.

4   Lift out the battery. Be careful - it's heavy. If equipped, remove the battery cover from the battery.

Battery tray

5   Remove the battery.

6   Release the wiring harness from the

retainers on the side of the battery tray, then remove the four bolts attaching the battery tray to the vehicle (see illustration).
7   Remove the battery tray from the vehicle.

Installation

8   If you are replacing the battery, make sure you get one that's identical, with the same dimensions, amperage rating, cold cranking rating, etc.
9   Installation is the reverse of removal. Connect the cable to the positive battery terminal first, then connect the ground cable to the negative battery terminal.

5   Battery cables and sensors - replacement

Battery cables

1   When removing the cables, always disconnect the cable(s) from the negative battery terminal first and hook it up last, or you might accidentally short out the battery with the tool you're using to loosen the cable clamps. Even if you're only replacing a cable for the positive terminal, be sure to disconnect the negative cable(s) from the battery first.
2   Disconnect the old cables from the battery or the mega-fuse terminal, then trace each of them to their opposite ends and disconnect them. Be sure to note the routing of each cable before disconnecting it to ensure correct installation.
3   If you are replacing any of the old cables, take them with you when buying new cables. It is vitally important that you replace the cables with identical parts.
4   Clean the threads of the solenoid or ground connection with a wire brush to remove rust and corrosion. Apply a light coat of battery terminal corrosion inhibitor or petroleum jelly to the threads to prevent future corrosion.
5   Attach the cable to the solenoid or

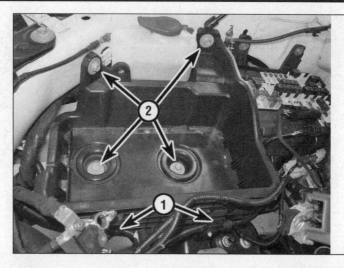

4.6 Battery tray mounting details
1   *Wiring harness retainers*
2   *Mounting bolts*

ground connection and tighten the mounting nut/bolt securely.
6   Before connecting a new cable to the battery, make sure that it reaches the battery post without having to be stretched.
7   Connect the cable to the positive battery terminal first, then connect the ground cable to the negative battery terminal.

Battery sensors

Battery current sensor

Note: *The battery current sensor is attached to the negative battery cable near the battery. Not all models are equipped with this sensor.*
8   Remove the nut attaching the negative battery cable to the terminal and disconnect both cables from the stud.
9   Detach the sensor from the battery tray.
10   Note the positioning of the battery current sensor. Mark the cable for correct installation of the new sensor.
11   Disconnect the battery current sensor electrical connector.
12   Remove the tape securing the sensor to the cable and remove the sensor by sliding it up and off of the cable.

13   Installation is reverse of removal. Orient the sensor on the cable using the reference mark and apply electrical tape to secure.

Alternator current sensor

Note: *The alternator current sensor is attached to the alternator B+ cable near the underhood junction box.*
14   Disconnect the negative battery terminal (see Section 3).
15   Remove the terminal cover from the side of the underhood junction box (see illustration).
16   Locate the alternator B+ cable. Remove the nut and disconnect the cable from the stud (see illustration).
17   Note the positioning of the alternator current sensor. Mark the cable for correct installation of the new sensor.
18   Disconnect the alternator current sensor electrical connector (see illustration).
19   Remove the tape securing the sensor to the cable and remove the sensor by sliding it up and off of the cable.
20   Installation is reverse of removal. Orient the sensor on the cable using the reference mark and apply electrical tape to secure.

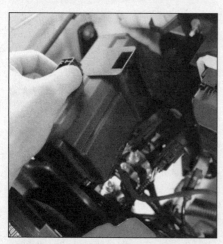

5.15 Detach the cover from the junction box to the rear of the battery

5.16 Alternator B+ cable retaining nut

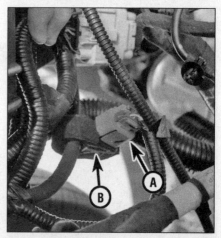

5.18 Alternator current sensor electrical connector (A) and sensor (B)

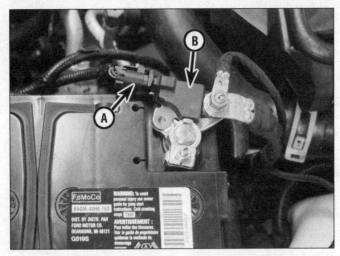

**5.22 Battery monitoring sensor electrical connector (A)
and sensor (B)**

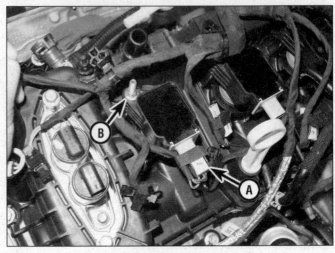

**6.4 Identifying coil components
(2.7L model shown, others similar)**

A)   *Connector with lock*   B)   *Coil bolt/stud*

Battery monitoring sensor

Note: *The battery monitoring sensor is part of the negative battery terminal clamp and is replaced as a unit.*

21   Disconnect the negative cable from the battery.

22   Disconnect the battery monitoring sensor electrical connector (see illustration).

23   Remove the nut and detach the negative battery cables from the negative terminal clamp.

24   Installation is reverse of removal.

---

6   Ignition coils - removal and installation

Removal

2.7L models

1   Remove the two nuts at the front of the engine cover. Lift up at the front and unhook the retainers at the rear of the cover to remove.

2   Disconnect the harness retainers from the coil fastener studs.

3   When working on the passenger (right) side ignition coils, disconnect the right Camshaft Position Sensor (CMP) connector. See Chapter 6, Section 11.

4   Slide the connector locks away from the coils to disengage and disconnect the connectors from the coils (see illustration).

Note: *Use compressed air to clear the ignition coil and surrounding area of debris prior to removing the coils.*

5   Remove the bolt/stud securing the ignition coil.

6   Pull the coil from the upper spark plug using a twisting motion to remove it from the cylinder head (see illustration).

3.5L and 5.0L models

7   Remove the engine cover as necessary to allow access to the ignition coils.

8   On 3.5L non-turbo models, when working on the passenger (right) side ignition coils, the upper intake manifold must be removed. See Chapter 2A, Section 5.

9   On 2016 and earlier 3.5L turbo models, remove the high-pressure fuel pump insulator cover retainer and the cover from the left rear

of the engine. Disconnect the high-pressure fuel pump electrical connector.

10   On 2017 and later 3.5L turbo models, disconnect the crankcase ventilation tube from the front of the driver (left) valve cover and disconnect the electrical connector. Position the tube out of the way to allow access to the ignition coils.

11   On all models, disconnect the ignition coil electrical connectors.

Note: *Use compressed air to clear the ignition coil and surrounding area of debris prior to removing the coils.*

12   On all models, remove the bolt securing the ignition coil, then pull the coil from the upper spark plug using a twisting motion to remove it from the cylinder head.

Installation

13   Installation is the reverse of the removal procedure with the following additions:

a)   *Prior to installing the coil, coat the interior of the rubber boot with silicone dielectric compound.*

b)   *Connect each coil electrical connector to its correct coil and make sure they are tight and secure.*

---

7   Alternator - removal and installation

1   Disconnect the cable from the negative battery terminal (see Section 3).

Removal

2.7L and 3.5L (non-turbo) models

2   On 2.7L models, remove the pipe between the turbocharger inlet ducts and the air filter housing (see Chapter 4).

3   On 3.5L models, remove the air filter housing (see Chapter 4).

4   On all models, remove the drivebelt (see Chapter 1).

6.6 Pull firmly using a twisting motion to remove the coil (2.7L model shown, others similar)

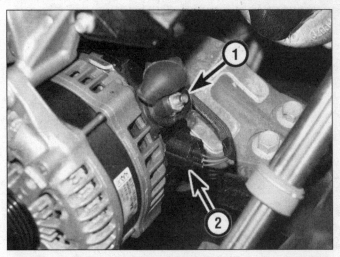

7.6 Alternator electrical connections (2.7L shown, others similar)

1   *B+ terminal*

2   *Alternator connector*

7.7 Alternator mounting nut and bolt (2.7L model shown, others similar)

5   On 2.7L models, disconnect the quick-connect fitting for turbocharger bypass tube from under the inlet tube.

6   Disconnect the electrical connector and the B+ cable from the alternator (see illustration).

7   Remove the upper nut and lower bolt attaching the alternator to the bracket (see illustration).

8   Remove the alternator from the vehicle.

3.5L turbocharged models

9   Raise the front of the vehicle and support it securely on jackstands.

10   On 2016 and earlier models, remove the two nuts at the front of the engine cover. Lift up at the front and unhook the retainers at the rear of the cover to remove.

11   Disconnect the Intake Air Temperature Sensor (IAT) (see Chapter 6, Section 7).

12   Detach the coolant reservoir hose from the intake duct.

13   Remove the pipe between the turbocharger inlet ducts and the air filter housing (see Chapter 4, Section 14).

14   Disconnect the quick-connect fitting for turbocharger bypass tube from under the driver's (left) inlet tube. Disconnect the four quick-connect fittings on top of the inlet tube.

15   Loosen the clamp for the driver's (left) inlet tube at the turbocharger and remove the inlet tube.

Note: *The clamp can be accessed through the inner fender liner on the driver's side front.*

16   On 2016 and earlier models, loosen the clamps at both the turbo and intercooler and remove the turbocharger outlet tube.

17   Remove the under vehicle cover and/or skid plate (as equipped).

18   Disconnect the quick-connect fitting for the turbocharger bypass tube from under the vehicle.

19   Remove the drivebelt (see Chapter 1, Section 26).

20   Remove the nut and remove the B+

8.4 Starter electrical connections (2.7L model shown, others similar)

cable from the alternator (see illustration 7.6).

21   Disconnect the electrical connector from the alternator.

22   Remove the upper nut and lower bolt attaching the alternator to the bracket (see illustration 7.7).

Note: *It may be necessary to also remove the stud for the alternator mounting nut to remove the alternator.*

23   Remove the alternator from the vehicle.

5.0L models

24   Remove the drivebelt (see Chapter 1, Section 26).

25   Remove the bolt and remove the drive-belt tensioner assembly.

26   Remove the nut and remove the B+ cable from the alternator (see illustration 7.6).

27   Disconnect the electrical connector from the alternator.

28   Remove the two lower mounting bolts and separate the alternator from the engine.

29   Remove the bolts attaching the alternator to the bracket.

30   Remove the alternator from the vehicle.

Installation

31   Installation is the reverse of removal. Tighten fasteners to the torque listed in this Chapter's Specifications.

32   Install the drivebelt and reconnect the cable to the negative terminal of the battery.

8   Starter motor - removal and installation

1   Disconnect the cable from the negative terminal of the battery (see Section 3).

2   Raise the vehicle and support it securely on jackstands.

3   Remove the under vehicle cover and/or skid plate (as equipped). Remove the transmission skid plate (if equipped).

4   Open the protective cap for the solenoid cable terminal and disconnect both cables from the starter solenoid (see illustration).

5   On 3.5L models, remove the nut from the lower starter mounting bolt stud and remove

the transmission cooler lines bracket from the stud.

Note: *On 3.5L and 5.0L models, a ground cable is attached to the lower starter mounting bolt (see illustration).*

6   On all models, remove the starter motor mounting bolts (see illustration) and detach the starter from the engine.

Note: *On 3.5L and 5.0L models, a ground cable is attached to the lower starter mounting bolt (see illustration).*

7   Installation is the reverse of removal. Tighten the starter mounting bolts to the torque listed in this Chapter's Specifications.

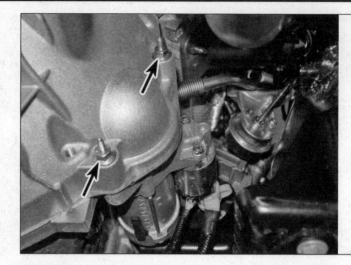

8.6 Remove the starter bolts (2.7L model shown, others similar)

Notes

Notes

Chapter 6
Emissions and engine control systems

Contents

	Section
Accelerator Pedal Position (APP) sensor - replacement	5
Camshaft Position (CMP) sensor - replacement	11
Catalytic converter	24
Crankshaft Position (CKP) sensor - replacement	10
Cylinder Head Temperature (CHT) sensor - replacement	9
Engine Coolant Temperature (ECT) sensor - replacement	6
Engine Oil Pressure (EOP) sensor - replacement	12
Evaporative emissions control (EVAP) system - general description and component replacement	23
Fuel rail pressure/temperature sensor - replacement	21
Fuel tank pressure (FTP) sensor - replacement	20
General information	1
Intake Air Temperature (IAT) sensor - replacement	7
Knock sensors - replacement	19
Manifold Absolute Pressure (MAP) sensor - replacement	8
Obtaining and clearing Diagnostic Trouble Codes (DTCs)	3
Oil pressure control solenoid - replacement	13
On Board Diagnosis (OBD) system	2
Oxygen sensors - general information and replacement	18
Positive Crankcase Ventilation (PCV) system	22
Powertrain Control Module (PCM) - removal and installation	4
Turbocharger Boost Pressure (TCPB) and Charge Air Cooler Temperature (CACT) sensor - replacement	15
Turbocharger bypass valve - replacement	16
Turbocharger wastegate vacuum sensor - replacement	17
Variable Camshaft Timing (VCT) variable force solenoid - removal and installation	14

Specifications

Torque specifications
Ft-lbs (unless otherwise indicated)

Note: One foot-pound (ft-lb) of torque is equivalent to 12 inch-pounds (in-lbs) of torque. Torque values below approximately 15 foot-pounds are expressed in inch-pounds, because most foot-pound torque wrenches are not accurate at these smaller values.

Cylinder head temperature sensor	
2.7L engine	106 in-lbs
3.5L engines	89 in-lbs
5.0L engine	97 in-lbs
ECT sensor (2.7L engine only)	142 in-lbs
Engine Oil Pressure (EOP) sensor	
2.7L engine	24
3.5L turbocharged and 5.0L engine	
Step 1	133 in-lbs
Step 2	Tighten an additional 185 degrees
Knock sensor bolts	177 in-lbs
VCT variable force solenoid bolts	
2.7L engine	97
3.5L non-turbo and 5.0L engines	
Step 1	71 in-lbs
Step 2	Tighten additional 20 degrees
3.5L turbocharged engine	89
CMP sensor mounting bolt	89 in-lbs
CKP sensor mounting bolt	89 in-lbs

1   General information

1   To prevent pollution of the atmosphere from incompletely burned and evaporating gases, and to maintain good driveability and fuel economy, a number of emission control systems are incorporated (see illustrations). They include the:

a) *On-Board Diagnostic (OBD) II system*
b) *Electronic Fuel Injection (EFI) system*
c) *Evaporative Emissions Control (EVAP) system*
d) *Positive Crankcase Ventilation (PCV) system*
e) *Catalytic converter(s)*

2   Before assuming that an emissions control system is malfunctioning, check the fuel and ignition systems carefully. The diagnosis of some emission control devices requires specialized tools, equipment and training. If checking and servicing become too difficult or if a procedure is beyond your ability, consult a dealer service department or other repair shop. Remember, the most frequent cause of emissions problems is simply a loose or broken wire or vacuum hose, so always check the hose and wiring connections first.

3   This doesn't mean, however, that emissions control systems are particularly difficult to maintain and repair. You can quickly and easily perform many checks and do most of the regular maintenance at home with common tune-up and hand tools.

Note: *Because of a Federally mandated warranty which covers the emissions control system components, check with your dealer about warranty coverage before working on any emissions-related systems. Once the warranty has expired, you may wish to perform some of the component checks and/or replacement procedures in this Chapter to save money.*

4   Pay close attention to any special precautions outlined in this Chapter. It should be noted that the illustrations of the various systems may not exactly match the system installed on your vehicle because of changes made by the manufacturer during production or from year-to-year.

5   A Vehicle Emissions Control Information (VECI) label is attached to the underside of the hood (see illustration). This label contains information regarding the types of emissions control systems installed on the vehicle. When servicing the engine or emissions systems, the VECI label on your particular vehicle should always be checked for up-to-date information.

2   On Board Diagnosis (OBD) system

General description

1   All models are equipped with the second generation OBD-II system. This system consists of an on-board computer known as the Powertrain Control Module (PCM), and information sensors, which monitor various functions of the engine and send data to the PCM. This system incorporates a series of diagnostic monitors that detect and identify fuel injection and emissions control system faults and store the information in the computer memory. This system also tests sensors and output actuators, diagnoses drive cycles, freezes data and clears codes.

2   The PCM is the brain of the electronically controlled fuel and emissions system. It receives data from a number of sensors and other electronic components (switches, relays, etc.). Based on the information it receives, the PCM generates output signals to control various relays, solenoids (fuel injectors) and other actuators. The PCM is specifically calibrated to optimize the emissions, fuel economy and driveability of the vehicle.

3   It isn't a good idea to attempt diagnosis or replacement of the PCM or emission control components at home while the vehicle is under warranty. Because of a federally-mandated warranty which covers the emissions system components and because any owner-induced damage to the PCM, the sensors and/or the control devices may void this warranty, take the vehicle to a dealer service department if the PCM or a system component malfunctions.

Scan tool information

4   Because extracting the Diagnostic Trouble Codes (DTCs) from an engine management system is now the first step in troubleshooting many computer-controlled systems and components, a code reader, at the very least, will be required (see illustration). More powerful scan tools can also perform many of the diagnostics once associated with expensive factory scan tools (see illustration). If you're planning to obtain a generic scan tool for your vehicle, make sure that it's compatible with OBD-II systems. If you don't plan to purchase a code reader or scan tool and don't have access to one, you can have the codes extracted by a dealer service department or an independent repair shop.

Note: *Some auto parts stores even provide this service.*

3   Obtaining and clearing Diagnostic Trouble Codes (DTCs)

Note: *Before outputting any DTCs stored in the PCM, thoroughly inspect ALL electrical connectors and hoses. Make sure that all electrical connections are tight, clean and free of corrosion. Make sure that all hoses are correctly connected, fit tightly and are in good condition (no cracks or tears).*

1.5 The Vehicle Emission Control Information (VECI) label contains such essential information as the types of emission control systems installed on the engine

2.4a Simple code readers are an economical way to extract trouble codes when the CHECK ENGINE light comes on

2.4b Hand-held scan tools like these can extract computer codes and also perform diagnostics

Information Sensors

Accelerator Pedal Position (APP) sensor - as you press the accelerator pedal, the APP sensor alters its voltage signal to the PCM in proportion to the angle of the pedal, and the PCM commands a motor inside the throttle body to open or close the throttle plate accordingly

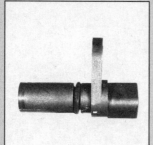

Camshaft Position (CMP) sensor - produces a signal that the PCM uses to identify the number 1 cylinder and to time the firing sequence of the fuel injectors

Crankshaft Position (CKP) sensor - produces a signal that the PCM uses to calculate engine speed and crankshaft position, which enables it to synchronize ignition timing with fuel injector timing, and to detect misfires

Engine Coolant Temperature (ECT) sensor - a thermistor (temperature-sensitive variable resistor) that sends a voltage signal to the PCM, which uses this data to determine the temperature of the engine coolant

Fuel tank pressure sensor - measures the fuel tank pressure and controls fuel tank pressure by signaling the EVAP system to purge the fuel tank vapors when the pressure becomes excessive

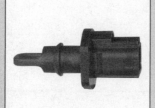

Intake Air Temperature (IAT) sensor - monitors the temperature of the air entering the engine and sends a signal to the PCM to determine injector pulse-width (the duration of each injector's on-time) and to adjust spark timing (to prevent spark knock)

Knock sensor - a piezoelectric crystal that oscillates in proportion to engine vibration which produces a voltage output that is monitored by the PCM. This retards the ignition timing when the oscillation exceeds a certain threshold

Manifold Absolute Pressure (MAP) sensor - monitors the pressure or vacuum inside the intake manifold. The PCM uses this data to determine engine load so that it can alter the ignition advance and fuel enrichment

Mass Air Flow (MAF) sensor - measures the amount of intake air drawn into the engine. It uses a hot-wire sensing element to measure the amount of air entering the engine

Oxygen sensors - generates a small variable voltage signal in proportion to the difference between the oxygen content in the exhaust stream and the oxygen content in the ambient air. The PCM uses this information to maintain the proper air/fuel ratio. A second oxygen sensor monitors the efficiency of the catalytic converter

Throttle Position (TP) sensor - a potentiometer that generates a voltage signal that varies in relation to the opening angle of the throttle plate inside the throttle body. Works with the PCM and other sensors to calculate injector pulse width (the duration of each injector's on-time)

Photos courtesy of Wells Manufacturing, except APP and MAF sensors.

Accessing the DTCs

1   The Diagnostic Trouble Codes (DTCs) can only be accessed with a code reader or a scan tool (see Section 2). Simply plug the connector of the tool into the Data Link Connector (DLC) or diagnostic connector (see illustration), which is located under the lower edge of the dash, just to the right of the steering column. Then follow the instructions included with the scan tool to extract the DTCs.

2   Once you have viewed all of the stored DTCs, look them up on the accompanying DTC chart.

3   After troubleshooting the source of each DTC, make any necessary repairs or replace the defective component(s).

Clearing the DTCs

4   Clear the DTCs with the scan tool in accordance with the instructions provided by the scan tool's manufacturer.

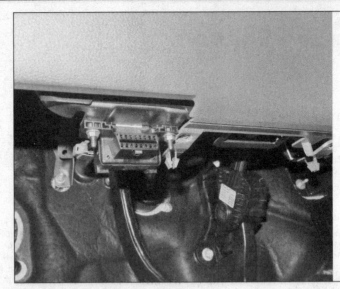

3.1 The 16-pin Data Link Connector (DLC), also referred to as the diagnostic connector, is located under the left part of the dash

Diagnostic Trouble Codes

Code	Probable cause
P0001	Fuel Volume Regulator Control Circuit/Open
P0003	Fuel Volume Regulator Control Circuit Low
P0004	Fuel Volume Regulator Control Circuit High
P000A	A Camshaft Position Slow Response (Bank 1)
P000B	B Camshaft Position Slow Response (Bank 1)
P0010	A Camshaft Position Actuator A Control Circuit/Open Bank 1
P0011	A Camshaft Position Timing - Over-Advanced (Bank 1)
P0012	A Camshaft Position Timing - Over-Retarded (Bank 1)
P0013	B Camshaft Position Actuator A Control Circuit/Open Bank 1
P0014	B Camshaft Position Timing - Over-Advanced (Bank 1)
P0015	B Camshaft Position Timing - Over-Retarded (Bank 1)
P0016	Crankshaft Position/Camshaft Position Correlation (Bank 1 Sensor A)
P0017	Crankshaft Position/Camshaft Position Correlation (Bank 1 Sensor B)
P0018	Crankshaft Position/Camshaft Position Correlation (Bank 2 Sensor A)
P0019	Crankshaft Position/Camshaft Position Correlation (Bank 2 Sensor B)
P0020	A Camshaft Position Actuator A Control Circuit/Open Bank 2
P0021	A Camshaft Position Timing - Over-Advanced (Bank 2)
P0022	A Camshaft Position Timing - Over-Retarded (Bank 2)

Code	Probable cause
P0023	B Camshaft Position Actuator A Control Circuit/Open Bank 2
P0024	B Camshaft Position Timing - Over-Advanced (Bank 2)
P0025	B Camshaft Position Timing - Over-Retarded (Bank 2)
P0030	Upstream oxygen sensor, bank 1, heater circuit
P0034	Turbocharger/Supercharger Bypass Valve A Control Circuit Low
P0035	Turbocharger/Supercharger Bypass Valve A Control Circuit High
P0036	HO2S Heater Control Circuit (Bank 1 Sensor 2)
P0037	HO2S Heater Control Circuit Low (Bank 1 Sensor 2)
P0038	HO2S Heater Control Circuit High (Bank 1 Sensor 2)
P0040	Upstream oxygen sensors swapped (crossed wiring harnesses)
P0041	Downstream oxygen sensors swapped (crossed wiring harnesses)
P0050	Oxygen sensor heater control circuit open or short, Bank 2, sensor 1
P0053	Oxygen sensor heater control circuit resistance, Bank 1, sensor 1
P0054	Oxygen sensor heater control circuit resistance, Bank 1, sensor 2
P0055	Oxygen sensor heater control circuit resistance, Bank 1, sensor 3
P0059	Oxygen sensor heater control circuit resistance, Bank 2, sensor 1
P0060	Downstream oxygen sensor heater circuit open or short, Bank 2, sensor 2
P0068	MAP / MAF - Throttle Position Correlation
P0071	Ambient Air Temperature Sensor Circuit A Range/Performance
P0072	Ambient Air Temperature Sensor Circuit A Low
P0073	Ambient Air Temperature Sensor Circuit A High
P0074	Ambient Air Temperature Sensor Circuit A Intermittent/Erratic
P007B	Charge Air Cooler Temperature Sensor Circuit Range/Performance (Bank 1)
P007C	Charge Air Cooler Temperature Sensor Circuit Low (Bank 1)
P007D	Charge Air Cooler Temperature Sensor Circuit High (Bank 1)
P060A	Internal Powertrain Control Module (PCM) error
P060B	Internal Powertrain Control Module (PCM) analog to digital processing error
P060C	Internal Powertrain Control Module (PCM) main processor error
P061B	Internal Powertrain Control Module (PCM) torque calculation error
P061C	Internal Powertrain Control Module (PCM) engine rpm calculation error

Diagnostic Trouble Codes (continued)

Code	Probable cause
P061D	Internal Powertrain Control Module (PCM) air mass error
P061F	Internal Powertrain Control Module (PCM) Throttle Actuator Controller (TAC) error
P0087	Fuel Rail/System Pressure - Too Low (Bank 1)
P0088	Fuel Rail/System Pressure - Too High (Bank 1)
P008A	Low Pressure Fuel System Pressure - Too Low
P008B	Low Pressure Fuel System Pressure - Too High
P0093	Fuel System Leak Detected - Large Leak
P0094	Fuel System Leak Detected - Small Leak
P0096	Intake Air Temperature Sensor 2 Circuit Range/Performance (Bank 1)
P0097	Intake Air Temperature Sensor 2 Circuit Low (Bank 1)
P0098	Intake Air Temperature Sensor 2 Circuit High (Bank 1)
P00AB	Intake Air Temperature Sensor 1 Circuit Range/Performance (Bank 2)
P00AC	Intake Air Temperature Sensor 1 Circuit Low (Bank 2)
P00AD	Intake Air Temperature Sensor 1 Circuit High (Bank 2)
P00BA	Low Fuel Pressure - Forced Limited Power
P00BB	Fuel Injector Insufficient Flow - Forced Limited Power
P00BC	Mass Or Volume Air Flow A Circuit Range/Performance - Air Flow Too Low
P00BD	Mass Or Volume Air Flow A Circuit Range/Performance - Air Flow Too High
P00BE	Mass Or Volume Air Flow B Circuit Range/Performance - Air Flow Too Low
P00BF	Mass Or Volume Air Flow B Circuit Range/Performance - Air Flow Too High
P00C1	Turbocharger/Supercharger Bypass Valve B Control Circuit Low
P00C2	Turbocharger/Supercharger Bypass Valve B Control Circuit High
P00C6	Fuel Rail Pressure Too Low - Engine Cranking (Bank 1)
P00CE	Intake Air Temperature Measurement System - Multiple Sensor Correlation (Bank 1)
P00D2	HO2S Heater Control Circuit Range/Performance (Bank 1 Sensor 2)
P00DF	Charge Air Cooler Coolant Temperature Sensor A Circuit Range/Performance
P00E0	Charge Air Cooler Coolant Temperature Sensor A Circuit Low
P00E1	Charge Air Cooler Coolant Temperature Sensor A Circuit High
P00E2	Charge Air Cooler Coolant Temperature Sensor A Intermittent/Erratic
P0100	Mass Or Volume Air Flow Sensor A Circuit

Code	Probable cause
P0101	Mass Or Volume Air Flow Sensor A Circuit Range/Performance
P0102	Mass Or Volume Air Flow Sensor A Circuit Low
P0103	Mass Or Volume Air Flow Sensor A Circuit High
P0104	Mass Or Volume Air Flow Sensor A Circuit Intermittent
P0106	Barometric (BARO) pressure sensor circuit, performance problem
P0107	Barometric (BARO) pressure sensor/MAP sensor circuit, low voltage
P0108	Barometric (BARO) pressure sensor/MAP sensor circuit, high voltage
P0109	Barometric (BARO) pressure sensor/MAP sensor circuit intermittent
P010A	Mass Or Volume Air Flow Sensor B Circuit
P010C	Mass Or Volume Air Flow Sensor B Circuit Low
P010D	Mass Or Volume Air Flow Sensor B Circuit High
P010E	Mass Or Volume Air Flow Sensor B Circuit Intermittent/Erratic
P010F	Mass Or Volume Air Flow Sensor A/B Correlation
P0111	Intake Air Temperature (IAT) sensor 1 circuit, range/performance problem
P0112	Intake Air Temperature (IAT) sensor 1 circuit, low input
P0113	Intake Air Temperature (IAT) sensor circuit, high input
P0114	Intake Air Temperature (IAT) sensor circuit, intermittent failure
P0116	Engine Coolant Temperature Sensor 1 Circuit Range/Performance
P0117	Engine Coolant Temperature Sensor 1 sensor circuit, low input
P0118	Engine Coolant Temperature Sensor 1 sensor circuit, high input
P0119	Engine Coolant Temperature Sensor 1 Circuit Intermittent/Erratic
P011E	Engine Coolant Temperature 1 / Ambient Air Temperature Correlation
P0120	Throttle / Pedal Position Sensor / Switch A Circuit
P0121	Throttle / Pedal Position Sensor / Switch A Circuit Range / Performance
P0122	Throttle / Pedal Position Sensor / Switch A Circuit Low
P0123	Throttle / Pedal Position Sensor / Switch A Circuit High
P0124	Throttle / Pedal Position Sensor/Switch A Intermittent
P0125	Insufficient Coolant Temp For Closed Loop Fuel Control
P0127	IAT2 sensor, problem with Charge Air Cooler
P0128	Coolant Thermostat (Coolant Temp Below Thermostat Regulating Temperature)

Diagnostic Trouble Codes (continued)

Code	Probable cause
P012B	Turbocharger inlet pressure sensor, circuit range/performance
P012C	Turbocharger inlet pressure sensor, circuit low
P012D	Turbocharger inlet pressure sensor, circuit high
P012E	Turbocharger inlet pressure sensor, circuit erratic
P0130	O2 Sensor Circuit (Bank 1 Sensor 1)
P0131	O2 Sensor Circuit Low Voltage (Bank 1 Sensor 1)
P0132	O2 Sensor Circuit High Voltage (Bank 1 Sensor 1)
P0133	O2 Sensor Circuit Slow Response (Bank 1 Sensor 1)
P0134	O2 Sensor Circuit No Activity Detected (Bank 1 Sensor 1)
P0135	O2 Sensor Heater Circuit (Bank 1 Sensor 1)
P0136	O2 Sensor Circuit (Bank 1 Sensor 2)
P0137	O2 Sensor Circuit Low Voltage (Bank 1 Sensor 2)
P0138	O2 Sensor Circuit High Voltage (Bank 1 Sensor 2)
P0139	O2 Sensor Circuit Slow Response (Bank 1 Sensor 2)
P013A	O2 Sensor Slow Response - Rich To Lean (Bank 1 Sensor 2)
P013B	O2 Sensor Slow Response - Lean To Rich (Bank 1 Sensor 2)
P013C	O2 Sensor Slow Response - Rich To Lean (Bank 2 Sensor 2)
P013E	O2 Sensor Delayed Response - Rich To Lean (Bank 1 Sensor 2)
P0141	O2 Sensor Circuit No Activity Detected (Bank 1 Sensor 2)
P0148	Fuel delivery error
P0150	Oxygen sensor heater control circuit resistance, Bank 2, sensor 1
P0151	Upstream oxygen sensor circuit, low voltage (left cylinder bank)
P0152	Upstream oxygen sensor circuit, high voltage (left cylinder bank)
P0153	Heated oxygen sensor circuit, slow response (left cylinder bank)
P0154	Upstream oxygen sensor heater circuit problem, Bank 2, sensor 1
P0155	Oxygen sensor, Bank 2, sensor 2, circuit open or short
P0156	Downstream oxygen sensor circuit problem (left cylinder bank)
P0158	Downstream oxygen sensor circuit, high voltage (left cylinder bank)
P0159	Downstream oxygen sensor circuit, slow response, Bank 2, sensor 2
P0161	Downstream oxygen sensor heater circuit problem, Bank 2, sensor 2

Code	Probable cause
P0171	System too lean (right cylinder bank)
P0172	System too rich (right cylinder bank)
P0174	System too lean (left cylinder bank)
P0175	System too rich (left cylinder bank)
P017C	Cylinder Head Temperature Sensor Circuit Low
P017D	Cylinder Head Temperature Sensor Circuit High
P017E	Cylinder Head Temperature Sensor Circuit Intermittent/Erratic
P0181	Fuel Temperature Sensor A Circuit Range/Performance
P0182	Fuel Temperature Sensor A Circuit Low
P0183	Fuel Temperature Sensor A Circuit High
P018B	Fuel Pressure Sensor B Circuit Range/Performance
P018C	Fuel Pressure Sensor B Circuit Low
P0192	Fuel Rail Pressure Sensor Circuit Low (Bank 1)
P0193	Fuel Rail Pressure Sensor Circuit High (Bank 1)
P0201	Injector no. 1 circuit malfunction
P0202	Injector no. 2 circuit malfunction
P0203	Injector no. 3 circuit malfunction
P0204	Injector no. 4 circuit malfunction
P0205	Injector no. 5 circuit malfunction
P0206	Injector no. 6 circuit malfunction
P0207	Injector no. 7 circuit malfunction
P0208	Injector no. 8 circuit malfunction
P0217	Engine coolant over-temperature
P0218	Transmission fluid over-temperature
P0219	Engine over speed condition
P0221	Throttle Position (TP) sensor B circuit range/performance problem
P0222	Throttle Position (TP) sensor B circuit, low input
P0223	Throttle Position (TP) sensor B circuit, high input
P0231	Fuel pump secondary circuit low
P0232	Fuel pump secondary circuit high

Diagnostic Trouble Codes (continued)

Code	Probable cause
P0234	Turbocharger/Supercharger A Overboost Condition
P0236	Turbocharger/Supercharger Boost Sensor A Circuit Range/Performance
P0237	Turbocharger/Supercharger Boost Sensor A Circuit Low
P0238	Turbocharger/Supercharger Boost Sensor A Circuit High
P023A	Charge Air Cooler Coolant Pump Control Circuit/Open
P023B	Charge Air Cooler Coolant Pump Control Circuit Low
P023C	Charge Air Cooler Coolant Pump Control Circuit High
P0243	Turbocharger/Supercharger Wastegate Actuator A
P0244	Turbocharger/Supercharger Wastegate Actuator A Range/Performance
P0245	Turbocharger/Supercharger Wastegate Actuator A Low
P0246	Turbocharger/Supercharger Wastegate Actuator A High
P0247	Turbocharger/Supercharger Wastegate Actuator B
P0248	Turbocharger/Supercharger Wastegate Actuator B Range/Performance
P0249	Turbocharger/Supercharger Wastegate Actuator B Low
P0250	Turbocharger/Supercharger Wastegate Actuator B High
P025A	Fuel Pump Module A Control Circuit/Open
P025B	Fuel Pump Module A Control Circuit Range/Performance
P025C	Fuel Pump Module A Control Circuit Low
P025D	Fuel Pump Module A Control Circuit High
P025E	Turbocharger/Supercharger Boost Sensor A Intermittent/Erratic
P026A	Charge Air Cooler Efficiency Below Threshold
P027B	Fuel Pump Module B Control Circuit Range/Performance
P028D	Charge Air Cooler Cooling Fan Control Circuit Low
P028E	Charge Air Cooler Cooling Fan Control Circuit High
P0297	Vehicle Overspeed Condition
P0298	Engine Oil Over Temperature Condition
P0299	Turbocharger/Supercharger A Underboost Condition
P02EE	Cylinder 1 Injector Circuit Range/Performance
P02EF	Cylinder 2 Injector Circuit Range/Performance
P02F0	Cylinder 3 Injector Circuit Range/Performance

Code	Probable cause
P02F1	Cylinder 4 Injector Circuit Range/Performance
P02F2	Cylinder 5 Injector Circuit Range/Performance
P02F3	Cylinder 6 Injector Circuit Range/Performance
P02FC	Cold Start Fuel Injection Control Circuit Low
P02FD	Cold Start Fuel Injection Control Circuit High
P0300	Random misfire detected
P0301	Cylinder no. 1 misfire detected
P0302	Cylinder no. 2 misfire detected
P0303	Cylinder no. 3 misfire detected
P0304	Cylinder no. 4 misfire detected
P0305	Cylinder no. 5 misfire detected
P0306	Cylinder no. 6 misfire detected
P0307	Cylinder no. 7 misfire detected
P0308	Cylinder no. 8 misfire detected
P0313	Misfire Detected With Low Fuel
P0315	PCM unable to learn crankshaft pulse wheel tooth spacing
P0316	Misfire occurred during first 1000 engine revolutions
P0320	Ignition engine speed input circuit malfunction
P0322	Ignition/Distributor Engine Speed Input Circuit No Signal
P0325	Knock/Combustion Vibration Sensor 1 Circuit (Bank 1)
P0326	Knock/Combustion Vibration Sensor 1 Circuit Range/Performance (Bank 1)
P0327	Knock/Combustion Vibration Sensor 1 Circuit Low (Bank 1)
P0328	Knock/Combustion Vibration Sensor 1 Circuit High (Bank 1)
P0330	Knock/Combustion Vibration Sensor 2 Circuit (Bank 2)
P0331	Knock/Combustion Vibration Sensor 2 Circuit Range/Performance (Bank 2)
P0332	Knock/Combustion Vibration Sensor 2 Circuit Low (Bank 2)
P0333	Knock/Combustion Vibration Sensor 2 Circuit High (Bank 2)
P0335	Crankshaft Position Sensor A Circuit
P0336	Crankshaft Position Sensor A Circuit Range/Performance
P0339	Crankshaft Position Sensor A Circuit Intermittent

Diagnostic Trouble Codes (continued)

Code	Probable cause
P0340	Camshaft Position (CMP) sensor circuit malfunction (right cylinder head)
P0341	Camshaft position sensor, A circuit, Bank 1, range or performance
P0344	Camshaft position sensor, A circuit, intermittent
P0345	Camshaft Position (CMP) sensor circuit malfunction (left cylinder head)
P0346	Camshaft position sensor, A circuit, range or performance
P0349	Camshaft position sensor, A circuit, Bank 2, intermittent
P0350	Ignition coil primary or secondary circuit malfunction
P0351-P0358	Ignition coil primary or secondary circuit malfunction, coils 1 through 8
P0365	Camshaft Position Sensor B Circuit (Bank 1)
P0366	Camshaft Position Sensor B Circuit Range/Performance (Bank 1)
P0369	Camshaft Position Sensor B Circuit Intermittent (Bank 1)
P0390	Camshaft Position Sensor B Circuit (Bank 2)
P0391	Camshaft Position Sensor B Circuit Range/Performance (Bank 2)
P0394	Camshaft Position Sensor B Circuit Intermittent (Bank 2)
P0400	EGR flow failure (outside the minimum or maximum limits)
P0403	EEGR electric motor windings or circuits to PCM shorted or open (6.8L engine)
P0420	Catalyst system efficiency below threshold (right cylinder bank)
P0430	Catalyst system efficiency below threshold (left cylinder bank)
P0442	EVAP control system, small leak detected
P0443	EVAP control system, canister purge valve circuit malfunction
P0446	EVAP control system canister vent solenoid circuit malfunction
P0451	Fuel tank pressure sensor circuit out of range or performance problem
P0452	Fuel tank pressure sensor circuit, low input
P0453	Fuel tank pressure sensor circuit, high input
P0454	Fuel tank pressure sensor circuit, noisy
P0455	EVAP control system, big leak detected
P0456	EVAP control system, very small leak detected
P0457	EVAP control system, leak detected (fuel filler neck cap loose or off)
P0460	Fuel level sensor circuit malfunction

Code	Probable cause
P0461	Fuel level sensor circuit range or performance problem
P0462	Fuel level sensor circuit, low input
P0463	Fuel level sensor circuit, high input
P0480	Fan 1, control primary circuit malfunction
P0481	Fan 2, control circuit, open or short
P0482	Medium Fan Control (MFC) primary circuit failure
P04DB	Crankcase Ventilation System Disconnected
P0500	Vehicle Speed Sensor A
P0501	Vehicle Speed Sensor A Range/Performance
P0503	Vehicle Speed Sensor A Intermittent/Erratic/High
P0504	Brake switch circuit, correlation to brake position switch
P0505	Idle Control System
P0506	Idle Control System - RPM Lower Than Expected
P0507	Idle Control System - RPM Higher Than Expected
P050A	Cold Start Idle Control System Performance
P050B	Cold Start Ignition Timing Performance
P050E	Cold Start Engine Exhaust Temperature Too Low
P0512	Starter relay circuit, short
P051B	Crankcase Pressure Sensor Circuit Range/Performance
P051C	Crankcase Pressure Sensor Circuit Low
P051D	Crankcase Pressure Sensor Circuit High
P0528	Fan Speed Sensor Circuit No Signal
P052A	Cold start cam position timing, Bank 1, over-advanced
P052B	Cold start cam position timing, Bank 1, over-retarded
P052C	Cold start cam position timing, Bank 2, over-advanced
P052D	Cold start cam position timing, Bank 2, over-retarded
P052F	Cold Start Fuel Pressure Performance Bank 1
P0544	Exhaust Gas Temperature Sensor Circuit (Bank 1 Sensor 1)
P0545	Exhaust Gas Temperature Sensor Circuit Low (Bank 1 Sensor 1)
P0546	Exhaust Gas Temperature Sensor Circuit High (Bank 1 Sensor 1)

Diagnostic Trouble Codes (continued)

Code	Probable cause
P054A	Cold Start Exhaust B Camshaft Position Timing Over-Advanced (Bank 1)
P054B	Cold Start Exhaust B Camshaft Position Timing Over-Retarded (Bank 1)
P054C	Cold Start Exhaust B Camshaft Position Timing Over-Advanced (Bank 2)
P054D	Cold Start Exhaust B Camshaft Position Timing Over-Retarded (Bank 2)
P0562	System voltage low
P0563	System voltage high
P0571	Brake switch, A circuit
P0572	Brake switch, A circuit, low voltage
P0573	Brake switch, A circuit, high voltage
P05FF	Brake Pressure Sensor / Brake Pedal Position Sensor Correlation
P0600	Serial communication link (PCM) error
P0602	Control module programming error
P0603	Powertrain Control Module (PCM) Keep-Alive-Memory (KAM) test error
P0604	Powertrain Control Module (PCM) Random (RAM memory corrupted
P0605	Powertrain Control Module (PCM) Read-Only-Memory (ROM) error
P0606	Powertrain Control Module (PCM), internal communication error
P0607	Powertrain Control Module (PCM), PCM needs reprogramming
P060A	Internal Control Module Monitoring Processor Performance
P060B	Internal Control Module A/D Processing Performance
P060C	Internal Control Module Main Processor Performance
P060D	Internal Control Module Accelerator Pedal Position Performance
P0610	Control Module Vehicle Options Error
P061A	Internal Control Module Torque Performance
P061B	Internal Control Module Torque Calculation Performance
P061C	Internal Control Module Engine RPM Performance
P061D	Internal Control Module Engine Air Mass Performance
P061E	Internal Control Module Brake Signal Performance
P061F	Internal Control Module Throttle Actuator Controller Performance
P0627	Fuel pump, A circuit, control/open
P062B	Internal Control Module Fuel Injector Control Performance

Code	Probable cause
P062D	Internal Control Module Vehicle Speed Performance
P062F	Powertrain Control Module (PCM) EEPROM error
P0630	VIN Not Programmed Or Incompatible - ECM/PCM
P0642	Reference voltage circuit, low voltage
P0643	Reference voltage circuit, high voltage
P064A	Fuel Pump Control Module A
P064D	Internal Control Module O2 Sensor Processor Performance (Bank 1)
P064E	Internal Control Module O2 Sensor Processor Performance (Bank 2)
P064F	Unauthorized Software/Calibration Detected
P0652	Sensor Reference Voltage B Circuit Low
P0653	Sensor Reference Voltage B Circuit High
P0657	Transmission solenoid actuator, supply voltage circuit open
P0660	Intake Manifold Tuning Valve Control Circuit/Open (Bank 1)
P0663	Intake Manifold Tuning Valve Control Circuit/Open (Bank 2)
P0685	ECM/PCM Power Relay Control Circuit/Open
P0686	ECM/PCM Power Relay Control Circuit Low
P0687	ECM/PCM Power Relay Control Circuit High
P0689	ECM/PCM Power Relay Sense Circuit Low
P068A	ECM/PCM Power Relay De-Energized - Too Early
P0690	Powertrain control module, power relay control circuit, high
P06A6	Sensor Reference Voltage A Circuit Range/Performance
P06A7	Sensor Reference Voltage B Circuit Range/Performance
P06A8	Sensor Reference Voltage C Circuit Range/Performance
P06B6	Internal Control Module Knock Sensor Processor 1 Performance
P06B8	Internal Control Module Non-Volatile Random Access Memory (NVRAM) Error
P06D1	Internal Control Module Ignition Coil Control Module Performance
P06E9	Engine Starter Performance
P0703	Brake Switch B Circuit
P0704	Clutch Switch Input Circuit
P0720	Output Shaft Speed Sensor Circuit

Diagnostic Trouble Codes (continued)

Code	Probable cause
P0721	Output Shaft Speed Sensor Circuit Range/Performance
P0722	Output Shaft Speed Sensor Circuit No Signal
P0723	Output Shaft Speed Sensor Circuit Intermittent
P0830	Clutch Pedal Switch A Circuit
P0833	Clutch Pedal Switch B Circuit
P08A9	Clutch Pedal Position Sensor A Circuit Low
P08AA	Clutch Pedal Position Sensor A Circuit High
P08B6	Clutch Pedal Position Sensor B Circuit Low
P08B7	Clutch Pedal Position Sensor B Circuit High
P08B9	Clutch Pedal Position Sensor A/B Correlation
P0A3B	Generator Over Temperature
P1001	KOER Not Able to Complete, KOER Aborted
P100F	Wastegate Control Pressure/BARO Correlation
P1011	Wastegate Control Pressure Sensor Circuit Range/Performance
P1012	Wastegate Control Pressure Sensor Circuit Low
P1013	Wastegate Control Pressure Sensor Circuit High
P1014	Wastegate Control Pressure Sensor Circuit Intermittent/Erratic
P1015	Wastegate Control Pressure Lower Than Expected
P1016	Wastegate Control Pressure Higher Than Expected
P101F	Cylinder Head Temperature Sensor 1 Out Of Self Test Range
P1021	Cylinder Head Temperature Sensor 2 Circuit Range/Performance
P1022	Cylinder Head Temperature Sensor 2 Circuit Low
P1023	Cylinder Head Temperature Sensor 2 Circuit High
P1024	Cylinder Head Temperature Sensor 2 Circuit Intermittent/Erratic
P1025	Cylinder Head Temperature Sensor 2 Out Of Self Test Range
P1026	Engine Coolant Temperature 1 / Cylinder Head Temperature 2 Correlation
P1030	Cylinder 1 Fuel Injector Heater Circuit Low
P1031	Cylinder 1 Fuel Injector Heater Circuit High
P1032	Cylinder 2 Fuel Injector Heater Circuit Low
P1033	Cylinder 2 Fuel Injector Heater Circuit High

Code	Probable cause
P1034	Cylinder 3 Fuel Injector Heater Circuit Low
P1035	Cylinder 3 Fuel Injector Heater Circuit High
P1038	Fuel Injector Heater Control Module Control Circuit
P1039	Fuel Injector Heater Control Module System Voltage
P103A	Fuel Injector Heater Control Module Monitor Circuit
P103B	Fuel Injector Heater Control Module Performance
P1060	Excessive Camshaft Chain Wear
P1061	Excessive Camshaft Chain Wear - Forced Limited Engine Speed
P1100	Mass Air Flow Sensor Circuit Intermittent
P1101	Mass Air Flow Sensor Out Of Self Test Range
P1112	Intake Air Temperature Circuit Intermittent
P1116	Engine Coolant Temperature Sensor Out Of Self Test Range
P1117	Engine Coolant Temperature Sensor Circuit Intermittent
P111B	Engine Coolant Warm-Up Not Detected
P1121	Throttle Position Sensor A Inconsistent With MAF/MAP Sensor
P1124	Throttle Position Sensor A Out Of Self Test Range
P1127	Exhaust Temperature Out Of Range, O2 Sensor Tests Not Completed
P115E	Throttle Actuator Control Throttle Body Air Flow Trim At Max Limit
P117A	Engine Oil Overtemperature - Forced Limited Power
P1184	Engine Oil Temperature Sensor Out of Self Test Range
P1260	Theft Detected, Vehicle Immobilized
P1270	Engine RPM Or Vehicle Speed Limiter Reached
P1285	Cylinder Head Over Temperature Condition
P1288	Cylinder Head Temperature Sensor Out Of Self Test Range
P1289	Cylinder Head Temperature Sensor Circuit High
P128A	Cylinder Head Temperature Sensor Circuit Intermittent/Erratic
P1290	Cylinder Head Temperature Sensor Circuit Low
P1299	Cylinder Head Over Temperature Protection Active
P130D	Engine Knock/Combustion Performance - Forced Limited Power
P1336	Crankshaft/Camshaft Sensor Range/Performance

Diagnostic Trouble Codes (continued)

Code	Probable cause
P1397	System Voltage Out Of Self Test Range
P1408	EGR Flow Out Of Self Test Range
P144A	EVAP System Purge Vapor Line Restricted/Blocked
P144C	EVAP System Purge Flow Performance During Boost
P1450	Unable To Bleed Up Fuel Tank Vacuum
P1500	Vehicle Speed Sensor
P1501	Vehicle Speed Sensor Out Of Self Test Range
P1502	Vehicle Speed Sensor Intermittent
P1548	Engine Air Filter Restriction
P1561	Brake Line Pressure Sensor Circuit
P1572	Brake Pedal Switch Circuit
P1575	Pedal Position Out Of Self Test Range
P1588	Throttle Control Detected Loss Of Return Spring
P160A	Control Module Vehicle Options Reconfiguration Error
P161A	Incorrect Response From Immobilizer Control Module
P162D	Internal Control Module Cruise Control Performance
P162E	Internal Control Module PTO Control Performance
P162F	Starter Motor Disabled - Engine Crank Time Too Long
P1633	Keep Alive Power Voltage Too Low
P1635	Tire/Axle Out of Acceptable Range
P1636	Inductive Signature Chip Communication Error
P1639	Vehicle ID Block Corrupted, Not Programmed
P1646	Linear O2 Sensor Control Chip (Bank 1)
P1647	Linear O2 Sensor Control Chip (Bank 2)
P164A	O2 Sensor Positive Current Trim Circuit Performance (Bank 1 Sensor 1)
P164B	O2 Sensor Positive Current Trim Circuit Performance (Bank 2 Sensor 1)
P164C	Internal Control Module Start-Stop Performance
P166A	Restraints Deployment Communication Circuit
P1674	Control Module Software Corrupted
P1698	Cold Start Fuel Pump Primary Circuit/Open

Code	Probable cause
P169B	Cold Start Fuel Pump Primary Circuit High
P169C	Cold Start Fuel Pump Secondary Circuit/Open
P1703	Brake Switch Out Of Self Test Range
P1793	Ignition Supply Malfunction
P1900	Output Shaft Speed Sensor Circuit Intermittent
P1934	Vehicle Speed Signal
P1935	Brake Switch/Sensor Signal
P193C	Steering Wheel Angle Signal
P193F	Vehicle Speed Signal Intermittent
P2004	Intake Manifold Runner Control Stuck Open (Bank 1)
P2005	Intake Manifold Runner Control Stuck Open (Bank 2)
P2006	Intake Manifold Runner Control Stuck Closed (Bank 1)
P2007	Intake Manifold Runner Control Stuck Closed (Bank 2)
P2008	Intake Manifold Runner Control Circuit/Open (Bank 1)
P2011	Intake Manifold Runner Control Circuit/Open (Bank 2)
P2014	Intake Manifold Runner Position Sensor/Switch Circuit (Bank 1)
P2019	Intake Manifold Runner Position Sensor/Switch Circuit (Bank 2)
P2070	Intake Manifold Tuning Valve Stuck Open (Bank 1)
P2071	Intake Manifold Tuning Valve Stuck Closed (Bank 1)
P2088	A Camshaft Position Actuator Control Circuit Low (Bank 1)
P2089	A Camshaft Position Actuator Control Circuit High (Bank 1)
P2090	B Camshaft Position Actuator Control Circuit Low (Bank 1)
P2091	B Camshaft Position Actuator Control Circuit High (Bank 1)
P2096	Post Catalyst Fuel Trim System Too Lean (Bank 1)
P2097	Post Catalyst Fuel Trim System Too Rich (Bank 1)
P2098	Post Catalyst Fuel Trim System Too Lean (Bank 2)
P2099	Post Catalyst Fuel Trim System Too Rich (Bank 2)
P2100	Throttle Actuator A Control Motor Circuit / Open
P2101	Throttle Actuator A Control Motor Circuit Range / Performance
P2107	Throttle Actuator A Control Module Processor

Diagnostic Trouble Codes (continued)

Code	Probable cause
P2109	Throttle / Pedal Position Sensor A Minimum Stop Performance
P2111	Throttle Actuator A Control System - Stuck Open
P2112	Throttle Actuator A Control System - Stuck Closed
P2118	Throttle Actuator A Control Motor Current Range / Performance
P2119	Throttle Actuator A Control Throttle Body Range / Performance
P2122	Throttle / Pedal Position Sensor / Switch D Circuit Low
P2123	Throttle / Pedal Position Sensor / Switch D Circuit High
P2127	Throttle / Pedal Position Sensor / Switch E Circuit Low
P2128	Throttle / Pedal Position Sensor / Switch E Circuit High
P2135	Throttle / Pedal Position Sensor / Switch A / B Voltage Correlation
P2138	Throttle / Pedal Position Sensor / Switch D / E Voltage Correlation
P2149	Fuel Injector Group B Supply Voltage Circuit/Open
P2163	Throttle / Pedal Position Sensor A Maximum Stop Performance
P2176	Throttle Actuator A Control System - Idle Position Not Learned
P2195	O2 Sensor Signal Biased / Stuck Lean (Bank 1 Sensor 1)
P2196	O2 Sensor Signal Biased / Stuck Rich (Bank 1 Sensor 1)
P2197	O2 Sensor Signal Biased / Stuck Lean (Bank 2 Sensor 1)
P2198	O2 Sensor Signal Biased / Stuck Rich (Bank 2 Sensor 1)
P219A	Bank 1 Air-Fuel Ratio Imbalance
P219B	Bank 2 Air-Fuel Ratio Imbalance
P219C	Cylinder 1 Air-Fuel Ratio Imbalance
P219D	Cylinder 2 Air-Fuel Ratio Imbalance
P219E	Cylinder 3 Air-Fuel Ratio Imbalance
P219F	Cylinder 4 Air-Fuel Ratio Imbalance
P21A0	Cylinder 5 Air-Fuel Ratio Imbalance
P21A1	Cylinder 6 Air-Fuel Ratio Imbalance
P21CF	Cylinder 1 Injector B Circuit/Open
P21D0	Cylinder 2 Injector B Circuit/Open
P21D1	Cylinder 3 Injector B Circuit/Open
P21D2	Cylinder 4 Injector B Circuit/Open

Code	Probable cause
P21D3	Cylinder 5 Injector B Circuit/Open
P21D4	Cylinder 6 Injector B Circuit/Open
P2227	Barometric Pressure Sensor A Circuit Range/Performance
P2228	Barometric Pressure Sensor A Circuit Low
P2229	Barometric Pressure Sensor A Circuit High
P2230	Barometric Pressure Sensor A Circuit Intermittent/Erratic
P2237	O2 Sensor Positive Current Control Circuit / Open (Bank 1 Sensor 1)
P2240	O2 Sensor Positive Current Control Circuit / Open (Bank 2 Sensor 1)
P2243	O2 Sensor Reference Voltage Circuit / Open (Bank 1 Sensor 1)
P2247	O2 Sensor Reference Voltage Circuit / Open (Bank 2 Sensor 1)
P2251	O2 Sensor Negative Current Control Circuit / Open (Bank 1 Sensor 1)
P2254	O2 Sensor Negative Current Control Circuit / Open (Bank 2 Sensor 1)
P2270	O2 Sensor Signal Biased / Stuck Lean (Bank 1 Sensor 2)
P2271	O2 Sensor Signal Biased / Stuck Rich (Bank 1 Sensor 2)
P2272	O2 Sensor Signal Biased / Stuck Lean (Bank 2 Sensor 2)
P2273	O2 Sensor Signal Biased / Stuck Rich (Bank 2 Sensor 2)
P2279	Intake Air System Leak
P2280	Air Flow Restriction/Air Leak Between Air Filter And MAF Bank 1
P2281	Air Leak Between MAF And Throttle Body
P2282	Air Leak Between Throttle Body And Intake Valve
P2300	Ignition Coil A Primary Control Circuit Low
P2301	Ignition Coil A Primary Control Circuit High
P2303	Ignition Coil B Primary Control Circuit Low
P2304	Ignition Coil B Primary Control Circuit High
P2306	Ignition Coil C Primary Control Circuit Low
P2307	Ignition Coil C Primary Control Circuit High
P2309	Ignition Coil D Primary Control Circuit Low
P2310	Ignition Coil D Primary Control Circuit High
P2312	Ignition Coil E Primary Control Circuit Low
P2313	Ignition Coil E Primary Control Circuit High

Diagnostic Trouble Codes (continued)

Code	Probable cause
P2315	Ignition Coil F Primary Control Circuit Low
P2316	Ignition Coil F Primary Control Circuit High
P2318	EVAP System Switching Valve Control Circuit/Open
P2450	EVAP System Switching Valve Performance/Stuck Open
P2510	ECM / PCM Power Relay Sense Circuit Range/Performance
P25B3	Turbocharger/Supercharger Wastegate A Stuck Open
P25B4	Turbocharger/Supercharger Wastegate A Stuck Closed
P25B5	Turbocharger/Supercharger Wastegate B Stuck Open
P25B6	Turbocharger/Supercharger Wastegate B Stuck Closed
P260F	EVAP System Monitoring Processor Performance
P2610	ECM/PCM Engine Off Timer Performance
P2626	O2 Sensor Positive Current Trim Circuit / Open (Bank 1 Sensor 1)
P2627	O2 Sensor Positive Current Trim Circuit Low (Bank 1 Sensor 1)
P2628	O2 Sensor Positive Current Trim Circuit High (Bank 1 Sensor 1)
P2629	O2 Sensor Positive Current Trim Circuit / Open (Bank 2 Sensor 1)
P2630	O2 Sensor Positive Current Trim Circuit Low (Bank 2 Sensor 1)
P2631	O2 Sensor Positive Current Trim Circuit High (Bank 2 Sensor 1)
P2632	Fuel Pump B Control Circuit/Open
P264F	Engine Serial Number Not Programmed Or Incompatible
P26C4	Internal Control Module Clutch Pedal Performance
P26EA	Fuel Pump Control Module B
P2A01	O2 Sensor Circuit Range / Performance (Bank 1 Sensor 2)
P2A07	O2 Sensor Circuit Range / Performance (Bank 2 Sensor 2)
P2AB7	Wastegate Position Sensor A Circuit
P2AB8	Wastegate Position Sensor A Circuit Low
P2AB9	Wastegate Position Sensor A Circuit High
P2ABA	Wastegate Position Sensor B Circuit
P2ABB	Wastegate Position Sensor B Circuit Low
P2ABC	Wastegate Position Sensor B Circuit High
P2ABD	Turbocharger/Supercharger Wastegate Actuator A Driver Current/Temperature Too High

Code	Probable cause
P2ABE	Turbocharger/Supercharger Wastegate Actuator B Driver Current/Temperature Too High
P2C27	Fuel Injector Group B Supply Sense Circuit Low
P2C28	Fuel Injector Group B Supply Sense Circuit High

4 Powertrain Control Module (PCM) - removal and installation

Caution: *To avoid electrostatic discharge damage to the PCM, handle the PCM only by its case. Do not touch the electrical terminals during removal and installation. If available, ground yourself to the vehicle with an anti-static ground strap, available at computer supply stores.*

Note: *The replacement of the PCM requires the new PCM to be programmed. This is a procedure that must be performed at a dealership or other properly equipped repair facility.*

1   If the PCM is to be replaced, it is best to have a dealership or qualified repair facility perform the Programmable Module Installation (PMI) procedure along with other required procedures. These procedures involve downloading the current data from the existing PCM and uploading it to the new PCM after installation as well as identifying the vehicle the PCM is installed in (as-built data). Take this into consideration prior to replacing the PCM.

2   The Powertrain Control Module (PCM) is located in the passenger's (right) side of the cowl, accessible from the engine compartment (see illustration).

3   Unlock the PCM connector latches and disconnect the electrical connectors from the PCM (see illustration).

4   Remove the two nuts and pull the PCM from the cowl (see illustration).

5   Installation is reverse of removal.

6   If a new (replacement) PCM is to be installed, the following programming procedures need to be performed after installation (these must be performed at a dealership or other qualified repair facility):

    a) *Module configuration.*
    b) *Anti-theft security access.*
    c) *Misfire monitor neutral profile correction.*

5 Accelerator Pedal Position (APP) sensor - replacement

1   To replace the APP sensor, see Chapter 4, Section 3.

6 Engine Coolant Temperature (ECT) sensor - replacement

Warning: *Wait until the engine is completely cool before beginning this procedure.*

Caution: *The ECT sensor is not to be re-used. Install only a NEW ECT sensor once it is removed.*

Note: *Only 2.7L models are equipped with an Engine Coolant Temperature (ECT) sensor.*

Note: *The Engine Coolant Temperature (ECT) sensor determines the coolant temperature. A problem in the CMP sensor circuit will set a diagnostic trouble code.*

1   Drain the cooling system (see Chapter 1).

2   Remove the fuel rails (see Chapter 4, Section 16), the water pump (see Chapter 3, Section 9) and the coolant outlet connector (coolant pipe) between the cylinder banks.

3   Disconnect the ECT sensor electrical connector.

4   Unscrew the ECT sensor from the engine and discard.

5   Installation is reverse of removal. Tighten the NEW ECT sensor to the torque listed in this Chapter's Specifications.

6   Refill the cooling system (see Chapter 1).

4.2 The PCM is located on the right side of the cowl

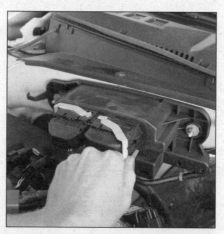

4.3 To disconnect the electrical connectors from the PCM, depress the lock tabs and swing open the levers

4.4 Remove the two nuts and pull the PCM from the cowl

7.1 Location of the IAT sensor (2.7L model shown)

8.2 Location of the MAP sensor (2.7L model shown)

9.2 The CHT sensor is located near the left-bank turbocharger (2.7L model shown)

7   Intake Air Temperature (IAT) sensor - replacement

Note: *Only 2.7L and 3.5L turbocharged models are equipped with an Intake Air Temperature (IAT) sensor. A problem in the IAT sensor circuit will set a diagnostic trouble code.*

1   The Intake Air Temperature (IAT) sensor is located on the intake air tube between the air filter housing and the air inlet ducts (see illustration).

2   Disconnect the electrical connector, then rotate the IAT sensor counterclockwise to release it from the intake air duct.

3   Installation is reverse of removal.

8   Manifold Absolute Pressure (MAP) sensor - replacement

Note: *The Manifold Absolute Pressure (MAP) sensor measures pressure within the intake manifold. A problem in the MAP sensor circuit will set a diagnostic trouble code.*

2.7L and 3.5L models

1   Remove the two nuts at the front of the engine cover. Lift up at the front and unhook the retainers at the rear of the cover to remove.

2   Locate the MAP sensor on the top of the intake manifold (see illustration) and disconnect the electrical connector.

3   Remove the mounting bolt and remove the MAP sensor.

4   Installation is reverse of removal. Lubricate the MAP sensor O-ring with clean engine oil prior to installation.

5.0L models

Note: *On 5.0L models, the MAP sensor is located on the rear of the intake manifold.*

5   Remove the intake manifold from the engine (see Chapter 2B, Section 5).

6   Locate the MAP sensor on the rear of the intake manifold and remove the fastener

to remove the sensor.

7   Installation is reverse of removal. Lubricate the MAP sensor O-ring with clean engine oil prior to installation.

9   Cylinder Head Temperature (CHT) sensor - replacement

Note: *The cylinder head temperature sensor is a major component of the Fail Safe Cooling system. This sensor varies the value of its voltage output in accordance with temperature changes. The change in the resistance values will directly affect the voltage signal from the CHT sensor. As the sensor temperature decreases, the resistance values will increase (voltage increases). If the cylinder head temperature exceeds 265-degrees F, the PCM disables half of the fuel injectors at a time. The cylinders that do not receive fuel act as cooling air pumps for the other cylinders. If the temperature exceeds 330-degrees F, the PCM disables all the fuel injectors. A problem in the CHT sensor circuit will set a diagnostic trouble code.*
Caution: *The CHT sensor is not to be reused. Install only a NEW CHT sensor once it is removed.*

2.7L models

1   Remove the two nuts at the front of the engine cover. Lift up at the front and unhook the retainers at the rear of the cover to remove.

2   Locate the CHT sensor in the driver cylinder head and disconnect the electrical connector (see illustration).

3   Unscrew the CHT sensor from the cylinder head and discard.

4   Installation is reverse of removal. Tighten the NEW CHT sensor to specification shown in this Chapter's Specifications.

3.5L non-turbo models

Note: *The CHT sensor is located under the*

lower intake manifold in the passenger's (right) cylinder head.

5   To remove the cylinder head temperature sensor, the upper and lower intake manifolds must be removed from the engine (see Chapter 2A, Section 5).

6   Locate the CHT sensor in the passenger's (right) cylinder head and unplug the electrical connector.

7   Unscrew the CHT sensor from the cylinder head and discard.

8   Installation is reverse of removal. Tighten the NEW CHT sensor to specification shown in this Chapter's Specifications.

3.5L turbocharged and 5.0L models

Note: *The CHT sensor is located at the rear of the passenger's (right) cylinder head, above the transmission bellhousing.*

9   Raise and support the front of the vehicle on jack stands and remove the passenger front wheel.

10   Remove the passenger's (right) front inner fender splash shield.

11   Locate the CHT sensor at the rear of the passenger's (right) cylinder head and unplug the electrical connector.

12   Unscrew the CHT sensor from the cylinder head and discard.

13   Installation is reverse of removal. Tighten the NEW CHT sensor to specification shown in this Chapter's Specifications.

10   Crankshaft Position (CKP) sensor - replacement

Note: *The crankshaft position sensor (CKP) determines the timing on each cylinder for the fuel injectors and ignition system. A problem in the crankshaft sensor circuit will set a diagnostic trouble code.*
Caution: *After installing the CKP sensor, a scan tool should be used to perform the Misfire Monitor Neutral Profile Correction procedure.*

10.3 Location of the CKP sensor (2.7L model shown; on 5.0L models the sensor is mounted higher up, behind the cylinder head)

10.10 Remove the fasteners securing the exhaust manifold heat shield

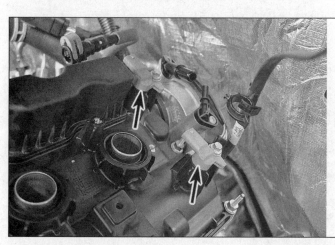

11.3 Locating the CMP sensors on 2.7L models (left [driver's side] bank shown)

2.7L and 5.0L models

1   Raise and support the front of the vehicle on jack stands and remove the passenger's (right) front wheel.
2   Remove the passenger's (right) front inner fender splash shield.
3   Locate the CKP sensor at the right-rear side of the engine block (see illustration).
4   If necessary, disconnect any harness retainers.
5   Disconnect the CKP sensor electrical connector.
6   Remove the bolt and pull the sensor from the engine block.
Note: *The CKP sensor is very long.*
7   Installation is reverse of removal. Tighten the bolt to the torque listed in this Chapter's Specifications.

3.5L models

8   Raise the front of the vehicle and support it securely on jackstands. Remove the under vehicle cover and/or skid plate (as equipped). Remove the transmission skid plate (if equipped).
9   If you're working on a turbocharged

model, remove the left (driver's side) turbocharger (see Chapter 4).
10   Remove the two fasteners and the heat shield located on the left rear (driver's) side of the engine block (see illustration).
11   Remove the CKP sensor access plug in the engine bellhousing.
12   Remove the bolt and pull the sensor out of the access hole.
13   Disconnect the crankshaft position sensor electrical connector.
Note: *The CKP sensor is very long.*
14   Installation is reverse of removal. Tighten the bolt to the torque listed in this Chapter's Specifications.

11   Camshaft Position (CMP) sensor - replacement

Note: *The Camshaft Position (CMP) sensor determines the position of the cylinder for ignition start-up signals and for sequential fuel injection signals to each cylinder. The engine is equipped with four CMPs, one for each camshaft. A problem in the CMP sensor circuit will*

set a diagnostic trouble code.
Note: *On 2.7L models, the CMPs are mounted on the top of the valve covers. On 3.5L turbocharged models, the driver's side (left) CMPs are mounted on the top of the valve cover at the rear of the engine, and the passenger (right) CMPs are mounted on the rear of the cylinder head. On 3.5L non-turbo and 5.0L models, the CMPs are mounted on the rear of the cylinder heads.*
1   On 2.7L and 3.5L turbocharged models, remove the two nuts at the front of the engine cover. Lift up at the front and unhook the retainers at the rear of the cover to remove.
2   On 3.5L non-turbo and 5.0L models, loosen the wheel lug nuts, raise and support the front of the vehicle on jackstands, then remove the front wheel for the sensor requiring replacement. Remove the inner fender splash shield (see Chapter 11).
3   On all models, locate and disconnect the electrical connector(s) from the camshaft position sensor(s) (see illustration).
4   Remove the bolt and pull the sensor out of the valve cover or cylinder head.
Note: *On 5.0L engines, the radio noise filter is attached to the engine by the driver's (left) side intake CMP sensor bolt.*
5   Lubricate the O-ring with clean engine oil prior to installation.
6   Installation is the reverse of removal.

12   Engine Oil Pressure (EOP) sensor - replacement

Note: *3.5L non-turbo models are not equipped with an Engine Oil Pressure (EOS) sensor.*
Note: *The Engine Oil Pressure (EOP) sensor determines the oil pressure. A problem in the EOP sensor circuit will set a diagnostic trouble code.*
Caution: *If the EOP sensor is to be reinstalled, apply sealant to the sensor threads.*

12.1 Remove the air cleaner outlet pipe (2.7L model shown)

12.5 Location of the EOP sensor (2.7L model shown)

13.2 Location of the oil pressure control solenoid (2.7L model shown)

2.7L models

Note: *On 2.7L models, the EOP sensor is located on the passenger's side cylinder head, near the turbocharger.*

1   Loosen the clamps and remove the air filter outlet duct attached the the air filter housing lid and the left and right air intake ducts (see illustration).

2   Loosen the right front wheel lug nuts, then raise the front of the vehicle and support it securely on jackstands. Remove the wheel and the inner fender splash shield (see Chapter 11).

3   Loosen the clamp at the turbocharger and remove the right air filter outlet pipe between the turbocharger inlet and the air filter outlet pipe (see Chapter 4, Section 17).

4   Loosen the clamps and remove the charge air cooler inlet pipe between the turbocharger outlet and the intercooler.

5   Locate and disconnect the EOP sensor electrical connector (see illustration).

6   Use a deep socket or wrench to unscrew the EOP sensor.

7   Installation is reverse of removal. Tighten the sensor to the torque listed in this Chapter's Specifications.

3.5L turbocharged and 5.0L models

Note: *On 3.5L turbocharged and 5.0L models, the EOP sensor is located on the oil cooler/filter adapter housing.*

8   Loosen the left-front wheel lug nuts, then raise and support the front of the vehicle on jackstands.

9   Remove the under vehicle cover and/or skid plate (as equipped).

10   On 3.5L turbocharged models, remove the driver's side inner fender splash shield (see Chapter 11).

11   On all models, locate the EOP sensor installed in the oil cooler adapter housing.

12   Disconnect the electrical connector and unscrew the EOP sensor to remove.

13   Installation is reverse of removal. Tighten the sensor to the torque listed in this Chapter's Specifications.

13   Oil pressure control solenoid - replacement

Note: *3.5L non-turbo models are not equipped with an Engine Oil Pressure (EOS) sensor.*

2.7L models

1   Raise and support the front of the vehicle on jackstands.

Note: *It may be necessary to remove the engine undercover.*

2   The oil pressure control solenoid is located near the crankshaft pulley at the bottom of the engine (see illustration).

3   Disconnect the electrical connector.

4   Remove the retainer bolt and remove the solenoid from the front of the engine.

5   Installation is the reverse of removal.

3.5L turbocharged models

6   The oil pressure control solenoid is located inside of the engine and requires the engine front cover to be removed to access and replace the solenoid. See Chapter 2A, Section 9.

7   Disconnect the electrical connector.

8   Remove the retainer and remove the solenoid from the front of the engine.

9   Installation is reverse of removal.

5.0L models

Note: *The oil pressure control solenoid is located on the left side of the engine, near the rear of the alternator.*

10   Loosen the left front wheel lug nuts, then raise and support the front of the vehicle on jackstands. Remove the wheel.

11   Remove the inner fender splash shield (see Chapter 11).

12   Locate the oil pressure control solenoid behind the alternator and disconnect the electrical connector.

13   Remove the retainer bolt and remove the solenoid from the side of the engine.

14   Installation is reverse of removal.

14   Variable Camshaft Timing (VCT) variable force solenoid - removal and installation

Note: *The Variable Camshaft Timing (VCT) variable force solenoid supplies force to actuate the VCT oil control valve. The engine is equipped with four VCTs. The PCM sends a signal based on engine speed and load, and the solenoid moves the VCT oil control valve to advance or retard or hold position. The camshaft is then re-positioned in relation to crankshaft timing to allow for optimum engine performance with lower emissions and reduced fuel consumption. A problem in the VCT sensor circuit will set a diagnostic trouble code.*

14.2a Identifying the driver's (left) bank VCT solenoids . . .

14.2b . . . and the passenger's (right) bank VCT solenoids
(2.7L model shown)

Note: *On 2.7L models, the VCTs are located on the top of the heads at the front of the engine. On 3.5L and 5.0L models, the VCTs are located under the valve covers, in the heads at the front of the engine.*

1   On 2.7L models, remove the two nuts at the front of the engine cover. Lift up at the front and unhook the retainers at the rear of the cover to remove.

2   On all models, locate and disconnect the VCT solenoid connectors (see illustrations).

3   On 3.5L and 5.0L models, remove the valve cover for the solenoid to removed (see Chapter 2A, Section 4 or Chapter 2B, Section 4).

4   Unscrew the bolts and remove the VCT from the cylinder head.

5   Installation is reverse of removal. Tighten the bolts to the torque listed in this Chapter's Specifications.

15   Turbocharger Boost Pressure (TCPB) and Charge Air Cooler Temperature (CACT) sensor - replacement

Note: *Only 2.7L and 3.5L (turbocharged) models are equipped with a combination Turbocharger Boost Pressure (TCPB) and Charge Air Cooler Temperature (CACT) sensor. A problem in the sensor circuit will set a diagnostic trouble code.*

1   Locate the TCPB/CACT sensor in the intake pipe between the intercooler and the throttle body (see illustration).

2   Disconnect the electrical connector and remove the fasteners.

3   Remove the TCPB/CACT sensor from the air intake pipe.

4   Installation is reverse of removal.

16   Turbocharger bypass valve - replacement

Note: *Only 2.7L and 3.5L (turbocharged) models are equipped with a Turbocharger bypass valve. A problem in the sensor circuit will set a diagnostic trouble code.*

1   Raise the vehicle and support it securely on jackstands.

2   Remove the under vehicle cover and/or skid plate (as equipped).

3   Locate the turbocharger bypass valve attached to the intercooler above the outlet pipe.

4   Disconnect the turbocharger bypass valve quick-disconnect fitting.

5   Disconnect the electrical connector (see illustration).

6   Remove the fasteners and the bypass valve from the intercooler (see illustration).

7   Installation is the reverse of removal.

15.1 Locating the Turbocharger Boost Pressure (TCPB) and
Charge Air Cooler Temperature (CACT) sensor
(2.7L shown; 3.5L similar)

16.6 Disconnect the electrical connector (1) and remove the two
bolts (2) attaching the bypass valve to the intercooler

17.2 Locating the wastegate vacuum sensor

17.4 Disconnect the vacuum line after unbolting the sensor

17 Turbocharger wastegate vacuum sensor - replacement

Note: *Only 2.7L and 3.5L (turbocharged) models are equipped with a wastegate vacuum sensor. A problem in the sensor circuit will set a diagnostic trouble code.*

1   Remove the two nuts at the front of the engine cover. Lift up at the front and unhook the retainers at the rear of the cover to remove.

2   Locate the wastegate vacuum sensor on the top of the intake manifold (see illustration) and disconnect the electrical connector.

3   Remove the mounting bolt and remove the wastegate vacuum sensor.

4   Disconnect the vacuum line that runs to the wastegates (see illustration).

5   Installation is the reverse of removal.

18 Oxygen sensors - general information and replacement

General information

1   All models covered by this manual have On-Board Diagnostics II (OBD-II) engine management systems, which means that they have the ability to verify the accuracy of the basic feedback loop between the oxygen sensor and the PCM. They accomplish this by using an oxygen sensor in front of the catalytic converter and an oxygen sensor behind the catalytic converter. By sampling the exhaust gas before and after the catalytic converter, the PCM can determine the efficiency of the converter and can even predict when it will fail.

2   The primary (upstream) oxygen sensor is located in the exhaust pipe or manifold and the secondary (downstream) oxygen sensor is located on or behind the catalytic converter. The upstream and downstream oxygen sensors on all models is a heated oxygen sensor. The PCM uses a supply wire and ground wire to control the power to the O2 sensor heater during warm-up.

Note: *The downstream oxygen sensors may also be referred to as Catalyst Monitor Sensor (CMS).*

3   Special care must be taken whenever a sensor is serviced.

a) *Oxygen sensors have a permanently attached pigtail and an electrical connector which should not be removed from the sensor. Damage or removal of the pigtail or electrical connector can adversely affect operation of the sensor.*

b) *Grease, dirt and other contaminants should be kept away from the electrical connector and the louvered end of the sensor.*

c) *Do not use cleaning solvents of any kind on an oxygen sensor.*

d) *Do not drop or roughly handle an oxygen sensor.*

e) *The silicone boot must be installed in the correct position to prevent the boot from being melted and to allow the sensor to operate properly.*

Replacement

Note: *Because it is installed in the exhaust manifold or pipe, which contracts when cool, the oxygen sensor may be very difficult to loosen when the engine is cold. Rather than risk damage to the sensor, assuming you are planning to reuse it in another manifold or pipe, start and run the engine for a minute or two, then shut it off. Be careful not to burn yourself during the following procedure.*

4   Raise the vehicle and support it securely on jackstands. Access the oxygen sensor harness and unplug the electrical connector (see illustrations).

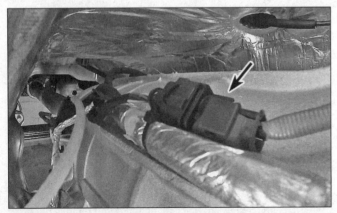

18.4a Oxygen sensor electrical connectors (top of transmission) - right cylinder bank (2.7L model shown)

18.4b Oxygen sensor electrical connectors (attached to a bracket near the rear of the transmission) - left cylinder bank (2.7L model shown)

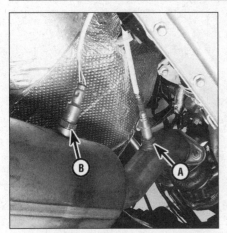

18.5a Upstream (A) and downstream (B) oxygen sensors - left cylinder bank shown, right bank similar (2.7L model shown)

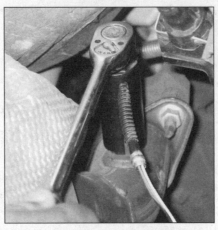

18.5b If available, use a slotted socket to remove the oxygen sensor

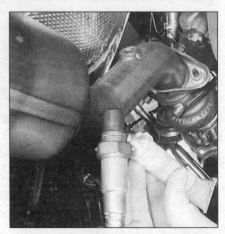

18.6 Applying anti-seize compound to an oxygen sensor (new sensors should already be coated)

5   Unscrew the sensor from the exhaust manifold or exhaust pipe (see illustration).
Note: *The best tool for removing an oxygen sensor is a special slotted socket, especially if you're planning to reuse a sensor. If you don't have this tool, and you plan to reuse the sensor, be extremely careful when unscrewing the sensor.*
6   If the old sensor is to be installed, apply anti-seize compound to the threads of the sensor to facilitate future removal (see illustration). The threads of new sensors should already be coated with this compound, but if you're planning to reuse an old sensor, recoat the threads. Install the sensor and tighten it securely.
7   Reconnect the electrical connector of the pigtail lead to the main wiring harness.
8   Lower the vehicle, test drive the car and verify that no trouble codes have been set.

19   Knock sensors - replacement

1   Wait until the engine is completely cool before beginning this procedure.
Note: *The knock sensors are located in the valley between the cylinder banks. The knock control system is designed to reduce spark knock during periods of heavy detonation. This allows the engine to use optimal spark advance to improve driveability. The knock sensors detect abnormal vibration in the engine and produce a voltage output which increases with the severity of the knock. The voltage signal is monitored by the PCM, which retards ignition timing until the detonation ceases. A problem in the knock sensor circuit will set a diagnostic trouble code.*
Note: *All models have two knock sensors that share a single wiring harness; they must be replaced as a pair.*
2   Relieve the fuel system pressure (see Chapter 4), then disconnect the cable from the negative terminal of the battery (see Chapter 5).
3   On 3.5L non-turbo models, disconnect the knock sensor harness electrical connector

located on the rear of the left (driver's side) cylinder head.
4   On 5.0L models, remove the intake manifold (see Chapter 2B, Section 5).
5   On 2.7L and 3.5L models, remove the fuel rails (see Chapter 4, Section 16).
6   On 2.7L models, remove the water pump (see Chapter 3) and coolant outlet connector (coolant pipe between the cylinder banks), then disconnect the Engine Coolant Temperature (ECT) sensor connector.
7   On all models, disconnect the electrical connector and remove the bolts securing the knock sensors to the cylinder banks, then remove the knock sensors.
8   Coat the threads of the knock sensor bolts with thread sealant. New sensor bolts are pre-coated with thread sealant; do not apply any additional sealant or the operation of the sensor may be affected.
9   Install the knock sensors and tighten the bolts to the torque listed in this Chapter's Specifications.
Caution: *Do not tighten the knock sensor bolt without a torque wrench. The knock sensor readings may be inaccurate or damage may occur to the knock sensor or engine block.*
10   Remainder of installation is the reverse of removal.

20   Fuel tank pressure (FTP) sensor - replacement

Warning: *Gasoline is extremely flammable, so take extra precautions when you work on any part of the fuel system. Don't smoke or allow open flames or bare light bulbs near the work area, and don't work in a garage where a gas-type appliance (such as a water heater or clothes dryer) is present. Since gasoline is carcinogenic, wear fuel-resistant gloves when there's a possibility of being exposed to fuel, and, if you spill any fuel on your skin, rinse it off immediately with soap and water. Mop up any spills immediately and do not store fuel-soaked rags where they could ignite. When you per-*

form any kind of work on the fuel system, wear safety glasses and have a Class B type fire extinguisher on hand. The fuel system is under pressure, so if any lines must be disconnected, the pressure in the system must be relieved first (see Chapter 4 for more information).
1   The fuel tank pressure (FTP) sensor is used to monitor the fuel tank pressure or vacuum during the OBD-II test portion for emissions integrity. This test scans various sensors and output actuators to detect abnormal amounts of fuel vapors that may not be purging into the canister or the intake system for recycling. The FTP sensor helps the PCM monitor this pressure differential (pressure vs. vacuum) inside the fuel tank. A problem in the fuel tank pressure sensor circuit will set a diagnostic trouble code.
Note: *The Fuel Tank Pressure (FTP) sensor is part of the vapor tube assembly and serviced as one unit.*
2   Remove the fuel tank (see Chapter 4, Section 7).
3   Disconnect the vapor tube from the quick-disconnect fittings and remove the vapor tube and FTP sensor (see illustration).
4   Installation is the reverse of removal.
5   Turn the ignition on and check for leaks.

20.3 Identifying the fuel pressure sensor and tube on top of the fuel tank

22.2 Locating the PCV valve (2.7L model shown)

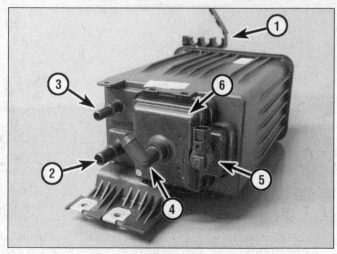

23.8 Identifying EVAP canister components

1	*EVAP line retainers*	4	*Canister vent line*
2	*Canister line to fuel tank*	5	*Canister vent solenoid*
3	*Canister line to engine*	6	*Canister filter*

**23.11 Remove the EVAP canister mounting
bolts and remove the canister**

21   Fuel rail pressure/temperature
sensor - replacement

1   The fuel rail pressure and temperature sensors are attached to the fuel rails. Fuel rail removal is required to remove the sensors. See Chapter 4, Section 16.

22   Positive Crankcase Ventilation
(PCV) system

Note: *The PCV valve on all models is located on the right-side valve cover.*
1   The Positive Crankcase Ventilation (PCV) system reduces hydrocarbon emissions by scavenging crankcase vapors. It does this by circulating fresh air from the air cleaner through the crankcase, where it mixes with blow-by gases and is then rerouted through a PCV valve to the intake manifold.
2   The PCV valve is located on the valve cover (see illustration).
3   To maintain idle quality, the PCV valve restricts the flow when the intake manifold vacuum is high. If abnormal operating conditions

(such as piston ring problems) arise, the system is designed to allow excessive amounts of blow-by gases to flow back through the crankcase vent tube into the air cleaner to be consumed by normal combustion.
4   Checking and replacement of the PCV valve is covered in Chapter 1.

23   Evaporative emissions control
(EVAP) system - general
description and component
replacement

Warning: *Gasoline is extremely flammable, so take extra precautions when you work on any part of the fuel system. Don't smoke or allow open flames or bare light bulbs near the work area, and don't work in a garage where a gas-type appliance (such as a water heater or clothes dryer) is present. Since gasoline is carcinogenic, wear fuel-resistant gloves when there's a possibility of being exposed to fuel, and, if you spill any fuel on your skin, rinse it off immediately with soap and water. Mop up any spills immediately and do not store fuel-soaked rags where they could ignite. When you perform any kind of work on the fuel system, wear safety glasses and have a Class B type fire extinguisher on hand. The fuel system is under pressure, so if any lines must be disconnected, the pressure in the system must be relieved first (see Chapter 4 for more information).*

General description

1   This system is designed to trap and store fuel vapors that evaporate from the fuel tank, throttle body and intake manifold during non-operation or idling, store them in the charcoal canister and then route them into the combustion chamber to be burned during engine operation.
2   The Evaporative Emission Control Sys-

tem (EVAP) consists of a charcoal-filled canister and the lines connecting the canister to the fuel tank, a fuel vapor management valve (VMV), a fuel tank pressure sensor, fuel filler cap, a canister vent solenoid, a fuel vapor vent valve, ported vacuum and intake manifold vacuum.
3   Fuel vapors are transferred from the fuel tank, throttle body and intake manifold to a canister where they are stored when the engine is not operating. When the engine is running, the fuel vapors are purged from the canister by a vapor management valve (VMV), which is PCM controlled and consumed in the normal combustion process. The fuel tank pressure sensor detects internal fuel tank pressure and relays the information to the PCM which in turn regulates the EVAP system purge controls.

Component replacement

Charcoal canister

Note: *The charcoal canister is located on the driver's side frame rail, forward of the fuel tank.*
4   Disconnect the negative battery cable (see Chapter 5, Section 3).
5   Raise and support the vehicle on jackstands.
6   Remove the transfer case skid plate (if equipped).
7   Remove the fuel filler cap to relieve the pressure inside the fuel tank.
8   Disconnect the charcoal canister quick-disconnect fittings and hose (see illustration).
9   Disconnect the charcoal canister vent solenoid electrical connector.
10   Detach the EVAP line retainers from the canister.
11   Remove the charcoal canister mounting bolts (see illustration).
12   Remove the charcoal canister from the vehicle.
13   Installation is the reverse of removal.

23.15 Rotate the vent solenoid clockwise to remove

23.19 Release the clips to remove the filter

Canister vent solenoid

Note: *The canister vent solenoid is located on the charcoal canister and is part of the lid it is connected to.*

14 Remove the charcoal canister from the vehicle.

15 Rotate the solenoid in a clockwise direction to remove from the canister (see illustration).

16 Installation is the reverse of removal. Ensure a click is heard when installing the solenoid to the canister.

Canister vent filter

Note: *The canister vent filter is located on the charcoal canister under the vent solenoid.*

17 Remove the charcoal canister from the vehicle.

18 Remove the canister vent solenoid from the canister.

19 Release the four tabs and remove the canister vent filter from the canister (see illustration).

20 Installation is the reverse of removal. Ensure a click is heard when installing the vent filter to the canister.

Canister purge valve

Note: *The canister purge valve is located on the left (driver's) side of the intake manifold, just behind the throttle body.*

21 On 2.7L and 3.5L turbocharged models, remove the engine cover.

22 On all models, disconnect the electrical connector and quick-connect fitting from the valve and intake manifold as necessary (see illustration).

23 On 2.7L and 3.5L turbocharged models, slide the valve from the retainer on the intake manifold.

24 On 3.5L non-turbo and 5.0L models, remove the two bolts and remove the purge valve from the intake manifold.

25 Installation is the reverse of removal.

---

24 Catalytic converter

Note: *Because of a Federally mandated extended warranty which covers emissions-re-*

23.22 Disconnect the purge valve hoses and connector to remove (2.7L model shown)

lated components such as the catalytic converter, check with a dealer service department before replacing the converter at your own expense.

General description

1 The catalytic converter is an emission control device added to the exhaust system to reduce pollutants from the exhaust gas stream. The three-way catalyst lowers the levels of oxides of nitrogen (NOx) as well as hydrocarbons (HC) and carbon monoxide (CO).

Check

2 The test equipment for a catalytic converter is expensive and highly sophisticated. If you suspect that the converter on your vehicle is malfunctioning, take it to a dealer or authorized emissions inspection facility for diagnosis and repair.

3 Whenever the vehicle is raised for servicing of underbody components, check the converter for leaks, corrosion, dents and other damage. Check the welds/flange bolts that attach the front and rear ends of the converter to the exhaust system. If damage is discovered, the converter should be replaced.

4 Although catalytic converters don't break too often, they can become plugged. The easiest way to check for a restricted converter is

to use a vacuum gauge to diagnose the effect of a blocked exhaust on intake vacuum.

a) Connect a vacuum gauge to an intake manifold vacuum source.

b) Warm the engine to operating temperature, place the transmission in Park (automatic) or Neutral (manual) and apply the parking brake.

c) Note and record the vacuum reading at idle.

d) Quickly open the throttle to near full throttle and release it shut. Note and record the vacuum reading.

e) Perform the test three more times, recording the reading after each test.

f) If the reading after the fourth test is more than one in-Hg lower than the reading recorded at idle, the exhaust system may be restricted (the catalytic converter could be plugged or an exhaust pipe or muffler could be restricted).

Replacement

5 Be sure to spray the nuts on the exhaust flange studs before removing them from the catalytic converter(s).

6 Remove the nuts and straps and separate the catalytic converter from the exhaust system.

7 Installation is the reverse of removal.

Notes

Chapter 7 Part A
Automatic transmission

Contents

	Section		Section
Automatic transmission overhaul - general information	14	Shift lever - removal and installation	3
Automatic transmission - removal and installation	13	Steering wheel paddle shifters - replacement	5
Auxiliary cooling - component removal and installation	10	Transmission auxiliary fluid pump - replacement	9
Diagnosis - general	2	Transmission Control Module (TCM)	
General information	1	(10-speed transmission) - replacement	8
Output shaft seal - replacement	11	Transmission mount - replacement	12
Shift cable - removal, installation and adjustment	4	Transmission Range (TR) sensor - description	
Shift interlock system - description, check and		and adjustment	6
actuator replacement	7		

Specifications

Fluid specifications
Type and capacity... See Chapter 1

Torque specifications
Ft-lbs (unless otherwise indicated)

Note: *One foot-pound (ft-lb) of torque is equivalent to 12 inch-pounds (in-lbs) of torque. Torque values below approximately 15 foot-pounds are expressed in inch-pounds, because most foot-pound torque wrenches are not accurate at these smaller values.*

Auxiliary fluid pump bolts	115 In-lbs
Output shaft nut (10-speed transmission with bolt-on output flange)	148
Output shaft flange	
Bolt (10-speed transmission)	81
Nut (6-speed transmission)	59
Torque converter-to-driveplate nuts	30
Transmission-to-engine bolts	35
Transmission cooler line bolt	22
Transmission crossmember-to-frame nuts/bolts	76
Transmission mount-to-crossmember nuts	76
Transmission mount-to-transmission bolts	66

1   General information

1   The transmission is a fully automatic, electronic-shift six-speed or 10-speed (some 2017 and later models) with a lock-up torque converter, known as a torque converter clutch, or TCC (the TCC provides a direct connection between the engine and the drive wheels for improved efficiency and fuel economy) and has selectable Tow/Haul mode and manual up/down shift features.

2   On 6-speed transmissions, the Powertrain Control Module (PCM) controls the transmission electronic functions. There is not a separate Transmission Control Module (TCM). On vehicles with auto stop/start, the transmission is equipped with an auxiliary pump on the passenger side of the case. This pump is used to maintain line pressure during shut-down on auto stop/start models.

3   On 10-speed models, a separate TCM controls the transmission electronic functions.

4   The transmission fluid dipstick is located under the vehicle on the right front side of the transmission. The dipstick is used to check fluid level and add fluid in the same fashion as a dipstick with a tube that is accessed through the engine compartment.

5   Because of the complexity of the clutches and the electronic and hydraulic control systems, and because of the special tools and expertise needed to overhaul an automatic transmission, diagnosis and repair of this transmission must be handled by a dealer service department or a transmission repair shop. The procedures in this Chapter are limited to general diagnosis, routine maintenance and adjustment: replacing the shift lever, replacing and adjusting the shift cable, and similar jobs. Serious repair work, however, must be done by a transmission specialist. But if the transmission must be rebuilt or replaced, you can save money by removing and installing it yourself, so instructions for that procedure are included as well.

Adaptive learning drive cycle

Note: *Perform on a level road surface. The engine and transmission must be at normal operating temperature. Ensure the transmission fluid is at the correct level.*

6   Check for the presence of any Diagnostic Trouble Codes (DTCs) stored in the PCM (see Chapter 6). If any DTCs are stored, write them down and clear them.

7   Warm the engine and transmission to operating temperature.

6-speed transmissions

8   With the transmission in Drive (D), accelerate moderately from a stop to 50 mph). Make sure the transmission shifts into 6th gear. With the transmission in in 6th gear, maintain vehicle speed and throttle position for a minimum of 15 seconds.

9   While maintaining a steady speed and throttle in 6th gear, lightly apply and release the brake to operate stop lights. Maintain the current speed and throttle position for a minimum of 5 seconds.

10   When safe, bring the vehicle to a complete stop and remain at idle with the transmission in Drive (D) and foot on the brake pedal for a minimum of 20 seconds.

11   Repeat steps 8, 9 and 10 an additional five times.

10-speed transmissions

12   Accelerate from a stop with about 15-percent throttle. Use care to make sure that the 1-2, 2-3, 3-4, 4-5, 5-6, 6-7, 7-8 shifts occur between 1300-1600 rpm.

13   Continue to accelerate (you can apply more throttle after the 7-8 upshift) until the vehicle reaches 55 mph and 8-9 and 9-10 shifts are made.

14   When safe, bring the vehicle to a complete stop and remain at idle with the transmission in Drive (D) and foot on the brake pedal for a minimum of 5 seconds.

15   Shift to Neutral (N) then to Reverse (R).

16   Repeat steps 11, 12, 13 and 14 and additional six (6) times.

2   Diagnosis - general

Note: *Automatic transmission malfunctions may be caused by five general conditions: poor engine performance, improper adjustments, hydraulic malfunctions, mechanical malfunctions or malfunctions in the computer or its signal network. Diagnosis of these problems should always begin with a check of the easily repaired items: fluid level and condition (see Chapter 1), and shift cable adjustment. Next, perform a road test to determine if the problem has been corrected or if more diagnosis is necessary. If the problem persists after the preliminary tests and corrections are completed, additional diagnosis should be done by a dealer service department or transmission repair shop. Refer to the* Troubleshooting *section at the front of this manual for information on symptoms of transmission problems.*

Note: *All of the vehicles covered in this manual require battery power to be available at all times to maintain strategy parameters which are stored in the keep alive memory (KAM). Therefore, whenever the battery is to be disconnected, first note the following to ensure that there are no unforeseen consequences of this action:*

a) *The KAM will lose the information stored in its memory when the battery is disconnected. This is a temporary condition.*

b) *Whenever the battery is disconnected, the information relating to operating values will have to be re-programmed into the unit's memory.*

c) *The PCM does this by itself, but until then, there may be a generally inferior level of performance. Once the PCM relearns these values it will return to normal operating condition.*

Preliminary checks

Note: *10-speed transmissions may skip gears when accelerating from a complete stop or decelerating to a stop. This is normal operation.*

1   Drive the vehicle to warm the transmission to normal operating temperature.

2   Check the fluid level as described in Chapter 1:

a) *If the fluid level is unusually low, add enough fluid to bring the level within the designated area of the dipstick, then check for external leaks (see below).*

b) *If the fluid level is abnormally high, drain off the excess, then check the drained fluid for contamination by coolant. The presence of engine coolant in the automatic transmission fluid indicates that a failure has occurred in the internal radiator walls that separate the coolant from the transmission fluid (see Chapter 3).*

c) *If the fluid is foaming, drain it and refill the transmission, then check for coolant in the fluid or a high fluid level.*

3   Check the engine idle speed.

Note: *If the engine is malfunctioning, do not proceed with the preliminary checks until it has been repaired and runs normally.*

4   Inspect the shift cable (see Section 4). Make sure it's properly adjusted and operates smoothly.

Fluid leak diagnosis

5   Most fluid leaks are easy to locate visually. Repair usually consists of replacing a seal or gasket. If a leak is difficult to find, the following procedure may help.

6   Identify the fluid. Make sure it's transmission fluid and not engine oil or brake fluid (automatic transmission fluid is a deep red color).

7   Try to pinpoint the source of the leak. Drive the vehicle several miles, then park it over a large sheet of cardboard. After a minute or two, you should be able to locate the leak by determining the source of the fluid dripping onto the cardboard.

8   Make a careful visual inspection of the suspected component and the area immediately around it. Pay particular attention to gasket mating surfaces. A mirror is often helpful for finding leaks in areas that are hard to see.

9   If the leak still cannot be found, clean the suspected area thoroughly with a degreaser or solvent, then dry it.

10   Drive the vehicle for several miles at normal operating temperature and varying speeds. After driving the vehicle, visually inspect the suspected component again.

11   Once the leak has been located, the cause must be determined before it can be properly repaired. If a gasket is replaced but the sealing flange is bent, the new gasket will not stop the leak. The bent flange must be straightened.

12   Before attempting to repair a leak, check to make sure the following conditions are corrected or they may cause another leak.

Note: *Some of the following conditions cannot be fixed without highly specialized tools and expertise. Such problems must be referred to a transmission repair shop or a dealer service department.*

3.11 Disconnect the TCS connector

3.12 Remove the shift lever bolt

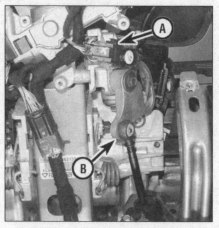

3.19 Disconnect the BTSI solenoid connector (A) and the shift cable (B)

Gasket leaks

13 Check the pan periodically. Make sure the bolts are tight, no bolts are missing, the gasket is in good condition and the pan is flat (dents in the pan may indicate damage to the valve body inside).

14 If the pan gasket is leaking, the fluid level or the fluid pressure may be too high, the vent may be plugged, the pan bolts may be too tight, the pan sealing flange may be warped, the sealing surface of the transmission housing may be damaged, the gasket may be damaged or the transmission casting may be cracked or porous. If sealant instead of gasket material has been used to form a seal between the pan and the transmission housing, it may be the wrong sealant.

Seal leaks

15 If a transmission seal is leaking, the fluid level or pressure may be too high, the vent may be plugged, the seal bore may be damaged, the seal itself may be damaged or improperly installed, the surface of the shaft protruding through the seal may be damaged or a loose bearing may be causing excessive shaft movement.

16 Make sure the dipstick tube seal is in good condition and the tube is properly seated. Periodically check the area around the speedometer gear or sensor for leakage. If transmission fluid is evident, check the O-ring for damage.

Case leaks

17 If the case itself appears to be leaking, the casting is porous and will have to be repaired or replaced.

18 Make sure the oil cooler hose fittings are tight and in good condition.

Fluid comes out vent pipe

19 If this condition occurs, the transmission is overfilled, there is coolant in the fluid, the case is porous, the dipstick is incorrect, the vent is plugged or the drain back holes are plugged.

3 Shift lever - removal and installation

Note: *The Transmission Control Switch (TCS) contains the tow/haul switch and upshift/downshift (SelectShift) buttons. Both are part of the shift lever/shift knob, and not serviceable separately.*

Shift knob - console mounter shifter

1 Set the parking brake.

2 Open the center console lid and pull firmly to release the clips attaching the trim panel around the shifter and cup holder, to the center console.

3 Remove the screws in the console center tray and pull firmly to release the clips attaching the shifter bezel to the center console.

4 Raise the shifter bezel enough to disconnect the electrical connectors and detach the shift boot clips. Remove the shifter bezel.

5 Turn the ignition on, press the brake pedal and move the shifter to the 1 position.

6 Disconnect the shift knob electrical connector.

7 Remove the screws attaching the shift knob to the shift lever assembly and remove the knob and boot.

8 The boot can be removed from the knob.

9 Installation is the reverse of removal.

Shift lever - column mounted shifter

10 Remove the steering column covers (see Chapter 11).

11 Unplug the electrical connector for the shift lever (see illustration).

12 Remove the shift lever bolt (see illustration).

13 Remove the shift lever.

14 Installation is the reverse of removal. Be sure to replace the shift lever bolt; do NOT use the old bolt.

Shift lever assembly

Column mounted shifter

Caution: *Before replacing the column shift lever assembly for no-start or hard-to-shift concern, verify the shift cable-to-bracket clips are seated fully at both the transmission and the shift lever assemblies. Cables that are not fully seated can be the cause of shift cable binding and may prevent the manual shaft from fully returning to the P position, causing a no-start condition.*

15 Set the parking brake.

16 Move the shift lever to the Neutral (N) position.

17 Remove the shift lever.

18 Disconnect the BTSI solenoid connector (see illustration).

19 Using a screwdriver, carefully pry the shift cable from the shift lever pivot (see illustration).

20 Remove and discard the three screws attaching the shift lever assembly to the steering column (see illustration).

21 Installation is the reverse of removal.

22 Use new bolts when installing the shift lever assembly to the column.

3.20 Remove the three screws to remove the shift lever mechanism

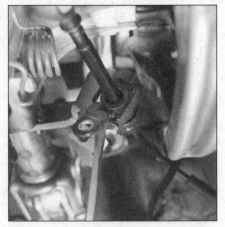

4.4 Remove the bolt and the cable retainer

4.5 Pry the cable from the shift lever assembly pivot

4.6 Remove the screw and the instrument panel lower trim

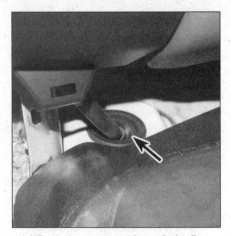

4.8 Push the grommet through the floor

4.10 Pry up the cable lock to release the cable

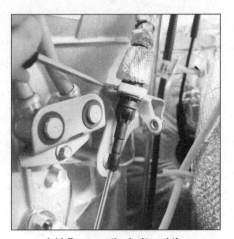

4.11 Remove the bolt and the cable retainer

Console mounted shifter

Note: *The BTSI solenoid is part of the shift lever assembly and not serviceable separately.*

23   Remove the shift knob.
24   Remove the four bolts attaching the shift lever assembly to the floor.
25   Remove the bolt attaching the shift cable to the shift lever assembly.
26   Using a screwdriver, carefully pry the shift cable from the shift lever pivot.
27   Disconnect the electrical connector from the rear of the shift lever assembly.
28   Remove the shift lever assembly from the vehicle.
29   Installation is the reverse of removal.
30   Adjust the shift cable (see Section 4).

---

4   Shift cable - removal, installation and adjustment

Removal and installation
Column mounted shifter

1   Remove the steering column covers (see Chapter 11).

2   Shift the transmission to Drive (D) position.
3   Remove the knee bolster and steering column reinforcement plate (see Chapter 11, Section 23).
4   Remove the bolt attaching the shift cable retainer to the bracket and remove the retainer (see illustration).
5   Using a screwdriver, carefully pry the shift cable from the shift lever pivot (see illustration).
6   Remove the instrument panel lower trim at the carpet by removing the screw on the driver's side and pull away enough to access the shift cable grommet in the floor (see illustration).

Console mounted shifter

7   Remove the shift lever assembly (see Section 3).

All models

8   Push the rubber grommet and shift cable through the floor (see illustration).
Note: *Pull the carpet back to access the cable as necessary.*
9   Raise the vehicle and place it securely on jackstands.

10   Clean the cable adjustment lock and carefully pry up on the end facing the rear of the vehicle to disengage the lock (see illustration).
11   Remove the bolt attaching the shift cable retainer to the bracket and remove the retainer at the transmission (see illustration).
12   Remove the cable housing clip from the vehicle floor.
13   Remove the cable from the vehicle, feeding the cable from the passenger compartment and out of the bottom of the vehicle.
14   Installation is the reverse of removal. Be sure to adjust the cable.

Adjustment
15   Working inside the vehicle, put the shift lever in the Drive (D) position.
16   Raise the vehicle and support it securely on jackstands.
17   Working at the transmission, with the shift cable adjustment lock unlatched, perform the following in order:

a) *Rotate the shift lever at the transmission clockwise until it stops.*
b) *Rotate the shift lever at the transmission counter-clockwise three (3) clicks to place in Drive (D).*

18   Lock the shift cable adjustment lock. Ensure an audible click is heard and pull on the lock and the cable to ensure it is fastened securely.

19   Move the shift lever through all gear positions and verify that the indicated positions correspond with the actual gear positions at the manual lever. Also verify that the engine will start only in Park and Neutral, and that the back-up lights come on when the shift lever is placed in Reverse. If necessary, readjust the cable until these conditions are met. It may also be necessary to adjust the transmission range sensor (see Section 6).

7.5 Move the brake shift interlock solenoid spindle outward

5   Steering wheel paddle shifters - replacement

Warning: *The models covered by this manual are equipped with a Supplemental Restraint System (SRS), more commonly known as airbags. Always disable the airbag system before working in the vicinity of any airbag system component to avoid the possibility of accidental deployment of the airbag, which could cause personal injury (see Chapter 12, Section 27).*

Note: *The up-shift paddle switch is located on the left side of the steering wheel and the downshift paddle switch is located on the right.*

1   Remove the driver's side airbag assembly (see Chapter 10, Section 11).

2   Disconnect the electrical connector for the switch to be replaced.

3   Remove the two screws and remove the paddle switch assembly.

4   Installation is the reverse of removal.

6   Transmission Range (TR) sensor - description and adjustment

Note: *The TorqShift transmission uses a transmission range sensor that is inside the transmission and requires a special tool for service. Replacement should be performed by a qualified repair facility.*

Description

1   The Transmission Range (TR) sensor, which is located inside the transmission at the manual lever, is an information sensor for the Powertrain Control Module (PCM). Among its functions are those normally handled by a conventional Park/Neutral switch: it prevents the engine from starting in any gear other than Park or Neutral, and closes the circuit for the back-up lights when the shift lever is moved to Reverse.

Adjustment

2   If the engine starts in any position other than Park or Neutral, the shift cable is either out of adjustment or the TR sensor is defective. The TR sensor is non-adjustable; adjust the shift cable to adjust the TR sensor operation (see Section 4).

7.13 Remove the BTSI solenoid bolt

7   Shift interlock system - description, check and actuator replacement

Description

1   The shift interlock system prevents the shift lever from being moved out of the Park position unless the brake pedal is depressed. The system consists of a Brake Transmission Shift Interlock (BTSI) solenoid mounted on the steering column or on the shifter assembly in the console. When the ignition key is turned to the Run position, the actuator is energized. When the brake pedal is depressed, the shift lever can be moved from Park.

Check

2   Check the following if the BTSI solenoid isnt working correctly:

a) *Fuses F18 (5A) in the Body Control Module (BCM) and F55 (40A) in the Battery Junction Box (BJB).*

b) *Brake lights operate when pedal is depressed.*

Override

Note: *The following procedure places the shift lever in Neutral (N). With the shift lever in neutral, the vehicle can be started and driven.*

3   Set the parking brake and turn the ignition off. Remove the key if applicable.

Column mounted shifter

4   Detach the shift lever boot from the column covers by pressing towards the front of the vehicle from the rear of the boot.

5   Move the brake shift interlock solenoid spindle outward (see illustration).

6   With the spindle held outward, press the brake pedal and move the shift lever to Neutral (N).

Console mounted shifter

7   Remove the rubber insert in the tray between the shift lever and cup holders.

8   Carefully pry the access cover off and remove.

9   Use a suitable tool to push the brake shift interlock solenoid lever forward.

10   With the spindle held forward, press the brake pedal and move the shift lever to Neutral (N).

Actuator replacement

Column mounted shifter

11   Remove the steering column covers (see Chapter 11).

12   Remove the shift lever mechanism (see Section 3).

13   Remove the BTSI solenoid bolt (see illustration).

7.14a Pry out the BTSI solenoid clip . . .

7.14b . . . and remove the BTSI solenoid

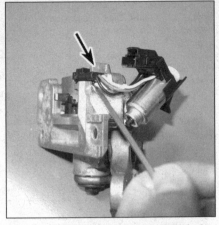

7.15 Press in on the spring-loaded pin for the park position switch

14 Carefully pry out the BTSI solenoid clip and pull the BTSI solenoid from the shift lever mechanism (see illustrations).
15 Press the spring loaded pin for the park position switch and rotate the switch clockwise to remove (see illustration).
16 Remove the BTSI solenoid and park position switch from the shift lever mechanism.
17 Installation is the reverse of removal.

Console mounted shifter

18 The BTSI solenoid is part of the shift lever assembly and not serviceable separately. If the BTSI actuator requires replacement, the shift lever assembly must be replaced. See Section 3.

8 Transmission Control Module (TCM) (10-speed transmission) - replacement

Note: *On 6-speed transmissions, the PCM controls transmission operation.*

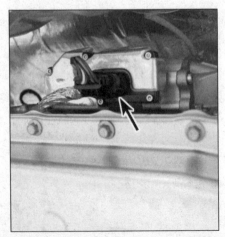

9.3 Disconnect the AUX pump connector

Note: *The TCM is located on a bracket attached to the passenger frame rail under the cab.*
1 Slide the connector lock tab away from the TCM to disengage.
2 Pull the connector straight off of the TCM or damage to the terminals may occur.
3 Remove the three nuts attaching the TCM to the frame.
4 Installation is reverse of removal.
Note: *If a new module is installed, module configuration must be restored and solenoid body strategy must be entered by a qualified repair center.*

9 Transmission auxiliary fluid pump - replacement

Note: *Vehicles with auto stop/start are equipped with an auxiliary fluid pump. On 6-speed transmissions, the pump is located on the right (passenger) side of the transmission. On 10-speed transmissions, the pump is located inside of the transmission. The following procedure covers removal and installation or pumps on 6-speed transmissions only.*
1 Raise and support the vehicle on jackstands.
2 Remove the transmission under cover and skid plate, if equipped.
3 Disconnect the auxiliary fluid pump connector (see illustration).
4 Heat the three Torx bolts using a heat gun to soften the thread sealant.
5 Place a drain pan under the pump to catch any fluid.
6 Remove the bolts and the auxiliary pump.
7 Remove and discard the gasket.
8 Installation is reverse of removal. Use a new gasket and torque the bolts to the torque listed in this Chapter's Specifications.
9 Check the automatic transmission fluid, adding as necessary (see Chapter 1).

10 Auxiliary cooling - component removal and installation

Cooler

1 Remove the grille (refer to Chapter 11, Section 12).
2 Place a drain pan underneath the vehicle to catch fluid. Disconnect the transmission cooler hoses.
3 Release the clips on each end of the cooler and pull the cooler up to remove it.
4 Installation is the reverse of removal.

Coolant by-pass valve/fluid warmer (5.0L models)

Warning: *Wait until the engine is completely cool before beginning this procedure.*
5 Raise and support the front of the vehicle on jackstands.
6 Remove the skid plates as necessary to access the components for removal.
7 Locate the by-pass valve/fluid warmer on the frame, above the stabilizer bar.
8 Remove the bolt and disconnect the cooler hoses from the by-pass valve.
9 Remove the bolt and disconnect the cooler line from the by-pass valve.
10 Remove and discard the sealing rings for the lines.
11 Remove the two bolts attaching the by-pass valve to the fluid warmer and remove the by-pass valve.
12 Remove the bolt and disconnect the cooler line from the fluid warmer.
13 Remove and discard the sealing rings for the lines and by-pass valve connection.
14 Clamp the coolant hoses for the fluid warmer to prevent coolant loss. Remove the hoses from the fluid warmer.
15 Remove the three bolts attaching the fluid warmer to the frame and remove the fluid warmer.
16 Installation is reverse of removal. Top off the transmission fluid and cooling system as necessary (see Chapter 1).

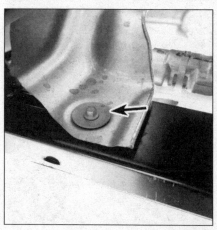

12.4 Remove the exhaust heat shield bolts

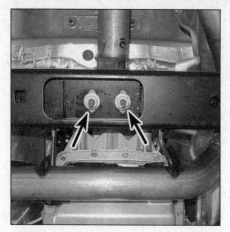

12.5 Remove the nuts attaching the mount to the crossmember

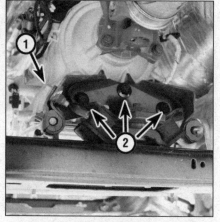

12.8 Remove the exhaust hanger cap (1) and the bolts (2) attaching the mount to the transmission (2WD shown)

17   Lubricate the sealing rings using clean engine oil during installation.

11   Output shaft seal - replacement

Note: *On 2WD non-Raptor 10-speed transmissions, the output shaft flange is attached using a bolt. On 2WD 6-speed transmissions, the output shaft flange is attached using a nut.*
1   Raise and support the vehicle on jackstands.
2   Remove the rear driveshaft (see Chapter 8, Section 2).
3   On 4WD models, remove the transfer case (see Chapter 7B, Section 6).
4   On 2WD models with a bolt-on output shaft flange, mark the flange and output shaft for proper alignment during installation. Remove the nut or bolt and remove the output shaft flange.
Note: *On models that use a retaining nut, and additional seal is located under the nut that also requires replacement.*
Caution: *On 2WD models that use a bolt, a special tool is required to remove the output shaft nut once the flange is removed.*
5   On all models, pry out the seal with a screwdriver or a seal removal tool. Don't damage the seal bore.
6   Lubricate the new seal lips with petroleum jelly.
7   Drive the seal into place with a large socket or section of tubing. The outside diameter of the socket should be slightly smaller than the outside diameter of the seal.
Note: *On 4WD 10-speed transmissions, use care when installing the new seal over the output shaft to prevent seal damage.*
8   On 2WD models with a bolt-on output shaft flange, line up the marks when installing the output shaft flange.
Caution: *On 2WD models that use a bolt, a special tool is required to install and torque the output shaft nut.*
9   On all models, installation is reverse of

removal. Use a new nut or bolt and for the output shaft flange and tighten to the specifications in this Chapter's Specifications.
10   On 2WD models with a nut attaching the output shaft flange, stake the nut in two places to prevent it from loosening.
11   Top off the transmission fluid as necessary.

12   Transmission mount - replacement

1   Raise and support the vehicle on jackstands.
2   Remove the transmission undercover and skip plate, if equipped.
3   Place a transmission jack or a floor jack under the transmission.
4   Remove the bolts attaching the exhaust heat shield to the crossmember (see illustration).
5   Remove the two nuts attaching the transmission mount to the crossmember (see illustration).
6   Remove four nuts and bolts and remove the transmission crossmember from the vehicle.
Note: *When removing the crossmember it may be necessary to use a knife or similar to cut the heat shield material where the frame and crossmember come together.*
7   Remove the bolt and the left (driver's) side exhaust hanger cap from the transmission mount (see illustration 12.9).
8   On 2WD models, remove three transmission mount bolts and slide the mount off of the exhaust hangers to remove (see illustration).
9   On 4WD models, remove two transmission mount bolts on each side of the mount (4 total) and slide the mount off of the exhaust hangers to remove.
10   Installation is reverse of removal. Tighten all fasteners to the torque values listed in this Chapter's Specifications.

13   Automatic transmission - removal and installation

Removal
1   Disconnect the cable from the negative battery terminal (see Chapter 5, Section 3).
2   On 3.5L turbocharged models and models with a 10-speed transmission, remove the engine cover and disconnect the oxygen sensor connector located at the rear of the left (driver's side) valve cover.
3   On models with a 10-speed transmission, disconnect the oxygen sensor connector located at the rear of the right (passenger's) valve cover.
4   On all models, Raise the vehicle and support it securely on jackstands.
5   Remove the starter (see Chapter 5, Section 8).
6   Remove the driveshaft(s) (see Chapter 8).
7   On 2WD models, remove the front stabilizer bar (see Chapter 10, Section 3).
8   On all models, remove any skid plates, if equipped.
9   On 10-speed models, remove the transmission pan heat shield and detach the insulated transmission cover.
10   Drain the transmission fluid (see Chapter 1).
11   Place a transmission jack or a floor jack under the transmission and secure the transmission to the jack with safety chains.
12   Disconnect the oxygen sensor connectors and remove the left (driver's side) catalytic converter assembly.
13   Remove the transmission mount (see Section 12).
14   Disconnect the oxygen sensor connectors and remove the right (passenger's side) catalytic converter assembly.
15   On 10-speed models, disconnect the vent tube at the top of the transmission, behind the bellhousing.
16   On all models, remove the shift lever shield (if equipped).

13.17 Remove the transmission fluid cooler line bolt

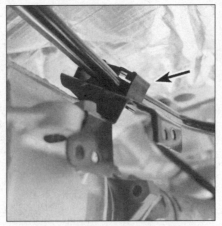

13.19 Disconnect the fuel line bracket from the transmission

13.22 Rotate the electrical connector housing and pull out of the transmission

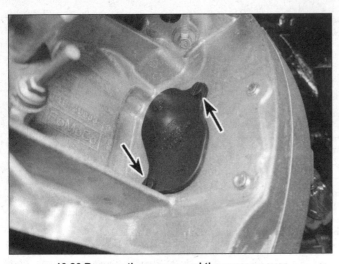

13.26 Remove the screws and the access cover (2.7L model shown)

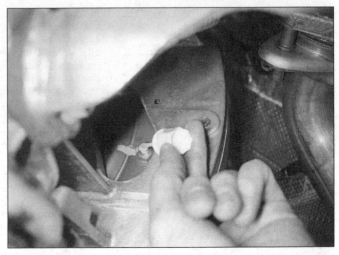

13.29 Mark the relationship between the torque converter and the driveplate for installation

17 Remove the transmission fluid cooler line bolt, release the lines from the bracket next to the oil pan and re-position the lines out of the way (see illustration). Discard the O-rings.
Note: *Remove any transmission mounting bolts or nuts to disconnect the cooling line bracket.*
18 Disconnect the shift cable from the adjuster (see Section 4). Remove the bolt and cable from the bracket (see illustration 4.11).
19 Disconnect the fuel line bracket bolt from the top of the rear of the transmission (see illustration).
20 4WD models, disconnect the transfer case vent tube.
21 Disconnect the transfer case shift motor electrical connector and harness clips.
22 On 6-speed models, working at the right rear of the transmission, rotate the transmission electrical connector housing and pull out of the transmission (see illustration).
23 On 10-speed models, working at the right rear of the transmission, slide the locking tab up on the transmission electrical connec-

tor and disconnect.
24 On models with auto stop/start, disconnect the auxiliary fluid pump connector above the transmission pan (see illustration 9.3).
25 On all models, disconnect the transmission electrical harness clips and position out of the way.
26 On 2.7L models, remove the two screws and the access cover (see illustration).
27 On 3.5L turbocharged and non-turbo models on the right (passenger's) side looking from the engine side of the bellhousing, remove the two screws and access cover.
28 On 5.0L models, remove the driveplate inspection cover at the bottom of the bell housing. On the left (driver's) side looking from the engine side of the bellhousing, remove the rubber access plug.
29 On all models, locate the nearest torque converter stud. Mark the relationship of the torque converter to the driveplate, then remove and discard the four torque converter retaining nuts. Rotate the engine using the

crankshaft bolt to bring each nut within reach through the access hole (see illustration).
30 Remove the ten bolts (seven on 5.0L models) attaching the transmission to the engine. The top bolts also secure the fuel line bracket (see illustrations).
31 Make a final check that all wires have been disconnected from the transmission, then move the transmission and jack toward the rear of the vehicle until the torque converter is separated from the driveplate. Secure the torque converter to the transmission so it won't fall out during removal.
32 On 2WD models, lower the transmission to remove from the vehicle.
33 On 4WD models, as the transfer case makes it difficult to remove, move the transmission towards the rear of the vehicle, then tilt the front of the transmission down and remove towards the front of the vehicle.
34 On 4WD models, remove the transfer case as necessary (see Chapter 7B, Section 6).

13.30a Remove the bottom bolt . . .

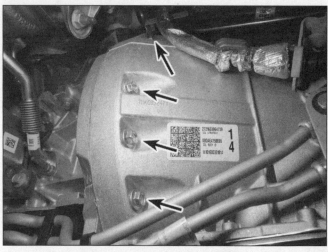

13.30b . . . the driver's (left) side bolts. . .

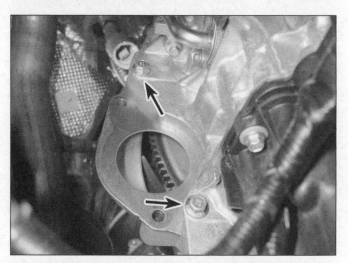

13.30c . . . the passenger's (right) side bolts. . .

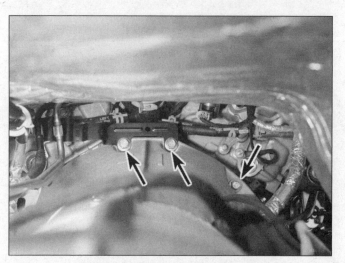

13.30d . . . and the top bolts and bracket

35 On models with auto stop/start, remove the auxiliary transmission fluid pump if necessary (see Section 9).

Installation

36 Installation is reverse of removal, noting the following points:

Note: *If a new transmission is installed, solenoid body strategy must be entered by a qualified repair center.*

a) Use new nuts for the engine and transmission mounts and install using hand tools.
b) Use new nuts for the torque converter.
c) Tighten all fasteners to the torque listed in this Chapter's Specifications.
d) Install new oil cooler line O-rings.
e) Flush the transmission cooler prior to installation.
f) If the transmission had a mechanical failure, replace the auxiliary oil cooler (see Section 10).

g) Lubricate the torque converter pilot hub (where the torque converter enters the crankshaft).
h) Adjust the shift cable (see Section 4).
i) After filling the transmission with new fluid, check the transmission fluid level at operating temperature (150 to 170 degrees) and top off as necessary. Use a scan tool to verify transmission fluid temperature.
j) If a new valve body has been installed, the solenoid body strategy must be updated by a qualified technician.
k) Perform the adaptive learn drive cycle (see Section 1).

14 Automatic transmission overhaul - general information

1 In the event of a fault occurring, it will be necessary to establish whether the fault is electrical, mechanical or hydraulic in nature, before repair work can be contemplated. Diagnosis requires detailed knowledge of the transmission's operation and construction, as well as access to specialized test equipment, and so is deemed to be beyond the scope of this manual. It is therefore essential that problems with the automatic transmission are referred to a dealer service department or other qualified repair facility for assessment.

2 Note that a faulty transmission should not be removed before the vehicle has been assessed by a knowledgeable technician equipped with the proper tools, as troubleshooting must be performed with the transmission installed in the vehicle.

Notes

Chapter 7 Part B
Transfer case

Contents

	Section		Section
Electric shift motor - replacement	2	Transfer case - removal and installation	6
General information	1	Transfer Case Control Module (TCCM) - replacement	3
Rear output shaft oil seal - replacement	5	Transfer case overhaul - general information	7
Shift range selector switch - replacement	4		

Specifications

Fluid specifications
Type and capacity .... See Chapter 1

Torque specifications
Ft-lbs (unless otherwise indicated)

Note: *One foot-pound (ft-lb) of torque is equivalent to 12 inch-pounds (in-lbs) of torque. Torque values below approximately 15 foot-pounds are expressed in inch-pounds, because most foot-pound torque wrenches are not accurate at these smaller values.*

Transfer case-to-transmission bolts	168 In-lbs
Transmission mount bolts	66
Electric shift motor bolts	89 In-lbs
Drain and fill plugs	133 In-lbs

1   General information

1   Borg-Warner 4469 and 4467 2-speed torque-on-demand transfer case are both Electronic shift-on-the-fly (ESOF) system.

Electronic shift-on-the-fly (ESOF) system

2   The electronic shift-on-the-fly (ESOF) system on 4WD vehicles allows the driver to engage 4WD High while the vehicle is moving. The hub locks are engaged automatically, and an electronic shift is initiated. A switch on the dash allows a selection of 2WD, 4WD High or 4WD Low. The vehicle must be at a complete stop, with the transmission in Neutral and the brake applied before 4WD Low can be engaged.

Neutral flat towing procedure

Note: *4WD vehicles system have the ability to be towed on all 4 wheels with the transfer case in neutral. The neutral flat towing activation procedure instructs the transfer case to place the shift motor into a neutral position. Having the transfer case in neutral prevents damage to the transmission while towing (for example: behind a motorhome).*
Caution: *2WD vehicles CANNOT be flat towed with any of the wheels on the ground. Damage to the transmission or vehicle may occur.*
Note: *An mechanical sound may be heard when the transfer case shifts into or out of the NEUTRAL position.*

Enable

Warning: *When the transfer case is in neutral for neutral flat towing, the vehicle may be able to roll - even with the transmission in park (P). Press the brake pedal while the transfer case is shifted to neutral. Failure to follow this instruction may result in personal injury or property damage.*
3   Turn the ignition ON - do not start the engine. If the vehicle has keyless start/stop, with your foot off of the brake pedal, press the

engine START/STOP button once.
4   Press the brake pedal and hold steady.
5   Rotate the shift range select switch into 2H position.
6   Shift the transmission shift lever to the neutral (N) position.
7   Rotate the shift range select switch exactly as follows: within 7 seconds, rotate from 2H to 4L and back to 2H 5 times.
8   When successful, the instrument cluster reads "NEUTRAL TOW LEAVE IN N" or "NEUTRAL TOW ENABLED LEAVE TRANSMISSION IN NEUTRAL". Repeat the procedure if one of these messages does not appear.

   a) *Leave the transmission in neutral and turn the ignition off while towing.*
   b) *The key will remain in the vehicle while towing. Use the keyless entry to lock and unlock the vehicle.*
   c) *If the vehicle has keyless start/stop, with your foot off of the brake pedal, press the engine START/STOP button once. The key does not need to remain in the vehicle while towing.*

9   Remove your foot from the brake pedal.

Disable

10   Turn the ignition ON - do not start the engine. If the vehicle has keyless start/stop, with your foot off of the brake pedal, press the engine START/STOP button once.
11   Press the brake pedal and hold steady.
12   Shift the transmission shift lever to any position except park (P) or neutral (N).
13   Remove your foot from the brake pedal.
14   When successful, the instrument cluster reads "NEUTRAL TOW DISABLED". Repeat the procedure if one of these messages does not appear.

2   Electric shift motor - replacement

Note: *The electric shift motor must be replaced as an assembly.*
1   Raise the vehicle and support it securely on jackstands (if necessary).

2   Remove the transfer case skid plate (if equipped).
3   Disconnect the shift motor electrical connector.
4   Remove the Gray/Brown wire terminal pin from the shift motor connector. This wire connects elsewhere on the transfer case and must be removed when replacing the electric shift motor.
5   Remove the shift motor bracket bolt.
6   Remove the three electric shift motor bolts.
7   Remove the electric shift motor.
8   Clean the grease from the motor adapter and apply a new coat of multi-purpose grease.
9   Apply a thin bead of silicone sealant to the transfer case-to-shift motor mating surface.
10   The remainder of installation is the reverse of removal.

3   Transfer Case Control Module (TCCM) - replacement

Note: *The TCCM is located below the passenger side of the instrument panel, near the A pillar, attached to the firewall/floor.*
1   Disconnect the negative battery cable (see Chapter 5, Section 3).
2   Remove the passenger kick panel trim.
3   Remove the passenger under dash panel to gain access to the TCCM.
4   Locate the TCCM and disconnect the electrical connectors (see illustration).
5   Loosen the lower nut and remove the upper nut, then slide the TCCM off the studs and out of the vehicle.
6   Installation is reverse of removal.

4   Shift range selector switch - replacement

1   Using a plastic trim tool, carefully pry the switch and switch bezel as an assembly from the instrument panel.
2   Unplug the electrical connector from the backside of the switch.
3   Installation is the reverse of removal.

5   Rear output shaft oil seal - replacement

Note: *Front output shaft oil seal replacement requires disassembly of the transfer case for replacement, and is not covered.*
1   Raise the vehicle and support it securely on jackstands.
2   Remove the transfer case skid plate as necessary to access the seal.
3   Remove the rear driveshaft (see Chapter 8).
4   Pry out the seal with a screwdriver or a seal removal tool. Don't damage the seal bore (see illustration).

3.4 Location of the transfer case control module

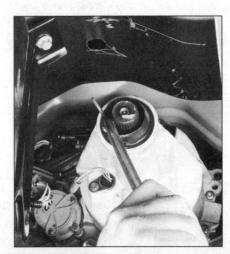

5.4 Carefully pry out the old seal

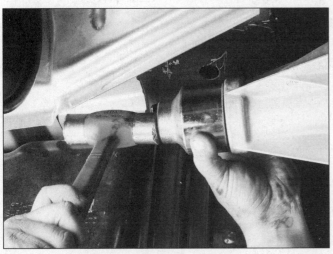

5.6 Drive the seal into place with a seal driver or a large socket

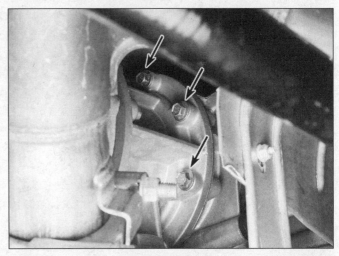

6.12 Remove and discard the bolts attaching the transfer case to the transmission

5   Lubricate the new seal lips with petroleum jelly.

6   Drive the seal into place with a seal driver or a large socket (see illustration). The outside diameter of the socket should be slightly smaller than the outside diameter of the seal.

7   Install the driveshaft (see Chapter 8).

8   The remainder of installation is the reverse of removal.

6   Transfer case - removal and installation

Removal

1   Raise the vehicle and support it securely on jackstands.

2   If equipped, remove the transfer case and transmission skid plate bolts, then remove the skid plates.

3   Drain the transfer case lubricant (see Chapter 1).

4   Remove the front and rear driveshafts (see Chapter 8).

5   Unplug the electric shift motor connector (see Section 2). Disconnect the harness clips.

6   Disconnect the vent hose from the top of the transfer case on the transmission side.

7   Support the transfer case with a jack - preferably a special jack with an adapter made for this purpose. Safety chains or tie-downs will help steady the transfer case on the jack.

8   Remove the bolts attaching the exhaust heat shield to the crossmember.

9   Remove the transmission crossmember from the vehicle.

Note: *When removing the crossmember it may be necessary to use a knife or similar to*

cut the heat shield material where the frame and crossmember come together.

10   Remove the driver side exhaust hanger bolt.

11   Remove the transmission mount bolts and remove the mount and bracket from the transfer case.

12   Remove and discard the nine transfer case bolts-to-transmission bolts (see illustration).

Note: *The bolts attaching the transfer case to the transmission are not to be reused.*

13   Make a final check that all wires and hoses have been disconnected from the transfer case, then move the transfer case and jack toward the rear of the vehicle until the transfer case is clear of the transmission. The transmission may require adjustment up or down to remove the transfer case. Keep the transfer case level as this is done. Once the input shaft is clear, lower the transfer case and remove it from under the vehicle.

Installation

14   Installation is the reverse of removal. Be sure to install a new mounting gasket and tighten the transmission-to-transfer case bolts to the torque listed in this Chapter's Specifications.

15   Fill the transfer case with the specified fluid (see Chapter 1), run the engine and check for fluid leaks.

7   Transfer case overhaul - general information

1   Overhauling a transfer case is a difficult job for the do-it-yourselfer. It involves the disassembly and reassembly of many small parts. Numerous clearances must be pre-

cisely measured and, if necessary, changed with select-fit spacers and snap-rings. As a result, if transfer case problems arise, it can be removed and installed by a competent do-it-yourselfer, but overhaul should be left to a transmission repair shop. Rebuilt transfer cases may be available - check with your dealer parts department and auto parts stores. At any rate, the time and money involved in an overhaul is almost sure to exceed the cost of a rebuilt unit.

2   Nevertheless, it's not impossible for an inexperienced mechanic to rebuild a transfer case if the special tools are available and the job is done in a deliberate step-by-step manner so nothing is overlooked.

3   The tools necessary for an overhaul include internal and external snap-ring pliers, a bearing puller, a slide hammer, a set of pin punches, a dial indicator and possibly a hydraulic press. In addition, a large, sturdy workbench and a vise or transfer case stand will be required.

4   During disassembly of the transfer case, make careful notes of how each piece comes off, where it fits in relation to other pieces and what holds it in place. Noting how they are installed when you remove the parts will make it much easier to get the transfer case back together.

5   Before taking the transfer case apart for repair, it will help if you have some idea what area of the transfer case is malfunctioning. Certain problems can be closely tied to specific areas in the transfer case, which can make component examination and replacement easier. Refer to the *Troubleshooting* section at the front of this manual for information regarding possible sources of trouble.

Notes

Chapter 8
Driveline

Contents

	Section		Section
Driveshaft(s) - removal and installation	2	Rear axle assembly - removal and installation	7
Driveshaft center support bearing - check and replacement	3	Rear axleshaft - removal and installation	8
Front axle assembly (4WD models) - removal and installation	6	Rear axleshaft bearing - replacement	10
Front driveaxles (4WD models) - removal and installation	5	Rear axleshaft oil seal - replacement	9
General information	1	Universal joints - replacement	4
Pinion oil seal - replacement	11		

Specifications

General

Differential lubricant type and capacity.. See Chapter 1

Torque specifications   **Ft-lbs** (unless otherwise indicated)

Note: *One foot-pound (ft-lb) of torque is equivalent to 12 inch-pounds (in-lbs) of torque. Torque values below approximately 15 foot-pounds are expressed in inch-pounds, because most foot-pound torque wrenches are not accurate at these smaller values.*

Driveaxle/hub nut*	30
IWE bolts	106
Differential pinion shaft locking bolt*	22
ELD coil connector adapter to differential bolt	62 inch-lbs
Differential housing cover bolts	33
Differential Allen head fill plug	38
Driveshaft flange bolts*	76
Front	55
Rear	76
Crossmember nuts and bolts	66
Center support bearing bolts*	35
Front axle	
Axle housing bushing bolt	
Front	129
Rear	111
Rear axle U bolt nuts** (Tighten U bolt nuts in an "X" pattern)	
Step 1	26
Step 2	52
Step 3	74
Step 4	98
Front CV joint to pinion flange cup bolts	41
Axle vent tube	159 inch-lbs

Manufacturer recommends using new fasteners

1   General information

1   The information in this Chapter deals with the components from the rear of the engine to the rear wheels, except for the transmission (and transfer case, if equipped), which is dealt with in the previous Chapter. For the purposes of this Chapter, these components are grouped into two categories: driveshaft and axles. Separate Sections within this Chapter offer general descriptions and checking procedures for components in each of the two groups.

2   Since nearly all the procedures covered in this Chapter involve working under the vehicle, make sure it's securely supported on sturdy jackstands or on a hoist where the vehicle can be easily raised and lowered.

2   Driveshaft(s) - removal and installation

Note: *The manufacturer recommends replacing driveshaft fasteners with new ones when installing the driveshaft.*

Removal
Rear

1   Raise the vehicle and support it securely on jackstands.

2   Use chalk, paint or a scribe to "index" the relationship of the driveshaft to the differential mating flange and to the transmission output shaft flange. This ensures correct alignment when the driveshaft is reinstalled (see illustrations).

3   Remove and discard the bolts securing the driveshaft flange to the differential pinion flange (see illustration).

Note: *The driveshaft to pinion fitting is a very snug fit. Do not hammer on any of the components to separate them. Use a prybar to work them apart.*

If equipped with a two piece driveshaft, remove the center support bearing bolts and discard them (see Section 3).

4   Some automatic transmissions have a splined slip yoke. Mark the relationship of the output shaft to slip yoke and simply slide the yoke out of the transmission.

5   Pry the universal joint away from its mating flange and remove the shaft from the flange. Be careful not to let the end caps for the universal joint to fall off (which would cause contamination and loss of the needle bearings).

Note: *Use electrical tape to temporarily hold the U joint caps into place.*

Front (4WD models)

6   Remove the transmission shield (if equipped)

7   Using a scribe, white paint or a hammer and punch, place marks on the driveshaft and differential flanges in line with each other. This is to make sure the driveshaft is reinstalled in the same position to preserve the balance.

8   Make alignment marks on the driveshaft and transfer case flanges.

9   Remove and discard the stabilizer bar clamp bolts and let it swing down out of the way of the front driveshaft.

10   Unbolt the CV joint to pinion flange cup bolts and discard them and retainers.

11   Remove and discard the bolts and retainers that attach the CV shaft to the transfer case.

12   Pry the CV shaft from the flange cups and remove it.

Note: *Wrap tape around the universal joint bearings at the axle end of the driveshaft so they won't fall off.*

Installation

13   Installation is the reverse of removal. If the shaft cannot be lined up due to the components of the differential or transmission having been rotated, put the vehicle in Neutral or rotate one wheel to allow the original alignment to be achieved. Make sure the universal joint caps are properly placed in the flange seat. Tighten the fasteners to the torque listed in this Chapter's Specifications.

Note: *Check the transmission fluid level if any fluid spilled out when the driveshaft was removed (see Chapter 1).*

2.2a Mark the relationship of the driveshaft U-joint to the differential pinion flange. . .

2.2b . . . and to the transmission output shaft flange

2.3 Insert a screwdriver through the U-joint to prevent the driveshaft from turning as you break loose the four U-joint-to-pinion flange bolts

3 Driveshaft center support bearing - check and replacement

Note: *Driveshaft center support bearing replacement requires the use of a hydraulic press. Remove the driveshaft and have a repair shop or automotive machine shop remove the bearing.*

Check

1 The center support bearing can be checked in a similar manner as the universal joints are examined. Check for looseness or deterioration of the flexible rubber mounting.

Replacement

2 Raise the vehicle and support it securely on jackstands.
3 Remove the driveshaft (see Section 2).
4 Remove the strap which retains the rubber cushion to the bearing support bracket (see illustration).
5 Separate the cushion, bracket and remove the rubber insulator.
6 Have the old bearing and dust slinger pressed off.
7 Install a new slinger and bearing.
8 Pack the space between the inner dust slinger and the bearing with lithium-base grease.
9 Carefully tap the bearing and slinger assembly onto the driveshaft journal until the components are tight against the shoulder on the shaft. Use a suitable piece of tubing to do this, taking care not to damage the shaft splines.
10 Lubricate the shaft splines with lithium-base grease.
11 Install the bearing rubber cushion, bracket and strap. The center support bearing bracket should be installed with the deep flange rearward.
12 Install the flange and retaining nut. Tighten the nut to the torque listed in this Chapter's Specifications.

13 The remainder of installation is the reverse of removal.

4 Universal joints - replacement

Single-cardan U-joints

Note: *A press or large vise will be required for this procedure. It may be advisable to take the driveshaft to a local dealer service department, service station or machine shop where the universal joints can be replaced for you, normally at a reasonable charge.*
1 Remove the driveshaft as outlined in Section 2.
2 Use a small pair of pliers to remove the snap-rings from the spider (see illustration).
3 Supporting the driveshaft, place it in position on a workbench equipped with a vise.
4 Place a piece of pipe or a large socket, having an inside diameter slightly larger than the outside diameter of the bearing caps, over one of the bearing caps. Position a socket with an outside diameter slightly smaller than that of the opposite bearing cap against the cap (see illustration) and use the vise or press to force the bearing cap out (inside the pipe or large socket). Use the vise or large pliers to work the bearing cap the rest of the way out.
5 Transfer the sockets to the other side and press the opposite bearing cap out in the same manner.
6 Pack the new universal joint bearings with grease. Ordinarily, specific instructions for lubrication will be included with the universal joint servicing kit and should be followed carefully.
7 Position the spider in the yoke and partially install one bearing cap in the yoke.
8 Start the spider into the bearing cap and then partially install the other cap. Align the spider and press the bearing caps into position, being careful not to damage the dust seals.
9 Install the snap-rings. If difficulty is

encountered in seating the snap-rings, strike the driveshaft yoke sharply with a hammer. This will spring the yoke ears slightly and allow the snap-rings to seat in the groove.
10 Install the grease fitting and fill the joint with grease. Be careful not to overfill the joint, as this could blow out the grease seals.
11 Install the driveshaft (see Section 2).

Double-cardan U-joints

12 Use the above procedure, but note that it will have to be repeated because the double-cardan joint is made up of two single-cardan joints. Also pay attention to how the spring, centering ball and bearing are arranged.
Note: *Some of the following conditions cannot be fixed without highly specialized tools and expertise. Such problems must be referred to a transmission repair shop or a dealer service department.*

5 Front driveaxles (4WD models) - removal and installation

Removal

1 Loosen the wheel lug nuts, raise the vehicle and support it securely on jackstands, then remove the wheel. Remove the dust cap from the hub/wheel bearing.
2 Remove the driveaxle/hub nut from the axle and discard it. Obtain a new one for installation.
3 Remove the brake disc (see Chapter 9).
4 Disconnect the vent and vacuum lines from the Integrated Wheel End (IWE), then remove the fasteners securing the IWE to the steering knuckle.
Note: *The IWE is the device bolted to the steering knuckle that couples the driveaxles to the wheel hub when 4WD mode is engaged.*
5 Remove the ABS sensor and bracket (see Chapter 9).
6 Remove the flexible brake hose bracket.
7 Remove the three IWE bolts.

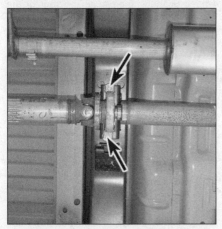

3.4 Remove the bolts securing the strap to the center support bearing

4.2 A pair of needle-nose pliers can be used to remove the universal joint snap-rings

4.4 To press the universal joint out of the driveshaft yoke, set it up in a vise with the small socket pushing the joint and bearing cap into the large socket

7.7a Driver's side

1 Vent hose   3 Brake lines
2 ABS sensor wires   4 Wire harness

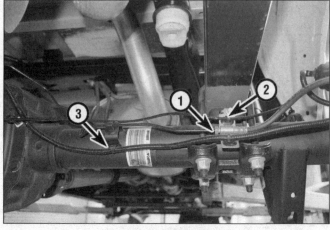

7.7b Passenger's side

1 Brake line   3 Wire harness
2 ABS sensor wire

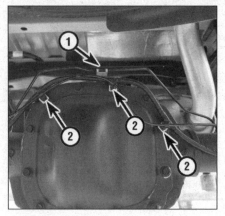

7.8 Differential housing bracket locations

1 Brake line brackets
2 ABS sensor and wire harness brackets

8 Separate the tie-rod end from the steering knuckle (see Chapter 10).
9 Separate the upper control arm from the steering knuckle (see Chapter 10).
10 Swing the steering knuckle/hub assembly out (away from the vehicle) until the end of the driveaxle is free of the hub.
11 Support the outer end of the driveaxle with a piece of wire to avoid unnecessary strain on the inner CV joint.
12 Remove the integrated wheel end (IWE) from the driveaxle outboard end.
13 Carefully pry the inner CV joint out of the differential or off of the axle shaft, as applicable.
14 Remove the driveaxle from the vehicle.

Installation

15 Install the integrated wheel end on the driveaxle outboard end. Apply 24 inches of vacuum to the vacuum supply port (the large port) of the IWE and hold the vacuum in that position until the bolts are tightened.
16 The remainder of installation is the reverse of removal, with the following points:

a) The upper balljoint-to-steering knuckle nut and the tie-rod end nut should not be reused. New ones should always be used. Be sure to tighten them to the torque listed in the Chapter 10 Specifications.
b) Tighten the integrated wheel end fasteners and the driveaxle/hub nut to the torque listed in this Chapter's Specifications). Be sure to use a new driveaxle/hub nut.
c) Connect the vent and vacuum lines for the integrated wheel end (IWE).
d) Install the wheel and lug nuts, lower the vehicle and tighten the lug nuts to the torque listed in the Chapter 1 Specifications.

6 Front axle assembly (4WD models) - removal and installation

1 Loosen the wheel lug nuts, raise the front of the vehicle and support it securely on jackstands placed under the frame. Block the rear wheels to keep the vehicle from rolling off the stands. Remove the front wheels.
2 Remove the lower shield, if equipped.
3 Remove the front driveshaft (see Section 2).
4 Remove the underbody shields, if equipped.
5 With the steering wheel in the straight ahead position, remove the steering shaft U-joint bolt and separate the shaft from the steering gear box (see Chapter 10).
Caution: Make sure that the steering shaft is not rotated with the steering gear removed or damage to the airbag clockspring assembly could occur. One method of preventing the steering shaft from rotating is to run the seat belt through the steering wheel and clip the seat belt buckles together.
6 Remove the driveaxles (see Section 5).
7 Remove the front crossmember.
8 Remove the axle tube bushing bolt and flange nut.

9 Use a transmission jack to support the axle, then remove the rear housing bushing bolts.
10 Remove the front housing bushing bolts.
11 Disconnect the front axle breather hose and move it aside out of the way.
12 Carefully lower the axle with the transmission jack.
13 Installation is the reverse of removal. Be sure to tighten all fasteners to the torque specifications listed in this Chapter's Specifications. Check the lubricant level after installation (see Chapter 1).

7 Rear axle assembly - removal and installation

Removal

1 If equipped with EPB (Electronic Parking Brake) system, deactivate the EPB (see Chapter 9).
2 Block the front wheels. Loosen the rear wheel lug nuts, then raise the rear of the vehicle and support it with jackstands placed under the frame rails.
3 Remove the rear wheels.
4 Disconnect the driveshaft from the rear axle and support it out of the way.
5 Disconnect the ABS sensors (see Chapter 9).
6 Disconnect the parking brake cable from the parking brake lever and the parking brake bracket from the axle assembly. If equipped with EPB, disconnect the electrical connection to the parking brake actuator (see Chapter 9).
7 Disconnect the brake lines, vent hose, wire harness brackets and the ABS sensor brackets from the axle assembly (see illustration).
8 Remove the brake line mounting bolt from the top side of the axle assembly and the brackets for the wire harness and ABS sensor (see illustration).
9 Disconnect the ELD connector from the left side of the differential housing.

7.12 Remove the nuts and U-bolts securing the axle to the springs

8.6a Position a large screwdriver between the rear axle case and a ring gear bolt to keep the differential case from turning when removing the pinion shaft lock bolt

8.6b Rotate the differential case 180-degrees and slide the pinion shaft out of the case until the stepped part of the shaft contacts the ring gear

10 Support the rear axle with a floor jack.

11 Remove the lower mounting bolts securing the rear shock absorbers to the axle (see Chapter 10).

12 With the jack(s) supporting the axle, remove and discard the nuts and U-bolts securing the axle to the springs (see illustration).

13 Lower the axle assembly and remove it from under the vehicle.

Installation

14 Installation is the reverse of the removal.

15 Tighten all fasteners to the torque settings listed in this Chapter's Specifications. Tighten the axle U-bolts in an "X" pattern.

16 Check and fill the axle with the specified lubricant (see Chapter 1).

17 Reactivate the EPB (if equipped) (see Chapter 9).

8   Rear axleshaft - removal and installation

1   Loosen the rear wheel lug nuts. Raise the rear of the vehicle, support it securely on jackstands and block the front wheels.

2   Remove the rear wheel.

3   Remove the brake disc (see Chapter 9).

4   Remove ABS sensor from the backing plate (see Chapter 9).

5   Drain the differential lubricant (see Chapter 1).

6   Remove the lock bolt from the differential pinion shaft. Slide the notched end of the pinion shaft out of the differential case as far as it will go (see illustrations).

7   Push the outer (flanged) end of the axleshaft in and remove the C-lock from the inner end of the shaft (see illustration).

8   Withdraw the axleshaft, taking care not to damage the oil seal in the end of the axle housing as the splined end of the axleshaft passes through it.

Note: *Have drain pan at the brake end of the axleshaft as you pull it out. Some oil will spill as you remove it.*

8.7 Push in on the axle flange and remove the C-lock from the inner end of the axleshaft

9   Installation is the reverse of removal. The manufacturer recommends that a new pinion shaft lock bolt be used, but if one is not available, coat the threads with a non-hardening thread locking compound. Install the pinion shaft lock bolt and tighten it to the torque listed in this Chapter's Specifications.

10   Refill the axle with the correct quantity and grade of lubricant (see Chapter 1). Tighten the wheel lug nuts to the torque listed in the Chapter 1 Specifications.

9   Rear axleshaft oil seal - replacement

1   Remove the axleshaft (see Section 8).

2   Pry the oil seal out of the end of the axle housing (see illustration).

3   Apply a film of multi-purpose grease to the oil seal recess and tap the new seal evenly into place with a hammer and seal installation tool (see illustration) or a large socket so the lips are facing in and the metal face is visible

9.2 Prying out the axleshaft oil seal with a seal removal tool

9.3 Using a seal driver to install the axleshaft oil seal - drive the seal in until it's flush with the bore

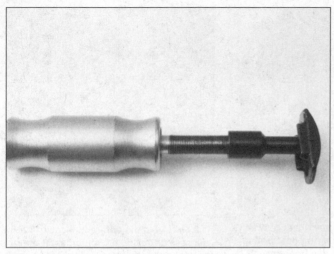

10.2 A typical slide hammer and axleshaft bearing remover attachment

10.3 Removing the axleshaft bearing with a slide hammer

10.4 Use a bearing driver or a large socket to tap the bearing evenly into the axle housing

from the end of the axle housing. When correctly installed, the face of the oil seal should be flush with the end of the axle housing.

4   Install the axleshaft (see Section 8).

---

10 Rear axleshaft bearing - replacement

1   Remove the axleshaft oil seal (see Section 9).

2   A bearing puller which grips the bearing from behind will be required for this job (see illustration).

3   Attach a slide hammer to the puller and extract the bearing from the axle housing (see illustration).

4   Clean out the bearing recess and drive in the new bearing with a bearing installer positioned against the outer bearing race (see illustration). Make sure the bearing is fully seated in the recess.

5   Install a new oil seal (see Section 9).

---

11 Pinion oil seal - replacement

Note: *This procedure applies to the front and rear pinion oil seals.*

1   Loosen the wheel lug nuts. Raise the front (for front differential) or rear (for rear differential) of the vehicle and support it securely on jackstands. Block the opposite set of wheels to keep the vehicle from rolling off the stands. Remove the wheels.

2   Disconnect the driveshaft from the differential pinion flange and support it out of the way with a piece of wire or rope (see Section 2).

3   Rotate the pinion a few times using a beam-type or dial-type inch-pound torque wrench to check the torque required to rotate the pinion (see illustration). Record it for use later.

4   Mark the relationship of the pinion flange to the shaft. It's also a good idea to count the amount of exposed threads as a reference when reinstalling the pinon flange (see illustration).

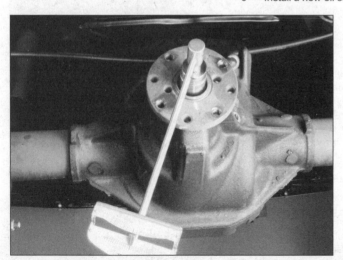

11.3 Use an inch-pound torque wrench to check the torque necessary to rotate the pinion shaft

11.4 Mark the relative positions of the pinion and flange before removing the nut

11.5 If you don't have a special flange holding tool to hold the pinion flange while loosening and backing off the pinion flange locknut, use a screwdriver inserted through a hole in the flange and jammed against the top of the reinforcing rib on the differential carrier

11.7 If the pinion flange is difficult to remove, pull it off with a two or three-jaw puller

5   A special tool (available at most auto parts stores) or a chain wrench can be used to keep the companion flange from moving while the self-locking pinion nut is loosened. A screwdriver or long punch inserted through one of the holes in the flange can also be used to immobilize the flange (see illustration).

6   Remove the pinion nut.

7   Withdraw the flange. It may be necessary to use a two-jaw puller engaged behind the flange to draw it off. Do not attempt to pry or hammer behind the flange or hammer on the end of the pinion shaft (see illustration).

8   Pry out the old seal and discard it (see illustration).

9   Lubricate the lips of the new seal and fill the space between the seal lips with wheel bearing grease, then tap it evenly into position with a seal installation tool or a large socket (see illustration). Make sure it enters the housing squarely and is tapped in to its full depth.

10   Install the pinion flange, lining up the marks made in Step 4. If necessary, tighten the pinion nut to draw the flange into place. Do not try to hammer the flange into position.

11   Apply a bead of RTV sealant to the ends of the splines visible in the center of the flange so oil will be sealed in.

12   Install the washer and a new pinion nut. Tighten a little at a time until the drag recorded previously is reached. As a check only, count the number of exposed threads showing just in case a burr on a thread is causing a false reading of the torque value.

13   Measure the torque required to rotate the pinion and tighten the nut in small increments (no more than 5 ft-lbs) until it matches the figure recorded in Step 3. To compensate for the drag of the new oil seal, the nut should be tightened a little more until the rotational torque of the pinion exceeds the earlier recording by 3 in-lbs. for the rear pinion and no more than 5 in-lbs. for the front pinion on 4WD drive vehicles.

14   Reinstall all components removed previously by reversing the removal Steps, tightening all fasteners to their specified torque values. Check the fluid level in the differential and adjust as needed.

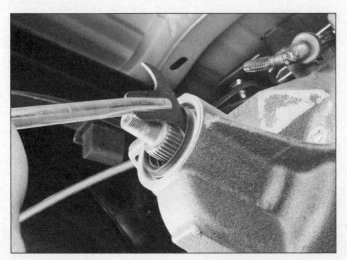

11.8 Pry out the old pinion seal with a seal removal tool

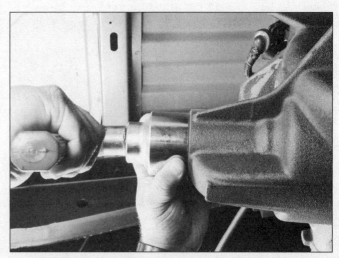

11.9 Lubricate the lips of the new pinion seal and seat it squarely in the bore, then drive it into the carrier with a seal driver or a large socket

Notes

Chapter 9   Brakes

Contents

	Section
Adjustable brake pedal and bracket - removal, installation and indexing	13
Anti-lock Brake System (ABS) - general information	3
Brake disc - inspection, removal and installation	6
Brake hoses and lines - inspection and replacement	10
Brake hydraulic system - bleeding	11
Brake light switch - replacement	14
Brake vacuum pump (2.7L V6 models) - removal and installation	15
Cable-actuated parking brake - component replacement	7

	Section
Disc brake caliper - removal and installation	5
Disc brake pads - replacement	4
Electronic Parking Brake (EPB) - general information, troubleshooting, deactivation/activation and component replacement	8
General information and precautions	1
Master cylinder - removal and installation	9
Power brake booster - check, removal and installation	12
Troubleshooting	2

Specifications

General

Brake fluid type	See Chapter 1
Disc brakes	
Brake pad minimum thickness	See Chapter 1
Disc minimum thickness	Cast into disc
Minimum pad lining thickness	See Chapter 1
Disc lateral runout limit	0.003 inch
Parking brakes	
Shoe lining minimum thickness	See Chapter 1

Torque specifications   Ft-lbs (unless otherwise indicated)

Note: *One foot-pound (ft-lb) of torque is equivalent to 12 inch-pounds (in-lbs) of torque. Torque values below approximately 15 foot-pounds are expressed in inch-pounds, because most foot-pound torque wrenches are not accurate at these smaller values.*

Brake hose banjo fitting bolt to caliper*	
Front	26
Rear	26
Caliper mounting bolts	
Front	27
Rear	24
Caliper mounting bracket bolts**	
Front	184
Rear without EPB	111
Rear with EPB	181
Caliper mounting bolts**	
Front	27
Rear	
Without EPB	27
With EPB	24

*Use new washers for banjo fittings
**Manufacturer recommends replacing with new fasteners

Torque specifications (continued)

Ft-lbs (unless otherwise indicated)

Note: *One foot-pound (ft-lb) of torque is equivalent to 12 inch-pounds (in-lbs) of torque. Torque values below approximately 15 foot-pounds are expressed in inch-pounds, because most foot-pound torque wrenches are not accurate at these smaller values.*

EPB actuator bolts**	71 inch-lbs
Disc dust shield bolts	
Front	155 inch-lbs
Rear with EPB	155 inch-lbs
Rear without EPB	124 inch-lbs
Master cylinder mounting nuts	18
Power brake booster mounting nuts	18
Power brake booster-to-adjustable pedal bracket nuts	18
ABS wheel speed sensor bolt	
Front	106 inch-lbs
Rear	133 inch-lbs
Vacuum pump mounting bolts (2.7L models only)	75 inch-lbs
Wheel lug nuts	See Chapter 1

**Manufacturer recommends replacing with new fasteners

---

1   General information

General

The vehicles covered by this manual are equipped with hydraulically operated front and rear brake systems. The front and rear brakes are disc type. Both the front and rear brakes are self adjusting. The disc brakes automatically compensate for pad wear.

Hydraulic system

The hydraulic system consists of two separate circuits. The master cylinder has separate reservoirs for the two circuits and, in the event of a leak or failure in one hydraulic circuit, the other circuit will remain operative.

Power brake booster

The power brake booster, utilizing engine manifold vacuum and atmospheric pressure to provide assistance to the hydraulically operated brakes, is mounted on the firewall in the engine compartment.

Parking brake

There are two types of parking brake systems used. One is a cable-operated parking brake system which utilizes a set of parking brake shoes inside the rear brake disc. They are manually operated by the driver with the parking brake pedal. The other is an Electronic Parking Brake (EPB) system which is operated automatically. The EPB system utilizes the rear brake pads and does not have separate parking brake shoes. Working on the rear brakes of the EPB system requires deactivation of the EPB. Failure to do so can result in personal injury. See Section 8 for detailed instruction on deactivation procedures.

Service

After completing any operation involving disassembly of any part of the brake system, always test drive the vehicle to check for proper braking performance before resuming normal driving. When testing the brakes, perform the tests on a clean, dry, flat surface. Conditions other than these can lead to inaccurate test results.

Test the brakes at various speeds with both light and heavy pedal pressure. The vehicle should stop evenly without pulling to one side or the other. Under hard braking, the ABS system may engage, resulting in brake pedal pulsation. This is considered normal operation.

Tires, vehicle load and wheel alignment are factors which also affect braking performance.

Precautions

There are some general cautions and warnings involving the brake system on this vehicle:

a) *Use only brake fluid conforming to DOT 4 specifications.*

b) *The brake pads and linings contain fibers which are hazardous to your health if inhaled. Whenever you work on brake system components, clean all parts with brake system cleaner. Do not allow the fine dust to become airborne. Also, wear an approved filtering mask.*

c) *Safety should be paramount whenever any servicing of the brake components is performed. Do not use parts or fasteners which are not in perfect condition, and be sure that all clearances and torque specifications are adhered to. If you are at all unsure about a certain procedure, seek professional advice. Upon completion of any brake system work, test the brakes carefully in a controlled area before putting the vehicle into normal service. If a problem is suspected in the brake system, don't drive the vehicle until it's fixed.*

d) *Used brake fluid is considered a hazardous waste and it must be disposed of in accordance with federal, state and local laws.* **DO NOT pour it down the sink, into septic tanks or storm drains, or on the ground.**

e) *Clean up any spilled brake fluid immediately and then wash the area with large amounts of water. This is especially true for any finished or painted surfaces.*

2 Troubleshooting

PROBABLE CAUSE	CORRECTIVE ACTION

No brakes - pedal travels to floor

1 Low fluid level 2 Air in system	1 and 2 Low fluid level and air in the system are symptoms of another problem - a leak somewhere in the hydraulic system. Locate and repair the leak
3 Defective seals in master cylinder	3 Replace master cylinder
4 Fluid overheated and vaporized due to heavy braking	4 Bleed hydraulic system (temporary fix). Replace brake fluid (proper fix)

Brake pedal slowly travels to floor under braking or at a stop

1 Defective seals in master cylinder	1 Replace master cylinder
2 Leak in a hose, line, caliper or wheel cylinder	2 Locate and repair leak
3 Air in hydraulic system	3 Bleed the system, inspect system for a leak

Brake pedal feels spongy when depressed

1 Air in hydraulic system	1 Bleed the system, inspect system for a leak
2 Master cylinder or power booster loose	2 Tighten fasteners
3 Brake fluid overheated (beginning to boil)	3 Bleed the system (temporary fix). Replace the brake fluid (proper fix)
4 Deteriorated brake hoses (ballooning under pressure)	4 Inspect hoses, replace as necessary (it's a good idea to replace all of them if one hose shows signs of deterioration)

Brake pedal feels hard when depressed and/or excessive effort required to stop vehicle

1 Power booster faulty	1 Replace booster
2 Engine not producing sufficient vacuum, or hose to booster clogged, collapsed or cracked	2 Check vacuum to booster with a vacuum gauge. Replace hose if cracked or clogged, repair engine if vacuum is extremely low
3 Brake linings contaminated by grease or brake fluid	3 Locate and repair source of contamination, replace brake pads or shoes
4 Brake linings glazed	4 Replace brake pads or shoes, check discs and drums for glazing, service as necessary
5 Caliper piston(s) or wheel cylinder(s) binding or frozen	5 Replace calipers or wheel cylinders
6 Brakes wet	6 Apply pedal to boil-off water (this should only be a momentary problem)
7 Kinked, clogged or internally split brake hose or line	7 Inspect lines and hoses, replace as necessary

Excessive brake pedal travel (but will pump up)

1 Drum brakes out of adjustment	1 Adjust brakes
2 Air in hydraulic system	2 Bleed system, inspect system for a leak

Excessive brake pedal travel (but will not pump up)

1 Master cylinder pushrod misadjusted	1 Adjust pushrod
2 Master cylinder seals defective	2 Replace master cylinder
3 Brake linings worn out	3 Inspect brakes, replace pads and/or shoes
4 Hydraulic system leak	4 Locate and repair leak

Brake pedal doesn't return

1 Brake pedal binding	1 Inspect pivot bushing and pushrod, repair or lubricate
2 Defective master cylinder	2 Replace master cylinder

Troubleshooting (continued)

PROBABLE CAUSE	CORRECTIVE ACTION

Brake pedal pulsates during brake application

PROBABLE CAUSE	CORRECTIVE ACTION
1 Brake drums out-of-round	1 Have drums machined by an automotive machine shop
2 Excessive brake disc runout or disc surfaces out-of-parallel	2 Have discs machined by an automotive machine shop
3 Loose or worn wheel bearings	3 Adjust or replace wheel bearings
4 Loose lug nuts	4 Tighten lug nuts

Brakes slow to release

PROBABLE CAUSE	CORRECTIVE ACTION
1 Malfunctioning power booster	1 Replace booster
2 Pedal linkage binding	2 Inspect pedal pivot bushing and pushrod, repair/lubricate
3 Malfunctioning proportioning valve	3 Replace proportioning valve
4 Sticking caliper or wheel cylinder	4 Repair or replace calipers or wheel cylinders
5 Kinked or internally split brake hose	5 Locate and replace faulty brake hose

Brakes grab (one or more wheels)

PROBABLE CAUSE	CORRECTIVE ACTION
1 Grease or brake fluid on brake lining	1 Locate and repair cause of contamination, replace lining
2 Brake lining glazed	2 Replace lining, deglaze disc or drum

Vehicle pulls to one side during braking

PROBABLE CAUSE	CORRECTIVE ACTION
1 Grease or brake fluid on brake lining	1 Locate and repair cause of contamination, replace lining
2 Brake lining glazed	2 Deglaze or replace lining, deglaze disc or drum
3 Restricted brake line or hose	3 Repair line or replace hose
4 Tire pressures incorrect	4 Adjust tire pressures
5 Caliper or wheel cylinder sticking	5 Repair or replace calipers or wheel cylinders
6 Wheels out of alignment	6 Have wheels aligned
7 Weak suspension spring	7 Replace springs
8 Weak or broken shock absorber	8 Replace shock absorbers

Brakes drag (indicated by sluggish engine performance or wheels being very hot after driving)

PROBABLE CAUSE	CORRECTIVE ACTION
1 Brake pedal pushrod incorrectly adjusted	1 Adjust pushrod
2 Master cylinder pushrod (between booster and master cylinder) incorrectly adjusted	2 Adjust pushrod
3 Obstructed compensating port in master cylinder	3 Replace master cylinder
4 Master cylinder piston seized in bore	4 Replace master cylinder
5 Contaminated fluid causing swollen seals throughout system	5 Flush system, replace all hydraulic components
6 Clogged brake lines or internally split brake hose(s)	6 Flush hydraulic system, replace defective hose(s)
7 Sticking caliper(s) or wheel cylinder(s)	7 Replace calipers or wheel cylinders
8 Parking brake not releasing	8 Inspect parking brake linkage and parking brake mechanism, repair as required
9 Improper shoe-to-drum clearance	9 Adjust brake shoes
10 Faulty proportioning valve	10 Replace proportioning valve

Troubleshooting (continued)
PROBABLE CAUSE   **CORRECTIVE ACTION**

Brakes fade (due to excessive heat)

1 Brake linings excessively worn or glazed	1 Deglaze or replace brake pads and/or shoes
2 Excessive use of brakes	2 Downshift into a lower gear, maintain a constant slower speed (going down hills)
3 Vehicle overloaded	3 Reduce load
4 Brake drums or discs worn too thin	4 Measure drum diameter and disc thickness, replace drums or discs as required
5 Contaminated brake fluid	5 Flush system, replace fluid
6 Brakes drag	6 Repair cause of dragging brakes
7 Driver resting left foot on brake pedal	7 Don't ride the brakes

Brakes noisy (high-pitched squeal)

1 Glazed lining	1 Deglaze or replace lining
2 Contaminated lining (brake fluid, grease, etc.)	2 Repair source of contamination, replace linings
3 Weak or broken brake shoe hold-down or return spring	3 Replace springs
4 Rivets securing lining to shoe or backing plate loose	4 Replace shoes or pads
5 Excessive dust buildup on brake linings	5 Wash brakes off with brake system cleaner
6 Brake drums worn too thin	6 Measure diameter of drums, replace if necessary
7 Wear indicator on disc brake pads contacting disc	7 Replace brake pads
8 Anti-squeal shims missing or installed improperly	8 Install shims correctly

Note: *Other remedies for quieting squealing brakes include the application of an anti-squeal compound to the backing plates of the brake pads, and lightly chamfering the edges of the brake pads with a file. The latter method should only be performed with the brake pads thoroughly wetted with brake system cleaner, so as not to allow any brake dust to become airborne.*

Brakes noisy (scraping sound)

1 Brake pads or shoes worn out; rivets, backing plate or brake shoe metal contacting disc or drum	1 Replace linings, have discs and/or drums machined (or replace)

Brakes chatter

1 Worn brake lining	1 Inspect brakes, replace shoes or pads as necessary
2 Glazed or scored discs or drums	2 Deglaze discs or drums with sandpaper (if glazing is severe, machining will be required)
3 Drums or discs heat checked	3 Check discs and/or drums for hard spots, heat checking, etc. Have discs/drums machined or replace them
4 Disc runout or drum out-of-round excessive	4 Measure disc runout and/or drum out-of-round, have discs or drums machined or replace them
5 Loose or worn wheel bearings	5 Adjust or replace wheel bearings
6 Loose or bent brake backing plate (drum brakes)	6 Tighten or replace backing plate
7 Grooves worn in discs or drums	7 Have discs or drums machined, if within limits (if not, replace them)
8 Brake linings contaminated (brake fluid, grease, etc.)	8 Locate and repair source of contamination, replace pads or shoes
9 Excessive dust buildup on linings	9 Wash brakes with brake system cleaner
10 Surface finish on discs or drums too rough after machining (especially on vehicles with sliding calipers)	10 Have discs or drums properly machined
11 Brake pads or shoes glazed	11 Deglaze or replace brake pads or shoes

Troubleshooting (continued)

PROBABLE CAUSE	CORRECTIVE ACTION

Brake pads or shoes click

PROBABLE CAUSE	CORRECTIVE ACTION
1 Shoe support pads on brake backing plate grooved or excessively worn	1 Replace brake backing plate
2 Brake pads loose in caliper	2 Loose pad retainers or anti-rattle clips
3 Also see items listed under Brakes chatter	

Brakes make groaning noise at end of stop

PROBABLE CAUSE	CORRECTIVE ACTION
1 Brake pads and/or shoes worn out	1 Replace pads and/or shoes
2 Brake linings contaminated (brake fluid, grease, etc.)	2 Locate and repair cause of contamination, replace brake pads or shoes
3 Brake linings glazed	3 Deglaze or replace brake pads or shoes
4 Excessive dust buildup on linings	4 Wash brakes with brake system cleaner
5 Scored or heat-checked discs or drums	5 Inspect discs/drums, have machined if within limits (if not, replace discs or drums)
6 Broken or missing brake shoe attaching hardware	6 Inspect drum brakes, replace missing hardware

Rear brakes lock up under light brake application

PROBABLE CAUSE	CORRECTIVE ACTION
1 Tire pressures too high	1 Adjust tire pressures
2 Tires excessively worn	2 Replace tires
3 Defective proportioning valve	3 Replace proportioning valve

Brake warning light on instrument panel comes on (or stays on)

PROBABLE CAUSE	CORRECTIVE ACTION
1 Low fluid level in master cylinder reservoir (reservoirs with fluid level sensor)	1 Add fluid, inspect system for leak, check the thickness of the brake pads and shoes
2 Failure in one half of the hydraulic system	2 Inspect hydraulic system for a leak
3 Piston in pressure differential warning valve not centered	3 Center piston by bleeding one circuit or the other (close bleeder valve as soon as the light goes out)
4 Defective pressure differential valve or warning switch	4 Replace valve or switch
5 Air in the hydraulic system	5 Bleed the system, check for leaks
6 Brake pads worn out (vehicles with electric wear sensors - small probes that fit into the brake pads and ground out on the disc when the pads get thin)	6 Replace brake pads (and sensors)

Brakes do not self adjust

Disc brakes

PROBABLE CAUSE	CORRECTIVE ACTION
1 Defective caliper piston seals	1 Replace calipers. Also, possible contaminated fluid causing soft or swollen seals (flush system and fill with new fluid if in doubt)
2 Corroded caliper piston(s)	2 Same as above

Drum brakes

PROBABLE CAUSE	CORRECTIVE ACTION
1 Adjuster screw frozen	1 Remove adjuster, disassemble, clean and lubricate with high-temperature grease
2 Adjuster lever does not contact star wheel or is binding	2 Inspect drum brakes, assemble correctly or clean or replace parts as required
3 Adjusters mixed up (installed on wrong wheels after brake job)	3 Reassemble correctly
4 Adjuster cable broken or installed incorrectly (cable-type adjusters)	4 Install new cable or assemble correctly

Rapid brake lining wear

PROBABLE CAUSE	CORRECTIVE ACTION
1 Driver resting left foot on brake pedal	1 Don't ride the brakes
2 Surface finish on discs or drums too rough	2 Have discs or drums properly machined
3 Also see Brakes drag	

3 Anti-lock Brake System (ABS) - general information

General information

1   The Anti-lock Brake System is designed to maintain vehicle steerability, directional stability and optimum deceleration under severe braking conditions on most road surfaces. It does so by monitoring the rotational speed of each wheel and controlling the brake line pressure to each wheel during braking. This prevents the wheels from locking up. The ABS system has taken on a lot more responsibilities than just controlling the brakes during a panic stop. Several different control modules communicate with the ABS controller to maintain vehicle road stability. The following electrical system are all involved in the function of the ABS system.

Electronic Stability Control

2   The Electronic Stability Control (ESC) aids in controlling lateral movement by modulating brake fluid pressure to each wheel.

Hill Descent Control

3   The Hill Descent Control aides in controlling low speed maneuvers down steep grades.

Hill Start Assist system

4   The Hill Start Assist system aides in controlling the vehicle from rolling while stationary on a steep slope. With the system activated, the vehicle will remain in place as you move your foot from the brake pedal and onto the accelerator.

Crash Avoidance System

5   Crash avoidance systems also use the ABS system to apply the brakes when the system is activated.

Trailer Sway Control System

6   Trailer sway control systems use the ABS system to maintain stability when pulling a trailer.

Adaptive Cruise Control System

7   The adaptive cruise control system also utilizes the ABS system to maintain the preset distance from the vehicle in front of you.

Torque Vectoring System

8   The torque vectoring system uses the ABS system to calculate wheel rotation in a turn and adjusts the brake fluid to the front and back brakes in order for the front of the vehicle to hug the inside of the turn better, which improves tire grip.

ABS components

9   The ABS system has three main components - the wheel speed sensors, the ABS control module and the hydraulic control unit

3.9 The hydraulic control unit for the Anti-lock Brake System is located in the left-front area of the engine compartment

3.18 Location of the front wheel speed sensor

(see illustration). Wheel speed sensors - located at each wheel, send a variable voltage signal to the control unit, which monitors these signals, compares them to its program and determines whether a wheel is about to lock up. When a wheel is about to lock up, the control unit signals the hydraulic unit to reduce hydraulic pressure (or increase) at that wheel's brake caliper. Pressure modulation is handled by electrically-operated solenoid valves.

10   If a problem develops within the system, an ABS warning light will glow on the dashboard. Sometimes, a visual inspection of the ABS system can help you locate the problem. Carefully inspect the ABS wiring harness. Pay particularly close attention to the harness and connections near each wheel. Look for signs of chafing and other damage caused by incorrectly routed wires. If a wheel sensor harness is damaged, the sensor must be replaced.

Warning: *Do NOT try to repair an ABS wiring harness. The ABS system is sensitive to even the smallest changes in resistance. Repairing the harness could alter resistance values and cause the system to malfunction. If the ABS wiring harness is damaged in any way, it must be replaced.*

Warning: *Repair or removal of either the ABS control module or hydraulic unit must start with the original controller and module in place and the data extracted. If the ABS controller has no communication with the scanner, the factory data (or more commonly called "AS BUILT DATA") will need to be downloaded into the replacement controller. This is something that should be left for either a dealership service department or other qualified repair facility.*

Caution: *Make sure the ignition is turned off before unplugging or reattaching any electrical connections.*

Diagnosis and repair

11   If a dashboard warning light comes on and stays on while the vehicle is in operation, the ABS system requires attention. Although special electronic ABS diagnostic testing

tools are necessary to properly diagnose the system, you can perform a few preliminary checks before taking the vehicle to a dealer service department or other repair shop.

   a) *Check the brake fluid level in the reservoir.*
   b) *Verify that the computer electrical connectors are securely connected.*
   c) *Check the electrical connectors at the hydraulic control unit.*
   d) *Check the fuses.*
   e) *Follow the wiring harness to each wheel and verify that all connections are secure and that the wiring is undamaged.*

12   If the above preliminary checks do not rectify the problem, the vehicle should be diagnosed and serviced by a dealer service department or a qualified independent repair shop.

Wheel speed sensor - removal and installation

Front wheel speed sensor

13   Loosen the wheel lug nuts, raise the front of the vehicle and support it securely on jackstands. Apply the parking brake.

14   Remove the front wheels.

15   Remove the brake disc (see Section 6).

16   Trace the wiring back from the sensor, detaching all brackets and clips while noting its correct routing, then disconnect the electrical connector.

17   Use compressed air to remove any debris around the speed sensor and mounting bolt.

18   Remove the mounting bolt and pull the sensor out from the steering knuckle (see illustration).

19   Installation is the reverse of the removal procedure. Tighten the mounting bolt to the torque listed in this Chapter's Specifications.

20   Install the wheel and lug nuts, tightening them securely. Lower the vehicle and tighten the lug nuts to the torque listed in the Chapter 1 Specifications.

Rear wheel speed sensor

21   Locate the speed sensor and follow the wire harness back to the electrical connector. Disconnect the connector and release the clips holding the wire harness.

22   Use compressed air to remove any debris from around the speed sensor bolt.

23   Remove the mounting bolt and pull the sensor out (see illustration).

24   Installation is the reverse of the removal procedure. Tighten the mounting bolt to the torque listed in this Chapter's Specifications.

25   Install the wheel and lug nuts, tightening them securely. Lower the vehicle and tighten the lug nuts to the torque listed in the Chapter 1 Specifications.

---

4   Disc brake pads - replacement

Warning: *Disc brake pads must be replaced on both wheels at the same time - never replace the pads on only one wheel. Also, the dust created by the brake system is harmful to your health. Never blow it out with compressed air and don't inhale any of it. An approved filtering mask should be worn when working on the brakes. Do not, under any circumstances, use petroleum-based solvents to clean brake parts. Use brake system cleaner only!*

1   Remove the cap from the brake fluid reservoir. If the brake fluid is at the MAX level, remove a third of the fluid.

Front disc brake pads

Caution: *Install new caliper slippers onto the caliper mounting bracket and new V-springs when installing new brake pads.*

2   Loosen the wheel lug nuts, raise the front of the vehicle and support it securely on jackstands. Apply the parking brake.

3   Remove the wheels. Work on one brake assembly at a time, using the assembled brake for reference if necessary.

4   Inspect the brake disc carefully as outlined in Section 6. If machining is necessary, follow the information in that Section to remove the disc, at which time the pads can be removed as well.

5   Push the piston back into its bore to provide room for the new brake pads. A C-clamp can be used to accomplish this (see illustration). As the piston is depressed to the bottom of the caliper bore, the fluid in the master cylinder will rise. Make sure that it doesn't overflow. If necessary, remove some of the fluid.

6   Follow the accompanying photos (illustrations 4.6a through 4.6n), for the actual pad replacement procedure. Be sure to stay in order and read the caption under each illustration.

7   When reinstalling the caliper, be sure to tighten the mounting bolts to the torque listed in this Chapter's Specifications. After the job has been completed, firmly depress the brake pedal a few times to bring the pads into contact with the disc. Check the level of the brake fluid, adding some if necessary. Check the operation of the brakes carefully before placing the vehicle into normal service.

3.23 Rear wheel speed sensor location

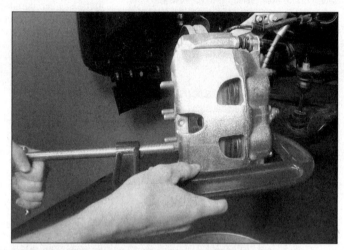

4.5 Before removing the caliper, be sure to depress the piston into the bottom of its bore in the caliper with a large C-clamp to make room for the new pads

4.6a Always wash the brakes with brake cleaner before disassembling anything

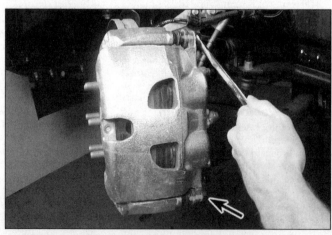

4.6b Remove the upper and lower caliper mounting bolts. . .

4.6c . . . then remove the caliper and use a piece of wire to support it. Never let the caliper hang by the brake hose

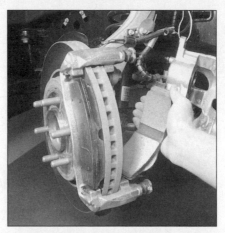

4.6d Remove the inner pad from the caliper mounting bracket. . .

4.6e . . . then remove the outer pad

4.6f Remove and discard the upper and lower pad retaining clips from the caliper mounting bracket

4.6g Inspect the caliper mounting bracket for burrs, deposits or other damage that may interfere with the brake pads moving properly during normal braking. Clean the mounting surfaces thoroughly

4.6h Pull out both guide pins and clean them off, then apply a coat of high-temperature brake grease to them. Also, inspect the guide pin dust boots. Damaged dust boots must be replaced

4.6i Install new brake pad retaining clips onto the mounting bracket

4.6j Install the inner pad

4.6k Install the outer pad

4.6l While holding the brake pads to the disc, place the caliper into position

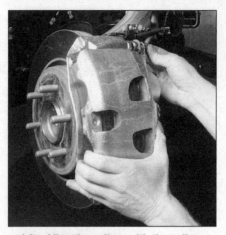

4.6m Align the caliper with the caliper bracket and hand start the caliper mounting bolts

4.6n Tighten the mounting bolts to the torque listed in this Chapter's Specifications

Rear disc brake pads

8   Loosen the wheel lug nuts, raise the rear of the vehicle and support it securely on jackstands. Block the wheels at the opposite end. Remove the wheels. Work on one brake assembly at a time, using the assembled brake for reference if necessary.

Caution: *On rear brake systems equipped with EPB (Electronic Parking Brake), the system must be deactivated before any work is performed on the rear brakes. See Section 8 for the EPB system deactivation and reactivation procedures.*

9   Inspect the brake disc carefully as outlined in Section 6. If machining is necessary, follow the information in that Section to remove the disc, at which time the pads can be removed as well.

Warning: *Push the piston back into its bore to provide room for the new brake pads. A C-clamp can be used to accomplish this only if your vehicle is not equipped with EPB. On EPB (Electronic Parking Brake) systems, use*

a scissor-type brake pad spreader tool or a caliper piston retractor tool to move the piston back into the caliper bore. As the piston is depressed to the bottom of the caliper bore, the fluid in the master cylinder will rise. Make sure that it doesn't overflow. If necessary, remove some of the fluid.

10   Follow the accompanying photos (illustrations 4.10a through 4.10o), for the actual pad replacement procedure. Be sure to stay in order and read the caption under each illustration.

11   When reinstalling the caliper, be sure to tighten the mounting bolts to the torque listed in this Chapter's Specifications. If equipped with the electronic parking brake system follow the procedures to active the EPB (see Section 8) before applying brake pressure. Firmly depress the brake pedal a few times to bring the pads into contact with the disc. Check the level of the brake fluid, adding some if necessary. Check the operation of the brakes carefully before placing the vehicle into normal service.

4.10a Always wash the brakes with brake cleaner before disassembling anything

4.10b Remove the caliper mounting bolts. Hold the guide pin with a wrench to prevent it from turning while loosening the bolt

4.10c Remove the caliper

4.10d Hang the caliper with a length of wire. Never let the caliper hang by the brake hose

4.10e Remove the inner brake pad

4.10f Remove the outer brake pad

4.10g Remove the lower brake pad retaining clip

4.10h Remove the upper brake pad retaining clip

4.10i Clean the mating area for the new retaining clips

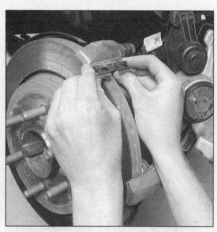

4.10j Install the new retaining clips

4.10k Install the outer pad onto the caliper mounting bracket

4.10l Install the inner brake pad

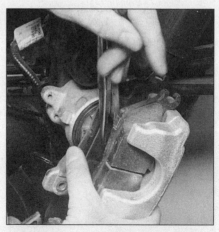

4.10m Using a pad spreader or caliper piston tool (for EPB systems, shown) or C clamp (for cable-operated parking brake systems), push the piston into the caliper to make room for the new pads

4.10n Remove the guide pins and lubricate them with high-temperature brake grease, then reinstall them

4.10o Place the caliper over the brake pads, then install the caliper mounting bolts and tighten them to the torque listed in this Chapter's Specifications

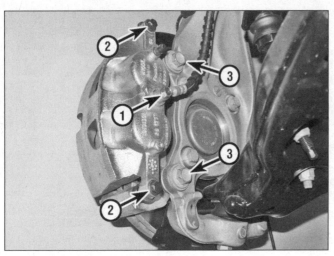

5.2a Front caliper mounting details

1   *Inlet fitting and bolt*
2   *Caliper mounting bolts*
3   *Caliper mounting bracket bolts*

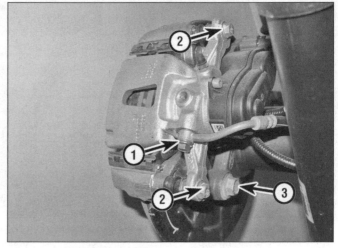

5.2b Rear caliper mounting details

1   *Inlet fitting and bolt*
2   *Caliper mounting bolts*
3   *Caliper mounting bracket bolt (upper bolt not visible)*

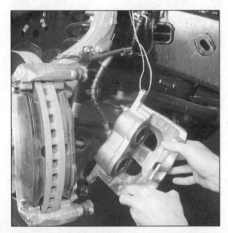

5.3 Hang the caliper with a length of wire. DON'T allow the caliper to hang by the brake hose! (typical shown)

5   Disc brake caliper - removal and installation

Warning: *Dust created by the brake system is harmful to your health. Never blow it out with compressed air and don't inhale any of it. An approved filtering mask should be worn when working on the brakes. Do not, under any circumstances, use petroleum-based solvents to clean brake parts. Use brake system cleaner only.*

Note: *If replacement is indicated (usually because of fluid leakage), it is recommended that the calipers be replaced, not overhauled. New and factory rebuilt units are available on an exchange basis, which makes this job quite easy. Always replace the calipers in pairs - never replace just one of them.*

Removal

1   Loosen the wheel lug nuts, raise the vehicle (front or rear) and place it securely on jackstands. Remove the wheels.

2   Remove the inlet fitting bolt and disconnect the brake hose from the caliper (see illustrations). Plug the brake hose to keep contaminants out of the brake system and to prevent losing any more brake fluid than is necessary.

Caution: *If the caliper is being removed for access to another component, don't disconnect the hose.*

3   Refer to Section 4 for the caliper removal procedure. If the caliper is being removed for access to another component, use a piece of wire to securely hang it out of the way (see illustration).

6.3 The brake pads on this vehicle were obviously neglected, as they wore down completely and cut deep grooves into the disc - wear this severe means the disc must be replaced

6.4a Use a dial indicator and rotate the disc to check disc runout

6.4b Using a swirling motion, remove the glaze from the disc surface with sandpaper or emery cloth

6.5a The minimum (discard) thickness of the brake disc is cast into the disc (rear disc shown, front similar)

6.5b Use a micrometer to measure disc thickness

Installation

4   Install the caliper by reversing the removal procedure.

5   Bleed the brake circuit according to the procedure in Section 11. Make sure there are no leaks from the hose connections. Test the brakes carefully before returning the vehicle to normal service.

6   Brake disc - inspection, removal and installation

Warning: *Dust created by the brake system is harmful to your health. Never blow it out with compressed air and don't inhale any of it. An approved filtering mask should be worn when working on the brakes. Do not, under any circumstances, use petroleum-based solvents to clean brake parts. Use brake system cleaner only.*

Inspection

1   Loosen the wheel lug nuts, raise the vehicle and support it securely on jackstands, then remove the wheels.

2   Remove the brake caliper as outlined in Section 5. After removing the caliper bolts, suspend the caliper out of the way with a piece of wire (see illustration 4.3).

3   Visually inspect the disc surface for score marks and other damage. Light scratches and shallow grooves are normal after use and may not always be detrimental to brake operation, but deep scoring requires disc removal and refinishing by an automotive machine shop. Be sure to check both sides of the disc (see illustration). If pulsating has been noticed during application of the brakes, suspect disc runout.

4   To check disc runout, place a dial indicator at a point about 1/2-inch from the outer edge of the disc (see illustration). Set the indi-

cator to zero and turn the disc. The indicator reading should not exceed the specified allowable runout limit. If it does, the disc should be refinished by an automotive machine shop.

Note: *The discs should be resurfaced regardless of the dial indicator reading, as this will impart a smooth finish and ensure a perfectly flat surface, eliminating any brake pedal pulsation or other undesirable symptoms related to questionable discs. At the very least, if you elect not to have the discs resurfaced, remove the glaze from the surface with emery cloth or sandpaper, using a swirling motion (see illustration).*

5   It's absolutely critical that the disc not be machined to a thickness under the specified minimum thickness. The minimum (or discard) thickness is cast or stamped into the inside of the disc (see illustration). The disc thickness can be checked with a micrometer (see illustration).

6.8 Use cutting pliers to remove any metal retaining washers from the wheel studs (if equipped)

7.3a Have an assistant pull the cable down as you install the 4 mm Allen wrench in the lock-out hole just behind the parking brake lever arm

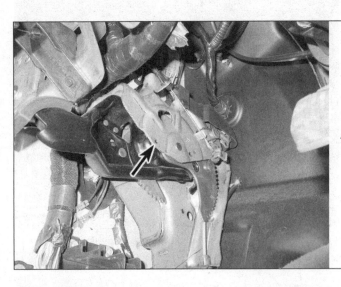

7.3b Place the 4 mm Allen wrench here to lock the pedal in place

Removal

Caution: *On rear brake systems equipped with EPB (Electronic Parking Brake) the system needs to be deactivated before any work is performed on the rear brakes. Go to the general information section (see Section 8) for detailed instructions and procedures for deactivating the EPB system.*

6   Remove the brake caliper as outlined in Section 5. It isn't necessary to disconnect the brake hose. After removing the caliper bolts, suspend the caliper out of the way with a piece of wire (see illustration 5.3).

7   Remove the two caliper mounting bracket bolts and detach the mounting bracket (see illustration 5.2a or 5.2b).

8   If equipped, remove the pressed-metal retaining washers and discard them (it is not necessary to reinstall them) (see illustration). Slide the brake disc off the hub or axle flange.

Installation

9   Clean the mounting surface between the wheel studs. Remove any rust scale or debris that could interfere with the mating surfaces of the disc to the spindle.

10   Place the disc in position over the wheel studs.

11   Install the caliper mounting bracket, tightening the bolts to the torque value listed in this Chapter's Specifications.

12   Install the caliper and tighten the bolts to the torque listed in this Chapter's Specifications.

13   Install the wheel, then lower the vehicle to the ground. Tighten the lug nuts to the torque listed in the Chapter 1 Specifications. Depress the brake pedal a few times to bring the brake pads into contact with the disc. Bleeding won't be necessary unless the brake hose was disconnected from the caliper. Check the operation of the brakes carefully

before driving the vehicle. Reactivate the EPB system (if equipped) by following the procedure in the electronic parking brake actuator section, (see Section 8) for detailed instructions.

7   Cable-actuated parking brake - component replacement

Warning: *Dust created by the brake system is harmful to your health. Never blow it out with compressed air and don't inhale any of it. An approved filtering mask should be worn when working on the brakes. Do not, under any circumstances, use petroleum-based solvents to clean brake parts. Use brake system cleaner only.*

Parking brake shoes - replacement

1   Loosen the rear wheel lug nuts. Raise the vehicle and support it securely on jackstands. Remove the wheels. Be sure to block the front tires.

2   Release the parking brake completely.

3   Have an assistant pull down on the parking brake cable from underneath the vehicle while you hold the parking brake pedal to its highest point. Insert a 4 mm Allen wrench or a 5/32 drill bit into the hole just behind the parking brake lever arm. This will hold the pedal up with the tension off of the cable. (see illustrations).

4   Remove the brake discs (see Section 6).

5   Clean the parking brake assembly with brake system cleaner before beginning any work. Follow illustrations 7.3a through 7.3m for replacement of the parking brake shoes. Be sure to stay in order and read the caption under each illustration.

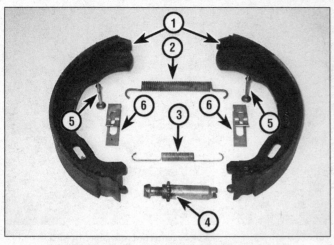

7.5a Parking brake shoes and component details

1   Parking brake shoes
2   Retracting spring
3   Adjusting screw spring
4   Adjusting screw assembly

5   Hold-down spring
    retainers
6   Hold-down clips

7.5b Wash down the brake assembly with brake cleaner; DO NOT blow it out with compressed air!

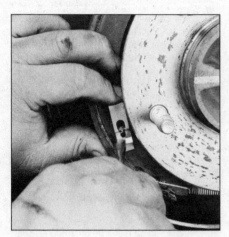

7.5c Remove the front hold-down clip . . .

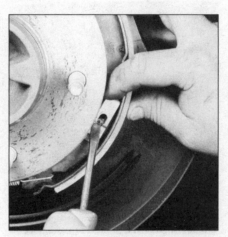

7.5d . . . and the rear hold-down clip

7.5e Remove the parking brake shoe adjuster . . .

7.5f . . . remove the lower return spring

7.5g Spread the parking brake shoes as shown and lift off the parking brake shoe assembly; if you're replacing the old shoes, remove the upper return spring and transfer it to the new shoes

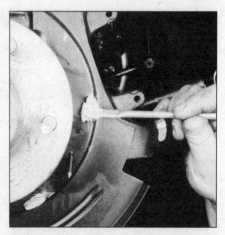

7.5h Lubricate the shoe contact points on the backing plate with high-temperature brake grease

7.5i With the upper return spring installed into the shoes as shown, spread the lower ends of the shoes apart and install the parking brake shoe assembly

7.5j Install the front shoe hold-down clip . . .

7.5k . . . and the rear shoe hold-down clip

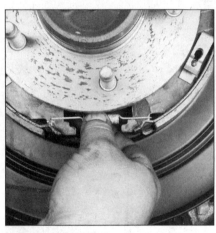

7.5l Install the lower return spring . . .

7.5m . . . and the adjuster (make sure the star wheel of the adjuster is pointing towards the front of the vehicle)

6   Clean the brake disc/parking brake drum and check it for score marks, deep grooves, hard spots (which will appear as small discolored areas) and cracks. If the disc/drum is worn, scored or out-of-round, it can be resurfaced by an automotive machine shop.

7   After the shoes have been installed, turn the adjusting screw so the disc just fits over the new shoes. When the disc is installed, the shoes should not rub as the disc is turned. If you have a brake shoe adjusting gauge, adjust the diameter of the shoes to 0.02-inch less than that of the drum surface of the rear brake disc.

8   Repeat this procedure for the other parking brake assembly.

9   Install the brake discs (see Section 6).

10   Remove the rubber plug from the brake backing plate and, using a screwdriver or brake adjusting tool, turn the adjusting screw star wheel until the parking brake shoes start to drag as the disc is turned, then back off the

star wheel until the shoes don't drag.

11   Remove the 4 mm Allen wrench from the parking brake lever.

12   Install the rear wheels and lug nuts, lower the vehicle and tighten the lug nuts to the torque listed in the Chapter 1 Specifications.

Parking brake cable - replacement

Note: *The parking brake cable system consists of three parts: An LH and an RH cable, and a front cable. The front cable is removed with the parking brake lever.*

13   Release the tension on the parking brake cables by having a helper pull down on the cable while you insert the Allen wrench into the locking hole as described in Step 3.

14   Press inward on the tabs securing the cable to the brake shoe actuator lever, then pull the cable free from the bracket.

15   Pull the tension spring back far enough to slip the cable end off of the parking brake control lever, then remove the cable.

16   Disconnect the cable from the equalizer bracket (where the LH and RH cables join together).

17   Press inward on the tabs that secure the cable to the frame bracket, then pull the cable free.

18   Snap open the plastic cable retainers and separate the LH and RH cables.

19   If you're removing the RH cable, remove the parking brake cable bracket bolt.

20   Installation is the reverse of removal.

Parking brake manual lever - replacement

21   Remove the tension on the parking brake cable as described in the parking brake shoe segment.

22   Remove the brake pedal bracket assembly. For adjustable pedal equipped vehicles see (Section 13).

23   From underneath the vehicle, disconnect the front parking brake cable from the cable union.

24   Remove the sill plate and driver's side kick panel.

25   Disconnect the parking brake warning light connection.

26   Pull up the carpeting and insulation to expose the parking brake cable.

27   Pull the front cable grommet from the cab floor, then remove the bolts securing the lever to the kick panel area. Remove the cable and lever together.

Note: *The front parking brake cable can now be removed from the parking brake lever for service and replacement.*

28   Installation is the reverse of removal.

29   Be sure to follow the steps to initiate the adjustable pedal system (see Section 13).

8   Electronic Parking Brake (EPB) - general information, troubleshooting, deactivation/ activation and component replacement

Warning: *Dust created by the brake system is harmful to your health. Never blow it out with compressed air and don't inhale any of it. An approved filtering mask should be worn when working on the brakes. Do not, under any circumstances, use petroleum-based solvents to clean brake parts. Use brake system cleaner only.*

Warning: *Do NOT perform any repairs to the rear braking system on a vehicle equipped with Electronic Parking Brake (EPB) unless you've deactivated the system. Follow the procedure outlined in this section.*

General information

1   The Electronic Parking Brake (EPB) system utilizes an actuator mounted on each rear brake caliper. The EPB control module monitors the functions of the actuators for the engagement and release. The control module also stores any trouble codes related to the EPB system. If a malfunction occurs in the EPB system, the controller will turn on the parking brake warning light in the instrument panel.

2   The red brake warning light is for hydraulic issues; the yellow brake warning light is for issues with the EPB system. In some cases, both the red and yellow warning lights can come on informing you of a problem with the EPB system. The yellow parking brake warning light will also come on when the EPB system is in the service mode.

Troubleshooting

System fault	Service procedure
Red warning light is on, never comes on, or is flashing	*Low on brake fluid, wiring, connections, faulty brake fluid level sensor, parking brake is on, brake booster vacuum sensor, EPB, IPC, or ABS concerns*
Yellow warning light is on or never comes on	*Faulty parking brake switch, connections, wiring, EPB module concerns*
Message center displays parking brake malfunction or "Service Parking Brake System Now"	*Have system checked for codes*
Message center displays "Parking Brake Limited Service Required"	*Have system checked for codes*
Message center displays "Maintenance Mode"	*System is in the service mode*
Rear brakes are dragging	*Service the rear brake system*
Parking brake system does not release or fails to engage	*Check for codes and have the system checked for network communication concerns*

EPB Deactivation procedure

a) *Turn the ignition to ON.*
b) *Continue to hold the accelerator pedal and EPB switch.*
c) *Turn the ignition to OFF, then within 5 seconds, turn the ignition to ON.*
d) *Turn the ignition OFF and release the EPB switch.*
e) *The EPB is now in the "inactive" or "service mode" and is safe to perform the service work needed.*

EPB Activation procedure

a) *After completing the service work, you'll need to reactivate the electronic parking brake system.*
b) *Turn the ignition on and hold the accelerator pedal to the floor as you move the EPB switch in the activate position (upwards).*
c) *Turn the ignition switch to the OFF position without releasing the accelerator pedal or the EPB switch.*
d) *Within 5 seconds turn the ignition switch to the ON position.*
e) *Release the accelerator pedal and EPB switch.*
f) *The EPB is now in "active" mode and is ready for use.*

Component replacement
EPB actuator

3   Loosen the rear wheel lug nuts. Raise the vehicle and support it securely on jackstands. Remove the wheels. Be sure to block the front tires.

4   Deactivate the EPB system by following the steps provided (see Section 8).

5   Disconnect the electrical connector from the actuator (see illustration).

6   Remove the two bolts securing the actuator to the caliper. Discard the bolts and obtain new ones for installation (see illustration).

Note: *On some models, the left hand caliper brake hose is overlapping the actuator. This routing of the hose prevents removal of the actuator. If so, the hose will need to be removed from the caliper. (This only applies to the left hand side and only on certain production models).*

7   Work the actuator off of the caliper by slightly twisting from left to right as you pull it outward.

8.5 Actuator electrical connector

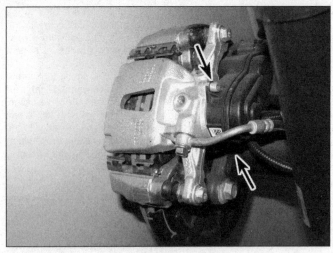

8.6 Actuator mounting bolts

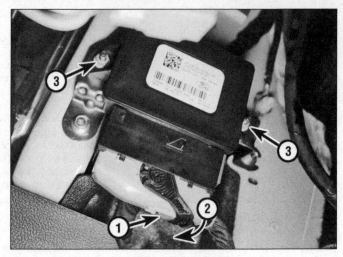

8.10 EPB module details

1   *Depress the safety tab*
2   *Then swing the connector lock open and unplug the connector*
3   *Mounting nuts*

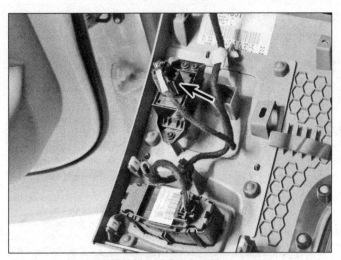

8.16 EPB switch electrical connector

8.17 EPB switch mounting screws

8   Discard the O-ring.
9   To install, replace the O-ring and fasteners. On the left-hand side (on the models needing the brake line removed) bleed the brake system after installation (see Section 11). Otherwise, installation is the reverse of removal. Use the Activation procedure to initiate the EPB system.

EPB module

10   Locate the module above the driver's-side kick panel (see illustration).
11   Disconnect the electrical connector.
12   Unscrew the two nuts and remove the module.
13   Installation is the reverse of removal. To clear the code and restore the EPB system, turn the ignition to ON and apply the parking brake twice within 5 seconds, pausing for a 1/2 second in the neutral position between each movement. Use a scan tool to clear the service code from the EPB module.

14   Perform the EPB activation procedure as described earlier in this Section.
Note: *A code may have been stored in the computer memory. Have the codes checked and cleared. Also, have the EPB Configuration routine checked (also known as the Apply and Release test).*

EPB control switch

15   Pull back sharply on the top of the driver's knee bolster and swing it down.
16   Disconnect the electrical connector from the EPB switch (see illustration).
17   Remove the screws securing the EPB switch to the knee bolster (see illustration).
18   Installation is the reverse of removal.
Note: *Whenever the EPB switch or module has been disconnected, a service code may be stored in the module.*
19   To clear the code and restore the EPB system, turn the ignition to ON and apply the

parking brake twice within 5 seconds, pausing for a 1/2 second in the neutral position between each movement. Use a scan tool to clear the service code from the EPB module.
Note: *The service light will not always come on because of the EPB system being disconnected, but a trouble code will be stored in the computer memory.*

---

9   Master cylinder - removal and installation

Removal

1   The master cylinder is located in the engine compartment, mounted to the power brake booster.
2   Using a large syringe or equivalent, siphon the brake fluid from the master cylin-

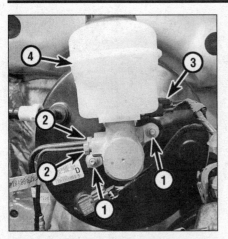

9.3 Master cylinder details

1 Mounting nuts
2 Brake line fittings
3 Fluid level warning switch connector
4 Fluid reservoir

9.9 The best way to bleed air from the master cylinder before installing it on the vehicle is with a pair of bleeder tubes that direct brake fluid into the reservoir during bleeding

9.14 Be sure to install a new rubber O-ring on the master cylinder (typical shown)

der reservoir and dispose of it properly.

Caution: *Brake fluid will damage paint. Cover all painted surfaces and avoid spilling fluid during this procedure. If fluid is spilled, rinse it off with plenty of water.*

3   Disconnect the electrical connector from the fluid level warning switch (see illustration).

4   On 4WD models, disconnect the front axle vent tube retainer from the master cylinder mounting stud on the brake booster.

5   Place rags under the fluid fittings and prepare brake hose caps or a plastic bag to cover the ends of the lines once they are disconnected. Loosen the fittings at the ends of the brake lines where they enter the master cylinder. To prevent rounding off the corners on these nuts, use a flare-nut wrench, which wraps around the nut. Pull the brake lines slightly away from the master cylinder and plug the holes with the brake line caps or wrap the master cylinder in the plastic bag to prevent contamination and spills.

6   Remove the nuts attaching the master cylinder to the power booster. Pull the master cylinder off the studs and out of the engine compartment. Again, be careful not to spill the fluid as this is done.

7   If a new master cylinder is being installed and is not equipped with a reservoir, transfer the reservoir from the old master cylinder to the new one using new seals. Remove the reservoir retaining pins and carefully pry the reservoir away from the old master cylinder. Use clean brake fluid to ease installation of the new seals and reservoir.

Caution: *Old brake fluid that has been opened and left on a shelf for a long period of time should not be used. Purchase new brake fluid instead. Brake fluid is hygroscopic and will absorb moisture from the air. If the brake fluid was left opened or unsealed, or is over a year old, it should be disposed of properly; it is unsafe for use.*

Installation

8   Bench bleed the new master cylinder before installing it. Mount the master cylinder in a vise, with the jaws of the vise clamping on the mounting flange.

9   Attach a pair of master cylinder bleeder tubes to the outlet ports of the master cylinder (see illustration).

10   Fill the reservoir with brake fluid of the recommended type (Chapter 1).

11   Slowly push the pistons into the master cylinder (a large Phillips screwdriver can be used for this) - air will be expelled from the pressure chambers and into the reservoir. Because the tubes are submerged in fluid, air can't be drawn back into the master cylinder when you release the pistons.

Note: *When bench bleeding, it's always best to find clear hoses for the brake lines. This way you'll be able to see the smaller bubbles as they leave the master cylinder and travel slowly up the tubing. Wait for the small bubbles to reach the end of the tubing before releasing the master cylinder piston.*

12   Repeat the procedure until no more air bubbles are present.

13   Remove the bleed tubes, one at a time, and install plugs in the open ports to prevent fluid leakage and air from entering. Install the reservoir cap.

14   Install the master cylinder over the studs on the power brake booster and tighten the attaching nuts only finger-tight at this time (see illustration).

Note: *Be sure to install a new O-ring into the sleeve of the master cylinder*

15   Thread the brake line fittings into the master cylinder. Since the master cylinder is still a bit loose, it can be moved slightly in order for the fittings to thread in easily. Be careful not to cross-thread or strip the fittings as they are installed.

16   Fully tighten the mounting nuts, then the brake line fittings. Tighten the nuts to the

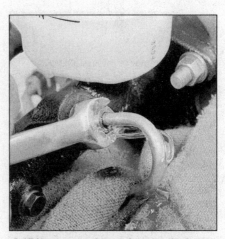

9.17 Have an assistant depress the brake pedal and hold it down, then loosen the fitting nut, allowing the air and fluid to escape; repeat this procedure on both fittings until the fluid is clear of air bubbles

torque listed in this Chapter's Specifications.

17   Fill the master cylinder reservoir with fluid, then bleed the master cylinder and the brake system as described in Section 11. To bleed the cylinder on the vehicle, have an assistant depress the brake pedal and hold the pedal to the floor. Loosen the fitting just enough to allow air and fluid to escape then tighten it lightly (see illustration). Repeat this procedure on both fittings until the fluid is clear of air bubbles and then tighten the fittings securely.

Caution: *Have plenty of rags on hand to catch the fluid - brake fluid will ruin painted surfaces. After the bleeding procedure is completed, rinse the area under the master cylinder with clean water.*

18   Bleed the remainder of the brake system (see Section 11).

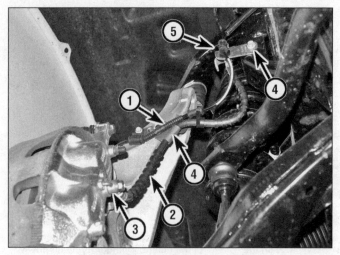

10.3a Front brake hose details

1   *Wheel speed sensor harness*
2   *Flexible brake hose*
3   *Brake hose-to-caliper banjo fitting*
4   *Brake hose brackets*
5   *Steel brake line-to-brake hose fitting (behind bracket)*

10.3b Rear brake hose details

1   *Brake hose-to-caliper banjo fitting*
2   *Brake hose*
3   *Steel brake line-to-brake hose fitting*

19   The remainder of installation is the reverse of removal. Test the operation of the brake system carefully before placing the vehicle into normal service.

Warning: *If you are in doubt about the effectiveness of the brake system, or the BRAKE or ABS light is on, DO NOT OPERATE THE VEHICLE. Have the vehicle towed to a dealer service department or qualified independent repair shop for further testing.*

10   Brake hoses and lines - inspection and replacement

Warning: *If air has found its way into the hydraulic control unit, the system must be bled with the use of a scan tool. If the brake pedal feels spongy even after bleeding the brakes, or the ABS light on the instrument panel does not go off, or if you have any doubts whatsoever about the effectiveness of the brake system, have the vehicle towed to a dealer service department or other repair shop equipped with the necessary tools for bleeding the system.*

1   About every six months, with the vehicle raised and placed securely on jackstands, the flexible hoses which connect the steel brake lines with the front and rear brake assemblies should be inspected for cracks, chafing of the outer cover, leaks, blisters and other damage. These are important and vulnerable parts of the brake system and inspection should be complete. A light and mirror will be needed for a thorough check. If a hose exhibits any of the above defects, replace it with a new one.

Flexible hoses

2   If you're replacing a front hose, loosen the wheel lug nuts, raise the front of the vehi-

cle and support it securely on jackstands. Clean all dirt away from the ends of the hose.
3   To disconnect a front brake hose from the metal line, unscrew the steel brake line fitting with a flare-nut wrench. For front brake hoses, remove the brake hose brackets (see illustrations).
4   Disconnect the hose from the caliper, discarding the sealing washers.
5   Using new sealing washers, attach the new brake hose to the caliper. Tighten the banjo fitting bolt to the torque listed in this Chapter's Specifications.
6   To reattach a brake hose to the junction, route the line to its original position, then tighten the fitting nut securely.
7   Bleed the brake system (see Section 11).

Metal brake lines

8   To disconnect a metal brake line from any fitting, unscrew the metal tube nut with a flare nut.
9   When replacing brake lines, be sure to use the correct parts. Don't use copper tubing for any brake system components. Purchase steel brake lines from a dealer parts department or auto parts store.
10   Prefabricated brake lines, with the tube ends already flared and fittings installed, are available at auto parts stores and dealer parts departments. These lines can be bent to the proper shapes using a tubing bender.
11   When installing the new line make sure it's well supported in the brackets and has plenty of clearance between moving or hot components.
12   After installation, check the master cylinder fluid level and add fluid as necessary. Bleed the brake system as outlined in Section 11 and test the brakes carefully before placing the vehicle into normal operation.

11   Brake hydraulic system - bleeding

Warning: *Wear eye protection when bleeding the brake system. If the fluid comes in contact with your eyes, immediately rinse them with water and seek medical attention.*

Warning: *Brake fluid that has been sitting around for a long time should not be used. Purchase new brake fluid instead. Brake fluid is hygroscopic and aborbs moisture from the air, which can cause the fluid to boil under heavy braking conditions, which will render the brakes useless. If the brake fluid is old or has been left unsealed, it should be disposed of properly; it is unsafe for use.*

Note: *Bleeding the brake system is necessary to remove any air that's trapped in the system when it's opened during removal and installation of a hose, line, caliper, wheel cylinder or master cylinder.*

1   It will probably be necessary to bleed the system at all four brakes if air has entered the system due to low fluid level, or if the brake lines have been disconnected at the master cylinder.
2   If a brake line was disconnected only at a wheel, then only that caliper must be bled.
3   If a brake line is disconnected at a fitting located between the master cylinder and any of the brakes, that part of the system served by the disconnected line must be bled.
4   Remove any residual vacuum from the brake power booster by applying the brake several times with the engine off.
5   Remove the master cylinder reservoir cap and fill the reservoir with brake fluid. Reinstall the cap.
Caution: *Check the fluid level often during the bleeding operation and add fluid as neces-*

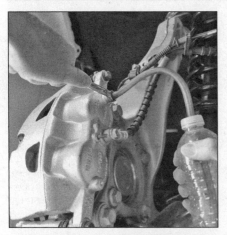

11.8 When bleeding the brakes, a hose is connected to the bleed screw at the caliper and submerged in brake fluid - air will be seen as bubbles in the tube and container (all air must be expelled before moving to the next wheel)

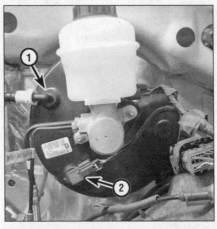

12.7 Disconnect the vacuum hose (1) from the fitting on the power booster and the booster sensor lead (2) (don't pull the rubber fittings out of the booster)

12.9 Squeeze the tabs and remove the retaining pin

sary to prevent the fluid level from falling low enough to allow air bubbles into the master cylinder.

6   Have an assistant on hand, as well as a supply of new brake fluid, an empty clear plastic container, a length of plastic, rubber or vinyl tubing to fit over the bleeder valve and a wrench to open and close the bleeder valve.

7   Beginning at the right rear wheel (the longest brake line from the master cylinder), loosen the bleeder screw slightly, then tighten it to a point where it's snug but can still be loosened quickly and easily.

8   Place one end of the tubing over the bleeder screw fitting and submerge the other end in brake fluid in the container (see illustration).

9   Have the assistant slowly depress the brake pedal and hold it in the depressed position.

10   While the pedal is held depressed, open the bleeder screw just enough to allow a flow of fluid to leave the valve. Watch for air bubbles to exit the submerged end of the tube. When the fluid flow slows, tighten the screw, then have your assistant release the pedal. **Caution:** *The assistant must not release the brake pedal with the bleeder screw open or air will be sucked back into the line.*

11   Repeat until no more air is seen leaving the tube, then tighten the bleeder screw and proceed to the left rear wheel, the right front wheel and the left front wheel, in that order, and perform the same procedure. Be sure to check the fluid level in the master cylinder reservoir frequently.

Models with EPB (Electronic Parking Brake)

12   Apply and release the parking brake five times.

13   Starting with the right-rear caliper, place

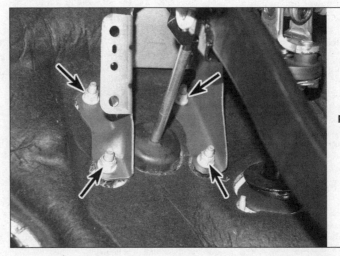

12.10 To detach the power brake booster from the firewall, remove these four nuts

one end of the tubing over the bleeder screw fitting and submerge the other end in brake fluid in the container. Loosen the bleeder screw 1/2 turn until no air bubbles exit the caliper.

14   Repeat Steps 12 and 13 as necessary, then perform the same procedure on the left rear caliper.

All models

15   Refill the master cylinder with fluid at the end of the operation.

16   Check the operation of the brakes. The pedal should feel solid when depressed, with no sponginess. If necessary, repeat the entire process.

Warning: *If you are in doubt about the effectiveness of the brake system, or the BRAKE or ABS light is on, DO NOT OPERATE THE VEHICLE. Have the vehicle towed to a dealer service department or qualified independent repair shop for further testing.*

12 Power brake booster - check, removal and installation

Operating check

1   Depress the brake pedal several times with the engine off and make sure that there is no change in the pedal reserve distance.

2   Depress the pedal and start the engine. If the pedal goes down slightly, operation is normal.

Airtightness check

3   Start the engine and turn it off after one or two minutes. Depress the brake pedal several times slowly. If the pedal goes down farther the first time but gradually rises after the second or third depression, the booster is airtight.

4   Depress the brake pedal while the engine is running, then stop the engine with the pedal

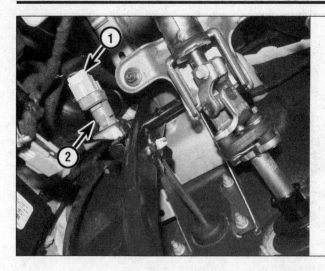

14.1 Brake light switch details

1 *Electrical connector*
2 *Brake light switch*

depressed. If there is no change in the pedal reserve travel after holding the pedal for 30 seconds, the booster is airtight.

Removal and installation

5 Disassembly of the power unit requires special tools and is not ordinarily performed by the home mechanic. If a problem develops, it's recommended that a new or factory rebuilt unit be installed.

6 In the engine compartment, remove the nuts attaching the master cylinder to the booster and carefully pull the master cylinder forward until it clears the mounting studs. Be careful not to bend or kink the brake lines. On 4WD models remove the front axle vent tube from the master cylinder to brake booster attachment bolt.

7 Disconnect the vacuum hose from the fitting on the power brake booster and vacuum sensor (see illustration).

8 Remove the brake light switch (see Section 14).

9 Remove the retaining pin and disconnect the pushrod from the brake pedal (see illustration).

Warning: *Discard the pin and obtain a new one for installation.*

15.2 Vacuum pump quick-connect fittings

10 Remove the nuts attaching the booster to the firewall (see illustration).

11 Carefully lift the booster unit away from the firewall and out of the engine compartment.

12 To install the booster, place it into position and tighten the retaining nuts to the torque listed in this chapter (see this Chapter's Specifications). Connect the pushrod to the brake pedal and install the NEW retaining pin.

13 Install the master cylinder. Reconnect the vacuum hose and vacuum sensor.

14 Test the operation of the brakes before placing the vehicle in normal service.

13 Adjustable brake pedal and bracket - removal, installation and indexing

Removal and installation

1 Move the pedals to the most forward position (towards the firewall).

Warning: *The brake pedal and accelerator pedal should be in the same position whether you are installing a new cable or pedal assembly. They should either be all the way forward or all the way rearward to avoid damaging the components.*

2 Remove the driver's side knee bolster trim.

3 Remove the four bolts securing the steering column reinforcement panel and remove it.

4 Disconnect the drive cable from the adjustable cable drive. Push in on the sides of the connector and pull the cable off.

5 Remove the brake light switch (see Section 14).

6 Remove the pin and brake booster rod from the brake pedal.

7 If equipped, remove the trailer lighting module from the brake booster bracket.

8 Remove the four booster to pedal assembly bracket nuts.

9 Push the brake booster towards the

engine and lift the pedal assembly out of the vehicle.

10 Installation is the reverse of removal, except the pedal assembly will need to be indexed to allow for full forward and rearward adjustment.

11 Torque all the fasteners to the torque listed in this Chapter's Specifications.

Indexing

Note: *The pedal assembly must be indexed whenever the pedal assembly is removed.*

12 With the adjustment cable disconnected from the brake pedal drive actuator, operate the accelerator pedal to the furthest rear (towards the driver) position.

13 Connect the drive cable to the brake pedal drive actuator.

14 Operate the pedals until the brake pedal pin that holds the pedal to the booster rod is aligned with the witness mark (small scribed line) on the side of the brake pedal bracket.

15 Disconnect the drive cable from the brake pedal once again.

16 Operate the accelerator pedal alone in the forward (towards the engine) until there is a 4 mm gap between the screw head attaching the assembly to the drive motor and the moving part of the accelerator pedal.

17 Now reconnect the cable to the brake pedal drive actuator.

18 Check the movement of the pedal assembly. There should be full movement forward and rearward on both pedals, and they should operate evenly with each other. If not, repeat the procedure.

14 Brake light switch - replacement

Warning: *Do not press or pull on the brake pedal while removing or installing the brake switch; otherwise it can be set out of adjustment or damage the switch.*

1 Disconnect the electrical connector from the switch (see illustration).

2 Rotate the switch a quarter-turn clockwise and remove the switch.

3 Installation is the reverse of removal.

15 Brake vacuum pump (2.7L V6 models) - removal and installation

Note: *The vacuum pump is mounted to the rear of the left cylinder head.*

1 Remove the engine cover (see Chapter 2A).

2 Detach the two vacuum hose quick-connect fittings from the pump (see illustration).

3 Loosen the left-front wheel lug nuts. Raise the front of the vehicle and support it securely on jackstands, then remove the wheel.

4 Remove the inner fender splash shield (see Chapter 11).

5   Pry off the wiring harness retainer from the back of the pump (see illustration).

6   Working through the fenderwell, remove the three vacuum pump mounting bolts and detach the pump from the rear of the cylinder head.

7   Clean the mating surfaces of all sealant.

8   Install new O-ring gaskets to the pump.

9   Apply a 1/8-inch bead of RTV sealant to the parting lines of the cylinder head and pump adapter.

10   Install the pump and mounting bolts. Tighten the bolts to the torque listed in this Chapter's Specifications.

Caution: *The pump must be installed within ten minutes of sealant application.*

11   The remainder of installation is the reverse of removal.

12   Install the wheel and lug nuts, then lower the vehicle. Tighten the lug nuts to the torque listed in the Chapter 1 Specifications.

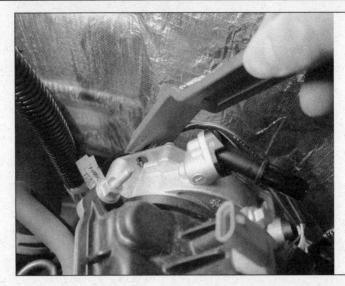

15.5 Detach the wiring harness from the pump

Notes

Chapter 10
Suspension and steering systems

Contents

	Section		Section
Balljoints - check and replacement	8	Steering column - removal and installation	12
General information	1	Steering gear - removal and installation	15
Hub and bearing assembly - replacement	7	Steering gear boots - replacement	14
Leaf springs - removal and installation	10	Steering knuckle - removal and installation	4
Lower control arm - removal and installation	6	Steering wheel - removal and installation	11
Shock absorber/coil spring (front) - removal, component replacement and installation	2	Tie-rod ends - removal and installation	13
		Upper control arm - removal and installation	5
Shock absorbers (rear) - removal and installation	9	Wheel alignment - general information	17
Stabilizer bar and bushings - removal and installation	3	Wheels and tires - general information	16

Specifications

Torque specifications

Ft-lbs (unless otherwise indicated)

Note: *One foot-pound (ft-lb) of torque is equivalent to 12 inch-pounds (in-lbs) of torque. Torque values below approximately 15 foot-pounds are expressed in inch-pounds, because most foot-pound torque wrenches are not accurate at these smaller values.*

Front suspension

Hub and bearing assembly mounting bolts*	129
Driveaxle/hub nut*	See Chapter 8
Stabilizer bar link nuts*	
2WD models	52
4WD models	59
Stabilizer bar bracket bolts*	46
Lower balljoint nut*	76
Upper balljoint nut*	46
Lower control arm-to-frame bolts/nuts*	258
Shock absorber-to-lower control arm nuts*	66
Shock rod-to-upper mount nut*	41
Shock absorber upper mounting nuts*	52
Upper control arm-to-frame bolts and nuts*	122
IWE mounting bolts	106 inch lbs.

Manufacturer recommends replacing with new fasteners

Torque specifications (continued)   **Ft-lbs** (unless otherwise indicated)

Note: *One foot-pound (ft-lb) of torque is equivalent to 12 inch-pounds (in-lbs) of torque. Torque values below approximately 15 foot-pounds are expressed in inch-pounds, because most foot-pound torque wrenches are not accurate at these smaller values. Torque specifications*

Rear suspension
Leaf spring
    Spring shackle-to-frame nut and bolt*.. 173
    Spring-to-frame nut and bolt*... 258
Leaf spring U bolt nuts* (Tighten in an "X" pattern)
    Step 1 26
    Step 2 52
    Step 3 74
    Step 4 98
Shock absorber upper and lower bolt and nut* 66
Note: *Manufacturer recommends replacing with new fasteners*

Steering
Steering wheel retainer bolt* 41
Shift selector arm bolt.. 159 inch-lbs
Upper steering column shaft bolt* 21
Steering column-to-dash support nuts* 22
Steering column-to-dash support bolts* 21
Steering gear mounting bolts/nuts* 184
Steering column shaft pinch bolt*.. 22
Outer tie-rod end nut 76
Note: *Manufacturer recommends replacing with new fasteners*

1.1a Front suspension and steering components - front view (2WD model shown, 4WD model similar)

1	Upper control arm	4	Tie-rod end	7	Steering gear
2	Upper balljoint	5	Lower balljoint	8	Steering gear boot
3	Steering knuckle	6	Lower control arm	9	Shock absorber/coil spring assembly

1.1b Front suspension components - rear view

1   Stabilizer bar
2   Stabilizer bar link

3   Lower control arm
4   Shock absorber/coil spring assembly

1.2 Rear suspension components

1   Leaf springs   *2   Shock absorber*   *3   Rear axle housing*

1   General information

Front suspension

1   The front suspension system is fully independent (see illustration). The steering knuckles are connected to the upper and lower control arms by balljoints. The control arms are bolted to the frame. The shock absorbers and coil springs are integral assemblies (coil-over shock); the upper ends are bolted to the frame and the lower ends are bolted to the lower control arms. All models use a front stabilizer bar to reduce body roll during cornering.

Rear suspension

2   The rear suspension uses shock absorbers and leaf springs (see illustration). The forward end of each spring is attached to a bracket on each frame rail. The rear of each spring is shackled to a bracket on the side of the frame rail.

Steering

3   All models are equipped with electric power-assisted rack-and-pinion steering systems. The steering gear is bolted to the crossmember and is connected to the steering knuckles by a pair of tie-rods.
4   The EPAS (Electronic Power Assist Steering) system takes the place of the conventional hydraulic power steering system. The EPAS communicates by way of a PSCM (Power Steering Control Module) on a high speed data line with various other modules. The PSCM sends these signals to the EPAS and operates the reversible electric motor at various torque and reaction levels for the different driving conditions and road hazards.
5   The PSCM compensates for the speed as well as pull or drift experienced in normal driving and maintains steering stability. Along with drift control, the electronic steering system allows for greater parking lot maneuverability by increasing the torque-to-turn ratio at slow speeds as well as decreasing the turning force for straight ahead highway driving.

Lane Keeping System (LKS)

6   LKS (Lane Keeping System) is integrated with the EPAS, which uses a forward facing camera to evaluate the road lines and edges and helps to maintain the vehicle within those barriers. The steering wheel will vibrate and a visual message is sent to the instrument cluster if the vehicle veers to one side or the other when the system is activated.

Precautions

7   Frequently, when working on the suspension or steering system components, you may come across fasteners which seem impossible to loosen. These fasteners on the underside of the vehicle are continually subjected to water, road grime, mud, etc., and can become rusted or frozen, making them extremely difficult to remove. In order to unscrew these stubborn fasteners without damaging them (or other components), be sure to use lots of penetrating oil and allow it to soak in for a while. Using a wire brush to clean exposed threads will also ease removal of the nut or bolt and prevent damage to the threads. Sometimes a sharp blow with a hammer and punch is effective in breaking the bond between a nut and bolt threads, but care must be taken to prevent the punch from slipping off the fastener and ruining the threads. Heating the stuck fastener and surrounding area with a torch sometimes helps too, but isn't recommended because of the obvious dangers associated with fire. Long breaker bars and extension, or cheater, pipes will increase leverage, but never use an extension pipe on a ratchet - the ratcheting mechanism could be damaged. Sometimes, turning the nut or bolt in the tightening (clockwise) direction first will help to break it loose. Fasteners that require drastic measures to unscrew should always be replaced with new ones.

Note: *Plain water poured over a rusty nut and allowed to soak will sometimes soften the rust between the threads better than penetrating oils can. It doesn't work every time, however it might be a good first effort before resorting to the oils or the hammer and chisel.*
Note: *Since most of the procedures that are dealt with in this Chapter involve jacking up the vehicle and working underneath it, a good pair of jackstands will be needed. A hydraulic floor jack is the preferred type of jack to lift the vehicle, and it can also be used to support certain components during various operations.*
Warning: *Never, under any circumstances, rely on a jack to support the vehicle while working on it. Also, whenever any of the suspension or steering fasteners are loosened or removed they must be inspected and, if necessary, replaced with new ones of the same part number or of original equipment quality and design. Torque specifications must be followed for proper reassembly and component retention. Never attempt to heat or straighten suspension or steering components. Instead, replace bent or damaged parts with new ones.*

2   Shock absorber/coil spring (front) - removal, component replacement and installation

Note: *It is possible to replace the shocks or springs individually but the unit will have to be disassembled by a qualified repair shop with the proper equipment, and this will add considerable cost to the project. You can compare the cost of replacing the complete assemblies yourself to the cost of replacing individual components (with the help of a shop).*

Removal

1   Loosen the front wheel lug nuts. Raise the vehicle and support it securely on jackstands. Remove the front wheels.
2   If you're working on a 4WD model, remove the brake disc (see Chapter 9).
3   Detach the ABS wheel speed sensor bracket and brake hose bracket from the steering knuckle (see illustration).
4   On 4WD models, remove the hub end cap and the driveaxle/hub nut.
5   Detach the tie-rod end from the steering knuckle (see Section 13).
6   On 4WD models, unbolt the Integrated Wheel End (IWE) from the steering knuckle (see Chapter 8).
7   Detach the upper control arm balljoint from the steering knuckle (see Section 5). If you're working on a 2WD model, support the upper end of the steering knuckle with wire (see illustration).
8   If you're working on a 4WD model, separate the lower control arm balljoint from steering knuckle (see Section 8) and remove the steering knuckle.
9   Remove and discard the stabilizer bar link upper nut (see Section 3).

2.3 ABS wheel speed sensor and brake hose bracket bolts

2.7 On 2WD models, tie the upper end of the steering knuckle to the upper control arm to prevent it from falling outward

2.10 Shock absorber lower mounting nuts

2.11 Shock absorber upper mounting nuts

10   Remove and discard the shock absorber lower mounting nuts (see illustration).

11   Remove and discard the shock upper mounting nuts (see illustration).

12   Push downward on the lower control arm, then maneuver the shock absorber/ coil spring assembly out from between the frame and the lower control arm (see illustration).

Component replacement

13   The coil spring must be separated from the shock absorber for replacement of the shock absorber unit, coil spring or upper mount. A heavy-duty spring compressor fixture will be required for this, and for this reason we recommend taking the shock absorber/ coil spring assemblies to a properly equipped repair facility to have this stage of the procedure completed.

Warning: *Never loosen the shock rod-to-upper mount nut without the unit mounted in a spring compressor fixture and the spring compressed!*

Installation

Warning: *The manufacturer states to discard removed suspension component fasteners (nuts and bolts) and replace them with new ones.*

14   Installation is the reverse of removal. Be sure to tighten the suspension fasteners to the torque listed in this Chapter's Specifications, the brake fasteners to the torque listed in the Chapter 9 Specifications , and the driveaxle/hub nut (4WD models) to the torque listed in the Chapter 8 Specifications. Tighten the wheel lug nuts to the torque listed in the Chapter 1 Specifications.

3   Stabilizer bar and bushings - removal and installation

Warning: *The manufacturer recommends to discard suspension component fasteners (nuts and bolts) and replace them with new ones.*

1   Loosen the front wheel lug nuts. Raise the vehicle and support it securely on jackstands. Remove the front wheels.

2   Remove the under-body splash shields.

3   Remove and discard the stabilizer bar link nuts (see illustration).

Note: *If only the stabilizer bar is to be removed, just remove the link upper nuts.*

4   Remove the stabilizer bar bracket nuts and brackets. Discard the bracket nuts and the bracket retainers/studs.

5   Remove the stabilizer bar. Inspect the

2.12 A prybar inserted through the lower control arm can be used to lever the arm downward to assist in removing the shock absorber/coil spring unit (2WD model shown)

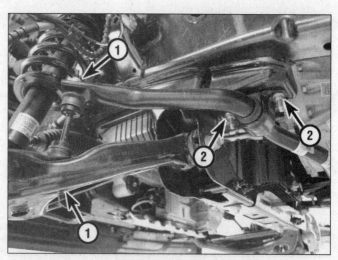

3.3 Stabilizer bar details

1   Stabilizer bar link nuts   2   Stabilizer bar bracket bolts

5.2 Separate the upper control arm from the balljoint with a balljoint separator or a two-jaw puller

5.4 Remove the fasteners and lift the upper arm off the frame bracket

rubber bushings for wear. Replace if necessary.

6   Installation is the reverse of removal. Be sure to tighten all fasteners to the torque values listed in this Chapter's Specifications.

4   Steering knuckle - removal and installation

Warning: *The manufacturer states to discard removed suspension component fasteners (nuts and bolts) and replace them with new ones.*

1   Apply the parking brake. Loosen the wheel lug nuts. Raise the front of the vehicle and support it securely on jackstands. Remove the wheel.
2   Remove the brake disc (see Chapter 9). Hang the caliper with a length of wire - don't let it hang by the brake hose.
3   Disconnect the tie-rod end from the steering knuckle (see Section 13).

6.4 Separate the balljoint from the lower control arm using a puller or a tool like this

4   On 4WD models, remove the driveaxle/hub nut cap and nut.
5   On 4WD models, remove the bolts securing the Integrated Wheel End (IWE) to the steering knuckle.
6   Remove and discard the upper and lower balljoint nuts. Detach the ball joints from the steering knuckle (see Section 5 and Section 6).
7   On 4WD models, support the front driveaxle before removing the steering knuckle.
8   Guide the steering knuckle out of the vehicle.
9   If needed, remove the disc dust shield and hub and bearing assembly (see Section 7) from the knuckle.
10   Installation is the reverse of removal. Tighten all suspension fasteners to the torque values listed in this Chapter's Specifications.
11   On 4WD models, tighten the driveaxle/hub nut to the torque listed in the Chapter 8 Specifications.
12   Tighten the wheel lug nuts to the torque listed in the Chapter 1 Specifications.

5   Upper control arm - removal and installation

Warning: *The manufacturer states to discard removed suspension component fasteners (nuts and bolts) and replace them with new ones.*

1   Apply the parking brake. Loosen the wheel lug nuts, raise the front of the vehicle and support it securely on jackstands. Remove the wheel.
2   Loosen the upper balljoint nut a few turns, then use a balljoint separator or puller to separate the balljoint from the steering knuckle (see illustration).
Caution: *Don't allow the steering knuckle to fall outward, as the brake hose may be damaged.*
3   Remove the shock absorber/coil spring

(see Section 2).
4   Remove and discard the fasteners, then detach the upper control arm from the frame (see illustration).
5   Inspect the bushings for wear and deterioration. If they're cracked or damaged, replace the control arm assembly.
6   Installation is the reverse of removal. Be sure to tighten all suspension fasteners to the torque listed in this Chapter's Specifications.
Note: *The pivot bolt nuts should be tightened with the vehicle at normal ride height. This can be done after the vehicle has been lowered to the ground or simulated by raising the lower control arm with a floor jack.*
7   It's a good idea to have the wheel alignment checked and, if necessary, adjusted.

6   Lower control arm - removal and installation

Warning: *The manufacturer states to discard removed suspension component fasteners (nuts and bolts) and replace them with new ones.*

1   Loosen the wheel lug nuts, raise the front of the vehicle and support it securely on jackstands. Apply the parking brake. Remove the wheel.
2   Detach the stabilizer bar link from the lower control arm (see Section 3).
3   Remove the shock absorber/coil spring lower mounting nuts (see Section 2).
4   Loosen the lower balljoint nut a few turns, then use a balljoint separator or puller to separate the balljoint from the steering knuckle. (see illustration). Once it has separated, remove and discard the nut.
5   Remove the pivot nuts and bolts from the control arm, then remove it from the frame (see illustrations).
6   Inspect the bushings for wear and deterioration. If they're cracked or damaged replace the control arm assembly.

6.5a Mark the flange and frame bracket around all pivot bolts and nuts so that they can be installed in their original positions

6.5b Control arm nut and bolt locations

7   Installation is the reverse of removal. Be sure to align the marks made in Step 5, and tighten all suspension fasteners to the torque listed in this Chapter's Specifications. **Note:** *The pivot bolt nuts should be tightened with the vehicle at normal ride height. This can be done after the vehicle has been lowered to the ground or simulated by raising the lower control arm with a floor jack.*
8   Have the wheel alignment checked and, if necessary, adjusted.

7   Hub and bearing assembly - replacement

Warning: *The manufacturer recommends to replace all removed suspension component fasteners (nuts and bolts).*
1   Apply the parking brake. Loosen the wheel lug nuts and raise the front of the vehicle. Support it securely on jackstands and remove the wheel.
2   Remove the brake disc (see Chapter 9).
3   On 4WD models, remove the hub dust cap and nut, then push the driveaxle through the hub splines as the hub and bearing assembly is removed in the next Step. **Caution:** *On 4WD models, be careful not to over extend the inner CV joint. Once the hub has been removed, support the outer end of the driveaxle with a length of wire or rope.*
4   Remove the four bolts securing the hub assembly to the steering knuckle. Then remove the hub assembly (see illustration).
5   Installation is the reverse of removal.
6   Replace all suspension fasteners that were removed with new fasteners and torque to the proper specifications (see this Chapter's Specifications).
7   Install the wheels, lower the vehicle and tighten the wheel lug nuts to the torque listed (see Chapter 1).

8   Balljoints - check and replacement

Check
1   Inspect the upper and lower balljoints for looseness whenever the vehicle is raised for any reason. You can check the balljoints with the suspension assembled as follows.
2   Raise the vehicle and support it securely on jackstands.
3   Wipe the balljoints clean and inspect the seals for cuts and tears. If a balljoint seal is damaged, replace the balljoint.
4   To check the upper balljoint, grab the upper control arm near the balljoint and attempt to move the arm up and down. Any noticeable play between the upper control arm and the steering knuckle indicates the need to replace the upper balljoint (see illustration).
5   To check the lower balljoint, attempt to move the wheel up and down while checking

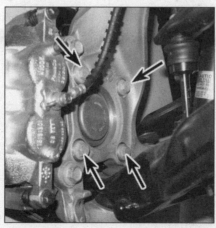

7.4 Hub bolt locations (2WD shown)

for play between the lower control arm and the steering knuckle. Any noticeable play indicates the need to replace the balljoint.

Upper ball joint - removal and installation
6   The upper balljoints on these models are not serviceable. If the balljoint must be replaced, the control arm and balljoint must be replaced as a single assembly (see Section 5) for removal and installation procedures for the upper control arm.

Lower ball joint - removal and installation
7   Apply the parking brake. Loosen the wheel lug nuts and raise the front of the vehicle. Support it securely on jackstands and remove the wheel.
8   Remove the steering knuckle (see Section 4).

8.4 Grab the upper control arm (A) and attempt to move it up and down while checking for any movement between the control arm and the steering knuckle (B)

9.2 Shock absorber mounting fasteners

9   Remove and discard the lower ball joint snap-ring.

10   Using a balljoint removal socket and press clamp (available at specialty tool retailers and some auto parts stores), press the balljoint out of the lower control arm from the top out through the bottom.

11   To install, use the balljoint installing socket and press clamp. Press the balljoint into place (from the underside of the control arm) making sure the balljoint presses firmly into the control arm and exposes the snapring groove on the opposite side of the control arm.

12   Install the new snap-ring.

13   Installation is the reverse of removal.

9   Shock absorbers (rear) - removal and installation

Warning: *The manufacturer recommends to replace all removed suspension component fasteners (nuts and bolts).*

1   Raise the rear of the vehicle, support it securely on jackstands and block the front wheels. Place a floor jack under the axle adjacent to the shock absorber being removed. Raise the jack just enough to take the load off the shock absorber.

2   Remove the nut and bolt securing the lower end of the shock absorber to the rear axle (see illustration).

3   Remove the nut and bolt securing the top of the shock absorber to the upper mounting bracket on the frame.

4   Installation is the reverse of the removal steps. Tighten the nuts and bolts to the torque listed in this Chapter's Specifications.

10   Leaf springs - removal and installation

Removal

Warning: *The manufacturer recommends to replace all removed suspension component fasteners (nuts and bolts).*
Note: *Removal of the left-side leaf spring requires that the gas tank be lowered (see Chapter 4). Right-side spring removal requires that the rear portion of the exhaust*

system (muffler) be removed.

1   Loosen the rear wheel lug nuts. Raise the rear of the vehicle, support it securely on jackstands placed under the frame rails and block the front wheels. Remove the wheel.

2   Remove the shock absorber lower mounting nut and bolt (see Section 9).

3   Support the rear axle with a floor jack nearest the spring to be removed. Remove the four U-bolt nuts, then remove the spring plate and U-bolts (see illustration). Now lower the jack far enough to relieve tension from the spring.

4   Remove the lower bolt and nut securing the shackle assembly to the frame bracket at the rear of the spring (see illustration).

5   Remove the spring hanger bolt and nut at the front of the spring (see illustration). Remove the spring.

6   Remove the shackle and spring as one unit from the vehicle.

7   If necessary, remove the nut and bolt and detach the shackle from the spring.

8   Inspect the spring shackle bushings for wear or distortion. If worn or damaged replace the shackle assembly.

9   Inspect the spring eye bushings for wear or distortion. If worn or damaged have them replaced by an automotive machine shop or other qualified repair facility.

10   On 4WD models, replace the spring spacer if needed. If the spacer has a single protrusion on one end in the center, it should face towards the front of the vehicle. If it has a single offset protrusion or two protrusions, it should face the rear of the vehicle.

Installation

11   Install the spring in the front bracket. Tighten the bolt and nut finger-tight.

12   Place the spring shackle in the frame bracket. Install the bolt and nut and tighten them finger-tight.

13   Raise the axle into contact with the spring making sure they are positioned correctly. Install the U-bolts and nuts and tighten them to the torque listed in this Chapter's

10.4 To detach the rear end of the leaf spring and shackle from the frame, remove the lower nut and bolt

10.5 To detach the front end of the leaf spring from its bracket, remove this nut and bolt

10.3 With the axle supported, remove the nuts from the U-bolts

11.3 Insert a narrow tool into the hole in each side of the steering wheel to release the spring steel retainers that secure the airbag

11.4a Lift the airbag module off of the steering wheel and tilt it towards you

11.4b Disconnect the electrical connectors from the airbag module by lifting the orange safety clip, then squeeze the two sides of the yellow connector and pull up to release

Specifications. Tighten the U-bolt nuts in a "X" pattern.

Note: *If equipped, be sure the spring spacer is in place.*

14   Install the wheel and lug nuts. Lower the vehicle to the ground and tighten the spring bracket bolt and nut and shackle-to-frame bracket bolt and nut to the torque values listed in this Chapter's Specifications.

---

11   Steering wheel - removal and installation

Warning: *The models covered by this manual are equipped with a Supplemental Restraint System (SRS), more commonly known as airbags. Always disable the airbag system before working in the vicinity of any airbag system component to avoid the possibility of accidental deployment of the airbag, which could cause personal injury (see, Chapter 12).*

Removal

1   Park the vehicle with the front wheels pointed straight ahead and the steering wheel centered. Disconnect the cable from the negative terminal of the battery (see Chapter 1).

2   Refer to Chapter 12 and disable the airbag system.

3   On each side of the steering wheel, insert a 3 mm Allen wrench (or other narrow tool) into the hole. Push the wire clip inward and slightly forward to gain good contact with the release spring. As the spring is pressed, pull the airbag module away from the steering wheel (see illustration).

4   Lift the airbag module off the steering wheel and disconnect the airbag and horn electrical connectors (see illustrations).

Caution: *When handling the airbag module, hold it with the trim side facing away from you. Set the airbag module down in a safe location with the trim side facing up.*

5   Remove the steering wheel retaining bolt

and mark the position of the steering wheel to the shaft (see illustration).

Note: *The steering wheel will only fit on one way, but marking it to the shaft will help during installation.*

6   Lift the steering wheel off the shaft.

7   Tape the inner rotor of the clockspring to the housing to prevent it from turning (see illustration).

Caution: *Don't hammer on the shaft or the steering wheel in an attempt to dislodge the wheel! While the steering wheel is removed, do NOT turn the steering shaft or rotor of the clockspring. If this happens, the clockspring will no longer be aligned properly, which could damage the ribbon within the clockspring, rendering the airbag inoperative. If the clockspring is accidentally moved, it must be centered before installing the steering wheel. A good tip would be to tape the inner and outer rings of the clockspring together to avoid any movement while the steering wheel has been removed.*

11.5 Remove the steering wheel bolt and mark the relationship of the steering wheel to the steering shaft

11.7 Tape the clockspring so it does not become uncentered

11.9a Clockspring mounting screws

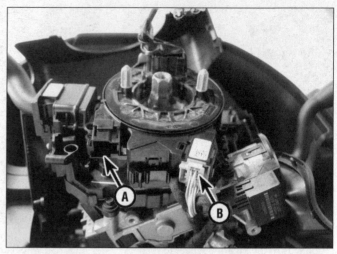

11.9b Clockspring electrical connectors

A   Connector location for steering wheel mounted audio controls
B   Main clockspring electrical connector

Clockspring - centering, removal and installation

Caution: *Only perform this procedure if the clockspring or steering shaft have been rotated while the steering wheel has been removed, or if the clockspring must be replaced.*

8   Verify that the front wheels are pointing straight ahead. Turn the clockspring housing counterclockwise by hand until it becomes hard to turn (don't apply too much force, though, because the cable could break). Turn the clockspring clockwise three complete turns until the electrical connector is in the 12 o'clock position.

9   If it's necessary to remove the clockspring from the steering column, remove the steering column covers (see Chapter 11). Remove the retaining screws and the electrical connectors from the bottom of the clockspring and then remove it (see illustrations).

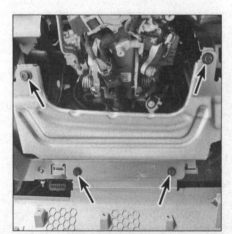

12.3 Steering column reinforcement panel mounting fasteners

Reverse the removal procedure to install the clockspring, but be sure it is centered.

Installation

10   To install the wheel, align the mark on the steering wheel hub with the mark on the shaft and slide the wheel onto the shaft. Install the bolt and tighten it to the torque listed in this Chapter's Specifications.

11   The remainder of installation is otherwise the reverse of removal. Be sure the electrical connectors are securely connected to the airbag module and the airbag module snaps securely into place.

12   Steering column - removal and installation

Warning: *The models covered by this manual are equipped with a Supplemental Restraint System (SRS), more commonly known as airbags. Always disable the airbag system before working in the vicinity of any airbag system component to avoid the possibility of accidental deployment of the airbag, which could cause personal injury (see Chapter 12).*

Warning: *The manufacturer states to discard removed steering component fasteners (nuts and bolts) and replace them with new ones.*

Removal

1   Park the vehicle with the wheels pointing straight ahead. Disconnect the cable from the negative terminal of the battery (see Chapter 1).

2   Remove the knee bolster from under the steering column (see Chapter 11).

3   Remove the steering column reinforcement panel from under the steering column (see illustration).

4   Remove the steering column covers (see Chapter 11).

5   If necessary, remove the SCCM (Steering Column Control Module) (see Chapter 12).

6   Remove the shift lever (see Chapter 7A). Also detach the shift cable from the column (see Chapter 7A).

7   If equipped, disconnect the power telescopic and tilt electrical connections.

8   Disconnect the deployable column electrical connector (see illustration).

9   Remove the pinch bolt from the upper steering column shaft (see illustration).

10   Disconnect any remaining electrical connectors from the steering column.

11   Remove the two nuts and two bolts securing the steering column to the dash support (see illustration).

12   Lower the column and pull it to the rear, making sure nothing is still connected.

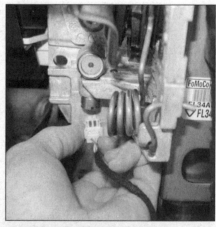

12.8 Unplug the deployable column electrical connector from the left side of the column

12.9 Remove the steering column shaft pinch bolt

12.11 Steering column mounting fasteners

Installation

13 Guide the steering column into position, connect the upper steering column shaft, then install the mounting fasteners, but don't tighten them yet.

Warning: *If the front wheels were turned while the steering shaft was disconnected, the clockspring must be re-centered or it will be damaged when the vehicle is put back into service (see Section 11).*

14 Tightening all the fasteners to the torque listed in this Chapter's Specifications.

Warning: *The manufacturer recommends installing all new fasteners for the steering column and related steering components.*

15 The remainder of the installation is the reverse of removal.

13 Tie-rod ends - removal and installation

Warning: *The manufacturer states to discard removed suspension component fasteners (nuts and bolts) and replace them with new ones.*

1 Loosen the wheel lug nuts, raise the vehicle and place it securely on jackstands. Remove the wheel.

2 Loosen the tie-rod end locknut and mark the position of the tie-rod end on the threaded portion of the tie-rod (see illustrations).

3 Loosen the nut from the tie-rod end balljoint stud, then separate the tie-rod end from the steering knuckle (see illustration).

Remove the nut and detach the tie-rod end from the steering knuckle arm.

Note: *Hold the ballstud on the tie-rod end with the appropriate tool if it turns while removing the nut.*

4 Unscrew the old tie-rod end and install the new one. Make sure the new tie-rod end is aligned with the mark you made on the threads of the tie-rod.

Note: *As you unscrew the tie-rod, count the number of turns. Thread the replacement tie-rod back on with the same number of turns. The turns and the index mark you made should match up together.*

5 Installation is the reverse of removal. Be sure to tighten all fasteners to the torque settings listed in this Chapter's Specifications.

13.2a Loosen the tie-rod end locknut

13.2b Mark the position of the tie-rod end on the threaded portion of the tie-rod

13.3 With the ballstud nut loosened, separate the tie-rod end from the steering knuckle using a suitable tool or puller

14.4 The outer clamp on the steering gear boot can be removed with pliers - the inner clamp must be cut off

15.5 Remove the pinch bolt. Mark the shaft to the steering universal joint for accurately indexing the shaft when reinstalling

14 Steering gear boots - replacement

1   If a steering gear boot is torn, dirt and moisture can damage the steering gear. Replace it.
2   Loosen the wheel lug nuts, raise the vehicle and place it securely on jackstands. Remove the front wheels.
3   Remove the tie-rod end and locknut (see Section 13).
4   Remove the boot clamps (see illustration) and slide the boot off the tie-rod.
5   Installation is the reverse of removal. Be sure to use new clamps on the boot.

15 Steering gear - removal and installation

Warning: *The models covered by this manual are equipped with a Supplemental Restraint System (SRS), more commonly known as airbags. Always disable the airbag system before working in the vicinity of any airbag system component to avoid the possibility of accidental deployment of the airbag, which could cause personal injury.*
Caution: *Before replacing the steering gear, the original unit must have its data uploaded onto a scanner and saved before it is removed from the vehicle, then it can be downloaded into the replacement power steering control module.*
Caution: *Always make sure the negative battery cable is disconnected before disconnecting any of the steering gear components. Failure to do so can result in damage to the EPAS (Electronic Power Assist Steering) system.*

1   Disconnect the cable from the negative terminal of the battery (see Chapter 5).
2   Loosen the front wheel lug nuts. Raise the vehicle and support it securely on jackstands. Remove the front wheels.
3   Remove the outer tie rod ends from the steering knuckles (see Section 13).
4   Remove the lower engine splash shields and guards.
5   Index the steering gear to the steering shaft, then remove the steering shaft pinch bolt (see illustration).
6   Disconnect the electrical connections to the Power Steering Control Module (PSCM). Move the wire harness out of the way so it does not get caught in the steering gear assembly as you remove it (see illustration).
7   Remove the large bolts securing the steering gear assembly to the cross member (see illustration).
8   Shift the steering gear assembly slightly to the driver's side, then lower the assembly out of the vehicle, taking great care not to damage the inner tie rod threads.
9   Installation is the reverse of removal. Use all new fasteners for any of the steering components. Torque all bolts and nuts to the proper torque specifications listed in this Chapter's Specifications.
10 Install the wheels and tighten the lug nuts to the torque listed in the Chapter 1 Specifications.

15.6 PSCM electrical connections

15.7 Steering gear assembly mounting bolts

16 Wheels and tires - general information

1   All vehicles covered by this manual are equipped with metric-size steel belted radial tires (see illustration). These models require the specific tire size, speed rating, load range and construction type to insure the correct ride, handling, speedometer/odometer calibration, tire/body clearance, wheel bearing tolerance and brake cooling characteristics. Use of other size or type of tires may affect all/one of these conditions. Don't mix different types of tires, such as radials and bias belted, on the same vehicle as handling may be seriously affected. It's recommended that tires be replaced in pairs on the same axle, but if only one tire is being replaced, be sure it's the same size, structure and tread design as the other.

2   Because tire pressure has a substantial effect on handling and wear, the pressure on all tires should be checked at least once a month or before any extended trips (see Chapter 1).

3   Wheels must be replaced if they're bent, dented, leak air, have elongated bolt holes, are heavily rusted, out of vertical symmetry or if the lug nuts won't stay tight. Wheel repairs that use welding or peening are not recommended.

4   Tire and wheel balance is important to the overall handling, braking and performance of the vehicle. Unbalanced wheels can adversely affect handling and ride characteristics as well as tire life. Whenever a tire is installed on a wheel, the tire and wheel should be balanced by a shop with the proper equipment.

17 Wheel alignment - general information

1   A wheel alignment refers to the adjustments made to the front and rear wheels so they're in proper angular relationship to the suspension and the ground (see illustration). Wheels that are out of proper alignment not only affect steering control, but also increase tire wear.

2   Getting the proper front and rear wheel alignment is a very exacting process, one in which complicated and expensive machines are necessary to perform the job properly. Because of this, you should have a technician with the proper equipment perform these tasks. We will, however, use this space to give you a basic idea of what is involved with front end alignment so you can better understand the process and deal intelligently with the shop that does the work.

3   Toe-in is the turning in of the front wheels. The purpose of a toe specification is to ensure parallel rolling of the front wheels. In a vehicle with zero toe-in, the distance between the front edges of the wheels will be the same as the distance between the rear edges of the wheels. The actual amount of toe-in is normally only a fraction of an inch. Toe-in adjustment is controlled by the tie-rod length. Incorrect toe-in will cause the tires to wear improperly by making them scrub against the road surface.

4   Camber is the tilting of the front wheels from vertical when viewed from the front of the vehicle. When the wheels tilt out at the top, the camber is said to be positive (+). When the wheels tilt in at the top the camber is negative (-). The amount of tilt is measured in degrees from the vertical and this measurement is called the camber angle. This angle affects the amount of tire tread which contacts the road and compensates for changes in the suspension geometry when the vehicle is cornering or traveling over an undulating surface. Camber is adjusted by loosening the lower control arm-to-frame bolts and moving the arm in (to increase camber) or out (to decrease camber).*

Note: * *Replacement eccentric bolts must first be installed.*

5   Caster is the tilting of the top of the front steering axis from the vertical. A tilt toward the rear is positive caster and a tilt toward the front is negative caster. Caster is also adjusted by loosening the lower control arm-to-frame bolts, but instead of moving the arm in or out, the outer end of the arm is moved toward the front (to increase caster) or toward the rear (to decrease caster).

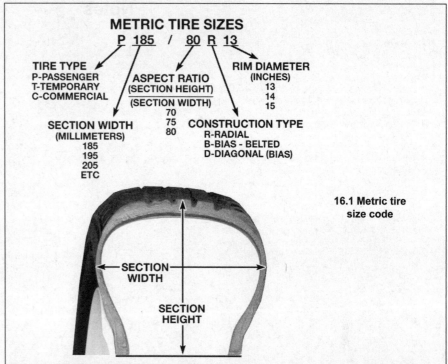

16.1 Metric tire size code

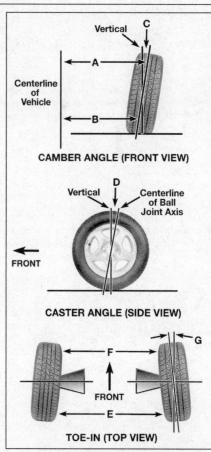

17.1 Front end alignment details

A minus B = C (degrees camber)
D = degrees caster
E minus F = toe-in (measured in inches)
G = toe-in (expressed in degrees)

Notes

Chapter 11 Body

Contents

	Section			Section
Body repair - major damage	4		Hood - removal, installation and adjustment	10
Body repair - minor damage	3		Hood latch and release cable - removal and installation	11
Bumpers - removal and installation	13		Hood support struts - removal and installation	9
Center console - removal and installation	28		Instrument panel - removal and installation	24
Cowl covers - removal and installation	27		Mirrors - removal and installation	20
Dashboard trim panels - removal and installation	23		Radiator grille and headlight housing trim - removal	
Door(s) - removal, installation and adjustment	16		and installation	12
Door latch, lock cylinder and handle - removal and installation	17		Repair minor paint scratches	2
Door trim panels - removal and installation	15		Seats - removal and installation	26
Door window glass - removal and installation	18		Steering column covers - removal and installation	25
Door window glass regulator - removal and installation	19		Tailgate - removal and installation	21
Fastener and trim removal	6		Tailgate latch, release handle, actuator and lock cylinder -	
Front fender - removal and installation	14		removal and installation	22
General information	1		Upholstery, carpets and vinyl trim - maintenance	5
Hinges and locks - maintenance	7		Windshield and fixed glass - replacement	8

1 General information

Warning: *The models covered by this manual are equipped with a Supplemental Restraint System (SRS), more commonly known as airbags. Always disable the airbag system before working in the vicinity of any airbag system components to avoid the possibility of accidental deployment of the airbags, which could cause personal injury (see Chapter 12).*

Certain body components are particularly vulnerable to accident damage and can be unbolted and repaired or replaced. Among these parts are the hood, doors, tailgate, liftgate, bumpers and front fenders.

Only general body maintenance practices and body panel repair procedures within the scope of the do-it-yourselfer are included in this Chapter.

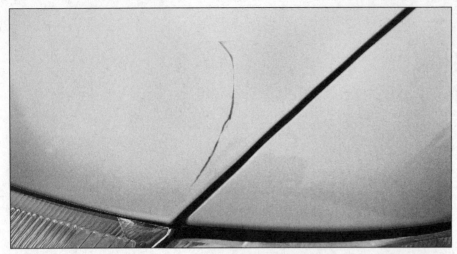

Make sure the damaged area is perfectly clean and rust free. If the touch-up kit has a wire brush, use it to clean the scratch or chip. Or use fine steel wool wrapped around the end of a pencil. Clean the scratched or chipped surface only, not the good paint surrounding it. Rinse the area with water and allow it to dry thoroughly

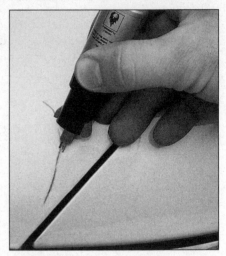

Thoroughly mix the paint, then apply a small amount with the touch-up kit brush or a very fine artist's brush. Brush in one direction as you fill the scratch area. Do not build up the paint higher than the surrounding paint

2   Repair minor paint scratches

No matter how hard you try to keep your vehicle looking like new, it will inevitably be scratched, chipped or dented at some point. If the metal is actually dented, seek the advice of a professional. But you can fix minor scratches and chips yourself. Buy a touch-up paint kit from a dealer parts department or an auto parts store. To ensure that you get the right color, you'll need to have the specific make, model and year of your vehicle and, ideally, the paint code, which is located on a special metal plate under the hood or in the door jamb.

3   Body repair - minor damage

Plastic body panels

The following repair procedures are for minor scratches and gouges. Repair of more serious damage should be left to a dealer service department or qualified auto body shop. Below is a list of the equipment and materials necessary to perform the following repair procedures on plastic body panels.

Wax, grease and silicone removing solvent
Cloth-backed body tape
Sanding discs
Drill motor with three-inch disc holder
Hand sanding block
Rubber squeegees
Sandpaper
Non-porous mixing palette
Wood paddle or putty knife
Curved-tooth body file
Flexible parts repair material

Flexible panels (bumper trim)

1   Remove the damaged panel, if necessary or desirable. In most cases, repairs can be car-

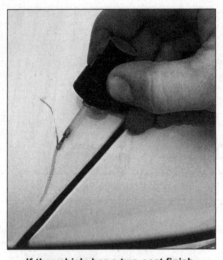

If the vehicle has a two-coat finish, apply the clear coat after the color coat has dried

ried out with the panel installed.
2   Clean the area(s) to be repaired with a wax, grease and silicone removing solvent applied with a water-dampened cloth.
3   If the damage is structural, that is, if it extends through the panel, clean the backside of the panel area to be repaired as well. Wipe dry.
4   Sand the rear surface about 1-1/2 inches beyond the break.
5   Cut two pieces of fiberglass cloth large enough to overlap the break by about 1-1/2 inches. Cut only to the required length.
6   Mix the adhesive from the repair kit according to the instructions included with the kit, and apply a layer of the mixture approximately 1/8-inch thick on the backside of the panel. Overlap the break by at least 1-1/2 inches.
7   Apply one piece of fiberglass cloth to the adhesive and cover the cloth with additional adhesive. Apply a second piece of fiberglass

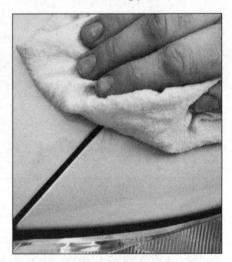

Wait a few days for the paint to dry thoroughly, then rub out the repainted area with a polishing compound to blend the new paint with the surrounding area. When you're happy with your work, wash and polish the area

cloth to the adhesive and immediately cover the cloth with additional adhesive in sufficient quantity to fill the weave.
8   Allow the repair to cure for 20 to 30 minutes at 60-degrees to 80-degrees F.
9   If necessary, trim the excess repair material at the edge.
10   Remove all of the paint film over and around the area(s) to be repaired. The repair material should not overlap the painted surface.
11   With a drill motor and a sanding disc (or a rotary file), cut a "V" along the break line approximately 1/2-inch wide. Remove all dust and loose particles from the repair area.
12   Mix and apply the repair material. Apply a light coat first over the damaged area; then continue applying material until it reaches a level

slightly higher than the surrounding finish.

13   Cure the mixture for 20 to 30 minutes at 60-degrees to 80-degrees F.

14   Roughly establish the contour of the area being repaired with a body file. If low areas or pits remain, mix and apply additional adhesive.

15   Block sand the damaged area with sandpaper to establish the actual contour of the surrounding surface.

16   If desired, the repaired area can be temporarily protected with several light coats of primer. Because of the special paints and techniques required for flexible body panels, it is recommended that the vehicle be taken to a paint shop for completion of the body repair.

Steel body panels

See photo sequence

Repair of dents

17   When repairing dents, the first job is to pull the dent out until the affected area is as close as possible to its original shape. There is no point in trying to restore the original shape completely as the metal in the damaged area will have stretched on impact and cannot be restored to its original contours. It is better to bring the level of the dent up to a point that is about 1/8-inch below the level of the surrounding metal. In cases where the dent is very shallow, it is not worth trying to pull it out at all.

18   If the backside of the dent is accessible, it can be hammered out gently from behind using a soft-face hammer. While doing this, hold a block of wood firmly against the opposite side of the metal to absorb the hammer blows and prevent the metal from being stretched.

19   If the dent is in a section of the body which has double layers, or some other factor makes it inaccessible from behind, a different technique is required. Drill several small holes through the metal inside the damaged area, particularly in the deeper sections. Screw long, self-tapping screws into the holes just enough for them to get a good grip in the metal. Now pulling on the protruding heads of the screws with locking pliers can pull out the dent.

20   The next stage of repair is the removal of paint from the damaged area and from an inch or so of the surrounding metal. This is easily done with a wire brush or sanding disk in a drill motor, although it can be done just as effectively by hand with sandpaper. To complete the preparation for filling, score the surface of the bare metal with a screwdriver or the tang of a file or drill small holes in the affected area. This will provide a good grip for the filler material. To complete the repair, see the Section on filling and painting.

Repair of rust holes or gashes

21   Remove all paint from the affected area and from an inch or so of the surrounding metal using a sanding disk or wire brush mounted in a drill motor. If these are not available, a few sheets of sandpaper will do the job just as effectively.

22   With the paint removed, you will be able to determine the severity of the corrosion and decide whether to replace the whole panel, if possible, or repair the affected area. New body panels are not as expensive as most people think and it is often quicker to install a new panel than to repair large areas of rust.

23   Remove all trim pieces from the affected area except those which will act as a guide to the original shape of the damaged body, such as headlight shells, etc. Using metal snips or a hacksaw blade, remove all loose metal and any other metal that is badly affected by rust. Hammer the edges of the hole in to create a slight depression for the filler material.

24   Wire-brush the affected area to remove the powdery rust from the surface of the metal. If the back of the rusted area is accessible, treat it with rust inhibiting paint.

25   Before filling is done, block the hole in some way. This can be done with sheet metal riveted or screwed into place, or by stuffing the hole with wire mesh.

26   Once the hole is blocked off, the affected area can be filled and painted. See the following subsection on filling and painting.

Filling and painting

27   Many types of body fillers are available, but generally speaking, body repair kits which contain filler paste and a tube of resin hardener are best for this type of repair work. A wide, flexible plastic or nylon applicator will be necessary for imparting a smooth and contoured finish to the surface of the filler material. Mix up a small amount of filler on a clean piece of wood or cardboard (use the hardener sparingly). Follow the manufacturer's instructions on the package, otherwise the filler will set incorrectly.

28   Using the applicator, apply the filler paste to the prepared area. Draw the applicator across the surface of the filler to achieve the desired contour and to level the filler surface. As soon as a contour that approximates the original one is achieved, stop working the paste. If you continue, the paste will begin to stick to the applicator. Continue to add thin layers of paste at 20-minute intervals until the level of the filler is just above the surrounding metal.

29   Once the filler has hardened, the excess can be removed with a body file. From then on, progressively finer grades of sandpaper should be used, starting with a 180-grit paper and finishing with 600-grit wet-or-dry paper. Always wrap the sandpaper around a flat rubber or wooden block, otherwise the surface of the filler will not be completely flat. During the sanding of the filler surface, the wet-or-dry paper should be periodically rinsed in water. This will ensure that a very smooth finish is produced in the final stage.

30   At this point, the repair area should be surrounded by a ring of bare metal, which in turn should be encircled by the finely feathered edge of good paint. Rinse the repair area with clean water until all of the dust produced by the sanding operation is gone.

31   Spray the entire area with a light coat of primer. This will reveal any imperfections in the surface of the filler. Repair the imperfections with fresh filler paste or glaze filler and once more smooth the surface with sandpaper. Repeat this spray-and-repair procedure until you are satisfied that the surface of the filler and the feathered edge of the paint are perfect. Rinse the area with clean water and allow it to dry completely.

32   The repair area is now ready for painting. Spray painting must be carried out in a warm, dry, windless and dust free atmosphere. These conditions can be created if you have access to a large indoor work area, but if you are forced to work in the open, you will have to pick the day very carefully. If you are working indoors, dousing the floor in the work area with water will help settle the dust that would otherwise be in the air. If the repair area is confined to one body panel, mask off the surrounding panels. This will help minimize the effects of a slight mismatch in paint color. Trim pieces such as chrome strips, door handles, etc., will also need to be masked off or removed. Use masking tape and several thickness of newspaper for the masking operations.

33   Before spraying, shake the paint can thoroughly, then spray a test area until the spray painting technique is mastered. Cover the repair area with a thick coat of primer. The thickness should be built up using several thin layers of primer rather than one thick one. Using 600-grit wet-or-dry sandpaper, rub down the surface of the primer until it is very smooth. While doing this, the work area should be thoroughly rinsed with water and the wet-or-dry sandpaper periodically rinsed as well. Allow the primer to dry before spraying additional coats.

34   Spray on the top coat, again building up the thickness by using several thin layers of paint. Begin spraying in the center of the repair area and then, using a circular motion, work out until the whole repair area and about two inches of the surrounding original paint is covered. Remove all masking material 10 to 15 minutes after spraying on the final coat of paint. Allow the new paint at least two weeks to harden, then use a very fine rubbing compound to blend the edges of the new paint into the existing paint. Finally, apply a coat of wax

4   Body repair - major damage

1   Major damage must be repaired by an auto body shop specifically equipped to perform body and frame repairs. These shops have the specialized equipment required to do the job properly.

2   If the damage is extensive, the frame must be checked for proper alignment or the vehicle's handling characteristics may be adversely affected and other components may wear at an accelerated rate.

3   Due to the fact that all of the major body components (hood, fenders, etc.) are separate and replaceable units, any seriously damaged components should be replaced rather than repaired. Sometimes the components can be found in a wrecking yard that specializes in used vehicle components, often at considerable savings over the cost of new parts.

These photos illustrate a method of repairing simple dents. They are intended to supplement *Body repair - minor damage* in this Chapter and should not be used as the sole instructions for body repair on these vehicles.

1 If you can't access the backside of the body panel to hammer out the dent, pull it out with a slide-hammer-type dent puller. Tap with a hammer near the edge of the dent to help 'pop' the metal back to its original shape, about 1/8-inch below the surface of the surrounding metal

2 Using coarse-grit sandpaper, remove the paint down to the bare metal. Clean the repair area with wax/silicone remover.

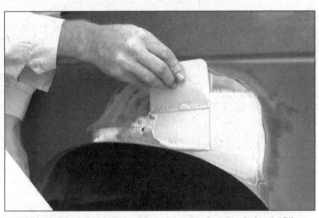

3 Following label instructions, mix up a batch of plastic filler and hardener, then quickly press it into the metal with a plastic applicator. Work the filler until it matches the original contour and is slightly above the surrounding metal

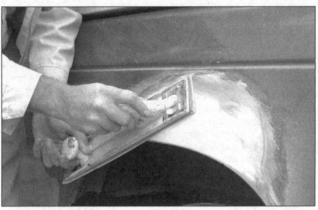

4 Let the filler harden until you can just dent it with your fingernail. File, then sand the filler down until it's smooth and even. Work down to finer grits of sandpaper - always using a board or block - ending up with 360 or 400 grit

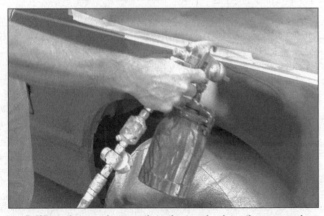

5 When the area is smooth to the touch, clean the area and mask around it. Apply several layers of primer to the area. A professional-type spray gun is being used here, but aerosol spray primer works fine

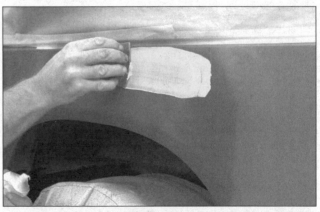

6 Fill imperfections or scratches with glazing compound. Sand with 360 or 400-grit and re-spray. Finish sand the primer with 600 grit, clean thoroughly, then apply the finish coat. Don't attempt to rub out or wax the repair area until the paint has dried completely (at least two weeks)

5   Upholstery, carpets and vinyl trim - maintenance

Upholstery and carpets

1   Every three months remove the floor-mats and clean the interior of the vehicle (more frequently if necessary). Use a stiff whiskbroom to brush the carpeting and loosen dirt and dust, then vacuum the upholstery and carpets thoroughly, especially along seams and crevices.

2   Dirt and stains can be removed from carpeting with basic household or automotive carpet shampoos available in spray cans. Follow the directions and vacuum again, then use a stiff brush to bring back the "nap" of the carpet.

3   Most interiors have cloth or vinyl upholstery, either of which can be cleaned and maintained with a number of material-specific cleaners or shampoos available in auto supply stores. Follow the directions on the product for usage, and always spot-test any upholstery cleaner on an inconspicuous area (bottom edge of a backseat cushion) to ensure that it doesn't cause a color shift in the material.

4   After cleaning, vinyl upholstery should be treated with a protectant. **Note:** *Make sure the protectant container indicates the product can be used on seats - some products may make a seat too slippery.* **Caution:** *Do not use protectant on vinyl-covered steering wheels.*

5   Leather upholstery requires special care. It should be cleaned regularly with saddle-soap or leather cleaner. Never use alcohol, gasoline, nail polish remover or thinner to clean leather upholstery.

6   After cleaning, regularly treat leather upholstery with a leather conditioner, rubbed in with a soft cotton cloth. Never use car wax on leather upholstery.

7   In areas where the interior of the vehicle is subject to bright sunlight, cover leather seating areas of the seats with a sheet if the vehicle is to be left out for any length of time.

Vinyl trim

8   Don't clean vinyl trim with detergents, caustic soap or petroleum-based cleaners. Plain soap and water works just fine, with a soft brush to clean dirt that may be ingrained. Wash the vinyl as frequently as the rest of the vehicle.

9   After cleaning, application of a high-quality rubber and vinyl protectant will help prevent oxidation and cracks. The protectant can also be applied to weather-stripping, vacuum lines and rubber hoses, which often fail as a result of chemical degradation, and to the tires.

6   Fastener and trim removal

Refer to illustration 6.4

1   There is a variety of plastic fasteners used to hold trim panels, splash shields and other parts in place in addition to typical screws, nuts and bolts. Once you are familiar with them, they can usually be removed without too much difficulty.

2   The proper tools and approach can prevent added time and expense to a project by minimizing the number of broken fasteners and/or parts.

3   The following illustration shows various types of fasteners that are typically used on most vehicles and how to remove and install them **(see illustration)**. Replacement fasten-

Fasteners

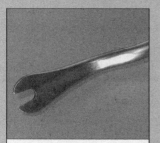

This tool is designed to remove special fasteners. A small pry tool used for removing nails will also work well in place of this tool

A Phillips head screwdriver can be used to release the center portion, but light pressure must be used because the plastic is easily damaged. Once the center is up, the fastener can easily be pried from its hole

Here is a view with the center portion fully released. Install the fastener as shown, then press the center in to set it

This fastener is used for exterior panels and shields. The center portion must be pried up to release the fastener. Install the fastener with the center up, then press the center in to set it

This type of fastener is used commonly for interior panels. Use a small blunt tool to press the small pin at the center in to release it . . .

. . . the pin will stay with the fastener in the released position

Reset the fastener for installation by moving the pin out. Install the fastener, then press the pin flush with the fastener to set it

This fastener is used for exterior and interior panels. It has no moving parts. Simply pry the fastener from its hole like the claw of a hammer removes a nail. Without a tool that can get under the top of the fastener, it can be very difficult to remove

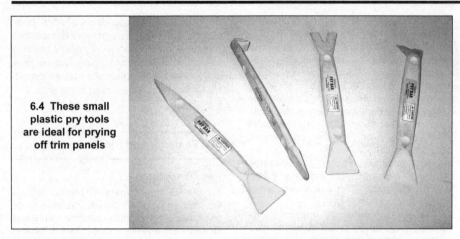

6.4 These small plastic pry tools are ideal for prying off trim panels

9.2 Use a small screwdriver to pry the clip out of its locking groove, then detach the end of the strut from the locating stud

ers are commonly found at most auto parts stores, if necessary.

4   Trim panels are typically made of plastic and their flexibility can help during removal. The key to their removal is to use a tool to pry the panel near its retainers to release it without damaging surrounding areas or breaking-off any retainers. The retainers will usually snap out of their designated slot or hole after force is applied to them. Stiff plastic tools designed for prying on trim panels are available at most auto parts stores (see illustration). Tools that are tapered and wrapped in protective tape, such as a screwdriver or small pry tool, are also very effective when used with care.

7   Hinges and locks - maintenance

1   Once every 3000 miles, or every three months, the hinges and latch assemblies on the doors, hood and trunk should be given a few drops of light oil or lock lubricant. The door latch strikers should also be lubricated with a thin coat of grease to reduce wear and ensure free movement. Lubricate the door and trunk locks with spray-on graphite lubricant.

8   Windshield and fixed glass - replacement

1   Replacement of the windshield and fixed glass requires the use of special fast-setting adhesive/caulk materials and some specialized tools. It is recommended that these operations be left to a dealer or a shop specializing in glass work.

9   Hood support struts - removal and installation

1   Open the hood and support it securely.
2   Using a small screwdriver, detach the retaining clips at both ends of the support strut, then pry or pull sharply to detach it from the vehicle (see illustration).
3   Installation is the reverse of removal.

10   Hood - removal, installation and adjustment

Note: *The hood is heavy and somewhat awkward to remove and install - at least two people should perform this procedure.*

Removal and installation

1   Use blankets or pads to cover the cowl area of the body and fenders. This will protect the body and paint as the hood is lifted off.
2   Disconnect any cables or wires that will interfere with removal.
3   Make marks or scribe a line around the hood hinge to ensure proper alignment during installation (see illustration).
4   Have an assistant support one side of the hood while you support the other. Remove the hood support struts (see Section 9) then simultaneously remove the hinge-to-hood bolts (see illustration).
5   Lift off the hood.
6   Installation is the reverse of removal.

Adjustment

7   Fore-and-aft and side-to-side adjustment of the hood is done by moving the hinge plate slot after loosening the bolts or nuts.
8   Scribe a line around the entire hinge plate so you can determine the amount of movement (see illustration 10.3).
9   Loosen the bolts or nuts and move the

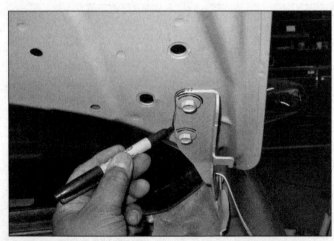

10.3 Make marks or scribe a line around the hood hinge using a marker

10.4 Support the hood with your shoulder while removing the hood bolts

hood into correct alignment. Move it only a little at a time. Tighten the hinge bolts and carefully lower the hood to check the position.

10 If necessary after installation, the entire hood latch assembly can be adjusted up-and-down as well as from side-to-side on the radiator support so the hood closes securely and flush with the fenders. To make the adjustment, scribe a line or mark around the hood latch mounting bolts to provide a reference point, then loosen them and reposition the latch assembly, as necessary. Following adjustment, retighten the mounting bolts (see Section 11 for hood latch mounting details).

11 Finally, adjust the hood bumpers (turning them in or out) on the radiator support so the hood, when closed, is flush with the fenders, and that the grille is supported by the lower bumpers (see illustration).

12 The hood latch assembly, as well as the hinges, should be periodically lubricated with white, lithium-base grease to prevent binding and wear.

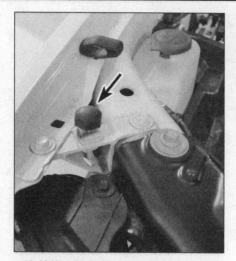

10.11 Hood adjustment bumpers - right side shown, left side identical

11.2 Hood latch mounting bolt locations

11 Hood latch and release cable - removal and installation

Latch

1 Scribe a line around the latch to aid alignment when reinstalling the latch assembly.

2 Remove the latch retaining bolts securing the latch to the radiator support (see illustration) and remove the latch.

3 Disconnect the hood release cable by disengaging the cable from the back of the latch assembly then disconnect the electrical connector, if equipped.

4 Installation is the reverse of the removal procedure.

Note: *Adjust the latch so the hood engages securely when closed and the hood bumpers are slightly compressed.*

Cable

5 Remove the hood latch as described earlier in this Section, then detach the cable from the latch. Remove the air intake duct/air filter housing (see Chapter 4) then remove the radiator cover (see illustration).

6 Remove the left side headlight housing assembly (see Chapter 12).

7 Attach a length of wire to the end of the cable (in the engine compartment). This will be used to pull the new cable back into the engine compartment.

8 Working in the engine compartment, detach the cable from all of its retaining clips. It may be necessary to cut some of the clips to free the cable.

9 Working under the instrument panel, remove the left kick panel (see Section 24), then remove fastener and detach the hood release handle (see illustration). Dislodge the grommet and pull the cable through the

firewall and into the cab.

10 Detach the wire from the old cable, then attach it to the end of the new cable.

Note: *Make sure the new cable is equipped with a grommet.*

11 Pull the new cable through the firewall and into the engine compartment. Seat the grommet in the firewall.

12 The remainder of installation is the reverse of removal.

12 Radiator grille and headlight housing trim - removal and installation

1 Open the hood.

2 Remove the air filter housing (see Chapter 4) and the radiator cover (see illustration 11.5).

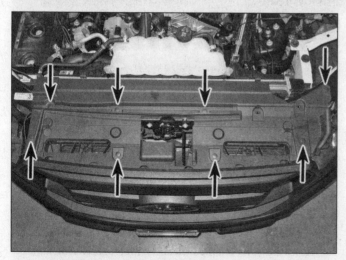

11.5 Remove the locking pins and remove the radiator cover

11.9 Hood release handle mounting bolt

12.3 Disconnect the electrical connectors from the top of the radiator grille

12.5a Remove the lower mounting screws at the front of the fenderwell. . .

12.5b . . .and the upper plastic push-pin. . .

3　Disconnect the electrical connectors from the radiator grille (see illustration) and the washer hose, if equipped.

4　Raise the front of the vehicle and support it securely on jackstands.

5　Working from inside both of the fenderwells, remove the mounting screws at the corners of the fenders. Remove the headlight housing trim panel plastic push-pin, then pry away the headlight housing trim panel to release it from the retaining clips and remove it (see illustrations).

6　Remove the air deflector push-pins (see illustration) and deflectors from each side of the grille.

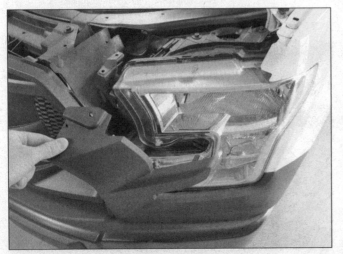

12.5c . . .then carefully pry the headlight housing trim free from the retaining clips to remove it

12.6 Air deflector push-pin locations - left side shown, right side identical

12.7 Radiator grille upper mounting bolt locations

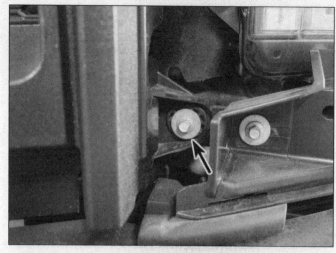

12.8 Grille lower mounting bolt locations - left side shown, right side identical

7   Remove the radiator grille upper mounting bolts (see illustration).
8   Remove the grille lower mounting bolts (see illustration).
9   Unclip the wiring harness at the top of the grille. Pull the grille upwards to disengage the locking pins along the top of the grille, then pull the grille outwards and remove it from the vehicle.
10   Installation is the reverse of removal.

13   Bumpers - removal and installation

Front bumper

1   Loosen the front wheel lug nuts, raise the front of the vehicle and support it securely on jackstands. Apply the parking brake. Remove the front wheels.
2   Remove the splash shield and skid plate from under the vehicle, if equipped.
3   Remove the inner fender splash shields (see illustration 14.2).
4   Remove the radiator grille (see Section 12).
5   Remove the air deflector push-pins along the top-inner edge of the bumper (see illustration).
6   From under the vehicle, remove the front bumper nuts (see illustration).
7   From under the vehicle, remove the bumper outer support rod bolts (if equipped).
8   Using a trim tool, pry the bumper trim panel out of the front bumper (see illustration).
9   Disconnect the electrical connector and remove the cruise control module from the

13.5 Remove the air deflector push-pins - 1 of 3 shown

13.6 Front bumper nut location - left side shown, right side identical

13.8 Carefully pry the bumper trim panel out of the bumper

13.10 Remove the nuts retaining the bumper to the frame brackets

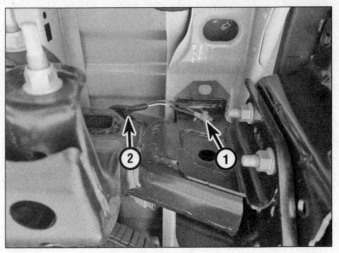

13.14 Remove the ground wire bolt (1) and the harness retainer (2)

13.15 Disconnect the rear bumper wiring harness connector

13.16 Remove the nuts, then lift away the rear bumper (left side shown, right side identical)

bumper, if equipped with adaptive cruise control.

10   With an assistant supporting the bumper, remove the nuts retaining the bumper (see illustration).

11   Lift the bumper away from the frame.

12   Installation is the reverse of removal.

Rear bumper

13   If necessary, raise the rear of the vehicle and support it securely on jackstands.

14   Remove the harness ground wire bolt and harness retainer from the frame, then swing it over the frame rail (see illustration).

15   Disconnect the rear bumper wiring harness electrical connector (see illustration). Make sure the wiring harness is free and won't get caught when lifting away the bumper.

16   With an assistant supporting the bumper, remove the nuts retaining the bumper to the frame, then remove the bumper (see illustration).

Note: *On some models, it may be necessary to lower the rear exhaust pipe down to create enough clearance room for the bumper to be removed.*

17   Installation is the reverse of removal.

14   Front fender - removal and installation

1   Raise the vehicle and support it securely on jackstands and remove the front wheel.

2   Remove the fasteners retaining the fender inner splash shield (see illustration). Also detach the wiring harness clips from the splash shield, noting their locations to ensure correct installation.

3   Remove the headlight housing (see Chapter 12).

14.2 Location of the inner fender splash shield fasteners

14.4a Using a trim tool remove the trim panel. . .

14.4b . . .then remove the two lower mounting bolts at the rear of the wheel opening

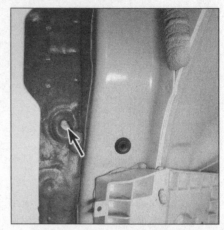

14.5 The inner fender fastener is surrounded by sealant

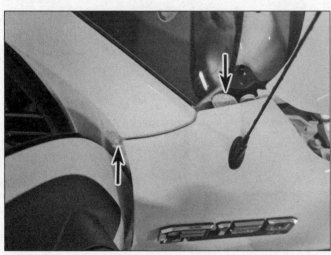

14.6 Location of the fender-to-cowl bolt and the fender-to-door pillar bolt

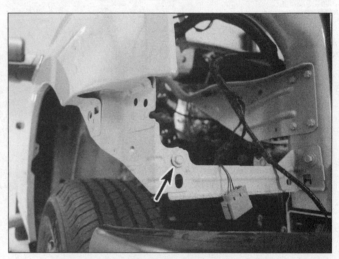

14.7 Remove the fender front mounting bolt

4   Remove the fender-to-rocker panel trim panel and bolts (see illustrations).

5   Remove the fender inner fastener (see illustration).

6   Remove the fender-to-cowl bolt and the fender-to-door pillar bolt (see illustration).

Note: *It will be necessary to lift the corner of the cowl panel up to access the fender-to-cowl bolt.*

7   Remove the fender front fastener (see illustration).

8   Remove the fender upper fasteners (see illustration).

9   Using a razor knife, cut the body sealer between the inner fender and the body (this is the same sealer surrounding the bolt in illustration 14.5).

10   Detach the fender. It's a good idea to have an assistant support the fender while it's being moved away from the vehicle to prevent damage to the surrounding body panels or

14.8 Fender upper fastener locations

15.1 Remove the door panel upper mounting screw

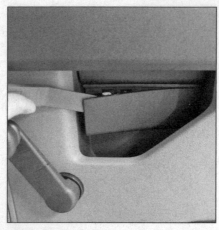

15.2a Pry the fastener cover out using a trim tool. . .

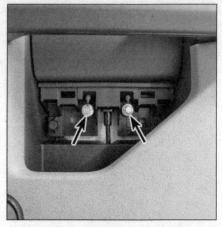

15.2b . . .then remove the retaining screws

15.3a Use a trim tool to separate the front of the handle cover. . .

15.3b . . .and remove the cover

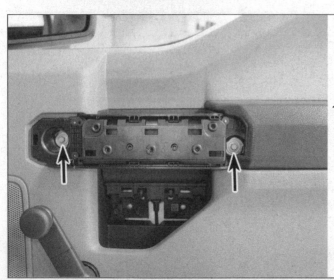

15.4 Remove the door trim panel fasteners that are exposed when the handle is removed

paint. If you're removing the right-side fender, disconnect the antenna electrical connector (see Chapter 12).

11   Installation is the reverse of removal. Some components (such as the antenna or foam baffle) may need to be transferred onto the new fender before installation.

15   Door trim panels - removal and installation

Front door trim panel

1   Remove the door sail panel (see illustration 20.1) then remove the upper mounting screw (see illustration).

2   Pry-out and remove the trim cover, then remove then panel retaining screws under the inside door handle (see illustrations).

3   Pry the inside door handle trim off (see illustrations).

4   Remove the door panel fasteners (see illustration).

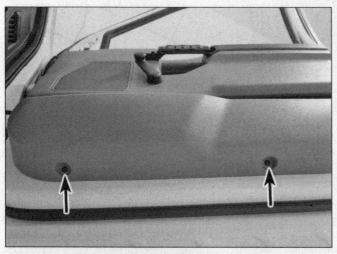

15.5 Lower trim panel fastener locations

15.6a Use a screwdriver to separate to the window handle cover. . .

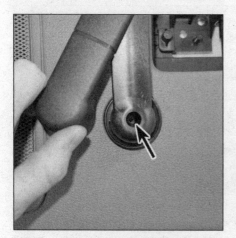

15.6b . . .then remove the window handle mounting screw (Torx head)

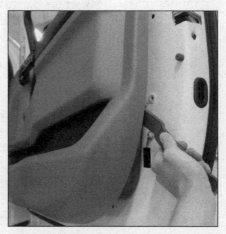

15.7 Disengage the fasteners along the outer edge of the panel

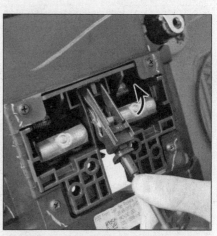

15.8 Disconnect the latch cable from the trim panel by pivoting it outward

5   Remove the door trim panel lower mounting fasteners (see illustration).

6   On manual window equipped models, use a screwdriver to separate to the window handle cover, then remove the window handle fastener (see illustrations).

7   Use a trim tool to disengage the door panel clips (see illustration), then raise the trim panel up and off of the door. Also disconnect any wiring harness connectors.

8   Disconnect the latch cable and remove the door trim panel (see illustration).

9   For access to the inside door components, carefully peel back and remove the plastic watershield (see illustration 19.1).

10   Installation is the reverse of removal.

Rear door trim panel (Super Cab and SuperCrew models)

11   Pry-off the small trim cover and remove the seat belt upper anchor bolt.

12   Pry-off and remove the door pillar trim covers.

13   Remove the inside door handle trim cover, then retaining bolts.

14   If equipped, pry-off the trim cover located underneath the grab handle, then remove the exposed panel bolts.

15   Pry-off the door grab handle trim cover, then remove the exposed bolts.

16   Remove the door trim panel lower retaining bolts.

17   If necessary on models equipped with manual crank windows, remove the rear window crank as described in Step 6.

18   Use a trim tool to disengage the clips on the outer edge of the panel, then pull the panel up and off of the door.

19   Disconnect any wiring harness connectors. Disconnect the door latch cable as described in Step 8, then remove the rear door trim panel from the vehicle.

20   For access to the inside door components, carefully peel back and remove the

plastic watershield.

21   Installation is the reverse of removal.

16   Door(s) - removal, installation and adjustment

Caution: *The door is heavy and somewhat awkward to remove and install - at least two people should perform this procedure.*

Front door

1   Pull or pry-out the grommet, then disconnect the electrical connector in the door opening.

2   Place a floor jack under the door or have an assistant on hand to support it when the hinge bolts are removed.

Note: *If a jack is used, place a few rags between it and the door to protect the door's painted surfaces.*

16.3a Remove the fastener from the door stop strap. . .

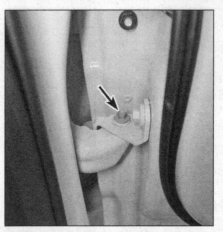

16.3b . . .then remove the door retaining bolt at each hinge (lower hinge shown)

16.5 Adjust the door lock striker by loosening the mounting bolts and gently tapping the striker in the desired direction

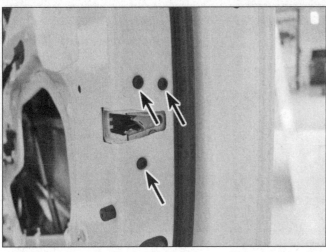

17.6 Remove the latch retaining bolts from the end of the door

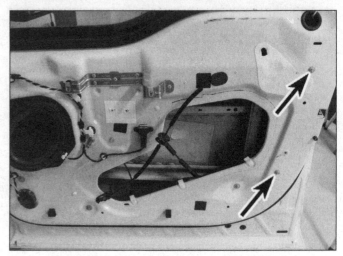

17.7 Remove the front window rear guide bolts

3   Scribe around the hinges with a marking pen to aid in alignment when installing, then remove the fasteners and carefully lift off the door (see illustrations).

4   Installation is the reverse of removal, making sure to align the hinges with the marks made during removal before tightening the bolts.

5   Following installation of the door, check the alignment and adjust the hinges, if necessary. Adjust the door lock striker, centering it in the door latch (see illustration).

Rear door (Super Cab and SuperCrew models)

Warning: *On Super Cab models (without a door stop strap), the rear door must only be removed/installed with the door open at 90-degrees. If the door is replaced at its full open (170-degree) position, damage to the internal door hinge spring may occur.*

6   Pry-off and remove the door hinge trim panel from the vehicle body, if equipped.

7   Working through the door opening, pull or pry the rubber electrical connector grommet out of the body. Pull wiring harness through the grommet hole and disconnect the electrical connector.

8   Remove the bolt securing the door stop strap, if equipped.

9   Mark around the door hinges with a pen or a scribe to facilitate realignment during installation.

10   Have an assistant help support the door while you remove the mounting bolts. On Super Cab models, remove the four mounting bolts along the inside of the door and carefully remove it with the door opened at 90-degrees only (see above Warning). On SuperCrew models, remove the hinge-to-door bolts and lift the door off.

11   Installation is the reverse of the removal.

12   Following installation of the door, check the alignment and adjust the hinges, if necessary. Adjust the door lock striker, centering it in the door latch (see illustration 16.5).

17   Door latch, lock cylinder and handle - removal and installation

Door latch (front)

1   Remove the front door trim panel and watershield as described in Section 15.

2   Remove the door speaker (see Chapter 12).

3   Disconnect the window from the regulator, then push the window fully upwards by hand and use tape to secure it in this position (see Section 18).

4   Remove the window regulator mounting nuts (see Section 19) and slide the regulator forward and out of the way.

5   Remove the outside door handle (see Steps 12 through 16).

6   Remove the bolts securing the latch to the door (see illustration).

7   Remove the window rear guide bolts (see illustration). Push the inside door handle

17.12 Remove the exterior front door handle bolt

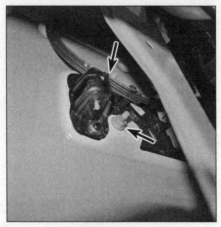

17.14 Remove the inside door handle fasteners

17.15 Slide the handle to the front while pulling outwards on the front of the handle

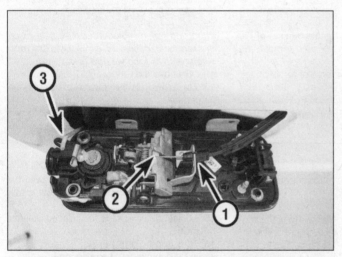

17.16 Remove the cable by releasing the cable body from the bracket (1), then unhook the cable end from the lever's slot (2). Also disconnect the lock cylinder rod (3) from the handle.

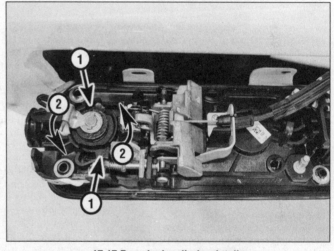

17.17 Door lock cylinder details

1   *Release the door lock cylinder retaining tabs by sliding them outward*
2   *Rotate the door lock cylinder counter-clockwise, then pull it out of the handle*

cable and also the lock rod into the inside of the door.

8   Working through the large access hole, position the latch as necessary to disconnect the electrical connectors, then remove the latch and window guide, together as an assembly, from the door.

9   Remove the necessary latch fasteners and disconnect the cables, then separate the latch from the window guide and related components. Transfer these components onto the new latch.

10   Installation is the reverse of removal.

Door lock cylinder and outside handle (front)

11   To remove the outside handle and door lock cylinder assembly, first remove the front door trim panel and watershield as described in Section 15.

12   Remove the plug on the end of the door,

then remove the handle retaining bolt (see illustration).

13   If equipped, disconnect the electrical connector from the outside handle.

14   Remove the remaining inside handle fasteners (see illustration).

15   Pull the front of the handle outwards and slide the handle to the front (see illustration) and out of the door.

16   Disconnect the necessary cables and rods, then remove the door handle (see illustration).

Note: *On some models, there may be more cables/rods to disconnect than what is shown, but can be disconnected in a similar manner.*

17   For the removal of the door lock cylinder, release the retaining tabs, rotate the door lock cylinder counter-clockwise, then slide the cylinder out of the handle (see illustration).

18   Installation is the reverse of removal.

Door latches (rear) - Super Cab models

Note: *Super Cab models are equipped with two rear door latches.*

Upper latch

19   Remove the rear door trim panel and splash shield (see Section 15).

20   Remove the upper latch bolts (near the top of the door).

21   Disconnect the cable and remove the latch.

22   Installation is the reverse of removal.

Lower latch

23   Remove the rear door trim panel and splash shield (see Section 15).

24   Disconnect the cables and remove the rear door inside handle.

25   Remove the three rear door lower latch bolts at the bottom of the door.

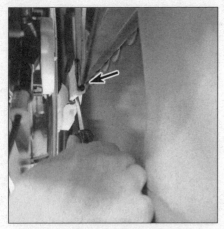

18.4 On both sides of the window, pry and release the glass retaining clips and separate the glass from the regulator

19.1 Carefully pull the watershield out and down, working your way around the opening

19.2 Tape the door window securely in place

26   Push any cables or grommets that are connected to the latch into the inside of the door, the disconnect any electrical connectors and guide the latch out of the door opening.
27   Installation is the reverse of removal.

Door latch (rear) - SuperCrew models

28   Remove the rear door trim panel and splash shield (see Section 15).
29   Remove the rear outside door handle (see Steps 36 through 39).
30   Separate the window glass from the window regulator and tape the window in the "fully up" position (see Section 19).
31   Remove the rear door window regulator mounting nuts, then position the regulator temporarily out of the way.
32   Remove the three latch bolts from the side of the door.
33   Remove the lower window guide bolt (on the side opposite of the speaker).
34   Push any cables or grommets that are connected to the latch into the inside of the door, the disconnect any electrical connectors and guide the latch assembly out of the door opening.
35   Transfer the necessary components from the old latch assembly onto the new latch. Installation is the reverse of removal.

Outside door handle (rear) - SuperCrew models

36   Remove the rear door trim panel and splash shield (see Section 15).
37   Remove the outside door handle access plug and mounting bolt from the side of the door.
38   Remove the two mounting nut access covers on the inside of the door (at the same height as the bolt previously removed), then remove the nuts.
39   Pull out on the handle and slide it rear-

ward, then position the handle outside of the door. Disconnect the cable, then remove the rear outside handle.
40   Installation is the reverse of removal.

18   Door window glass - removal and installation

Front

1   Remove the door trim panel and watershield (see Section 15).
2   Lower the window.
3   Pry the inner weather seal out of the window opening, then raise the window halfway.
4   Release the glass retaining clips to separate the window glass from the window regulator (see illustration).
5   Remove the window glass by lifting it upward by hand and tilting it forward, then guide the glass out of the door.
6   To install, lower the glass into the door, slide it into position while aligning the tabs into the regulator, making sure it clips securely in place.
7   On models with power windows, carry out the power window initialization procedure listed at the end of this Section.
8   The remainder of installation is the reverse of removal.

Rear (Super Cab and SuperCrew models)

9   Follow Steps 1 through 3, but on the rear door.
10   Raise the window for access to the regulator clips, then release the retaining clips with a screwdriver.
Note: *On Super Cab models, the rearmost window glass guide will have to be removed with the window raised in the upward position. Also, if the regulator/motor is already dam-*

aged and being replaced, it may help to cut the regulator cables to allow for extra room when removing the window glass.
11   Remove the window.
12   Installation is the reverse of the removal procedure.
13   On models with power windows, carry out the power window initialization procedure listed at the end of this Section.

Power window initialization

14   Start the engine, then lift and hold the power window switch until the window is fully closed.
15   Once the window is fully closed, release the switch.
16   Lift and hold the power window switch again for a minimum of one second.
17   Press and hold the power window switch down until the window is completely open, then release the switch.
18   Lift and hold the power window switch until the window is fully closed.
19   Test the automatic window operation - one touch down to open and one touch up to close. If the operation is not correct, repeat Steps 14 through 18.

19   Door window glass regulator - removal and installation

Note: *The rear door window regulator is removed in a similar manner as the front regulator; the only main difference being that the rear door speaker may need to be removed to allow for better access (depending on the model).*
1   Remove the door trim panel (see Section 15) and watershield (see illustration).
2   Unclip and separate the window glass from the regulator (see Section 18). Push the glass all the way up and tape it securely to the door frame (see illustration).

3   Remove the window regulator-to-door and track mounting fasteners (see illustrations), then carefully guide the regulator assembly out of the access hole.
4   On power window equipped models, unplug the electrical connector.
5   Transfer any working regulator components (such as the motor) to the new assembly if necessary.
6   Installation is the reverse of removal.

20   Mirrors - removal and installation

Outside Mirror
1   Using a trim tool, remove the door trim sail panel (see illustration).
2   On power mirrors, unplug the electrical connector(s).
3   Remove the nuts/bolts and detach the mirror from the door (see illustration).
4   To remove the mirror glass, first position the mirror glass fully inwards and upwards. Gently pry the glass out with a standard screwdriver from the correct location, which is from the lower outside corner. Be careful not to damage the mirror glass.
5   To remove the mirror glass, first position the mirror glass fully inwards and upwards. Gently pry the glass out and separate it from the mirror motor with a flat bladed screwdriver from the correct location, which is from the lower outside corner. Be careful not to damage the mirror glass.
Note: *On vehicles with long-arm (double) mirrors, the lower mirror can be removed by hand, without the use of a screwdriver to pry it out.*
6   The mirror motor (if equipped) is located underneath the glass and can be replaced at this time if necessary, by removing the three mounting screws and disconnecting the electrical connectors.
7   Installation is the reverse of removal.

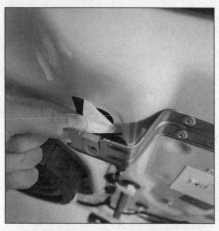
19.3a Peel the tape back to locate the window regulator-to-upper front track mounting fastener

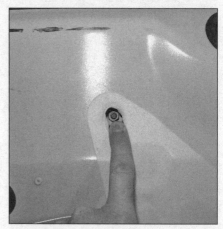
19.3b Peel or puncture the foam tape to locate window regulator-to-upper rear track mounting fastener

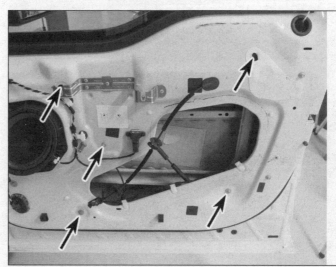
19.3c Location of the window regulator-to-door fasteners

20.1 Carefully pry out the sail panel

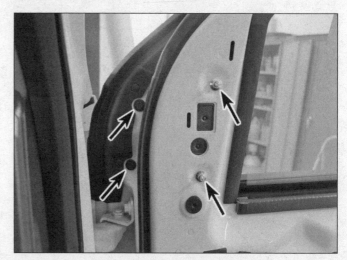
20.3 Remove the mirror retaining fasteners

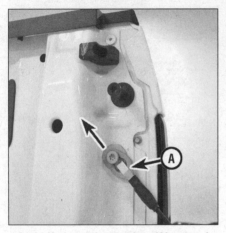

21.1 Lift the spring retainer (A) out and slide the cable end bracket off of the pin

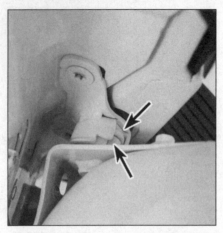

21.2 Align the flat on the right-side hinge pin with the slot in the hinge pocket and lift the tailgate off the vehicle

Interior (Rearview) Mirror

8   These model vehicles may be equipped with several different types of rearview mirrors - many of which require special factory service tools for replacement. To avoid potential damage to the mirror mounts or related components, this job is best left to be completed by a dealer service department.

21   Tailgate - removal and installation

1   Open the tailgate and detach the support cables (see illustration).
2   Lower the tailgate until the flat on the right side hinge-pin aligns with the slot in the hinge pocket. Lift the right-hand side of the tailgate out of the pocket (see illustration). With the help of an assistant to support the weight, withdraw the left hinge pin from the body (being pulled straight out on this side) and remove the tailgate from the vehicle.
3   Installation is the reverse of removal.

22   Tailgate latch, release handle, actuator and lock cylinder - removal and installation

1   Lower the tailgate and remove the tailgate access cover (see illustration).

Latch

Note: *The top (outermost) latch fastener will need to be replaced upon installation.*
2   Remove the latch mounting fasteners (see illustration). It may be necessary to use an impact-driver to loosen them.
3   Disconnect the control rod from the latch control assembly (for the side being replaced) (see illustration), then remove the latch with the rod from the tailgate.

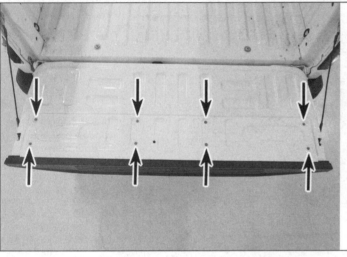

22.1 Remove the cover screws to access the inside of the tailgate

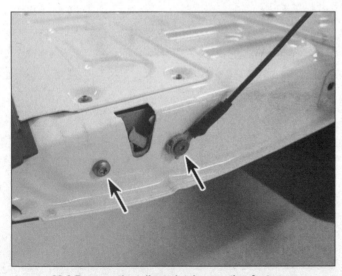

22.2 Remove the tailgate latch mounting fasteners

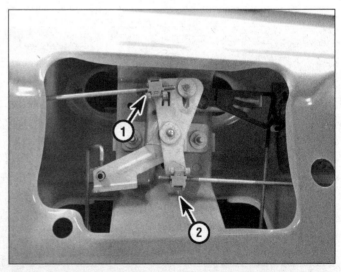

22.3 Unclip the necessary latch rod out of the retaining clip on the latch control assembly

| 1   Right side latch rod | 2   Left side latch rod |

4   If replacing the latch, transfer the control rod onto the new latch, securing it with the retaining clip.
5   Installation is the reverse of removal. Install a new top (outer) latch bolt.

Release handle
6   Remove the tailgate access cover (see illustration 22.1).
7   Remove the release handle mounting nuts (see illustration).
8   Remove the handle from the tailgate body, positioning it outward for better access to the inner handle components.
9   On mechanical handle models, disconnect the control rods (see illustration) and rear view camera electrical connector, if equipped.
10   On models without mechanical handles, disconnect the various electrical connectors to the handle.
11   Remove the handle from the tailgate.
12   Transfer the necessary inner handle components to the new handle.
13   Installation is the reverse of removal.

Latch control actuator assembly
14   Remove the tailgate access cover screws and cover (see illustration 22.1).
15   Disconnect the control rods and remove the assembly retaining nuts (see illustration).
16   Disconnect the electrical connector(s) to the actuator, if equipped, then remove the assembly from the tailgate.
17   Installation is the reverse of removal.

Automatic actuator (if equipped)
18   Remove the latch control actuator assembly (see Steps 14 through 16).
19   Remove the auto actuator-to-control assembly fasteners and separate the actuator from the control assembly.
20   Installation is the reverse of removal.

Lock cylinder
21   Remove the release handle (see Steps 6 through 11).
22   Remove the lock cylinder retaining nut then slide out the lock from the tailgate handle.
23   Installation is the reverse of removal.

23 Dashboard trim panels - removal and installation

Warning: *The models covered in this manual are equipped with a Supplemental Restraint System (SRS), more commonly known as air bags. Always disable the airbag system before working in the vicinity of any airbag system component to avoid the possibility of accidental deployment of the airbags, which could cause personal injury (see Chapter 12).*
1   Disconnect the cable from the negative

22.7 Release handle nut location - 1 of 2 shown

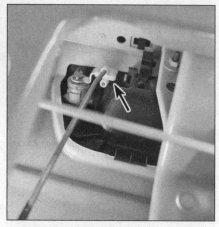

22.9 Disconnect the handle lock cylinder rod (shown) and release rod (not shown, but similar)

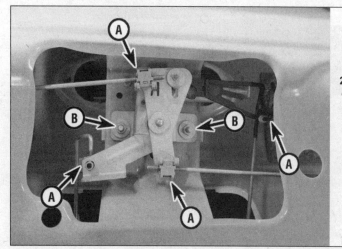

22.15 Disengage the control actuator-to-latch and lock rods (A) and remove the control actuator retaining nuts (B)

battery terminal (see Chapter 5, Section 4).
2   If equipped, remove the center console where necessary (see Section 28).

Knee bolster
3   Use a dull, flat-bladed tool around the top of the knee bolster to release the clips, then lower the panel, disconnect the electrical connectors and remove the panel fasteners (see illustrations).
4   Installation is the reverse of removal.

23.3a Carefully release the clips and pull the panel off

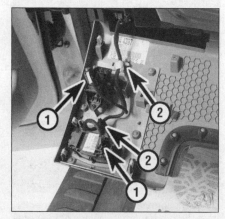

23.3b Disconnect the electrical connectors (1) and release the harness clips (2) from the panel

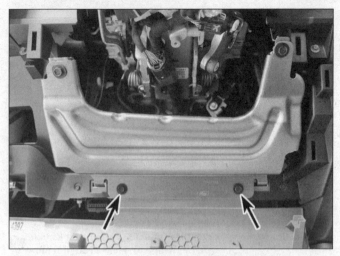

23.3c Remove the bolts and knee bolster panel

23.6 Instrument cluster finish panel mounting screw locations

23.7 Using a trim tool, pry the trim panel out from the instrument panel

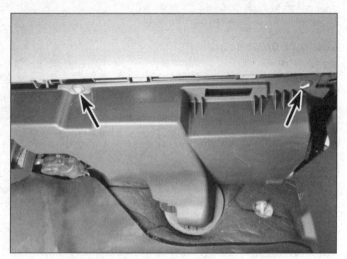

23.9 Right side lower panel fastener locations

23.10 Disconnect the electrical connector from the module on the inside of the panel

23.12a Use a pair of pliers and compress the locking tabs. . .

Instrument cluster finish panel

5   Remove the knee bolster (see Step 5).
6   Remove the panel mounting screws (see illustration).
7   Carefully pry the finish panel out and remove it (see illustration).
8   Installation is the reverse of removal.

Right side (glovebox) lower panel

9   Remove the plastic push pins the (see illustration), then remove the right side lower panel.
10   Disconnect the electrical connector from the module, if equipped (see illustration).
11   Installation is the reverse of removal.

Glove box

12   Remove the glove box hinge pins (see illustrations).

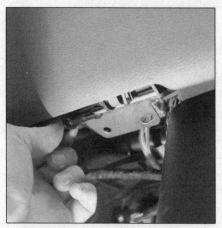

23.12b . . .then pull the hinge pins out - right side shown, left side identical

23.13 Push the end of the damper down and forward to disconnect it from the glove box

23.14 Push both sides in until the stops are released (right side shown, left side similar)

23.15 Lower the glove box until the hinges are free of the pivots, then pull off the glovebox

23.18 Pry the storage compartment trim panel off

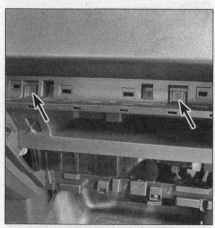

23.19a Remove the storage compartment fasteners. . .

13   Open the glove box door and remove the glove compartment dampener by pushing the end of the damper down and forward (see illustration).

14   Push the sides of the glove box inwards until the stops (see illustration) are released.

15   Lower the glove box and remove it from the hinges (see illustration).

16   Installation is the reverse of removal.

Glove box storage compartment

17   Open the glove box.

18   Use a trim stick (if necessary) to pry the storage compartment rubber trim panel off (see illustration).

19   Remove the two screws, pull the glove box storage compartment out (releasing it from the clips), then disconnect the electrical connector (see illustrations).

20   Installation is the reverse of removal.

23.19b . . .pull the storage compartment out of the instrument panel, releasing it from the retaining clips. . .

23.19c . . .then disconnect the electrical connector.

23.21 Lift the mat out from the upper storage compartment

23.22 Location of the upper storage compartment screws

23.23 Pry the storage compartment out of the instrument panel

24.2a Remove the screw covers and A-pillar mounting screws. . .

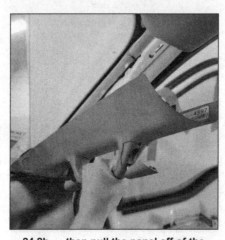

24.2b . . .then pull the panel off of the A-pillar and disconnect the tweeter electrical connector (if equipped)

24.6 Use a flat-bladed tool or trim stick to remove the instrument panel end caps

Upper dashboard storage compartment

21   Remove the mat from the upper storage compartment (see illustration).
22   Remove the two screws from the upper storage compartment (see illustration).
23   Use a plastic trim tool to pry the storage compartment out of the instrument panel (see illustration).
24   Installation is the reverse of removal.

24   Instrument panel - removal and installation

Warning: *The models covered by this manual are equipped with a Supplemental Restraint System (SRS), more commonly known as airbags. Always disable the airbag system before working in the vicinity of any airbag system component to avoid the possibility of accidental deployment of the airbags, which could cause personal injury (see Chapter 12).*
Caution: *This is a difficult procedure for the home mechanic. There are many hidden fasteners, difficult angles to work in and many electrical connectors to label and disconnect/*

connect. We recommend that this procedure be done only by an experienced do-it-yourselfer.
Note: *During removal of the instrument panel, make careful notes of how each piece comes off, where it fits in relation to other pieces and what holds it in place. If you note how each part is installed before removing it, getting the instrument panel back together again will be much easier. Label the electrical connectors and keep track of where each fastener belongs for installation.*
1   Disconnect the cable from the negative battery terminal (see Chapter 5, Section 4). Turn the front wheels to the straight-ahead position and lock the steering column.
2   Remove the A-pillar trim panels (see illustrations) and disconnect the electrical connector to the tweeters (see Chapter 12), if equipped.
3   If equipped, remove the center console (see Section 28).
4   Remove the steering wheel (see Chapter 10).
5   Remove the knee bolster (see Section 23).
6   Remove the instrument panel end caps (see illustration).

7   Remove the scuff plate from each door opening (see illustration).
8   Remove the side kick panels at each end (see illustrations) and pull the weather stripping off the front of each door opening.
9   Remove the front driver and passenger seats, then the front center seat (see Section 26).
10   Remove the floor console (see Section 28), if equipped.
11   On models without floor consoles, remove the lower trim panel (see illustrations).
12   On models equipped with a steering column mounted shift lever, remove the steering column covers (see Section 25).
13   Remove the steering column support (see illustration).
14   Remove the select lever cable mounting bolt then pop the end of the cable off of the selector ballstud (see illustration). Separate the shift cable from the bracket by lifting the rear plastic tabs with a screwdriver and sliding it off the metal bracket.
15   Remove the floor covering fasteners, where necessary, and pull the covering back (see illustrations).

24.7 Carefully pry up and remove the scuff plates

24.8a Pry up the rear of the kick panel. . .

24.8b . . . then pull the kick panel off

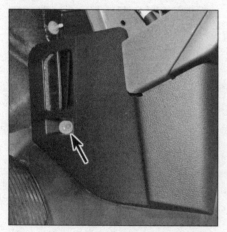

24.11a Remove the lower trim panel fastener. . .

24.11b . . .then pull out the trim panel to release it from the clips

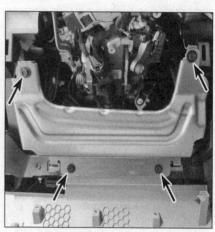

24.13 Steering column support plate bolt locations

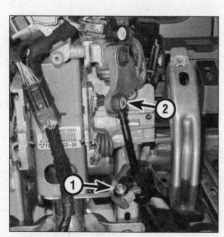

24.14 Remove the select lever cable mounting bolt (1) then gently pop the cable end off the selector ballstud (2) with a screwdriver

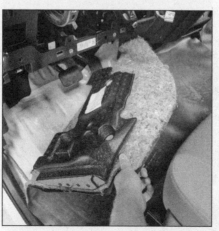

24.15a Pull the floor covering back from the left. . .

24.15b . . .and right side

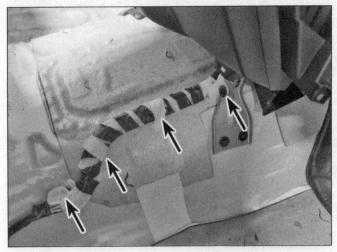

24.17 Release the plastic harness retainers along the floorboard

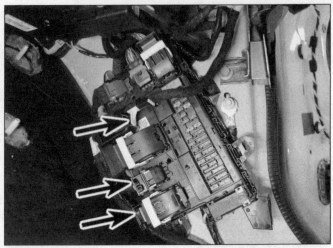

24.19a Disconnect these electrical connectors from the right side kick panel area. . .

24.19b . . .and from behind the glove box. . .

24.19c . . .and at the left side of the glove box opening, remove the electrical connectors and instrument panel mounting bolt (1). . .

24.19d . . .then disconnect the electrical connectors from the left side kick panel

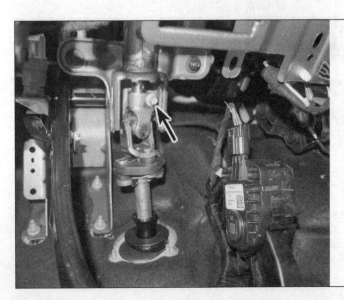

24.20 Remove the upper steering column shaft pinch bolt

16   If equipped, remove the plastic retainers for the floor ducts and remove the ducts.

17   Remove the wiring harness retainers along the floorboard (see illustration). Also disconnect the electrical connectors, where equipped.

18   Remove the plastic push pin retainers on the insulator panel under the glovebox and remove the insulator (see Section 23).

19   Disconnect the instrument panel electrical connectors (see illustrations). Note: A number of electrical connectors must be disconnected in order to remove the instrument panel. Most are designed so that they will only fit on the matching connector (male or female), but if there is any doubt, mark the connectors with masking tape and a marking pen before disconnecting them.

20   Remove the pinch bolt and disconnect the upper steering column shaft (see illustration). Check the steering column removal Warnings in Chapter 10, Section 12.

24.21a Remove the access panel from each side of the dashboard. . .

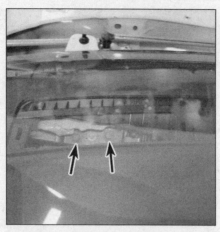

24.21b . . .and remove the instrument panel top mounting bolts (viewed from the outside looking through the windshield)

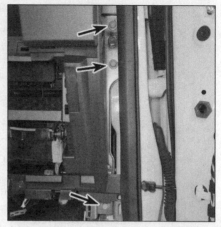

24.22a Remove the fasteners from the right side. . .

24.22b . . . and the left side. . .

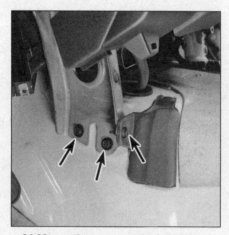

24.22c . . . then remove the instrument panel left side center bracket fasteners. . .

24.22d . . . and right side center bracket fasteners.

21   Remove the access panels from the top of the dashboard and remove the mounting bolts (see illustrations).
22   Remove the fasteners securing the instrument panel (see illustrations).
23   Pull the instrument panel towards the rear of the vehicle and disconnect any remaining electrical connectors interfering with removal, if necessary. Make absolutely sure that all the necessary electrical connectors are disconnected.
24   Once all the electrical connectors have been confirmed to be disconnected, rotate the instrument panel assembly to be face-down, then carry it out through the driver's door opening.
Note: *This is a two-person job.*
25   Installation is the reverse of removal.

25   Steering column covers - removal and installation

Warning: *The models covered by this manual are equipped with a Supplemental Restraint System (SRS), more commonly known as airbags. Always disable the airbag system before working in the vicinity of any airbag system component to avoid the possibility of accidental deployment of the airbags, which could cause personal injury (see Chapter 12).*
1   Extend the steering wheel fully and lock it in its lowest position.
2   Release the front cover clips with a screwdriver (see illustration). The left and right side cover clips can be accessed without removing the steering wheel by rotating the steering wheel as necessary.

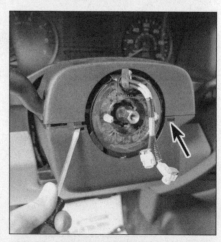

25.2 Disengage the steering column cover clips at each side - steering wheel has been removed for clarity

25.3 Separate and remove the upper cover - arrows indicate the remaining clips fastening to the lower cover

25.4a Remove the lower steering column cover fasteners. . .

25.4b . . . then guide the cover off of the column height adjustment lever

26.2a To disconnect the electrical connector, depress the safety tab. . .

26.2b . . . then swing open the lever to release the connector

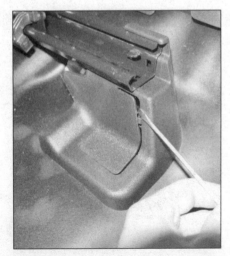

26.3a Use a small screwdriver to remove the bolt cover. . .

3   Separate the cover halves, then disengage the clips at the rear of the upper cover and remove the upper cover (see illustration).
4   Remove the fasteners from the lower steering column cover and guide the cover off of the column adjustment lever (see illustrations).
5   Installation is the reverse of removal.

---

26   Seats - removal and installation

Warning: *Some models are equipped with seat belt pre-tensioners, which are pyrotechnic (explosive) devices that tighten the seat belts during an impact of sufficient force. Always disable the airbag system before working in the vicinity of any restraint system component to avoid the possibility of accidental deployment of the airbag(s) and seat belt pre-tensioners, which could cause personal injury (see Chapter 12).*

Front seat

1   Disconnect the cable from the negative battery terminal (see Chapter 5).
2   Working underneath the front section of the seat, locate and disconnect the electrical connector(s) (see illustrations).
Note: *Position the seat all the way forward and all the way to the rear (as necessary) to access the front and rear seat retaining bolts. On models with automatic seat position adjustment, the electrical connector(s) can be disconnected after the seat retaining bolts have been removed.*
3   Detach any bolt trim covers and remove the retaining bolts (see illustrations).
4   Lift the seat out of the vehicle. This step may be easier with the help of an assistant.
5   Installation is the reverse of removal.

Center front seat

6   Remove the passenger's side seat (see Steps 1 through 4).

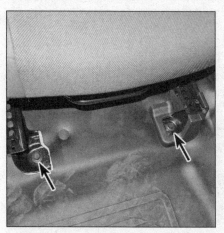

26.3b . . . then remove the bolts at the front. . .

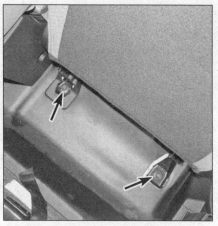

26.3c... and the rear of the seat

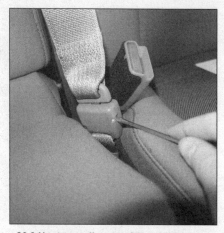

26.8 Use a small screwdriver to depress the locking tab and disconnect the seat belt from the anchor

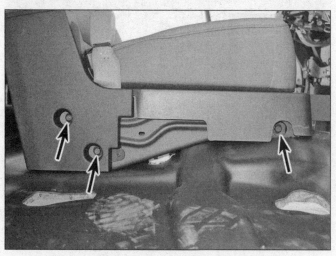

26.10 Right side mounting bolt locations

26.11a Remove the bolt from the rear side of the seat. . .

7   Position the driver's seat all the way forward and all the way to the rear to allow access to the center seat left side retaining bolts.

8   Depress the locking tab (see illustration) and disconnect the center seat belt from the seat belt anchor, if equipped.

9   Disconnect the electrical connector from the right side of the seat, if equipped.

10   Remove the mounting bolts from the right side of the seat (see illustration).

11   Remove the mounting bolts from the left side of the seat (see illustrations).

12   Lift the seat out of the vehicle.

13   Installation is the reverse of removal.

Rear seats
Super Cab models
Right side seat

14   Pull the cushion release handle and slightly raise the seat cushion.

15   Remove the front bolts, then lower the seat cushion.

16   Pull the seat back release strap and fold the seat back downward.

17   Remove the outer safety belt lower anchor-to-seat bolt.

18   Remove the seat rear mounting nuts and remove the right side seat.

19   Installation is the reverse of removal.

Left side seat

20   Remove the right side seat first (see Steps 14 through 18).

21   Pull the cushion release handle and slightly raise the seat cushion.

22   Remove the front bolts, then lower the seat cushion.

23   Remove the safety belt lower anchor-to-seat bolt.

24   Pull the seat back latch handle on the backside of the seat and fold the seat back downward.

25   On models equipped with a subwoofer, remove the subwoofer (see Chapter 12).

26.11b . . . then the front side of the seat

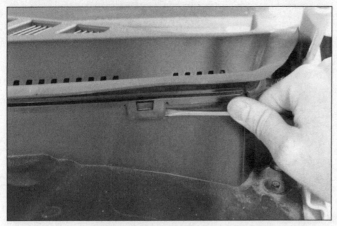

27.2a Using a small screwdriver, release the clips along the front of the cowl

27.2b Left side cowl clip locations

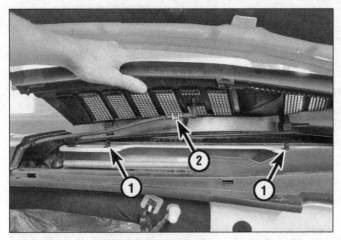

27.3 Lift up the cover and disengage the rear retaining clips (1), then disconnect the washer hose (2)

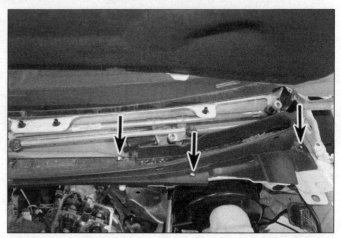

27.4 Remove the pushpin fasteners and outer screw, then lift the lower cover from the cowl

26 Disconnect the rear seat heater electrical connector, if equipped.

27 Remove the seat rear mounting nuts and with the help of an assistant, remove the left side rear seat.

28 Installation is the reverse of removal.

SuperCrew models

Right side seat

29 Pull the cushion release handle and slightly raise the seat cushion.

30 Remove the front bolts, then lower the seat cushion.

31 Pull the seat back release strap and fold the seat back down.

32 Release the hook-and-loop strap holding the spare tire jack to the seat and remove the jack.

33 On models equipped with inflatable (SRS) safety belts, first disable the SRS system (see Chapter 12), then remove the safety belt lower anchor bolt cover and remove the bolt.

34 On models without inflatable safety (SRS) belts, remove the safety belt lower

anchor-to-seat bolt (there should be no cover over the bolt).

35 Disconnect the rear seat heater electrical connector and also the inflatable belt connector, if equipped.

36 Remove the seat rear mounting nuts and remove the right side seat.

37 Installation is the reverse of removal.

Left side seat

38 Remove the right side seat first (see Steps 29 through 36).

39 Pull the cushion release handle and slightly raise the seat cushion.

40 Remove the front bolts, then lower the seat cushion.

41 On models equipped with inflatable (SRS) safety belts, first disable the SRS system (see Chapter 12), then remove the safety belt lower anchor bolt cover and remove the bolt.

42 On models without inflatable safety (SRS) belts, remove the safety belt lower anchor-to-seat bolt (there should be no cover over the bolt).

43 Raise the seat cushion slightly then

release the seat back latch on the backside of the seat and fold the seat back down.

44 On models equipped with a subwoofer, remove the subwoofer (see Chapter 12).

45 Disconnect the rear seat heater electrical connector, if equipped.

46 Remove the seat rear mounting nuts and with the help of an assistant, remove the left side rear seat.

47 Installation is the reverse of removal.

27 Cowl covers - removal and installation

1 Remove the windshield wiper arms (see Chapter 12, Section 12).

2 Starting with the left side, release the upper cowl clips (see illustrations).

3 Lift the upper cover up to disengage the retaining clips at the rear, then disconnect the windshield washer hose (see illustration).

4 Remove the pushpins and outer screw on the left side cowl cover (see illustration), then remove the lower cowl cover.

27.5 Release the clips at the front edge of the right side cowl cover

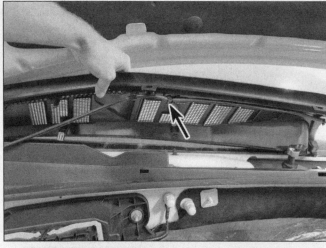

27.6 Disconnect the washer hose from the right side upper cowl cover

5   Release the clips securing the right side cowl upper cover (see illustration).
6   Lift the upper cover up, making sure to disengage the clips at the rear, and disconnect the windshield washer hose (see illustration).
7   Remove the pushpins and outer screw on the right side lower cowl cover (see illustration), then remove the cover.
8   Installation is the reverse of removal.

28   Center console - removal and installation

Note: *Not all vehicles are equipped with a center console*
1   Using a trim tool, pry out and remove the center console side trim panels.
Note: *The left side panel has a retaining screw at the front.*
2   At the front of the console, remove the small trim panels from the left and right corners using a trim tool.
3   If equipped, remove the console-mounted gear selector lever (see Chapter 7A).
4   Using a trim tool and working from the rear to the front, pry the top shifter panel/floor console top panel up, disengaging the clips around the perimeter of the panel.

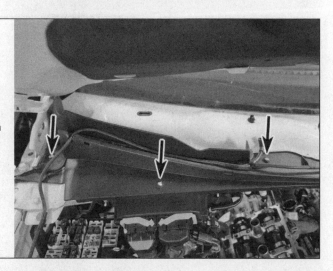

27.7 Remove the pushpin fasteners and outer screw, then lift the lower cover from the cowl

Note: *There are two retaining clips at the front, and are disengaged by pulling the top panel rearward after the other clips have been released.*
5   Remove the cup holder panel and fasteners.
Note: *The front seats will have to be positioned forward and rearward, as necessary, to allow access to all of the center console mounting bolts.*
6   Remove the center console mounting bolts along the bottom sides of the console. Also, disconnect the bottom electrical connector. Once the mounting bolts have been removed, slide the console assembly slightly rearward to access the front electrical connector(s).
7   Disconnect the electrical connectors at the front of the console, then guide the center console assembly out of the vehicle.
8   Installation is the reverse of removal.

Notes

Chapter 12
Chassis electrical system

Contents

	Section
Airbag system - general information	27
Antenna and cable - removal and installation	14
Bulb - replacement	21
Circuit breakers - general information	4
Cruise control system - general information	23
Daytime Running Lights (DRL) - general information	26
Electrical troubleshooting - general information	2
Front Controls Interface Module (FCIM)/Front Controls Interface Display Module (FCDIM), radio and speakers - removal and installation	13
Fuses and fusible links - general information	3
General information	1
Headlight bulb - replacement	16
Headlight housing - removal and installation	18
Headlight lens refurbishing	19
Headlights - adjustment	17

	Section
Horn - replacement	20
Ignition switch and key lock cylinder - replacement	9
Instrument cluster - removal and installation	11
Instrument panel switches - replacement	10
Key fob - programming, battery replacement, key fob strength testing/driver's door keypad - removal and installation	6
Mirrors - description	22
Power door lock and keyless entry system - description and check	25
Power window system - description and check	24
Rear window defogger - check and repair	15
Relays - general information and testing	5
Steering column switches - replacement	8
Turn signal and hazard flasher - check and replacement	7
Wiper motor - check and replacement	12
Wiring diagrams - general information	28

Specifications

Torque specifications
Ft-lbs (unless otherwise indicated)

Note: *One foot-pound (ft-lb) of torque is equivalent to 12 inch-pounds (in-lbs) of torque. Torque values below approximately 15 foot-pounds are expressed in inch-pounds, because most foot-pound torque wrenches are not accurate at these smaller values.*

Passenger airbag mounting nuts* .... 80 in-lbs

* Manufacturer recommends replacing the original fasteners with new fasteners.

1   General information

1   The electrical system is a 12-volt, negative ground type. Power for the lights and all electrical accessories is supplied by a lead/acid-type battery which is charged by the alternator.

2   This Chapter covers repair and service procedures for the various electrical components not associated with the engine. Information on the battery, alternator, distributor and starter motor can be found in Chapter 5.

3   It should be noted that when portions of the electrical system are serviced, the negative battery cable should be disconnected from the battery to prevent electrical shorts and/or fires.

2   Electrical troubleshooting - general information

1   A typical electrical circuit consists of an electrical component, any switches, relays, motors, fuses, fusible links or circuit breakers related to that component and the wiring and connectors that link the component to both the battery and the chassis. To help you pinpoint an electrical circuit problem, wiring diagrams are included at the end of this Chapter.

2   Before tackling any troublesome electrical circuit, first study the appropriate wiring diagrams to get a complete understanding of what makes up that individual circuit. Trouble spots, for instance, can often be narrowed down by noting if other components related to the circuit are operating properly.

If several components or circuits fail at one time, chances are the problem is in a fuse or ground connection, because several circuits are often routed through the same fuse and ground connections.

3   Electrical problems usually stem from simple causes, such as loose or corroded connections, a blown fuse, a melted fusible link or a failed relay. Visually inspect the condition of all fuses, wires and connections in a problem circuit before troubleshooting the circuit.

4   If test equipment and instruments are going to be utilized, use the diagrams to plan ahead of time where you will make the necessary connections in order to accurately pinpoint the trouble spot.

5   The basic tools needed for electrical troubleshooting include a circuit tester or

voltmeter (a 12-volt bulb with a set of test leads can also be used), a continuity tester, which includes a bulb, battery and set of test leads, and a jumper wire, preferably with a circuit breaker incorporated, which can be used to bypass electrical components (see illustrations). Before attempting to locate a problem with test instruments, use the wiring diagram(s) to decide where to make the connections.

Voltage checks

6   Voltage checks should be performed if a circuit is not functioning properly. Connect one lead of a circuit tester to either the negative battery terminal or a known good ground. Connect the other lead to a connector in the circuit being tested, preferably nearest to the battery or fuse (see illustration). If the bulb of the tester lights, voltage is present, which means that the part of the circuit between the connector and the battery is problem free. Continue checking the rest of the circuit in the same fashion. When you reach a point at which no voltage is present, the problem lies between that point and the last test point with voltage. Most of the time the problem can be traced to a loose connection.
Note: *Keep in mind that some circuits receive voltage only when the ignition key is in the Accessory or Run position.*

Finding a short

7   One method of finding shorts in a live circuit is to remove the fuse and connect a test light in place of the fuse terminals (fabricate two jumper wires with small spade terminals, plug the jumper wires into the fuse box and connect the test light). There should be voltage present in the circuit. Move the suspected wiring harness from side-to-side while watching the test light. If the bulb goes off, there is a short to ground somewhere in that area, prob-

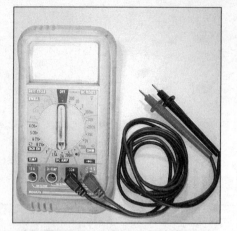

2.5a The most useful tool for electrical troubleshooting is a digital multimeter that can check volts, amps, and test continuity

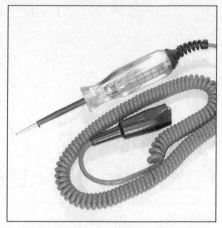

2.5b A simple test light is a very handy tool for testing voltage

ably where the insulation has rubbed through.
Note: *Before starting to look for a short, walk around the vehicle and look for any obvious body damage that may have something to do with any wiring. Also, check below the vehicle for any unusual wiring that is not attached. If there isn't anything obvious, try to find out which half of the car the short is located. Once you have determined which half of the car it is in, then keep dividing the car in half and half again until you locate the short.*

Ground check

8   Perform a ground test to check whether a component is properly grounded. Disconnect the battery and connect one lead of a continuity tester or multimeter (set to the ohms scale), to a known good ground. Connect the other lead to the wire or ground connection being tested. If the resistance is low (less than 5 ohms), the ground is good. Or, use a test

light hooked to a good positive voltage source (such as the battery positive post). If the test light does not go on, the ground is not good.
Note: *In reverse of the method described, if you have determined that a lead is supposed to be a ground by way of the wiring diagram, and you are absolutely sure it is a ground lead, a test light can prove it out. By attaching the test light to a known good ground, and if the circuit you are working on is in working order, and you touch it to the known "bad" ground lead, the test light will light up. Meaning, that particular wire is looking for a ground source and your test light provided the ground path. Double check that it is supposed to be a ground lead and find out where it is supposed to be attached.*

Continuity check

9   A continuity check is done to determine if there are any breaks in a circuit - if it is pass-

2.6 In use, a basic test light's lead is clipped to a known good ground, then the pointed probe can test connectors, wires or electrical sockets - if the bulb lights, the circuit being tested has battery voltage

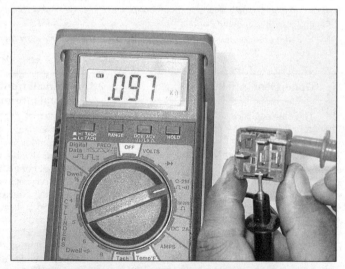

2.9 With a multimeter set to the ohms scale, resistance can be checked across two terminals - when checking for continuity, a low reading indicates continuity, a high reading or infinity indicates high resistance or lack of continuity

ing electricity properly. With the circuit off (no power in the circuit), a self-powered continuity tester or multimeter can be used to check the circuit. Connect the test leads to both ends of the circuit (or to the "power" end and a good ground), and if the test light comes on, the circuit is passing current properly. If the resistance is low (less than 5 ohms), there is continuity. If the reading is 10,000 ohms or higher, there is a break somewhere in the circuit. The same procedure can be used to test a switch, by connecting the continuity tester to the switch terminals. With the switch turned On, the test light should come on (or low resistance should be indicated on a meter) (see illustration).

Finding an open circuit

10   When diagnosing for possible open circuits, it is often difficult to locate them by sight because the connectors hide oxidation or terminal misalignment. Merely wiggling a connector on a sensor or in the wiring har-

ness may correct the open circuit condition. Remember this when an open circuit is indicated when troubleshooting a circuit. Intermittent problems may also be caused by oxidized or loose connections.

11   Electrical troubleshooting is simple if you keep in mind that all electrical circuits are basically electricity running from the battery, through the wires, switches, relays, fuses and fusible links to each electrical component (light bulb, motor, etc.) and to ground, from which it is passed back to the battery. Any electrical problem is an interruption in the flow of electricity to and from the battery.

Connectors

12   Most electrical connections on these vehicles are made with multiwire plastic connectors. The mating halves of many connectors are secured with locking clips molded into the plastic connector shells. The mating halves of large connectors, such as some of

those under the instrument panel, are held together by a bolt through the center of the connector.

13   To separate a connector with locking clips, use a small screwdriver to pry the clips apart carefully, then separate the connector halves. Pull only on the shell, never pull on the wiring harness as you may damage the individual wires and terminals inside the connectors. Look at the connector closely before trying to separate the halves. Often the locking clips are engaged in a way that is not immediately clear. Additionally, many connectors have more than one set of clips.

14   Each pair of connector terminals has a male half and a female half. When you look at the end view of a connector in a diagram, be sure to understand whether the view shows the harness side or the component side of the connector. Connector halves are mirror images of each other, and a terminal shown on the right side end view of one half will be on the left side end view of the other half.

Electrical connectors

Most electrical connectors have a single release tab that you depress to release the connector

Some electrical connectors have a retaining tab which must be pried up to free the connector

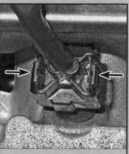

Some connectors have two release tabs that you must squeeze to release the connector

Some connectors use wire retainers that you squeeze to release the connector

Critical connectors often employ a sliding lock (1) that you must pull out before you can depress the release tab (2)

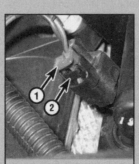

Here's another sliding-lock style connector, with the lock (1) and the release tab (2) on the side of the connector

On some connectors the lock (1) must be pulled out to the side and removed before you can lift the release tab (2)

Some critical connectors, like the multi-pin connectors at the Powertrain Control Module employ pivoting locks that must be flipped open

3.1a The engine compartment fuse/ relay box is mounted to the top of the right inner fenderwell in the engine compartment - it contains miniaturized fuses, cartridge-type fusible links, relays and circuit breakers

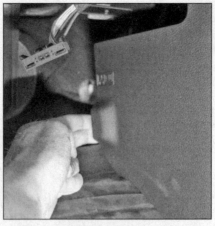

3.1b Remove the access panel from the right kick panel. . .

3.1c. . . then remove the fuse box cover to gain access to the fuses in the BCM

3   Fuses and fusible links - general information

Fuses

1   The electrical circuits of the vehicle are protected by a combination of fuses, circuit breakers and fusible links. Fuse blocks are located under the instrument panel and in the engine compartment (see illustrations).

2   Each of the fuses is designed to protect a specific circuit (or circuits), and the various circuits are identified on the fuse panel cover.

3   Miniaturized fuses are employed in the fuse blocks. These compact fuses, with blade terminal design, allow fingertip removal and replacement. If an electrical component fails, always check the fuse first. The best way to check a fuse is with a test light. Check for power at the exposed terminal tips of each fuse. If power is present on one side of the fuse but not the other, the fuse is blown. A blown fuse can also be confirmed by visually inspecting it (see illustration).

4   Be sure to replace blown fuses with the correct type. Fuses of different ratings are physically interchangeable, but only fuses of the proper rating should be used. Replacing a fuse with one of a higher or lower value than specified is not recommended. Each electrical circuit needs a specific amount of protection. The amperage value of each fuse is molded into the fuse body.

5   If the replacement fuse immediately fails, don't replace it again until the cause of the problem is isolated and corrected. In most cases, this will be a short circuit in the wiring caused by a broken or deteriorated wire.

Fusible links

6   Some circuits are protected by fusible links. The links are used in circuits which are not ordinarily fused, or which carry high current.

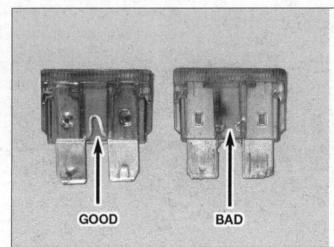

GOOD **BAD**

3.3 When a fuse blows, the element between the terminals melts - the fuse on the right is blown, the fuse on the left is good

7   Cartridge type fusible links are located in the engine compartment fuse and relay box and are similar to a large fuse. After disconnecting the negative battery cable, simply unplug and replace a fusible link with one of the same amperage.

4   Circuit breakers - general information

1   Circuit breakers protect certain circuits, such as the power windows or heated seats. Depending on the vehicle's accessories, there may be one or two circuit breakers, located in the fuse/relay box in the engine compartment (see illustration 3.1a).

2   Because the circuit breakers reset automatically, an electrical overload in a circuit-breaker-protected system will cause the circuit to fail momentarily, then come back on. If the circuit does not come back on, check it immediately.

3   For a basic check, pull the circuit breaker

up out of its socket on the fuse panel, but just far enough to probe with a voltmeter. The breaker should still contact the sockets.

4   With the voltmeter negative lead on a good chassis ground, touch each end prong of the circuit breaker with the positive meter probe. There should be battery voltage at each end. If there is battery voltage only at one end, the circuit breaker must be replaced.

5   Some circuit breakers must be reset manually.

5   Relays - general information and testing

General information

1   Several electrical accessories in the vehicle, such as the fuel injection system, horns, starter, and fog lamps use relays to transmit the electrical signal to the component. Relays use a low-current circuit (the control circuit) to open and close a high-current circuit (the

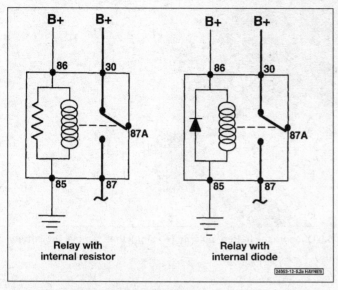

5.2a Typical ISO relay designs, terminal numbering and circuit connections

5.2b Most relays are marked on the outside to easily identify the control circuits and the power circuits - four terminal type shown

power circuit). If the relay is defective, that component will not operate properly. Most relays are mounted in the engine compartment fuse/relay box, with some specialized relays located above the interior fuse box in the dash (see illustrations 3.1a and 3.1c). If a faulty relay is suspected, it can be removed and tested using the procedure below or by a dealer service department or a repair shop. Defective relays must be replaced as a unit.

Testing

2   Most of the relays used in these vehicles are of a type often called "ISO" relays, which refers to the International Standards Organization. The terminals of ISO relays are numbered to indicate their usual circuit connections and functions. There are two basic layouts of terminals on the relays used in these vehicles (see illustrations).

3   Refer to the wiring diagram for the circuit to determine the proper connections for the relay you're testing. If you can't determine the correct connection from the wiring diagrams, however, you may be able to determine the test connections from the information that follows.

4   Two of the terminals are the relay control circuit and connect to the relay coil. The other relay terminals are the power circuit. When the relay is energized, the coil creates a magnetic field that closes the larger contacts of the power circuit to provide power to the circuit loads.

5   Terminals 85 and 86 are normally the control circuit. If the relay contains a diode, terminal 86 must be connected to battery positive (B+) voltage and terminal 85 to ground. If the relay contains a resistor, terminals 85 and 86 can be connected in either direction with

respect to B+ and ground.

6   Terminal 30 is normally connected to the battery voltage (B+) source for the circuit loads. Terminal 87 is connected to the ground side of the circuit, either directly or through a load. If the relay has several alternate terminals for load or ground connections, they usually are numbered 87A, 87B, 87C, and so on.

7   Use an ohmmeter to check continuity through the relay control coil.

a) Connect the meter according to the polarity shown in the illustration for one check; then reverse the ohmmeter leads and check continuity in the other direction.

b) If the relay contains a resistor, resistance will be indicated on the meter, and should be the same value with the ohmmeter in either direction.

c) If the relay contains a diode, resistance should be higher with the ohmmeter in the forward polarity direction than with the meter leads reversed.

d) If the ohmmeter shows infinite resistance in both directions, replace the relay.

8   Remove the relay from the vehicle and use the ohmmeter to check for continuity between the relay power circuit terminals. There should be no continuity between terminal 30 and 87 with the relay de-energized.

9   Connect a fused jumper wire to terminal 86 and the positive battery terminal. Connect another jumper wire between terminal 85 and ground. When the connections are made, the relay should click.

10   With the jumper wires connected, check for continuity between the power circuit terminals. Now, there should be continuity between terminals 30 and 87.

11   If the relay fails any of the above tests, replace it.

6   Key fob - programming, battery replacement, key fob strength testing/driver's door keypad - removal and installation

Key fob - programming

Note: This procedure is for the RKE (Remote Key Entry) type key fobs and not for the IKT (Integrated Key Transmitter) type. The IKT is automatically programmed when the PATS (Passive Anti-Theft System) is programmed.

Note: IKT transmitters can only be programmed with a scan tool. Two working keys are required.

Note: When programming the RKE transmitter ALL remotes must be present and in working order.

1   Programming can be done with a scanner or with the following procedure.

Caution: DO NOT touch the brake pedal when programming the RKE or this will end the program procedure.

2   Using the door lock switch on either door, cycle the locks to the Unlock position.

3   Rapidly cycle the ignition key from Off to On 8 times within 10 seconds ending with the 8th time in the On position. If successful, the door locks will Lock and Unlock once.

4   Within 20 seconds, press any button on the RKE transmitter that is being programmed to the vehicle.

5   The doors should Lock and then Unlock to confirm the programming was successful.

6   Repeat the same procedure of pressing any button on the next remote to be programmed up to a maximum of four remotes. Each time a successful programming of the next remote is accepted, the door locks will Lock and Unlock.

6.8 Gently pry the two halves of the fob apart

6.9 Observe the battery polarity (+/- sign), then remove the battery

6.17 Pry the retainer clip forward to remove it

6.18 Grasp the keypad module and remove it from the door, then disconnect the electrical connector

7   To end the programming session, turn the key to Off. The session will automatically end when a maximum of four RKE fobs are programmed, or 20 seconds have passed without any RF input from the remote(s).

Key fob - battery replacement

8   Use a thin coin or small flat bladed screwdriver to separate the two halves of the key fob (see illustration).
9   Check that the polarity is correct, then remove the old battery (see illustration).
10   Use the correct battery (Battery number CR2032).
11   Replace the battery and check operation of the remote. If needed, reprogram the remote.

Key fob - strength testing

12   The key fob remote has an operating distance of 30 feet. Each time a button on the fob is pushed a signal is received by the TPMS (Tire Pressure Monitor System). This signal is then passed onto the BCM (Body Control

Module) where it is then processed to unlock or lock the doors.
13   The fob battery can be checked with an volt meter after it has been removed from the key fob. It should have 2.5 volts.
14   If for some reason your key fob fails to operate even after you've tried a replacement battery, take your key fob to a repair shop that has a tire monitor reset tool. Most of these tools have an RF strength indicator test as part of their diagnostics features. The technician can check whether or not your key fob is in working order or not. If there is no RF signal, the key fob is more than likely faulty. If the signal is weak, chances are the battery needs to be replaced.

Driver's door key pad - removal and installation

15   Remove the driver's door panel (see Chapter 11).
16   Raise the window to the fully closed position.
17   Pull the retainer clip toward the front of

the door to remove it (see illustration).
18   Slightly push the keypad module out of the door far enough to get your fingers behind it from the outside (see illustration).
19   Leave the connector to hang outside of the door so that it doesn't fall back inside.
20   Installation is the reverse of removal.

7   Turn signal and hazard flasher - check and replacement

Warning: *The models covered by this manual are equipped with a Supplemental Restraint System (SRS), more commonly known as airbags. Always disconnect the negative battery cable(s) and wait two minutes before working in the vicinity of any airbag system component to avoid the possibility of accidental deployment of the airbag, which could cause personal injury (see Section 27).*

1   The turn signal and hazard flashers are an integral part of the BCM (Body Control Module) and are not serviced separately. If the

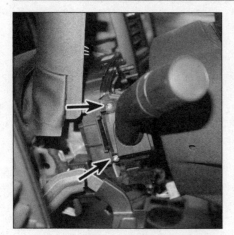

8.4 Multi-function switch mounting fasteners (steering wheel removed for clarity)

8.16 Steering Column Control Module (SCCM) (A)

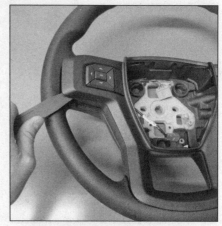

8.22 Carefully pry the switch bezel up from the steering wheel

BCM has been determined as the fault, the unit will need to be replaced and programmed to the vehicle. See a qualified independent repair facility or dealer repair department for replacement and programming.

2   When the flasher unit is functioning properly, an audible click can be heard during its operation. If the turn signal indicator (on the instrument panel) on one side of the vehicle flashes much more rapidly than normal, a faulty turn signal bulb is usually indicated.

3   If both turn signals fail to blink, the problem may be due to a blown fuse, a faulty flasher unit, a broken switch, a loose or open connection or a faulty Body Control Module. If a quick check of the fuse box indicates that the turn signal fuse has blown, check the wiring for a short before installing a new fuse.

---

8   Steering column switches - replacement

Warning: *The models covered by this manual are equipped with a Supplemental Restraint System (SRS), more commonly known as airbags. Always disconnect the negative battery cable(s) and wait two minutes before working in the vicinity of any airbag system component to avoid the possibility of accidental deployment of the airbag, which could cause personal injury (see Section 27).*

Multi-function switch

1   Disconnect the cable from the negative battery terminal (see Chapter 5).

2   Remove the steering column covers (see Chapter 11).

3   Remove the steering column control switch (see Steps 11 through 14), if equipped.

4   Remove the Torx screws for the multi-function switch. Pull the multi-function switch off of the steering column (see illustration).

5   Installation is the reverse of removal.

Adjustable pedal switch

6   Remove the knee bolster (see Chapter 11).

7   Carefully lift the hooked clips that secure the adjustable pedal switch to the knee bolster. Remove it by pulling it away from the steering column.

8   Installation is the reverse of removal.

Cruise control switch

9   The cruise control switch is mounted on the steering wheel. To remove the switch, use a flat-bladed trim tool and pry the switch out of the steering wheel starting on the outside edge. Once the switch is free disconnect the electrical connectors but don't let the wires fall back into the wheel.

10   Installation is the reverse of removal.

Steering column control switch

11   Remove the steering column covers (see Chapter 11).

12   Rotate the steering wheel 90-degrees counterclockwise.

13   Remove the switch mounting screws.

14   Depress the two retaining tabs and remove the switch from the column.

15   Installation is the reverse of removal.

Steering column control module - SCCM

16   The SCCM (Steering Column Control Module) collects the input signals from all of the various steering column switches and routes the data signals to the appropriate next module(s). The adjustable pedals also run through the SCCM. The SCCM is located under the steering column covers (see illustration).

17   To replace the SCCM requires downloading the information from the original SCCM and then reinstalling that information into the

8.23 Disconnect the electrical connector to the steering wheel switch

replacement SCCM. This requires the use of the proper scanner and diagnostic tools. See your local dealer or qualified independent repair facility for any repair or diagnostics regarding the SCCM operation.

Heated steering wheel module - removal and installation

Caution: *The HSWM (Heated Steering Wheel Module) is mounted behind the driver's knee bolster trim panel. Replacing the HSWM requires programming of the replacement module. This task cannot be carried out without the proper scanning and diagnostic tools. See your local dealer or qualified independent repair facility for proper configuration.*

18   Remove the driver's side knee bolster trim panel (see Chapter 11).

19   Disconnect the electrical connector from the HSWM and remove the fasteners.

20   Installation is the same as removal. Have the HSWM reconfigured by a qualified repair facility.

\9.3 To disconnect the electrical connector from the ignition switch, depress this release tab and pull the connector out

9.4 Depress the release tabs on top and bottom of the switch, then pull the switch out

9.13a Disconnect the electrical connector to the PATS transceiver...

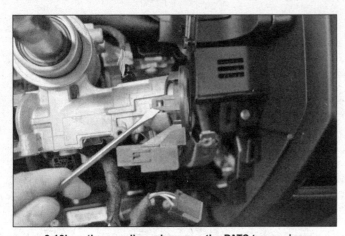

9.13b ... then unclip and remove the PATS transceiver

9.15 To remove the ignition lock cylinder, place the key in the "ACC" position, push in on the release tab with a small screwdriver or a small punch and pull the cylinder straight out

Steering wheel multi-function switch

21   Remove the driver's airbag module (see Chapter 10).

22   Use a trim tool to carefully pry the steering wheel trim bezel off of the steering wheel (see illustration).

23   Disconnect the electrical connectors to the switches (see illustration).

24   Remove the steering wheel switch(es) fasteners and remove the switch(es) from the bezel.

25   Installation is the reverse of removal.

9   Ignition switch and key lock cylinder - replacement

Warning: *The models covered by this manual are equipped with a Supplemental Restraint System (SRS), more commonly known as airbags. Always disconnect the negative battery cable(s) and wait two minutes before working in the vicinity of any airbag system component to avoid the possibility of accidental deploy-*

ment of the airbag, which could cause personal injury (see Section 27).

1   Disconnect the cable from the negative battery terminal (see Chapter 5, Section 3).

Ignition switch - non-keyless models

2   Remove the steering column covers and the tilt-column handle, if equipped (see Chapter 11).

3   Unplug the ignition switch electrical connector (see illustration).

4   Press in on the two tabs securing the ignition switch to the steering column (see illustration).

5   Pull the switch away from the column to remove it.

6   The remainder of the installation is the reverse of removal. Check for proper operation of the ignition switch in the lock, start and accessory positions.

Ignition switch - keyless models

7   Remove the knee bolster panel (see Chapter 11).

8   Disconnect the electrical connector to

the start/stop switch.

9   Depress the two tabs from the back side of the switch and push the switch out from the knee bolster panel.

10   The remainder of installation is the reverse of removal.

Lock cylinder - non-keyless models

11   Disconnect the cable from the negative battery terminal (see Chapter 5, Section 3).

12   Remove the steering wheel covers (see Chapter 11).

13   Disconnect the electrical connector to the PATS (Passive Anti-Theft System) transceiver. Use a small pick (such as a dental pick tool) and raise the two locking tabs far enough to allow the transceiver to be disconnected (see illustrations). Then remove the PATS transceiver.

14   Turn the key to the ACC position.

15   Insert a 1/8-inch punch or small blade screwdriver into the access hole. Depress the punch while pulling out on the lock cylinder to remove it from the steering column housing (see illustration).

10.7 Turn the panel over and disconnect the electrical connector from the switch

10.17 Disconnect the electrical connector from the backside of the USB hub trim panel

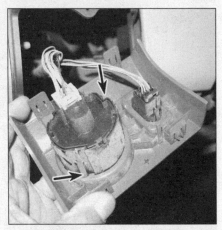

10.22 Press in on these tabs to remove the pro trailer backup assist switch

16   To install the lock cylinder, make sure the switch is in the ACC position and align the locking tab while pushing the cylinder into place.

17   Rotate the key back to the Off position. This will allow the retaining pin to extend itself back into the locating hole in the steering column housing.

18   Turn the lock to ensure that operation is correct in all positions.

19   The remainder of installation is the reverse of removal.

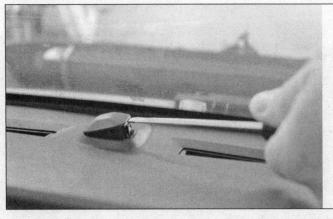

10.24 Pry the sensor up and out of the instrument panel

10   Instrument panel switches - replacement

Warning: *The models covered by this manual are equipped with a Supplemental Restraint System (SRS), more commonly known as airbags. Always disconnect the negative battery cable(s) and wait two minutes before working in the vicinity of any airbag system component to avoid the possibility of accidental deployment of the airbag, which could cause personal injury (see Section 27).*

Hazard flasher switch

1   Disconnect the cable from the negative battery terminal (see Chapter 5, Section 3).

2   Remove the Front Controls Interface module (FCIM) (see Section 13).

3   Working on the backside of the FCIM panel, squeeze the tabs on the hazard flasher switch and pull the switch out from the panel.

4   Installation is the reverse of the removal procedure.

Headlight/fog light switch and panel dimmer switch

5   Disconnect the cable from the negative battery terminal (see Chapter 5, Section 3).

6   Remove the knee bolster panel (see Chapter 11).

7   Disconnect the electrical connector (see illustration) from the back of the switch.

8   Press in on the tabs to remove the switch from the knee bolster.

9   Installation is the reverse of the removal procedure.

4WD selector switch (MSS - Mode Selector Switch)

10   Disconnect the cable from the negative battery terminal (see Chapter 5).

11   Using a trim tool, carefully pry the MSS from the left-side center trim and vent panel.

12   Disconnect the electrical connector to the switch.

13   Installation is the reverse of the removal procedure.

Rear defogger switch

14   The rear defogger switch is part of the HVAC control module; see Chapter 3 for removal.

Universal Serial Bus (USB) hub

15   Disconnect the cable from the negative battery terminal (see Chapter 5).

16   Using a trim tool carefully pry the USB hub trim plate from the center trim panel.

Note: *On models equipped with a floor console, the USB hub is mounted inside the console enclosure and is removed in the same way as the one mounted in the instrument panel.*

17   Disconnect the USB hub electrical connectors (see illustration).

18   Installation is the reverse of the removal procedure.

Pro Trailer Backup assist selector switch

19   Disconnect the cable from the negative battery terminal (see Chapter 5).

20   Remove Front Controls Interface (FCIM) Module (see Section 13).

21   Remove the left side center trim panel and HVAC vent panel (see Chapter 11).

22   Press in on the two locking tabs and push the control knob out of the trim panel (see illustration).

23   Installation is the reverse of the removal procedure.

Sunload sensor

24   Using a small screwdriver or trim tool pry the sensor up and out of the instrument panel (see illustration).

10.25 Disconnect the electrical connector to the sensor

10.29 Disconnect the electrical connector to the sensor

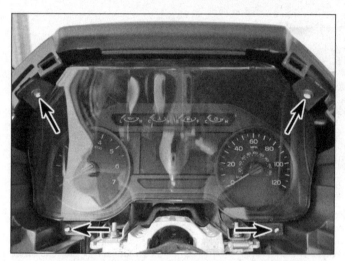

11.5 Instrument cluster mounting screw locations

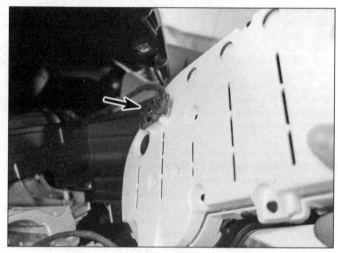

11.6 Disconnect the instrument cluster electrical connector

25   Disconnect the electrical connector to the sensor and remove the sensor (see illustration).

26   Installation is the reverse of removal.

In-vehicle temperature and humidity sensor

27   Remove the knee bolster (see Chapter 11).

28   Locate the sensor on the back side of the instrument cluster trim panel.

Note: *If the sensor is to difficult to access from the back side of the instrument panel, remove the instrument cluster trim panel (see Chapter 11).*

29   Disconnect the electrical connector (see illustration) to the sensor and unclip the sensor from the instrument panel.

30   Installation is the reverse of removal.

11 Instrument cluster - removal and installation

Warning: *The models covered by this manual are equipped with a Supplemental Restraint System (SRS), more commonly known as airbags. Always disconnect the negative battery cable(s) and wait two minutes before working in the vicinity of any airbag system component to avoid the possibility of accidental deployment of the airbag, which could cause personal injury (see Section 27).*

1   Disconnect the cable from the negative battery terminal (see Chapter 5).

Note: *If you are replacing the instrument cluster, the information stored in the old instrument cluster must be uploaded to a scanner to be reinstalled in the replacement cluster. Consult a dealer service department or other properly equipped repair facility before proceeding.*

2   Remove the knee bolster panel (see Chapter 11).

3   Lower the steering column to the lowest position and pull out the knee bolster trim panel to release the retaining clips.

4   Remove the instrument cluster bezel (see Chapter 11).

5   Remove the four screws securing the instrument cluster to the dash assembly (see illustration).

6   Pull the instrument cluster out and unplug the electrical connector from the backside (see illustration), then remove the cluster from the instrument panel.

7   Installation is the reverse of removal.

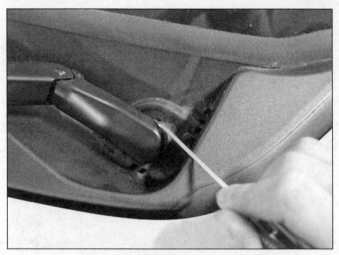

12.7 Release the wiper locking tab using a small screwdriver or pick and pull the wiper arm off the wiper motor shaft

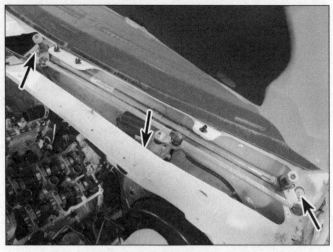

12.9 Wiper assembly mounting bolts

12 Wiper motor - check and replacement

Wiper motor circuit check

Note: *Refer to the wiring diagrams for wire colors in the following checks. When checking for voltage, probe a grounded 12-volt test light to each terminal at a connector until it lights; this verifies voltage (power) at the terminal. If the following checks fail to locate the problem, have the system diagnosed by a dealer service department or other properly equipped repair facility.*

Note: *There are some general voltage and ground tests that can be made to check the operation of the wiper system. To test it properly requires the use of a scanner with bi-directional capabilities. If the following outlined generic tests do not lead to a result, take your vehicle to the appropriate repair facility for diagnostics and repairs.*

1   If the wipers work slowly, make sure the battery is in good condition and has a strong charge (see Chapter 5). If the battery is in good condition, remove the wiper motor and operate the wiper arms by hand. Check for binding linkage and pivots. Lubricate or repair the linkage or pivots as necessary. Reinstall the wiper motor. If the wipers still operate slowly, check for loose or corroded connections, especially the ground connection. If all connections look OK, replace the motor.

2   If the wipers fail to operate when activated, check the fuse (see Section 3). If the fuse is OK, connect a jumper wire between the wiper motor's ground terminal and ground, then retest. If the motor works now, repair the ground connection. If the motor still doesn't work, turn the wiper switch to the HI position and check for voltage at the motor.

3   If there's voltage at the connector, remove the motor and check it off the vehicle with fused jumper wires from the battery. If the motor now works, check for binding linkage (see Step 1). If the motor still doesn't work, replace it. If there's no voltage to the motor, check for voltage at the wiper control relays. If there's voltage at the wiper control relays and no voltage at the wiper motor, have the switch tested. If the switch is OK, the wiper control relay is probably bad. See Section 5 for relay testing.

4   If the interval (delay) function is inoperative, check the continuity of all the wiring between the switch and wiper control module.

5   If the wipers stop at the position they're in when the switch is turned off (fail to park), check for voltage at the park feed wire of the wiper motor connector when the wiper switch is Off but the ignition is On. If no voltage is present, check for an open circuit between the wiper motor and the fuse panel.

Wiper motor replacement

6   Disconnect the cable from the negative battery terminal (see Chapter 5).

7   Mark the positions of the wiper arm(s) on the windshield, then remove the wiper arm(s) (see illustration).

8   Remove the cowl cover (see Chapter 11).

9   Disconnect the wiper motor wiring harness connector and remove the three bolts securing the windshield wiper motor/linkage assembly and remove the assembly (see illustration).

10   Mark the location of the wiper crank arm to the linkage assembly and wiper motor shaft. Remove the wiper motor crank arm nut and separate the crank arm from the motor (see illustration).

11   Remove the fasteners securing the motor to the linkage assembly (see illustration).

12   Installation is the reverse of removal. Tighten all the fasteners securely.

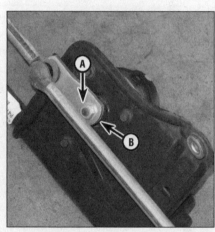

12.10 Crank arm nut and match marks

A   Crank arm nut
B   Match mark the crank arm to the wiper motor shaft and to the bracket before removing the crank arm

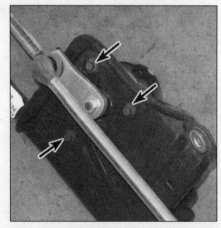

12.11 Remove the fasteners

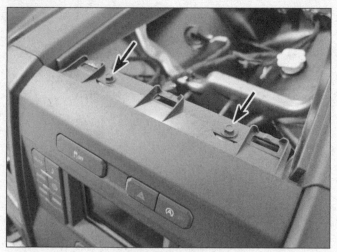

13.5a FCIM fastener locations

13.5b Use a trim tool to carefully pry the FCIM out of the instrument panel

13.6 Disconnect the electrical connectors from the rear of the FCIM

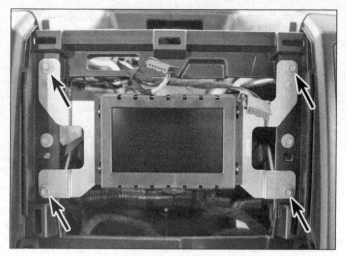

13.7 FCDIM fastener locations

13   Front Controls Interface Module (FCIM)/Front Controls Interface Display Module (FCDIM), radio and speakers - removal and installation

Warning: *The models covered by this manual are equipped with a Supplemental Restraint System (SRS), more commonly known as airbags. Always disconnect the negative battery cable(s) and wait two minutes before working in the vicinity of any airbag system component to avoid the possibility of accidental deployment of the airbag, which could cause personal injury (see Section 27).*

1   Disconnect the cable from the negative battery terminal (see Chapter 5).

Front Controls Interface Module (FCIM)

2   Using a trim tool, pry out the instrument panel center speaker grille, if equipped.
3   Remove the rubber mat from the bottom of the tray.
4   Remove the instrument panel storage tray fasteners and tray (see Chapter 11).
5   Remove the FCIM mounting bolts (see illustrations) and pry the interface module forward. Disconnect the electrical connectors and remove the FCIM from the instrument panel.
6   Disconnect the electrical connectors and remove the (FCIM) from the instrument panel and remove the (FCIM) module from the panel (see illustration).

Front Control/Display Interface Module (FCDIM)

7   Remove the FCIM (see Steps 2 through 6), then remove the (FCDIM) fasteners (see illustration).
8   Disconnect the electrical connector and remove the (FCDIM) from the instrument panel (see illustration).
9   Installation is the reverse of removal.
10   Verify that all controls operate correctly.

Radio - Audio Control Module (ACM)

Warning: *If you are replacing the ACM (Audio Front Control Module) with a new one, upload the ACM configuration into a scan tool so that it can be reloaded into the replacement unit. This will have to be done by an appropriately equipped repair facility.*

13.8 Disconnect the electrical connector from the rear of the FCDIM

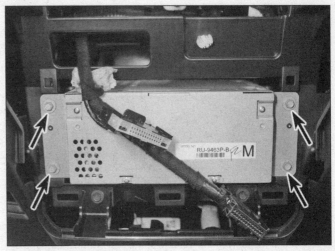

13.12 Remove the radio receiver mounting fasteners

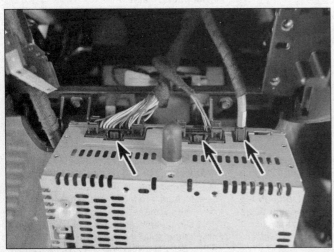

13.13 Disconnect the electrical connectors and antenna cable

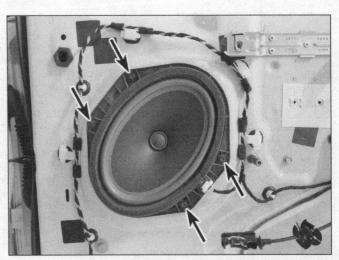

13.16 Door speaker mounting fastener locations

Note: *If equipped with the base AM/FM radio, it does not need to be programmed.*

11   Remove the FCIM (see Steps 2 through 6).

12   Remove the fasteners securing the radio to the dash (see illustration).

13   Pull the unit out far enough to disconnect the electrical connections and antenna lead (see illustration).

14   Installation is the reverse of removal.

Speakers

Door speakers

15   Remove the door trim panel (see Chapter 11).

16   Remove the mounting fasteners (see illustration), withdraw the speaker, unplug the electrical connector (see illustration) and

remove the speaker from the vehicle.

17   Installation is the reverse of removal.

Instrument panel center speaker

18   Using a trim tool, pry out the instrument panel center speaker grille.

19   Remove the mounting fasteners, withdraw the speaker, unplug the electrical connector and remove the speaker from the vehicle.

20   Installation is the reverse of removal.

Tweeter speaker

21   Remove the A-pillar trim panel (see Chapter 11).

22   Disconnect the electrical connector to the tweeter (see illustration).

23   Remove the mounting screws and tweeter from the trim panel.

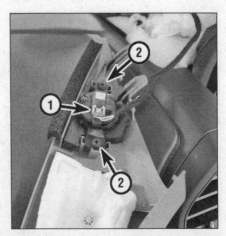

13.22 Tweeter speaker details

1   *Electrical connector*
2   *Mounting screws*

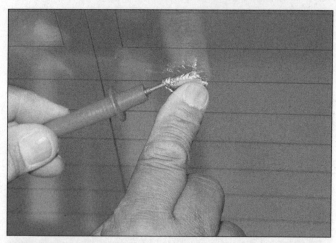

15.4 When measuring the voltage at the rear window defogger grid, wrap a piece of aluminum foil around the positive probe of the voltmeter and press the foil against the wire with your finger

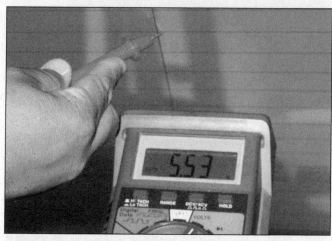

15.5 To determine if a heating element has broken, check the voltage at the center of each element - if the voltage is 5- or 6-volts, the element is unbroken - if the voltage is 10- or 12-volts, the element is broken between the center and the ground side - if there is no voltage, the element is broken between the center and the positive side

Subwoofer speaker

24   Fold down the rear seat.

25   Disconnect the electrical connector to the subwoofer.

26   Remove the mounting bolts and subwoofer from the cab.

---

14   Antenna and cable - removal and installation

Antenna

1   Remove the right side inner fender splash shield (see Chapter 11).

2   Unscrew the antenna mast and the base on the passenger's side fender.

3   Lower the glove box door to access the antenna cable, then disconnect the cable from the clips along the front of the heater/blower motor housing.

4   Working in the fender, remove the antenna mounting bolt and lower the antenna mast base from the fender.

5   Disconnect the antenna cable connection and pull the lead out through the grommet into the fender and remove the antenna base and cable.

6   Installation is the reverse of removal.

Antenna cable

7   Remove the FCIM, FCDIM and radio (see Section 13), then disconnect the antenna lead from the rear side of the radio.

8   Lower the glove box completely and remove the right side kick panel to gain access to the antenna cable.

9   Pull the antenna with back through the grommet and disconnect the antenna cable lead from the antenna mast lead connection.

10   Installation is the reverse of removal.

---

15   Rear window defogger - check and repair

1   The rear window defogger consists of a number of horizontal elements baked onto the glass surface.

2   Small breaks in the element can be repaired without removing the rear window.

Check

3   Turn the ignition switch and defogger system switches to the On position. Using a voltmeter, place the positive probe against the defogger grid positive terminal and the negative probe against the ground terminal. If battery voltage is not indicated, check the fuse, defogger switch and related wiring. If voltage is indicated, but all or part of the defogger doesn't heat, proceed with the following tests.

4   When measuring voltage during the next two tests, wrap a piece of aluminum foil around the tip of the voltmeter positive probe and press the foil against the heating element with your finger (see illustration). Place the negative probe on the defogger grid ground terminal.

5   Check the voltage at the center of each heating element (see illustration). If the voltage is 5- or 6-volts, the element is OK (there is no break). If the voltage is 0-volts, the element is broken between the center of the element and the positive end. If the voltage is 10- to 12-volts the element is broken between the center of the element and ground. Check each heating element.

6   Connect the negative lead to a good body ground. The reading should stay the same. If it doesn't, the ground connection is bad.

7   To find the break, place the voltmeter negative probe against the defogger ground terminal. Place the voltmeter positive probe with the foil strip against the heating element at the positive terminal end and slide it toward the negative terminal end. The point at which the voltmeter deflects from several volts to zero is the point at which the heating element is broken (see illustration).

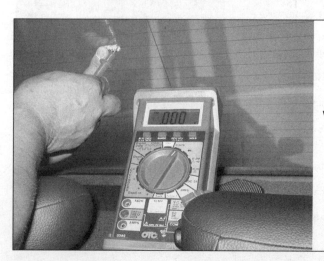

15.7 To find the break, place the voltmeter negative lead against the defogger ground terminal, place the voltmeter positive lead with the foil strip against the heating element at the positive terminal end and slide it toward the negative terminal end - the point at which the voltmeter reading changes abruptly is the point at which the element is broken

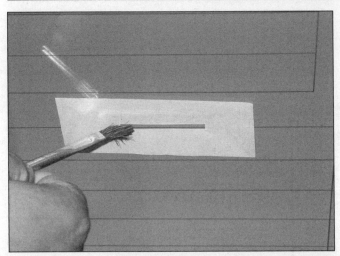

15.13 To use a defogger repair kit, apply masking tape to the inside of the window at the damaged area, then brush on the special conductive coating

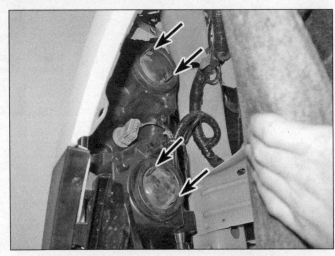

16.3a Locate the bulb covers on the backside of the housing and pull the covers off using the tabs…

16.3b … to access the low and high beam bulbs

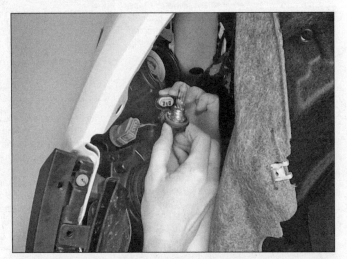

16.4 Disconnect the electrical connector and twist the bulb socket out of the housing

Repair

8   Repair the break in the element using a repair kit specifically recommended for this purpose, available at most auto parts stores. Included in this kit is plastic conductive epoxy.
9   Prior to repairing a break, turn off the system and allow it to cool off for a few minutes.
10   Lightly buff the element area with fine steel wool, then clean it thoroughly with rubbing alcohol.
11   Use masking tape to mask off the area being repaired.
12   Thoroughly mix the epoxy, following the instructions provided with the repair kit.
13   Apply the epoxy material to the slit in the masking tape, overlapping the undamaged area about 3/4-inch on either end (see illustration).
14   Allow the repair to cure for 24 hours before removing the tape and using the system.

16 Headlight bulb - replacement

Warning: *Halogen gas filled bulbs are under pressure and may shatter if the surface is scratched or the bulb is dropped. Wear eye protection and handle the bulbs carefully, grasping only the base whenever possible. Do not touch the surface of the bulb with your fingers because the oil from your skin could cause it to overheat and fail prematurely. If you do touch the bulb surface, clean it with rubbing alcohol.*
Note: *This procedure is for halogen bulbs only. If equipped with LED headlights, the housing must be replaced as a complete assembly.*
Note: *Turning the wheel towards the opposite side of the headlight housing you're working on to give better access the to the headlight panel without having to remove the wheel well liner or front wheel.*
1   Working inside the fenderwell, locate the headlight trim panel directly behind the headlight housing and remove the screws and plastic push-pin fasteners and pull the panel out of the way.
2   On models equipped with fender mouldings, remove the two moulding screws then release the three moulding retainers on the inside of the moulding and move the front section of fender moulding out away from the fender.
3   Remove the bulb cover(s) from the back of the headlight housing (see illustrations).
4   Rotate the headlight bulb(s) from the back side of the headlight housing, a quarter turn counterclockwise to remove (see illustration).
Caution: *Always replace the headlamp with the same type of bulb. Some aftermarket bulbs that claim to give off a more intense field of light may actually do that. However, the way most of these bulbs accomplish the higher intensity is with a higher current flow. This puts a heavy strain on the factory wiring and connec-*

17.1 Location of the headlight adjustment screw

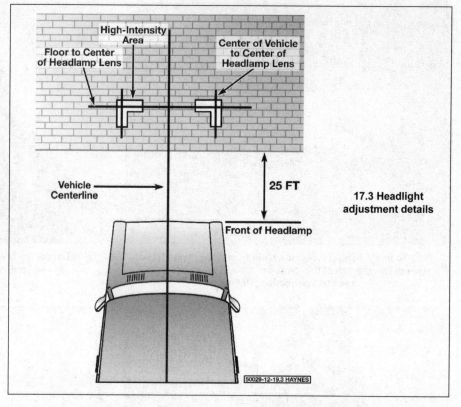

High-Intensity Area

Floor to Center of Headlamp Lens

Center of Vehicle to Center of Headlamp Lens

Vehicle Centerline

25 FT

17.3 Headlight adjustment details

Front of Headlamp

50029-12-19.3 HAYNES

tions that were never designed to carry an excessive current as required by some of these aftermarket bulbs. This also includes the HID aftermarket systems. There is a risk changing from the factory systems to any aftermarket lighting system.

5   Installation is the reverse of removal.

17   Headlights - adjustment

Note: *The headlights must be aimed correctly. If adjusted incorrectly they could blind the driver of an oncoming vehicle and cause a serious accident or seriously reduce your ability to see the road. The headlights should be checked for proper aim every 12 months and any time a new headlight is installed or front end body work is performed. It should be emphasized that the following procedure is only an interim step which will provide temporary adjustment until the headlights can be adjusted by a properly equipped shop.*

1   Location of the adjustment screws, only the vertical aiming can be adjusted (see illustration).

2   There are several methods of adjusting the headlights. The simplest method requires

masking tape, a blank wall and a level floor.

3   Position masking tape vertically on the wall in reference to the vehicle centerline and the centerlines of both headlights (see illustration).

4   Position a horizontal tape line in reference to the centerline of all the headlights.

Note: *It may be easier to position the tape on the wall with the vehicle parked only a few inches away.*

5   Adjustment should be made with the vehicle parked 25 feet from the wall, sitting level, the gas tank half-full and no heavy load in the vehicle.

6   Starting with the low beam adjustment, position the high intensity zone so it is two inches below the horizontal line and two inches to the side of the headlight vertical line, away from oncoming traffic. Adjustment

is made by turning the adjusting screw clockwise to raise the beam and counterclockwise to lower the beam.

7   With the high beams on, the high intensity zone should be vertically centered with the exact center just below the horizontal line.

Note: *It may not be possible to position the headlight aim exactly for both high and low beams. If a compromise must be made, keep in mind that the low beams are the most used and have the greatest effect on safety.*

18   Headlight housing - removal and installation

Note: *Turning the wheel towards the opposite side of the headlight housing your're working on to give better access the to the headlight trim panel without having to remove the inner fender liner or front wheel.*

1   Working inside the fenderwell, locate the headlight trim panel directly behind the headlight housing and remove the screws and plastic push-pin fasteners and pull the panel out of the way.

2   On models equipped with fender mouldings, remove the two moulding screws, then release the three moulding retainers on the inside of the moulding and move the front section of fender moulding out away from the fender.

3   Remove the headlight housing trim panel (see Chapter 11, Section 12).

4   Remove the plastic push-pins and mounting screws from inside the inner fender liner (see illustration).

5   Remove the plastic push-pin from under

18.4 Remove the plastic push-pin from the fender

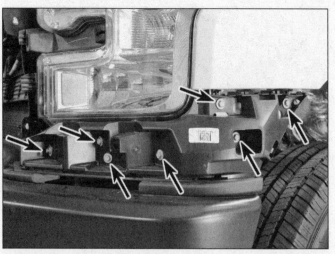

18.7a Remove the headlight trim panel bracket bolts...

18.7b ... then release the tabs and separate the bracket halves

18.9 Headlight assembly mounting bolt locations

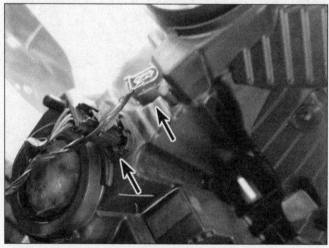

18.10 Disconnect the electrical connections and remove the housing

the inner portion of the headlight housing.

6 Remove the headlight trim (see Chapter 11).

7 Remove the headlight housing trim panel bracket bolts, then release the retaining tabs and slide the bracket away from the body (see illustrations).

8 Disconnect the electrical connector to the marker light (see illustration 21.5).

9 Remove the three bolts securing the headlight assembly to the core support (see illustrations).

10 Pull the housing from the radiator core support and disconnect the electrical connectors (see illustration).

11 Unclip the harness (see illustration) from the housing and remove the headlight housing.

12 Installation is the reverse of removal.

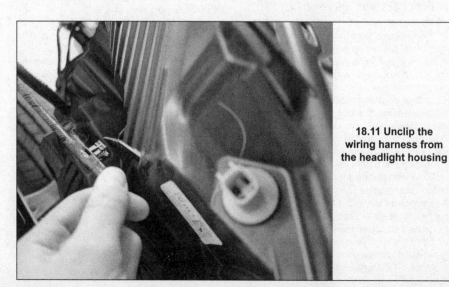

18.11 Unclip the wiring harness from the headlight housing

19.1 Cloudy headlight lenses are ugly and reduce the amount of
light projected

19.3 Mask off the surrounding area and apply the compound with
the buffer

19.4 The result should be a lens that is almost as clear as new

20.2 Location of the horns

19   Headlight lens refurbishing

1   The plastic lens on most headlight assemblies are susceptible to U.V. damage from the sun as well as being out in the weather. There are several companies that make restoration kits to restore the plastic lens back to their original condition. There are also a few home remedies that have been proven somewhat effective too, such as toothpaste buffed onto the lens as well as some bug sprays that dissolve the opaque and clouded surface of the headlight lens (see illustration).
2   Most restoration kits are a three-step process that requires a variable speed hand drill to perform the various steps. When starting a headlight restoration project, be sure to be in a well ventilated area and where you don't have anything you don't want the buffing chemicals and compounds to be sprayed on.
3   Mask off the area around the headlight assembly to avoid any painted surfaces from being damaged with the drill or the compounds in the restoration kit. Have plenty of clean rags handy to wipe up any spills and to perform the final buffing (see illustration).
4   Follow all the directions in the restoration kit as described in the instructions. We also recommend adding a top coat of wax or a suitable U.V. protectant as a final finish coat (see illustration).

20   Horn - replacement

1   Remove the radiator grille (see Chapter 11).
2   Disconnect the electrical connector(s) from the horn(s) (see illustration).
3   Remove the horn mounting nut(s) and separate the horn(s) from the bracket.
4   Installation is the reverse of removal.

21   Bulb - replacement

Fog light

1   Lift and support the front end of the vehicle (if necessary).
2   Locate the fog light bulb socket and disconnect the electrical connector.
3   Twist the bulb socket counterclockwise to remove. The defective bulb can then be removed from the socket and replaced.
4   Installation is the reverse of removal.

Front turn signal and marker lights

Marker light bulb

5   Open the hood and locate the marker bulb at the inside corners of the headlights (see illustration). Twist the bulb socket a counterclockwise and remove the socket. The

Bulb removal

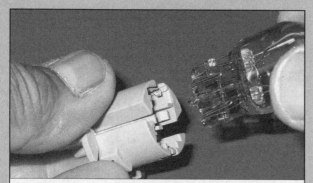

To remove many modern exterior bulbs from their holders, simply pull them out

On bulbs with a cylindrical base ("bayonet" bulbs), the socket is spring-loaded; a pair of small posts on the side of the base hold the bulb in place against spring pressure. To remove this type of bulb, push it into the holder, rotate it 1/4-turn counterclockwise, then pull it out

If a bayonet bulb has dual filaments, the posts are staggered, so the bulb can only be installed one way

To remove most overhead interior light bulbs, simply unclip them

defective bulb can then be removed from the socket and replaced.

Turn signal bulb

6   Raise the front of the vehicle and support it securely on jackstands, then rotate the wheel towards opposite side.

Note: *Turning the wheel towards the opposite side gives better access to the headlight trim panel without having to remove the inner fender liner.*

7   Working inside the fenderwell, locate the trim panel directly behind the headlight housing, then remove the screws and plastic push-pin fasteners and pull the panel out of the way.

Note: *On models equipped with fender mouldings, remove the two moulding screws, then release the three moulding retainers on the inside of the moulding and move the front section of fender moulding out away from the fender.*

8   Twist the bulb socket from the back side of the headlight housing counterclockwise to remove. The defective bulb can then be removed from the socket and replaced (see illustration).

9   Installation is the reverse of removal.

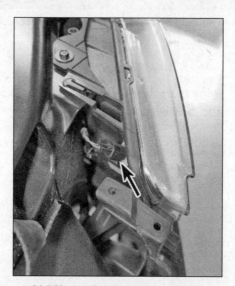

21.5 Marker light location - radiator support trim panel removed for clarity

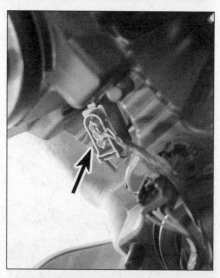

21.8 Turn signal bulb location - marker light location is on the opposite side

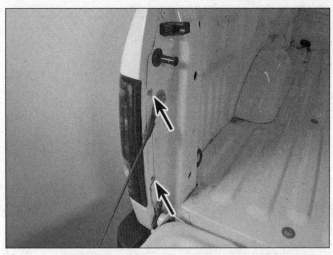

21.11a Remove the rear taillight housing mounting screws…

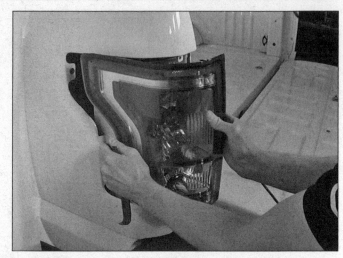

21.11b … then grip the housing firmly and pull it away from the body

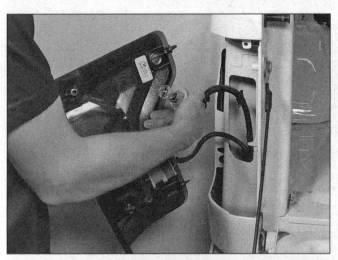

21.12 Remove the taillight housing for access to the bulb holders

21.15 Location of the bulb holder from under the vehicle

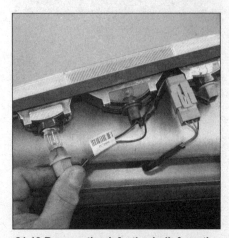

21.19 Remove the defective bulb from the high-mounted brake light assembly

Rear turn signal, brake, tail and back-up lights

10   Open the tailgate.

11   Remove the retaining screws securing the rear taillight housing, then pull the taillight assembly outward to access the taillight bulbs (see illustrations).

12   Twist the bulb socket, then remove the bulb holder from the housing (see illustration).

13   The defective bulb can then be removed from the socket and replaced.

14   Installation of the taillight housing is the reverse of removal.

License plate light

15   The license plate light bulbs can be accessed from the rear of the bumper in two ways. The first, carefully pry the light housing out using a flat-bladed screwdriver, then pull the bulb assembly from the bumper. The second is from under the vehicle; locate the bulb holder (see illustration).

16   Twist the bulb holder 1/4-turn to remove it from the housing. The defective bulb can then be pulled straight out of the socket and replaced.

17   Installation is the reverse of removal.

High-mounted brake light

18   Remove the lens retaining screws and pull the lamp assembly outward to access the bulbs.

19   Twist the bulb socket a quarter turn counterclockwise, then remove the bulb assembly from the housing (see illustration).

20   The defective bulb can then be pulled straight out of the socket and replaced.

Dome, courtesy, map and cargo lights

21   These lights are LED units and are not serviceable.

Outside mirror bulb replacement

22   Rotate mirror glass all the way inward.
23   Using a small flat bladed screwdriver, reach into the outside edge between the mirror and the mirror housing and release the plastic clip by pushing the clip forward.
24   Grasp the lens cover as you apply pressure to the clip so that the lens doesn't fall.
25   Rotate the lens outward to free the two front tabs.
26   Replace the bulbs by pulling straight out away from the housing.
27   Installation is the reverse of removal
Note: *On models equipped with puddle lights, pry the light out from the base of the mirror then disconnect the electrical connector and remove the light assembly. The bulb is not serviceable and the light assembly must be replaced as a unit.*

Instrument cluster illumination

28   To gain access to the instrument cluster illumination lights, the instrument cluster will have to be removed (see Section 11). The bulbs are fixed into position inside the instrument cluster. Take the instrument cluster to the appropriate repair facility that is equipped to repair the cluster.

22   Mirrors - description

Outside rear view mirrors

Note: *These models are equipped with a Body Control Module (BCM), (which doubles as the main interior fuse box). Several systems are linked to a centralized control module that allows simple and accurate troubleshooting, but only with a professional-grade scan tool. The Body Control Module governs the door locks, the power windows, the ignition lock and security system, the interior lights, the Daytime Running Lights system, the horn, the windshield wipers, the heating/air conditioning system and the power mirrors. In the event of malfunction with this system, have the vehicle diagnosed by a dealership service department or other qualified automotive repair facility.*
1   The electric rear view mirrors use two motors to move the glass; one for up and down adjustments and one for left-right adjustments. Some vehicles are equipped with heated (defog), power folding, power telescopic, and memory mirrors as well. These mirrors are an integral part of the power seat memory unit and the navigation systems as well as incorporated with the Body Control Module (BCM). If there is a problem with these systems it is advised to seek out a qualified independent repair facility or your local dealer.
2   The control switch has a selector portion which sends voltage to the left or right side mirror. With the ignition in the ACC position and the engine OFF, roll down the windows and operate the mirror control switch through all functions (left-right and up-down) for both the left and right side mirrors.
3   Listen carefully for the sound of the electric motors running in the mirrors.
4   If the motors can be heard but the mirror glass doesn't move, there's probably a problem with the drive mechanism inside the mirror. Power mirrors have no user-serviceable parts inside - a defective mirror must be replaced as a unit.
5   If the mirrors don't operate and no sound comes from the mirrors, check for a blown fuse.
6   If the fuses are OK, remove the mirror control switch. Have the switch continuity checked by a dealer service department or other qualified shop.
Note: *If the mirrors are continuously moved 10 times in a row the system will shut down the power to the mirrors for 3 1/2 minutes allowing the motor to cool off. In extreme cases it can keep the power off for up to 30 minutes.*
7   Check the ground connections.
8   If the mirror still doesn't work, remove the mirror and check the wires at the mirror for voltage.
9   If there's not voltage in each switch position, check the circuit between the mirror and control switch for opens and shorts.
10   If the mirror is inoperative, try holding the switch in one of the directions and swing the door open and closed. If there is a break in the door jamb you may occasionally make contact long enough to avoid removing the mirror from the door for further testing. This will also give you some clue as to where the break is rather than testing things in one given position.
Note: *If there's voltage, remove the mirror and test it off the vehicle with jumper wires. Before testing, check the wiring diagram for the correct leads that have to be used for each position. Applying voltage to the wrong leads can damage the mirror drive motors. Replace the mirror if it fails this test.*

Interior mirror

11   The inside mirror removal can be found in Chapter 11.
12   The vehicle maybe equipped with one or more of the following interior mirror features.

a) *Basic interior mirror with manual flip lever for dimming.*
b) *Automatic mirror dimming to reduce night time glare.*
c) *Auto dimming with video display.*
d) *Compass*

Note: *The video display is turned on by the navigation system anytime the vehicle is put into reverse. In vehicles with the touch screen, the image is not in the mirror but on the touch screen video display.*
Note: *The interior mirror with the built-in compass has an internal compass module as part of the mirror assembly. It cannot be removed or serviced. For calibration procedures see your owner's manual for details.*

23   Cruise control system - general information

1   The Powertrain Control Module (PCM) controls the cruise control system electronically via the electronic throttle control system. If you have problems with the cruise control system, check for the presence of trouble codes stored in the PCM (see Chapter 6, Section 3). If that doesn't turn up any problems, have it checked by a dealer service department or other qualified repair shop.

24   Power window system - description and check

Note: *These models are equipped with a Body Control Module (BCM) incorporated with the window system. Several systems are linked to a centralized control module that allows simple and accurate troubleshooting, but only with a professional-grade scan tool. The Body Control Module governs the door locks, the power windows, the ignition lock and security system, the interior lights, the Daytime Running Lights system, the horn, the windshield wipers, the heating/air conditioning system and the power mirrors. In the event of malfunction with this system, have the vehicle diagnosed by a dealership service department or other qualified automotive repair facility.*
1   The power window system operates electric motors, mounted in the doors, which lower and raise the windows. The system consists of the control switches, the motors, regulators, glass mechanisms, the Body Control Module (BCM) and associated wiring.
2   The power windows can be lowered and raised from the master control switch by the driver or by remote switches located at the individual windows. Each window has a separate motor that is reversible. The position of the control switch determines the polarity and therefore the direction of operation.
3   The window motor circuits are protected by a fuse. Each motor is also equipped with an internal circuit breaker; this prevents one stuck window from disabling the whole system.
4   The power window system will only operate when the ignition switch has activated the Retained Accessory Power (RAP) relay. In addition, many models have a window lock-out switch at the master control switch which, when activated, disables the switches at the rear windows and, sometimes, the switch at the passenger's window also. Always check these items before troubleshooting a window problem related to any of the other windows besides the driver's window. Window lock-out does not affect the driver's window.
5   These procedures are general in nature, so if you can't find the problem using them,

take the vehicle to a dealer service department or to an independent repair facility that specializes in electrical repairs.

6   If the power windows won't operate, always check the fuse and circuit breaker first.

7   If only the rear windows are inoperative, or if the windows only operate from the master control switch, check the rear window lockout switch for continuity in the unlocked position. Replace it if it doesn't have continuity.

8   Check the wiring between the switches and fuse panel for continuity. Repair the wiring, if necessary.

9   If only one window is inoperative from the master control switch, try the other control switch at each individual window.

Note: *This doesn't apply to the driver's door window.*

10   If the same window works from one switch, but not the other, check the switch and/or wiring for continuity.

11   If the switch tests OK, check for a short or open in the circuit between the affected switch and the window motor.

12   If one window is inoperative from both switches, remove the switch panel from the affected door. Check for voltage at the motor (refer to Chapter 11 for door panel removal) while the switch is operated.

Note: *There are voltage and ground signals present at the switch connector. However, on 2010 and later models, there are also two data lines to the BCM that are not true positive/ negative signals. Be sure you are testing the correct leads. Do not apply voltage or ground to any leads you are not sure of. Seek professional help in diagnosing any problems with the window circuits if you are unsure.*

13   If voltage is reaching the motor, disconnect the glass from the regulator. Move the window up and down by hand while checking for binding and damage. Also check for binding and damage to the regulator. If the regulator is not damaged and the window moves up and down smoothly, replace the motor. If there's binding or damage, lubricate, repair or replace parts, as necessary.

14   If voltage isn't reaching the motor, check the wiring in the circuit for continuity between the switches and the BCM, and between the BCM (if applicable) and the motors. You'll need to consult the wiring diagram. If the circuit is equipped with a relay, check that the relay is grounded properly and receiving voltage.

15   Test the windows to confirm proper repairs.

Note: *To verify if the motor is getting the needed voltage or ground, a simple but effective test is to sit in the car with the ignition on, open a door and look at the dome light. Then operate the switch to the faulty window. If you see the dome light dimming slightly this is a good indication that the motor is getting power and is probably a stuck motor or faulty wiring. Do not hold the switch on for very long when a motor is stuck or wiring is in question or more damage may occur. Finally, in some cases, a good rap on the door panel in the general area*

of the window motor - while the key is on and the window switch is depressed in the direction the window needs to move - will free up a stuck motor temporarily. You can damage the door panel or more internal components if you hit it too hard or are too aggressive.

Window express down programming

Note: *Any time the battery or window motor are disconnected, you will need to perform this procedure to reestablish the auto feature.*

16   Lower the window to its lowest position, holding the switch in the Down position for an additional five seconds.

17   Raise the window to its highest position, holding the window switch in the Up position for an additional five seconds.

18   Verify proper operation.

25 Power door lock and keyless entry system - description and check

Note: *These models are equipped with a Body Control Module (BCM). Several systems are linked to a centralized control module that allows simple and accurate troubleshooting, but only with a professional-grade scan tool. The Body Control Module governs the door locks, the power windows, the ignition lock and security system, the interior lights, the Daytime Running Lights system, the horn, the windshield wipers, the heating/air conditioning system and the power mirrors. In the event of malfunction with this system, have the vehicle diagnosed by a dealership service department or other qualified automotive repair facility.*

1   The power door lock system operates the door lock actuators mounted in each door. The system consists of the switches, actuators, lock and unlock relays, Body Control Module (BCM) and associated wiring. Diagnosis can usually be limited to simple checks of the wiring connections and actuators for minor faults that can be easily repaired.

2   Power door lock systems are operated by bi-directional solenoids located in the doors. The lock actuators are mounted as part of the door latch. Remove the door latch for access to the door lock actuator. The lock switches have two operating positions: Lock and Unlock. These switches send a signal to the BCM, which in turn sends a signal to the door lock relays, the relays then send the needed voltage to each of the door lock solenoids.

3   If you are unable to locate the trouble using the following general steps, consult your dealer service department or qualified independent repair shop.

4   Always check the circuit protection first. Some vehicles use a combination of circuit breakers and fuses.

5   Check for voltage at the switches. If no voltage is present, check the fuse first. If the fuse is good then check the wiring between

the fuse panel and the switches for an open lead.

6   If voltage is present, test the switch for continuity. Replace it if there's not continuity in both switch positions. There should be a voltage input and, when switch is depressed, voltage should be going out on the appropriate lead. Follow the wiring diagram for the actual wire and position on the switch. To remove the switch, use a flat-bladed trim tool to pry out the door/window switch assembly.

7   If the switch has continuity, check the wiring between the switch, BCM, door lock relay and the door lock solenoid.

8   If all but one of the lock solenoids operates, remove the trim panel from the affected door and check for voltage at the solenoid while the lock switch is operated. One of the wires should have positive voltage in the Lock position; the other lead should have positive voltage in the Unlock position.

9   If the inoperative solenoid is receiving positive voltage on one lead and negative on the other, the solenoid is most likely defective. Check the connections for good contact; if the connection is good, replace the solenoid.

10   If the inoperative solenoid isn't receiving voltage or ground, check for an open or short in the wire between the lock solenoid and the relay. A good method of non-destructive testing is to squeeze the rubber corrugated tubing and search with your fingers for an individual wire. Follow the wire as far as possible and feel for any breaks in the leads.

Note: *It's not uncommon for wires to break in the portion of the harness between the body and door (opening and closing the door fatigues and eventually breaks the wires).*

11   On the models covered by this manual, power door lock system communication goes through the Body Control Module. If the above tests do not pinpoint a problem, take the vehicle to a dealer or qualified shop with the proper scan tool to retrieve trouble codes from the BCM. Replacing of some components may result in programming issues. To avoid replacing good components always test thoroughly before any parts are deemed faulty.

Keyless entry system

12   The keyless entry system consists of a remote control transmitter that sends a coded infrared signal to a receiver, which then operates the door lock system.

13   Replace the battery when the transmitter doesn't operate the locks at a distance of 10 feet. Normal range should be about 65 feet.

14   For more information on key fob battery replacement, programming and additional keys see Section 6.

26 Daytime Running Lights (DRL) - general information

1   The Daytime Running Lights (DRL) system illuminates the headlights whenever the engine is running. The only exception is with

the engine running and the parking brake engaged. Once the parking brake is released, the lights will remain on as long as the ignition switch is on, even if the parking brake is later applied.

2   The DRL system supplies reduced power to the headlights so they won't be too bright for daytime use, while prolonging headlight life.

---

27   Airbag system - general information

General information

1   All models are equipped with a Supplemental Restraint System (SRS), more commonly known as airbags. This system is designed to protect the driver, and the front seat passenger, from serious injury in the event of a head-on or frontal collision. It uses an electronic crash sensor (ESC) (also known as the Restraints Control Module [RCM] on later models) mounted on the center tunnel behind the instrument panel. The airbag assemblies are mounted on the steering wheel and the right side of the passenger's side dash. Seat belt pre-tensioners are also incorporated. These are pyrotechnic devices controlled by the Restraints Control Module (RCM) that reduce the slack in the seat belts during an impact of sufficient force to trigger the airbags.

Airbag module

Driver's side

2   The airbag inflator module contains a housing incorporating the cushion (airbag) and inflator unit, mounted in the center of the steering wheel. The inflator assembly is mounted on the back of the housing over a hole through which gas is expelled, inflating the bag almost instantaneously when an electrical signal is sent from the system. A "clockspring" on the steering column under the steering wheel carries this signal to the module.

3   This clockspring assembly can transmit an electrical signal regardless of steering wheel position. The igniter in the airbag converts the electrical signal to heat and ignites the powder, which inflates the bag.

Passenger's side

4   The airbag is mounted above the glove compartment and designated by the letters SRS (Supplemental Restraint System). It consists of an inflator containing an igniter, a reaction housing/airbag assembly and a trim cover.

5   The airbag is considerably larger than the steering wheel-mounted unit and is supported by the steel reaction housing. The trim cover is textured and painted to match the instrument panel and has a molded seam which splits when the bag inflates.

Electronic crash sensor (ESC)/Restraints Control Module (RCM) diagnostic unit

6   This unit supplies the current to the airbag system (and seat belt pre-tensioners, on models so equipped) in the event of the collision, even if battery power is cut off. It checks this system every time the vehicle is started, causing the "SRS" light to go on and then off, if the system is operating properly. If there is a fault in the system, the light will go on and stay on, flash, or the dash will make a beeping sound. If this happens, the vehicle should be taken to your dealer immediately for service.

Servicing components near the SRS system

7   There are times when you need to remove the steering wheel, the instrument cluster, the radio, the heater/air conditioning control assembly or other components that are near airbag components. At these times you'll be working around components and wire harnesses for the SRS system. Do not use electrical test equipment on airbag system wires; it could cause the airbag(s) to deploy. ALWAYS DISABLE THE SRS SYSTEM BEFORE WORKING NEAR THE SRS SYSTEM COMPONENTS OR RELATED WIRING.

Disarming the system and other precautions

Warning: *Failure to follow these precautions could result in accidental deployment of the airbag and personal injury.*

8   Whenever working in the vicinity of the steering wheel, instrument panel or any of the other SRS system components, the system must be disarmed. To disarm the system:

Disabling

Warning: *If the SRS light on the instrument panel does not turn off after 30 seconds of turning the key to the On position, do not proceed. Have the SRS system diagnosed by a dealer service department or other properly equipped shop.*

9   Turn off all accessories on the vehicle and disconnect any memory-saver devices. Turn off the ignition switch.

10   Disconnect the cable from the negative terminal of the battery (see Chapter 5).

11   Wait at least two minutes before proceeding with any work.

Enabling

12   To enable a functional SRS system, simply reconnect the battery. When turning the key to the On position, do so from outside the vehicle, reaching between the steering wheel and the instrument panel.

Warning: *When the battery cable is connected or the ignition switch is turned to On, no one should be in front of any airbag module, in case of accidental deployment.*

13   To test if the SRS system is working properly, turn the ignition switch from On to Off for ten seconds, then back to On. The warning light should illuminate for six seconds and go out.

14   The warning light indicates a problem with the SRS system if the light blinks, stays illuminated continuously, or fails to illuminate in one minute. If one of these conditions exists, have your system checked with a scan tool at a dealership.

Precautions

15   Whenever handling an airbag module, always keep the airbag opening (the trim side) pointed away from your body. Never place the airbag module on a bench or other surface with the airbag opening facing the surface. Always place the airbag module in a safe location with the airbag opening facing up.

16   Never measure the resistance of any SRS component or use any electrical test equipment on any of the wiring or components. An ohmmeter has a built-in battery supply that could accidentally deploy the airbag.

17   Never use electrical welding equipment on a vehicle equipped with an airbag without first disconnecting the airbag electrical connectors, located under the steering column near the combination switch connector (driver's airbag) (see Chapter 10) and behind the glovebox (passenger's airbag). On models with seat belt pre-tensioners, the pretensioner electrical connectors are located behind the B-pillar trim panels and/or under the seats, depending on the model.

18   Never dispose of a live airbag module or seat belt pre-tensioner. Return it to a dealer service department or other qualified repair shop for safe deployment and disposal.

Airbag module - removal and installation

Driver's side airbag module and clockspring

19   Refer to *Steering wheel - removal and installation* in Chapter 10 for the driver's side airbag module and clockspring removal and installation procedures.

Passenger's side airbag module

20   Disarm the airbag system as described previously in this Section.

21   Lower the glove box door fully to gain access to the airbag by pressing the glovebox door tabs and pushing down, then unplug the electrical connector and remove the airbag module mounting nuts and bolts. Be sure to heed the precautions outlined previously in this Section.

22   Carefully slide a flat-bladed screwdriver under the right bottom edge of the airbag panel and lift up. Separate the panel from the clips.

23   Installation is the reverse of the removal procedure. Tighten the airbag module mounting screws securely.

28 Wiring diagrams - general information

1   Since it isn't possible to include all wiring diagrams for every year covered by this manual, the following diagrams are those that are typical and most commonly needed.

2   Prior to troubleshooting any circuits, check the fuse and circuit breakers (if equipped) to make sure they're in good condition. Make sure the battery is properly charged and check the cable connections (see Chapter 1).

3   When checking a circuit, make sure that all connectors are clean, with no broken or loose terminals. When unplugging a connector, do not pull on the wires. Pull only on the connector housings themselves.

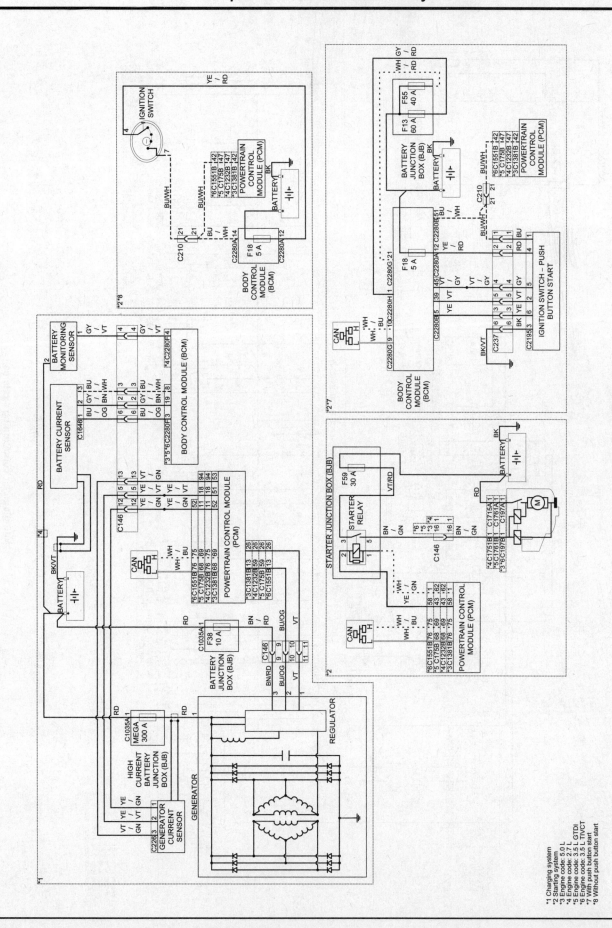

Starting and charging systems

*1 Charging system
*2 Starting system
*3 Engine code: 5.0 L
*4 Engine code: 2.7 L
*5 Engine code: 3.5 L GTDI
*6 Engine code: 3.5 L TIVCT
*7 With push button start
*8 Without push button start

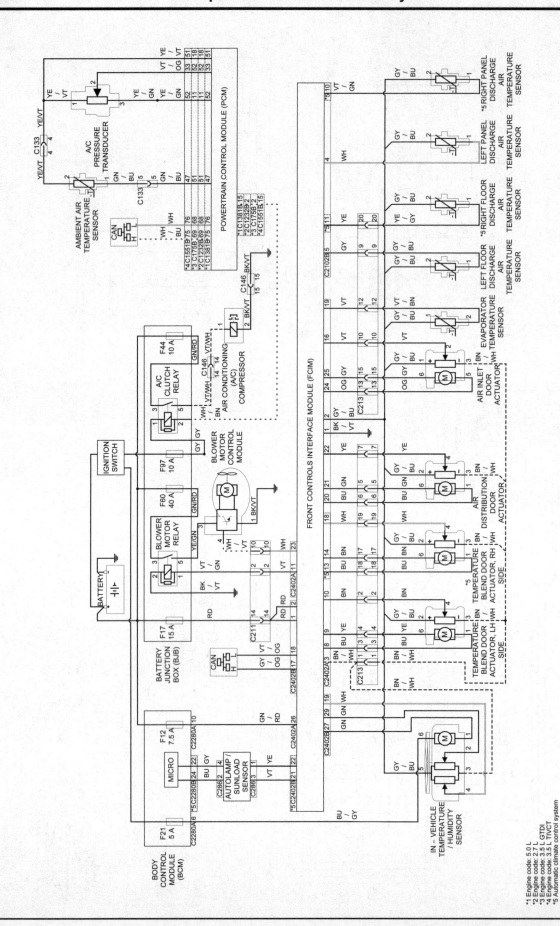

Heating and air conditioning systems

*1 Engine code: 5.0 L
*2 Engine code: 2.7 L GTDI
*3 Engine code: 3.5 L GTDI
*4 Engine code: 3.5 L TiVCT
*5 Automatic climate control system

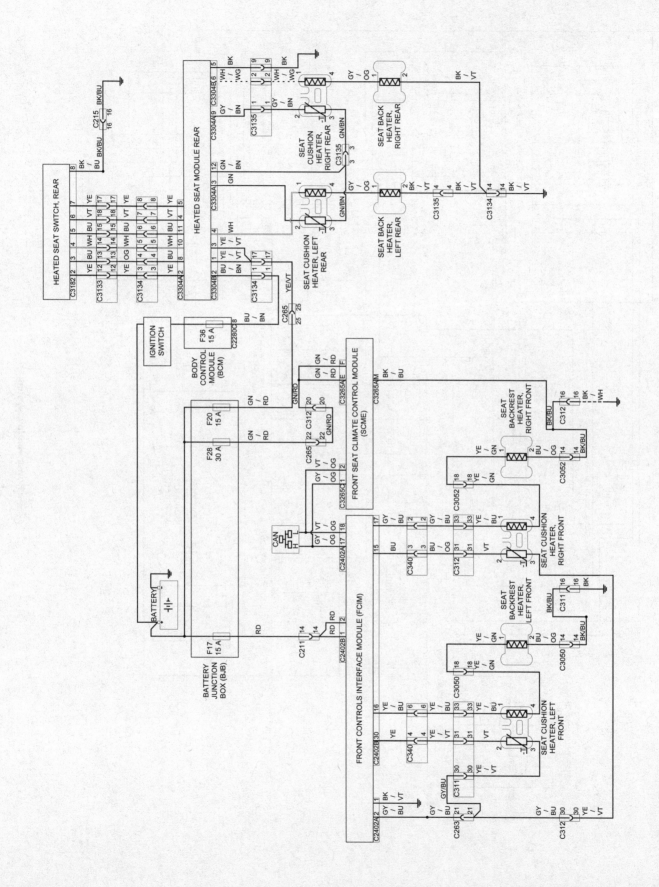

Heated seating system

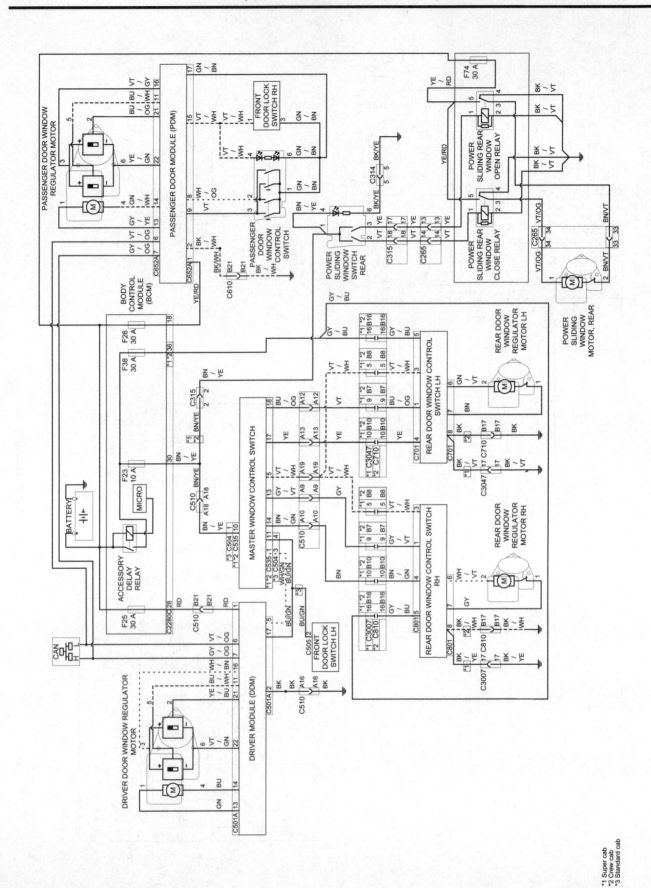

Power window system

*1 Super cab
*2 Crew cab
*3 Standard cab

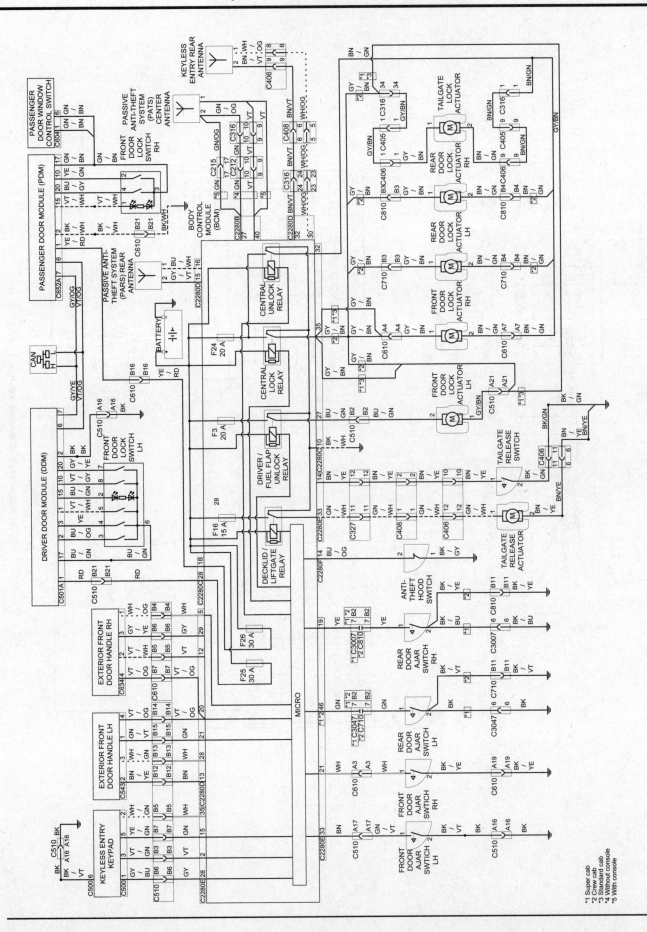

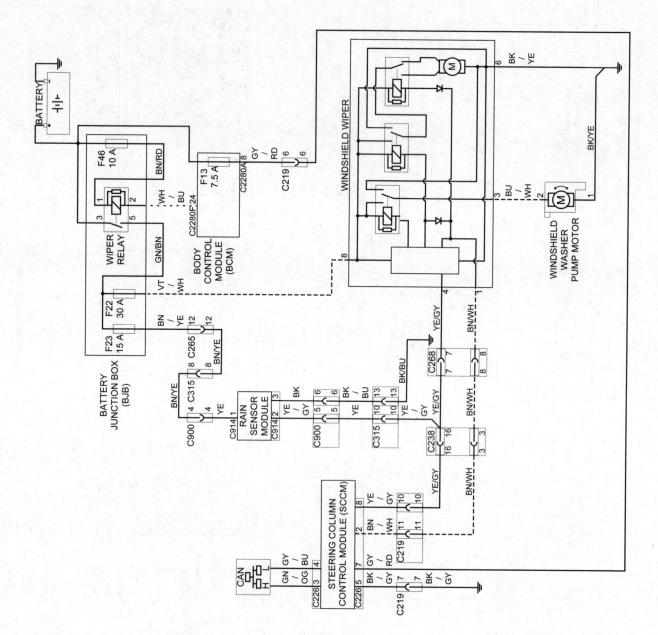

Windshield wiper and washer system

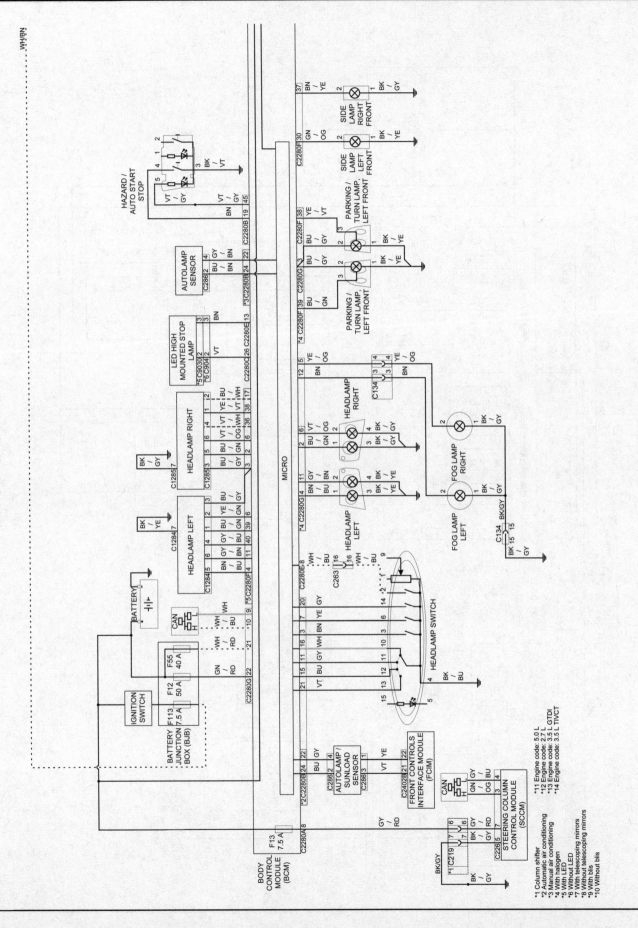

Exterior lighting system (1 of 2)

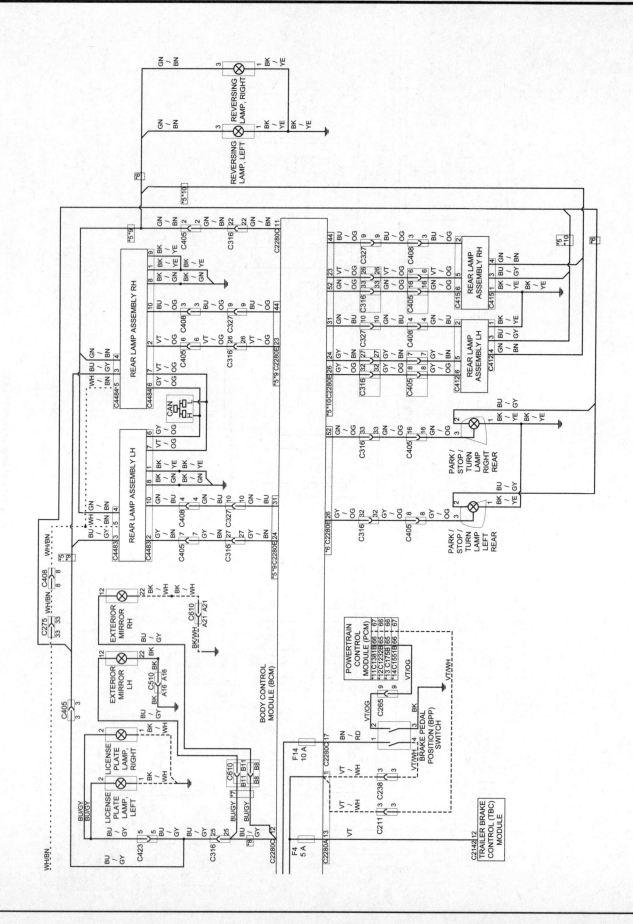

Exterior lighting system (2 of 2)

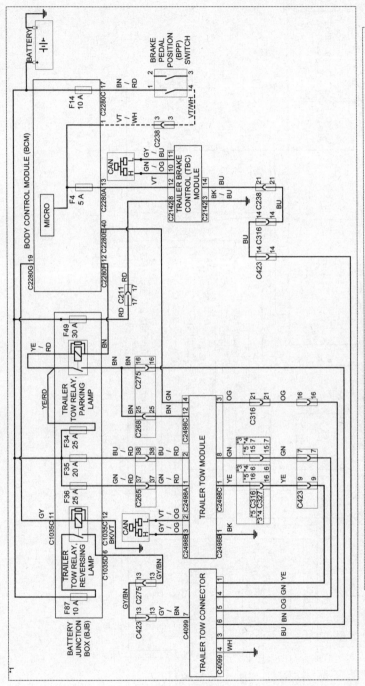

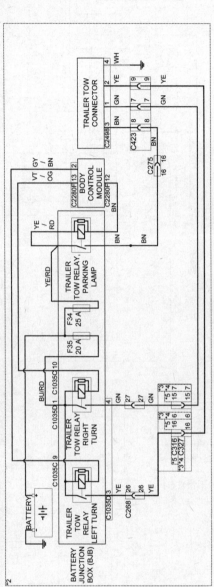

Trailer wiring system

*1 7-way trailer row
*2 4-way trailer row
*3 Super cab
*4 Crew cab
*5 Standard cab

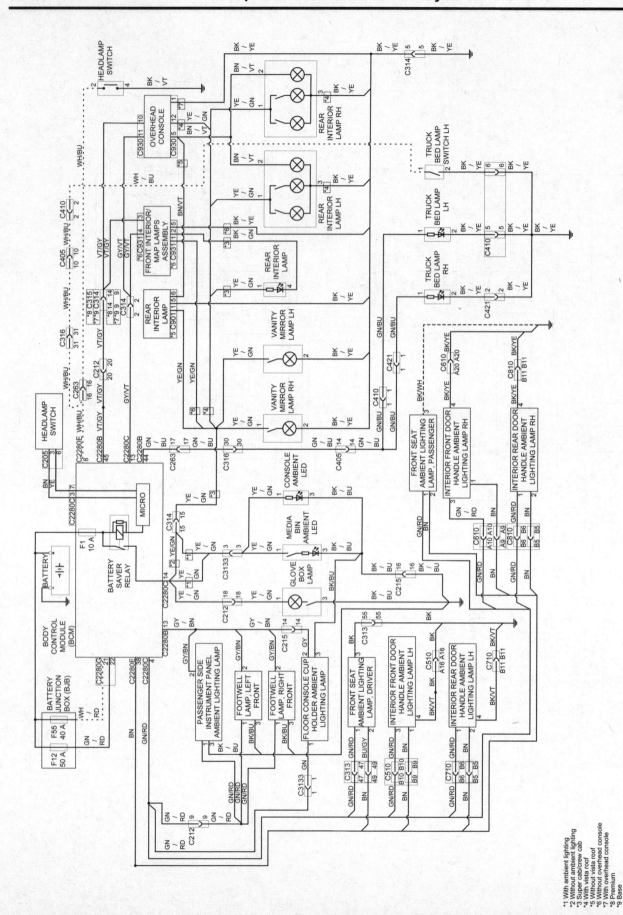

Interior lighting system

*1 With ambient lighting
*2 Without ambient lighting
*3 Super cab/screw cab
*4 With vista roof
*5 Without vista roof
*6 Without overhead console
*7 With overhead console
*8 Premium
*9 Base

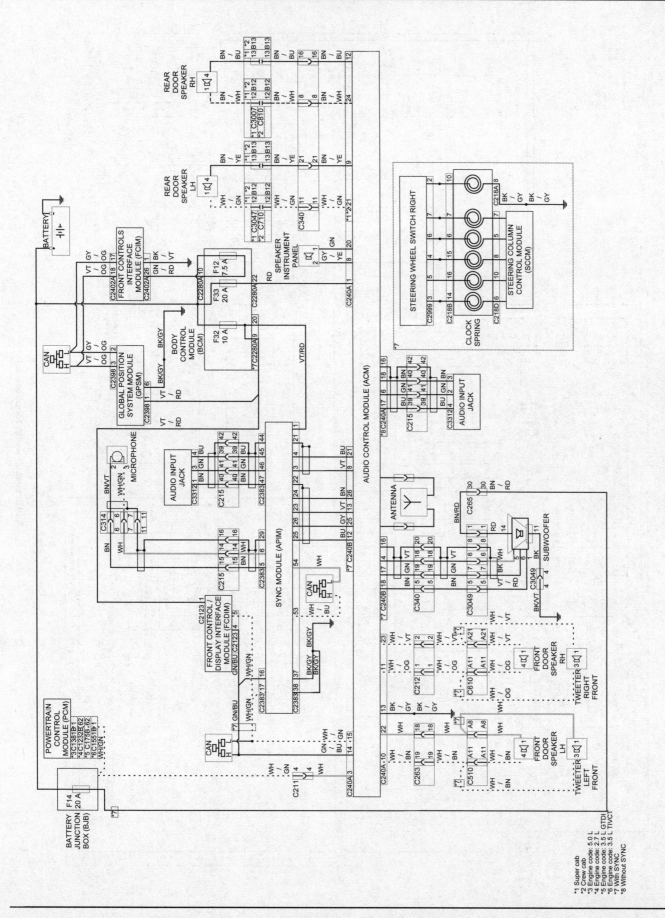

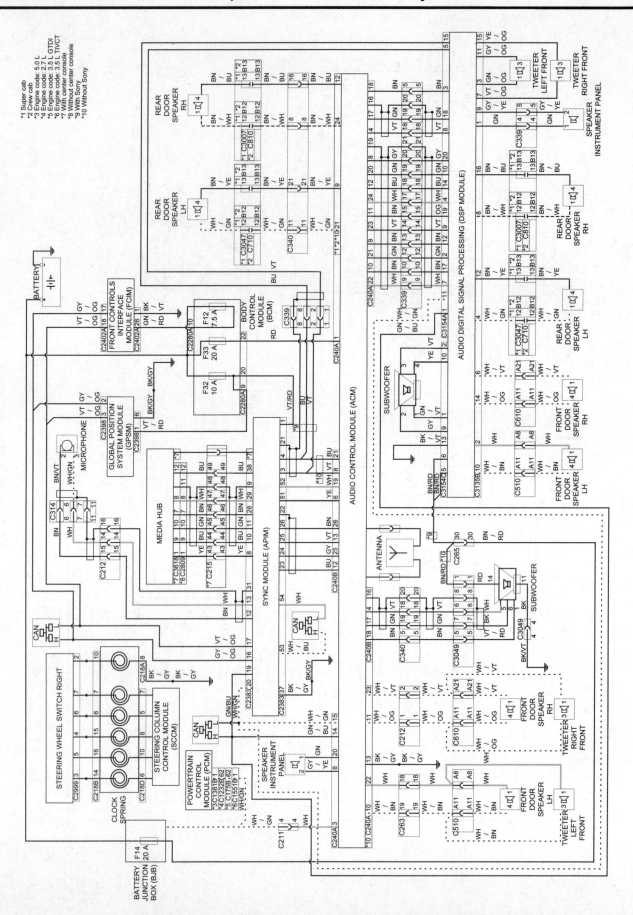

Audio system - with touchscreen

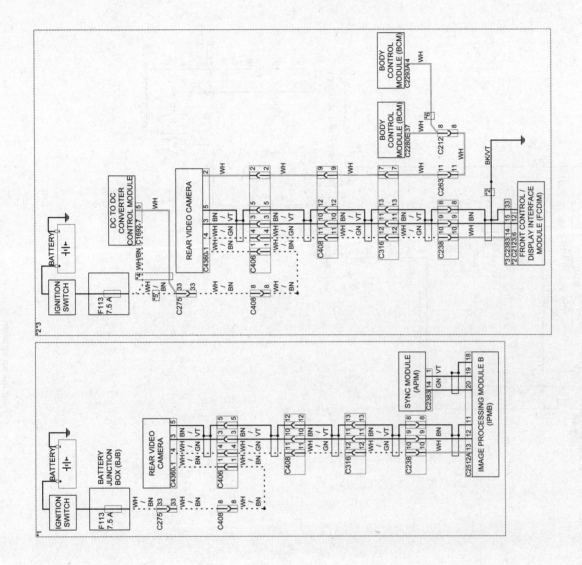

Rear-view camera system

*1 With 360 camera
*2 Without 360 camera SYNC 1
*3 Without 360 camera SYNC 2
*4 With start-stop
*5 Without start-stop
*6 With inverter

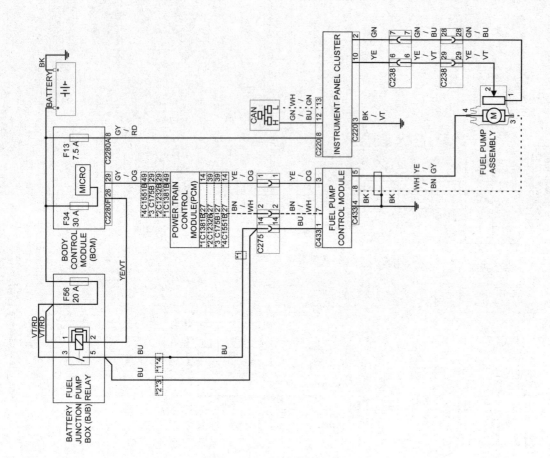

Fuel pump system

*1 Engine code: 5.0 L
*2 Engine code: 2.7 L
*3 Engine code: 3.5 L GTDI
*4 Engine code: 3.5 L TIVCT

BATTERY JUNCTION BOX (BJB)

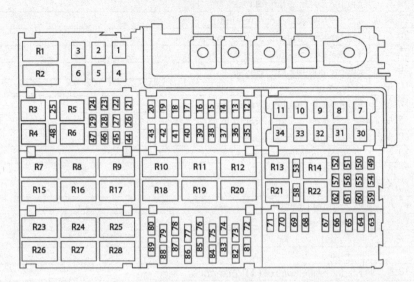

FUSE/RELAY	VALUE	DESCRIPTION
F1	-	Not used
F2	-	Not used
F3	-	Not used
F4	40 A	Rear window defrost grid
F5	-	Not used
F6	-	Not used
F7	-	Not used
F8	-	Not used
F9	60 A	ABS module
F10	50 A	Body control module (BCM)
F11	60 A	Body control module (BCM)
F12	20 A	Audio digital signal processing (DSP) module, subwoofer amplifier
F13	25 A	Transfer case control module
F14	10 A	Spot lamp module (SLM)
F15	15 A	Front controls interface module (FCIM)
F16	10 A	Steering column lock relay
F17	10 A	Multi-contour sear relay
F18	15 A	Rear heated seat / snow plow relay, Heated seat module rear
F19	-	Not used
F20	-	Not used
F21	30 A	Windshield wiper
F22	15 A	Rain sensor module
F23	25 A	Engine cooling fan relays, Engine cooling fan motor 2
F24	-	Not used
F25	-	Not used
F26	30 A	Driver seat module (DSM), Seat control switch, driver side front
F27	30 A	Seat control switch, passenger side front
F28	30 A	Front seat climate control module (SCME)
F29	-	Not used

Chapter 12 Chassis electrical system

F30	50 A	Engine cooling fan relay 3
F31	25 A	Trailer tow relay, parking lamp
F32	20 A	Trailer tow module, Trailer tow relays
F33	25 A	Trailer tow module
F34	50 A	Engine cooling fan relay 1
F35	10 A	Generator
F36	10 A	Integrated wheel end (IWE) solenoid
F37	15 A	Transfer case control module (TCCM)
F38	10 A	Telescoping mirror relays
F39	30 A	Transmission fluid pump
F40	25 A	Horn relay
F41	10 A	A/C clutch relay
F42	10 A	PCM power relay
F43	10 A	Wiper relay
F44	-	Not used
F45	-	Not used
F46	30 A	Trailer brake control (TBC) module
F47	30 A	Power running board (PRB) module
F48	-	Not used
F49	30 A	DC to DC converter control module. Body control module (BCM), Fuses 6,7,12,13,32,33
F50	40 A	Body control module (BCM)
F51	20 A	Fuel pump relay
F52	30 A	Electronic park brake module
F53	15 A	Exterior mirrors
F54	30 A	Electronic park brake module
F55	30 A	Starter relay
F56	40 A	Blower motor relay
F57	30 A	ABS module
F58	-	Not used
F59	-	Not used
F60	25 A	Transfer Case control module (TCCM)
F61	-	Not used
F62	30 A	Power sliding rear window open and close relay
F63	-	Not used
F64	-	Not used
F65	-	Not used
F66	10 A	Trailer tow relay, reversing lamp
F67	-	Not used
F68	20 A	Power point 1, instrument panel
F69	20 A	Power point 2, instrument panel, Power point, console front
F70	20 A	Power point, console rear, Power point, seat
F71	20 A	Power point, console center
F72	25 A	Power train control module (PCM), 10 A also used
F73	-	Not used
F74	25 A	Evap valves, Fuel vapor vent valve, Heated oxygen sensor, Variable camshaft timing solenoids, Intake manifold tuning valves
F75	-	Not used

Fuses and relays (2 of 5)

F76	10 A	A/C clutch relay, Engine cooling fan relays, Active grille shutters, Turbocharger Bypass valve (TCBY), Temperature control valve, transmission fluid warmer, Westgate control solenoid, oil pressure control solenoid, Cabin heater coolant pump
F77	-	Not used
F78	20 A	Ignition coil -on-plugs, 15 A also used
F79	-	Not used
F80	-	Not used
F81	10 A	Power steering control module (PSCM)
F82	-	Not used
F83	10 A	ABS module
F84	-	Not used
F85	10 A	Powertrain control module (PCM)
F86	10 A	Transfer case control module, Cruise control module (C-CM)
F87	10 A	Transmission fluid pump
F88	-	Not used
F89	7.5 A	DC to DC converter control module, Video cameras, Rear lamp assemblies
R1	-	Telescoping exterior rear view mirror retract relay
R2	-	Telescoping exterior rear view mirror retract relay
R3	-	Not used
R4	-	Not used
R5	-	A/C clutch relay
R6	-	Fuel pump relay
R7	-	Engine cooling fan relay 1
R8	-	Power sliding rear window open relay
R9	-	Blower motor relay
R10	-	Wiper relay
R11	-	PCM power relay
R12	-	Starter relay
R13	-	Not used
R14	-	Multi-contour sear relay
R15	-	Not used
R16	-	Power sliding rear window close relay
R17	-	Not used
R18	-	Rear window defrost relay
R19	-	Trailer tow relay, parking lamp
R20	-	Not used
R21	-	Steering column lock relay
R22	-	Horn relay
R23	-	Engine cooling fan relay 3
R24	-	Not used
R25	-	Rear heated seat / snow plow relay
R26	-	Not used
R27	-	Not used
R28	-	Engine cooling fan relay 2

BODY CONTROL MODULE (BCM)

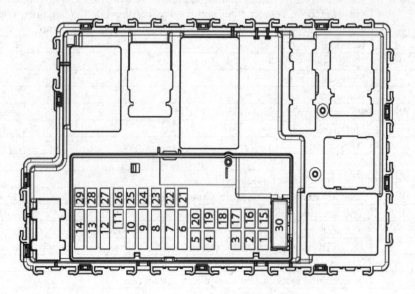

FUSE/RELAY	VALUE	DESCRIPTION
F1	10 A	Battery saver relay
F2	7.5 A	Driver seat module (DSM), Seat control switch, driver side front
F3	20 A	Driver / Fuel flap unlock relay, Double / Aux lock relay
F4	5 A	Trailer brake control (TBC) module, Powertrain control module (PCM), Brake pedal Position (BPP) switch
F5	20 A	Not used
F6	10 A	Not used
F7	10 A	Security horn relay or not used
F8	10 A	Intrusion sensor or not used
F9	7.5 A	Gateway module, Front controls interface module (FCM), Steering column control module (SCCM), Instrument panel cluster (IPC)
F10	10 A	Brake pedal position (BPP) switch, Gateway module
F11	15 A	Decklid / liftgate relay, Child lock relay
F12	5 A	Head Up display (HUD) module, Ignition switch-push button start, Ignition switch
F13	5 A	Floor shifter, Overdrive cancel switch, Telematics module
F14	5 A	In-vehicle temperature / humidity sensor, Head Up display (HUD) module
F15	10 A	Master window control switch, DC / AC inverter module, Roof opening panel module, Power sliding window switch, rear
F16	20 A	Central lock relay, Central unlock relay
F17	30 A	Driver door module (DDM)
F18	30 A	Passenger Door module (PDM)
F19	30 A	Roof opening panel module, sunshade module
F20	-	Not used
F21	-	Not used
F22	-	Not used
F23	15 A	Adjustable pedal switch
F24	10 A	Global position system module (GPSM), Sync module (APIM), Radio transceiver module (RTM), Front control / display interface module (FCDIM)
F25	20 A	Audio control module (RCM)

F26	30 A	Ignition relay
F27	10 A	Restraints control module (RCM)
F28	15 A	Auto-diming interior mirror, Heated seat module rear, Image processing module B (IPMB), Heated steering wheel module (HSWN)
F29	15 A	Battery junction box (BJB)
F30	30 A	Rear door window control switches

Notes

Index

A

About this manual, 0-5
Accelerator Pedal Position (APP) sensor
    replacement, 6-23
    replacement and adjustment, 4-4
Adjustable brake pedal and bracket - removal, installation and indexing, 9-22
Air bypass valve - removal and installation, 4-15
Air conditioning and heater
    blower/control module - replacement, 3-13
    control module - removal and installation, 3-15
Air conditioning and heating system - check and maintenance, 3-5
Air conditioning
    compressor - removal and installation, 3-15
    condenser - removal and installation, 3-16
    evaporator core - removal and installation, 3-16
    pressure cycling switch - replacement, 3-16
    receiver-drier (desiccant bag) - removal and installation, 3-15
    thermostatic expansion valve (TXV) - general information, 3-17
Air filter
    check and replacement, 1-23
    housing - removal and installation, 4-10
Airbag system - general information, 12-23
Alternator - removal and installation, 5-6
Antenna and cable - removal and installation, 12-14
Anti-lock Brake System (ABS) - general information, 9-7
Automatic transmission fluid
    and filter change, 1-24
    fluid level check, 1-12
Automatic transmission, 7A-1
    Automatic transmission - removal and installation, 7A-7
    Automatic transmission overhaul - general information, 7A-9
    Auxiliary cooling - component removal and installation, 7A-6
    Diagnosis - general, 7A-2
    General information, 7A-2

    Output shaft seal - replacement, 7A-7
    Shift cable - removal, installation and adjustment, 7A-4
    Shift interlock system - description, check and actuator replacement, 7A-5
    Shift lever - removal and installation, 7A-3
    Steering wheel paddle shifters - replacement, 7A-5
    Transmission auxiliary fluid pump - replacement, 7A-6
    Transmission Control Module (TCM) (10-speed transmission) - replacement, 7A-6
    Transmission mount - replacement, 7A-7
    Transmission Range (TR) sensor - description and adjustment, 7A-5
Automotive chemicals and lubricants, 0-18
Auxiliary cooling - component removal and installation, 7A-6

B

Balljoints - check and replacement, 10-9
Battery
    and battery tray - removal and installation, 5-4
    disconnection and reconnection, 5-4
    cables and sensors - replacement, 5-5
    check, maintenance and charging, 1-15
Block heater - replacement, 3-18
Body, 11-1
    Body repair - major damage, 11-3
    Body repair - minor damage, 11-2
    Bumpers - removal and installation, 11-9
    Center console - removal and installation, 11-29
    Cowl covers - removal and installation, 11-28
    Dashboard trim panels – removal and installation, 11-19
    Door latch, lock cylinder and handle - removal and installation, 11-14
    Door trim panels - removal and installation, 11-12
    Door window glass - removal and installation, 11-16
    Door window glass regulator - removal and installation, 11-16

Door(s) - removal, installation and adjustment, 11-13

Fastener and trim removal, 11-5

Front fender - removal and installation, 11-10

General information, 11-1

Hinges and locks - maintenance, 11-6

Hood - removal, installation and adjustment, 11-6

Hood latch and release cable - removal and installation, 11-7

Hood support struts - removal and installation, 11-6

Instrument panel - removal and installation, 11-22

Mirrors - removal and installation, 11-17

Radiator grille and headlight housing trim – removal and installation, 11-7

Repair minor paint scratches, 11-2

Seats - removal and installation, 11-26

Steering column covers - removal and installation, 11-25

Tailgate - removal and installation, 11-18

Tailgate latch, release handle, actuator and lock cylinder - removal and installation, 11-18

Upholstery, carpets and vinyl trim - maintenance, 11-5

Windshield and fixed glass - replacement, 11-6

Booster battery (jump) starting, 0-16

Brake check, 1-21

Brake fluid change, 1-25

Brakes, 9-1

Adjustable brake pedal and bracket - removal, installation and indexing, 9-22

Anti-lock Brake System (ABS) - general information, 9-7

Brake disc - inspection, removal and installation, 9-13

Brake hoses and lines - inspection and replacement, 9-20

Brake hydraulic system - bleeding, 9-20

Brake light switch - replacement, 9-22

Brake vacuum pump (2.7L V6 models) - removal and installation, 9-22

Cable-actuated parking brake - component replacement, 9-14

Disc brake caliper - removal and installation, 9-12

Disc brake pads - replacement, 9-8

Electronic Parking Brake (EPB) - general information, troubleshooting, deactivation/ activation and component replacement, 9-17

General information and precautions, 9-2

Master cylinder - removal and installation, 9-18

Power brake booster - check, removal and installation, 9-21

Troubleshooting, 9-3

Bulb - replacement, 12-18

Bumpers - removal and installation, 11-9

Buying parts, 0-9

C

Cabin air filter replacement, 1-22

Cable-actuated parking brake - component replacement, 9-14

Camshaft Position (CMP) sensor - replacement, 6-25

Camshaft(s) - removal, inspection and installation, 2B-10

Camshafts and tappets/roller followers and lash adjusters - removal, inspection and installation, 2A-15

Catalytic converter, 6-31

Center console - removal and installation, 11-29

Chassis electrical system, 12-1

Airbag system - general information, 12-23

Antenna and cable - removal and installation, 12-14

Bulb - replacement, 12-18

Circuit breakers - general information, 12-4

Cruise control system - general information, 12-21

Daytime Running Lights (DRL) - general information, 12-22

Electrical troubleshooting - general information, 12-1

Front Controls Interface Module (FCIM)/Front Controls Interface Display Module (FCDIM), radio and speakers - removal and installation, 12-12

Fuses and fusible links - general information, 12-4

General information, 12-1

Headlight bulb - replacement, 12-15

Headlight housing - removal and installation, 12-16

Headlight lens refurbishing, 12-18

Headlights – adjustment, 12-16

Horn - replacement, 12-18

Ignition switch and key lock cylinder - replacement, 12-8

Instrument cluster - removal and installation, 12-10

Instrument panel switches - replacement, 12-9

Key fob - programming, battery replacement, key fob strength testing/driver's door keypad - removal and installation, 12-5

Mirrors - description, 12-21

Power door lock and keyless entry system - description and check, 12-22

Power window system - description and check, 12-21

Rear window defogger - check and repair, 12-14

Relays - general information and testing, 12-4

Steering column switches - replacement, 12-7

Turn signal and hazard flasher - check and replacement, 12-6

Wiper motor - check and replacement, 12-11

Wiring diagrams - general information, 12-24

Chassis lubrication, 1-15

Circuit breakers - general information, 12-4

Conversion factors, 0-19

Cooling, heating and air conditioning system, 3-1

Air conditioning and heater blower/control module - replacement, 3-13

Air conditioning and heater control module - removal and installation, 3-15

Air conditioning and heating system - check and maintenance, 3-5

Air conditioning compressor - removal and installation, 3-15

Air conditioning condenser - removal and installation, 3-16

Air conditioning evaporator core - removal and installation, 3-16

Air conditioning pressure cycling switch - replacement, 3-16

Air conditioning receiver-drier (desiccant bag) - removal and installation, 3-15

Air conditioning thermostatic expansion valve (TXV) - general information, 3-17

Block heater - replacement, 3-18

Coolant temperature sending unit - general information, 3-12

Cooling fan and shroud - removal and installation, 3-8

Cooling module - removal and installation, 3-10

Expansion tank - removal and installation, 3-8

General information, 3-2

Heater core - removal and installation, 3-13

Interior cabin heater coolant pump - removal and installation, 3-14

Oil cooler - removal and installation, 3-17

Radiator - removal and installation, 3-9

Thermostat - replacement, 3-7

Troubleshooting, 3-3

Water pump - removal and installation, 3-11

Cooling system

check, 1-19

servicing (draining, flushing and refilling), 1-23

Cowl covers - removal and installation, 11-28

Crankshaft - removal and installation, 2C-14

Crankshaft Position (CKP) sensor - replacement, 6-24

Crankshaft pulley

and crankshaft front seal - replacement, 2A-9

and front oil seal - removal and installation, 2B-6

Cruise control system - general information, 12-21

Cylinder compression check, 2C-4

Cylinder Head Temperature (CHT) sensor - replacement, 6-24

Cylinder heads - removal and installation

V6 engines, 2A-10

V8 engine, 2B-12

D

Dashboard trim panels – removal and installation, 11-19

Daytime Running Lights (DRL) - general information, 12-22

Diagnosis - general, 7A-2

Differential lubricant

change, 1-30

lubricant level check, 1-22

Disc brake

caliper - removal and installation, 9-12

pads - replacement, 9-8

Door latch, lock cylinder and handle - removal and installation, 11-14

Door trim panels - removal and installation, 11-12

Door window glass

regulator - removal and installation, 11-16

removal and installation, 11-16

Door(s) - removal, installation and adjustment, 11-13

Drivebelt check and replacement, 1-26

Driveline, 8-1

Driveshaft center support bearing - check and replacement, 8-3

Driveshaft(s) - removal and installation, 8-2

Front axle assembly (4WD models) - removal and installation, 8-4

Front driveaxles (4WD models) - removal and installation, 8-3

General information, 8-2

Pinion oil seal - replacement, 8-6

Rear axle assembly - removal and installation, 8-4

Rear axleshaft - removal and installation, 8-5

Rear axleshaft bearing - replacement, 8-6

Rear axleshaft oil seal - replacement, 8-5

Universal joints - replacement, 8-3

Driveplate - removal and installation, 2A-20

E

Electric shift motor - replacement, 7B-2

Electrical troubleshooting - general information, 12-1

Electronic Parking Brake (EPB) - general information, troubleshooting, deactivation/ activation and component replacement, 9-17

Emissions and engine control systems, 6-1

Accelerator Pedal Position (APP) sensor - replacement, 6-23

Camshaft Position (CMP) sensor - replacement, 6-25

Catalytic converter, 6-31

Crankshaft Position (CKP) sensor - replacement, 6-24

Cylinder Head Temperature (CHT) sensor - replacement, 6-24

Engine Coolant Temperature (ECT) sensor - replacement, 6-23

Engine Oil Pressure (EOP) sensor - replacement, 6-25

Evaporative emissions control (EVAP) system - general description and component replacement, 6-30

Fuel rail pressure/temperature sensor - replacement, 6-30

Fuel tank pressure (FTP) sensor - replacement, 6-29

General information, 6-2

Intake Air Temperature (IAT) sensor - replacement, 6-24

Knock sensors - replacement, 6-29

Manifold Absolute Pressure (MAP) sensor - replacement, 6-24

Obtaining and clearing Diagnostic Trouble Codes (DTCs), 6-2

Oil pressure control solenoid - replacement, 6-26

On Board Diagnosis (OBD) system, 6-2

Oxygen sensors - general information and replacement, 6-28

Positive Crankcase Ventilation (PCV) system, 6-30

Powertrain Control Module (PCM) - removal and installation, 6-23

Turbocharger Boost Pressure (TCPB) and Charge Air Cooler Temperature (CACT) sensor - replacement, 6-27

Turbocharger bypass valve - replacement, 6-27

Turbocharger wastegate vacuum sensor - replacement, 6-28

Variable Camshaft Timing (VCT) variable force solenoid - removal and installation, 6-26

Engine, in-vehicle repair procedures

V6 engines

Camshafts and tappets/roller followers and lash adjusters - removal, inspection and installation, 2A-15

Crankshaft pulley and crankshaft front seal - replacement, 2A-9

Cylinder heads - removal and installation, 2A-10

Driveplate - removal and installation, 2A-20

Engine front cover - removal and installation, 2A-11

Engine mounts - check and replacement, 2A-21

Exhaust manifolds - removal and installation, 2A-9

General information, 2A-4

Intake manifold(s) - removal and installation, 2A-7

Oil pan - removal and installation, 2A-19

Oil pump - removal and installation, 2A-20

Rear main oil seal - replacement, 2A-20

Repair operations possible with the engine in the vehicle, 2A-4

Timing chains and sprockets - removal and installation, 2A-12

Valve clearance (3.5L Duratec and 2016 and earlier 3.5L EcoBoost engines) - check and adjustment, 2A-4

Valve covers - removal and installation, 2A-5

V8 engine
  Camshaft(s) - removal, inspection and
    installation, 2B-10
  Crankshaft pulley and front oil seal - removal
    and installation, 2B-6
  Cylinder heads - removal and installation, 2B-12
  Engine mounts - check and replacement, 2B-15
  Exhaust manifolds - removal and
    installation, 2B-6
  Flywheel/driveplate - removal and
    installation, 2B-15
  General information, 2B-4
  Intake manifold - removal and
    installation, 2B-5
  Oil pan - removal and installation, 2B-13
  Oil pump - removal and installation, 2B-14
  Rear main oil seal - replacement, 2B-15
  Repair operations possible with the engine in
    the vehicle, 2B-4
  Roller followers and valve lash adjusters -
    removal, inspection and installation, 2B-10
  Timing chain cover - removal and
    installation, 2B-7
  Timing chains, tensioners and sprockets -
    removal, inspection and installation, 2B-8
  Top Dead Center (TDC) for number one piston
    - locating, 2B-4
  Valve covers - removal and installation, 2B-4
  Variable Camshaft Timing (VCT) system -
    general information, 2B-10
Engine - removal and installation, 2C-7
Engine Coolant Temperature (ECT) sensor -
  replacement, 6-23
Engine electrical systems, 5-1
  Alternator - removal and installation, 5-6
  Battery - disconnection and reconnection, 5-4
  Battery and battery tray - removal and
    installation, 5-4
  Battery cables and sensors - replacement, 5-5
  General information and precautions, 5-2
  Ignition coils - removal and installation, 5-6
  Starter motor - removal and installation, 5-7
  Troubleshooting, 5-2
Engine front cover - removal and
  installation, 2A-11
Engine mounts - check and replacement
  V6 engines, 2A-21
  V8 engine, 2B-15
Engine oil and filter change, 1-12
Engine Oil Pressure (EOP) sensor -
  replacement, 6-25

Engine overhaul
  disassembly sequence, 2C-8
  reassembly sequence, 2C-18
Engine rebuilding alternatives, 2C-6
Engine removal - methods and
  precautions, 2C-6
Evaporative emissions control (EVAP) system
  - general description and component
  replacement, 6-30
Exhaust manifolds - removal and installation
  V6 engines, 2A-9
  V8 engine, 2B-6
Exhaust system
  check, 1-18
  servicing - general information, 4-16
Expansion tank - removal and installation, 3-8

F

Fastener and trim removal, 11-5
Fluid level checks, 1-8
Flywheel/driveplate - removal and
  installation, 2B-15
Fraction/decimal/millimeter equivalents, 0-20
Front axle assembly (4WD models) - removal
  and installation, 8-4
Front Controls Interface Module (FCIM)/Front
  Controls Interface Display Module (FCDIM),
  radio and speakers - removal and
  installation, 12-12
Front driveaxles (4WD models) - removal and
  installation, 8-3
Front fender - removal and installation, 11-10
Fuel and exhaust systems, 4-1
  Accelerator Pedal Position (APP) sensor -
    replacement and adjustment, 4-4
  Air bypass valve - removal and installation, 4-15
  Air filter housing - removal and installation, 4-10
  Exhaust system servicing - general
    information, 4-16
  Fuel level sending unit - replacement, 4-10
  Fuel lines and fittings - general information and
    disconnection, 4-5
  Fuel pressure regulator - removal and
    installation, 4-10
  Fuel pressure relief procedure, 4-4
  Fuel Pump Driver Module (FPDM) -
    replacement, 4-10
  Fuel pump/fuel pressure - check, 4-4

Fuel pump/fuel pump module - removal and installation, 4-8
Fuel rails and injectors - removal and installation, 4-11
Fuel tank - cleaning and repair, 4-8
Fuel tank - removal and installation, 4-7
General information and precautions, 4-3
High-pressure fuel pump - removal and installation, 4-9
Intercooler - removal and installation, 4-15
Throttle body - removal and installation, 4-10
Troubleshooting, 4-3
Turbocharger(s) - removal and installation, 4-13
Wastegate control actuator - replacement and adjustment, 4-15
Fuel rail pressure/temperature sensor - replacement, 6-30
Fuel system check, 1-19
Fuel tank pressure (FTP) sensor - replacement, 6-29
Fuses and fusible links - general information, 12-4

G

General engine overhaul procedures, 2C-1
Crankshaft - removal and installation, 2C-14
Cylinder compression check, 2C-4
Engine - removal and installation, 2C-7
Engine overhaul - disassembly sequence, 2C-8
Engine overhaul - reassembly sequence, 2C-18
Engine rebuilding alternatives, 2C-6
Engine removal - methods and precautions, 2C-6
General information - engine overhaul, 2C-3
Initial start-up and break-in after overhaul, 2C-18
Oil pressure check, 2C-4
Pistons and connecting rods - removal and installation, 2C-9
Vacuum gauge diagnostic checks, 2C-5

H

Headlight
adjustment, 12-16
bulb - replacement, 12-15
housing - removal and installation, 12-16
lens refurbishing, 12-18

Heater core - removal and installation, 3-13
High-pressure fuel pump - removal and installation, 4-9
Hinges and locks - maintenance, 11-6
Hood
latch and release cable - removal and installation, 11-7
removal, installation and adjustment, 11-6
support struts - removal and installation, 11-6
Horn - replacement, 12-18
Hub and bearing assembly - replacement, 10-9

I

Ignition coil
check and replacement, 1-29
removal and installation, 5-6
Ignition switch and key lock cylinder - replacement, 12-8
Initial start-up and break-in after overhaul, 2C-18
Instrument
cluster - removal and installation, 12-10
panel - removal and installation, 11-22
panel switches - replacement, 12-9
Intake Air Temperature (IAT) sensor - replacement, 6-24
Intake manifold - removal and installation
V6 engines, 2A-7
V8 engine, 2B-5
Intercooler - removal and installation, 4-15
Interior cabin heater coolant pump - removal and installation, 3-14

J

Jacking and towing, 0-17

K

Key fob - programming, battery replacement, key fob strength testing/driver's door keypad - removal and installation, 12-5
Knock sensors - replacement, 6-29

L

Leaf springs - removal and installation, 10-10
Lower control arm - removal and installation, 10-8

M

Maintenance schedule, 1-7
Maintenance techniques, tools and working
    facilities, 0-9
Manifold Absolute Pressure (MAP) sensor -
    replacement, 6-24
Master cylinder - removal and installation, 9-18
Mirrors
    description, 12-21
    removal and installation, 11-17

O

Obtaining and clearing Diagnostic Trouble
    Codes (DTCs), 6-2
Oil cooler - removal and installation, 3-17
Oil pan - removal and installation
    V6 engines, 2A-19
    V8 engine, 2B-13
Oil pressure
    check, 2C-4
    control solenoid - replacement, 6-26
Oil pump - removal and installation
    V6 engines, 2A-20
    V8 engine, 2B-14
On Board Diagnosis (OBD) system, 6-2
Output shaft seal - replacement, 7A-7
Oxygen sensors - general information and
    replacement, 6-28

P

Pinion oil seal - replacement, 8-6
Pistons and connecting rods - removal and
    installation, 2C-9
Positive Crankcase Ventilation (PCV)
    system, 6-30
    check and replacement, 1-27
Power brake booster - check, removal and
    installation, 9-21

Power door lock and keyless entry system -
    description and check, 12-22
Power window system - description and
    check, 12-21
Powertrain Control Module (PCM) - removal and
    installation, 6-23

R

Radiator - removal and installation, 3-9
Radiator grille and headlight housing trim –
    removal and installation, 11-7
Rear axle assembly - removal and
    installation, 8-4
Rear axleshaft
    bearing - replacement, 8-6
    oil seal - replacement, 8-5
    removal and installation, 8-5
Rear main oil seal – replacement
    V6 engines, 2A-20
    V8 engine, 2B-15
Rear output shaft oil seal - replacement, 7B-2
Rear window defogger - check and repair, 12-14
Recall information, 0-7
Relays - general information and testing, 12-4
Repair minor paint scratches, 11-2
Repair operations possible with the engine in
    the vehicle
    V6 engines, 2A-4
    V8 engine, 2B-4
Roller followers and valve lash adjusters -
    removal, inspection and installation, 2B-10

S

Safety first!, 0-21
Seat belt check, 1-18
Seats - removal and installation, 11-26
Shift
    cable - removal, installation and adjustment, 7A-4
    interlock system - description, check and
        actuator replacement, 7A-5
    lever - removal and installation, 7A-3
    range selector switch - replacement, 7B-2
Shock absorber/coil spring (front) - removal,
    component replacement and installation, 10-6
Shock absorbers (rear) - removal and
    installation, 10-10

Spark plug check and replacement, 1-28
Stabilizer bar and bushings - removal and installation, 10-7
Starter motor - removal and installation, 5-7
Steering
gear - removal and installation, 10-14
gear boots - replacement, 10-14
knuckle - removal and installation, 10-8
wheel - removal and installation, 10-11
wheel paddle shifters - replacement, 7A-5
Steering and suspension check, 1-20
Steering column
removal and installation, 10-12
covers - removal and installation, 11-25
switches - replacement, 12-7
Suspension and steering systems, 10-1
Balljoints - check and replacement, 10-9
General information, 10-6
Hub and bearing assembly - replacement, 10-9
Leaf springs - removal and installation, 10-10
Lower control arm - removal and
installation, 10-8
Shock absorber/coil spring (front) - removal,
component replacement and installation, 10-6
Shock absorbers (rear) - removal and
installation, 10-10
Stabilizer bar and bushings - removal and
installation, 10-7
Steering column - removal and installation, 10-12
Steering gear - removal and installation, 10-14
Steering gear boots - replacement, 10-14
Steering knuckle - removal and installation, 10-8
Steering wheel - removal and installation, 10-11
Tie-rod ends - removal and installation, 10-13
Upper control arm - removal and
installation, 10-8
Wheel alignment - general information, 10-15
Wheels and tires - general information, 10-15

T

Tailgate - removal and installation, 11-18
**Tailgate latch, release handle, actuator and lock
cylinder - removal and installation, 11-18**
Thermostat - replacement, 3-7
Throttle body - removal and installation, 4-10
Tie-rod ends - removal and installation, 10-13
**Timing chain cover - removal and
installation, 2B-7**

Timing chains
and sprockets - removal and installation, 2A-12
tensioners and sprockets - removal, inspection
and installation, 2B-8
Tire and tire pressure checks, 1-10
Tire rotation (every 6000 miles or 6 months), 1-17
**Top Dead Center (TDC) for number one piston -
locating, 2B-4**
Transfer case, 7B-1
Electric shift motor - replacement, 7B-2
General information, 7B-2
Rear output shaft oil seal - replacement, 7B-2
Shift range selector switch - replacement, 7B-2
Transfer case - removal and installation, 7B-3
Transfer Case Control Module (TCCM) -
replacement, 7B-2
Transfer case overhaul - general information, 7B-3
Transfer case lubricant
change (4WD models), 1-31
level check (4WD models), 1-22
**Transmission auxiliary fluid pump -
replacement, 7A-6**
**Transmission Control Module (TCM) (10-speed
transmission) - replacement, 7A-6**
Transmission mount - replacement, 7A-7
**Transmission Range (TR) sensor - description
and adjustment, 7A-5**
Tune-up and routine maintenance, 1-1
Air filter check and replacement, 1-23
Automatic transmission fluid and filter change, 1-24
Automatic transmission fluid level check, 1-12
Battery check, maintenance and charging, 1-15
Brake check, 1-21
Brake fluid change, 1-25
Cabin air filter replacement, 1-22
Chassis lubrication, 1-15
Cooling system check, 1-19
Cooling system servicing (draining, flushing and
refilling), 1-23
Differential lubricant change, 1-30
Differential lubricant level check, 1-22
Drivebelt check and replacement, 1-26
Engine oil and filter change, 1-12
Exhaust system check, 1-18
Fluid level checks, 1-8
Fuel system check, 1-19
Ignition coil check and replacement, 1-29
Introduction, 1-8
Maintenance schedule, 1-7

Positive Crankcase Ventilation (PCV) system
   check and replacement, 1-27
Seat belt check, 1-18
Spark plug check and replacement, 1-28
Steering and suspension check, 1-20
Tire and tire pressure checks, 1-10
Tire rotation (every 6000 miles or 6 months), 1-17
Transfer case lubricant change
   (4WD models), 1-31
Transfer case lubricant level check
   (4WD models), 1-22
Tune-up general information, 1-8
Underhood hose check and replacement, 1-18
Windshield wiper blade inspection and
   replacement, 1-17
**Turbocharger Boost Pressure (TCPB) and
Charge Air Cooler Temperature (CACT)
sensor - replacement, 6-27**
Turbocharger
   bypass valve - replacement, 6-27
   wastegate vacuum sensor - replacement, 6-28
Turbocharger(s) - removal and installation, 4-13
**Turn signal and hazard flasher - check and
replacement, 12-6**

U

Underhood hose check and replacement, 1-18
Universal joints - replacement, 8-3
**Upholstery, carpets and vinyl trim -
maintenance, 11-5**
**Upper control arm - removal and
installation, 10-8**

V

V6 engines, 2A-1
   Camshafts and tappets/roller followers and
      lash adjusters - removal, inspection and
      installation, 2A-15
   Crankshaft pulley and crankshaft front seal -
      replacement, 2A-9
   Cylinder heads - removal and installation, 2A-10
   Driveplate - removal and installation, 2A-20
   Engine front cover - removal and installation, 2A-11
   Engine mounts - check and replacement, 2A-21
   Exhaust manifolds - removal and installation, 2A-9
   General information, 2A-4

   Intake manifold(s) - removal and installation, 2A-7
   Oil pan - removal and installation, 2A-19
   Oil pump - removal and installation, 2A-20
   Rear main oil seal - replacement, 2A-20
   Repair operations possible with the engine in the
      vehicle, 2A-4
   Timing chains and sprockets - removal and
      installation, 2A-12
   Valve clearance (3.5L Duratec and 2016 and
      earlier 3.5L EcoBoost engines) - check and
      adjustment, 2A-4
   Valve covers - removal and installation, 2A-5
V8 engine, 2B-1
   Camshaft(s) - removal, inspection and
      installation, 2B-10
   Crankshaft pulley and front oil seal - removal and
      installation, 2B-6
   Cylinder heads - removal and installation, 2B-12
   Engine mounts - check and replacement, 2B-15
   Exhaust manifolds - removal and installation, 2B-6
   Flywheel/driveplate - removal and
      installation, 2B-15
   General information, 2B-4
   Intake manifold - removal and installation, 2B-5
   Oil pan - removal and installation, 2B-13
   Oil pump - removal and installation, 2B-14
   Rear main oil seal - replacement, 2B-15
   Repair operations possible with the engine in the
      vehicle, 2B-4
   Roller followers and valve lash adjusters -
      removal, inspection and installation, 2B-10
   Timing chain cover - removal and installation, 2B-7
   Timing chains, tensioners and sprockets -
      removal, inspection and installation, 2B-8
   Top Dead Center (TDC) for number one piston -
      locating, 2B-4
   Valve covers - removal and installation, 2B-4
   Variable Camshaft Timing (VCT) system -
      general information, 2B-10
Vacuum gauge diagnostic checks, 2C-5
**Valve clearance (3.5L Duratec and 2016 and
earlier 3.5L EcoBoost engines) - check and
adjustment, 2A-4**
Valve covers - removal and installation
   V6 engines, 2A-5
   V8 engine, 2B-4
Variable Camshaft Timing (VCT)
   system - general information, 2B-10
   variable force solenoid - removal and
      installation, 6-26
Vehicle identification numbers, 0-6

W

Wastegate control actuator - replacement and adjustment, 4-15

Water pump - removal and installation, 3-11

Wheel alignment - general information, 10-15

Wheels and tires - general information, 10-15

Windshield and fixed glass - replacement, 11-6

Windshield wiper blade inspection and replacement, 1-17

Wiper motor - check and replacement, 12-11

Wiring diagrams - general information, 12-24

Haynes Automotive Manuals

NOTE: If you do not see a listing for your vehicle, consult your local Haynes dealer for the latest product information.

ACURA
- 12020 **Integra** '86 thru '89 **& Legend** '86 thru '90
- 12021 **Integra** '90 thru '93 **& Legend** '91 thru '95
  - **Integra** '94 thru '00 - see HONDA Civic (42025)
  - **MDX** '01 thru '07 - see HONDA Pilot (42037)
- 12050 **Acura TL** all models '99 thru '08

AMC
- **Jeep CJ** - see JEEP (50020)
- 14020 **Mid-size models** '70 thru '83
- 14025 **(Renault) Alliance & Encore** '83 thru '87

AUDI
- 15020 **4000** all models '80 thru '87
- 15025 **5000** all models '77 thru '83
- 15026 **5000** all models '84 thru '88
  - **Audi A4** '96 thru '01 - see VW Passat (96023)
- 15030 **Audi A4** '02 thru '08

AUSTIN-HEALEY
- **Sprite** - see MG Midget (66015)

BMW
- 18020 **3/5 Series** '82 thru '92
- 18021 **3-Series** incl. Z3 models '92 thru '98
- 18022 **3-Series** incl. Z4 models '99 thru '05
- 18023 **3-Series** '06 thru '10
- 18025 **320i** all 4 cyl models '75 thru '83
- 18050 **1500 thru 2002** except Turbo '59 thru '77

BUICK
- 19010 **Buick Century** '97 thru '05
  - **Century** (front-wheel drive) - see GM (38005)
- 19020 **Buick, Oldsmobile & Pontiac Full-size** (Front-wheel drive) '85 thru '05
  - **Buick Electra, LeSabre and Park Avenue; Oldsmobile Delta 88 Royale, Ninety Eight and Regency; Pontiac Bonneville**
- 19025 **Buick, Oldsmobile & Pontiac Full-size** (Rear wheel drive) '70 thru '90
  - **Buick Estate, Electra, LeSabre, Limited, Oldsmobile Custom Cruiser, Delta 88, Ninety-eight, Pontiac Bonneville, Catalina, Grandville, Parisienne**
- 19030 **Mid-size Regal & Century** all rear-drive models with V6, V8 and Turbo '74 thru '87
  - **Regal** - see GENERAL MOTORS (38010)
  - **Riviera** - see GENERAL MOTORS (38030)
  - **Roadmaster** - see CHEVROLET (24046)
  - **Skyhawk** - see GENERAL MOTORS (38015)
  - **Skylark** - see GM (38020, 38025)
  - **Somerset** - see GENERAL MOTORS (38025)

CADILLAC
- 21015 **CTS & CTS-V** '03 thru '12
- 21030 **Cadillac Rear Wheel Drive** '70 thru '93
  - **Cimarron** - see GENERAL MOTORS (38015)
  - **DeVille** - see GM (38031 & 38032)
  - **Eldorado** - see GM (38030 & 38031)
  - **Fleetwood** - see GM (38031)
  - **Seville** - see GM (38030, 38031 & 38032)

CHEVROLET
- 10305 **Chevrolet Engine Overhaul Manual**
- 24010 **Astro & GMC Safari Mini-vans** '85 thru '05
- 24015 **Camaro V8** all models '70 thru '81
- 24016 **Camaro** all models '82 thru '92
- 24017 **Camaro & Firebird** '93 thru '02
  - **Cavalier** - see GENERAL MOTORS (38016)
  - **Celebrity** - see GENERAL MOTORS (38005)
- 24020 **Chevelle, Malibu & El Camino** '69 thru '87
- 24024 **Chevette & Pontiac T1000** '76 thru '87
  - **Citation** - see GENERAL MOTORS (38020)
- 24027 **Colorado & GMC Canyon** '04 thru '10
- 24032 **Corsica/Beretta** all models '87 thru '96
- 24040 **Corvette** all V8 models '68 thru '82
- 24041 **Corvette** all models '84 thru '96
- 24045 **Full-size Sedans** Caprice, Impala, Biscayne, Bel Air & Wagons '69 thru '90
- 24046 **Impala SS & Caprice and Buick Roadmaster** '91 thru '96
  - **Impala** '00 thru '05 - see LUMINA (24048)
- 24047 **Impala & Monte Carlo** all models '06 thru '11
  - **Lumina** '90 thru '94 - see GM (38010)
- 24048 **Lumina & Monte Carlo** '95 thru '05
  - **Lumina APV** - see GM (38035)
- 24050 **Luv Pick-up** all 2WD & 4WD '72 thru '82
  - **Malibu** '97 thru '00 - see GM (38026)
- 24055 **Monte Carlo** all models '70 thru '88
  - **Monte Carlo** '95 thru '01 - see LUMINA (24048)
- 24059 **Nova** all V8 models '69 thru '79
- 24060 **Nova and Geo Prizm** '85 thru '92
- 24064 **Pick-ups** '67 thru '87 - Chevrolet & GMC
- 24065 **Pick-ups** '88 thru '98 - Chevrolet & GMC

- 24066 **Pick-ups** '99 thru '06 - Chevrolet & GMC
- 24067 **Chevrolet Silverado & GMC Sierra** '07 thru '12
- 24070 **S-10 & S-15 Pick-ups** '82 thru '93, **Blazer & Jimmy** '83 thru '94,
- 24071 **S-10 & Sonoma Pick-ups** '94 thru '04, including **Blazer, Jimmy & Hombre**
- 24072 **Chevrolet TrailBlazer, GMC Envoy & Oldsmobile Bravada** '02 thru '09
- 24075 **Sprint** '85 thru '88 **& Geo Metro** '89 thru '01
- 24080 **Vans** - Chevrolet & GMC '68 thru '96
- 24081 **Chevrolet Express & GMC Savana** Full-size Vans '96 thru '10

CHRYSLER
- 10310 **Chrysler Engine Overhaul Manual**
- 25015 **Chrysler Cirrus, Dodge Stratus, Plymouth Breeze** '95 thru '00
- 25020 **Full-size Front-Wheel Drive** '88 thru '93
  - **K-Cars** - see DODGE Aries (30008)
  - **Laser** - see DODGE Daytona (30030)
- 25025 **Chrysler LHS, Concorde, New Yorker, Dodge** Intrepid, **Eagle** Vision, '93 thru '97
- 25026 **Chrysler LHS, Concorde, 300M, Dodge** Intrepid, '98 thru '04
- 25027 **Chrysler 300, Dodge Charger & Magnum** '05 thru '09
- 25030 **Chrysler & Plymouth Mid-size** front wheel drive '82 thru '95
  - **Rear-wheel Drive** - see Dodge (30050)
- 25035 **PT Cruiser** all models '01 thru '10
- 25040 **Chrysler Sebring** '95 thru '06, **Dodge** Stratus '01 thru '06, **Dodge** Avenger '95 thru '00

DATSUN
- 28005 **200SX** all models '80 thru '83
- 28007 **B-210** all models '73 thru '78
- 28009 **210** all models '79 thru '82
- 28012 **240Z, 260Z & 280Z** Coupe '70 thru '78
- 28014 **280ZX** Coupe & 2+2 '79 thru '83
  - **300ZX** - see NISSAN (72010)
- 28018 **510 & PL521 Pick-up** '68 thru '73
- 28020 **510** all models '78 thru '81
- 28022 **620 Series Pick-up** all models '73 thru '79
  - **720 Series Pick-up** - see NISSAN (72030)
- 28025 **810/Maxima** all gasoline models '77 thru '84

DODGE
- **400 & 600** - see CHRYSLER (25030)
- 30008 **Aries & Plymouth Reliant** '81 thru '89
- 30010 **Caravan & Plymouth Voyager** '84 thru '95
- 30011 **Caravan & Plymouth Voyager** '96 thru '02
- 30012 **Challenger/Plymouth Saporro** '78 thru '83
- 30013 **Caravan, Chrysler Voyager, Town & Country** '03 thru '07
- 30016 **Colt & Plymouth Champ** '78 thru '87
- 30020 **Dakota Pick-ups** all models '87 thru '96
- 30021 **Durango** '98 & '99, **Dakota** '97 thru '99
- 30022 **Durango** '00 thru '03 **Dakota** '00 thru '04
- 30023 **Durango** '04 thru '09, **Dakota** '05 thru '11
- 30025 **Dart, Demon, Plymouth Barracuda, Duster & Valiant** 6 cyl models '67 thru '76
- 30030 **Daytona & Chrysler Laser** '84 thru '89
  - **Intrepid** - see CHRYSLER (25025, 25026)
- 30034 **Neon** all models '95 thru '99
- 30035 **Omni & Plymouth Horizon** '78 thru '90
- 30036 **Dodge and Plymouth Neon** '00 thru '05
- 30040 **Pick-ups** all full-size models '74 thru '93
- 30041 **Pick-ups** all full-size models '94 thru '01
- 30042 **Pick-ups** full-size models '02 thru '08
- 30045 **Ram 50/D50 Pick-ups & Raider and Plymouth Arrow Pick-ups** '79 thru '93
- 30050 **Dodge/Plymouth/Chrysler RWD** '71 thru '89
- 30055 **Shadow & Plymouth Sundance** '87 thru '94
- 30060 **Spirit & Plymouth Acclaim** '89 thru '95
- 30065 **Vans - Dodge & Plymouth** '71 thru '03

EAGLE
- **Talon** - see MITSUBISHI (68030, 68031)
- **Vision** - see CHRYSLER (25025)

FIAT
- 34010 **124 Sport Coupe & Spider** '68 thru '78
- 34025 **X1/9** all models '74 thru '80

FORD
- 10320 **Ford Engine Overhaul Manual**
- 10355 **Ford Automatic Transmission Overhaul**
- 11500 **Mustang** '64-1/2 thru '70 **Restoration Guide**
- 36004 **Aerostar Mini-vans** all models '86 thru '97
- 36006 **Contour & Mercury Mystique** '95 thru '00
- 36008 **Courier Pick-up** all models '72 thru '82
- 36012 **Crown Victoria & Mercury Grand Marquis** '88 thru '10
- 36016 **Escort/Mercury Lynx** all models '81 thru '90
- 36020 **Escort/Mercury Tracer** '91 thru '02

- 36022 **Escape & Mazda Tribute** '01 thru '11
- 36024 **Explorer & Mazda Navajo** '91 thru '01
- 36025 **Explorer/Mercury Mountaineer** '02 thru '10
- 36028 **Fairmont & Mercury Zephyr** '78 thru '83
- 36030 **Festiva & Aspire** '88 thru '97
- 36032 **Fiesta** all models '77 thru '80
- 36034 **Focus** all models '00 thru '11
- 36036 **Ford & Mercury Full-size** '75 thru '87
- 36044 **Ford & Mercury Mid-size** '75 thru '86
- 36045 **Fusion & Mercury Milan** '06 thru '10
- 36048 **Mustang V8** all models '64-1/2 thru '73
- 36049 **Mustang II** 4 cyl, V6 & V8 models '74 thru '78
- 36050 **Mustang & Mercury Capri** '79 thru '93
- 36051 **Mustang** all models '94 thru '04
- 36052 **Mustang** '05 thru '10
- 36054 **Pick-ups & Bronco** '73 thru '79
- 36058 **Pick-ups & Bronco** '80 thru '96
- 36059 **F-150 & Expedition** '97 thru '09, F-250 '97 thru '99 **& Lincoln Navigator** '98 thru '09
- 36060 **Super Duty Pick-ups, Excursion** '99 thru '10
- 36061 **F-150** full-size '04 thru '10
- 36062 **Pinto & Mercury Bobcat** '75 thru '80
- 36066 **Probe** all models '89 thru '92
  - **Probe** '93 thru '97 - see MAZDA 626 (61042)
- 36070 **Ranger/Bronco II** gasoline models '83 thru '92
- 36071 **Ranger** '93 thru '10 **& Mazda Pick-ups** '94 thru '09
- 36074 **Taurus & Mercury Sable** '86 thru '95
- 36075 **Taurus & Mercury Sable** '96 thru '05
- 36078 **Tempo & Mercury Topaz** '84 thru '94
- 36082 **Thunderbird/Mercury Cougar** '83 thru '88
- 36086 **Thunderbird/Mercury Cougar** '89 thru '97
- 36090 **Vans** all V8 Econoline models '69 thru '91
- 36094 **Vans** full size '92 thru '10
- 36097 **Windstar Mini-van** '95 thru '07

GENERAL MOTORS
- 10360 **GM Automatic Transmission Overhaul**
- 38005 **Buick Century, Chevrolet Celebrity, Oldsmobile Cutlass Ciera & Pontiac 6000** all models '82 thru '96
- 38010 **Buick Regal, Chevrolet Lumina, Oldsmobile Cutlass Supreme & Pontiac Grand Prix** (FWD) '88 thru '07
- 38015 **Buick Skyhawk, Cadillac Cimarron, Chevrolet Cavalier, Oldsmobile Firenza & Pontiac J-2000 & Sunbird** '82 thru '94
- 38016 **Chevrolet Cavalier & Pontiac Sunfire** '95 thru '05
- 38017 **Chevrolet Cobalt & Pontiac G5** '05 thru '11
- 38020 **Buick Skylark, Chevrolet Citation, Olds Omega, Pontiac Phoenix** '80 thru '85
- 38025 **Buick Skylark & Somerset, Oldsmobile Achieva & Calais and Pontiac Grand Am** all models '85 thru '98
- 38026 **Chevrolet Malibu, Olds Alero & Cutlass, Pontiac Grand Am** '97 thru '03
- 38027 **Chevrolet Malibu** '04 thru '10
- 38030 **Cadillac Eldorado, Seville, Oldsmobile Toronado, Buick Riviera** '71 thru '85
- 38031 **Cadillac Eldorado & Seville, DeVille, Fleetwood & Olds Toronado, Buick Riviera** '86 thru '93
- 38032 **Cadillac DeVille** '94 thru '05 **& Seville** '92 thru '04 **Cadillac DTS** '06 thru '10
- 38035 **Chevrolet Lumina APV, Olds Silhouette & Pontiac Trans Sport** all models '90 thru '96
- 38036 **Chevrolet Venture, Olds Silhouette, Pontiac Trans Sport & Montana** '97 thru '05
  - **General Motors Full-size Rear-wheel Drive** - see BUICK (19025)
- 38040 **Chevrolet Equinox** '05 thru '09 **Pontiac Torrent** '06 thru '09
- 38070 **Chevrolet HHR** '06 thru '11

GEO
- **Metro** - see CHEVROLET Sprint (24075)
- **Prizm** - '85 thru '92 see CHEVY (24060), '93 thru '02 see TOYOTA Corolla (92036)
- 40030 **Storm** all models '90 thru '93
  - **Tracker** - see SUZUKI Samurai (90010)

GMC
- **Vans & Pick-ups** - see CHEVROLET

HONDA
- 42010 **Accord CVCC** all models '76 thru '83
- 42011 **Accord** all models '84 thru '89
- 42012 **Accord** all models '90 thru '93
- 42013 **Accord** all models '94 thru '97
- 42014 **Accord** all models '98 thru '02
- 42015 **Accord** '03 thru '07
- 42020 **Civic 1200** all models '73 thru '79
- 42021 **Civic 1300 & 1500 CVCC** '80 thru '83
- 42022 **Civic 1500 CVCC** all models '75 thru '79

(Continued on other side)

Haynes North America, Inc., 859 Lawrence Drive, Newbury Park, CA 91320-1514 • (805) 498-6703 • http://www.haynes.com

Haynes Automotive Manuals (continued)

NOTE: If you do not see a listing for your vehicle, consult your local Haynes dealer for the latest product information.

42023 **Civic** all models '84 thru '91
42024 **Civic & del Sol** '92 thru '95
42025 **Civic** '96 thru '00, **CR-V** '97 thru '01,
     Acura Integra '94 thru '00
42026 **Civic** '01 thru '10, **CR-V** '02 thru '09
42035 **Odyssey** all models '99 thru '10
     Passport - see ISUZU Rodeo (47017)
42037 **Honda Pilot** '03 thru '07, **Acura MDX** '01 thru '07
42040 **Prelude CVCC** all models '79 thru '89

HYUNDAI
43010 **Elantra** all models '96 thru '10
43015 **Excel & Accent** all models '86 thru '09
43050 **Santa Fe** all models '01 thru '06
43055 **Sonata** all models '99 thru '08

INFINITI
     G35 '03 thru '08 - see NISSAN 350Z (72011)

ISUZU
     Hombre - see CHEVROLET S-10 (24071)
47017 **Rodeo, Amigo & Honda Passport** '89 thru '02
47020 **Trooper & Pick-up** '81 thru '93

JAGUAR
49010 **XJ6** all 6 cyl models '68 thru '86
49011 **XJ6** all models '88 thru '94
49015 **XJ12 & XJS** all 12 cyl models '72 thru '85

JEEP
50010 **Cherokee, Comanche & Wagoneer Limited**
     all models '84 thru '01
50020 **CJ** all models '49 thru '86
50025 **Grand Cherokee** all models '93 thru '04
50026 **Grand Cherokee** '05 thru '09
50029 **Grand Wagoneer & Pick-up** '72 thru '91
     Grand Wagoneer '84 thru '91, Cherokee &
     Wagoneer '72 thru '83, Pick-up '72 thru '88
50030 **Wrangler** all models '87 thru '11
50035 **Liberty** '02 thru '07

KIA
54050 **Optima** '01 thru '10
54070 **Sephia** '94 thru '01, **Spectra** '00 thru '09,
     Sportage '05 thru '10

LEXUS
     ES 300/330 - see TOYOTA Camry (92007) (92008)
     RX 330 - see TOYOTA Highlander (92095)

LINCOLN
     Navigator - see FORD Pick-up (36059)
59010 **Rear-Wheel Drive** all models '70 thru '10

MAZDA
61010 **GLC Hatchback** (rear-wheel drive) '77 thru '83
61011 **GLC** (front-wheel drive) '81 thru '85
61012 **Mazda3** '04 thru '11
61015 **323 & Protegé** '90 thru '03
61016 **MX-5 Miata** '90 thru '09
61020 **MPV** all models '89 thru '98
     Navajo - see Ford Explorer (36024)
61030 **Pick-ups** '72 thru '93
     Pick-ups '94 thru '00 - see Ford Ranger (36071)
61035 **RX-7** all models '79 thru '85
61036 **RX-7** all models '86 thru '91
61040 **626** (rear-wheel drive) all models '79 thru '82
61041 **626/MX-6** (front-wheel drive) '83 thru '92
61042 **626, MX-6/Ford Probe** '93 thru '02
61043 **Mazda6** '03 thru '11

MERCEDES-BENZ
63012 **123 Series Diesel** '76 thru '85
63015 **190 Series** four-cyl gas models, '84 thru '88
63020 **230/250/280** 6 cyl sohc models '68 thru '72
63025 **280 123 Series** gasoline models '77 thru '81
63030 **350 & 450** all models '71 thru '80
63040 **C-Class:** C230/C240/C280/C320/C350 '01 thru '07

MERCURY
64200 **Villager & Nissan Quest** '93 thru '01
     All other titles, see FORD Listing.

MG
66010 **MGB** Roadster & GT Coupe '62 thru '80
66015 **MG Midget, Austin Healey Sprite** '58 thru '80

MINI
67020 **Mini** '02 thru '11

MITSUBISHI
68020 **Cordia, Tredia, Galant, Precis &**
     Mirage '83 thru '93
68030 **Eclipse, Eagle Talon & Ply. Laser** '90 thru '94
68031 **Eclipse** '95 thru '05, **Eagle Talon** '95 thru '98
68035 **Galant** '94 thru '10
68040 **Pick-up** '83 thru '96 **& Montero** '83 thru '93

NISSAN
72010 **300ZX** all models including Turbo '84 thru '89
72011 **350Z & Infiniti G35** all models '03 thru '08
72015 **Altima** all models '93 thru '06
72016 **Altima** '07 thru '10
72020 **Maxima** all models '85 thru '92
72021 **Maxima** all models '93 thru '04
72025 **Murano** '03 thru '10
72030 **Pick-ups** '80 thru '97 **Pathfinder** '87 thru '95
72031 **Frontier Pick-up, Xterra, Pathfinder** '96 thru '04
72032 **Frontier & Xterra** '05 thru '11
72040 **Pulsar** all models '83 thru '86
     Quest - see MERCURY Villager (64200)
72050 **Sentra** all models '82 thru '94
72051 **Sentra & 200SX** all models '95 thru '06
72060 **Stanza** all models '82 thru '90
72070 **Titan pick-ups** '04 thru '10 **Armada** '05 thru '10

OLDSMOBILE
73015 **Cutlass** V6 & V8 gas models '74 thru '88
     For other OLDSMOBILE titles, see BUICK,
     CHEVROLET or GENERAL MOTORS listing.

PLYMOUTH
     For PLYMOUTH titles, see DODGE listing.

PONTIAC
79008 **Fiero** all models '84 thru '88
79018 **Firebird** V8 models except Turbo '70 thru '81
79019 **Firebird** all models '82 thru '92
79025 **G6** all models '05 thru '09
79040 **Mid-size Rear-wheel Drive** '70 thru '87
     Vibe '03 thru '11 - see TOYOTA Matrix (92060)
     For other PONTIAC titles, see BUICK,
     CHEVROLET or GENERAL MOTORS listing.

PORSCHE
80020 **911** except Turbo & Carrera 4 '65 thru '89
80025 **914** all 4 cyl models '69 thru '76
80030 **924** all models including Turbo '76 thru '82
80035 **944** all models including Turbo '83 thru '89

RENAULT
     Alliance & Encore - see AMC (14020)

SAAB
84010 **900** all models including Turbo '79 thru '88

SATURN
87010 **Saturn** all S-series models '91 thru '02
87011 **Saturn Ion** '03 thru '07
87020 **Saturn** all L-series models '00 thru '04
87040 **Saturn VUE** '02 thru '07

SUBARU
89002 **1100, 1300, 1400 & 1600** '71 thru '79
89003 **1600 & 1800** 2WD & 4WD '80 thru '94
89100 **Legacy** all models '90 thru '99
89101 **Legacy & Forester** '00 thru '06

SUZUKI
90010 **Samurai/Sidekick & Geo Tracker** '86 thru '01

TOYOTA
92005 **Camry** all models '83 thru '91
92006 **Camry** all models '92 thru '96
92007 **Camry, Avalon, Solara, Lexus ES 300** '97 thru '01
92008 **Toyota Camry, Avalon and Solara and**
     Lexus ES 300/330 all models '02 thru '06
92009 **Camry** '07 thru '11
92015 **Celica Rear Wheel Drive** '71 thru '85
92020 **Celica Front Wheel Drive** '86 thru '99
92025 **Celica Supra** all models '79 thru '92
92030 **Corolla** all models '75 thru '79
92032 **Corolla** all rear wheel drive models '80 thru '87
92035 **Corolla** all front wheel drive models '84 thru '92
92036 **Corolla & Geo Prizm** '93 thru '02
92037 **Corolla** models '03 thru '11
92040 **Corolla Tercel** all models '80 thru '82
92045 **Corona** all models '74 thru '82
92050 **Cressida** all models '78 thru '82
92055 **Land Cruiser** FJ40, 43, 45, 55 '68 thru '82
92056 **Land Cruiser** FJ60, 62, 80, FZJ80 '80 thru '96
92060 **Matrix & Pontiac Vibe** '03 thru '11
92065 **MR2** all models '85 thru '87
92070 **Pick-up** all models '69 thru '78
92075 **Pick-up** all models '79 thru '95
92076 **Tacoma, 4Runner, & T100** '93 thru '04
92077 **Tacoma** all models '05 thru '09
92078 **Tundra** '00 thru '06 **& Sequoia** '01 thru '07
92079 **4Runner** all models '03 thru '09
92080 **Previa** all models '91 thru '95
92081 **Prius** all models '01 thru '08
92082 **RAV4** all models '96 thru '10
92085 **Tercel** all models '87 thru '94
92090 **Sienna** all models '98 thru '09
92095 **Highlander & Lexus RX-330** '99 thru '07

TRIUMPH
94007 **Spitfire** all models '62 thru '81
94010 **TR7** all models '75 thru '81

VW
96008 **Beetle & Karmann Ghia** '54 thru '79
96009 **New Beetle** '98 thru '11
96016 **Rabbit, Jetta, Scirocco & Pick-up** gas
     models '75 thru '92 & Convertible '80 thru '92
96017 **Golf, GTI & Jetta** '93 thru '98, **Cabrio** '95 thru '02
96018 **Golf, GTI, Jetta** '99 thru '05
96019 **Jetta, Rabbit, GTI & Golf** '05 thru '11
96020 **Rabbit, Jetta & Pick-up** diesel '77 thru '84
96023 **Passat** '98 thru '05, **Audi A4** '96 thru '01
96030 **Transporter 1600** '68 thru '79
96035 **Transporter 1700, 1800 & 2000** '72 thru '79
96040 **Type 3 1500 & 1600** all models '63 thru '73
96045 **Vanagon** all air-cooled models '80 thru '83

VOLVO
97010 **120, 130 Series & 1800 Sports** '61 thru '73
97015 **140 Series** all models '66 thru '74
97020 **240 Series** all models '76 thru '93
97040 **740 & 760 Series** all models '82 thru '88
97050 **850 Series** all models '93 thru '97

TECHBOOK MANUALS
10205 **Automotive Computer Codes**
10206 **OBD-II & Electronic Engine Management**
10210 **Automotive Emissions Control Manual**
10215 **Fuel Injection Manual** '78 thru '85
10220 **Fuel Injection Manual** '86 thru '99
10225 **Holley Carburetor Manual**
10230 **Rochester Carburetor Manual**
10240 **Weber/Zenith/Stromberg/SU Carburetors**
10305 **Chevrolet Engine Overhaul Manual**
10310 **Chrysler Engine Overhaul Manual**
10320 **Ford Engine Overhaul Manual**
10330 **GM and Ford Diesel Engine Repair Manual**
10333 **Engine Performance Manual**
10340 **Small Engine Repair Manual, 5 HP & Less**
10341 **Small Engine Repair Manual, 5.5 - 20 HP**
10345 **Suspension, Steering & Driveline Manual**
10355 **Ford Automatic Transmission Overhaul**
10360 **GM Automatic Transmission Overhaul**
10405 **Automotive Body Repair & Painting**
10410 **Automotive Brake Manual**
10411 **Automotive Anti-lock Brake (ABS) Systems**
10415 **Automotive Detailing Manual**
10420 **Automotive Electrical Manual**
10425 **Automotive Heating & Air Conditioning**
10430 **Automotive Reference Manual & Dictionary**
10435 **Automotive Tools Manual**
10440 **Used Car Buying Guide**
10445 **Welding Manual**
10450 **ATV Basics**
10452 **Scooters 50cc to 250cc**

SPANISH MANUALS
98903 **Reparación de Carrocería & Pintura**
98904 **Manual de Carburador Modelos**
     Holley & Rochester
98905 **Códigos Automotrices de la Computadora**
98906 **OBD-II & Sistemas de Control Electrónico**
     del Motor
98910 **Frenos Automotriz**
98913 **Electricidad Automotriz**
98915 **Inyección de Combustible** '86 al '99
99040 **Chevrolet & GMC Camionetas** '67 al '87
99041 **Chevrolet & GMC Camionetas** '88 al '98
99042 **Chevrolet & GMC Camionetas**
     Cerradas '68 al '95
99043 **Chevrolet/GMC Camionetas** '94 al '04
99048 **Chevrolet/GMC Camionetas** '99 al '06
99055 **Dodge Caravan & Plymouth Voyager** '84 al '95
99075 **Ford Camionetas y Bronco** '80 al '94
99076 **Ford F-150** '97 al '09
99077 **Ford Camionetas Cerradas** '69 al '91
99088 **Ford Modelos de Tamaño Mediano** '75 al '86
99089 **Ford Camionetas Ranger** '93 al '10
99091 **Ford Taurus & Mercury Sable** '86 al '95
99095 **GM Modelos de Tamaño Grande** '70 al '90
99100 **GM Modelos de Tamaño Mediano** '70 al '88
99106 **Jeep Cherokee, Wagoneer & Comanche**
     '84 al '00
99110 **Nissan Camioneta** '80 al '96, **Pathfinder** '87 al '95
99118 **Nissan Sentra** '82 al '94
99125 **Toyota Camionetas y 4Runner** '79 al '95

Over 100 Haynes motorcycle manuals also available

7-12

Haynes North America, Inc., 859 Lawrence Drive, Newbury Park, CA 91320-1514 • (805) 498-6703 • http://www.haynes.com